The Language of Herz's *Esther:*

A Study in Judeo-German Dialectology

The Language of Herz's *Esther:*
A Study in Judeo-German Dialectology

Edited by

ROBERT M. COPELAND

and

NATHAN SÜSSKIND

The University *of Alabama Press*
University, Alabama

Library of Congress Cataloging in Publication Data

Copeland, Robert M. 1907-
  The language of Herz's Esther.

  Bibliography: p.
  1. Herz, Joseph, 1776-1828. Ester. 2. Herz,
Joseph, 1776-1828—Language—Dialects. 3. Yiddish
language—Dialects—Germany. I. Süsskind, Nathan,
1911- joint author. II. Herz, Joseph, 1776-
1828. Ester. 1976. III. Title.
PJ5129.H4416E834   839'.09'22   75-34184
ISBN 0-8173-6902-3

To our two MALKAS

CONTENTS

Preface

The authors of the Commentary on Herz's _Esther_ pride
themselves in presenting to a wide reading public a hitherto
relatively unknown literary genius. For almost a century and
a half (since 1828) he was overlooked and unappreciated. Even
though he did have friends who urged him to bring out the
second edition (1854) of his "trifles", these friends could
not have really grasped all his humor, else they would have
urged him to write more, new, "trifles" rather than just re-
print his old ones.

He had the makings of a great writer of comedies. Unfortunately he tailored his "trifles" to a very limited
audience by the deliberate use of "dialect" of his own con-
coction, and by only "hinting" cryptically at a risqué humor
to avoid shocking the unintiated.

He wrote for the first generation of "emancipated", "enlightened" Jews of the Aufklärung period in Germany, for those
especially who were still well versed in Jewish religious lore,
who still knew Yiddish but were more at home in German. Such
an audience was small enough then (1828) and is almost non-
existent now. When one adds the autistic nature of the dialect and the deliberate mystification of his humor, it becomes
clear why he has been neglected and why there is an absolute

need for the Commentary.

The Commentary thus is the key to what is intrinsically great art and a delight to read.

Esther is also a most important historical document: it reflects the human drama of a submerged ethnic group in the grip of dynamic emergence into the mainstream of civilization with the concomitant psychological dilemmas, the identity crises involved in the cultural transition and linguistic assimilation of the German Jews--from pious speakers of Jüdisch-Deutsch praying for the Messiah to bring them back to Jerusalem--to cosmopolitan, emancipated, assimilated would-be "Germans of the Mosaic faith."

Their Jüdisch-Deutsch was, of course, the origin of what had become, on non-German speech-territory,--Yiddish. Esther should thus constitute a milestone in the development of Yiddish. To the uninitiated, however, it could sooner become a stumbling stone: the Commentary points up every inauthentic case of "dialect" concocted by Herz for the pur- pose of spoofing, and we label it "inauth. h.c." (=inauthen- tic-, humoris causa). Yet in spite of this, and in spite of Esther's remaining without much direct influence, it is important for the history of Yiddish as well as the history of Jewish literature and the Jewish theater. It is part of the great movement of the secularization of Jewish life and literature and the best example typifying its time and genre.

The genre is the Purim Play and the time the Period of Enlightenment or Emancipation.

The Purim Play had long been part of the religion-- ordered, carnival-like Purim merriment--celebrating the last minute miraculous escape of all the Jews from complete annihi- lation at the hands of their neighbors as decreed by the

Persian King Ahasuerus upon the urging of his prime minister
Haman. Queen Esther, whose Jewishness had been hidden from
both King and Minister, manages—at the risk of her life—to
convince the King of his mistake. The tables are turned on
Haman: he and the attackers of the Jews are destroyed. The
story is told in the Book of Esther in the Bible.

In the last two thousand years Jewish life was almost
perennially as precarious as in the times of Esther—only
that, unlike on that Purium, the reprieve at the last moment
came only sometimes, and then the community decreed its own
"Little Purim." It was not only shver (hard) to be a Jew
(as the Yiddish proverb has it) but also dangerous to life
and limb. But harder even than to be a Jew was it for him to
be merry in a worldly way. The only happiness a Jew could
expect was otherworldly. Only on Purim, the anniversary
celebrating God's ever-sure dependability to save the just,
could the Jew give release to his pent-up yearning for care-
free merriment, and then it was boundless!

The extra-sober puritanical Rabbis decreed intoxication
on Purim—to a point where the drunk cannot distinguish between "Curse Haman!" and "Bless Mordecai!"[1]. Also decreed (in
the Bible) are gifts to friends and the poor. The poor fell
upon the idea of singing for their gifts as they went from
house to house. So, soon organized groups of amateur enter-
tainers emerged. They dramatized the story of Esther, at
first straight, but then more often burlesqued in the carnival
spirit. Sketches lampooning personalities and conditions in
the community vied with the Esther burlesque. For variety,

---

[1] Talmud (Megillah 7b); Schulchan Aruch: Orach Chayim 695,3.

other stories and themes, usually those well-known from Bible and Midrash, alternated with Esther (e.g., "Joseph and his Brothers," "The Sacrifice of Isaac"). From these traditions then evolved the professional Jewish Theater (in Yiddish and other languages).[2]

But long before there developed a professional Jewish stage, writers indulged in daydreaming about it and composed dramatic works, many of them comedies. The Purim comedy lent itself especially for the purposes of the "Enlighteners" (Maskilim): bitter social critique and didactic endeavors for uplift and education. Humor was more than a mannerism that characterized most Jewish literature of the Enlightenment; it was a major weapon. And for Purim the humor could be as broad as one wished, or almost... There is the story of the Purim Play published (1708) in Frankfurt a/M that was so shocking that the Jewish communal authorities made sure they obtained every available copy and burned it![3] The elegance and crypticism of Herz's humor saved it from burning --at the cost of its impact.

Our work, presented in photo-offset because typesetting would be so complicated and would lead to countless errors, consists of three parts of which we offer only two at this time. We hope that the publication of these will increase the market for the largest and weightiest part, the Analysis of the Language ("A"). Its potential interest is limited to linguists only. We refer to A in our linguistic comments and

---

[2] B. Gorin: Di Geschichte fun Idishen Teater, p. 41ff.; Sch. Ernst, "Rabbinical Attitudes to the Theater," Archiv far Geshichte, Teater un Drame, ed. J. Schatzsky, I (New York, 1930) pp. 34-47

[3] Gorin, p. 50.

will consider furnishing Xeroxes at cost to any who would want
them.

> The rest: 1. The original ("O") in Hebrew characters,
> by photo-offset.
> 2. The Transliteration ("T") of "O" in a
> specially adapted Roman alphabet.
> 3. The Commentary ("C").
> 4. Lexicology ("L"), a dictionary of all
> "difficult" words.

Esther will be of interest toGerman Jews in general;
lovers of Yiddish, its literature and history; students of
Jewish history, religion and folklore; linguists in general
and students of German dialects in particular; lovers of
humor; students of the theater and, folklore; and the clergy
of all faiths.

It is indeed a privilege and a pleasure to register
here our sincerest gratitude to the late Dr. Taylor Starck,
Kuno Francke Professor of German, and to the late Dr. Harry
A. Wolfson, Littauer Professor of Jewish History and Literature, both of Harvard University, for their guidance of
Dr. Copeland's doctoral dissertation of which our work is an
extension; to Professor Judah A. Joffe, of blessed memory,
for advice and the loan of his copy of Esther; to Professor
Harry Zohn, Chairman of the Department of Germanic and Slavic
Languages at Brandeis University, for suggesting the idea of
this publication and for his constant encouragement; to Dr.
Fred Grubel and the Leo Baeck Institute, for their interest,
their financial aid, and their efforts in behalf of publication; to Dr. Menahem Schwelzer and Dr. Herman Dicker, of the
Library of the Jewish Theological Seminary, for a loan of
their copies of Esther; to our typists, Mrs. Edith M. Rothen-

berg, secretary of the German Department at the College of the City of New York, Mr. Donald Steele, graduate student of Semitics at Harvard University, Mrs. Mitsue Miyata Frey, Research Associate of the African Studies Association, Brandeis University, and finally to Professor Irving Greenberg, Chairman of the Jewish Studies Department, College of the City of New York, for his enthusiastic encouragement.

R.M.C.

N.S.

PART   I

Text and Transliteration

Key

I. Transliteration of German words.

A. Consonants

ב = b   כ = ch   פ = f

ג = g   final ך = ch   final ף = f

ד = d   ל = l   צ = z

ה = h   מ = m   final ץ = z

ו = w   final ם = m   ק = k

וו = w   נ = n   ר = r

ז = s   final ן = n   ש = sch (שט = st) in
                                        (שפ = sp) all
ט = t   ס = ṡ   positions

י = j   פ = p

B. Vowel Letters

אַ = a

אָ = o

ע = e

אִי, י = i

אוּ, ו = u

C. Diphthongs

אַיי, יי = ai

אוי, וי = oi

II. Transliteration of Hebrew Words, according to the Ashkenazic Pronounciation.

A. Consonants--the same as under I.A., with the following additions:

א = ' at the middle or end, but not at the beginning of a word; in the latter case it is not to be designated.

ע = ʻ at the beginning, middle and end of a word.

ב	= v	שׁ = ṡ	Note:	Dogesch forte indicates con-
ח	= ḥ	תּ = th		sonantal gemina-
כ	= k	ת = ś		tion.
ק	= Ḳ			

B. Vowel Points

$$\text{———} \;,\; \text{———} = a$$
$$\text{—}\;,\; \text{—}: = o$$
$$\text{ֹו}\;,\; \text{֮} = \hat{o}$$

$$: \;,\; \text{—}\;,\; \text{—}: = e$$
$$\text{ֹי}\;,\; \text{——} = \hat{e}$$
$$\text{ֹי}\;,\; \text{——} = i$$
$$\text{ֹו}\;,\; \text{֮} = u$$

III. Transliteration of proper names which occur in the Bible follows the form used in the German Bible.

IV. Hebrew words are underlined with a German translation in footnote. Hebrew words that have made their way into German or are intelligible to the German reader are underlined, but not translated.

V. Biblical Hebrew phrases are translated according to Luther's version of the Boble.

VI. French words are transliterated, underlined, and given their modern French equivalents in footnotes.

VII. Capitalization and punctuation are according to the method used in German texts of the same period.

אסתר.
אָדער
דיא בעלאָהנטע טוגענד.

—·→→✦←·—

איינע פאָזע אין פיער אבשניטטען

נעבסט

איינינען נאָך ניכט געדרוקקטען געדיכטען

מין יידיט-דייטטער אונדמאַרט

פאָן

יוסף הערץ.

Zweite vermehrte Auflage.

Fürth, 1854.
Verlag von S. B. Gusdorfer.
Druck der J. Sommer'schen Buchdruckerei.

ESTHER

oder

Di belohnte Tugend

******

Aine Posse in fier Abschnitten

nebst

Ainigen noch nicht gedrukkten Gedichten

in jidisch=daitscher Mundart

fon

Joseph Herz

Zweite vermehrte Auflage

Fürth, 1854
Verlag von S. B. Gusdorfer
Druck der J. Sommer'schen Buchdruckerei

פֿאָרוואָרט דעז פֿערפֿאַסערז·

מיט דיעזענוועניגען בלעֶטטערן איבערגעבע איך דעם פּובלֿיקום
אייגע פּרֹאֶבע אייגער לֿיטערֹאַריטעגן קלֿייגיגקייטען , דיא איהר ענט=
שטעהען דער היעטערן לֿויגע איסֿיגער שטוגדען, וואֶ דיא פֿאֶנטֹאַזֿיע
איהרע בילֿדער איט בוגדען פֿאֶרבען מֹאַהלֿטע, לֿו פֿערדֹאֶנקען הֹאַט.

דיעזעֶ ווערקלֿען איזט לֿו געריגגֿפֿיגֿ, אום פֿיעלֿ דעֶריבער זֿאַגֿען
לֿו קעגגען; נור פֿיגדע איך פֿיר גֹאֶטהיג , איין ערמֹאַגגערונג לֿו
בריגגֿען, דֹאַם מיך לֿו יעגער לֿייט, אַלֿז איך עם גיעֶדערטריעב, ווייט
ענטפֿעֶרנט, עֶ מין דרוק ערטיעגען לֿו לֿאַסֿסֿען, זֿמֹלֿבֿעֶ נור אַלֿז
אייגע בעזֿוסֿטיגֿעגֿעגֿדע אוגטערֹאהֹאֶלֿטוגג פֿיר איך בעטרֹאֶבֿטֿעֶטֿע, אויד
נור דורך דֿאַ דריגֿעגֿעגֿדע ביטטעֶגֿ אייגער פֿֿריינדֿע איך ענטֿשֿלֿאֶם,
עֶ דעם דרוקקעֶ לֿו איבערגעבֿעֶן. דֿאהעֶר ביטטעעֶ מיך, דֹאַם דיעזעֶ
פּרֹאֶדוקטע מין יעדעֶם געבֿילֿדֿעֶטֿעֶן לֿעזֿער נור פֿֿרֹאֶזֿהֿיֿן אויך הֿיעֶטֿעֶר=
קייט פֿעֶרברֿיֿטֿעֶן מֶלֿלֿ, דֹאַם עֶ איט טֿאֶלֿאֶגֿג אויד נֿאֶבֿילֿטֿ אויפֿֿ=
געגֿאָמֿמֿעֶן וועֶרדֿעֶ.

פֿֿירדֿאַ, בחדש חשון תקפֿ״ח לֿפֿֿ״ק.

יוסף הערֿץ·

דעֶם פֿֿיעֶלֿוֿייֿטֿיֿגֿעֶן פֿעֶרלֿֿאֶגֿגֿעֶן דעֶז פּובלֿֿיקוֿאֶ לֿוֿ ענטֿשֿפֿֿרֿעֶלֿֿבֿעֶן,
הֹאֶט זֿיך דעֶר פֿעֶרלֿֿעֶגֿגֿעֶר ענטֿשֿלֿֿאֶמֿמֿעֶן , דיעֶו ווֿעֶרֿקֿלֿֿעֶן מֿין אייגער
נֿוֿייֿטֿעֶן אויֿפֿֿלֿֿאֶגֿגֿעֶ ערטֿייֿגֿעֶן לֿֿו לֿֿאֶזֿמֿעֶן, אויד אייֿגֿעֶ בֿיֿו יֿעֶטֿלֿֿט נֿֿאֶך
אֿוֿנֿגֿעֶדֿרֿוֿקֿקֿעֶטֿעֶ געֶדֿיֿכֿטֿעֶ דֿעֶו פֿעֶרֿמֿאֶסֿמֿעֶרֿז בֿייֿלֿֿוֿפֿֿיֿגֿעֶן.

—∞—

Forwort des Ferfasers

Mit diesenwenigen Blettern ibergebe ich dem Publikum
aine Probe mainer literarischen Klainigkaiten, di ihr Ent-
stehen der haitern Loine misiger Stunden, wo di Fantasi Ihre
Bilder mit bunden Farben mahlte, zu ferdanken hat.

Dieses Werkchen ist zu geringfigig, um fiel dariber
sagen zu kennen: nur finde ich fir nethig, in Erinnerung zu
bringen, das ich zu jener Zait, als ich es niederschrieb,
wait entfernt, es in Druk erschainen zu lassen, Solches nur
als aine belustigende Unterhaltung fir mich betrachtete, und
nur durch das dringende Bitten mainer Frainde mich entschlos,
es dem Drukke zu ibergeben. Daher bitte ich, da dieses
Produkt in jedem gebildeten Zirkel nur Frohsin und Haiter-
kait ferbraiten soll, das es mit Schonung und Nachsicht oif-
genommen werde.

Firda be-.ôdesch ^H.eschwen THKP" ^H. LP"K[1]

Joseph Herz

Dem fielsaitigen Ferlangen des Publikums zu entsprechen, hat sich der Ferleger entschlossen, dies Werkchen
in ainer zwaiten Oiflage erschainen zu lassen, und ainige
bis jetzt noch ungedrukkten Gedichten des Ferfasers baizu-
figen.

————************————

[1] Fürth im Monat d. 20. Okt.—d. 19. Nov. 5588 AM=1828 C.E.

פּערזאָנען.

אהשוורוש, קעניג פֿון
פּערזיען.

המן, זײַן מיניסטער.

מרדכי, מײַן פֿרמואער
עדזער יהודי.

אסתר, זײַנע ניכטע.

אײן מעדלען, בײַ
אסתר.

הרבונה, מײַן הָאפֿמאַן.

רעקאַ, זײַנע פֿרוי.

צעטילפֿע, מיהרע
טאָכטער.

צעפֿירעטע, די אַמַגד.

יוקל, דער משרת.

התך, הָאפֿבעדינטער.

קאָראַ, מאַקאַ,

זאָקאַ, ציירע,

געטפֿיזיננען דער אסתר.

מירצאַ, אוטטער דער
ציירע.

בגתן, תרש, הָאפֿזײַטע.

אַפֿראַצעגע, מײַנע
הָאפֿדמואע.

טהירצע, פֿיגסי,

פֿאַקסי, פֿרויען פֿון
שושן.

צווייא גאַלאַנס

סידי, מײַנע פֿרוי, די
גריבען פֿערקופֿטע.

מאַלינע, מײַנע אַמַגד.

פֿאָרגעגהאָע שושין'ס.

דרייא ווייבער.

אײן קנאבע.

אײַן קינד.

קאָהר פֿאָן קיערערן.

אײן האהן.

Personen

Ahasveros, Kenig in
Persien.
Haman, sain Minister.
Mardachai, ain frommer
Edler Jehudi[1].
Esther, saine Nichte.
Ain Medchen, bai
Esther.
Harbona, ain Hofman.
Reka, saine Froi.
Zetulpe, ihre
Tochter.
Zefirete, die Magd.
Jukl, der Meschores[2].
Hathach, Hofbedienter.
Kora, Moka,
Soka, Zaire.
Geśpilinnen der Esther.

Mirza, Mutter der
Zaire.
Bigthan, Theres, Hoflaite.
Afrozene, aine
Hofdame.
Thirze, Figśi
Fakśi, Froien in
Susan.
Zwai Galanś
Śidi, aine Froi, di
Griben ferkoift.
Maline, aine Magd.
Vornehme Susan'ś.
Drai Waiber.
Ain Knabe.
Ain Kind.
Kohr fon Kindern.
Ain Hahn.

————————***********————————

1. Jude.
2. Diener.

ערזטער אַבשניטט.

(ציממער אים פֿאַללאָט.)

חרבונה

(קאָממט אויז איינער זייטענטהירע.)

טיהן פֿאָטט איז דיא ארורה;
דיא האָט דען גהאַט אַ צורה,
וויא מֿהן אויגנטניטטנער קאָרפּעם.
וואַ טייטט, וויא האָט ער ניט אעהר תרבית?
ווען דער אמהן זאַהאַגט: קואַאע!
דמאַרל דיא פֿרמה ניט — ברואַאע.
דער מלך, טיקט דו נעביך מין בעטטען
זיא זאַלל אַ ביסלע נמקעט קואאע, און דיא געטטען
לאָסטן זאַהאַגען: ווען מיך אַהַג.
איז געווויהס גטטעקט מין מצה = טמאַג?
שטות — האָט עבים דיא גהאַטטן
נויטהווענדיגע משא ומתן
האָט אעגן דיא היהנער דיא טווענן נויל בינדען.
זוי מֿהגע קען דעך דיא גאַנלע קהילה פֿערזינדען.
וואָמַ טייטט —ווען דער מלך עבעם בעפֿיהאָט?
אויל דער האָב מיך טוין לאַהג געניהאָט;

1

Erster Abschnitt

(Zimmer im Pallast.)

Harbona

(kommt ois ainer Saitenthire.)

Schihn fott is di Aruroh[1]:

Di hot doch ghat a Zuroh[2],

Wi ahn oisgschnittner Karpeṡ.

Was taitsch, wi hot mer nit mehr Tharbuṡ[3]?

5   Wen der Mahn saagt: kumme!

Darf di Frah nit--brumme.

Der Melech[4], schikt doi nebich in besten

Si soll a biṡle naket kumme, un di Gesten

Loṡt'n saagen: wen ich mag.

10   Is gewihṡ gstekt in Mazzoh=Taag[5]?

Stuṡ[6]--hot ebiṡ doi ghattn

Noithwendige Maṡṡo u--Maththon[7].

Hot meṡn di Hihner di Schwenz noif binden.

Soi ahne ken doch di ganze Kehiloh[8] fersinden.

15   Waas taitsch--wen der Melech[4] ebeṡ befihlt?

Oif der hob ich schoin lang gezihlt:

---

1. Zänkerin. 2. Gesicht. 3. Sitten--Tharbuṡ] Tharbiṡ--an
impure rhyme with karpeṡ. 4. König. 5. ungesäuerter Teig--
"Anderseits gilt demjenigen, der bei einer gewöhnlichen Arbeit
einen unnötigen Eifer zeigt und daher nicht die geringste
Unterbrechung gestatten will, der spöttische Zuruf: Knetest
Du etwa einen Mazzeteig, dass Du Deine Arbeit nicht auf einen
Augenblick verlassen darfst?..Das Kneten des Mazzeteigs darf
nämlich nicht unterbrochen werden, er möchte sonst in Sauerteig
"übergehen." Tendlau, Prov.#194. 6. Dummheit. 7. Unterhaltung. 8. Gemeinde.

דער איהר עזוז=קאָט איז יי גיאאער היע!
אָבער אין טטעקט זי טיהן אין דיזע בריה
געלט, מאָלע וויַן פערגיהט איהר'ס לאָבען
אין אַדאַם ושתי גיהט זיַן קראָבען.

אחשורוש.

(קאָמט אויז זיַנעס קאַבנעט.)

חרבונה, האָט ושתי טאָהן
פיר איהרען פרעלפען, דען פּערדיהנטען לאָהן?
אויַ! דער טטעגלע זאָלל מאַן זיַן ריכטען —
געה! — מאַן זאָלל איהר'ז בעריכטען.

חרבונה.

גרויסער קיניג, און מעכטיגער הערר!
בעהאָררטער, פֿון הונדערט און זיעבענאונדנaleaציך
מדינות.
לאָסט איך ריהטען, אַ בעאָר ווטaleaÝ טאיך נער
איהר וויסט, ביַ איר איז קאָהן — מינות
איהר העטט גאַטטעס רעכט.
פון ושתי וואָר עס געווissטaleaÝ שלעכט,
דאָס זיא, אויַ מייער פערלאַנגע
ניט גלייַך, הער איז גאַנגע —
עס איז אָבער, ושתי ניט מאַהן,
זיא ניט פֿאָלגט איהרען אמאַהן;
גיהט מאַל מייער מדינות אויַ,
איהר וועט זעהן, קאָהן אמאַהן גיט ניקס אין הויז! —

Der ihr <u>Asus</u>=kat[1] is joi nimmer hie!

Ober iz stekt si schihn in di Brih

Gelt, alle wail fergiht ihr'ṡ Lachen

Iz Madam Vasthi giht si krachen.

    Ahasveros
   (kommt ois sainem Kabnet.)

5 Harbona, hat Vasthi schohn

 Fir ihren Frefel, den ferdihnten Lohn?

 Oif der stelle soll man si richten--

 Geh!--Man soll mir's berichten.

    Harbona.

 Groiser Kinig, un mechtiger Herr!

10 Beharrscher, fun hundert un siebenunzwanzig
         <u>Medinôṡ</u>.[2]

 Loṡt mich rihten, a baar Wattlich ner

 Ihr wiṡt, bai mir is kahn--<u>Minôṡ</u>[3]

 Ihr hett Gotteṡ Reht.

 Fun Vasthi wor es gewaltig schlecht,

15 Daṡ si, oif aier Ferlange

 Nit glaich, her is gange--

 Eṡ is ober, Vasthi mit alahn,

 Di nit folgt ihren Mahn:

 Giht all aier <u>Medinôṡ</u>[2] ois

20 Ihr wat sehi, kahn Mahn gilt nikṡ in Hois!--

1. Dreistigkeit.
2. Provinzen.
3. Ketzerei.

און פֿון הודה, ביז כּוש אן ענד
פֿיהרען דיא ווײבער, דאַז רעגיאַמענט.
זיא פֿרײגען ניקס, נוך גאָטט אונ דיא וועלט,
וואָפֿען נאָר נוי דאַז געלד,
פֿאָר פּוץ, אונ נײע קלײדער ;
פֿאָר קונצערטען, אונ טריהאַטהער !
וואַקעגס מעה, מען דיא מרעמע געוינדער !
טראַגען פֿאָר אַ כּפרה, דיא קינדער
האַלטען דיה אאַהן פֿאָר אַ הונד ;
דער האָט נעביך, קאַהן רוהיגע שטונד ;
דער אוז לאָפֿען — דער אוז רעננע
מין ווינד, מין ווצטטער, אונ מין רײהגען,
אוז פֿערפֿריהרען, אוז פֿערברעננע,
פֿון האָן אמס, אויך דיא מנדערע ניהגען.
דיוערט דאַז דינג נאָך לענגער פֿאָטט
העס מיר הס ושלום דיה גרעסטען מפֿאָטט !
דרום אײן האַרר, אונ קיניג !
ביטט מיך אונטערטהיניג :
לאָסט טרײבען אַ דיקרײהט,
עה עם וואַטט צו שפֿיהט ;
די נײן לעסמען מיר שטעזלֿען :
וואַז פֿון הײט אַהן, דיא אעננער האַבן וועזלֿען
איסמען דיא ווײבער גלײך טוין —
וואַ ניט, קריעגט יעדע וויא ושתּי מיהר לויהן.
מיהר וואַט זעהי, דאַז ווײבעררעגיאַמענט,
הוים דו ביזאָלֿ זײן ענד.

1*

Un fun Hôduh,[1] bis Kusch[2] an End

Fihren di Waiber, das Regiment.

Si froigen niks, noich Gott un di Welt,

Woffen nor nois das Geld,

5 For Puz, un naie Klader:

For Kunzerten, un Trihather!

Zwakens ah, an di areme Gesinder!

Schlagen for a Kapporoh,[3] di Kinder

Halten dihn Mahn for a Hund:

10 Der hot nebich, kahn ruhige Stund:

Der mus lafen--der mus renne

In Wind, in Wetter, un in Rihgen,

Mus ferfrihren, mus ferbrenne,

Fun ahn Mes, oif di andere zihgen.

15 Doiert das Ding noch lenger fott

Hem mir Has ve-Scholôm[4] dihn gresten Spott!

Drum main Harr, un Kinig!

Bitt ich unterthinig:

Lost schraiben a Dikriht,

20 Eh es watt zu spiht:

Doi nain lesen mir stellen:

Was fun haint ahn, di Menner habn wellen

Missen di Waiber glaich toin--

Wu nit, kriegt jide wi Vasthi ihr Loihn.

25 Ihr wat sehi, das Waiberregiment,

Hoit doi ball sain End.

---

1. Indien--Hôddu] Hoduh--cf. Esther I, 1.   2. die Mohren.
3. Versöhnung--for a discussion of the various meanings of
Kapporoh vid. Part II #286.   4. Gottbehüt!

אחשורוש•

טעהן! חרבונה טעהן!

דאַז זעלֶז, וואָן אַוו געטעהען.

אמַן טיקֶ' עס וואָלֶ' דער טטעלֶזע גלֶייך

רוזֶ פֿער קורֶיער, אֶין אֶייֶגען רֶייך

אֶויך הֶיער אֶין שושַן, רופֶע אַמַן עס אֶויז:

דאַס דער אַמַן נור מֶיֶט העֶרר אֶין הֶויז.

אֶין וֶילֶזע ערטטרעֶעקעֶע זֶיך מֶהֶכֶיג אֶויזֶנַאַהֶעע

פֿאַן דער בעֶטטֶזערֶין, בֶיז נֶור עדֶענֶ-דֶמַאֶע. —

יענֶט געה . . . .

חרבונה•

(נעהֶט אֶייֶנֶעע שֶריטֶטֶע פֿאָרֶוֶוערֶטס, קעהרֶט אֶבֶ'ער ווֶידֶער אֶום)

הֶמַאֶט! — דֶי פֿאַמַאֶֶט אֶיר עבֶעס אֶין;

ווֶאֶ וֶועהֶרֶט דעֶן — אַ אֶין?

ווֶין יֶוטֶט אַבֶעֶנֶעֶע דֶי קוהֶריֶהֶר,

אֶי הֶערֶט זֶו, אֶון פֿאַמֶלֶֶיֶגֶט אֶיר:

אֶייֶער רֶונֶז אֶיז זֶו געֶטֶיֶלֶֶזֶט,

אֶייֶער וֶואֶכֶנֶט אֶיז וֶואֶרֶען ערֶפֶֿילֶֶזֶט

ושתי העֶען אֶיר געֶטֶיקֶט לֶוֶין שֶטֶן,

אַבֶער מֶיהֶר זֶייֶט זֶו גֶוֶטֶען,

נַאֶך אַ געֶזֶוֶדֶער אֶמֶהֶן — אַ קֶצֶין

זֶו — ווֶאַז וֶועֶזֶֶזֶען אֶיר אֶונֶז מֶוֶהֶלֶין

דֶי יעֶהֶרֶלֶיֶך פֶֿערֶטֶטֶרֶייֶבֶעֶן

דֶיֶהֶן מֶהֶרֶעֶאַנֶען, ווֶי דֶיֶהֶן — רֶייֶבֶעֶן!

דֶי לֶייֶט, דֶי פֿעֶרֶגֶעֶהֶט גֶאַר געֶטֶווֶיֶנֶֶד.

Ahasveros.

Schehn! Harbona schehn!

Das soll, un mus geschehen.

Man schik' es oif der Stelle glaich

Rum per Kurier, in mainen Raich

5   Oich hier in Susan, rufe man es ois:

Das der Man nur ist Herr in Hois,

Main Wille erstrekke sich ohne Oisnahme

Fon der Bettlerin, bis zur Edeldame.-

Jezt geh...

Harbona.

(geht ainige Schritte forwerts, kehrt aber wider um)

10   Halt!--Doi falt mir ebes ain:

Wi wehrs den--a main?

Wail just abgenge di Kuhrihr,

Soi hert zu, un foligt mir:

Aier Rôges[1] is nu gstillt,

15   Aier Wunsch is woren erfillt

Vasthi hem mir geschikt zu'n Soton,[2]

Aber ihr sait zu guten,

Noch a gsunder Mahn--a Kozin[3]

Nu--Was wellen mir uns uhzin

20   Di Jehrlich ferstraichen

Dihn ahremen, wi den--raichen!

Di Zait, di fergeht gar gschwind.

1. Verdriesslichkeit.
2. Satan.
3. Herrscher.

מיהר העטט, קײַהן קינד, און קײַהן רינד,
עס איז אסור דאָך ניט טיהן
זוי ַהַמָהן, דו רוסן לו גיהן —
און חויב מיהר טוין ַא מלך זײַט,
וואָטט מיך דאָך עפֿטַערט לַַמֵג — דיא נייט!
און ווען מיהר מיך זייט גַאַנֹל פֿון דיא וויבער
פורש?
ווער זַאָֹֹל דען מיבער הונדערט יַהָר מאַוו — זײַן
מייער יורש — ?
העטטעט מייער הַאַרֹֹע הַאַך זו געדיבט
ווער היעבעט דען מייער טַאַהַטע, מויֹל דיא וועֹט
געברויבט?
און העטט, מייער טַאַהַטע מייער אטאָאע ניט געטוואַע,
וואָו ווערט דען מיהר העררקָואַע? —
און העטט דער ניט גהַהָט מַַך ַא זוהן
זינעט מיהר דען חַאָֹעווזיֹן מויפַֹֿן טרוהן?
מיהר זײַט אין דיא בעטטע מיַהֹר אונבטַריע,
מיהר קעננט נאָך הַאַבען דיא זכיה
לו קרידֹהגען ַאן בן זכר
דיהן מיהר ַאַֹֹו פֿין בחור,
אונטער דיא חופֿה וואַטט פֿיהרען
און דער זיך איט תירה און חכמה, וואַט ניהרען.
דרום הָאַרר קיניג, ביטט מיך!

אחשורוש.

טטײַֹן חרבונה! נור ניבֿטס פֿאַָן מיינעס שידיך.

Ihr hett, kahn Kind, un kahn Rind

Es is osur[1] doch nit schihn

Soi alahn, doi rum zu gihn---

Un oib ihr schoin a Melech[2] sait,

5 Watt aich doch efters lang---di Zait!

Un wen ihr aich sait ganz fun di Waiber

poresch[3]?

Wer soll den iber hundert Jahr amoil--sain

aier Joresch[4]?

Hettet aier Harrle aach soi gedoicht

Wer hiebet den aier Taate, oif di Welt

gebroicht?

10 Un hett, aier Taate aier Memme nit genumme,

Wu wert den ihr herkumme?---

Un hett der nit ghat aach a Suhn

Sizet ihr den allewail oif'n Truhn?

Ihr sait in di beste Johr unbschrie,

15 Ihr kennt noch haben di Sechijjoh[5]

Zu krihgen an Ben Sochor[6]

Dihn ihr als fain Bohur[7],

Unter di Huppoh[8] watt fihren

Un der sich mit Thoroh[9] un Hochmoh[10], watt zihren

20 Drum Harr Kinig, bitt ich!

Ahasveros.

Still Harbona! Nur nichts fon ainem Schiddich[11].

---

1. bei meiner Seele--The fundamental idea is that of a prohibition. 2. König. 3. trennt. 4. Erbe. 5. Glück.
6. Mannesstamm. 7. Jüngling. 8. Traghimmel. 9. geistliche
Gelehrsamkeit. 10. weltliche Bildung. 11. Verlobungsantrag
A colloquial form of normalized Hebrew Schidduch.

חרבונה∙

גאָטט בעהיהט איך פֿאָר שדכנות

דוי האָב איך נו פֿיען נאמנות

דאַז איך זעלֹזען, פֿון אַ בעסער גידידיך ווּיהגעןַ

העלֹפֿען, חם ושלום זעהן — בעטריגען.

דרום הערט מיר נו ווּאַז איך דוי זאַג

לאָסטט בעקאַמנט אַמעֹבען, דעֹרך טרואַוען טאָג

און מין זאַלֹ' מייער מדינות טרייבען:

זוי פֿיעֹן אַמדֹיך נאָר זען אויפֿגֹוֹטרייבען,

פֿון פֿוֹפֿגעהי, בי לואַמֹניג יאָהר

זאַלֹן אער דיהן מלך טטעעֹלֹזען פֿאָר

און ווּעֹלֹע מיך ווֹאַט געעאַמוֹלֹזען טעהן,'

און ווֹאַט האַבעֹן, מין מייער מאַג — חג,

דיא נעאַט מיהר דעֹרפֿוֹהן

און זעטֹלֹט זיא אויפֿ'ן טרוֹהןֹ.

אַיך געבט מאַוֹיֹע מאֹט

מויב מיהר מיך, ניט באַזֹן נמֹריט לֹאַבֹט;

דען, ווֹיך יעֹדע ווֹעֹן דיא ערטֹטע זיין

דיא קֹואַאָע ווֹעֹֹן, נאַך שושן ריין

זוי לֹאַאַפֿען זיא ווּאַן זיא קעֹננען,

נאָר פֿאָטֹט — ווּאָן זיא געֹנגע און טֹטעֹגעֹנעֹ.

מֹהֹע טֹפֿריֹנגֹט, מֹיבער טֹטֹאַהֹן און טֹטֹאַק

האַֹב נאַֹקֹיט פֿאָֹטֹט, מין אֹונטֹעֹרמֹאַק.

דיא מאֹנֹדֹעֹרע, מֹיז ערֹטֹט האַֹֹב מֹיינֹגֹטֹניֹהֹרֹט,

דעֹרֹלֹו אֹין גֹרעֹסֹטֹעֹן טֹטֹאַהֹט פֿריֹיֹהֹרֹט,

Harbona

Gott behiht mich for Schadchonus:[1]

Doi hob ich zu fiel Ne'emonus:[2]

Das ich sellet, fun a baar Gildilich wihgen,

Helfen, H.as ve--Scholôm[3] ahn--betriegen.

5　Drum hert mir zu was ich doi sag

Lost bekannt machen, dorch Trummel Schlag

Un in all' aier Medinôs:[4] schraiben:

Soi fiel Madlich nor sen oifzutraiben,

Fun fufzehi, bis zwanzig Jahr

10　Soll mer dihn Melech[5] stellen for

Un welche aich wat gefallen schehn,

Un wat haben, in aier Aagen--H.ên[6],

Di nemt ihr derfuhn

Un setzt si oif'n Truhn.

15　Iz gebt amoile acht

Oib ihr aich, nit ball narisch lacht:

Den, wail jede will di erste sain

Di kumme will, nach Susan rain

Soi laafen si waas si kenne,

20　Nor fott--wi si genge un stenne.

Ahne springt, iber Stahn un Stok

Halb nakit fott, in Unterrok.

Di andere, is erst halb aingschnihrt,

Derzu in gresten Staat frisihrt,

1. Ehestiftershonorar.
2. Vertrauenswürdigkeit.
3. Gott behüt!
4. Provinzen.
5. König.
6. Gunst.

וואָפֿפֿט און זיך גטוינער, אַ גרוי: טוהך,
און טיהסט פּאָטט, אין אַהן טאָפֿפֿעג, אין אַהן — טוהך.
אַהנג ווֹוינט אין דער מדינה ווייט
די האָט מורא, זי פֿערזויאט די נייט
די טֹיהסט, אין דער גטוינדיגקֹט
כֹין, אין קיטטעגֹע פֿון דער אַאַד.
האָט דערנֹ, אַ הערערעגווינקערֹע אֹיֹ
איט בלֹאעם, און גזרות רעות דרֹיֹ!
די פֿאָהרט איט ֹיהר פֹֿערד עקסטרע פֿאָטט,
און עטטאַאיהרטם ניט, וואַ: אַאַך קֹטט;
די אַאַדער, וואַאַד געביך לֹ פֿום אין זֹאַד,
און טרֹאַגט, ֹיהר בינדֹעֹ, אין דער האַאַד!
די אין גרֹיֹע אֹעננטעֹ געעֹגע,
קעעֹגע זיך געביך גֹאַר ניט — פֿאָטטברעעֹגע —
אֹיך בעעניֹד קֹאַהֹן ווֹיטער,
אַ אַ אין שושן די פֿולֹאַאַבֹערם, און די טנֹיֹדער;
די קרֹיהגען די העעֹד פֿאָֹֹ לֹ טוֹין
און דרֹיֹפֿאָֹעֹם — אַאַֹבֹערֹֹיֹן!
דֹאַם וואַֹטט זֹין אַ געעֹֹאַֹפֹֿער! אַ גטֹאַֹטֹער!
אַ געבֹֹיֹטער, אַ געטֹאַֹטֹער!
אַ געֹאַֹֹ! אַ געוויֹאַאַֹגֹ!
אַ געֹאַֹרֹאַֹ! אַ געטיֹאַאַֹגֹ!
דען געֹויהֹם, קֹואַֹא זֹי פֿיֹעֹ נקבות הער,
ווֹא דער זֹאַֹד, אַֹן פֹֿאָֹרט פֹֿון אֹעֹער,
כֹו — אֹונֹטֹער די אַֹאַֹֹֹיך אַֹֹֹֹֹע,
וואַֹט ֹיהֹר מנשכה, דֹאַֹ געֹ֓ינֹע אַ — כלה?

Wofft um sich gschwind, a grois Tuhch,

Un schihšt fott, in ahn Toffel, in ahn--Schuhch.

Ahne woint in der Medinoh[1] wait

Di hot Moro'[2], si fersoimt di Zait

5   Di schlihft, in der Gschwindigkat

Nain, in Kittele fun der Mad.

Hot derzu, a Herrenwinkerle oif

Mit Blumeš, un Gesêrôš ro'ôš[3] droif!

Di fahrt mit fihr Pferd ekštre Pošt,

10   Un estemihrtš nit, was aach košt:

Di ander, waad nebich zu Fuš in Sand,

Un tragt, ihr Bindele, in der Hand!

Di in groise Mentel genge,

Kenne sich nebich gar nit--fottbrenge--

15   Ich benaid kahn waiter,

Als in Susan di Puzmacherš, un di Schnaider:

Di krihgen di Hend foll zu toin

Un draifacheš--Macherloin!

Daš watt sain a Geplapper! A Gschnatter!

20   A Gebloiter, a Getatter!

A Gelaf! a Gewimmel!

A Gelarme! a Getimmel!

Den gewihš, kumme soi fiel Nekêvôš[4] her,

Wi der Sand, an Port fun Meer,

25   Nu--unter di Madlich alle,

Watt ihr Menaške?[5] doch gfinne--a Kalloh?[6]

---

1. Provinz. 2. Furcht. 3. Schlechte Dekrete. 4. Frauenzimmer. 5. kleiner Manasseh--The name of the firstborn son
of the biblical Joseph--vid. Genesis--41, 51; 46, 20.
6. Braut.

מון חיי'ס מַאך ניט, וואָ טהוטם?

העם איר אַ ביסעלע קהאט איט זי — וואוער וואָה!

אהשורוש.

וואָהאָמען! דו אימַבסט איר ווידער אוטה;

דיין פַּארטאָנַג געפַאלַט איר גוט.

גיה לאָז דיא דעקרעטע טרייבען,

איך וויל דיא ליט, איט ינאַגען איר פַארטרייבען.

(ביידע אויף פַּערשיעדענע זייטען אב.)

───────

(ח רב ו נ ה'ס וואָהנשטובע. ר ע ק אַ זיצט אונד קלויבט
לינזען. צט ו ל פ ע זיצט אם קלאַפיר, אייַ קליינעס קינד
הינטערם טיש, מעהרערע קינדער בעשעפטיגען זיך לערמענד
אים צימער.)

רעקאַ.

אער וואַס גאַר ניאאער ווע אער ואָל קאָלבען?

אער קאאט וואנבטריע — רוק;

אייַ קינד.

אעאאע! ס' מַרמַקסטמַקסטסערקסאָע האָט איך
געטאָבען,

רעקאַ.

וואַ: ס' קריהגט! וועַ איך איבערַ קום!

Un is's aach nit, was thuts?

Hem mir a bisle khat mit si--unser Uhz!

> Ahasveros.

Wohlan! Du machst mir wider Muth:

Dain Forschlag gefallt mir gut.

5 Gih las di Dekrete schraiben,

Ich will di Zait, mit Jagen mir fertraiben.

> (Baide oif ferschiedene Saiten ab.)

(Harbona's Wohnstube. Reka sizt und kloibt

Linsen. Ztulpe sizt am Klafir, ain klaines Kind

hinterm Tisch, mehrere Kinder bescheftigen sich lermend

im Zimmer.)

> Reka.

Mer waas gar nimmer was mer soll kochen?

Mer kummt unbschrie--rum:

> Ain Kind.

Nemme! s'Arakstakskserksle hot mich
>>>>>>>>>>>>> gstochen,

> Reka.

10 Sag: s'krihgt! Wen ich ibern kum!

צעטולפּע•

זען געװיס װידער מיבערן קלאָפֿיהר געװיסען, דיא גאָססענ־
יונגען!

דאָס טוין װידער אַ זײט גסטרונגע איז?

(זיא שפּיעלט אונד זיננט, אַללע קינדער שטיממען מיט איין)

אַנדרע װאָאַ האָפּטו דען גענען

דאַ דיך אַן יעאאערליך טאַטט?

ניקס אַן אַ לעבֿעֿלֿעֿ אַפּֿענ

און אַ פּאַאר ליפּֿעֿלֿיך װאַטט.

חרבונה

(קאָממט צור טהירע חעריין.)

דאַאַ איז יוי חזיר ניט דערלאַאבט?

אער אַאַהנגט דאָך חם ושלום אער פֿערטאַבט.

װאָריס זײט איהר גאָסעניוגגים ניט אין חדר?

װאָטט, מיך וַאַגם אײער רבי, בלי נדר!

(נו רעקאַ:)

דוי, אַמַך, טוב װעק דײן סחורה,

רעקאַ•

אױ ! הײנט איז זיא אװו־בחסד, דיא שררה,

איך — דער איז עבעם װידערואַטאַטיק!

קעננסט מעהן מאַהגעגבליק װאַטטען, מיך בין גלײך דוי פֿאַטטיק.

Zetulpe.

Sen gewiṡ wider ibern Klafihr gewiṡen, di Gaṡenjungis!

Daṡ schoin wider a Sait gṡprunge is?

(Si spielt und singt, alle Kinder stimmen mit ain)

Madle waas hoṡtu den geṡn

Das dich so jemmerlich taṡt?

5   Nikṡ as a Leffele Suppen

Un a paar Zipfelich Waṡt

Harbona

(kommt zur Thire herain.)

Das is joi.$\overset{H}{\underset{.}{}}$asir[1] nit derlaabt?

Mer mahnt doch $\overset{H}{\underset{.}{}}$as ve-Scholôm[2] mer fertabt.

Worim sait ihr Gaṡenjungiṡ nit in $\overset{H}{\underset{.}{}}$eder?[3]

10   Watt, ich sagṡ aier Rabbi,[4] beli Neder[5]

(Zu Reka:)

Doi, mach, tub wek dain Ṡehôroh,[6]

Reka

Oi! Haint is si un=be-$\overset{H}{\underset{.}{}}$eṡed,[7] di Scheroroh,[8]

Sich[9]--Der is ebeṡ widerwottik!

Kennṡt ahn Ahgenblik watten, ich bin glaich doi fattik.

---

1. Schwein--A strengthening of the negative--_vid_. Tendlau,
Prov. #105. 2. Gott behüh! 3. Schule. 4. Lehrer. 5. ohne
Gewahr!--The fundamental idea is: without being held res-
ponsible. 6. Waren. 7. ungnädig. 8. Gebieterin. 9. Sich]'ich.

חרבונה׃

גיה נו, ברענג מיר מֶהֹנ גטװינד דינט אונד פֿיהֹדער׳,
איך אום דו טרײבען מ פֿאַר דיקריהטער —

רעקאַ׃

נו — װאָס װאָטט מיהר דו װידער נײַן טטעלֶלֶן?
דֶאַס איט מין דער טוהֹן ניט טאװהֹנ — װעלֶלֶן!
דו הָעֶטטום, פֿאָר מיער אױן זֶינֹט מַאֹך קָאֹהן בריהטעﬞ,
מיהר קעננט מַאֹך בעֶטטיהֹן, מײַער טטיהֹטעﬞ —
מיהר װעלֶטוﬞ נֶעהר ניט זײַן,
און טיטט מַאֶֶלֶנﬞ דער פֿאַרֶﬞ אין טוהֹך נין.

חרבונה׃

טין רעבֶט, טעט מיך נָאָר רעבֶט לֶױבעﬞ;
׳ס װאָטט מיך דָאֹך מ רינֶﬞ פֿאָרﬞגטױבעﬞ.
דעﬞ מין דיהﬞ דיקריהֹט דו, אום מיך קיינֹטטעֶלֶﬞ:
דֶאַס מיהר פֿוﬞ הײַנֹט מ טין מעסֹט, װֶﬞ מיר מעֶננער װעﬞלֶﬞ.

רעקאַ׃

זעֶבֹט מיהר, דָאﬞ העﬞלֶﬞפֹט מיך פֿיﬞﬞ,
דו דערﬞן, פֿרױﬞﬞ מיר װײַבער — מ הױﬞלﬞטטיהﬞﬞ,
זַאﬞ מַאױﬞﬞ, מיﬞ הﬞﬞﬞ און מיﬞ קרﬞﬞ,
און װעﬞ מיך מַאﬞﬞ ניט װיﬞﬞﬞ, װﬞﬞﬞ קעננטטﬞ מיﬞﬞ דעﬞ טﬞﬞ?

Harbona.

Gib zu, breng mir ahns gschwind Dint und Fihder,

Ich muś doi schraiben a paar Dikrihter--

Reka.

Nu--Waś watt ihr doi wider nain stellen?

Daś mit in der Schuhl nit schmuhsen--sellen!

5 Doi hośtuś, for aier Moil ligt aach kahn Brihtle,

Ihr kennt aach bestihn, aier Stihtle--

Ihr welts nehr nit sain,

Un schitt alles der Frah in Schuhch nain.

Harbona.

Schoin recht, tet aich nor recht loiben:

'ś watt aich doch a Rigel forgschoiben.

Den in dihn Dikriht doi, muś ich nainstellen:

Daś ihr fun haint an toin meśt, was mir Menner wellen.

Reka.

Secht ihr, das helft aich fiel,

Doi dernoich, froigen mir Waiber--a Huzelstihl,

15 Sag amoil, main Haz un main Kroin,

Un wen ich doch nit will, waas kennstu mir den toin?

נו, — אין אנדערן? דוא טרייבט דעך נוועה?

חרבונה ּ

דער מלך וועל נעוואע א פראה.
דו האב מיך מיהן דיא עצה גיהבען,

רעקא ּ

ער זעל נעוואע אונזער צעטולפע לוהבען !

חרבונה ּ

א איין גיה איר מיט דער טארבטער נעהר,
מיט דער מיז אמך טאן עבבעס דער אעהר!
דיא מיז, וויא זיא מלוטעויין בעוונות מלוע זעננע —
וילט זיא דען אעהר ניין מין צאינה וראינה?
מין תהלים אדער מעמדות,
ווין דאז מוואטטאההענגעהאנגט, אוז דער אודע מיז !
מיך דארל' איך דעך דו גלייך מויפטעזילנלען,
טוט זיא שבת ניקז, וויא מיבער ביצער זיטלען.
דער שטן מיז אדענטזיך אין זיא דריננע,
מיך אעלבט נאר וויסטסען, וואוז זיא טיהגעס דרמן געפיננע?
ווֹאז טוט דו מלז פֿער שטות דריננע טטיהן?
וויא דער האוזען טוט לו דער גריהטען גיהן,
לבסוף דעננע זיא זיך נעוואע ;
וואטט ער א טאאטטע, אוז זיא א אעואע !
דו האסטו דאז מעשה, פֿון א ביז ת.

Nu--in andern? Du schraibst doch zwah?

       Harbona.

Der <u>Melech</u>[1] will nemme a Frah.

Doi hob ich ihn di <u>ʿÊzoh</u>[2] gihben,

       Reka.

Er soll nemme unser Zetulpe lihben!

       Harbona.

5   A main gih mir mit der Tochter nehr,

Mit der is aach schon ebbeṡ der Mehr!

Di is, wi si allewail <u>ba-ʿAwônôs</u>[3] alle senne--

Sicht si den mehr nain in <u>Zeʾɛnoh ve-Ruʾɛnoh</u>[4]

In <u>Thehilim</u>[5] oder <u>Maʿamodôṡ</u>,[6]

10 Wail das umstahnsgsagt, ois der Mude is!

Ich darf mich doch doi glaich oifschlizzen,

Tut si <u>Schabboṡ</u>[7] niks, wi iber Bicher sitzen.

Der <u>Šoton</u>[8] is odentlich in si drinne,

Ich mecht nor wiṡṡen, waas si Schihneṡ dran gfinne?

15 Was tut doi als for <u>Štuṡ</u>[9] drinne stihn?

Wi der Hansel tut zu der Grihtel gihn,

<u>Le-be-sôf</u>[10] denne si sich nemme:

Watt er a Taate, un si a Memme!

Doi hoṡtu das <u>Maʿaṡeh</u>[11] fun <u>A</u> (A) bis <u>Š</u> (Z)

---

1. König. 2. Rat. 3. Durch Missetaten. 4. Title of the popular Bible text of the Pentateuch used especially by women. 5. Psalmen. 6. Special prayers said by pious Jews after the morning service. 7. Sabbat. 8. Satan. 9. Dummheit. 10. Am Ende. 11. Erzählung.

טטיהט יוי כלומר אַ אוין עבעם דריננע פֿון אַ גרוהל,
פֿון אַ פֿאַטט מָדער אַ גרויַען האַרר;

רעקאַ•

גיה דוא זיאָפֿען! דו שבשן! דו נאַרר!
וואַז איז דיר דרֹאָהן קשה? פֿון דיינעטוויהגען
קעננעט זיא חטטה גריע לעפֿל אַמֹל קריהגען!
התך האָט מיהר געֹרעֹט זי אַ גוטען שידיך,
וואָריַם האָטטו דיהן ניט געטוין? זאַג אַ אוין? מיך ביטטיך!

חרבונה•

נֹאהֹן — נֹאהֹן — גֹאָטט בעהיֹט!
דיא טויֹגֹט פֿאָר קֹאָהֹן גֹוֹטען ייד.
דיא פֿיהרֹט זיך דֹאָך אוֹל — אַ פֹֿתֹלי=בפרה!
געהֹט האַֹלפֿאַֹמֹט טֹלֹינֹקֹע טֹֹאַנֹקֹע רֹוֹם וויא אַ שררה.
פֿרֹמֹה זֹיהבֹען אַֹמֹאַֹג:
וואַז פֹֿערֹריֹבֹלֹט זיא דֹען, דֹיֹהֹן לֹיֹעֹבֹען לֹאַנֹגֹען טֹאַֹג?
לֹאַֹסֹט זיא זֹיך פֹֿאַֹן אוֹנֹד דֹען אֹיֹעֹהֹר עבֹעֹם וועהרֹען?
נֹיֹקֹז אוֹל דֹער וועֹֹגֹט טוֹט זיא דֹאָך בֹענֹגֹעהֹרֹען! —
זיא קֹען אוֹן וואַֹֹאַז אוֹאֹטֹטֹאַֹהֹגֹגֹֹאֹגֹט — נֹיֹקֹם!
אֹיֹז זֹאַֹך זי אַ פֹֿעֹרֹטֹֹיֹטֹטֹע בשמים ביֹקֹם
וויא זֹיא אַֹלֹֹנֹעֹוֹויֹֹֹֹא זֹעֹנֹנֹע
— אַֹלֹֹעֹם ווֹֹן זֹיא ווֹֹֹסֹמֹען — נֹיֹֹקֹם טֹוֹט זֹיֹא קֹעֹננֹע!
אַֹלֹֹעֹם פֹֿאַֹנֹגֹט זֹֹיֹא זֹֹאַֹן, אֹוֹן לֹֹאַֹסֹט'ם גֹֹלֹייֹך לֹיֹגֹֹען.
הֹיֹינֹט טֹטֹעֹֹקֹט מֹיֹהֹר אֹין קֹֹאָֹפֿ אֹוֹהֹֹלֹֹען, — אֹֹאַֹֹריֹנֹג טֹֹיֹקֹֹען.

Stiht joi kelômar[1] a moil ebeś drinne fun a Gruhf,

Fun a Faśt oder a groisen Harr;

   Reka.

Gih du simpel! Du <u>Schabbaschon</u>[2] Du Narr!

Was is dir drahn <u>koschoh</u>?[3] Fun dainetwihgen

5 Kennet si <u>.hotscheh</u>[4] groie Zepf aach krihgen!

Hathach hot ihr geret soi a guten <u>Schiddich</u>[5]

Worim hośtu dihn nit getoin? Sag a moil? Ich bittich!

   Harbona.

Nahn--nahn--Gott behit!

10 Di toigt for kahn guten Jid.

Di fihrt sich doch oif--a Pfuzi--<u>Kapporoh</u>[6]

Geht allfott schlinke schlanke rum wi a <u>Scheroroh</u>[7].

Frah lihben saag:

Was ferricht si den, dihn lieben langen Tag?

Lośt si sich fon uns den mehr ebeś wehren?

15 Niks oif der Welt tut si doch begehren!--

Si ken un waas umstahnsgsagt--niks!

Is aach soi a ferschitte <u>Beśomim</u>[8] Bikś

Wi si allewaile senne--

Alleś will si wiśśen--nikś tut si kenne!

20 Alleś fangt si ahn, un lośst'ś glaich ligen.

Haint stekt ihr in Kopf Muhlen--moring Stiken.

---

1. das heisst. 2. Tölpel! 3. schwer. 4. wenigstens.
5. Verlobung. 6. Versöhnung--<u>Vid</u>. Part II #286.
7. Gebieterin. 8. Gewürze--"Eine verschüttete Gewürzbüchse.--
So nannte man einen Menschen, der in Kenntnis und Wissen-
schaft wohl hier und da Manches genascht, aber nirgends ein
Gründliches gelernt hat, so wie die verschüttete Gewürzbüchse
nur eine Mischung von unbestimmten Gerüchen, aber keine
wirkliche Gewürze enthält."--Tendlau, <u>Prov</u>. #153.

איצטלט האָט זיא אין אמַאג ניט זַאגטן!
טוט זיא אַוזפַאטעט דאַ! קלאַפיר גאָר טאָזַאגטן.
גריזזסט איר דיה קאַפאל פאַמַל איט אוודיזזנגע זיעדער.
לאָסט זיך דו הערהאַזיטען אַלזע איהדער.
און אסור קען זיא אַ רעבט בריפַזע טרייבען;
איז ניט אין טטאַער, אַ פאַמטטען שעה אויל מַהן פלַחַל
זו בלייבען.
טוטטעזט אַזזַפאַטעט רוט אין אַ זַאַג קלַאַר, אַ זיידענגען
טפעענזער —
דיא טויגט זו אַ פרַמַה?‏ — וויא מיך זו אַ זמַחַלטעענזער.

רעקאָ·

גיה איר וועג! זאָם איר נאָר רוה!
נַאַהן, אער זאָסט זיא גענויז אויפַוזמַאקסמען וויא אַ קוה?
דו האָסט רעבט! — וועננס דיר גויבַענגעט,
וואַמַז מיך, וויא זיא נעביך מיהר נַיט פַערברעענגעט; —
פַזן דריעעטווייהגען, קעננט זיא ניט טרייבען, און ניט
זיהסמען,
דאַ! איז טונסט, פַאָר מַזטערס אודע געוויהסמען.
אַזזעווייזַזע גיזדען דיא פַאַפפערזיך ניאַוער;
אין גיטס גטיקטע פרויעזיאַוער —
וואַ! מיז נַמַך דער איעהר?‏ זיא קאָטטען מַהן געזַד;
דערגזיהגעגען, זען זיא אענטגען פַאָר דער — וועזַט.
אויל דיא קעפַל טטעענזַזען זיא זיך דמַך אין גמַאן שושו,
מיבער דער טעאַבטער מיהר גמַנג, און מיהר — לשון?‏
אי! זיא דען ניט אַ פערטוויהן, וויא אַ פריגעסמין.

Itzt hot si in maag nit sagen!

Tut si allfott das Klafir nor schlagen.

Grillst mir dihn Kopf foll mit unsilige Lieder.

Lost sich doi herhalten alle Mihder.

5 Un osur[1] ken si a recht Brifle schraiben:

Is nit in Stand, a Fattel Scho'oh[2] oif ahn Plaz
                              zu blaiben.

Schusselt allfott rum in a lang Klad, a saidenen
                                Spenzer--

Di toigt zu a Frah?--wi ich zu a Saaltenzer.

       Reka.

Gih mir weg! Los mir nor Ruh!

10 Nahn, mer lost si gewis oifwaksen wi a Kuh?

Du host recht!--Wens dir noichgenget,

Waas ich, wi si nebich ihr Zait ferbrenget:--

Fun dainetwihgen, kennt si nit schraiben, un nit
                                lihsen,

Das is schunst, for Alters Mude gewihsen.

15 Allewaile gilden di Popperlich nimmer:

Izt gits gschikte Froiezimmer---

Was is noch der Mehr? Si kosten ahn Geld:

Dergihgen, sen si Menschen for der--Welt.

Oif di Kepf stellen si sich doch in ganz Susan,

20 Iber der Tochter ihr Gang, un ihr--Loschon[3]?

Is si den nit a Perschoihn, wi a Prinzessin.

1. bei meiner Seele. 2. Stunde. 3. Sprache.

װאו זיח היהנקאוואט, אעבט אער זיח — אויפֿפֿרעסטען.
דו טוסט נאָר אַלֿלֿפֿאַטט אן מיהר קיהרֿפֿען!
'ט טעט ניט, זיח טיעבעט מין אַ אויזֿלֿאַךֿ — טזֿיהֿפֿען.
זיח מארװעט יױ נעביך, דיהן גאָנֿגֿען טמאַג!
דיר מיג מָבער נאָר אַ דעֿרֿן מין אַין מַהג,
דאָם זיח לֿוֿטטיֿג מין, װון טוט זינֿגֿען,
אַ ביסֿלֿע טאַנֿלֿֿנֿען, אַ ביסֿלֿע טפֿרינֿגֿען.
זיח זאָלֿל געװיהם גאָר ניאאער לֿאַבֿען?
נוהן — װי לֿאָם גֿלֿיֿךֿ אַ פֿוטטרַמֿרֿהַֿן, מיבער מיהר אַמֿהֿר אַמֿלֿֿבֿען!

חרבונה.

װידער גאָטט ניג געׂרעט — איין אױל זאָלֿל לֿיהֿגֿען —
מָבער מיהר װאַטט טון איטאַנֿאַכֿט חרטה קריהגֿען.

רעקאָ.

שטות! דו װאַחֿטסט װידער מַלֿלֿעם.
טװייג נאָר טטיֿלֿל, טו מיר דיהן גֿאַּחַֿלֿֿלֿעם! —
האָסט װײטער קַמֿהֿן זֿמֿריֿג מיח דיַח?
דוי דרֿוֿ אֿמֿךֿ דיר נאָר קַמֿהֿן מיה.
העסט מַעֿךֿ פֿיעֿן גֿטייֿדֿער געטﬧין
דו העסט זיח אױזֿגֿיהֿבֿﬨﬥ טﬧין —
מָבער מיךֿ װﬧַחַﬦם, דﬧַﬦ ק﬩ﬗנסﬨﬧ מיבﬧﬦ דיﬧﬡ האַﬥ ניﬨ
בר﬩﬘ﬗﬣﬥ.
דﬧﬧ ק﬩ﬗ﬩ﬦﬥﬧﬨ מﬧהﬠ דיﬧﬡ אﬧﬡﬖﬧﬗﬦﬧﬦﬡﬗﬤ נﬧַﬦ מﬧﬢﬠﬠשּׁﬣﬠﬧﬗﬠﬤ! —

חרבונה.

נﬧ — מיﬠﬦ האָﬢﬦ חﬗﬔﬧ, מיﬠﬦ האָﬢﬦ זﬧ ﬠﬧﬤﬧﬧﬥﬧﬥﬧﬤ!

Wu si hihnkummt, mecht mer si--oiffressen.

Du tust nor allfott an ihr kihfen!

's tet noit, si tiebet in a Moisloch--schlihfen.

Si arwet joi nebich, dihn ganzen Tag!

5   Dir is ober nor a Dorn in Ahg,

Das si lustig is, un tut singe,

A bisle tanzen, a bisle springe.

Si soll gewihs gar nimmer lachen?

Nuhn--Soi los glaich a Futtrahl iber ihr machen!

      Harbona.

10   Wider Gott nig geret--main Moil soll lihgen--

Ober ihr watt schoin mitanant $\overset{H}{.}arotoh$[1] krihgen.

      Reka.

$\underline{Stus}$![2] Du saast wider alles.

Schwaig nor still, tu mir dihn Gfalles!--

Host waiter kahn Sorig wi di?

15   Doi drum mach dir nor kahn Mih.

Hest aach fiel gschaider getoin

Du hest si oisgihben schoin--

Ober ich waas, das kenstu iber dain Haz nit brenge.

Du kennst ahn di Oiszehrung nor ahnhenge!--

      Harbona.

20   Nu--Ich hob $\overset{H}{.}\underline{eschek}$[3], ich hob soi gewellt!

1. Reue. 2. Dummheit. 3. Lust.

'ס·זען זײ חכֿמֿע אחמֿדﬞיך נﬞון מיֿלך בשטטעלﬞט;

וואﬞ מﬞס איז דﬞו נאﬞ ך דﬞער מֿעהֿר?

'ס קוואﬞ ע מֿעהֿר בכֿבֿודﬞ=ע אחמֿדﬞיך הֿער;

לﬞאﬞ סט מﬞער זֿﬞ א מֿ אﬞ ך הֿיהֿן גﬞיהֿן דﬞער לﬞו.

רעקאﬞ·

דﬞﬞ ﬞ ין עצֿה ברﬞיך מֿיך! ביֿ סט מֿ אﬞ גﬞרﬞﬞﬞﬞ ﬞ ﬞ ﬞ זﬞ ער חכֿם, דﬞו!

דﬞﬞ ﬞ יהֿן איז ניֿ ט לﬞו העלﬞ פﬞ ען, אﬞ ונ ניֿ ט לﬞו רﬞוﬞﬞﬞﬞﬞ יֿ טען,

דﬞער טﬞ ﬞ ﬞ וﬞﬞ עﬞﬞﬞ נﬞ ט אﬞ נﬞ דﬞ טﬞ ﬞ ﬞﬞ ﬞ יך, וויֿ א מﬞ פﬞ אﬞ ﬞ ם מﬞﬞﬞ וﬞﬞ הֿגﬞ ע — בﬞﬞﬞ וﬞ ﬞ ﬞﬞ יﬞﬞﬞﬞﬞ דﬞ ען,

וואﬞ ﬞﬞﬞﬞ ﬞﬞ ﬞ ﬞ רﬞ ﬞ יגﬞ נﬞ יﬞﬞ ﬞﬞ ﬞ ט, דﬞ עﬞﬞﬞﬞﬞ ﬞﬞﬞﬞﬞ וﬞﬞﬞ ﬞ פﬞ ﬞ יﬞﬞﬞﬞ הﬞ זﬞﬞﬞﬞﬞ עﬞﬞﬞ ט מﬞﬞﬞﬞﬞ יﬞﬞ ﬞ ﬞﬞ ר;

לﬞﬞﬞﬞ אﬞ ﬞ ﬞﬞﬞ ﬞ סﬞﬞ דﬞﬞﬞﬞﬞ יﬞﬞﬞﬞﬞ א טﬞﬞﬞﬞﬞﬞﬞ ﬞﬞﬞﬞﬞ ﬞ אﬞﬞﬞﬞﬞ ﬞ ﬞ ﬞﬞﬞﬞﬞ ﬞﬞﬞ ﬞ בﬞﬞﬞﬞ ﬞﬞ ﬞ ﬞﬞﬞﬞ טﬞﬞﬞﬞ ﬞ ﬞﬞﬞﬞﬞﬞ עﬞﬞﬞﬞﬞ ﬞ ﬞ ﬞ ר רﬞﬞﬞﬞ ﬞﬞﬞ ﬞﬞ ﬞ וﬞﬞﬞﬞﬞﬞ ﬞﬞ ﬞ נ טﬞﬞ ﬞﬞ ﬞ ﬞ רﬞﬞﬞﬞﬞ ﬞﬞ ﬞ אﬞﬞﬞﬞﬞﬞ ﬞﬞﬞ ﬞ גﬞﬞﬞﬞﬞﬞ ﬞﬞ ﬞ ﬞ ﬞﬞﬞﬞ ﬞ ﬞﬞﬞﬞﬞﬞ ﬞ ﬞﬞﬞﬞﬞ ﬞ ﬞ ﬞ נ וויֿ ﬞﬞ ﬞﬞ ﬞ א מֿ אﬞ ﬞ זﬞﬞ ﬞ ﬞﬞﬞﬞ ﬞ ﬞﬞﬞ יֿ ﬞ בﬞﬞﬞﬞﬞﬞ ﬞﬞﬞ ﬞﬞﬞﬞ עﬞﬞﬞﬞﬞ ﬞﬞﬞ ר ביֿ ער.

שטעלﬞ ﬞ ﬞﬞﬞ ﬞ ן זֿ ﬞﬞ ﬞ ﬞﬞﬞﬞ ﬞﬞ ﬞ ﬞ ﬞﬞﬞﬞﬞﬞﬞ ﬞﬞﬞ א דﬞﬞﬞﬞﬞ וﬞﬞﬞ ﬞ דﬞ וﬞﬞﬞ ﬞ הֿיֿ הֿﬞﬞﬞﬞﬞﬞ ﬞ ﬞﬞﬞ ן פﬞ אﬞ ﬞﬞﬞﬞ ﬞﬞﬞﬞ ﬞﬞﬞ רﬞﬞﬞﬞﬞﬞﬞﬞﬞ ﬞﬞ כﬞﬞ ﬞ ל הֿקֿהֿל,

אﬞ ונ בﬞﬞﬞﬞﬞ ﬞ ﬞ יﬞﬞﬞﬞﬞﬞﬞ ﬞ ﬞ ﬞﬞﬞﬞﬞﬞ עﬞﬞﬞﬞ ﬞﬞ ט זﬞﬞ ﬞ ﬞ ﬞﬞ ﬞﬞﬞﬞ ﬞ ﬞ ﬞﬞﬞﬞ יﬞﬞﬞﬞﬞﬞﬞﬞﬞ א וויֿ א מֿ אﬞ ﬞ ﬞ שﬞﬞﬞﬞ ﬞ ﬞ טﬞﬞ ﬞﬞﬞﬞ ﬞﬞﬞ יֿ ﬞ קﬞﬞﬞﬞﬞﬞﬞﬞﬞ ﬞﬞﬞ ﬞ ﬞﬞﬞﬞﬞﬞﬞ עﬞﬞﬞﬞ ﬞﬞﬞ סﬞ חﬞ וﬞﬞﬞﬞﬞﬞﬞ ﬞﬞﬞ רﬞﬞﬞﬞﬞ ﬞﬞ ﬞ ﬞﬞﬞﬞﬞﬞ הֿ — פﬞ אﬞ ﬞ הֿﬞﬞﬞ ﬞ ן.

מﬞﬞﬞﬞ אﬞ ﬞ בﬞﬞﬞﬞﬞ ﬞ ﬞﬞﬞﬞ ﬞﬞﬞ ﬞ עﬞﬞﬞﬞﬞﬞ ר זﬞﬞﬞﬞﬞ ﬞﬞﬞ ﬞﬞ ﬞ ﬞﬞ י גﬞﬞﬞﬞﬞ ﬞﬞﬞﬞﬞ ﬞ עﬞﬞﬞﬞﬞﬞ ﬞﬞ ﬞ נﬞﬞﬞﬞ ﬞﬞﬞ גﬞﬞﬞﬞ ﬞﬞﬞ ﬞﬞﬞ ﬞﬞﬞ עﬞﬞﬞﬞ חﬞﬞﬞﬞ ﬞﬞ ﬞ זﬞﬞﬞﬞﬞﬞ ﬞﬞﬞ זﬞﬞﬞﬞ ﬞﬞﬞﬞﬞﬞﬞﬞﬞ ﬞﬞﬞﬞ יֿ ﬞ ן זﬞﬞ ﬞﬞﬞﬞﬞﬞﬞ ﬞﬞ ﬞﬞﬞﬞﬞﬞ ﬞﬞﬞﬞﬞ אﬞﬞﬞﬞﬞﬞﬞ ﬞﬞ כﬞﬞﬞﬞﬞ ﬞﬞﬞﬞﬞﬞﬞ ﬞ ﬞ ﬞﬞ ען;

איט דﬞﬞﬞ ﬞ יהֿﬞﬞﬞﬞ ﬞ ן טﬞﬞﬞﬞ ﬞﬞﬞ ﬞﬞﬞ ﬞﬞﬞ מﬞﬞﬞﬞ אﬞ ﬞﬞﬞ ﬞﬞﬞ וﬞﬞﬞﬞﬞ ﬞﬞﬞ ﬞ בﬞﬞﬞﬞﬞ ﬞﬞﬞﬞﬞﬞﬞﬞ עﬞﬞﬞﬞ ﬞﬞ ﬞﬞﬞﬞﬞ ﬞﬞ ﬞﬞ זﬞﬞﬞﬞﬞﬞﬞﬞﬞ ﬞﬞﬞﬞﬞﬞ ﬞﬞﬞﬞﬞﬞ ﬞﬞﬞﬞﬞﬞ ﬞ עﬞﬞﬞﬞﬞ ﬞﬞﬞ קﬞﬞﬞﬞﬞﬞﬞﬞ ﬞﬞﬞﬞﬞ ﬞﬞﬞﬞﬞﬞﬞﬞﬞ ﬞﬞﬞﬞﬞ ﬞﬞﬞﬞﬞﬞ ﬞ ען קﬞﬞﬞﬞ ﬞﬞﬞﬞﬞﬞﬞﬞﬞ ﬞﬞﬞﬞﬞﬞ ﬞﬞﬞﬞﬞ ﬞﬞﬞﬞﬞﬞﬞﬞﬞﬞﬞ ﬞﬞﬞﬞﬞ ﬞﬞﬞﬞﬞ ﬞﬞ ﬞ ﬞﬞﬞﬞﬞ ﬞﬞﬞﬞﬞﬞ ﬞﬞﬞﬞﬞﬞ ﬞﬞﬞﬞﬞ ן איֿ ר מﬞﬞﬞﬞ אﬞﬞﬞﬞﬞ ﬞﬞﬞﬞﬞﬞ זﬞﬞﬞﬞ ﬞﬞﬞﬞﬞﬞ ﬞﬞﬞﬞﬞﬞﬞ עﬞﬞﬞﬞﬞ ﬞﬞﬞ מﬞﬞﬞﬞ אﬞﬞﬞﬞﬞ ﬞﬞﬞﬞﬞﬞﬞﬞ עﬞﬞﬞﬞﬞ ﬞﬞﬞ ס אﬞ מﬞﬞﬞﬞ אﬞﬞﬞﬞﬞ ﬞﬞﬞﬞﬞﬞ ﬞﬞﬞ ﬞﬞﬞﬞﬞ ﬞﬞ לﬞﬞﬞﬞﬞ ﬞﬞﬞﬞﬞﬞﬞﬞ ﬞﬞﬞﬞﬞﬞﬞﬞﬞﬞ ﬞﬞﬞﬞﬞﬞﬞﬞ ﬞﬞﬞ ﬞﬞﬞﬞﬞ ﬞﬞﬞﬞﬞ ﬞﬞﬞ ﬞﬞﬞﬞﬞﬞﬞ ﬞﬞﬞﬞﬞﬞ עﬞﬞﬞﬞﬞﬞ ﬞﬞﬞﬞﬞ ﬞﬞ ﬞﬞﬞﬞﬞﬞﬞﬞ ﬞﬞﬞ ן!

איך זﬞﬞﬞﬞﬞ ﬞﬞ ﬞ עﬞﬞﬞﬞﬞ ﬞﬞﬞﬞﬞﬞﬞ ﬞﬞﬞ ﬞﬞ לﬞﬞﬞﬞﬞﬞ ﬞﬞﬞﬞ דﬞﬞﬞﬞﬞ וﬞﬞﬞ ﬞﬞ ﬞ וﬞﬞﬞﬞﬞ ﬞﬞﬞﬞﬞﬞﬞﬞﬞﬞ גﬞﬞﬞﬞﬞﬞﬞﬞﬞﬞﬞ ﬞﬞﬞﬞﬞﬞ ﬞﬞﬞﬞﬞ ﬞﬞ י דﬞﬞﬞﬞﬞﬞ וﬞﬞﬞ ﬞﬞﬞ גﬞﬞﬞﬞﬞ ﬞﬞﬞ ﬞﬞﬞﬞﬞﬞﬞﬞﬞﬞ ﬞﬞﬞﬞﬞ ﬞﬞﬞﬞﬞﬞﬞ ﬞ יﬞﬞﬞﬞﬞﬞﬞ ﬞﬞﬞﬞﬞ ﬞﬞﬞ ﬞ ﬞﬞﬞﬞﬞ ﬞﬞ ﬞﬞﬞﬞﬞﬞﬞﬞﬞ ﬞﬞ ﬞﬞﬞﬞ ﬞﬞﬞﬞﬞ ך פﬞ ﬞ ﬞﬞﬞﬞﬞﬞ עﬞﬞﬞﬞﬞﬞ רﬞﬞﬞﬞﬞﬞﬞﬞﬞ ﬞﬞﬞﬞ ﬞﬞﬞﬞﬞ קﬞﬞﬞﬞ ﬞﬞﬞﬞﬞﬞﬞﬞﬞ רﬞﬞﬞﬞﬞﬞﬞﬞ ﬞﬞﬞ וﬞﬞﬞﬞﬞﬞﬞ ﬞﬞﬞﬞﬞ ﬞﬞﬞﬞﬞ אﬞﬞﬞﬞﬞﬞﬞﬞ ﬞﬞﬞﬞﬞ ﬞﬞﬞﬞﬞ ﬞﬞ עﬞﬞﬞﬞﬞﬞ...!

דﬞﬞﬞﬞﬞ אﬞﬞﬞﬞﬞ ﬞﬞﬞﬞﬞﬞﬞﬞ רﬞﬞﬞﬞﬞﬞﬞﬞ ﬞﬞﬞ ל' זﬞﬞﬞﬞ ﬞﬞﬞﬞﬞﬞﬞﬞﬞ י מﬞﬞﬞﬞ אﬞﬞﬞﬞﬞ ﬞﬞﬞﬞﬞﬞ יﬞﬞﬞﬞﬞﬞﬞﬞﬞﬞ ﬞﬞﬞ ר מﬞﬞﬞﬞ אﬞ ﬞﬞﬞﬞﬞ ﬞﬞﬞﬞﬞﬞ טﬞﬞﬞﬞﬞ ﬞﬞﬞﬞﬞﬞﬞﬞﬞ רﬞﬞﬞﬞﬞﬞﬞﬞ ﬞﬞﬞ יﬞﬞﬞﬞﬞﬞﬞﬞﬞﬞ ﬞﬞﬞﬞﬞﬞ ﬞﬞﬞ ט נﬞﬞﬞﬞ ﬞﬞﬞﬞﬞﬞﬞﬞﬞ יﬞﬞﬞﬞﬞﬞﬞﬞﬞﬞ ﬞﬞﬞﬞﬞ ﬞﬞﬞﬞﬞ בﬞﬞﬞﬞﬞﬞﬞﬞ עﬞﬞﬞﬞﬞﬞ ﬞﬞﬞ ר קﬞﬞﬞﬞﬞ ﬞﬞﬞﬞﬞﬞﬞﬞﬞ וﬞﬞﬞﬞﬞﬞﬞ ﬞﬞﬞ וﬞﬞﬞﬞﬞﬞ ﬞﬞﬞﬞﬞ אﬞﬞﬞﬞﬞﬞﬞﬞ ﬞﬞﬞ ע.

(דﬞﬞﬞﬞﬞ יﬞﬞﬞﬞﬞﬞﬞﬞﬞ א מﬞﬞﬞﬞ אﬞﬞﬞﬞﬞ ﬞﬞﬞﬞﬞﬞﬞﬞﬞ גﬞﬞﬞﬞﬞﬞ ﬞﬞﬞ ר שﬞﬞﬞﬞﬞﬞ ﬞﬞﬞﬞﬞﬞﬞﬞ טﬞﬞﬞﬞﬞﬞ ﬞﬞﬞ עﬞﬞﬞﬞﬞﬞﬞ ﬞﬞﬞ קﬞﬞﬞﬞﬞﬞ ﬞﬞﬞﬞﬞ ט דﬞﬞﬞﬞﬞ עﬞﬞﬞﬞﬞﬞﬞﬞ ﬞﬞﬞ ן קﬞﬞﬞﬞﬞ ﬞﬞﬞﬞ אﬞﬞﬞﬞﬞﬞﬞﬞ ﬞﬞﬞ פﬞﬞﬞﬞﬞ ﬞﬞﬞ ﬞﬞﬞﬞﬞﬞﬞﬞﬞﬞﬞ פﬞﬞﬞﬞﬞﬞﬞ צﬞﬞﬞﬞﬞ ﬞﬞﬞﬞﬞﬞ וﬞﬞﬞﬞﬞﬞﬞ ﬞﬞﬞ ר קﬞﬞﬞﬞﬞﬞﬞ יﬞﬞﬞﬞﬞﬞﬞﬞﬞﬞ עﬞﬞﬞﬞﬞﬞﬞ ﬞﬞﬞ נﬞﬞﬞﬞﬞﬞﬞﬞ טﬞﬞﬞﬞﬞﬞﬞ הﬞﬞﬞﬞﬞ יﬞﬞﬞﬞﬞﬞﬞﬞﬞ רﬞﬞﬞﬞﬞﬞﬞﬞﬞ ﬞﬞﬞ ע הֿﬞﬞﬞﬞﬞﬞﬞﬞﬞﬞ עﬞﬞﬞﬞﬞ ﬞﬞﬞ רﬞﬞﬞﬞﬞﬞﬞﬞﬞﬞﬞﬞ ﬞﬞﬞ ﬞﬞﬞﬞﬞﬞﬞﬞﬞﬞﬞ ﬞﬞﬞﬞﬞﬞ ﬞﬞﬞﬞﬞﬞﬞ יﬞﬞﬞﬞﬞﬞﬞﬞﬞﬞ ﬞﬞﬞﬞﬞ יﬞﬞﬞﬞﬞﬞﬞﬞﬞﬞﬞﬞ ﬞﬞ ן,

וויֿ נﬞﬞﬞﬞﬞﬞ ﬞﬞﬞ קﬞﬞﬞﬞﬞﬞﬞ ﬞﬞﬞ ט צﬞﬞﬞﬞﬞﬞﬞﬞ עﬞﬞﬞﬞﬞﬞ ﬞﬞﬞ ע טﬞﬞﬞﬞﬞﬞﬞﬞ וﬞﬞﬞﬞﬞﬞﬞﬞ לﬞﬞﬞﬞﬞﬞﬞﬞﬞ פﬞﬞﬞﬞﬞﬞﬞ ﬞﬞﬞ ע, דﬞﬞﬞﬞﬞ יﬞﬞﬞﬞﬞﬞﬞﬞﬞﬞ ﬞﬞﬞ ע גﬞﬞﬞﬞﬞﬞﬞﬞﬞﬞ עﬞﬞﬞﬞﬞﬞﬞ ﬞﬞﬞ ט הֿﬞﬞﬞﬞﬞﬞﬞﬞﬞ יﬞﬞﬞﬞﬞﬞﬞﬞﬞﬞﬞ ﬞﬞ ן צﬞﬞﬞﬞﬞﬞ ﬞﬞﬞ ו איֿ הﬞﬞﬞﬞﬞﬞﬞﬞﬞﬞ ר, קﬞﬞﬞﬞﬞ ﬞﬞﬞﬞﬞ אﬞﬞﬞﬞﬞﬞﬞﬞ ﬞﬞﬞ וﬞﬞﬞﬞﬞﬞﬞﬞﬞ מﬞﬞﬞﬞﬞ ﬞﬞ ט

דﬞﬞﬞﬞﬞ אﬞﬞﬞﬞﬞﬞﬞﬞ ﬞﬞﬞ ן צﬞﬞﬞﬞﬞﬞﬞﬞﬞﬞ וﬞﬞﬞﬞﬞﬞﬞﬞﬞﬞﬞﬞ רﬞﬞﬞﬞﬞﬞﬞﬞ ﬞﬞﬞ יﬞﬞﬞﬞﬞﬞﬞﬞﬞﬞﬞﬞ קﬞﬞﬞﬞ.)

חרבונה·

דﬞﬞﬞﬞﬞ אﬞﬞﬞﬞﬞﬞﬞﬞ ﬞﬞﬞﬞﬞ ﬞﬞﬞﬞﬞﬞ וﬞﬞﬞﬞﬞﬞﬞ מﬞﬞﬞﬞﬞ אﬞ ﬞ איז מﬞﬞﬞﬞ אﬞﬞﬞﬞﬞﬞﬞﬞﬞ גﬞﬞﬞﬞﬞﬞ ﬞﬞﬞ טﬞﬞﬞﬞﬞﬞﬞ אﬞﬞﬞﬞﬞ ﬞﬞﬞﬞﬞﬞﬞﬞ וﬞﬞﬞﬞﬞﬞﬞﬞﬞ הﬞﬞﬞﬞﬞﬞﬞﬞﬞ ﬞﬞﬞﬞﬞﬞﬞﬞﬞﬞﬞﬞﬞ ﬞﬞﬞﬞﬞ ס! דﬞﬞﬞﬞﬞ אﬞﬞﬞﬞﬞﬞﬞﬞ ﬞﬞﬞﬞﬞﬞﬞﬞﬞ וﬞﬞﬞﬞﬞﬞﬞﬞﬞ איז מﬞﬞﬞﬞﬞ אﬞﬞﬞﬞﬞﬞﬞﬞﬞﬞ גﬞﬞﬞﬞﬞﬞﬞﬞﬞ ﬞﬞﬞ עﬞﬞﬞﬞﬞﬞﬞﬞﬞ בﬞﬞﬞﬞﬞﬞﬞﬞﬞﬞﬞﬞ אﬞﬞﬞﬞﬞﬞﬞﬞﬞﬞﬞ ﬞﬞﬞﬞﬞﬞﬞﬞ בﬞﬞﬞﬞﬞﬞﬞﬞﬞ ﬞﬞﬞ עﬞﬞﬞﬞﬞﬞﬞﬞﬞ ﬞﬞﬞ ن!

דﬞﬞﬞﬞﬞ אﬞﬞﬞﬞﬞﬞﬞﬞﬞﬞﬞﬞﬞﬞ איז מﬞﬞﬞﬞﬞ אﬞﬞﬞﬞﬞﬞﬞﬞﬞﬞﬞﬞﬞﬞﬞﬞ גﬞﬞﬞﬞﬞﬞﬞﬞﬞﬞ עﬞﬞﬞﬞﬞﬞﬞ=מﬞﬞﬞﬞﬞﬞﬞﬞﬞﬞﬞﬞﬞﬞﬞﬞﬞﬞﬞ שﬞﬞﬞﬞﬞﬞﬞﬞﬞﬞﬞﬞﬞﬞﬞﬞﬞﬞﬞﬞ חﬞﬞﬞﬞﬞﬞﬞﬞﬞﬞﬞﬞﬞﬞﬞﬞﬞﬞﬞﬞﬞ ﬞﬞﬞ יﬞﬞﬞﬞﬞﬞﬞﬞﬞﬞﬞﬞﬞﬞﬞﬞﬞﬞﬞﬞﬞﬞ ﬞﬞﬞ ת! דﬞﬞﬞﬞﬞ אﬞﬞﬞﬞﬞﬞﬞﬞﬞﬞﬞﬞﬞﬞﬞﬞ וﬞﬞﬞﬞﬞﬞﬞﬞﬞﬞﬞﬞ איז מﬞﬞﬞﬞﬞ אﬞﬞﬞﬞﬞﬞﬞﬞﬞﬞﬞﬞﬞﬞﬞﬞ גﬞﬞﬞﬞﬞﬞﬞﬞﬞﬞﬞﬞﬞﬞﬞﬞﬞﬞﬞﬞﬞ עﬞﬞﬞﬞﬞﬞﬞﬞﬞﬞﬞﬞﬞﬞﬞﬞﬞﬞﬞﬞﬞ לﬞﬞﬞﬞﬞﬞﬞﬞﬞﬞﬞﬞﬞﬞﬞﬞﬞﬞﬞﬞ אﬞﬞﬞﬞﬞﬞﬞﬞﬞﬞﬞﬞﬞﬞﬞﬞﬞﬞﬞﬞﬞﬞﬞﬞ פﬞﬞﬞﬞﬞﬞﬞﬞﬞﬞﬞﬞﬞﬞﬞﬞﬞﬞﬞﬞ פﬞﬞﬞﬞﬞﬞﬞﬞﬞﬞﬞﬞﬞﬞﬞﬞﬞﬞﬞﬞ עﬞﬞﬞﬞﬞﬞﬞﬞﬞﬞﬞﬞﬞﬞﬞﬞﬞﬞﬞﬞ ﬞﬞﬞ ن!

צעטולפע·

הֿﬞﬞﬞﬞﬞﬞ עﬞﬞﬞﬞﬞﬞ ﬞﬞﬞ רﬞﬞﬞﬞﬞﬞﬞﬞﬞﬞ עﬞﬞﬞﬞﬞ ﬞﬞﬞ ן זﬞﬞﬞﬞ ﬞﬞﬞﬞﬞﬞﬞﬞﬞ י לﬞﬞﬞﬞﬞﬞﬞﬞﬞﬞﬞ יﬞﬞﬞﬞﬞﬞﬞﬞﬞﬞﬞﬞ עﬞﬞﬞﬞﬞﬞﬞﬞﬞﬞﬞﬞﬞ בﬞﬞﬞﬞﬞﬞﬞﬞﬞﬞﬞﬞﬞ עﬞﬞﬞﬞﬞﬞﬞﬞﬞ אﬞﬞﬞﬞﬞﬞﬞﬞﬞﬞ וﬞﬞﬞﬞﬞﬞﬞﬞ טﬞﬞﬞﬞﬞﬞﬞﬞﬞﬞ טﬞﬞﬞﬞﬞﬞﬞﬞ עﬞﬞﬞﬞﬞﬞ ﬞﬞﬞﬞﬞﬞﬞ ר:

'ŝ sen joi alle Maadlich zun <u>Melech</u>[1] bestellt:

Waaŝ is doi noch der Mehr?

'ŝ kumme mehr <u>be-Chovod</u>=e[2] Maadlich her:

Loŝt mer si aach hihn gihn der zu.

      Reka.

5   Dain ʿÊzoh[3] broich ich! Biŝt a groiser H̩ochom[4], du!

Dihn is nit zu helfen, un nit zu roiten,

Der schwezt ondtlich, wi a Faŝ uhne--Boiden,

Worim nit, daas fihlet mir:

Loŝ di Tochter rum tragen wi a Zoiber[5] Bier.

10   Stell si doi hihn for <u>kol-ha-Kohol</u>[6],

Un biet si wi a Stikle <u>Ŝehôroh</u>[7]--fahl.

Ober soi genge alle sain Sachen:

Mit dihn Schambelle ken mer alleŝ machen!

Ich soll doi glaich ferkrumme...!

15   Darf si mir a Schritt niber kumme.

      (Di Magd stekt den Kopf zur Kichenthire herain,
      winkt Zetulpe, dise geht hin zu ihr, kommt
      dan zurik.)

      Harbona.

Dass is a Gschmuhŝ! Daas is a Gebabbel!

Daas is a Ge=<u>Maschhiŝ</u>[8]! Daas is a Gezappel!

      Zetulpe.

Heren Si liebe Mutter!

1. König.
2. ehrliche.
3. Rat.
4. Kluger.
5. Zoiber] soiber.
6. Die ganze Gemeinde.
7. Ware.
8. Zerstörung.

דיא לעפֿיהרעטטעג, אעלֿט אַ בֿיסֿלֿע — בֿאטטער.

רעקאַ•

דוי קֿאָך דיר! אוֹן זֿאָך דיר! אסור נֿיאַאַער ריהרען.
לֿאָם דיר פֿון אַהן נֿאַנֿדערן וֿאַטֿטֿטֿאַפֿֿט פֿיהרען.

חרבונה•

פֿרעה! אֿאָך נֿיט, דֿאַס מֿיך אֿיך אַן דיר קֿיהֿן —

רעקאַ•

וֿאַת? דו אֿתֿאַֿסֿט נֿאָך: בֿיער קֿום רֿויֿז, שלֿמֿיאֿל! —
אֿיך גֿיהֿסֿט דֿו אֿיר נֿיֿט גֿלֿיֿיֿך דֿוֿי נֿויֿז,
קֿרֿאַֿ מֿיך דיר דֿיֿן קֿלֿאָֿמֿלֿֿנֿערֿס גֿאַֿר רֿויֿז.
(זֿיֿא שֿיֿטֿטֿעֿט אֿֿלֿֿלֿֿע לֿיֿנֿזֿעֿן אֿיֿבֿער אֿיֿהֿן הֿער.)

חרבונה•

(שֿיֿטֿטֿעֿלֿט זֿיֿך, אֿוֿנֿד לֿוֿיֿפֿֿט פֿֿאָֿרֿט. אֿיֿם אֿבֿגֿעֿהֿן פֿֿאַֿר זֿיֿך:)
מֿוֿי וֿיֿה! בֿֿיֿא אֿיֿר קֿוֿאַֿאַֿט דֿֿאַֿֿ דֿיֿקֿרֿיֿהֿֿט,
מֿוֿאַֿטֿטֿֿאַֿהֿכֿסֿֿאַֿֿֿגֿֿﬞﬞﬞﬞﬞﬞﬞﬞﬞ, טֿוֿן לֿו טֿֿפֿֿיֿהֿֿט! —

רעקאַ• (וֿיֿיֿנֿֿט.)

אֿיֿך לֿֿאַֿמֿֿֿﬞﬞﬞﬞﬞﬞﬞﬞﬞﬞ עֿר פַֿֿֿﬞﬞﬞﬞﬞﬞﬞﬞטֿֿט, אֿוֿן לֿֿﬞﬞﬞﬞﬞﬞﬞﬞﬞﬞﬞאָֿסֿֿט אֿיֿך זֿﬞﬞﬞﬞﬞﬞﬞﬞיֿֿﬞﬞﬞﬞﬞﬞﬞﬞלֿֿֿֿֿﬞﬞﬞﬞﬞﬞﬞﬞﬞﬞﬞﬞﬞﬞﬞﬞﬞﬞﬞﬞﬞﬞﬞﬞﬞﬞﬞﬞﬞﬞﬞﬞﬞﬞﬞﬞﬞﬞﬞﬞﬞﬞﬞﬞﬞﬞﬞﬞﬞﬞﬞﬞﬞﬞﬞﬞ עֿֿֿﬞﬞﬞﬞﬞﬞﬞﬞﬞﬞﬞﬞﬞﬞﬞﬞﬞﬞﬞﬞﬞﬞﬞﬞﬞﬞﬞﬞﬞﬞﬞﬞﬞﬞﬞﬞﬞﬞﬞﬞﬞﬞנֿֿﬞﬞﬞﬞﬞﬞﬞﬞﬞﬞﬞﬞﬞﬞﬞﬞﬞﬞﬞﬞﬞﬞﬞﬞﬞﬞﬞﬞﬞﬞﬞﬞ,
גֿלֿיֿיֿך אֿעֿלֿט מֿיֿך מֿיֿהֿן דֿוֿי — אֿוֿיֿפֿֿטֿֿלֿֿֿﬞﬞﬞﬞﬞﬞﬞﬞﬞﬞﬞﬞﬞﬞﬞﬞﬞﬞﬞﬞﬞﬞﬞﬞﬞﬞﬞﬞﬞﬞﬞﬞﬞﬞﬞﬞﬞﬞﬞﬞﬞﬞﬞﬞﬞﬞﬞﬞﬞﬞﬞﬞﬞﬞﬞﬞﬞﬞﬞﬞﬞﬞﬞﬞﬞﬞﬞﬞﬞﬞﬞﬞﬞﬞﬞﬞﬞﬞﬞﬞﬞﬞﬞﬞﬞﬞ עֿֿֿﬞﬞﬞﬞﬞﬞﬞﬞﬞﬞﬞﬞﬞﬞﬞﬞﬞﬞﬞﬞﬞﬞﬞﬞﬞﬞﬞﬞﬞﬞﬞﬞﬞﬞﬞﬞﬞﬞﬞﬞﬞﬞﬞﬞנֿֿֿﬞﬞﬞﬞﬞﬞﬞﬞﬞﬞﬞﬞﬞﬞﬞﬞﬞﬞﬞﬞﬞﬞﬞﬞﬞﬞﬞﬞﬞﬞﬞﬞﬞﬞﬞﬞﬞﬞﬞﬞﬞﬞﬞﬞﬞﬞﬞﬞﬞﬞﬞﬞﬞﬞﬞﬞﬞﬞﬞﬞﬞﬞﬞﬞﬞﬞﬞﬞﬞﬞﬞﬞﬞﬞﬞﬞﬞﬞﬞﬞﬞﬞﬞﬞﬞﬞﬞﬞﬞﬞﬞﬞנֿﬞﬞ.
וֿֿֿֿֿֿֿﬞﬞﬞﬞﬞﬞﬞﬞﬞﬞﬞﬞﬞﬞﬞﬞﬞﬞﬞﬞﬞﬞﬞﬞﬞﬞﬞﬞﬞﬞﬞﬞﬞﬞﬞﬞﬞﬞﬞﬞﬞﬞﬞﬞﬞﬞﬞﬞﬞﬞﬞﬞﬞﬞﬞﬞﬞﬞﬞﬞﬞﬞﬞﬞﬞﬞﬞﬞﬞﬞﬞﬞﬞﬞﬞﬞﬞﬞﬞﬞﬞﬞﬞﬞﬞﬞﬞﬞﬞﬞﬞﬞ

Di Zefihrette, mecht a bisle--Butter.

>Reka.

Doi koch dir! Un soch dir! Osur[1] nimmer rihren.
Los dir fun ahn nandern Wattschaft fihren.

>Harbona.

Frah! Mach nit, das ich mich an dir kihl--

>Reka.

5 Waas? Du machst noch: Boier kum rois, Schlemihl[2]!--
Iz gihst du mir nit glaich doi nois,
Kraz ich dir dain Klozzers gar rois.

>(Si schittet alle Linsen iber ihn her.)

>Harbona.

(schittelt sich, und loift fort. Im abgehn for sich:)
Oi wih! Bai mir kummt daas Dikriht,
Umstahnsgsagt, schoin zu spiht!--

>Reka (waint.)

10 Iz laaft er fott, un lost mich sizzen,
Glaich mecht ich ihn doi--oifschlizzen.
Waas is ihn ober koschoh[3]
Dihn Boiswicht!--dihn Roscho[4]!
Er lost mich zapple--alah?
15 Waas ligt ihn den drahn:

---

1. bei meiner Seele.
2. Cf. Numbers: I, 6--Schelumiel the son of Zurishaddai; for
   connotation vid. Part II #481.
3. schwer.
4. Bösewicht.

מיך דאָל' איך וויא צו הוכד צו הוכד מַה רייסען!
אָבער וואָטט — מיך וויֹלֹין טוין תרבית וויסען.
מיך וויֹלֹ'ן וויסען, וואָאָס לֹו וויסען איז —
מיך זעו איך דוי הער געשיַ,
און טוב, מין יגון ואנחה אין נייט פֿערברענגען?
און זיך לֹו, וויא אַנדערע ווייבער שפֿאַזיהרען גענגען?
שפֿאַרר איך וויא זאָהן מַהנויטטוֹיטֹער אַלֹלֹפֿאָטט מיין?
נמהָן, מיך וויֹלֹ'ן קמהֹן זאָטטער נמַרר אווהר זיין.
להכעים! נאָם מיכֹ'ן אַלֹלֹעם ליגען, אַלֹלֹעם שטיהן —
און טוב צו ביסלֹע שפֿיעלֹען — גיהן.

צעטולפֿע.

נ'הבע אוטטער! טהון זיא זיך ניט זוי בעטריהבען.

סידי (קאָממט.)

אַדָאם רעקֹא קאָמֹפֿט זיא קמהֹן טיהנע גריהבען?

רעקֹא.

אָ וויה! דאַאַ זען הורג־זיך! דיא זען קֹאַהן!
דוי איז יוי גאַר ניקֹס דרמַהן!

סידי.

וואַאַ פֿאָלֹלֹט מיהר אויין? דאַאַ זען קֹאַהנגע?
(זיא העלט אייַנע אין דיא העַע.)

רעקֹא.

כו, וואַאַ קֹאַסֹט דען זוי מַהנגע?

2

Ich daf mich wi a Hund ah raiśen!

Ober watt--ich will'n schoin Tharbuś[1] waiśen.

Ich will'n waiśen, waaś zu waiśen is--

Ich sez mich doi her gewis,

5   Un tub, in <u>Jogôn ve-Anohoh</u>[2] mein Zait ferbrenge?

Un sich zu, wi andere Waiber spazihren genge?

Sparr mich wi ahn Ahnsittler allfott ain?

Nahn, ich will kahn sotter Narr mehr sain.

<u>Le-ha-Chʻiś</u>[3]! Loś ich'n alleś ligen, alleś śtihn--

10   Un tub a biśle śpielen--gihn.

        Zetulpe.

Lihbe Mutter! Thun Si sich nit soi betrihben.

      Śidi (kommt.)

Madam Reka kaaft Si kahn schihne Grihben?

      Reka.

O wih! Daas sen <u>Hôreg</u>=lich[4]! Di sen klahn!

Doi is joi gar nikś drahn!

      Śidi

15   Waas fallt Ihr ain? Daas sen klahne?

    (Si helt aine in di Hehe)

      Reka.

Nu, waas kost den soi ahne?

---

1. Sitten--<u>Vid</u>. p. 1, 1.4 of text.
2. Leid und Ächzen.
3. zum Trotz.
4. Zwerglein.

סידי.

דיא אַנדער׳ס ממוכנתה דוי דערזיעבען
האָט מיר וועלֿזען, זוי זאָלֿ איך זיהבען, מ באַגלֿנען
זיהבען.
איך האָב מיהר קאָהנע געלֿאָססען דרום.
מבער היינט מיז דראָנטטיק, איך ווילֿ אמאַלֿען דאַז איך
האַם קומ.
מיהר לאָם מיך מאַהנע אום מאַהן גראָטען.

קאָהר פֿאָן קינדערן.

יו! יו! אטאָאאט זיהבען!
קאַהל׳ אווז פֿון דער סידי גריהבען.

רעקאָ.

טווײגט טטוט מאָדער מיך טאָלֿג מיך אווֿל דיא גמאָטען.

(צו צעטולֿפֿע.)

דוי גרײוו מאָך! —
זאָלֿ איך דיר מאַך מאַהנע קאַמאָפֿען?
(זיא זולֿט גענסגריבען אויז.)

צעטולֿפֿע.

נײן זיא ווײסען דמאָך,
איך קאַן דאַריוֿ ניבט טאָמפֿען.
דיא פֿעטטטיגע זאַבלֿען, דעננען איר קײן גוט.
(דיא קינדער דרעננגען זיך לֿערמענד אום פֿידי העדום.)

Šidi

Di Madam Memuchanthoh[1] doi dernieben

Hot mir wellen, soi soll ich lihben, a Bazzen
                                    gihben.

Ich hob ihr kahne gelossen drum.

Ober haint is Donstik, ich will machen das ich
                                    ham kum.

5   Ihr los ich ahne um ahn Groschen.

        Kohr fon Kindern.

Joi! Joi! Memme lihben!

Kahf uns fun der Šidi Grihben.

        Reka.

Schwaigt stum oder ich schlag aich oif di Goschen.

        (zu Zetulpe.)

Doi groise Soch!--

10 Soll ich dir aach ahne kaafen?

        (Si sucht Gensgriben ois.)

        Zetulpe.

Nain Si waisen doch,

Ich kan daroif nicht schlafen.

Di fettige Sachen, denen mir kain Gut.

        (Di Kinder drengen sich lermend um Šidi[2] herum.)

1. cf. Esther I, 14.
2. Šidi] pidi.

רעקאָ•

וואַרט נאָהר, איך קום ווידער איבעריך איט דער
רוהט,
דו וואַרט אַין כפרה! העטט מיהר מַהנע איט
מַנאַנדער, טהאַטויי;
סידי ניהט נוי מיט דיא קוך, אַין אַמַאַד נַמַהַטוי. —

(סידי אַב.)

טעטס ברוּט אוּיז דער טוּבזַאַד הער דערלו,
פּרעסט דרוּיזען, לַמָּט איר נַמָר היננע רוה,
(זיא טהיילט בראַד אונטער דען קינדערן אוּיז, יעדעז
רוּיפט מיט איינעם שטוק אין דער האַנד הערום.)
קַמַהן מנוחה הַמָט אוּעהר מַהן נַמַהגעענבליק;
גַמַטט, וויא איז איר דער קַמַפֹ :וי טיק!
וואַמַ טטיהט אער אוּיז, מוואַבטריע איט דיא קינדער!

צעטולפע•

(שיבט דיא קינדער צו טהירע הינוּיז.)

אַמַ נוּי! מיך וווֹלֹ דו פַמָן וויטער
אַין מַריע גטוּיכד פרמַוויהרעַן
אַין וּמָלֹ זיך נור מַהנם פַמָן מיך — ריהרען?
(זיא זעצט זיך אַן דאַז קלאַפֿיר, שפילט אונד זינגט:)
"קינד וויֹלֹסט דו רוהיג טוֹלַמָטען,
"פַמָלֹגע איינען — ברויך:
"טעענדלע וויא איט מַפַמָטען
"אַיט . . . .

Reka.

Watt nohr, ich kum wider iberich mit der
                                        Ruht,

Doi watt main Kapporoh[1]! Hett ihr ahne mit
                                        ander, thaltsi.

Śidi giht nois in di Kuch, main Maad zahltSi.---

        (Śidi ab.)

Tetś Broit ois der Schublad her derzu,

5   Freśt droisen, lośt mir nor hinne Ruh,

        (Si thailt Brod unter den Kindern ois, jedes
        loift mit ainem Stuk in der Hand herum.)

Kahn Menuhoh[2] hot mehr ahn Nahgenblik:

Gott, wi is mir der Kopf soi tik!

Waas stiht mer ois, umbschrie mit di Kinder!

        Zetulpe.

        (Schibt di Kinder zu Thire hinois.)

Masch nois! Ich will doi fon Winter

10   Ain Arie gschwind prowihren

Iz soll sich nur ahnś fon aich--rihren?--

        (Si sezt sich an das Klafir, spilt und singt:)

„Kind willśt du ruhig schlafen,

„Folge mainen--Broich:

„Tendle wi mit Affen

15   „Mit...........

---

1. Versöhnung--Vid. Part II #286.
2. Ruhe.

דאָז קינד.

(הינטער דעם טישע פֿעללט שנעלל איין:)

איין בוך! — אָ ווײ איין בוך! איין בוך!

רעקאָ.

צעפֿירעטטע! גטווינד, 'ס קינד װיל אױפֿ'ן
היעפֿענזע —

צעפֿירעטטע.

גלײך. צעטולפֿע, זאָנג, זיא איר מ נװיהעפֿענזע;
אמאך זיא פֿאָטט, איך װיל מײנברעננע.

צעטולפֿע.

איך ווײס פֿיעל, ווּ זיא זעננע.

צעפֿירעטטע.

(צעשט דאז קינד פֿאָרט. איס פֿאָרטגעהן צו צעטולפֿע.)
דיא זינט אָבער מאך װיא מאהגעגמאהגעגעט;
דיא טטיהט ניט מול, װענס מול מיהר המהגעגמט.
אײנטווײהגעגן, זאָס זיא 'ס בלײבען —
(אַב.)

רעקאָ.

(רופֿט צום פֿענסטער הינויז:)
װאַטט איך װיל מײער גמסטענטטרמאַך טוין פֿער־
טרײבען.

Das Kind.

(hinter dem Tische fellt schnell ain:)

Main Boich!---O wih main Boich! Main Boich!

Reka.

Zefirette! Gschwind, 's Kind will oif'n
                              Hiefelle--

Zefirette.

Glaich. Zetulpe, lang Si mir a Zwihfelle:

Mach Si fott, ich will ainbrenne.

Zetulpe.

5   Ich wais fiel, wu si senne.

Zefirette

(zešt das Kind fort. Im fortgehn zu Zetulpe.)

Di sizt ober aach wi ahngenahgelt:

Di stiht nit oif, wenš oif ihr hahgelt.

Maintwihgen, loš Si 's blaiben---

(ab.)

Reka

(ruft zum Fenster hinois:)

Watt ich will aier Gaššenstraach schoin fer=
                              traiben.

(צו צעטולפּע•)

און דו, קלײַפּער נוֹבער ווײַטער,
מֶהר זֶעבער אוֹן מנחה — מיֹ גטײַדער!

צעטולפּע•

טָאן רעבֿט! מיך ווער גלײך דֶא פֿאַטטיק זײַ,

רעקאַ•

יוֹ דערמיך טוֹופּפֿערטם דיא אַמֶאוֹזעֶן ווֹדער נֹין —

דרייא ווייבער•

(רופֿעֶן צור טהירע הערײַן:)

ר ע ק אַ! גיהט זֹא מַ ביזֶע איט דו רוֹם?

רעקאַ•

יוֹ — מיך בֿין פֿרוֹי, דַאס מיך מַ ביזֶע פֿון איר קום.
(אב.)

צעטולפּע•

(שׁפּרינגט אויף פֿאַם קלאַפֿיר.)

אין האָט דֶעך מֶאַמֶלֶע דֶא גֶעקיהל זֶהַן ענג;
בֵּיח דער אֹיזֶט אַלֶֹֹעם אֹואגֶעוֶֶענגד.
דַאַ זֶענגד אַבֶֿער עטוֶֶאַ פֿאַססעֶן;
ווָארוֹם ווֹל זֹא אֹיך נֹיט מֶעך הֹיהן לָאססעֶן?
נו יֶא! דַאַ ווֹעהר טֶענגֶֶער ווֹֹ טֶעהֶן,
וֶֶען אֹיך נֹיט הֹיהן זֶעלֹֹט גֶעהֶן.
אַבֿער דֹיא ווָארֶן מֹין מֹיהר זֶֹיהבֶֿעֶן נֹיט פֶֿעטטיק;

(zu Zetulpe.)

Un du, klimper noicher waiter,

Ohr lieber iz Min.oh^{h} ^{1} -- is gschaider!

Zetulpe.

Schon recht! Ich wer glaich da fattik sain,

Reka.

Joi dernoich schlupperts di Mamsel wider nain--

Drai Waiber.

(rufen zur Thire herain:)

5   Reka! Giht Si a bisle mit doi rum?

Reka.

Joi--Ich bin froi, das ich a bisle fun mir kum.

(ab.)

Zetulpe.

(springt oif fom Klafir.)

Iz hat doch amale das Gekihf ahn End:

Bai der ist alles umgewend.

Das send aber etwas Possen:

10   Worum will si mich nit aach hihn lossen?

Nu ja! Das wehr schenner wi schehn,

Wen ich nit hihn sellt gehn.

Ober di warrn in ihr Lihben nit fettik:

1. Nachnittagsgottesdienst.

דיא זענד עטװאס װיטטערװעטטיק!
װאַרום ער װילל נין — װילל זיא גרייד יו —
װען ער זאַלבסט גרײהן — זאַלבט זיא בליא —
איך האַם זיא אַבער אַבגאַשפּאלען, װן טװייג שטילל.
דערנאַך טוה איך דאַך ערטט װאַז איך װילל.
אמאַל האָט געװיהם אַללע טאמאַך דאַז גליק?
נאַהן — נין — קאַהן געהע גיך האַללטען איך נאריק
מיך אױם געהר אַנטטעבילען איט דער אַאַלבט,
דאַם זיא דיהן װעבלטער פײן זאַלבט —
פונקטע מום װ פיער
זאַלל ער פאַאפערן אַן דיה טהיר. —

(נאַך איינער קורצען פױזע.)

װען מיך היינט נאַבלט װר העטט
דען אַװאַגאַנג איט אַעגטעען אין בעטט,(*)
קעננטיב'ס, אײן ביםאַע דמאַריך געהן;
דען געװיהם טוטם די שטעהן,
װיא ער אער זיך ביא דיא הױלט זאַלל אױפֿפֿיהרען
דמ קעננט איך אַללעם היינט נאַבלט פאַרמאָװיהרען.
אַבער װאַ העבלמט! װאַ זאַלל מיך טױן?
דיא ביבלױטיהקען זענד אַללע לו טױן,
מיך װילל נור דאַהער געהן אין דער העללוױג,
אונד איר אַבלערנען װ פאַאר טענגע שטענלאַיג.

(זיא געהעט אַן דען שפיגעל.)

האַרליך צעטטולפע — דו ברױםבט ניכטם װיטער.

(*) קינגגעט װערק איבער דען אַװאַגאַנג איט אַעגטעען.

Di send etwaś witterwettik!

Waaś er will nain---will si graid joi---

Wen er saacht grihn---saacht si bloi---

Ich laś si aber abzapple, un schwaig still.

5 Dernach tuh ich doch erśt was ich will.

Man hat gewihś alle Taach das Glik?

Nahn--nain--Kahn zehe Gail halten mich zurik.

Ich muś nehr anśtellen mit der Maacht,

Daś si'ś dihn Wechter fain saacht--

10 Punkte um a fier

Soll er pompern an dihn Thir.--

      (Nach ainer kurzen Poise)

Wen ich haint Nacht nur hett

Den Umgang mit Menschen in Bett. *)

Kenntich'ś, ain biśle dorich gehn:

15 Den gewihś tuts doi stehn,

Wi mer sich bai di Hoiche soll oiffihren

Das kennt ich alleś haint Nacht prowihren.

Aber was helfśt! Was soll ich toin?

Di Biblitihken send alle zu schoin:

20 Ich will nur daher gehn in der Helling,

Und mir ablernen a paar schene Stelling.

      (Si gehet an den Śpigel.)

Herrliche Zetulpe--Du broichst Nichtś waiter.

---

* Knigges Werk über den Umgang mit Menschen.-Adolf von
Knigge, 1752-1796. Über den Umgang mit Menschen, 1788.

און ווען ערטט ד׳ערכו קאַמאַען אײן קֿוייַדר.
אײן וייסליק, אײן טפֿילֿנֿלֿען;
און מֿאַן דיא הֿענד, אײן פֿינגֿערֿליֿך בֿלֿוֿלֿען.
דער וֿאָֿרֿט דֿאַז אֿוֿנד, און דיא מֿוֿלֿבֿען מֿוֿפֿרֿיֿסֿעֿן,
ווען איך וֿאָֿר חֿאַֿל אֿײֿן חֿפֿצֿית וֿיֿיֿסֿען.
און ווען ער אֿײן גֿזֿלֿט ערֿטֿט טֿיֿט —
פֿאַהֿרֿט ער גֿאָֿר לֿוֿיֿז דער הֿוֿיֿט !
מֿיֿבֿער אֿײן גֿטֿיֿקֿלֿיֿבֿקֿײֿט, דֿוֿי וֿוֿעֿרֿד ער קֿלֿאָֿנֿלֿען ;
דֿוֿי אֿיֿט וֿוֿלֿזֿ אֿיֿבֿלֿ׳ן דֿיֿא לֿיֿט פֿ׳ערֿקֿאָֿנֿלֿען.
מֿיֿך וֿוֿיֿסֿ׳ן אֿײֿן אֿוֿהֿלֿען, אֿײֿן טֿטֿיֿקֿקֿען,
טֿפֿיֿעֿן אֿיֿטֿ׳ן אֿפֿאָֿרֿיֿאֿט אֿוֿן אֿ בֿיֿזֿלֿע לֿוֿיֿקֿקֿען.
זֿעֿלֿ אֿיֿך אֿאַֿך הֿיֿהֿן אֿן קֿלֿאַֿפֿיֿהֿר,
אֿוֿנֿד טֿפֿיֿעֿן אֿוֿיֿזֿ׳ן פֿוֿאֿפֿעֿרֿנֿיֿקֿקֿעֿן, דֿיֿא אֿוֿבֿעֿרֿטֿהֿיֿר.
מֿוֿיֿפֿ׳ן קֿאָֿפֿ׳ לֿ וֿוֿעֿרֿד ער זֿיֿך דֿרֿיֿעֿבֿער טֿטֿעֿלֿ׳זֿעֿן ;
און קֿאָֿהֿן אֿ נֿדֿעֿרֿע אֿעֿהֿר הֿהֿ אֿזֿעֿהֿי וֿוֿעֿלֿזֿ׳ען.
דֿיֿא וֿוֿעֿרֿען דֿיֿא טֿיֿיֿעֿבֿעֿלֿ׳יֿך,
טֿפֿיֿלֿזֿ׳יֿג, וֿוֿיֿא דֿיֿא גֿיֿעֿבֿעֿלֿ׳יֿך,
דער לֿו פֿ׳ערֿנֿיֿהֿגֿען,
אֿוֿנֿד בֿ חֿ אַֿלֿ׳ עֿטֿוֿוֿאַ אֿ נֿדֿעֿרֿטֿט קֿרֿיֿהֿגֿ׳עֿן !

(אֿײן עֿקֿסֿטֿאַֿסֿ׳ע.)

אַֿבֿעֿר הֿעֿטֿט נֿעֿר דֿעֿן פֿ חֿ אַֿמֿהֿסֿמֿעֿר ;
טֿעֿט נֿעֿר רֿעֿלֿ׳ט טֿיֿהֿבֿען.
אֿחֿשֿ ורֿוֿש דֿער גֿר אָֿסֿעֿר !
וֿוֿעֿרֿד אֿיֿך דֿעֿרֿהֿיֿהֿבֿ׳ען.
יֿ חֿ אֿיֿך, אֿיֿך אֿ וֿס ער נֿע אַ אַ נֿע,
אֿיֿך קֿ אָֿפֿ אֿין טֿרֿיֿוֿוֿ אָֿפֿ׳ה !

Un wen eršt derzu kommen main Klaidr.

Main Waišzaich, main Spizzen:

Un an di Hend, main Fingerlich blizzen.

Der wart das Mund, un di Oichen oifraišen,

5   Wen ich war all main $\overset{H}{.}$afozôs[1] waišen.

Un wen er main Gsicht eršt schoit---

Fahrt er gar ois der Hoit!

Iber main Gschiklichkait, doi werd er klozzen:

Doi mit will ich'n di Zait ferkozzen.

10   Ich waiš'n main Muhlen, main Stikken.

Spiel mit'n Mariasch un a bisle Zwikken.

Sez mich aach hihn an Klafihr,

Und spiel oiš'n Pumpernikkel, di Uberthir.

Oif'n Kopf werd er sich drieber ste-len:

15   Un kahn andere mehr ahnsehi wellen.

Di weren di Schnieblich,

Spizzig, wi di Giebelich,

Der zu ferzihgen,

Und ball etwas anderst krihgen!

(in Ekštaše.)

20   Aber hett ner den Pohšer:

Tet ner recht tihben.

Ahasveros der Grošer!

Werd mich derhihben.

Ja mich, mich muš er nemme,

25   Ich kom in Triumfh!

---

1. Sachen.

פֿרייא דיך טאַמאַטע, פֿרייא דיך אטאאאע!
מייער צעטולפֿע מיזט — טרואפֿן׳.

(אֲב.)

צוויטער אבשניטט.

מרדכי׳ס וואָהנונג.

(א ס ת ר זיצט אונד נעהעט. ר׳ מ ר ד כ י שטעהעט
אם פֿענזטער אונד לערנט. איין מעדכען פֿאַן צעהען
ביז צוועלף יאהר זיצט אונד שניידעט צווייבעל אין
איינעם טאָפֿף היניין.)

מרדכי.

וואָס טוט אער טון וידער מויזקלייגנ֗ע?
די קלאָהנם פֿריג אַ אויל די מונטען דאַ יינגֿע.
(דאַז מעדכען לויפֿט אן דאַז פֿענזטער, רופֿט הינונטער, דאַן צו
ר׳ מ ר ד כ י.)

מעדכען.

יי דמאַז האָטט מאַך ניט געהערט.
וואַטט מיך זיך זעלבסט, וואַז אער בעגעהרט.

מרדכי.

בֿ֗ייב נאָר דו, עם וואַררען קואָע זיין

Frai dich Taate, frai dich Memme!

Aier Zetulpe ist---Trumpf.

>(ab.)

>Zweiter Abschnitt

Mardachai's Wohnung.

(Esther sizt und nehet. $\underline{R}$'[1] Mardachei stehet

am Fenster und lernt. Ain Medchen fon zehen

bis zwelf Jahr sizt und schnaidet Zwaibel in

ainen Topf hinain.)

>Mardachai

Was tut mer schoin wider oisklingle?

Du Klahns froig a moil doi unten das Jingle.

(Das Medchen loift an das Fenster, ruft hinunter, dan zu

$\underline{R}$'[1] Mardachai.)

>Medchen.

5 Joi daas hott aach nit gehert.

Watt ich sich selbst, was mer begehrt.

>Mardachai.

Blaib nor doi, es warren kumme sain

---

1. An abbreviation for Reb (Herr) from Hebrew <u>Rabbi</u>--found
throughout the text-henceforth to be underlined but not
placed in a footnote.

25

פֿרעאָדע קואידיזאַנדען רייַ,

איט גאַנגעןטפֿרינגערליך מאָדער דאָקקען
אין דער בלוינ גלאָקקען?
וואַז טוט אער איט דיהן הבל הבלים
מאַלֹע נמאַגענבֿיק מאַהן אַנדערער חלום!
אום אער מאַלֹע שטות דען גוקקען?
דעננע דיך דיין באַזאַר קלײַנערליך מאַך טיין יוקקען?

(ער זיהעט זיך אום.)

איז כה אחיה! דאָך געלאָפֿפֿען פּאָטט,
דוּ העטטיר׳ס טטיהן טוין דאָט
איט׳ן אין געלאַררעאַע.
גאָטט זאָלֹ זיך דערבאַרעאַע!
וואַהַז איז דחאַז מאַלֹעוויין פֿאָר אַ דור.
גיהט זי ניקם אין קאַמפֿל רום נמָר
וויא שטזת, און נמאַרענטסמפּאָטסטען,
און וויא אער איז רעכֿט אויגעלאָמַסטען.
ניקם אַז וואוילֹוטט, און פֿאַרגניגען,
פֿון מאַהן וואַטטטסהויא אין אַנדערן ליהגען!
פֿרעטסטען, זיפֿטען, פֿונגען, טפֿיהלֹען,
מין ליהבען האַרר גאָטט, דיא טהיג מאַבטטיהלֹען.
ניקם וויא לֹוטער חוצפה - ליהדלֹיך זינגע
כל עולם מין גזיבֿט נין טפֿרינגע.
אַ ספר מהכלֹוזעהי מיז מאַהן עבירה!
מאַלֹע נמאַהגענבֿיק מאַהן אַנדערע גזירה;
דוי מיז אַ קמַרווע, דוי אַ קרעכלֹאָע,
דוי אַ קואידיע, דוי אַ טעעלֹאָע.

Fremde Kumidianden rain,

Mit Gagelspringerlich oder Dokken

In der bloie Glokken?

Waas tut mer mit dihn <u>Havel Havolim</u>[1]

5 Alle Nagenblik ahn anderer <u>H̱.alôm</u>[2]!

Muš mer alle <u>Štuš</u>[3] den gukken?

Denne dich dain baar Kraizerlich aach schoin jukken?

    (Er sihet sich um.)

Is <u>Kôh ehjeh</u>[4]! doch geloffen fott,

Doi hettir'š stihn schoin dot

10 Mit'n in Gelarreme.

Gott soll sich derbareme!

Waas is daas allewail for a <u>Dôr</u>[5].

Giht si nikš in Kopf rum nor

Wi <u>Štuš</u>[3], un Narrenšpoššen,

15 Un wi mer is recht oisgeloššen.

Nikš as Woillušt, un Fergnigen,

Fun ahn Wattšhois in andern zihgen!

Freššen, soifen, puzzen, spihlen,

In lihben Harr Gott, di Thig abstihlen.

20 Nikš wi loiter <u>H̱.uzpoh=lihdlich</u>[6] singe

<u>Kol'Ôlom</u>[7] in Gsicht nain springe.

A <u>Šêfer</u>[8] ahnzusehi is ahn'<u>Avêroh</u>[9]!

Alle Nahgenblik ahn andere <u>Gesêroh</u>[10]!

Doi is a Karwe, doi a Krenzle,

25 Doi a Kumidie, doi a Tenzie.

1. Vanites Vanitatum. 2. Traum. 3. Dummheit. 4. So
möge ich leben. 5. Generation. 6. freche Lieder.
7. Jedermann. 8. Buch. 9. Sünde. 10. Dekret.

פֿאָר איבעראיוטה וויסטען זיא גאָר גיאאער וואַאם זיא
וועלֿלען?
ניהרען זיך וויא דיא מאָפֿפֿען,
אמאָהנע זיא העט זיך מאָלֿמען דערטהמפֿפֿען.
(דאַז מערכען אונד ה ת ך שטירצען צור טהירע העריין.)

מערכען•

נו העטט מיהרם געהערט וואַאז זיא וועלֿלען?
אאָריינג אין מאָלֿמער פֿריה . . . . . .

אסתר• (איינפֿאַללֿעלֿער)

נוהן, — איז א היההנגיהבעטטם היע?

מערכען•

נוהן עבעס מאַדערטט. דיא העדט :
דער מלך ווילֿל, דער בעגעהרט,
דאַם אאָריינג אין מאָלֿמער פֿריה,
זיי פֿיעל אמאַמֿדֿיך זען אין שישן היע
אין טלֿאָם כול' קוֹאאע זעלֿלֿען,
און זעלֿלֿען זיך פֿאָר מיהן טטעלֿלֿען.
מאָלֿלע פֿון פֿופֿלֿעהי ביז לואַהנליג יֿהֿר
אום אער מיהן טטעלֿלֿען פֿאָר,
און איז מֿהֿנע דרוכטער דיא גמֿאָלֿט 'ל,
זיי ווֿלֿל ער זיא גלֿייך פֿאָר אַ פֿראַה בעהאַלֿטען.

אסתר•

אוי! ווער דוי דאַאַ: מזל האָט!

For Ibermuth wissen si gar nimmer waas si
wellen?

Zihren sich wi di Affen,

Mahne si hem sich allahn derschaffen.

    (Das Medchen und Hathach stirzen zur Thire herain.)

        Medchen.

Nu hett ihrs gehert waas si wellen?

5 Moring in aller Frih...........

        Esther. (ainfallend)

Nuhn,--Is a Hihngihbets hie?

        Medchen

Nahn ebes anderst. Doi hert:

Der <u>Melech</u>[1] will, der begehrt,

Das moring in aller Frih,

10 Soi fiel Maadlich sen in Susan hie

In Schlos noif kumme sellen,

Un sellen sich for ihn stellen.

Alle fun fufzehibis zwangig Johr

Mus mer ihn stellen for,

15 Un is ahne drunter di gfallt'n,

Soi will er si glaich for a Frah behalten.

        Esther.

Oi! Wer doi daas <u>Massol</u>[2] hot!

---

1. König.
2. Glück.

מרדכי.

נו, 'ס קומט מעלעם פֿון גאָטט.

מבֿער מיך גלאַמב מאַן דער גטיכטע קמהן וואָטט,

גיה נו, דרעהן מיז ניקט,

דמאַז מיז מ חלום, דמאַז מיז מ גיקם!

מעדכען.

— זעבֿט בייא דיהן בלוזען היאואען פֿון מעלואבֿטינגען

מרדכי.

דו הער דיא דיא שבֿועות פֿון דיהן ניעדערטרעבֿטיגען,

בייט גלייך טטילל, דוא קלאַהנם הורג=זעו, דו!

נו, אסתרלע, וואַמ זמאַגסט דען דו דערלו?

אסתר.

וואַמ טייטט, וואַמ מיך דערלו זמאַג?

מיך טוועהרן בייא דיהן פֿריאפֿענזטטמאַג,

און בייא דיהן וועלקערהמלן פֿון גאָטט,

מיך גלאַמב פֿון דער גאַננע גטיבֿטע קמהן וואָטט.

דמאַ האָט געוויהם מאַהנער געהמאַלטן פֿאָר מ נמרר;

יוי מ מלך, זוי מ גרויזער המַרר

כעמט גלייך זוי מאַהנע, כעהר מן הבא בידו;

דמאַ וועהר עבֿעם מ נייע אודע.

זעםט מיך כעהר מיט דיא חלומית גיהן,

אָמריס טוט ניקם דערפֿוהן מין וואַלעגנבֿלעטטעלע טטיהן?

זמאַגט, וואַריס טטיהטם ניט מין דער לייטינג?

Mardachai.

Nu, 's kummt alles fun Gott.

Ober ich glaab an der Gschichte kahn Wott,

Gih zu, drahn is niks,

Daas is a $\overset{H}{.}$alôm[1], daas is Giks!

Medchen.

5   Secht bai dihn bloisen Himmel fun Allmechtigen--

Mardachai.

Doi her di Schevu'ôs[2] fun dihn Niedertrechtigen,

Bist glaich still, du klahns Horeg=le[3], du!

Nu Estherle, waas saagst den du derzu?

Esther.

Waas taitsch, waas ich derzu saag?

10 Ich schwehr'n bai dihn Frimfelistag,

Un bai dihn Welkerholz fun Gott,

Ich glaab fun der ganze Gschichte kahn Wott.

Das hot gewihs ahner gehalten for a Narr:

Joi a Melech[4], soi a groiser Harr

15 Nemt glaich soi eine, nehr min ha-bo' be-Jodô[5]:

Daas wehr ebes a naie Mude.

Lest mich nehr mit di $\overset{H}{.}$alômôs[6] gihn,

Worim tut niks derfuhn in Wuchenblettle stihn?

Saagt, worim stihts nit in der Zeitung?

1. Traum.
2. Schwüre.
3. Mörderin.
4. König.
5. zufällig.
6. Träume.

התך (צו אסתר·)

‫נעכטן, דעמאלט איז ווידער מאווין א גטיידינג;
אחשורוש האָט זיך היינט ערטט רעטמאל פֿיהרט,
דרום האָט אערם היע ערטט פופֿליניהרט.
נאָבער דרוקקען האָט אערם נאָך ניט געקענט,
‫וואטוי זעהי אמאריוג קוואוטט אין קרוטפֿענגדענט.
‫נו וועגם נאָבער א אויׁע טטיהט די דריננע,
‫וואטוי זיך דאָך אסור קיאאער — בזיננע.‬

אסתר·

‫וואָרים ניט ? — איך בין איך נאָך מו.‬

החך·

‫יו — אער ווארט מיהר דרמאהנבערעננע א טאאזׁל.
‫'ן מלך דמו' אער ניט זיין זיׁ ווידערטפיניג;
‫א אין זיׁי זיׁי ניט זיׁ איינגענזינניג.
‫ביה זיׁי נו, אסתר, אאָך זיׁי קאהן ;עטטע פאָטטען.‬

אסתר (צו מרדכי·)

‫ויא, אונקעל! מיך ;עלֹזט מיך פֿערלאָטטען?
‫ווער ;מאָל מיך דען דיׁ וואטטטמאָֹבט פֿיהרען?
‫ווער מיׁער קאֹֹפיה אמאֹבען? דמו פֿיער טיהרען?
‫ווער מיׁק, קאֹמֹבען, ניהע, טטריקקען טטאָמֹבֿען?
‫מיׁער ברמֹדעהויב און קאֹמאֹדער אויזקלאָמֹבֿען?
‫ווער מיׁק וועטטען, בעהגֹ'ע, אוטנגע?
‫מאָלֹוע פֿרייטיג נולאַיטטטֹאַ רוׁ לֹמאַנגע‬

Hathach (zu Esther.)

SichtSi, daas is wider amoil a Gschaiding:

Ahasveros hot sich haint erst resolfihrt,

Drum hot mers hie erst puplizihrt.

Ober drukken hot mers noch nit gekent,

5 WatSi sehi moring kummts in Kruspendent.

Nu wens ober a moile stiht doi drinne,

WatSi sich doch o$\underset{\cdot\cdot}{\text{sur}}$[1] nimmer-bsinne.

Esther.

Worim nit?--Ich bsin mich noch als.

Hathach.

Joi--mer wart Ihr drahnbrenne a Schmalz.

10 'n Melech[2] daf mer nit sain soi widerspinig:

A main sai Si nit soi aigensinning.

Gih Si zu, Esther, mach Si kahn sette Possen.

Esther (zu Mardachai.)

Wi, Unkel! Ich sellt aich ferlossen?

Wer soll aich di Wattschaft fihren?

15 Wer aier Kofih machen? daas Faier schihren?

Wer aich, kochen, nihe, strikken stopfen?

Aier Bradehoif un Klaader oisklopfen?

Wer aich weschen, behgle, mange?

Alle Fraitig Noichmittag rois lange

---

1. bei meiner Seele.
2. König.

מייער טוהזאָאַנטען און קרהַהגען?
און װער דאַ עססן אין מיהבעלע טרהַגען?
הַ, נאַ — ביא מיך װיֹן מיך בלייבן
עװיג פֿריאָפֿען װענקען — און פֿאַרבען — רייבן.

מרדכי·

אסתרלע טװיג! דו אַמַבסט מיך זױ װאַך
טונסט, װיא אַ בוטטערװעקקןע!
גאָאַב איר מיך גיהבעט פֿיל דרום מַך
קעננט מיך דיך נעהר פֿערטטענקןע.
מבער װאַ העלפֿטם, מיך דאַפֿם ניט טױן;
אין קינד!'ס גענהט אסור ניט מַהן.
זיך'ס קואַט איר'ס גרײנע מַך טױן
װען מיך דענק נעהר — דרהַהן.

(ער װישט זיך דיא אױגען.)

אסתר·

האַט, מונקען! איר ב' טפֿרינגט דאַװ האַ
װעלט איר קואַט אַך דאַװ גרײנע.
נו דו ליגט טױן, פֿון אין װייגע
אַ פֿעננען טרעהרן, מױפֿן פֿריאָפֿענליך פֿאַהַן —

(זיא װישט זיך עבענפֿאַללאָ **דיא** אױגען).

מרדכי·

אַך! איר טטענע דיא האַר נו בהַרינג!
מיא איר דיא טרעהרען לאַמַפֿען — לונטער:

Aier Schuhlmantel un Krahgen?

Un wer das Essen in Ihfele tragen?

A, na--Bai aich will ich blaiben

Ewig Frimfel welkern--un Farbel--raiben.

> Mardachai.

5 Estherle schwaig! Du machst mich soi waach

Schunst, wi a Butterwekkle!

Glaab mir ich gihbet fiel drum aach

Kennt ich dich nehr ferstekkle.

Ober waas helfts, ich dafs nit toin:

10 Main Kind! 's geht <u>osur</u>[1] nit ahn.

Sich 's kummt mir 's Graine aach schoin

Wen ich denk nehr-drahn.

> (Er wischt sich di Oigen.)

> Esther.

Halt, Unkel! Mir z'springt daas <u>Haz</u>[2]

Secht mir kommt aach daas Graine.

15 Nu doi ligt schoin, fun main Waine

A Fezzen Trehrn, oifn Frimfelich Plaz--

> (Si wischt sich ebenfalls di Oigen).

> Mardachai.

Och! Mir stene di Hor zu Barig!

Wi mir di Trehren laafen--runter:

1. bei meiner Seele.
2. Haz] Ha

מערבען.

(ווישט זיך עבענפֿאַלל'ז דיא אויגען.)

נאה, דיא נװיהפֿטען בײגען גאָר נו חרינ.

דאם אער דו גרײנע אוס מיז קַמַן װואונדער.

התך.

זעבט מ אױן, דיא נװיהפֿטען טעגנעט,

האפֿ מיך געאומהגט דיא צרות זעגנעט,

דאם אונו דיא מאגען זי מיבער[מַ]מַפֿט.

מערכען.

(צײגט אױפֿ דיא צװיבעל.)

דוי ליגען דיא צרות דרינגע מין המַַמפֿטען.

און דיא שברי לב ליגען מַחך דערבײ'א,

דיא אַמַבען דאם איר גרײנע אעטטען אַזַ'ע דרײ'ם!

התך.

אין אום מיך ערטט אוּבער דַה גרײנע לַמַבען.

(אַללע פֿיער לאַבען לױט.)

מַבער װַחַ! העלפֿטט, דו מיז ניקט נו אַמַבען.

אסתר פֿמַלנ זיא איר, און גיה זיא מַחך גױל.

װַחַ! האָט זיא פֿאָר מ היצאית דרױן?

נַאַרלַ'י, װַחַ האַט זיא נו פֿערלַ'יהרען?

זיא זיא קַמַהן טַמַטבעלַ'י, טוב זיא זיך ניט זי ניהרען.

מ אענט אום דַה זײיגע טון:

מ קַלַמַיגקַמַט אױפֿ פֿ קַמפֿ' מ קרין,

װו מ געפֿטער מין דער הַמד,

Medchen.

(wischt sich ebenfalls di Oigen.)

Nah, di Zwihfel baisen gar zu arig.

Daś mer doi graine muś is kahn Wunder.

Hathach.

Secht a moil, di Zwihfel tenneś,

Hob ich gemahnt di Zorôŝ[1] senneś,

5   Daś uns di Aagen soi iberlaafen.

Medchen.

(zaigt oif di Zwibel.)

Doi ligen di Zorôŝ[1] drinne in Haafen.

Un di Schivrê Lêv[2] ligen aach derbai,

Di machen daś mir graine meśśen alle drai!

Hathach.

Iz muś ich erśt iber das Graine lachen.

(Alle fier lachen loit.)

10   Ober waas helftś, doi is nikś zu machen.

Esther folg Si mir, un gih Si aach noif.

Waas hot Si for a Hôzoꞌ ôs[3]   droif?

Narrli, was hot Si zu ferlihren?

Sai Si kahn Schotcheli, tub Si sich nit soi zihren.

A Mensch mus das seinige toin:

A Klanigkat oif'n Kopf a Kroin,

Un[4] a Zepter in der Hand,

1. Unglücksschläge.
2. Herzbrechen.
3. Ausgabe-plural of noun used collectively.
4. Un] U

און לֹו געביעטטען, איבער לײַט און לַאנד.

זאַגט זיא, װער זיא דען אַהער װערטה

דאַז זיא געגנעעט, אויף גאָטטעס ערד,

װען זיא זיך טעט נאָך לענגער בזיננע

אַ זאָטטע לאָטטעריע לֹו געװיננע? —

אסתּר.

נו זוי אײך זוי קַמהן אונטערטיעד,

אַ טרוהן, אָדער אַ בזַרבּעסבּריעד!

אַ איהנַקיזשװענלֹן, אָדער אַ קרוין,

בײם אײך זוי עז לײַבט געטון.

פֿאָר מײך זוי דאַז נאָר אַ געטפּאַם,

אחשורוש טטיהט מַבּער פֿיעל לֹו הוױך דיא נחַם.

זוי — דער האָט קַמהן קלַמהן — טטאָלֹן,

דער װאָט לַמַאָפֿעט, אײך פֿון װעלֹקערהאָלֹן

דוי נעאַאע, און אויף 'ן טרוהן געטװיעד זעלֹעס?

נמהן, װי פֿיעל חסד טו אײך איר ניט טעעלֹעס.

אײך האָב זוי יוי ניקס פֿאָרנע און ניקס היגטען.

התּך.

סװיע זיא, טוב זיא זיך נאָר ניט פֿערזינדען.

דען אַ מלך זיבט ניט נעהר אױהר אױפֿ 'ן געלֹד,

װיא 'ס מאָלֹעװוין בעזוונית מיז בײם דער װעלֹט!

גיה זיא נו, זיא מיז אַ נמַרלֹי,

עס האָט מַן געזאַגט עליו השׁלום אײן המַרלֹי

אַ טפֿריבװאָטעט, און דנַאַ טיהגנֹך:

Un zu gebieten, iber Lait un Land.

Saag Si, wer Si den mehr werth

Das Si genget, oif Gottes Erd,

Wen Si sich tet noch lenger bsinne

5   A sotte Loterie zu gewinne?--

        Esther.

Nu joi aich is kahn Unterschied,

A Truhn, oder a Barchesbried!

A Mihlkiwelle, oder a Kroin,

Bai aich is es laicht getoin.

10   For aich is das nor a Gspas,

Ahasveros stiht ober fiel zu hoich di Naas.

Joi--Der hot kahn klahn--Stolz,

Der wat laafen, mich fun Welkerholz

Doi nemme, un oif'n Truhn gschwind sezzen?

15   Nahn, soi fiel Ḥ.esed[1] tu ich mir nit schezzen.

Ich hob joi Niks forne un Niks hinten.

        Hathach.

Schwaig Si, tub Si sich nor nit fersinden.

Den a Melech[2] sicht nit nehr oif'n Geld,

Wi's allewail be-ʿAwônôs[3] is bai der Welt!

20   Gih Si zu, Si is a Narrli,

Es hot als gsagt ʿolov ha-Scholôm[4] main Harrli

A Sprichwott, un daas tihglich:

---

1. Gunst.
2. König.
3. durch ihre Missetaten.
4. selig, cf. requiescat in pace.

„מזלע חס ושלום זען אײהגגֹיך."
אַיר עענטען דאַפֿאַפֿען אוי גאַר ניקס לאַבּען.
װען גאָטט וויל, קען ער מזלעם אַהבּען.
לאָס זיא זיך נעהר ניט זײן לאַהאַד,
יא מיז מווּאבּטריע דיק אוּנד בראָד.
איז אַ אַנדׂע וויא אַ קאַטטען,
קען מאַך רײהן איט גרוֹפֿען פֿון פֿאַטטען.
האָטט ברוך השם מיהר גראַהאַדע גענﬞיﬠדער.
איז ניט אוּנגטיקט מין דיﬡ פֿיהדﬠר.
מָהרט אוּנד ﬦﬠנט, מאַך רﬠ﬽ﬡﬞט גוﬞט.
האָט אַ בּמאַר ﬠמﬡﬡﬠן, וויﬡ איﬡיך אוּן בּלוֹט.
קﬠן גוﬞט קﬡﬡﬠן, וועﬡﬞﬡﬡ אוּן ﬡﬠﬡﬠ,
איז מאַך מ﬽﬽﬽﬽טﬡﬞט מווﬡﬞבּטﬡﬞﬠ
גﬡﬡﬡﬠﬠﬡ אוּן ﬽ﬡﬡﬞט,
אוּן אַ קﬡﬠﬡﬞﬡﬠﬡﬞﬠﬠﬡﬞט פֿוﬡﬞ דﬠﬠר משפחה — קיﬡﬞ —

מרדכי.

וואַאַ! ז﬽﬽ﬞ﬽ מﬡﬞך טﬡﬞן, 'ﬡ איﬡ אַ גﬠﬠﬞירה!
מﬡך אוּﬡﬞ דﬡﬞך ﬽ﬡבּﬠﬠ הﬡﬞﬡﬞﬞﬡﬞﬡﬡﬠﬡﬞ, הﬡﬞﬞ קﬡﬞﬡﬞﬡﬞﬡ בﬠﬞﬠﬠﬡﬠﬠﬞﬠﬠﬞﬠﬠ.
דﬠﬠﬠﬞ טﬡﬞﬡﬞﬠﬡﬞﬠﬠﬠﬡﬞﬡﬠﬞﬠ אַ בﬡﬞﬠﬡﬠﬞ פֿﬠﬡﬠﬠﬞ מﬠﬞﬠﬠ,
מﬡך גﬡﬠﬡﬠﬞﬠﬡﬠﬞﬡﬡﬞﬠﬠﬠﬠﬠﬡ לטובה, אﬡﬞﬠ דﬡﬠﬡﬞ כﬠﬞﬡﬠﬡ
ז﬽﬽﬽ﬡ מﬠﬞﬠﬠﬠﬞﬠ בﬡﬞﬠﬠﬞﬠﬠﬠ ﬡﬠﬡﬞﬠ ניﬞﬠﬞﬠﬠ, וﬠﬠﬠﬠﬡﬞﬠﬠ דוﬞ בﬡﬞﬠﬠﬠﬠ,
אַ ייﬠﬞﬠﬠﬠ, מﬞﬠﬡﬠﬠﬠﬠﬠﬞ אַ קﬠﬠﬠﬡﬠﬠﬞﬠﬠ,
אַ טﬡﬠﬠﬡﬞﬠﬡﬞﬠﬠﬠ מﬠﬠﬠﬠﬠﬞﬠﬠﬞﬠﬠ אַ ﬡﬠﬠﬠﬡﬞﬠﬠ,
אַ פﬡﬞﬠﬠﬠﬠﬠﬠﬞﬠﬠﬡﬞﬠﬡﬞ, מﬠﬠﬠﬠﬞﬠﬠ אַ אﬡﬞﬠﬠﬞﬠﬠ,
אﬡך הﬡﬞﬠﬠ גﬠﬞ דﬠﬠﬡﬞﬠﬠﬠ גﬠ אﬡﬞﬠ טﬠﬠﬞﬠ.

Alle H.as ve--Scholôm[1] sen mihglich.

Mir Menschen daffen ois gar niks lachen.

Wen Gott will, ken er alles machen.

Los Si sich nehr nit sain laad,

5 Si is umbschrie dik und brad.

Is a Madle wi a Kasten,

Ken aach rihden mit Grufen un Fasten.

Hott boruch ha-Schêm[2] Ihr graade Gelieder.

Is nit ungschikt in di Fihder.

10 Ohrt und laient, aach recht gut.

Hot a baar Bakken, wi Milich un Blut.

Ken gut kochen, weschen un nihe,

Is aach allfott umbschrie

Gsund un frisch,

15 Un a Klanigkat fun der Mischpo.oh[3]--Kis[4].

        Mardachai

Waas soll ich toin, s is a Gesêroh[5]!

Ich mus dich ober hinschikken, hob kahn Berêroh[6].

Drum stih nor a bisle frih oif,

Ich gih selbst le-Tôvoh[7], mit dir noif

20 Saag ober bai Laib nit, wer du bist,

A Jid, oder a Krist,

A Tarrik oder a Haad,

A Prinzessin, oder a Maad,

Ich hob zu droif main Taʿam[8].

1. Gott behüt! 2. gesegnet sei sein Name. 3. Familie.
4. Cf. Esther II, 5. 5. Dekret. 6. Wahl. 7. zum Guten.
8. Beweggrund.

אין גיה איך צו מעריב בזמנה, קום גלייך ווידער אהם.
התך גיהט מיהר ניט מאך איט?
וואס טייטט, ווארים ניט?

(ביידע אב.)

אסתר (אליין.)

גיה איך ניט?
גיה איך יוי?
גיה איך איט?
בלייב איך דוי?
וויא מיכ׳ס מאך,
זמאג מהנם איר,
אב דיא זמך,
מיך פראמביער?
פראמביער מיכ׳ס
און גיה פאטט;
פערלויער מיכ׳ם,
איז פון גאטט!
קענן מאך זיין
מיך געווינכ׳ם,
נעמא׳ן מיין,
מון איך בינם.
צו איינטוויהגען,
איך גיה פאטם.
דיהנען ווענגען
גיב איר — גאטט! —
3

Iz gih ich zu Ma'ariv[1] bi-Semanoh[2], kum
                              glaich wider ham.

Hathach giht ihr nit aach mit?

Was taitsch, worim nit?

       (baide ab.)

       Esther (allain.)

    Gih ich nit?

5   Gih ich joi?

    Gih ich mit?

    Blaib ich doi?

    Wi ich's mach,

    Saag ahns mir,

10   Ob di Sach,

    Ich probier?

    Probier ich's

    Un gih fott:

    Ferlier ich's

15   Is fun Gott!

    Ken aach sain

    Ich gewinn's,

    Nemm'n ain,

    Un ich bins.

20   Nu maintwihgen,

    Ich gih fott.

    Dainen Siegen

    Gib mir--Gott!--

1. Abendgottesdienst. 2. zur Zeit.

שטינ[ל] וועד קאאט, איז טיין ווידער די דער אונקען?

צירע.

(שטירצט אונגעשטים הערייץ.)

ביסט זוי מאַהאַן? אין דער דוגקען!

אין האָן אין אַ יאָריגג ניקס מעהנלניהגעגן:

אין גאַנ[ל] שושן קען אין קאַן ?מאטטען אחרינ(ע

קריהגען!

אסתר.

נו, ליהג מאהן דין עטערנעג[ל]עם קלאַמאַר,

צירע.

וי די האָב אין אַ בוקקען דרינג עיה[ל]ענברחאַד.

אסתר.

ליהג דין קיא דאַמַ;עטטעם מאַהן.

צירע.

גיה וועג, ערוויננער אין ניט די דרמאַהן,

דאַמַ: מי אַ געאאַך! דאַמַ: מי אַ טאַ[ל]יע!

וי ?מאָ[ל]] וער מאהן דין ?מן אמאַ[ל]קען כליה?

דאַמַ: הורג ?[ל]ע! דער ע[ל]ענד! דער ווארק!

האָט איר'ם אין גרוגד ניין פאַעדדמאַרם!

אין האַ איר'ם מָבער פעעטט מאַך פאַמַרגענואאע:

פוָן היע טוט איר ניקם מן [ל]ייב אעהר קאאע.

אסתר.

וי ליהג מאהן דין טולבעם,

Still wer kummt, is schoin wider doi der Unkel?

      Zaire.

      (stirzt ungestim herain.)

Bist soi alahn? in der Dunkel!

Iz ho ich moring niks ahnzuzihgen:

In ganz Susan ken ich kahn sotten Marine

                        krihgen!

      Esther.

5   Nu, zihg ahn dain eternelles Klaad,

      Zaire.

Joi doi hob ich a Bukkel drinne eihlenbraad.

      Esther.

Zihg dain nai Dafetes ahn.

      Zaire.

Gih weg, erinner mich nit doi drahn,

Daas is a Gemach! Daas is a Talie!

10 Soi soll mer ahn sain Sach machen <u>kaljeh</u>[1]?

Daas <u>Hôreg</u>-le[2]! Der Elend! Der Worm!

Hot mir's in Grund nain ferdorm!

Ich ho mir's ober fest aach forgenumme:

Fun hie tut mir niks an Laib mehr kumme.

      Esther.

15 Soi zihg ahn dain Tuches,

---

1. Verderben--a colloquial pronounciation of a Hebrew word
<u>kelojoh</u> (Vernichtung).
2. Mörderin.

דעהאַ מיז אַ פרעלטטיג ווינטערקלאַמאַר.

צײרע.

נאַ, דעהאַ מיז אַ גענג פֿאַר רוחות,
דעהאַ האָט טעַן יעדע אַטאַר,
יעדע קעלֿי מון מאָטע פֿרחה.

קאָראַ, מאָקאַ, וואָקאַ.

(שטירצען צור טהירע העריין.)

וואַט איין כפרה! וואו טטעקט דען מיהר נואַה?

קאָראַ.

נו העטט מיהרם מאַך טוין געהערט?
אָבער דאָהאַ מיז מאַויל דער איה ווערטה!
דעהאַ וואַטט אַ נויֿגעהי אמאַבען;
האָסטו טוין בײם אַנאַנדער דיין זעעבען ואַבַען?

אסתר.

* — קאָלע האָר זעַן באַלֿ געבאַטט.

מאָקאַ.

מיך האָ ווי זוי לו טוין כאָך אַ גאַטנער לאַסט.
איי שווון היהטוע דעהאַ קעננט'ר,

אללע דרייאַ.

די דעהאַ אים דיא גיהלע בענדער?
דעמו לאָסט דו דיר אסור דעמך ניט ענדעמך!
אואַסט זעהי דיא שלומיאל= טע פֿערטענדער'ן.

Daas is a prechtig Winterklaad.

      Zaire.

Na, daas is a Gang for Ruhôs[1],

Daas hot schon jede Maad,

Jede Kechi un alte Frah.

       Kora, Moka, Soka.

      (stirzen zur Thire herain.)

5   Wat main Kapporoh[2]! Wu stekt den ihr zwah?

       Kora.

Nu hett ihrs aach schoin gehert?

Ober daas is amoil der Mih werth!

Daas watt a Noifsehi machen:

Hostu schoin bai anander dain Sieben Sachen?

       Esther.

10 Joi--Koze Hor sen ball gebast.

       Moka.

Ich ho joi zu toin noch a ganzer Last.

Main schwaz Hihtle daas kennt'r,

      Alle Drai.

Doi daas mit di gihle Bender?

Daas lost du osur[3] doch nit endern!

Wast sehi di Schlumielte[4] ferschender'n.

1. Geister.
2. Versöhnung--Vid. Part II #286.
3. bei meiner Seele.
4. Vid. Part II #481.

מאָקאַ·

דמאַ! לאָם מיך וויא איר וויא דער צעטולפֿע מיהרם אונאַבען.

זאָקאַ·

גיה וועג! דוא האָסט ליטער קרוואָע — זאַבען.
האָסטו ניט געאהי וויף'ן לעלטון ביזאָהן
וויא זיא וואוזגעאהי האָט, זין מיהר טמאַה!?

צוירע·

ספֿרים! האָטם דוי רעבט טענלער גיהבען?

מאָקאַ·

וואן וויא? — פנים־זיך זון פֿערליהבען.

קאָראַ·

דמאַ וואָר דער מ טעטאמט, וואן מ פֿרחאָלט;
דמאַ האָן אין זוב האָט מאָהן געזאָמלט.

מאָקאַ·

וואחמס טייטט, נאהבואָר קעננם ניט זיין אין פֿאַרים.

אסתר· (פֿאָר זיך.)

וויא איז איר זאָמר מיך וזי מיאוס!

צוירע·

זאַמגמט, לאָמט מיך מאוולע פֿרוינגען:
ווער האָט מיך דאן מאַז וויזפֿגעלויגען?

        Moka.

Daas los ich mir wi der Zetulpe ihrs machen.

        Soka.

Gih weg! Du host loiter krumme--Sachen.

Hostu nit gsehi oif'n leztn Bahl

Wi si oisgsehi hot, in ihr Schahl?

        Zaire.

5 Apripu[1]! Hots doi recht Tenzer gihben?

        Moka.

Un wi?--Ponim[2]--lich zun ferlihben.

        Kora.

Daas wor dir a Staat, un a Pracht:

Daas Haz in Laib hot ahn gelacht.

        Moka.

Waas taitsch, nuhbler kenns nit sain in Paris.

        Esther. (for sich.)

10 Wi is mir for aich soi mi'us[3]!

        Zaire.

Saagt, lest aich amoile froigen:

Wer hot aich den als oifgezoigen?

1. A propos.
2. Gesichtchen.
3. widerwärtig.

זאָקאָ·

װאַז· **טיטט**? װער װאָז װױפֿגעלױגען האָט?
איר העם געטמאַנט, אין זאַהנעם פֿאָטט.

מאָקאָ·

זיא העם זיך יױ יױ מאָרגדליך אױס װאָז געריסמעַן.
דיהן ניעַן טריהער האָם איך אַ אױזע נעהי טאָאַנען
איסמעַן.
װעַן מיך איך האָב װעַזֿזען אַ ביסזֿע נעהר היהױנזעַזֿזען
האָם איך גֿױך װידער מאַהנער געהאָם ביין פֿעַזֿזען!

קאָראָ·

אוין איך האָב גאָר נים קעַננע אַן זיזֿזען דעָנקעַן ;
,,אאַװזעַן! װאָזֿזען זיא איר דװאַז פֿעַרגניגעַן טעָנקעַן"?
איא אַזֿזע איױם קװאַאַ אַ סטודעַנט, אָדער אַ נמפֿעַליהר ;
אוין העם נים געַרױהם ביז איך איט זי אַנגאַמטיהר.

מאָקאָ·

דױ, העטם מיהר נאַעַהי דיהן טיהן סטודעָנט?
עַר האָם איך אָסור, נים מאַװין געָנקעַננט —
יוסט האָם עַר איר געאַאַבֿם זױ טיהנע קװאַפֿיאָענדַר
העאַאַין נעָביך אַ הױלֿזער ניהבעַן אַן אױזיקטטעָנדַר,
דאַס איך געָאַאַהנט האָב גֿױך עַר בֿױט.

צײרע

אין דאַל מיך מָבעָר גיהן, 'ס איז — נייט.

       Soka.

Waas taitsch? Wer uns oifgezoigen hot?

Mir hem getanzt, in ahnem fott.

       Moka.

Si hem sich joi orndlich um uns gerissen.

Dihn naien Triher ho ich a moile zehi tanzen

                        missen.

5 Wen ich mich hob wellen a bisle nehr hihnsezzen

Hot mich glaich wider ahner ghat bain Fezzen!

       Kora.

Un ich hob gar nit kenne an sizzen denken:

„Mamsel! Wollen Si mir daas Fergnigen schenken?"

Is alle Minut kumme a Student, oder a Nafezihr:

10 Un hem nit geruht bis ich mich mit si angaschihr.

       Moka.

Doi, hett ihr gsehi dihn schihn Student?

Er hot mich osur[1], nit amoil gekennt--

Just hot er mir gemacht soi schihne Kumplimender

Hemsin nebich a Huzzer gihben an Musikstender,

15 Das ich gemahnt hob glaich er blait.

        Zaire.

Iz daf ich ober gihn, 's is--Zait.

---

1. bei meiner Seele.

וואָקאָ•

דיא צעטילפע האָט מידער קמהן פום גיט געטעגלאָט.

מאָקאָ•

זיא האָט געהאַגט זיא האָט גיט געוואונט.

וואָקאָ•

יו! איין זיא איז געבליהבען יום טוב = טיק.

מירצאָ•

(האָט דיא לעצטען ווערטע געהערט.)

זיא ריהטען טוין פון פסח. וואָטט מאַך דוי זיין הין
צו נאַגעגבליק.
האָב אסור נאָך קמהן יום טוב=טיק טאאַלן!

(צו איהרער טאָלטער צייר ע.)

גיהסטו גלייך המאַט? איך ברעך דיר'ן האַם!
דו קריהגסט, קוס נעהר האָאַם
ער — טלאַהאַגט דיך קרום פון לאַהסן.
סטרהאַקט דיך אין געאַנלען נאָבעגד דוי הער.
איט דער אָך איז עבעם דעראָהער?
אָאָר מאַלע וויל מיך זיא נעהר בחרפה אַנאַלען,
כל עולם וויל מיך דערליה=לען מיהר זאַבען.
דער מיהר גלייבעם איז ניאאַער היע —
גאָטט! וואָ מיך איט דער חויזטיה מאַלע פריה.
בי אער זיא נון בעטט רוז ברענגט וואָטס נייע.
דערנוך טרעטטטו דיא קינדער, בי זיא גרינע —

Soka.

Di Zetulpe hat wider kahn Fuš nit gštellt.

Moka.

Si hot gsaagt si hot nit gewelt.

Soka.

Joi! Wail si is geblihben Jôm Tôv[1]=tik.

Mirza.

(hat di lezten Worte gehert.)

Si rihten schoin fun Pešah[2]. Watt aach doi sain in
a Negenblik.

5   Hob ošur[3] noch kahn Jôm Tôv[1]=tik Schmalz!

(zu ihrer Tochter Zaire.)

Gihštu glaich haam? Ich brech dirn Halš!

Du krihgšt, kum nehr haam

Er--schlaagt dich krum un lahm.

Štrakt dich in ganzen Nobend doi her.

10 Mit der Soch is ebeš der Mehr?

For alle will ich si nehr be--Herpoh[4] machen,

Kol'Ôlom[5] will ich derzihlen ihr Sachen.

Der ihr Glaicheš is nimmer hie--

Gott! Waš ich mit der oisstih alle Frih.

15 Bis mer si zun Bett rois brengt wotš naine.

Dernoch tretztsi di Kinder, bis si graine--

1. festlich--"Sie bleibt unberührt, kommt nicht an den Mann.
--beim Tanze--sie bleibt sitzen." Tendlau, Prov. #540.
2. Passah.
3. bei meiner Seele.
4. in Scham.
5. Jedermann.

ביז אער זיא בון מהרען ברענגט וואוס מאלעואין נעווי.

דער מיהר מויספֿיהרונג הא מיך נאך ניט געווהי.

המזבע טיהג טוטי מן זיך טנאקקלע און פוגנען,

און ווען דיא אמאאוען פֿמטיק מיא, לו'ן פֿענטטער נוז=

טער — גונגען.

זולט ריבער, זולט ניבער, וואו זיא הערבֿליגען.

טוטמעלט מין היז רויל און רמה, מעלֿע שטיהגען.

ניהט מין דער קוק, דיא גזינדער מה לו טרעלנען.

איטטועג, טוט זיך דיא גריהטֿען מן טיט נער זעלנען.

איבער מעלֿע וויל זיא בעפֿיהלנען, וויל זיא געביהטען.

און אסור קען זיא ם קמל מויל מויסטען למקקען? —

(איין קנאבע מיט איינער האנדלאטערנע.)

ק נ א ב ע ּ

נו, וויא לאנג טעט מיהר'ך נאך ריבער המקקען?

ער ניהט דער המאס רוק, מין מהן ברואוע!

מ י ר צ א ּ

טוין רעלט, מיך וואר גלייך המאס קואוע.

איבער מהן און מיך זיין, פֿאָרנע און היגטען.

ער אמאהנט געווויהס מיך און מיך גמר מ טינדען?

וואמט — נען מיט, מ בוטטערוענקלע, און 2 לויט

נואריקליך.

(צו דעם מערקען.)

מין וואר? אהשורוש וויל וידער מ פֿרמה נעאוע?

וואריקליך?

Bis mer si zun Ohren brengt watṡ alemoil zehi.

Der ihr Oiffihrung ho ich noch nit gsehi.

Halbe Tihg tutsi an sich schnokkle un puzzen,

Un wen di Mansel fatik is, zu'n Fenster nun=
                                    ter--guzzen.

5   Sicht riber, sicht niber, wu si herfligen.

Schuṡelt in Hois roif un rah, alle Stihgen.

Giht in der Kuch, di Gsinder ah zu trezzen.

Mittag, tut sich di Grihfen an Tisch ner sezzen.

Iber alle will si befihlen, will si gebihten.

10   Un oṡur[1] ken si a Kaz ois'm Oifen lokken?--

                (ain Knabe mit ainer Hondlaterne.)

                Knabe.

Nu, wi lang tet ihr ich noch riber hokken?

Er giht der haam rum, in ahn Brumme!

                Mirza.

Schoin recht, ich war glaich haam kumme.

Iber ahl muṡ ich sain, forne un hinten.

15   Er mahnt gewihṡ ich muṡ mich gar a schinden?

Watt--nem mit, a Butterwekle, un 2 Loit
                                    Zwariklich.

                (zu dem Medchen)

Is wohr? Ahasveros will wider a Frah nemme?
                                    Wariklich?

1. bei meiner Seele.

ק אָ ר אַ•

גיהט דיא צייערע מַאך אָמֶריגַ פֿריה?

(ה תך אונד ר' מרדכי קאַממען, התך מיט
איינעם האהן אויף דעם אַרם•)

מדעכעו•

אוי! ר' התך קואַאָט דער גיגעריגיה!

מרדכי•

חצופה ≠!ֶ!ע! קריהגמט גלֵיך מַהנע אויפֿ'ֶ ן אויֵ —

מ יר צ אַ•

אַמַנטאָ≠כֵ ע! דמַאו איו אַ גיהגער וויא אַ גויֵ.

(דער האהן קרעהעט•)

גיגערערעגגיע! גיגערערעגגיע!

מ אָ ק אַ•

דו הער! דער קמַרֵ קֵענ אָבער קריהע?

התך•

דו היהבסין מַאויֵ, דער איו אַ מציאה;

מירצאַ•

אוי! אוי! וויא דער ווי טווֶעהר איו.

צ יי ר ע•

אפשר איו ער גמַר מעובֿרת? —

40

Kora.

Giht di Zaire aach moring frih?

    (Hathach und R' Mardachai kommen, Hathach mit

    ainem Hahn oif dem Arm.)

    Medchen[1]!

Oi! R Hathach kummt der Gigerigih!

    Mardachai.

Hazufoh[2]=le! krihgst glaich ahne oif'n Moil---

    Mirza.

Manschoche! Daas is a Gihger wi a Goil.

        (Der Hahn krehet.)

5 Gigerregie! Gigerregie!

    Moka.

Doi her! Der Karl ken ober krihe?

    Hathach.

Doi hihbšin amoil, der is a Mezi'oh[3]:

    Mirza.

Oi! Oi! Wi der soi schwehr is.

    Zaire.

Efschor[4] is er gar me`ubbereš[5]?--

1. Medchen] Mdechen.
2. Unverschämtes Mädchen.
3. Gewinn.
4. vielleicht.
5. schwanger.

מירצאַ.

גיה וועג, טוויינ נעהר דּו אומָקקעןֶ;
האָסט יטט זי פיעל שכל' וויא דוּ דער גאָגעןֶ.

מערכעןֶ.

אָבער וואָ טוט ער דער איט? לאָסטערֶן דען לחַבֿעֶןֶ?
מָדער טסטערֶן וידער פֿערקמאַפֿעֶןֶ?

אסתר.

די וואָהר, די אסור קמַהֶן שקרֶן;
וחַוַ טוט ער מיִן אמת איטֶ' — גיהגער?

החכ.

וחַוַ טייטטֶ? וחַוַ מיך איטֶ'ן גיהגער טובֿ?
ערטטֶזיך גיט ער דּו גוטע היהנערזוב;
דערמולטעט, די האָט געוויהם פֿערגעטסטעןֶ:
וחַוַ ווֶיֶן די אוֹיפֶֿ'ן טאָמֶס דען עטטעֶן?
זען איר דען ניט קמַהֶן יידעֶן?
די לאָסט זיך'ֶן כשר אָחַבֿעֶן, רופֿעֶן און זיעדעֶן.
אָמֶרינֶג טוטטין מיֶן מֶ פֿמַפֿיער מיזוויקֶלע,
חַזֶלע איטטוחַנֶג און מֶבֿעָנדֶם עטטיי מֶ טטיקקֶלע,
דחַזַ מיז מיהֶר מֶ פוואָאער, דער מיז ניט קלמֶהֶןֶ;
דיִי גאַנֶלע וחוֹך האָטֶי זוּ גוטעֶן — דרמַהֶןֶ.

(דער האָן קרעהעט.)

גיגערערעגגיע! גיגערערעגגיע!

(מירצאַ'ס מאַן שטעקט דען קאָפֿף צור טהירע העריין.)

41

Mirza.

Gih weg, schwaig nehr du Mokkel:

Host just soi fiel Sêchel[1] wi doi der Gogel

Medchen.

Aber was tut Er der mit? LostEr'n den laafen?

Oder tutEr'n wider ferkaafen?

Esther.

5   Is wohr, is osur[2] kahn Scheker[3]:

Waas tut Er in Emes[4] mit'n--Gihger?

Hathach.

Waas taitsch? Waas ich mit'n Gihger tub?

Erstlich git er a gute Hihnersub:

Dernoichet, Si hot gewihs fergessen:

10   Waas will Si oif'n Schlos den essen?

Sen mir den nit kahn Jiden?

Si lost sich'n Koschor[5] machen, rupfen un sieden.

Moring tutSin in Papier ainwikle,

Alle Mittag un Obends estSi a Stikkle,

15   Daas is Ihr a Pummer, der is nit klahn:

Di ganze Wuch hotSi zu guten--drahn.

(Der Hahn krehet.)

Gigerregie! Gigerregie!

(Mirza's Man stekt den Kopf zur Thire herain.)

1. Verstand.
2. bei meiner Seele.
3. Lüge.
4. Wahrheit.
5. gesetzlich brauchbar und erlaubt.

נו טטענלט זיהר מיך נאך דיו הער ביז אמעריגג פריה?

וויא מאָכֿט אוט אער נאָך טיקקען נאָך מיך?

מירצא·

נו יוי, וואֶטט, איר קוֿאאֿע גלֿייך.

צירע! גֿי נו, אמֿך פֿאֶטט, מיך ביטטיק!

דיא מעדכען·

וואֶטט מ בֿיסלֿע מיר גענגע איטטיק.

(אלללע אֶב.)

מרדכי·

מיך וויֿל מאֶך נאֶך עבעס — טוֿין.

(ער געהעט אֶב.)

מעדכען·

זוי גאֶטט! 'ס שֿולֿחַנֿט זֿיעבען טוֿין.

(לוֿיפֿט אֶב.)

————

דריטטער אַבשנ·טט·

פֿרייער פֿלאטץ.   ר' מ ר ד כ י קאֶממט אין מאֶנטעל אונד ברייטע הויבע. עו איזט מאֶרגענס.

מרדכי·

הֿאֶטט! הֿאֶטט! 'ס מיז קאֶלֿט,

Nu stellt ihr aich noch doi her bis Moring frih?

Wi oft mus mer noch schikken noch aich?

Mirza.

Nu joi, watt, mir kumme glaich.

Zaire! Gi zu, mach fott, ich bittich!

Di Medchen.

5   Watt a bisle mir genge mittich.
                         (alle ab.)

Mardachai.

Ich will aach noch ebes--toin.
                         (Er gehet ab.)

Medchen.

Oi Gott! 's schlaagt sieben schoin.
                         (loift ab.)

Dritter Abschnitt.

Fraier Platz. R Mardachai kommt in Mantel und

        braite Haibe. Es ist Morgens.

        Mardachai.

Hutsch! Hutsch! 's is kalt,

אייער וועטט נו גוטען — מאַט.

מיך קען מאַך ניאַאער רעכט פֿאָמט.

(ער זעצט זיך.)

נו סטיהט מאַזֿעם בײַיע גאָטט.

טוט איר נאָר אײַן אסתרלי רעכט אַנט.

אָרנדײַך בין מיך אוגע המַד.

דיאַ זכיה וועַן מיך נער היהבעט,

דעם מ'יב'ם נאָך בכבוד אויזגיהבעט.

נו, נו, ווען גאָטט וויל הָטוּ'ין;

דער רשע זעזֿעט עבעט — קאָמטין,

דער המן איט זיין ניקסנוטליגע פֿרחה,

(בגתן אונד תרש קאָממען אין מעֶנטעל נעהיללט. דיא
שטראַסע הערוונטער, אונד זינד אים געשפרעבֿע בעגריפֿפֿען.)

ווער זעֶן דען מָבער דיאַ נוזֿחה?•

דיאַ טזֿײכען ײ ווי דיאַ גנבים בײַיע דער לבנה.

זעֶנס אפֿשר גאַר — טפֿיֶנע?

(זיא קאָממען נעהער.)

די הער וויאַ זיאַ סודית אַמַבֿען;

ווי סודית זעַן, גיטס קָהן גוטע — אַבֿען.

מיך אעַבֿט נער וויסמען, וואַמַז זיאַ וועזֿעֶן.

וואַמַט מיך וויֶלֿ מיך טזֿײֶפֿעֶן סטעֶנֿעֶן,

מיך אַמַך גטוויִנד דיאַ אַמַבֿגעֶן נו, און טו טינאַרבֿען,

תאָמר ײ קען מיך עבעם הָעַרכעֶן.

ער מאַלט זיך שלאַפֿעֶן. בגתן אונד תרש שפרעבֿעֶן וואַז
ציוזאַממעֶן, אונד געהעֶן פֿאָראיבער. מרדכי שפרינגט אויף.

נו ײ, דאַז איז דער איה ווערהרט,

Mer watt zu guten--alt.

Ich ken aach nimmer recht fott.
(Er setzt sich.)

Nu štiht alleš bai Gott.

Tut mir nor main Estherli recht ant.

5   Orndlich bin ich une Hand.

Di Sechijjoh[1] wen ich ner hihbet.

Daš ich'š noch be-Chovôd[2] oisgihbet.

Nu, nu, wen Gott will hots'in:

Der Roscho˓[3] sellet ebeš--klotsin,

10   Der Haman mit sain nikšnutzige Frah,

(Bigthan und Theres kommen in Mentel gehillt. di
Straše herunter, und sind im Gespreche begriffen.)

Wer sen den ober di zwah?

Di schlaichen joi wi di Ganovim[4] bai der Levonoh[5].

Sennš efschor[6] gar--Špione?

(Si kommen neher.)

Doi her wi si Šôdôš[7] machen:

15   Wu Šôdôš[7] sen, gitš kahn gute--Sachen.

Ich mecht ner wišsen, waas si wellen.

Watt ich will mich schloifen štellen,

Ich mach gschwind di Aagen zu, un tu schnorchen,

Thômar[8] joi ken ich ebeš horchen.

Er macht sich schlafen. Bightan und Theres sprechen was
zusammen, und gehen foriber. Mardachai springt oif.

Nu joi, das is der Mih wehrt,

---

1. Glück, 2. in Ehre. 3. Bösewicht. 4. Diebe. 5. Mond.
6. vielleicht. 7. Geheimnisse. 8. Im Fall--Literally=
should you say.

דו האָב איך טיהנע זאַלבן געהערט.

דיא אָנהנע מאַך דמו צרפת לשון

פֿערטטיהט קאַהנער היע אין שושן.

איר ניקם, דיר ניקם, אין מלך וועללען זיי פֿער־
גיפֿטען.

וואָטט, אייך אום אער נאָך היינט אין זיפֿטען

מון העלסטען גאַזינג העננע,

דיא נוירבלט, אום איך גליך, חויפֿ׳ן טלאָם היהא
ברעננע.

(אָב.)

(מאַדאַם פינסי אונד מאַדאַם פֿאַקסי בעעעגננען זיך אײ־
נאַנדער.)

פינסי.

ווי, מיהר דיהנער, אאַדאַם פֿאַקסי!

פֿאַקסי.

איך עאָפֿעהלע אייך, אאַדאַם פינסי.

פינסי.

וויא גיהטט? וואָאַ אאַבט מיהר — גוונדהאַטט?

פֿאַקסי.

ניט גוט, חואָטטאָהנסגזאָגט, מעללאָטט זיי — אָטט!

פינסי.

און אעללאָטט וואָטט זיי חואבטריע, טיק מון ברזאַדער.

Doi hob ich schihne Sachen gehert.

Di mahne aach das <u>Zorfaś Loschôn</u>[1]

Ferstiht kahner hie in Susan.

Mir nikś, dir nikś, in <u>Melech</u>[2] wellen si fergiften.

5 Watt, aich muś mer noch haint in Liften

An hechśten Galing henge,

Di Noichricht, muś ich glaich, oif'n Schloś hihnbrenge.

      (ab.)

(Madam Figśi und Madam Fakśi begegnen sich ainander.)

      Figśi.

Ai, ihr Dihner, Madam Fakśi!

      Fakśi.

Ich empfehle mich, Madam Figśi.

      Figśi.

10 Wi gihtś? Waas macht ihr--Gsundhatt?

      Fakśi.

Nit gut, umśtahnśgsagt, allfott soi--matt!

      Figśi.

Un allfott watt si umbschrie, tik un brader.

1. französische Sprache.
2. König.

פֿאָקסי.

יוי, 'ס װאַרטען איר מאַך צו ענג צוּ אײן קלאַמאַדער.
איך אַמאָהן אַלע פֿאָטטט, דיא בחור פֿאַלזען איר רונטער.
אױ עז דען מאַבער מ װאָוגדער ?
איך קען יוי גאַר ניקם אעהר געניעסען !
הי בין איך אַלעװײל בײן קונטיטער געװיהסען,
האַ איר נער עבבעם געמאַנגט אין אױן צו נעאאע.
דו אַמאָנגע זיח צו, װען זיח מפעטיט מאַך העאאע.

(זיא רײלט איהר אײנע טיטטע קאָנפֿעקט.)

פיגסי.

מאַ, נאַ, איך װילן זיח ניט בערמאַבען.
איבערהויפט, איך אום מאַ עבעם מאָפֿטיגם האָבען.
איך אאַ מאַ געודע טנעקקען, פֿאָר איר איך אין
אַמאָהן ;
די העאאער דיח גאַנגע װאָוך מאַללעװילע — דרמאָהן.
הי עספעטן איר אַללע נמבעל אָון מאַלע פֿריה,
ער מאָהנע, איך אַנדערטט המאַללעם צו 'ן קאָפֿיה.
סודסם טוב איך מאָבער 'ם גאַנגע יאָהר ניקם פֿערמאָבען.
אױ, זילטוי, דיא מאַרערענבאָרגער לעהקאָלבען,
דיח גענגע בײח איר צו גוטען ניט מױז,
דיח האָב איך צו גוטען אַלעפֿאָטט אין הויז.
מאַך אין דער קװאידיע דרינגע, איההקאָװין
אַמטס איר זי — מאָרגדליך ניט װאָװיל,
האַ איר פֿאָר הונגער דער המלװאָררט סטיינגם,
דו גאַ איך דערלאױטען נוױ, װען אער — גײגט,

Faksi.

Joi, 's warren mir aach zu eng all main Klaader.

Ich mahn allfott, di Bahn fallen mir runter.

Is es den ober a Wunder?

Ich ken joi gar niks mehr geniesen!

5   Doi bin ich allewail bain Kuntiter gewihsen,

Ho mir ner ebbes gelangt in Moil zu nemme.

Doi lange Si zu, wen Si Apetit aach hemme.

     (Si raicht ihr aine Tutte Konfekt.)

      Figsi.

Na, na, ich will Si nit beraaben.

Iberhoipt, ich mus als ebes Mopitigs haben.

10   Ich mach als gsunde Schnekken, for mir un main Mahn:

Doi hemmer di ganze Wuch allemoile--drahn.

Doi essen mir alle Nobez un alle Frih,

Er ahne, ich andert hallem zu'n Kofih.

Schunst tub ich ober 's ganze Johr niks fersuchen.

15   Joi, sichtSi, di Narrenborger Lihkuchen,

Di genge bai mir zu guten nit ois

Di hob ich zu guten allfott in Hois.

Aach in der Kumidie drinne, ihnmoil,

Wats mir soi--orndlich nit woil,

Das mir for Hunger der Hazworrm staigt,

20   Doi gih ich derzwischen nois, wen mer--gaigt,

און פֿון איר איז גוטלעכיך אײן טראטען.

שוינסט אָבער טוב איך פֿאָר דער סחורה ניקם פֿרנאטצן.

אפֿריפֿו, טוטוי הײנט ניט מין טהיאטער גיהן?

הײנט איז דער איהוואערט, הײנט וואוס — טיהן.

פֿאַקסי•

נאהן, אמאדאם פֿינ;זי מיך ווער טוועהרלץך קעננע,

אין אײלע הינטען טוט געביך פֿלעגנע!

פֿיגסי•

טו זיא זיך מעהן איהגעיבקאט מעהן און גיה זיא איט,

זיא וואטט זעהי, 'ם רייט'יר ניט —

פֿאַקסי•

נו איך ווילן זעהי זען איך קען.

וואהלי גיהבען זיא הײנט — דען?

פֿיגסי•

וואטוי, לאוי איך ערטט בזיננע,

איך בין דערל: געוויהסען מאָט טאָן דריננע.

יא זוי — ׳ן פֿואפֿערניקקעל, פֿון טיולער —

דיא אוזיק, זטאַגען זיא, איז פֿון או אילוער —

זעלוט זיא זעהי, וואהס זיא העט פֿאָר דעקלוערמאליוגע,

און וויא זיא פֿעלבטען דריננע איט קאהוהגנע.

פֿאַקסי•

אהאי, אין דיהן סטיק הײנט וואט געטאסען?

Un fill mir mit Gutzelich main Taschen.

Schunst ober tub ich for der Sehôroh[1] nikś frnaschen.

Apripu[2], tutSi haint nit in Thiater gihn?

Haint is der Mihwehrt, haint watś-schihn.

      Fakśi.

5 Nahn, Madam Figśi ich war schwehrlich kenne,

Main Maile hinten tut nebich flenne!

      Figśi.

Tu Si sich ahn Mihglichkat ahn un gih Si mit,

Si watt sehi, 'ś rait Ir nit--

      Fakśi.

Nu ich will sehi wen ich ken.

10 Waas gihben si haint--den?

      Figśi.

WatSi, loSi mich erst bsinne,

Ich bin derzu gewihśen oft schon drinne.

Ja, soi--'n Pumpernikkel, fun Schiller--

Di Musik, saagen si, is fun a Miller--.

15 Sellt Si sehi waaś si hem for Dekleraziune,

Un wi si fechten drinne mit Kanuhne.

      Fakśi.

Waas, in dihn Stik haint wat gschośśen?

---

1. Waren. 2. A propos.

נו יוי — דאַזוי זען פֿאָר מיר דיא רעכטע פֿאַסטען?
ווען מיך מע פיקסטוהן זיך, פֿאַנג איך חולשת טיער,
נאַהן איך בלײב דער האַאַם, דאַזוי מיז ניקס פֿאַר מיר!

פיגסי.

גיה זיא לו, זיא זיא קאַהן קינד;
דיא קאָמידיאַנטען טיהסען דאָך נעהר — בלינד.

פֿאָקסי.

אײנטוויהגען, בלינד היהן, בלינד הער.

(מאַראַם טהירצע קאַממט דיא שטראַסע הערונטער.)

פיגסי.

גוט אַאָרינג, טהירצע, וואַ מיז דו דעראַעהר?
וואַ קואַאַט זיא זוי פֿריה טוין הער?

טהירצע.

אײנם האָב מיך האַך אעסמען נוי\ דו פֿיהרען.
מיך האָ מורא, דאַזוי הורג = זע טוט מער דערפֿרײהרן.
ווען מיך איך גלײך מוי\פֿ\ן קאַמף\ העטט געטעללט,
האָטט\ם ניקס וואַהראַם מאַהכליהעגען — געוועלט.
דער ווינד בלייסטם נאָר זו לוי\;
דיא אַמאָבען זיא זיך מאָבער אַלֿלטוויין ניקס דרוי.
ווען זיא זיך נאָר קעגגע טיהן גאַמאַמנט מאַהנליהגען,
איז מ חידוש, ווען זיא דערנוי\ פֿלִים מון קאַטטאַהח
קריהגען?
מיך וויאָר מאַך מ אַמאָדוע, מיך וויער מאַך קאַהן — **סטמּק**

Nu joi--Daas sen for mir di rechte Possen?

Wen ich a Pikstuhl sich, fall ich H.ôlesches[1] schier,

Nahn ich blaib der haam, daas is niks for mir!

       Figsi.

Gih Si zu, sei Si kahn Kind:

5   Di Kumidianten schihsen doch nehr--blind.

       Faksi.

Maintwihgen, blind hihn, blind her.

    (Madam Thirze kommt di Strase herunter.)

       Figsi.

Gut Moring, Thirze, was is doi der Mehr?

Wu kummt Si soi frih schoin her?

       Thirze.

Mains hob ich aach mess noif doi fihren.

10 Ich ho Môro'[2], daas Hôreg[3]=le tut mer derfrihren.

Wen ich mich glaich oif'n Kopf hett gstellt,

Hott's niks waarms ahnzihgen--gewellt.

Der Wind bloists nor soi ois:

Doi machen si sich ober alle Wail niks drois.

15 Wen si sich nor kenne schihn galant ahnzihgen,

Is a Hidusch[4], wen si dernoich Flis un Katahrn krihgen?

Ich wor aach a Madle, ich wor aach kahn--Stok

---

1. in Ohnmacht fallen.   2. Furcht.   3. Mörderin.
4. ausserordentliche Sache.

איך האָב געטראַגען אײן געטעפּטען אונטערראָק,
אַ טיעפֿע הויב, װיאַ איער חילט האָט — קינדבעטטיסעעליך,

אַ גוונדען בּרוטסטפֿלעק, און היפֿטען קיסעעליך.
דרײאַ טיקקע, טוועהרע, װאַטערעאַ רעק,
און חויבּען דריבער אַ געטרחאַפֿטען — פֿלעק;
געװאַאַלקטע סטריאפֿל, און בּױערן טוהך,
ביז מען האַאַ נולֹ לו געטטעקט דחאַ טוהך.
אָבּער חילט העאַזי יױ לױטער פֿלֹהטען —
די קריהגען זיא עבּעם אַ בּיללֹע, איט אַ אוטהעעל;
די קען איער זעהי, װיא זיא זין פֿאַריהם
געגגע און סטעגגע, פֿון קאַמפֿל, ביז מן דיא פֿיהם.
רײכאַך זעססען זיא איהר קלֹחאַדער — טעילֹלֹע —
די טעהנסטע זאַבּען טוט איר אײנם פֿאַרבּילֹלֹע,
חיזט העזן זיא זאַלֹע נמהגעננבּיק אַ נמאַדרע גזירה.

פֿאַקסי.

נו װאַאַ זאַלֹל איער טוין, האָט איער דען אַ ברירה?
זיא געננגע מהן יױ ניט פֿון האַאַ,
ביז איער זיא אַנֹלֹכען לֹאָסט, װאַאַ זיא װעגֹלען מאַאַ?
אײנס אַנאַלֹט עבּעם הײנט אַ טטחאַט.
פֿון סטיק רונטער, האָט מיהנס מהן אַ קלֹחאַר.
ס זילֹט, חװאַבּטריע, אָבּער אַאַך חױ הײנט;
נאָר טחאַר, װענ'ס דיא און מהנטײנט.
איט דיהן לֹההדער חי חאַך עבּעם דעראָאַר.
מאַלֹעם קעננ'ים; ניקם אױ'ן לו טוועהר. ـ

Ich hob getragen main gstepten Unterrok,

A tiefe Hoib, wi mer izt hot--Kindbettschisselich,

A gsunden Brustflek, un Hiften Kisselich.

Drai tikke, schwehre, waareme Rek,

5 Un oiben driber a gstraaften--Flek:

Gewalkte Strimpf, un Boiern Schuhch,

Bis an Hals noif zu gstekt daas Tuhch.

Ober izt hemsi joi loiter Fluhtel--

Doi krihgen si ebes a Bichle, mit a Muthel:

10 Doi ken mer sehi, wi si in Parihs

Genge un stenne, fun Kopf, bis an die Fihs.

Doinoch lessen si ihr Klaader--schnizzle--

Di schehnste Sachen tut mir mains ferbizzle,

Izt[1] hem si alle Nahgenblik a nandre Geseroh[2].

        Faksi.

15 Nu waas soll mer toin, hot mer den a Bereroh[3]?

Si genge ahn joi nit fun Hals,

Bis mer si machen lost, waas si wellen als?

Mains macht ebes haint a Staat.

Fun Stik runter, hot ihns ahn a Klaad.

20 's sicht, umbschrie, ober aach ois haint:

Nor schaad, wen's di Sun ahnschaint.

Mit dihn Luhder is aach ebes der Mehr.

Alles kenn'is: niks is'n zu schwehr.--

1. izt] ist.
2. Dekret.
3. Wahl.

געזֹאלט זיא זעהי, װיא מיהנם אוהֹט װון סטיקט,
זײן טאֲאֲטע הֹאֲט מיהנם ערטא אַ בײטען געטריקט,
זי איט זײד, און קוהֹלעהֹרטע פענעהרֿלֿיך,
דאֲ אַ אֲאֲטטער אוהר היע מיז, גֹלֿאֲהֹב איך טװעהרֿלֿיך.
אֲאֲלֿזערהֹאֲמֲנד חיית, און עופית זען דרויֿלֿ;
אװֹל מֲהֹן זײט הֹאֲט 'ס געאֲאֲבט דוהֹכבֲמֲך, אױֿל דער
אַנדער אֲאֲנֲכהֹוֿלֿ.
'ס איז פֿאֲנֿלֿ חיית; ניקט װיא קוטטיערֿן און לֿאֲבֿען —
אַ האֲלֿזֿעֲסֿ עֹולֿם, קען מיהֹנם משוגע אֲאֲבֿען.
בין ערוב, ס' הֲאֲט דיא חוצפה, און ריהד קֿאֲהֹן אֲאֲ=
דער װאֲטט,
אַז לֿיטער פֿרֿאֲנֿלֿעט, איט'ן מלך אין מֲהֹנעֲסֿ פֿאֲטט.

טהירצע·

אײנטֿװֿיהֹגֿען, דוי לֿיגֿט איר אֲאֲך ניקט דרֿמֲהֹן,
אֲב אֵײֿנֿס קריהֹגֿט אױֿל דֿיטט, אֲאֲדֿער פֿרֿאֲנֿלֿעט אַ
אֲאֲהֹן —

(אֲב אֲיט פֿיגֿסֿי·)

פֿאֲקֿסֿי·

דער מיז אֲאֲך 'ס קֿטורת טוין געטװֿיגֿען.

(אֵײֿנֿע אֲאֲגֿר קֿאֲאֲמֿט.)

אװֿי, מֹאֲלֿינֿע! דוי גֿעהֹט הער, לֿעטט'ך פֿרֿויֿגֿען;
— װֹאֲטט, אֿיר גֿעֲנֿגֿע אֿיט אַנֿאֲנֿדֿער אֲאֲלֿע לֿוֿאֲה —
זֿיט מֿיהֹר דֿען נֿיֹאֲאֿער הֿיֹנֿטֿען בֿיֿם מֿיֿער פֿרֿמֲה?
4

Sellt Si sehi, wi ihns muhlt un stikt,

Sain Taate hot ihns erst a Baitel gstrikt,

Soi mit Said, un kuhlehrte Pehrlich,

Das a sotter mehr hie is, glaab ich schwehrlich.

5   Allerhand $\overset{H}{.}$ajjôs[1], un 'Ôfôs[2] sen droif:

Oif ahn Sait hot's gemacht Duhnbach, oif der
                              ander Mahnhoif.

's is foll $\overset{H}{.}$ajjôs[1]; niks wi Kuttern un Lachen--

A hallem 'Ôlom[3], ken ihns meschuggo'[4] machen.

Bin 'Oruv[5]'s hat di $\overset{H}{.}$uzpoh[6], un rihd kahn ander Wott,

10   As loiter Franzesch, mit'n Melech[7] in ahnem fott.

          Thirze.

Maintwihgen, doi ligt mir aach niks drahn,

Ob mains krihgt oif Daitsch, oder Franzesch a
                                        Mahn--

     (ab mit Figsi.)

          Faksi.

Der is aach 's Ketôres[8] schoin gstoigen[9]!

     (Aine Magd kommt.)

Oi, Maline! Doi geht her, lest'ch froigen:

15   --Watt, mir genge mit annander alle zwah--

Sait ihr den nimmer hinten bai aier Frah?

1. Tiere. 2. Vögel. 3. Welt. 4. wahnsinnig. 5. verbürge.
6. Frechheit. 7. König. 8. Weihrauch. 9. "Das
Räucherwerk (Ketoreth), der Weihrauch, den man ihm streute,
der Dunst und Duft seines Glückes ist ihm schon zu Kopf
gestiegen." Tnedlau, Prov. #263.

מאַגד.

נעהן, איך דיהן מעלעווין פֿאָרנע בין — שכר.
(זיא געהען אַב.)
(צוויי גאַללאַנס קאָממען.)

ערזטער.

דוא ביסט מיר אַ פֿײַנער בחור —
דוא ביסט נאָך אַ אמהן פֿון וואָטט.
זאַנג, וואָריס ביסטו ניט היהן קואאַע דאָט?
דאַז וואָר מיר אַ העל און אַ יעלבט;
מיר העם דיר געטטעער איבער דער וידער געלעלבט.

צווייטער.

ברודער! פֿערבלייה, עס טהוט מיר רעבט לייד.
מיך המטטע וומהרהאַפֿטיג ניט לייט.
מיך המטטע נאָטהווענדיגע — געטעפֿטען —

ערזטער.

דיא נעאַע דיר מאַך דיין כוחות, און דיין זעלטען!
בריטערלסע מיר וויטסען דאָך טוין —
דו האָסט מעלעפֿאָטטט דיא הענדפֿאָען — לו טוין.
גאָטטט בעהיט, דו רייטסט בעהריג מויז?
דו ביסט מאָויל אַ גרויסער טפעעקולעֿמנט,
אוֹך נעהר רעבט סודות דרויז,
דו וואַמסט דעך, דיין טטיקלֿיך זען מיר בעקמעננט.

צווייטער.

אויֿ עהר! מיך וואָר לו היוז,

Magd.

Nahn, ich dihn alle Wail forne bain------Ṡechur[1].

   (Si gehen ab.)

   (Zwai Gallanṡ kommen.)

       Erster.

Du biṡt mir a fainer Bohur[2]--

Du biṡt noch a Mahn fun Wott.

Saag, worim biṡtu nit hihn kumme dot?

5 Das wor dir a Hez un a Jacht:

Mir hem dir gester iber der wider gelacht.

       Zwaiter.

Bruder! Ferzaih, eṡ thut mir recht laid.

Ich hatte wahrhaftig nit Zait.

Ich hatte nothwendige--Gescheften--

       Erster.

10 Di nemme dir aach dain Kôhos[3], un dain Seften!

Briderle mir wiṡṡen doch schoin--

Du hoṡt allfott di Hendfoll--zu toin.

Gott behit, du raiṡt Barig ois?

Du biṡt amoil a groiser Ṡpekulant,

15 Mach nehr recht Sôdôṡ[4] drois,

Du waaṡt doch, dain Stiklich sen mir bekannt.

       Zwaiter.

Oif Ehr! Ich wor zu Hois,

---

1. A colloquial pronounciation of Hebrew Ṡechar.--Lohn.
2. Jüngling.
3. Kräfte.
4. Geheimnisse.

איך בין ניט קאאוע, נון ליאאער. כוּוּ.

ערזטער.

ערליהן 'ס רעכט, לייגענם נעהר ניט ;
איך האב דיך דאך גוועהי גיהן איט —
(ער אַנט איהם עטװאָ אינז אָהר.)

צװייטער.

דעמאָ איז מאַן מײנפּאַנן ; האָסט גוויהם מין טטמאַר.
איך זאַנן דערלו וועירען, וועין'ם איז וואַר.

ערזטער.

טװיין געהר טטינן, ברױכסט איר נאָקם ערליהזען.

צװייטער.

זיך, דוי דרױבען וועין איך דאַנפּעט װיהזען,
דוי זיך וױא 'ם דוי לוגיהט, װיא טמאַנן,
מאַנע פֿענטטער לינען איט נקיבות פֿאַנן.

ערזטער.

נו, גיה היהן, אמאַך זיא מ ביסמע דיא קוהר.

צװייטער.

(געהט אויף דען פֿאַללאַטט צו, אונד ציהט דען הוט.)
מהאאוען! טע װהו זוהעט זע באַן טוהר.
האָסט גוועהי, װיא זיא איך זוי פֿריינדליך גריסען.

ערזטער.

אמאַט, איך זאַם דיא דיא קאַוזוהגג מבטיהסען.

4 *

Ich bin nit kumme, zu'n Zimmer nois.

       Erster.

Erzihl's recht, laigens nehr nit:

Ich hob dich doch gsehi gihn mit--

    (Er sagt ihm etwas ins Ohr.)

       Zwaiter.

Daas is an Ainfall: host gewihs in Staar.

5   Ich soll derzu weren, wen's is war.

       Erster.

Schwaig nehr still, broichst mir niks erzihlen.

       Zwaiter.

Sih, doi droiben wen ich dafet wihlen.

Doi sich wi's doi zugiht, wi toll,

Alle Fenster ligen mit Nekêvôs[1] foll.

       Erster.

10 Nu gih hihn, mach si a bisle di Kuhr.

       Zwaiter.

    (Geht oif den Pallast zu, und ziht den Hut.)

Mamsel! Sche wu suhet le bon Schuhr[2].

Host gsehi, wi si mich soi fraindlich grisen.

       Erster.

Watt, ich los di Kanuhne abschihsen.

1. Frauenzimmer.   2. Je vous souhaite le bonjour.

צווייטער.

טע זוויא װאָטער דרעה=זיאָפּען זערװיהטעזהר!

ערזטער.

נו גיה נו, טטעגאָ דיך נאָך מַ יאָהר דוּ הער?
גיה לעהבער איט ריין, טפּיהזָען איר מַ פּאַרטיה,
נוּ'ן עסמען איז דמַך נאָך נו פּריה.

צווייטער.

ניין — ניין, היט עס איך בײא לייטען:
איך אום גלײך נאָך טיט — װעג רייטען.

ערזטער.

האַ! האַ! אוסט שיין װידער דאָט נול;
נו נו, איך גיב דיר איין המַנד דרויל,
'ם נאָטט דיר קאָהנער דאָ קאָיהטפָע איז'ן המַאָטען,
דיא מציאה טוט דיר ניט פליטה לַמַטאָען.
זמַאָג מיהר װיהגען איינער מַ גרוהם.
איך גיה איט דיא ריין, אמַאָלבֶאָן איר מַ פּרטַאָלבאָהם.

צווייטער.

אייגטוויהגען, דו לאָסט איר יוּ דמַך קאָהן רה!
אבער ניט לַעגגער, מַ מַ המַאָבע שעה.
(אַב אינז קאַפּפָעעאָהויז.)

מרדכי.

(קאָממט דיא שטראַסע הערונטער.)
דיא לוּחה העס מַאַך מיהר לויהן.

Zwaiter.

<u>Sche</u> <u>swi</u> <u>woter</u> <u>dreh-simpel</u> <u>serwihtehr!</u>[1]

Erster.

Nu gih zu, stell dich noch a Johr doi her?

Gih lihber mit rain, spihlen mir a Partih,

Zu'n Eṡṡen is doch noch zu frih.

Zwaiter.

5   Nain----nain, hait eṡ ich bai Zaiten:

Ich muṡ glaich nach Tisch--weg raiten.

Erster.

Ha! Ha! Muṡt schoin wider dot noif:

Nu, nu, ich gib dir main Hand droif,

'ṡ nascht dir kahner das Klihṡle ois'n Haafen,

10 Di <u>Mezi'oh</u>[2] tut dir nit <u>Pelêtoh</u>[3] laafen.

Saag ihr wihgen mainer a Gruhṡ.

Iz gih mit doi rain, machen mir a Franzefuhṡ.

Zwaiter.

Maintwihgen, du loṡt mir joi doch kahn Ruh!

Aber nit lenger, as a halbe <u>Scho'oh</u>[4].

(ab ins Kaffeehois.)

Mardachai.

(kommt di Straṡe herunter.)

15 Di zwah hem aach ihr Loihn,

---

1. Je suis votre très--simple serviteur.
2. billiger Einkauf.
3. auf der Flucht.
4. Stunde.

בנתן אונד תרש העננגע מען גאזינג טוין.

דיהן המין אעצלט מיך ערטט די זעהי.

נו, וועמז ניט מיז קען נאָך גטעהי.

התך. (קאממט)

ר' מרדכי! חייער אסתר לאָסט אייך גריהסען,

מיהבען בין מיך דרויבען בייא מיהר געוויהסען.

מרדכי. (שנעלל).

התך! זמחַגט איר גטוינד,

וועמז אמאַלט, וויא גיהטס דיהן גוטען קינד?

התך.

וועמז טיטט? וועמז זיא אמאַלט?

מואבטריע! זיא טטיפט, קוטטוערט און זאַלט.

זעלאָט מיהר נאָהר זעהי, וויא זיא מין גמאָד און זיבער גיהט,

און וויא פרעלצטיג דאָס בייא מיהר טטיהט.

די טטעננע אייך עבעס קוואהטער און טיהנע טיטטיך,

לאָן אבפוללען זיגען דרויל גמאָדיגע קעהרוויטליך,

מאַך טטעננע דרויל פאַהלעמהגנע היעפלעיך איט טאאעקקען,

דערניהבען טטיהט אַ גמאָדיג לעפּאַהרע בעקקען;

דמאַ איז אסיר גאָר ניט צו טעננען,

דמאַ האָט זיא נאָהר, אַ ביסעל דיא הענד צו נעללען.

אויפּן ערדטבוידען קעננעט אער עסמען.

העפלעבעוואַהניגע טטיהן, האַנדברעכַאַד איט גמאָדיגע טרעטסען,

Bigthan und Theres henge an Galing schoin.

Dihn Haman mecht ich erst doi sehi.

Nu, waas nit is ken noch gechehi.

        Hathach. (kommt)

R' Mardachai! Aier Esther lost aich grihsen,

5   Ihben bin ich droiben bai ihr gewihsen

        Mardachai. (schnell.)

Hathach! saagt mir gschwind,

Waas macht, wi gihts dihn guten Kind?

        Hathach.

Waas taitsch? Waas si macht?

Umbschrie! Si stift, kuttert un lacht.

10 Sellt ihr nohr sehi, wi si in Gold un Silber

                        gibt,

Un wi prechtig das bai ihr stiht.

Doi stenne aich ebes Kumuhter un schihne Tischlich,

Zu'n abpuzzen ligen droif goldige Kehrwischlich,

Aach stenne droif pozelahnene Hiefelich mit

                    Schmekken,

15 Dernihben stiht a goldig lefohre Bekken:

Das is osur[1] gar nit zu schezzen,

Das hot si nohr, a bisle di Hend zu nezzen.

Oif'n Erdsboiden kennet mer essen.

Helfebahnige Stihl, handbraad mit goldige

                    Tressen,

---

1. bei meiner Seele!

צו נעהר דיא שפיהלט דיא טענסטע מופערשטיקקליק,
איבערנויגען מיט פֿאָהר דאַס ניט דרויף זב לי דיא
אַיקליק —

אין דיא טפֿיגען קען איער זיך זעהי פֿון מונטן ביז
אויבען.

און אין דער היהך דוי הענגע דרויבען
דיא פֿאָרטרעטטער רום פֿון דיא אַלֿטע שררות,
דערנווויטען טטענגע שטאַהניגע עבודי זרות.
אין עקק שטיהט אַ פֿאַפֿעניע פֿון אַ נויפֿען.
און אַ קאָנעביע, 'ס דאָל' יוי אַ מלכה דרויף טלויפֿען,
געאווגלנעטער זען מיך מוי' דיא מענד,
אער מאַלֿ ניט אַחהנע, מא דיא זען פֿון אַנטענע־
הענד.

וויא דיא קינדער ישראל מויז מצרים געאנגע,
און דיא מרגלים דיא ווינטרויבען ברענגע.
נאָך אעהר פֿאָלֿבֿע מאַלֿטע געטיטיס,
און מאַך, וואַז ערטט געטעהי פֿאַר וויבען מיז;
זוי פֿון דער פֿראָהלנעטע רעוואָוואָהנאֿניהן,
און וויא נאַפֿמאָליהן קואַאט פֿון טרוהן.
איט יההווויהֿנען מיז זיא גאַבֿן בעהענגט,
דיא האָט מיהר אחשורוש טון געטענקט.
אַ טנוהר פֿעהרליק האָט מיא אַהן,
דיא מיז לפחות מאה אלפים ווערטה מאַלַהן,
ר' מרדכי ליעב! דיא העט מיך אַ גריהם,
דאַצֿ זען פֿווואַערם, וויא דיא מצה = קלֿיהם —
ווען מיא זיך ריהרט, ווען מיא זיך ריהגט,

A Nuhr di spihlt di schenṡte Uperštikklich,
Iberzoigen nit Flohr, daṡ nit droif sevlen[1] di Miklich--
In di Spigel ken mer sich sehi fun untn bis oiben.
Un in der Hihch doi henge droiben
Di Portretter rum fun di alte Scherorôṡ[2],
Derzwischen stenne štahnige Avôdê Sorôṡ[3].
In Ekk stiht a Poppele fun a Noifen.
Un a Kanebie, 'ṡ daf joi a Malkoh[4] droif schloifen.
Gemulzeter sen aich oif di Wend,
Mer soll nit mahne, aṡ di sen fun Menschen=hend.
Wi di Kinder Jiṡroêl[5] ois Mizrajjim[6] genge,
Un di Meragglim[7] di Waintroiben brenge.
Noch mehr solche alte Gschichtiṡ,
Un aach, was eršt gschehi for Woichen is:
Soi fun der franzesche Rewulaziuhn,
Un wi Napoliuhn kummt fun Truhn.
Mit Juhwihlen is si ganz behengt,
Di hot ihr Ahasveros schoin gschenkt.
A Schnuhr Pehrlich hot si ahn,
Di is le-Pehôṡ Mêoh Alofim[8] werth alahn,
R' Mardachai lieb! Di hem aich a Grihṡ,
Daas sen Pummerṡ, wi di Mazzoh=klihṡ[9]--
Wen si sich rihrt, wen si sich rihgt,

1. sevlen] sevli--scheissen. 2. Gebieter.
3. Götzenbilder. 4. Königin. 5. Israel. 6. Ägyptien.
7. Späher. 8. zum wenigsten ein hundert tausend.
9. ungesäuerte Klösse.

קוואט אללעם זו זאַמפען און פריהגט;
וואַז זיא בעפיהלט, וואַז זיא דען וויל,
פאר אימה, איז אללעם אייסזיך טטיל,
אחשורוש קואט מיהר גאַר ניאָער פון דער זייט,
און פערברענגט מיט מיהר זיין צייט.
דער האקט איבער מיהר, און טוטזי ארנדליך אויזברי=
טען,
מיהר וואַטט זעהי ר' מרדכי, זו גוטען! —

מרדכי.

התך! דאַו טטיהט נאַך ווייט מין פעלד,
דאַו קואַט וויל' דיהן די מויבען מהן;
דער קען אללעם אַרבען אין דער וועלט,
דער אמאַבט קלאַהנע גרויז, און גרויזע קלאַהן.

התך.

איך האַבם אַבער פאַר געוויהם געהערט,
דאַם אחשורוש נאַר זיא די בעגעהרט,
און די אַנדערע זאַל' אער אַזוע ווידער האאימאַגגען.

חרבונה (קאָממט געלייפען, שלענט די הענדע איבערן
קאָפף צוזאַממען.)

זאַמט מוג טרייע, זאַמט מוג קלאַגען,
גאַטט זאַל' זיך מרחם זיין! איר ווערן אַלזע דערטלאַנגען.

מרדכי.

חוק גאַטטם וויללען! וואַז איז די דערזאָעהר?

Kummt alles zu laafen un frihgt:

Waas si befihlt, waas si den will,

For Êmoh[1], is alles maislich still,

Ahasveros kummt ihr gar nimmer fun der Sait,

5   Un ferbrengt mit ihr sain Zait.

Der hokt iber ihr, un tutsi orndlich oisbruten,

Ihr watt sehi R' Mardachai, zu guten!-----

        Mardachai.

Hathach! Daas stiht noch wait in Feld.

Daas kummt oif dihn doi oiben ahn:

10 Der ken alles machen in der Welt,

Der macht klahne grois, un groise klahn.

        Hathach.

Ich hobs ober for gewihs gehert,

Das Ahasveros nor di begehrt,

Un di andere soll mer alle wider hamjaagen.

      Harbona (kommt geloifen, schlegt die Hende ibern

           Kopf zusammen.)

15 Lost uns schraie, lost uns klagen,

Gott soll sich merahêm[2] sain! Mir warrn alle derschlagen.

        Mardachai.

Um Gotts willen! Waas is doi der Mehr?

1. Furcht. 2. barmherzig.

חרבונה! זאַגט: װאָריס דעט מיהר דען זיי זעהר ?

חרבונה.

ר' מרדכי ליהב! װמַחַז איז דמַחַז פאָר אַ צרה,
איר זַרעאָע יידען, זען נעביך מַזַזע אַ כפרה!
המן, דער רשע, מון זין ניקסולינגע זרש,
העט מסירות מַהַקניהבען ביַא אחשורוש.
דער הַט דרין' אונזער אונטערגַאַנג בעטלַאָסעען,
גאָטט ערבאַרעם, איר װאָרן מַזַזע דערטאָסעען,
אער הַאקט אונז לו קרעפפלַיך,
אער לאַפפטט אונז מין טרעעפלַיך
דמַחַז בלוט מה — מון טיעד
אונז מַזַזע, איט װייב מון קינד!

מרדכי.

טטיזל! טעט נאָר ניט זיי אויזגעלאָסעען.

התך. (שרייעט.)

מוי װיה! אויך בין טוין דערטאָסעען
איך בין טוין אַ קרעפפלַזע,
איך בין טוין אַ לעעפלַזע,
איך בין טוין אַ טרעעפלַזע.
מוי װיה! מוי װיה! אין קעפפלַזע.

(לויפט אב.)

מרדכי.

דוי גיהט נאָר איט ריין מין דער טטוב.

Harbona! Saagt: worim det ihr den soi sehr?

       Harbona.

<u>R</u>' Mardachai lihb! Waas is daas for a <u>Zoroh</u>[1],

Mir areme Jiden, sen nebich alle a <u>Kapporoh</u>[2]!

Haman, der <u>Roscho</u>ᶜ[3], un sain nikśnuzige Seres,

5   Hem <u>Meśirôś</u>[4] ahngihben bai Ahasveros.

Der hot droif unser Untergang beschlośśen,

Gott erbarm, mir warrn alle derschośśen,

    Mer hakt uns zu Krepflich,

    Mer zapft uns zu Trepflich

10   Daas Blut ah--un schind

    Uns alle, mit Waib un Kind!

       Mardachai.

Still! Tet nor nit soi oisgelośśen.

       Hathach. (schraiet)

Oi wih! Ich bin schoin derschossen

    Ich bin schoin a Krepfle,

15   Ich bin schoin a Zepfle,

    Ich bin schoin a Trepfle.

Oi wih! Oi wih! main Kepfle.

      (loift ab.)

       Mardachai.

Doi giht nor mit rain in der Stub,

1. Unglück.

2. Sühnopfer.

3. Bösewicht.

4. Anklagen.

מיך ווָל זעהי, ווַחַז מיך דערלָז טוב,
דוי הויזען לָחַמַפט דמָך חַלָזעם לַחַאוע.
(ער געהעט אין דאָ הויז, הרבונה פָּאלָגט איהם.)

הרבונה׃

הוי וויה! וויא טטעקקען מיר מין חַ מרמה.
(ציממער אים פָּאללַאזט. אַיגע שׁעַגע קָאממט, אים ג־עוטען
שׁטאַאט געקליידעט, אונטער בײדען אַרמען בילכער.)
מיך בעעניד דיר, אסתר! ניכֿט דיין גלֿיקֿ;
וילָזיג, געגן געהע מיך — גוריק,
אײנען לֿיעבען ריגחַלֿדינַמַ הַגַב׳ מיך וויעדער,
אײנען הערלֿיבֿען געטהע, מונד בירגערס לֿיעדער,
הַמַ, טיקזַלֿ! נוז טפרעבֿ׳ מיך דיר הַמַהַז;
מיך געה׳ מוגד לֿעוי׳ טילֿזערס — רעויגחַלֿימַז!
(אב.)
(אײנע אַגדערע שׁעַגע קָאממט, מיט אײנער גיטאַררע אינד
אײנעז פַאק נָאטעגבלעטטער א־נטער דעם ארם.)
כוז, ווָהַהֿוַחַז! זַמ אום מיך טיידען,
הַמ בחַרבחַר! מָהַגע גלֿיבֿעז,
ניבֿט אײן אָמַנַחַרט! ניבֿט אײן היידען
קָאנטעז דמַ פָעזועגהַהערֿ ערווײבֿעז.
זַמ קַמַאוט, מיהר גרַמָסעז גיסטער! דעז נור בייז חיך
חיט זֿעוֿיגקֿייט, חיז — וומַגגע;
נור מיהר זייד אײן היאַאעז רייכֿ,
זייט אײן זֿיבֿט — אײגע זַמַגגע.
(אב.)
(עז קָאממט ווירדער אײנע, מיט אײגעם שׁפֿיגעל אין דער הַאגד.)

Ich will sehi, waas ich derzu tub,

Doi hoisen laaft doch alles zamme.

     (Er gehet in das Hois, Harbona folgt ihm.)

        Harbona.

Oi wih! Wi stekken mir in a <u>Mirmoh</u>[1].

     (Zimmer im Pallast. Aine Schene kommt, in gresten

        Staat geklaidet, unter baiden Armen Bicher.)

Ich benaid dir, Esther! nicht dain Glik:

5   Willig, gern gehe ich--zurik,

Mainen lieben Rinaldino hab' ich wieder,

Mainen herrlichen Gethe, und Birgers Lieder,

Ha, Schiksal! Nun sprech' ich dir Hohn:

Ich geh' und les' Schillers--Resignazion!

        (ab.)

     (Aine andere Schene kommt, mit ainer Gitarre und

        ainen Pak Notenbletter inter dem Arm)

10 Nun, wohlahn! so muś ich schaiden,

Ha Barbar! ohne glaichen,

Nicht main Mozart! nicht main Haiden.

Konten das Felsenherz erwaichen.

So kommt, ihr grosen Gaiśter! Den nur bai aich

15 Ist Seligkait, ist--Wonne:

Nur ihr said main Himmel Raich,

Sait main Licht--maine Sonne.

        (ab.)

(Es kommt wider aine, mit ainem Spigel in der Hand.)

1. Verrat.

מאָנט איר דען ניבט דער שפיגעל,
דאָס נאַטור ניבט איט גיינע
איר אויפֿגעדריקט דער טענההייט זיעגעל,
אונד איר פֿערזיהען טויזענד ריינע,
אונד דאָך האָט ער איך ניבט בעגעהרט,
קיין געווירדיגט, איך נו בעטראַבטען.
וואָהלאָן! ווער ניבט נו טעגלֶנן וייס — אין ווערטה,
דען קאַן מיך נור — פֿערמאָבטען.

(שטאָלץ אב.)

(איין מעדלען, גאַנץ שליבט געקליידעט, קאָמט.)
איינטווייהנגעגען, מיך גיה ווילֶיג, אונפֿערדרדאָסמען,
פֿון דוי, וויידער פֿאָטט.
מין היאאען ווערן דיא מיהאן געטהאָסמען,
מאַנגט ער דאָך הֶוו מין טפריבוואַמעט.
דרום גיה מיך האַך מין דער טיינֶען
וויידער המאַם, נו אין — אטאאע,
וועגס ווער גאָטטעם וויֶנֶען,
העט ער איך טין אטסמען — נעאאע.

(אב.)

צעטולפֿע.

(קאָממט העראויז, גאַנץ עלעגאַנט געקליידעט.)
וייס? אין איר זאַלֶל אמֶן זיך ניט פֿערֶעבען?
איר, איר, האָט ער מין קאָרעב געבבען!
און דאָם רוהם=פֿיהפעגֶע, דאַו גאַמאָלֶֶֹ'ט'ן!
יוטט דאַו דאַו רֶֶוֹ=נעהסֶֹוֹ ווֶֹֹוֹ ער בעהאַלֶֶֹטען!
וואָריק? וואַאֶ איוֹט איט דעהן דען דעראָעהר?
פֿון וייס פֶֿאָר אַ פֶֶֹֹֿאָיֶע איוֹ מיהגס דען הער?

Sagt mir den nicht der Spigel,

Das Natur nicht mit Gaize

Mir oifgedrikt der Schenhait Siegel,

Und mir ferlihen toisend Raize,

5   Und doch hat er mich nicht begehrt,

Koim gewirdigt, mich zu betrachten,

Wohlahn! Wer nicht zu schezzen wais--main Werth,

den kan ich nur--ferachten.

       (stolz ab.)

      (Ain Medchen, ganz schlicht geklaidet, kommt.)

Maintwihgen, ich gih willig, unferdrossen,

10   Fun doi, wider fott.

In Himmel warrn di Ihen gschlossen,

Saagt mer doch als ain Sprichwott.

Drum gih ich aach in der Stillen

Wider haam, zu main--Memme,

15   Wens wer Gottes Willen,

Het er mich schoin messen--nemme.

      (ab.)

      Zetulpe.

(kommt herois, ganz elegant geklaidet.)

Wais? In mir soll man sich nit ferleben?

Mir, mir, hat er ain Koreb geben!

Un das Ruhs=pihpele, das gfallt'n!

20   Just das Roz=nehsle will er behalten!

Worim? Waas ist mit dehn den der Mehr?

Fun wais for a Familie is ihns den her?

ווער זענד זיין היהנער, און זיין גענס ?
וואו מיזט מיהנט דען הער? ווער קענג'ם ?
אין האט ער דיא קין דערװיטט —
דא האט ער וואהז רעכטם וועג גפיטט ?
דען דרעק קאן אמן דעך פֿון מיהן רונטער טהבען,
יא מין מייכפֿאנן זאלן א אנגט האבען,
דאז הייסט א גוטע, דאז מיז א גטאמק ;
וויא אהנער, דער רום גיט איט'ן לווארעלבומק.
פֿערזעבט זיך מין דען ניבבעם, מין דען בוזוויטט:
אין דען עזענד, מין דען מפּפֿענגזעטט.

(זיא געהעט פֿאר דעם שפיגעל.)

גאטט בעעהיהט !
ווען מיך איך בעטרעבט,
מיז דאך א נונטערטיער.
וויא טייג אונד נאעבט.
וויס פֿאר א וויסינג האט א מין הױט,
און וויא גאַלאַנט בין מיך געבויט ;
אין העגדזע, אין פֿיסזע,
אין אייגע, אין ניסזע.
אין מויבען, אין לעהן,
אין חן - גריהבזע — וויא טעהן.
אין מרעם, אין האנז,
וויא טעהן מיזט ניבט חנז.
און פֿאן אין אנדרע זאבען,
דאז וויל מיך גאר קאהן לארעזע אאבען.
אבער דער קריפפען מיזט דאך גאנט פֿערוואקסען.

Wer send sain Hihner, un sain Genś?

Wu ist ihnś den her? Wer kenn'ś?

Iz hat er di Kiz derwischt--

Da hat er waaz Rechtś weg gfischt?

5   Den Dreck kan man doch fun ihn runter schaben.

Soi ain Ainfall soll a Mensch haben,

Das haiśt a Guśte, das is a Gschmak:

Wi ahner, der rum git mit'n Zwarechsak.

10   Ferlebt sich in den Nibbeś, in den Boiswicht:

In den Elend, in den Affengsicht.

                (Si gehet for dem Spigel.)

Gott behiht!

Wen ich mich betracht,

Is doch a Nunterschied.

15   Wi Taig und Nacht.

Waiś for a Waiśing hat main Hoit,

Un wi galant bin ich geboit:

        Main Hendle, main Fiśle,

        Main Maile, main Niśle.

20   Main Oichen, main Zehn,

        Main .ên=Gribble[1]--wi schehn.

        Main Arem, main Hals,

        Wi schehn ist nicht als.

        Un fon main andre Sachen,

25   Da will ich gar kahn Lareme machen.

Aber der Krippel ist doch ganś ferwakśen.

1. Schöngrübchen.

דאָ אשטײט דאָך ווי משיגע — פֿאַקטסען.
דער מלֹרוך! דיא גריהנע ביר!
דאָ וויֹל זיך אעטסטען איט איר?
אָבער וואַטט, איך וויֹל דיר טוין געבען,
איך וויֹל דיר וייסטען: אחשורוש זאַל זיך וון דיר
פֿערֹעהרבען.

(אין עקסטאַסע.)

פֿיער און פֿלֹאַם וויֹל איך טבֿרינֿנען,
אויז לֹאַסטען מן דיר איין אוטה —
להכעים קויל איך איר נאָך אַ גאַרנעטטאָר טפֿיֹנֿנען,
און פֿון דער אאַדאַם וורמה — אַ הוט.
האַ, נו טויט וויֹל איך דיך טרעלֿנֿנען.
דיך, מוכד היע דיא אאַדֿיֹך אלֹוֹען;
שבֿת טוה איך אײַן נײַא היעטטאָע אויפֿעֿנֿנען,
און גיה דריננע נו דער — כלה —

(שנעֿלֹל אבֿ.)

_____

(מרדכי'ס וואָהנונג, ער זיצט אונד לערנט.)

מאי טעמא? — וואַז איז דער טעים?

המן (שטעיקט דען קאָפֿף צור טהירע העריין.)

אײן זעעל, ער איז דערהאַווטם.

מרדכי.

ניקט אעהר נאַהן, בלֹיבט איר אָבער קשה?
(ער ערבליקט הֹמן.)

Das macht doch wi <u>meschuggo</u>ʻ[1]--Faksen.

Der Allroin! Di grihne Bir!

Das will sich messen mit mir?

Ober watt, ich will dir schoin geben,

5 Ich will dir waisen: Ahasveros soll sich in dir

ferlehben.

(in Ekstase)

Faier un Flam will ich sprizzen,

Ois lassen an dir main Muth--

<u>Le-ha-Chʻis</u>[2] koif ich mir noch a Garnetur Spizzen,

10 Un fun der Madam Muroh--a Hut.

Ha, zu Toit will ich dich trezzen.

Dich, und hie di Madlich alle:

<u>Schabbos</u>[3] tuh ich main nai Hietle oifsezzen,

Un gih drinne zu der---<u>Kalloh</u>[4]--

(schnell ab.)

(Mardachai's Wohnung, er sitzt und lernt.)

15 <u>Maʼi Taʻamo</u>ʼ[5]--Waas is der <u>Taʻam</u>[6]?

Haman (stekt den Kopf zur Thire herain.)

Main Seel, Er is derhaam.

Mardachai.

Niks mehr nahn, blaibt mir ober <u>koschoh</u>[7]?

(Er erblikt Haman)

1. wahnsinnig.
2. zum Trotz.
3. Sabbat.
4. Braut.
5. Warum.
6. Grund.
7. schwer eingehend.

מ' ווה! וואהז וויל דער דו, דער רשע?

המן.

ער איז אָבער אַ פֿלייסיגט אשענדזע.

מרדכי.

דער האָט ווידער קיין גזעהי מין קעגדזע,
מיז טיין ווידער שיכור,
דער כופר בעיקור.

(לויט.)

נו — וואהז זאָלל דען זיין?
וואהז פֿיהרט דיהן המרן צו איר ריין?

המן.

הער ער! האָט ער דען ניט אַ פֿרייד.
ווען ער אויל אַן טעהן גיזע רייט?

מרדכי.

וויא? וואהז? מיך זאָלל רייטען?
יס דענקען איך מיך גאַר ניט דיא לייטען,
דאַז מיך קואאע בין אַן אַ גויל,
אַס וויא מין אין יהובען אַ נאהנליגם אויל.
האָ מיך איך גזעלט מיל' אין טאהמטע זיין פֿאַערד,
און דוי בין מיך גול קואאע — פֿערקעהרט,
פֿום, האָ מיך גההאטעט, 'ן טוואהל טטאָן 'ן נמחם,
דוי וואָר מיך נמך אַ קלָמַהַן יינגלע דער המחם.
אילט אָבער בין מיך לאורך ימים אַ נחלטער יד,

O wih! Waas will der doi, der Roscho^c[1]?

      Haman.

Er is ober a flaisigs Mendle.

      Mardachai.

Der hot wider nain gsehi in Kendle,

Is schoin wider schikkôr[2],

5   Der Kôfer be-^{c}Ikôr[3].

      (loit.)

Nu--waas soll den sain?

Waas fihrt dihn Harrn zu mir rain?

      Haman.

Her Er! Hot Er den nit a Fraid.

Wen Er oif an schehn Gaile rait?

      Mardachai.

10 Wi? Waas? Ich soll raiten?

's denken mich gar nit di Zaiten,

Das ich kumme bin of a Goil,

As wi in main Lihben anahnzigs Moil.

Ho ich mich gsezt oif main Taate sain Pferd.

15 Un doi bin ich nuf kumme--ferkehrt,

Pums, ho ich ghatt, 'n Schwanz staz 'n Zaam,

Doi wor ich noch a klahn Jingle der haam.

Izt ober bin ich le-Ôrech Jomim[4] a nalter Jid,

---

1. Bösewicht.
2. betrunken.
3. Gottesleugner.
4. möge es viele Tage fortdauern!

בייא איר איז נו'ן רייטען חלשעווין נו שפיעט.

המן·

עס טהוט איר, מיין מייד,
זעלבסט הערנאָ'ך לייד —
ווך האָב' בײן קענינ
אייך פֿאָמ'רן געבעטען אונטערטהאַנינ.
'ס העלפֿט אַבער מאווין ניקס,
ער אום רייטען, איינער זיקס !

מרדכי·

נו יוי, וואַאַוּ זאָנט 'ן המַרן דרחזהן;
ווען איך חם ושלום ברעך אַ בַמהן ?
מַדער מיך טלאַנ איר מין קאָפּל' אַ לאָך ;
ער איז מין טטואַנד מאַך נאָך,
חון טוט חודשה אַ קוואידיע דרוי אמאַכען,
חון האַלט זיך דערנו דיא זײטען פֿאַר לאַכען.
זאַמַנט: ווארים זאָלן מיך יוטט רייטען ?
וואַאַ זאָל דען דער שטות בעדײטען ? —

המן·

מאַלע וועטטער ! עז אום מַבער זיין,
פֿאַמאָנט איר, חון ווילאָינט מיין.
דער קעניג טהוט'ן דאָך וואַס גוטס;
געוט, אוענדזע ! ער טהוטס ?

מרדכי·

וואַאַ האָב מיך מָבער געטוין,

Bai mir is zu'n Raiten allewail zu Špiet.

Haman.

Eš thut mir, main Aid,

Selbšt herzlich laid--

Ich hab' bain Kenig

5 Oich for'n gebetn unterthenig.

'š helft aber amoil nikš

Er muš raiten, mainer Sikš!

Mardachai.

Nu joi, waas ligt 'n Harrn drahn:

Wen ich H̥aš ve-Scholôm[1] brech a Bahn?

10 Oder ich schlag mir in Kopf a Loch:

Er is in Štand aach noch,

Un tut H̥udsche[2] a Kumidie drois machen,

Un halt sich derzu di Saiten for Lachen.

Saagt: Worim soll ich jušt raiten?

15 Waas soll den der Štuš[3] bedaiten?--

Haman.

Alle Wetter! Es muš aber sain,

Folgt mir, un willigt ain.

Der Kenig thut'n doch waš Gutš.

Gelt, Mendle! Er thutš?

Mardachai.

20 Waas hob ich ober getoin,

1. Gott behüt!
2. wenigstens--Vid. variant 12, 5; identity 69, 4.
3. Dummheit.

דאָס אויך קריהג זוי אַ גרויזאַמען זין?

הָמָן.

ער איז מיר אַבער, אויך אַ טיראַער.
וויסט מיהר'ם יעצט דען ניאַער,
דאָס מיהר ערטט קירלאָיך העטט
אונגערן קעניג דאָס ֶעבען גערעטט?
'ס האָט מויך קיינס אַהער דעראַן געדאַכט,
דוי האָט אַבער דער קעניג גוואַגט:
דער מרדכי, דער האָט מיר עררעטט דמו ֶעבען;
האָט אַמאָן מיהן מויך מיין טרינקגעלאָד געגעבען?
טהו זיך מיינער אונז מיינאַן זעהן,
מיך גלויב האַז, ער אוס מיין בוך נאָך טטעהן. —
בֶין וועטטער! די טטיהט ער מויך ווירקֶיך דריכנע.
דער קעניג טוט זיך ערטט אַ ביזֶע בזינע:
„מיך זֶהאַגט מיר אַבער, מיהר גוטען ֶיט,
„ווהז אמך מיך דען אמן פֿאָר אַ פֿרייד?
„מיט ווהז זַאֶן מיך מיהן בעגעהרען?"
חאַלֶען מיינער אַמייסטעטעט מיך אַהערען?
אַהַגט' מיך דאַרויֶ' לוין קעניג.
מיך אמך דען פֿאַרטֶאַנג אונטערטהעניג:
אַמָן ֶיהגט מיהן פרעבֶטיגע קֶיידער אַן,
אן זעלט מיהן מויֶ דעם קעניגס פֿפֿערד,
חאָ מיינער רופֿט: „דיס איזט דער מצן,
„רען דער קעניג צו עהרען בענעהרט."
חֶאָ, זֶהאַגט דער קעניג, געהסט דו מיר אַבער הייניג,

Das ich krihg soi a groisaamen Loin?

   Haman.

Er is mir aber, oich a Schlimmer.

Wist ihr's jezt den nimmer,

Das ihr erst kirzlich hett

5 Unsern Kenig das Leben gerett?

's hat oich kains mehr daran gedacht,

Doi hat aber der Kenig gsagt:

Der Mardachai, der hat mir errett das Leben:

Hat man ihn oich ain Trinkgeld gegeben?

10 Thu sich ainer um ainmal sehn,

Ich gloib als, er mus in main Buch noch stehn.--

Blitz Wetter! Doi stiht er oich wirklich drinne.

Der Kenig tut sich erst a bisle bsinne:

„Iz saagt mir aber, ihr guten Lait,

15 „Was mach ich den Man for a Fraid?

„Mit was soll ich ihn beehren?"

Wollen Aier Majestet mich anheren?

Sagt' ich daroif zu'n Kenig.

Ich mach den Forschlag unterthenig:

20 Man zihgt ihr prechtige Klaider an,

Un sezt ihn oif des Kenigs Pferd,

Un ainer ruft: „Dis ist der Man,

„Den der Kenig zu ehren begehrt."

Iz, saagt der Kenig, gehst du mir aber aiig,

אונד נעאוסט מיינט פֿאַן אין טעגסטע גיליק,
אונד דו טוסט איר דען מרדכי :עלבסט רוף פֿיהרען,
אונד וויא דו גזאָגט, פֿאָר מיהן הער פובליהירען.

מרדכי.

נו — און טונסט ניקט וויטער?
וועלט מיהר וויא איר אהזבען אַ געגגליטען רייטער?
נו יוי, אאַך דו דיהן עולם אַ פורים ⸗ שפיעל;
נאהן — נאהן — דו נעמ איך ניט וויא פֿיעל.
גאָטט בעהיט! אמָך דו מין מיקום אַ שפעקטאהקעל,
רייט רום מין ברמאטעהויב, און אַ ניטאהקעל.

המן.

ער הערט דעך, אמן ֿענגט מיהן מעדערע קלײדער מַן;
אמַן ֿהאסט מיהן געווזין וויא מין בעטעלֿאמַן
מין דער שטאַדט רייטען רום?
דמַ וועד דעך מ טאַנד פֿאָרֿן פובליקום.
דם נעמ ער גור מ וויֿן דיא פֿיטע,
דיֿ רופֿט מיינער אױֿ העברעאיט, אונד איך אױֿ
דיֿטע.
(ער גיבט איהם אײנע ראלֿע פֿאפיער.)

מרדכי.

נו? און דמאַ: מיֿ מאַֿעם?
דוי האָב איך פֿאָר וויא נוך 'ן דלות!
תאמר יוי טאَחאַגט איך דער גוין חם ושלום טויט!
און ווען דער שטות מאַך גערויט,

Und nimmst ains fon main schenste Gailich,

Und du tust mir den Mardachai selbst rum fihren,

Und wi du gsagt, for ihn her publizihren.

      Mardachai.

Nu---Un schunst niks waiter?

5 Welt ihr ois mir machen a nenglischen Raiter?

Nu joi, mach doi dihn 'Ôlom[1] a Purim[2]-Spiel:

Nahn--nahn--doi nem ich nit wi fiel.

Gott behit! Mach doi in Mokôm[3] a Spektahkel,

Rait rum in Braatehoib, un a Zitahkel.

      Haman.

10 Er hert doch, man legt Ihn andere Klaider an:

Man last Ihn gewis wi ain Bettelman

In der Stadt raiten rum?

Das wer doch a Schand for'n Publikum.

Da nem Er nur a Wail di Paitsch,

15 Dies ruft ainer oif Hebreisch, und ich oif

                    Daitsch.

    (Er gibt ihm aine Rolle Papier.)

      Mardachai.

Nu? Un daas is alles?

Doi hob ich for wi noich 'n Dalôs[4]!

Th ômar[5] joi schlaagt mich der Goil Has ve-Scholôm[6] toit!

Un wen der Stus[7] aach geroit,

1. Leute: literally--world.
2. Purimspiel.
3. Stelle.
4. Armut.
5. im Fall.
6. Gott behüt!
7. Dummheit.

װאַם איז די אײן רוח דען?
דאָם איך אָמָרינג ניקט נוך גיהן קען,
און אום מַבֿט טאָג דערהמַמ
מין בעסט ליגען, און בין קרום און לַמהם.

המן.

און זָאָל מיהן געװיז גאָר אין דער קוטטען
אין דער שטאָדֿט זָא רום לַמסמען רטטען?

מרדכי.

נו, די לַמבֿט ער דרוז?
די פַֿמָלֿט אער דֿאָך ניט רוז!
דען קען אער טיהן דרינגע טלױפֿען;
מַבער מָבֿפֿין גוין, דאַל' אער יו ניט טנױפֿען!
אין מַהן נװַהגעגנבֿזיק ליגט אער הונטען — פוטט.
האמר אין אמת, זעגט ער איך מין מַ קוטט?

,המן.

ער מיז װַמֿהרלֿיך מַ נעררטער אָמַן;
אָמַן געהט מיהן הַמָֿט מַן זַמטטען מַן.

מרדכי.

נו יו — און נור פֿאָרוּזֿט, טוט ער איך נמֿך הינטען
איט מַ טטריקקֿע מַן זַמטטען מַההנבינדען.
מַבער מַהדערטט טו מיל'ם מַמַך ניט;
דער גוין אום מַמַך גיהן טריטט פֿאָר טריטט.
5

Waas is doi main Ruah[1] den?

Daß ich moring niks noich gihn ken,

Un muß acht Tag derhaam

In Bett ligen, un bin krum un lahm.

     Haman.

5 Man soll ihn gewis gar in der Kutschen

In der Stadt so rum lassen rutschen?

     Mardachai.

Nu, doi lacht Er drois?

Doi fallt mer doch nit rois!

Den ken mer schihn drinne schloifen:

10 Ober off'n Goil, daf mer joi nit schnoifen!

In ahn Nahgenblik ligt mer hunten--putsch.

Th' ômar[2] in Emes[3], sezt Er mich in a Kutsch?

     Haman.

Er is wahrlich a nerrscher Man:

Man neht Ihn halt an Sattel an.

     Mardachai.

15 Nu joi--un zur Forsicht, tut Er mich noch hinten

Mit a Strikkle an Sattel ahnbinden.

Ober anderst tu ich's aach nit:

Der Goil muß aach gihn Schritt for Schritt.

1. Geist. 2. im Fall. 3. Wahrheit.

װאן נאָך עבעס, אַפריִ,

ער ביִד דאָך דיִהן גיֹןע דיִם מאַגען נו?

הָמָן.

איך אאַב' ער אַבער, אָדער — . . . .

(ער קנאַללט מיט דער פײטשע.)

מרדכי.

נו — נו — אאַך דער האַרר קאַהן זאָטטען מאַרעאיִע,

גאָטט זאָלל זיך דער בַמַרעאיִע!

װאַהַז זען דאַאַ פאָר נאַריִטע — ניִטטען:

— אוס מיך אין אײן מאָלטע טאַג נאָך רײטטען! —

(בײדע אָב.)

פֿיערטער אַבשניטט.

(ח ר ב ו נ ה'ס װאָהנשטובע. רעקאַ זיצט אַם טישע, פֿאַר איהר ליִגט אײנע דיִקע תפלה אױפֿגעשלאָגען, זיא בעטעט. צעטולפֿע איִם גרעטען נעגליִשע. בײדע האַבען דען קאָפֿף פֿערבונדען. יוקל שטעהעט אַם אָפֿען, האָט אײנען רונדען הוט אױף דעם קאָפֿע, אונד אײנע װײסע קאַפֿפֿע דאַרונטער. אללע דרייַא װײנען.)

רעקאַ.

אָך!

צעטולפֿע.

אַך!

Un noch ebes, <u>apripu</u>[1],

Er bind doch dihn Gaile di Aagen zu?

        Haman.

Iz mach' Er aber, oder————

    (Er knallt mit der Paitsche.)

        Mardachai.

Nu——Nu——Mach der Harr kahn sotten Lareme,

5   Gott soll sich der bareme!

Waas sen daas for narrische——Zaiten:

Mus ich main alte Tag noch raiten!——

        (Beide ab.)

———————————

    Fierter Abschnitt.

(Harbona's Wohnstube, Reka sizt am Tische,
for ihr ligt aine dike <u>Thefiloh</u>[2] oifgeschlagen, si
betet. Zetulpe im gresten Neglische. Baide haben

10   den Kopf ferbunden. Jukl stehet am Ofen, hat
ainen runden Hut oif dem Kopfe, und aine waise
Kappe darunter. Alle drai wainen.)

      Reka.

Och!

      Zetulpe.

Ach!

1. A propos.
2. Gebetbuch.

יוקל.

אָך! אָך!

צעטולפע.

זיעבע אוטטער, טהאָן זיך ניט זוי האַרעאַ־

רעקאַ.

גאָטט זאָלל זיך מיבער אונז דערבאַרעאַ!

יוקל.

אָך גאָטט! וויא פֿבאָמפערט איין אַזאַ גען.

צעטולפע.

זיעבע אוטטער, וואָז זאָלל מיך דען פֿאַר אַ תחינה
זאַגען ?

רעקאַ.

גענט, מיך קריהבט דיר 'ס קעלצע אין בוקקען מיך,
מיך האָסטו מורא, דאַז חית=לע גיהט דרויל;
וועגס וואַסער מען האַלל קוואַט, וואַטט מיהר אַזלע פֿרום.

יוקל.

מיך אַמאָהן פֿאַר הונגער, מיך פֿערקום!
דאַמאָז מיז אַ נאַריגער תענית היינט.

רעקאַ.

יוקל! וואַטט איין כפרה מון — גרײנט.

5*

Jukl.

Och! Och!

Zetulpe.

Liebe Mutter, thun Si sich nit soi hareme

Reka.

Gott soll sich iber uns derbareme!

Jukl.

Och Gott! Wi pfopert main Maagen.

Zetulpe.

5 Liebe Mutter, was soll ich den for a Thehinoh[1]
                                                saagen?

Reka.

Gelt, iz krihcht dir's Kezle in Bukkel noif,

Iz hoṡtu Môroׁ[2], das Ḥ.ajjaṡ=le[3] giht droif:

Wen's Waṡer an Hals kummt, watt ihr alle frum.

Jukl.

Ich mahn for Hunger, ich ferkum!

10 Daas is a nariger Thaᶜaniṡ[4] haint.

Reka.

Jukl! Watt main Kapporoh[5] un--graint.

---

1. demütiges Gebet. 2. Furcht. 3. Tierchen. 4. Fasten.
5. Sühnopfer, Vid. Part II #286.

יוקל.

די הערצן זיא, אמאאיען, וויא'ס אין אײן בױך די רוא־
פעלט,
וויא דער אטאאיע מיהר קאָפיהיהקריהגגען, אין דער
רעהר דאָט פואפעלט. —

רעקא.

טוויינגט נעהר טטום, איהר וואהכ־טעם!

צעטולפע.

פּפּוי, טאַק! האַט ער דען גאַר קײן — טאַמאַס?
דאַאַ גיבּט בּײא מיהן, וואַ זײן בּויערן וואָהנען,
ער פֿלײהגען! — ער גראָביאַהן!
אבער בּײא איר, בּײא דער אמאאיען — חרבונה,
דאַ געהן זײן אונפֿלאַהטיגקײטען ניט צאַהן.
יס היגדערט'ן געוויס, ווען ער זײן הוט
אין ליאאער רונטער טהוט?

יוקל.

נו, מיך וואָלן זיא אימ'ן היגטערן ליאאער בעלעטטיגען,
אמאאיען!

צעטולפע.

איך העטט'ן באַלד וואָ גזאַבּט, 'ס איז איר גאַר צו העלן. —

רעקא.

דיא טאָבּטער מיז ריאך נון מאַהל־ליהגגען משוגע!

Jukl.

Doi heren Si, Mansel, wi's in main Boich doi rum=

pelt,

Wi der Memme ihr Kofihkrihgle, in der

Rehr dot pumpelt--

Reka.

Schwaigt nehr Stum, ihr uhn=Ta‘am[1]!

Zetulpe.

Pfui, Schak! Hat Er den gar kain---Schaam?

5   Daas gilt bai Ihn, wu Sain Boiern wohnen,

Er Flihgel!--Er Grobiahn!

Aber bai mir, bai der Mamsel--Harbona,

Da gehn Sain Unflahtigkaiten nit ahn.

'ś hindert'n gewiś, wen Er Sain Hut

10   In Zimmer runter thut?

Jukl.

Nu, ich will Si mit'n Hintern nimmer beleśtigen,

Mamsel!

Zetulpe.

Ich hett'n ball was gsacht, 'ś is mir nor zu hell.--

Reka.

Di Tochter is doch zu'n Ahnlihgen meschuggo‘[2]!

1. Unschmackhafte.
2. wahnsinnig.

בעוונותינו הרבים! בייא דער מבוקה,
בייא דיהן טאָים-מזל! בייא דער צרה!
האַסטו ניקם אַנדערטש נו טוון, דו שררה?
זוי וואָר חודשה מאַך אין כפרה!

(זיא בעטעט ווייטער.)

ייעבער גאָטט! לאָס אונו זכות אבות געניסען. —
אָו וויה! דערט מיהר ניט, ער טוט טיהסען.
דו הערט אווי׳ דיא גאַס דאַו געריייא.
מאַו־אעבטינער גאָטט! טטיה אונו דאַך בייא.
טפרעןֵ דין גרויסע האַנד מיבער אונו אוי —
יוקל! לאַאַפֿט נאָר געטווינד אַ ביסלע טוי,
זעצט׳ך נאָר אוט נוין אין אטאהן,
גיהט נו, תאַטור טרעטפַאַט מיהר'ן זאַה.
אַו׳ מאַהנאַין וואָפַּט׳ן מאַהנם אין לאַרעאַע אוט.
גאָטט! מיך אַזאַה פֿאָר צרות, איך פֿערקום!

(זיא לייפֿט אים צימטער אויף אונד אב.)

(יוקל וילל הינויו, חרבונה טריטט העריין, זיא
שטאַסען צוזאַמטען.)

חרבונה.

דער חטור האָט איר דו גיהבען אַ האַלנער,
דער קריהגט אַ אוין זיין — טויופאָללער.

(ער שפרילבט גאַנץ אויזגעלאָזען הערום אונד וינגט.)

„האַפוַא, אַאַריַאַנעַנאָע! דריה דיך אַ אוין אום,
„דריה דיך האַוין אוט אונד אונד אום,
„דאַם איך“ . . . .

Ba-ʿAwônôsênu ho-rabbim[1]! Bai der Mevukoh[2],
Bai dihn Schlim=Massol[3]! Bai der Zoroh[4]!
Hoṡtu nikṡ anderṡt zu toin, du Scheroroh[5]?
Soi war ḥudsche[6] aach main Kapporoh[7]!

    (Si betet waiter.)

5 Lieber Gott! Loṡ uns Sechuṡ Ovôs[8] geniṡen.--
O wih! Hert ihr nit, mer tut schihṡen.
Doi hert oif di Gaṡ das Gschrai.
Allmechtiger Gott! Stih uns doch bai.
Spraz dain groise Hand iber uns ois--
10 Jukl! laaft nor gschwind a biṡle nois,
Secht'ch nor um noich main Mahn,
Giht zu, thʾômar[9] trefft ihr'n ahn.
Of ahnmoil woft'n ahnṡ in Lareme um.
Gott! Ich mahn for Zorôṡ[10] ich ferkum!

    (Si loift im Zimmer oif und ab.)
(Jukl will hinois, Harbona tritt herain, si
stoṡen zusammen.)

    Harbona.
15 Der Hamôr[11] hot mir doi gihben a Huzzer,
Der krihgt a moil sain--Oispuzzer.

    (Er spricht ganz oisgelassen herum und singt.)
„Hopsa, Marianele! Drih dich a moil um,
„Drih dich amoil um und um,
„Daṡ ich"........

---

1. Durch unzere zahlreichen Missetaten. 2. Elend.
3. Unglück. 4. Not. 5. Gebieterin. 6. wenigstens.
7. Sühnopfer. 8. das Verdienst der Väter.
9. im Falle. 10. Not. 11. Esel.

קינדערלעך! איהר האָפֿט לוסטיג זײַן;
הערט נאָר אױ׳ לו גרײַנע — .
פֿרומה! שבת לײהגסטו אַ געװנדען װאָטט מין דיװ זאַר־
וװעגן נײן,
און אַמבּסט אַ קוגען, איט רעטײנע —
מין ׳גיהט נאָר לו, און בײסט אַהן.

רעקאַ.

און גאָטטעם װילֿזען, אַהן!
װאַטײ אַמבּסטו פֿאָר אַ פֿאָסמען?
דו ביסט דאָך גאַנֿל אױיגעלאָסמען?
דו האָסט דיך געװײהם שיכור גאַמאַפֿען?
מָדער האָט אױזער לעטטען אפֿשר געטראָמאַפֿען?

חרבונה.

ניקט — גאָמאַפֿען,
ניקט — געטראָמאַפֿען;
אָבער געלמאָפֿען
בין אך אַז װיא.
דו װאַטסט דאָך, הײנט פֿריה,
נאַך טוהן, גיה מיך אַ ביסֿע אױיא.
װיא מיך היהנקוס, מֿן ר׳ מרדכי זײַן הױז,
מיז דיר די אַ גטעיה, — קַהן נױטען העטט אער
טוספֿען קעננע.
מיך האָב געאַמאַהנט, ׳ס טוט חס ושלום — ברעננע.
מֿן ׳ מהױיװ װאָטט אַ גטרײיװ: „אין ברעננע זײַן.‟

Kinderlich! Ihr daft lustig sain:

Hert ner oif zu zu graine--.

Frah! Schabbos[1] lihgstu a gesunden Wost in di Ar=
wesn nain,

Un machst a Kugel, mit Rezaine--

5 Iz giht nor zu, un baist ahn.

     Reka.

Um Gottes willen, Mahn!

Waas machstu for a Possen?

Du bist doch ganz oisgelossen?

Du host dich gewihs Schikkôr[2] gsoffen?

10 Oder hot unser Zettel efschor[3] getroffen?

     Harbona.

Niks--gsoffen,

Niks--getroffen:

Ober geloffen

Bin ich as wi.--

15 Du waast doch, haint frih,

Noich Schuhl, gih ich a bisle ois.

Wi ich hihnkum, an R' Mardachai sain Hois,

Is dir doi a Gstih,--kahn Noitel hett mer
tupfen kenne.

Ich hob gemahnt, 's tut H.as ve-Scholôm[4]--brenne.

20 Of ahnmoil watt a Gschrai: „Iz brenge si'n"

1. Sabbat. 2. betrunken. 3. vielleicht. 4. Gott behüt!

מיך האָב פֿערטאַננע: אין העננעוּין —
פֿאָר טרעקקען, האָב מיך געאוּהנט, מיך בלייא מאָפֿין
פֿאָן !
איר האָט נאָר וי געאקלאָפֿפֿט דאַאָ האַן,
מיך זיך היהו, זיך הער,
ווּאוּ מיך פֿינד אַ בעקמאַננטען נעהר.
אָל מַהגאוּין קואַאַט לֹו שפֿריננע התך,
מון זאַאַגט: ,,מיהר וויסט גאַר ניקט נאָך,
,,העטס אפֿשר נאָך גאַר ניט געהערט,
,,פֿון ר' מרדכי זיין חסד, איט'ן פֿעערד ?
,,דוּ דריננע העאַאוּין,
,,מַאוֹלעוּין שטריהלוֹען, מון קעאַאַעוּין,
,,טענננע'ן איט זַאַנד מון זַאַאַל אַבפֿיהגען,
,,אוּן אַ וויס העאַאוּד מַהאַליהגען.
,,דוּ גיהט עט ריין,
,,זיא וואַרן טוין איט'ן פֿאָטיג זיין.״ —
נו, וויא מיך דיר ניין קום אין חדר,
פֿראַח זיהבען ! דוּ טטיהט דיר
איין ר' מרדכי — דוּ העטט'ן ניאַאַער געקעננט,
אַרנדזיך וויא פֿייער העטס זיין באַקקען געברעננט,
אוֹפֿפֿערעזיהרט, מין גרעסטען טטמאַט,
מין אַ רויט טאַהרלאָך קלאַאַר,
דאַאָ וואָר_'רונד רום בזעסטען
איט ברמאַטע, גאָדיגע טרעטסען,
מון פֿון מונטען ביז הויבען
געטיקט, איט בלוואַם, מון טריבען ;

Ich hob ferstanne: Iz hengesi'n--

For Schrekken, hob ich gemahnt, ich blai off'n

Plaz!

Mir hot nor soi geklopft daas Haz,

Ich sich hihn, sich her,

5   Wu ich find a Gekannten nehr.

Of ahnmoil kummt zu springe Hathach,

Un saagt: „Ihr wist gar niks noch,

„Hets efschor[1] noch gar nit gehert:

„Fun R' Mardachai sain $\overset{H}{.}$esed[2], mit'n Pferd?

10 „Doi drinne hemmsi'n,

„Allewail strihlen, un kemmesi'n,

„Tenne'n mit Sand un Saaf abfihgen,

„Un a wais Hemmed ahnizihgen.

„Doi giht mit rain,

15 „Si warrn schoin mit'n fatig sain."

Nu, wi ich dir nain kum in $\overset{H}{.}$eder[3],

Frah lihben! Doi stiht dir

Main R' Mardachai- du hest'n nimmer gekennt,

Ordnlich wi Faier hem sain Bakken gebrennt,

20 Uffresihrt, in gresten Staat,

In a roit scharloch Klaad,

Daas wor rund rum bsessen

Mit braate, goldige Tressen,

Un fun unten bis oiben

25 Gstickt, mit Blummes, un Troiben:

1. vielleicht. 2. Glück. 3. Zimmer.

היבען און טריבען, אַזוי די די טאַטען,
זען גטפרונגע [עווען און האַטען;
אַל די נוואַה רמָק = טיהם,
טטיהם אין [יעבענסגריהם
דער ;יעבעניעהריגע קריעג.
מבער היגטען, — אַזַ[ע: ביה: זַמַ[ַ[וועג זין —
העאאיַ גטאַאַלט 'ם יקרות ניין.
אַ נאַפפַע[אַגריהנע אַטאַהַסענע וועסטע,
די וועָן דו גַעהי היהבעסט, העסטע
דיך גטטעַזַט אַפַן קמַפ'[;
די וואַר אַזַ[עוויַ[פַאַר אַ קנמַפ'[
אַ גרויַער בריַ[[[ימַאַד. — פַאָרעג אויפַ[ן נמַהבעַ[
מיַ גטטיקט, אַ ביַיערע אַיט אַ גאַהבעַ[,
דיַא גיהט גוו אַיז אין היַים.
בעסמער נונטמער וויַדער מיַ מַהנער אַיט אַ טַאַ[[אַמיַי,
דער [יגט אין טמַהַ[ען און בַ[זיַט זיך אַ טוט,
נונטער אַ גריַהנען בוט.
אַ ביַס[ע פַּון אַיהן ווער
וואַהַ[ען טוַי'[און — בעק.
פַאָרעג טטיהט אַ גרויַער — ביַערנהוַי'[,
אַ פַעג[[[ען הונד גיהט מַזַטיַנג דרוַי'[. —
דערנוילבַ[ט העאאיַ'[ן מַבער מַזַך [וַ'[ן גטפַאַהם
אַ פַעַ[[[ען בויך גטאַאַַזַט, ביַ מַן דער נַאַהם.
[ו [עטַ[ט נאַך, דיַ גיהַ[ע [יַדערע הויַ[ען,
נונטער מונד רונטער גטטיקט אַיט ניהגעַ[יַך און רויַען.
אַ פַאַמַר קוהַארַ[ער[טטיַפַסַזַיַך, אַיט [אַנגע טפַמַהרען,

Hiben un triben, ois di Taschen,

Sen gšprunge Lewen un Haschen:

Of di zwah Rok=schihš,

Stiht in Liebensgrihš,

5 Der siebenjehrige Krieg.

Ober hinten,--alles Bihs soll weg sain--

Hemmsi gemacht 's Jakruš[1] nain.

A napfelgrihne atlošene Wešte,

Di wen du gsehi hihbešt, hešte

10 Dich gštellt of'n Kopf:

Doi wor allemoil for a Knopf

A groiser Brilljand.--Forne oif'n Nahbel

Is gštikt, a Baiere mit a Gahbel.

Di giht nois in Hai.

15 Bešser nunter wider is ahner mit a Schallmai,

Der ligt in Schaaden un bloist sich a Tusch,

Unter a grihnen Busch.

A bišle fun ihn wek

Waaden Schoif un--Bek.

20 Forne štiht a groiser--Boiernhoif,

A fezzen Hund giht Achting droif.--

Dernoichet hemmsi'n ober aach zu'n Gšpahš

A fezzen Boich gemacht, bis an der Nahš.

Zu letzt noch, di gihle lidere Hoisen,

25 Runter und runter gštikt mit Nihgelich un Roisen.

A paar Kuhrierstifelich, mit lange Spohren,

1. Würde.

איך זָאג דיר: דו העסט דרוי'ל גטװאָרען,
ס' איז אַ װאָהרער גטװעהלײהר. —

צעטולפע.

בײא אײן זיעבען, מיך פֿערגעב איך מיך'ן טיער!

חרבונה.

װיא זיא דערנויך איט'ן פֿאָטטיג װאָהרען,
העט מיהן רויזגעטראָגען זעקס טװאַלע אָזאָהרען.
הינטין כיך זען מַבֿט הײטוקען, איט לֹאַנגע טפיסע.

רעקא.

אין טוטס איר באַנג, דאַס איך ניט בין דעָמטען גע=
װיסען.
מָבער איר גיהטס מַלֹזאָוין . . . .

חרבונה.

אין הַאָט אער געברוידֿט 'ן גוין,
נו, דער װאָר אַ ביזֹעע הויך;
און ר' מרדכי, איט זיין טיקקען בוידֿ,
װאַחַו זיך ניט לֹו העלֹפֿען, װון לֹו רויטען,
דער טֹלֹאַחַגט בײא המן אָל דיא סטוייטען;
„גיהט הער,“ זמַאַגט ער, „און זייט אײן פֿוהסע.
סטיהלֹעע!“
פואם, װאָר דער **רשע** לֹין דער היהך, איט דער
מחילה.

Ich saag dir: Du hest droif gschworen,

'š is a wahrer Gawehlihr.--

       Zetulpe.

Bai main Lieben, ich ferleb mich in'n schier!

       Harbona.

Wi si dernoich mit'n fattig wohren,

5   Hem ihn roisgetragen sekš schwaze Mohren.

Hintin noich sen acht Haituken, mit lange Špišen.

       Reka.

Iz tutš mir bang, das ich nit bin doten ge=
                      wišen.

Ober mir gihtš allemoil...

       Harbona.

Iz hot mer gebroicht 'n Goil,

10   Nu, der wor a bisle hoich:

Un <u>R</u>' Mardachai, mit sain tikken Boich,

Waas sich nit zu helfen, un zu roiten,

Der schlaagt bai Haman of di Štoiten:

„Giht her," saagt er, „un sait main Fuhse.
                        štihle!"

15   Pumš, wor der <u>Roscho'</u> [1] in der Hihch, mit der
                      <u>Mehiloh</u>[2] !

1. Bösewicht.
2. Arsch--An euphemism--literally "I beg your pardon."

חון חין מַהן טפרײנגלֹע,
װאָר ער דרױבען, װיא מַ ײנגלֹע!

רעקאָ•

דאַזַ איז מַ זכיה!

חרבונה•

איר העטַ מָבער עבֿער פֿיפֿאַט גטריע !
מַלֹעם האָט געױבעןט, און געױלֹט,
המן מָבער האָט פֿאָר רונז נאָר זּי גטֹולֹט.
פֿאַראוזַ איז געריטטען מ פרעבֿקטיגער הערמָזֹד,
דער האָט דיר נאָר זּי גטטרמָלֹט פֿון גמֹזֹד.
דערנוױך זען קואַא טרואפעטטען און בוזגען.

צעטטולֹפֿע•

פֿאָטער !ַ לֹאָסען זיא זיך עטװאַזַ פֿרױגען :
זען דען קאָהן מַפֿפֿעלֹיהר איט געריטטען ?
קאָהן קואיהם ? — קאָהן טטודרענטען ?

חרבונה•

װאַזַ דייטט ? מַלֹזֹע זענױ איט'ן,
און העטַ געאַאָט ניקס װיא קופֿלֹיאַענטטען.
מַפֿפֿעלֹיהרם, יענערמַהֹם, און געאַאהנגע,
איט חויבער = און אונטערגרנעװװערהר, און איט פֿמַהנגע.
חין דער איטט זען קואַא מַלֹזֹע = טיהסען.
קינדערֹיך ! איט דיהן אוזֹוג מִ⁜ עבֿעם דעראעהר
געװיהוזען.

Un in ahn Springle,

Wor er droiben, wi a Jingle!

Reka.

Daas is a <u>Sechijjoh</u>[1]!

Harbona.

Mir hem ober ebeṡ fifat gschrie!

5 Alleṡ hot gejubelt, un gejuchzt,

Haman ober hot for <u>Rôges</u>[2] nor soi gschluchzt.

Forois is geritten a prechtiger Herold,

Der hot dir nor soi gṡtrotzt fun Gold.

Dernoich sen kumme Trumpeten un Boigen.

Zetulpe.

10 Fater! Laṡen Si sich etwas froigen:

Sen den kahn Affezihr mit geritten?

Kahn Kumihṡ?--Kahn Studenten?

Harbona.

Waas daitsch? Alle sensi mit'n,

Un hem gemacht niks wi Kuplimenten.

15 Affezihrṡ, Jenerahlṡ, un Gemahne,

Mit Oiber=un untergewehr, un mit Fahne.

In der Mitt sen kumme sekṡ Galle=schihṡen.

Kinderlich! mit dihn Ufzug is ebeṡ der Mehr
                                        gewihsen.

1. Glück. 2. Verdrieselichkeit.

איך זמָלָם אַלָע חודש פֿערדיהנע, וואַמַ: דיא התונה
קאָטט.

רעקאַ·

דערנוֹיך דער אמַן, דערנוֹיך דער — וואָטט!

חרבונה·

דיא אָענסטען העסן זיך נאָר זוי געהוֹיבען;
גיווֹלָלען זען זיח אוֹך דיא דעבֿטער דרוֹיבען.

רעקאַ·

דו האָב מיך מאָבער אַלָו נאָך ניט געהערט,
וויח ר' מרדכי קואַאע אַיז לוֹ'ן חסד איט'ן פֿבֿערד?

חרבונה·

דו זעל דיך הער לוֹאיר.
מאָבער מַהן גאָמַלָלָעם טוואיר,
לאָמ איך אוֹיריהטען, און פֿריג דערנוֹיך. —

יוקל·

איך אוֹס'ן מַאָך רייטען זעהי, און זין גרוֹיזען בוֹיך.

(אָב.)

צעטולפֿע·

דמַאַ: איז איר אוֹיך אין רעלָטער רייטער.

רעקאַ·

לאָמ דיך פֿון דער ניט מַרר אַמַבֿבען, פֿערליהה וויטער!

Ich solls alle $\overset{H}{\underset{.}{ô}desch}$[1] ferdihne, waas di $\overset{H}{\underset{.}{a}sunoh}$[2]

koš̌t.

        Reka.

Dernoich der Man, dernoich der--Wošt!

        Harbona.

Di Menschen hem sich nor soi gehoiben:

Gsizzen sen si uf di Dechter droiben.

        Reka.

5   Doi hob ich ober als noch nit gehert,

Wi <u>R</u>' Mardachai kumme is zu'n $\overset{H}{\underset{.}{e}šed}$[3] mit'n Pferd?

        Harbona.

Doi sez dich her zumir.

Ober ahn Gfalleš tumir,

Loš mich oisrihten, un froig dernoich.--

        Jukl.

10   Ich muš'n aach raiten sehi, un sain groisen Boich.

     (ab.)

        Zetulpe.

Daas is mir oich ain rechter Raiter.

        Reka.

Loš dich fun der nit arr machen, ferzihl waiter!

1. Monat. 2. Hochzeit. 3. Glück.

(וויא זעצען זיך ביידע.)

חרבונה.

דו וואַמסט דאָך: זייט דיא אשתּר דוי דרויבען מיר,
דוי מיר האַלבפאַטעט, אַ געלעק, אַ גענקיס,
דוי גיהטס יוי לו, ווי בײַם קיניג מַטיסהויל,
דאַמַ הערט יוי נאָר ניט מויל,
דאַ גבּרעט און דאַמַ מויפבּגעטראַג,
מוי טאַג אמאַבּט אער נאַבּט, און מוי נאַבּט טאַג;
דער ווין קוואאט ניט פון דיא טיטען,
מאַלע מיטט הויט אער פון קעלזער אַ בוטעלזיע
פריטען.
מאַהן חברותה טיך דער מַנדער קוואאט לו'ן טפיהלען.

צעטולפע.

מען דיהן שוטה אעלבט מיך מיך נאָר — קיהלען!
דאַ ער זיך פּאָען זוי מין גרילל לאַמסט אוהלען.

רעקא.

וואַמַ טוסטו דעראויט, דו קעהרסט מאַך אַ קיצין;
האַב קאַהן זאַריג, דו בלײַבסט ניט מיבער.

חרבונה.

וואַטט, מיך רו' דיין חברותה מאַך נאָך ריבער,
נוילעט מיר דיא קאַטט — פּערפּאָלל.
זאַג נאָר, ווי מיך זוי פּאָטטיג וואַרן זאָל?

(ער וויל פאָרט.)

(Si sezen sich baide.)

Harbona.

Du waaśt doch: Sait di Eśther droiben is,

Doi is allfott, a Gelek, a Gekiś,

Doi gihtś joi zu, wi bai Kinig Atiśhoif,

Daas hert joi gar nit oif,

5   Das Gfreś un daas Oifgetrag,

Ois Tsg macht mer Nacht, un ois Nacht Tag:

Der Wain kummt nit fun di Tischen,

Alle Minut hoilt mer fun Keller a Butellie

                                 Frischen.

Ahn <u>.avruśoh</u>[1] noich[2] der ander kummt zu'n spihlen.

    Zetulpe.

10 An dihn <u>Schôteh</u>[3] mecht ich mich nor--kihlen!

Daś er sich fon soi ain Grill laśt uhzen.

    Reka.

Waas tuśtu dermit, du kehrśt aach a <u>Kozin</u>[4]:

Hob kahn Sorig, du blaibśt nit iber.

    Harbona.

Watt, ich ruf dain <u>.avruśoh</u>[1] aach noch riber,

15 Noichet is di Katt-ferfoll.

Saag nor, wi ich soi fattig warrn soll?

             (Er will fort.)

1. Gesellschaft. 2. noich] tich. 3. Narr. 4. Herrscher.

רעקאָ·

נו, נו — איך שוויג שוין, פֿערליהן נאָר וויטער.

חרבונה·

אַבער שטיל איטאַננאַנד ־יטיר! —
אַווו בין איך דען געבלֿיעבען? יוֹ בייא דער אשתר.
זיא אונ אחשורוש העט ניט מיינטװיֿעגען קעננע
געטטער.

ער װאָפֿפֿט זיך היהן, ער, װאָפֿפֿט זיך הער,
און מַהגאווין צַוואַגט ער:

„מיינטװעֿעגען קען יעך דעֿך ניט צעהר:
„פֿרְמָה! זָאַג איר מַאווין דאַ ספר הזכרונות העֿר."
די האָסטום, צוּוַאַגט זיא, מיך גיה נאָר, און צוויג
שטיֿלן —

אחשורוש נעאאאטט בוך, צעטלט אויך זיין בריֿלן,
ניהגט ביז איבער דיא מָאהרען רונטער דאַ קעפפֿלע,
און פֿאַנגט פֿאָר זיך צַהן לו פֿלעפֿפֿלֿע.
װיא ער טוט צַוויֿע זיא דריננע בֿעטטערן,
פֿאַנגט ער צַהן לו טריֿע: די העטטער'ן
שטעהן, איין מרדכי — דריננע,
־לֿטטו פֿרמֿה, װער זֿלֿט טוט גַפֿיננע.
זיך: דער האָט מיר דעררעטט דַ צַא לֿיהבען,
און האָבּ'ן נַעך ניט צַ אווין צַ טרינקגעלֿד גיהבען —
־צַהג איין הַזָל! און איין קרוין!
וואַאו צַגֿל מיך דיהן פֿאָר צַ כבוד צַהן טוֿיק?
אֿינטװיהגען, צַוַאגט זיא, טיקק'ן צַ שלח מנות.

Reka.

Nu, nu--Ich schwaig schoin, ferzihl nor waiter.

Harbona.

Ober still mitannand saitir!--

Wu bin ich den geblieben? Joi bai der Esther!

Si un Ahasveros hem nit ainschloifen kenne

gester.

5   Er wofft sich hihn, er wofft sich her,--

Of ahnmoil saagt er:

„Ainschloifen ken ich doch nit mehr:

„Frah! Lang mir amoil das Sêfer ha-Sich ronôs[1] her!"

Doi hostus, saagt si, iz gih nor, un schwaig

still--

10 Ahasveros nemmts Buch, setzt oif sain Brill,

Zihgt bis iber di Ohren runter das Kepple,

Un fangt for sich ahn zu plepple.

Wi er tut a waile soi drinne blettern,

Fangt er ahn zu schraie: Doi hetter'n

15 Stehn, main Mardachai--drinne,

Sichstu Frah, wer sucht tut gfinne.

Sich: der hot mir derrett daas Lihben,

Un hob'n noch nit a moil a Trinkgeld gihben--

Saag main Haz! Un main Kroin!

20 Waas soll ich dihn for a Kovôd[2] ahn toin?

Maintwihgen, saagt si schikk'n a Schala.h Monôs[3].

1. Buch der Chronika--Cf. Esther II, 23.
2. Ehre.
3. Austeilung der Geschenke.

 דו האָסט מאַבער איט מאַהן גאַר קמאַהן רחמנית!
דו טוסט מאַהן גאַר ניקם עטטעאַיהרען;
מיך קען איך אסור פאַר טאַיוֹל ניט ריהרען,
יוֹטט האַב מיך וועלֹזזען מאַהנפאַמַנגע, אַ ביסמַע זו טוהזען,
פאַמַנגט ער מאַהן, פֿון זיין מרדכי זו טאַוּהסטען.
וואָ איז איר פאַר דיין מרדכי זוי מיאוּס,
פֿאַמַנגט אסתר, אין מאַהן רוגז — כלומר־קיהם. —
אייכטוּוויהגגען אֹמַך מיהן זיהם מאָדער זוּבער מיין.
רוֹל לֿיעבער דיין תכשיט־זע, דיין המן ריין,
דער ווֹמַעם דמַך יוי מַזֹלזעם —
פֿריוג לֿיעבער דיהן, טוב איר דיהן גֹמַהֹלזזעם.
לֿאָסטערֹן קוואַע אַ ביסמַע רוֹיל,
ער מַראַעט דרוגטען כמַך אין הוֹיל.
אין האַט דער מלך בעמָיֹנַען:
טטמַאַנדע ביע זָמַלֹל אַערֹן המן הוֹילֿען.
המן לֿמַסט מַזֹלזעם טטיהן אוֹן לֿיגגען,
לֿמַאַפֿט טפמַהרען טטרמַמַך, טוט זיך ביז אוֹיל דיוא ערד
ביקקען.
אחשורוש פֿרויגט: וואָמַז טוסטו דרוגטען כמַך זוי
טפֿיהט,
"מיך בוי זו נמַר אַ גמַליינג, פֿוֹפֿלֹנֹיג מיהֹלֹן הויך, פֿאַר
אַ ייד."
כו, פֿמַמַנגט אחשורוש, דמַמַז האַט ביז אַמַרינג מַמַך
כמַך גיט.
אין פֿמַמַנג מאַוין — דו ביסט דמַך אין מַזֹלזען גטַייד —
"דוי ווֹמַטט ווידער עבעם גטַיידם רמַז קוואַאַג,"

Du hoṡt ober mit ahn gar kahn <u>Rachamonuṡ</u>[1]!

Du tuṡt ahn gar nikṡ eṡtemihren:

Ich ken mich <u>oṡur</u>[2] for Schloif nit rihren,

Juṡt hob ich wellen ahnfange, a biṡle zu tuhsen,

5 Fangt er ahn, fun sain Mardachai zu schmuhṡen.

Wi is mir for dain Mardachai so <u>miuṡ</u>[3],

Saagt Esther, in ahn <u>Rôges</u>[4]--<u>kelômar=kihṡ</u>[5].--

Maintwihgen mach ihn sihṡ oder soiber ain.

Ruf lieber dain <u>Tachschit=le</u>[6] dain Haman rain,

10 Der waaṡ doch joi alleṡ--

Froig lieber dihn, tub mir dihn Gfalleṡ.

Loṡter'n kumme a biṡle roif,

Er arwet drunten noch in Hoif.

Iz hot der <u>Melech</u>[7] befoilen:

15 Stande bie soll mer'n Haman hoilen.

Haman loṡt alleṡ stihn un ligen,

Laaft ṡpohren ṡtraach, tut sich bis oif di Erd
                                    bikken.

Ahasveros froigt: Waas tuṡtu drunten noch soi
                                    ṡpiht,

"Ich boi nor a Galing, fufzig Ihlen hoich, for a Jid."

20 Nu, saagt Ahasveros, daas hot bis moring aach
                                    noch Zait.

Iz saag amoil.--du biṡt doch in Allen gschaid--

"Doi watt wider ebeṡ Gschaidṡ rois kumme,"

1. Mitleid.
2. bei meiner Seele.
3. widerlich.
4. Verdriesslichkeit.
5. Scheinkäse, <u>Vid</u>. Part II #292.
6. Kleinod--Used ironically--<u>cf</u>. Tendlau, <u>Prov</u>. #49.
7. König.

פֿאַנגט המן אָהן, פֿאָר זיך צו בּרואוע.
נו, ״פֿאַנגט דער מלך, ״מאַך מיר מאויף, לאָם הערען:
מאָהן דיהן מיך אעצט רעבּט עהרען,
און גיהבּען אַ גרויסען לוין,
״מאַך: װאָהם ״פאָלל איך זיי מאָהן דען טוין?
איך פֿערגעעסנע המן דיא רונצלוע;
דער רשע פֿאַנגט אָהן צו טאוונצוע.
און ״מאַכט זיי מיר זיך ניין:
,,װער קען דען דאַצו מאָדערטעט זיין,
,,װיא איך?
,,יי געװיהם, ער אמאַהנט מיך. —
און ״מאַכט צו'ן מלך ,,װיהן מיהר זיי צו עהרען בּעי=
געעהרט,
,,דיהן זעטלט אער אזוי' אייער טעגסטען פֿפּערד,
,,טוט'ן אָפּפֿ'ן קאָפּֿ' דיא קרוין,
,,לאָסטן אייער קאָמאַדער דערצו מאַהנטיין,
,,פֿיהרטן זוי היע רום, אין גאַנצען מאָט,
,,און אַ גאַנל הויבּער רופֿט אַ זוי, װאָטט פֿאָר װאָטט:
,,,,דאַצו איז דער אמאַן, דיהן דער קיניג צו עהרען
בּעעגעהרט,,,,
,,און דער זעלבּסט אוס פֿיהרען דאַצו פֿפּערד."
נו — ״מאַכט אחשורוש — 'ם המאַסט מאַהנער
מרדכי היע,
צו דיהן גיהסטו אָארינג, מיט מאַללע פֿריה,
װאו ער װאוינט, מיט זיין הויז,
און פֿונט מיר'ן נאָר זוי רוז;

Fangt Haman ahn, for sich zu brumme.

Nu, saagt der Melech[1], saag mir amoil, los heren:

Ahn dihn ich mecht recht ehren,

Un gihben a groisen Loihn,

5   Saag: waas soll ich soi ahn den toin?

Iz fergenge Haman di Runzle:

Der Roscho^c[2] fangt ahn zu schmunzle.

Un saagt soi in sich nain:

„Wer ken den daas anderst sain,

10   „Wi ich?

„Joi gewihs, er mahnt mich.--

Un saagt zu'n Melech[1] „wihn ihr so zu ehren be=gehrt,

„Dihn setzt mer uf aier schensten Pferd,

„Tut'n off'n Kopf di Kroin,

15   „Lost'n aier Klaader derzu ahntoin,

„Fihrt'n soi hie rum, in ganzen Ott,

„Un a ganz Hoicher ruft a soi, Wott for Wott:

„„Daas is der Man, dihn der Kinig zu ehren
                        begehrt""

„Un der selbst fihren daas Pferd."

20   Nu--saagt Ahasveros--'s haast ahner
                    Mardachai hie,

Zu dihn gihstu moring, in alle Frih,

Wu er woint, in sain Hois,

Un puzt mir'n nor soi rois:

1. König.
2. Bösewicht.

פֿיהרסט'ן היע רום אָפֿפֿ'ן פֿפֿערד ;

דאַז דו קאָהן וואַרטע דער פֿוה פֿאַלאָט אויף דער **ערד.**

שוטסט קום איך דיר איט'ן גרויזען קול,

און לאָז דיר אויפֿבֿריהנען אַ בוקקען פֿאַלל.

איך שטויז רעכֿט וואויל. בֵּן נומי!

קום פֿין בּיי ניישען אָמְעְרינג פֿריה. —

חמן גיהט מילט אין מהן רונז פֿאַטט,

דערהאַזם זעהאַנגט ער פֿון זין חרפּה קאָהן וואָטט.

דיען זרש ליגט טוין אין מהן ברוואאע,

דאַם ער טוט זו לאַכן — ניט קוואאע.

רעקאָ.

נו, דיא האָטט'ן מאַך ניט גיההבען קאָהן איגרונע.

חרבונה.

זוי, געעלאָנקט האָטוי, דאַם אוי' וואָר דיא גאַכלע
שכונה.

היינט, אין מאַלער פֿריה, האָט ער זיך פֿאָטט געטויבען,

און אין דיא ניט נישט פֿון ר' מרדכי געוויבען.

דוי האָסט מילעט דיא גאַכלע געטיכטע פֿון גוין.

רעקאָ.

בַּם איין לֵיהבען! איך קעננט זי הערען נאָך הונדערט מיו.

חרבונה.

נאָהן, מיך אום פֿאָטט, קום מַבער בְּאַלל ווידער האַאַם.

(אב.)

Fihrŝt'n hie rum off'n Pferd:

Das doi kahn Watle der fuhn fallt oif der Erd.

Schunŝt kum ich dir mit'n groisen Kôl[1],

Un loŝ dir oifzihlen a Bukkel foll.

5   Iz schloif recht woil. Bon Nui!

Kum fain bai Zaiten moring frih.--

Haman giht izt in ahn Rôgeŝ[2] fott,

Derhaam saagt er fun sain Herpoh[3]-kahn Wott.

Den Seres ligt schoin in ahn Brumme,

10   Daŝ er tut soi lang--nit kumme.

            Reka.

Nu, Di hott'n aach nit gihben kahn Migrune.

            Harbona.

Joi, gezankt hotsi, daŝ uf wor di ganze

                              Schechunoh[4].

Haint, in aller Frih, hot er sich fott gschlichen,

Un is di Zait nit fun R' Mardachai gewichen.

15   Doi hoŝtu izet di ganze Gachichte fun Goil.

            Reka.

Ba main Lihben! Ich kennt si heren noch hundert Moil.

            Harbona.

Nahn, ich muŝ fott, kum ober ball wider haam.

            (ab.)

1. Stimme.
2. Verdriesslichkeit.
3. Schande.
4. Nachbarschaft.

רעקאַ.

וואֶו שטעקט דען דער יוקל, דער אוכ=טעם? —

צעטולפֿע.

דער זיהט דיא רייטערייַן דאֶך מויך.

יוקל.

(שפרינגט פֿערגניגט צור טהירע העריין.)

איך האֶננען מאַך גזעהי, אין זיין גרויזמוען בויך.
זיעבע אוזואוגַן! דאַז איז מיהר אֶבער מעהנער,
מין האַלבעם עולם גיטם גענוייהם זוי קאֶהנער;
דאַאַז איז אַ טיקעגניט, דאַאַז איז אַ פואאער —
זוי מעהנער אוז אַ נחת זיין מין זואאער,
מין דיא גרויזע הילבלען.
אוּל! ווען מיך דראַהן דענק, אוס מיך טוין טווילבלען.

(ער פֿעלבלט זיך מיט דעם הוטע אינם געזיכט.)

רעקאַ.

נו יוי, משרת אַמַך ווינד —

יוקל.

מיך זמאַג מיהר, 'ן טאַמַטע זייַער איז דערגיהגען
מַהן קינד!
דוי קען מיך מיהר אַ טוועהרער דרויל טוין.

רעקאַ.

טוויגט נאֶר אוכ=טעם, מיט מייַער גטווועהר.

Reka.

Wu stekt den der Jukl, der Un=ta'am[1]?---

Zetulpe.

Der siht di Raiterai doch oich.

Jukl.

(springt fergnigt zur Thire herain.)

Ich honnen aach gsehi, in sain groisamen Boich.

Liebe Mamsel! Das is Ihr ober ahner,

5   In Hallem ʿôlom[2] gitś gewihś soi kahner:

Daas is a Tikenisch, daas is a Pummer--

Soi ahner mus a Nahas[3] sain in Summer,

In di groise Hizzen.

Uf! Wen ich drahn denk, muś ich schoin schwizzen.

(Er fechelt sich mit dem Hute ihm Gesicht.)

Reka.

10   Nu joi, Meschoreś[4] mach Wind---

Jukl.

Ich saag Ihr, 'n Taate Sainer is dergihgen
                                        ahn Kind!

Doi ken ich Ihr a Schwehrer droif toin.

Reka.

Schwaig nor Un=ta'am[5], mit aier Gschwehr.

---

1. Geschmacklose. 2. Welt. 3. Bequemlichkeit. 4. Diener.
5. Geschmackloser.

מיך גְלָחַבֵּי מִיךְ טויִן.

„יוהלי"

דוּ הִינטען, אַמאָזען! דוּ וואָהר עבעס דעראָעהר,
דוּ הָאט זיך עבעס — געטוין.
אַמאָזען! דמאַז וואָהר מיהר מַ טפּעקטאַהעקען,
דוּ מיז איט זײן גרױסען בוקקען, דער פּרִיטעטע
במַקקעען
דיא זײט נויך געוָאפֿען איט זײן פּרִיטעטער.
אָל מַהכאַוין טוט ער מַ קלִיטטער;
פוטט, זִיגט ער אין מַהכער לֶענגג, מין דרעק.
מִין הָאט ער מָבער בעקוואאע עבעס טזָען,
אַזָזע געטסעגיאָנגעטע העעם געהױט אוֹיפֿן נויל
מִיך הָאָב מַאך געטלָאַגען דיבְטיג דרוין.
ר׳ מרדכי מָבער הָאט זיך זוי דערזָאַלט,
וויח׳ן פּרִיטטעבמַקקעען דער בוקקען איז אױפֿגעע
קרמַלט.
נו, אַמאָזען! דוּ מיז מיהר מַ מרמה רױ געואָפֿיגען,
דוּ וואָהר דרִיננע, וואַחַם 'י יִם הָאט מױ געואַפֿיגען:
מַ קאָפֿפֿעקיסען, מַ נונטערבעטעט, מַ דעקבעטטעניהך,
מ היהנערטטיג, מַ במַער קוריהרטטיגעעך, זעקט במַער
טיהך.
מַ רונטער הוט, מַ נחַלטע בריק, מַ פֿױגענַהיי:זע,
נָוחַה במַער הױזען, מַ איהַקיוועעען, מַ בוטטער
קרייסטָע.
מָבער נחַה — מין ערטט דמַז דמַז גערייח,

Ich glaabs aich schoin.

       Jukl.

Doi hinten, Mamsel! Doi wohr ebes der Mehr,

Doi hot sich ebes--getoin.

Mamsel! Daas wohr Ihr a Spektahkel,

5   Doi is mit sain groisen Bukkel, der Pritsche=
                                   bakkel

Di Lait noich geloffen mit sain Pritscher.

Of ahmoil tut er a Klitscher:

Putsch, ligt er in ahner lengs, in Drek.

Iz hot er ober bekumme ebes Schleg,

10   Alle Gassenjunges hem gehoit oif'n noif

Ich hob aach gschlagen dichtig droif.

R' Mardachai ober hot sich soi derlacht,

Wi'n Pritschebakkel der Bukkel is oifge=
                                 kracht.

Nu, Mamsel! Doi is Ihr a Mirmoh[1] rois geloffen,

15   Doi wohr drinne, waas 's Jam[2] hot ois gewoffen:

A Kopfekisen, a Nunterbett. a Dekbettzihch,

A Hihnerstaig, a baar Kurihrstifelich, seks[3] baar
                                     Schihch.

A runter Hut, a nalte Brik, a Foigelhaisle,

Zwah baar Hoisen, a Mihlkiwele, a Butter=
                                   kraisle.

Ober nahn--Iz erst daas Gschrai,

1. Trug--The fundamental concept is that of something falsely
   concealed; a camouflage; a cachet.
2. Meer.
3. seks] sekt.

אוּן דער נָאררעסאָע, דער דוּ היז געוויהזען,
ווּיא רויז גפֿאַללען איז, אַ טיװעטע הײַז,
אַ בוּנד סטרוּי, אוּן אַ נאָכטער — ביהזען.
איט אַ גיפֿענגמַההבען, אוּן אַ זוּטסעַט טאַל.
אַמאַוּען! בײַא אַיין גיהבבען! זײַא דאַן
קינטער גיהן, 'ס איז דער איה ווערטה,
ט' משובות לָיגט אַלָזעם נָאך אוּיף דער ערד,

צעטולפֿע.

דאַז פֿעהלסט איר, געה הינטער אוּיף דען געאומבאַריג.

יוקל.

הערגען זײַא לו, מיין קאַטו ערטט אַריג;
אַלַזעװוּיין געהט ערטט אַהן דער גטפֿעההם:
ווּיא אַיך קיין קאַאַע איך דיא אָאָרעגריפֿיטע גאַס,
דוּ זיבֿט לו המן זײַן הוּיז
דיא פֿרחה אוּנד דיא טאַלבֿטער לוּין פֿענטטער רוּיז.
זיך, דוּ קאַט דער פֿאַפֿאַם לו רייטען,
זמאַגט זרש, איך זילֿ'ס דעאָרבֿ'ן טפֿיקטיהֿ'ל פֿון ווײַטען,
אוּן דער אַזטע מרדכי פֿיהרט'ן גוּין, דער גיהט
דערניההבעם
וואַטט, וזאַהגם דיא טאַלבֿטער, דיהן אוּילֿ איך אַ טרינק
געאַד גיהבבען,
אוּען ער דוי הער קאַוּט, טיטט איך אין געאוזַאררעט
פֿאָפֿבן גונטער אַיין — נאַהבֿט = טאַזרעעט.
בחרי אַף טוטוי אין דער קוּך נוּיז לָזאהבֿען,

6*

Un der Larreme, der doi is gewihsen,

Wi rois gfallen is, a Schiwele Hai,

A Bund Stroi, un a nalter--Bihsen.

Mit a Noifegahbel, un a Suttel Schaf.

5   Mamsel! Bai main Lihben! Si daf

Ninter gihn, 's is der Mih werth,

's[1] Meschuvôs[2] ligt alles noch oif der Erd,

        Zetulpe.

Das fehlt mir, geh hinter oif den Gensbarig.

        Jukl.

Heren Si zu, iz kumts erst arig:

10   Alleweil geht erst ahn der Gspahs:

ai   Wi mir nain kumme in di moregrifische Gas,

Doi sicht zu Haman sain Hois

Di Frah und di Tochter zu'n Fenster roiz.

Sich, doi kumt der Papa zu raiten,

15 Saagt Seres, ich sich's dorch'n Spiktihf fun waiten,

Un der alte Mardachai fihrt'n Goil, der giht

                   dernihben

Watt, sahgt di Tochter, dihn will ich a Trink=

                   geld gihben,

Wen er doi her kumt, schitt ich in Gelarrem

Offn nunter main--Nahcht=scharrem.

Bo.ori-Of[3] tutsi in der Kuch nois lahfen,

---

1. 's] t'.
2. Holter di Polter.
3. der Zorn entbrannt-- Vid. Exodus 11, 8.

הָאקט זיך אוֹיֿלין גרעסטען ליאאגם הַמַדֿלֿפֿעַן.
זרש רוֿפֿט נויֿ: טיק דיך,
קינד! אמָך פֿאָטמט, מיך ביטט דיך,
גטוויֿנד בר׳ענג דאַז משיבות ריֿן,
דיהן מַהגענגביֿק אמֿרן זיֿ דרוֹגטען זיֿן. —
וויֿ מרדכי גו היֿן קוֹאָט פֿאָרין הוֹיֿ,
גיט ער המן מָ פֿואָפֿ, און זַמַהגט: מיֿן טרייֿ וווֹיֿ!
וויֿ דער גו טוֹט דיהן ערטטען טרייֿ,
פֿוֹטט! הָמ ער מיֿן גזֿילֿט גהָמט דיֿ קיֿעריֿ!
דָמ דיֿ בריה זי מיֿ חיבערן רוֹגטער געוֹאָפֿֿען.

רעקאַ•

דָמַ־ה הָמַהסט: קָמֿהן לֿעטֿען, און דָך — געטרוֹאָֿפֿ׳ן.

יוקל•

נו, דער פֿוֹטטַמַגד, דער רו אֿוֹ געוויֿהטען . . . .

רעקאַ•

נַמַהן, איט וויֿן אֿמֿרט אֿערֿן בעגיֿהטען,
דיהן בוֹזֿוויֿלֿט, דיהן רשע.

יוקל•

מָבֿער דיֿ חדפה, דיֿ בושה,
הָמ קָמַהגער גהָמטטֿען זיֿט גה אֿווֹ דער תיבה אֿזֿ
געָאנֿגע
מיֿן הָמ ער נו משחית'ן מַהנגֿמַמַנגֿע,
און הָמ נויֿ געָאאָֿזֿט, נו זיֿן זֿיֿט, מָ אֿואֿפֿֿען:

Hokt sich oif'n greśten Zimmes Haafen.

Seres ruft nois: Schik dich.

Kind! Mach fott, ich bitt dich,

Gschwind breng das Meschuvôs[1] rain,

5 Dihn Ahgenblik warrn si drunten sain.--

Wi Mardachai nu hihn kumt for'n Hois,

Git er Haman a Pumpf, un sahgt: Iz schrai ois!

Wi der nu tut dihn erśten Schrai,

Putsch! Hot er in Gsicht ghat di Kaierai!

10 Daś di Brih soi is ibern runter geloffen.

       Reka.

Dahs hahśt: kahn Zetel, un doch--getroffen.

       Jukl.

Nu, der Zustand, der doi is gewihśen....

       Reka.

Nahn, mit Wain wart mer'n begihśen,

Dihn Boiswicht, dihn Roschoʿ[2].

       Jukl.

15 Ober di .·erpoh[3], di Buschoh[4],

Hot kahner ghatten, sait Noah ois der Têvoh[5]

              is gange

Iz hot er zu maschhiś'n[6] ahngfange,

Un hot noif gemacht, zu sain Lait, a Mumfel:

---

1. Abfall.
2. Bösewicht.
3. Scham.
4. Schande.
5. Arche.
6. drohen.

»אַט נאָר דוא עלענדסגלוּיע! דוא נעססעננאַמעהד! דוא
נאַספּעןּ!

נאָם איך דערנוּיך הַאַוּן נאָר קוּאאע;
דוא ווארסט דיין חלק טוין בעקוּאאע.
פאָר טרעעקקעו איז דיא טאָבטער און דיא פרחה,
נוּן פענגסטעֶר נײן גפאַלֶלעֶן חולשת מלוּע לוּוּה!
ר' מרדכי האָט זיך מבער דוּ דרחה ניקם געקעהט,
דער האָט זיך דערטאָקקעֶלט פאָר לאָבעֶן, מאָפּין
פערעד.

מין האָט עֶר גטריע : המן! ווּאוּ וויטעֶר?
אמַ פאָמַט! איר ווּעֶלֶעֶן וויטעֶר.
ווּיא דער נוּג אַן טאַָם היהן איז קוּאאע,
הנאַוּאַן זעֶנקם שררות אין עאַפּאַנג געֶנוּאאע.
דאַט העאַוּזי געאַוּבט, פאָן רייִיג אַ טאָָהר,
דוּ זעֶן גטטאַננע דער פאַר:
זווּעֶלוֹן קלוָהַנע אַמאָהדלִיך,
דיא העֶן מַהֶנגֶהֶהֶט מיהֶר יום טוב קלָמָהדלִיך,
אִיט נוּיל גטאַטַלטע מַרווּעֶלִיך,
און העֶן געֶטראַנעֶן בלוּאא = קאָרווּעֶלִיך,
געֶבוּנדעֶן אִיט רוּטע בענדלִיך,
מין מיהֶר ווּיסע העֶנדלִיך.
מוֹל אַ טטעֶהלוָהֶט פּוָן בריהדער
זעֶן גטטאַנגע אוּיזנַנטעֶן, העֶן געֶנגע לִיעֶרעֶר,
און העֶן דערלוֹ געבלוּיזעֶן אִיט טרוּאפיהטעֶן,
אִיט פוּיגעֶן, גיִנגעֶן און אִיט פּלוָהטעֶן.

Watt nor du elendsgloie! du Gassenmahd! du
Zumpfel!

Los mich dernoich haam nor kumme:
Du warst dain $\overset{H}{\cdot}$elek[1] schoin bekumme.

For Schrekken is di Tochter un di Frah,
5 Zu'n Fenster nain gfallen $\overset{H}{\cdot}$olesches[2] alle zwah!

R' Mardachai hot sich ober doi drahn niks gekeht,
Der hot sich derschokkelt for Lachen, off'n
Pferd.

Iz hot er gschrie: Haman! Wu saiter?

Masch fott! Mir wellen waiter.

10 Wi der Zug an Schlos hihn is kumme,
Hemm'n seks Scheroros[3] in Empfang genumme.

Dot hemmsi gemacht, fun Raisig a Tohr,
Doi sen gstanne der for:

Zwelf klahne Mahdlich,
Di hem anghat ihr Jôm-Tôv[4] Klahdlich,

Mit noif gschatzte Arwelich,

Un hem getragen Blumme=karwelich,

Gebunden mit roite Bendlich,

In ihr waise Hendlich.

20 Of a Stehlahsche fun Brihder
Sen gstanne Musiganten, hem gsunge Lieder,

Un hem derzu gebloisen mit Trumpihten,

Mit Poigen, Gaigen un mit Flihten.

1. Teil.
2. in Ohnmacht fallend.
3. Gebieterinnen.
4. Fest-.

דערלאזיטען העט גטאָססען דיא קאַנוהנע,
און געבלוזען העט דיא פאָטטיליהנע
אָל מיהר האַררנער.
קאַמפּיהר העט זיא רונטער גטפיהלט פֿון דיא
טאַררנער.
דיא טאַאפּורם העט מין גטאָנגען מול דיא טרואאען,
דיא וואָן העט אַמך גʼעקטעלזהרט.
דרויבען אזז אסתר גטטאָננע מין דיהן גרעסטען
געטואאען,
און העט רונטער — גʼמפʼלעטיהרט —
דיא העט זיך פאָר לאָלבען דיא זייטען געהאַזטען,
וויא זיא העט גזעהי ʼן לוטטאַמד פֿון דיהן האָטען
המן, און מיהר מונקען פאָמרʼן טאָאָם פאַאָרביא רייטען,
אַן דיהן בעגאָמסטעננע המן זין נאַריטע גזיבטער טנידען,
דרויבען העט זיא דאַז כלה · זיער גזונגען,
און הונטען אזז דער המזווזטט — רואנגטפרהנגע.
דער העט מיהר גאאַלט, וזידער זין טטיקלזך.

רעקאַ.

וויא אזז דער רʼ מרדכי מואבטריע! זו גʼזיקלזך.

יוקל.

מזל העט זיך אעסטען המן היהכוואָפּפּען אָל דיא ערד,
דאַס רʼ מרדכי העט רונטער גקעננט פֿון פפערד,
דיהא צאַהגעגנבלזק זען קוואאע צו טיהטסען

Derzwischen hem gschossen di Kanuhne,

Un gebloisen hem di Postiljuhne
of ihr Harrner.

Klafihr hem si runter gspihlt fun di
Tarrner.

5 Di Tampurs hem iz gschlagen oif di Trummel,

Di Wach hot aach g'eksezshrt.

Droiben is Esther gstanne in dihn gresten
Getummel,

Un hot runter--g'apletihrt--

Di hot sich for Lachen di Saiten gehalten,

10 Wi si hot gsehi 'n Zustand fun dihn alten

Haman, un ihr Unkel for'n Schlos forbai raiten,

Un dihn begossenen Haman sain narische Gsichter schnaiden,

Droiben hem si das Kalloh[1]=lied gsunge,

Un hunten is der Hanswost--rumgsprunge.

15 Der hot ihr gmacht, wider sain Stiklich.

Reka.

Wi is der R' Mardachai umbschrie! soi glikklich.

Jukl.

Iz hot sich mesen Haman hihnwoffen of di Erd,

Das R' Mardachai hot runter gekennt fun Pferd,

Dihn Ahgenblik sen kumme zu schihsen

---

1. Brautlied.

18

:עקט הַלײַטוֹקקען, ווִיא דִיא רִיהזען,
זײ גְרױס, מִיך קעננם גָאַר נִיט זּו זַאַהגען,
דִיא העאאַ'ן טוֹיל מִין הַצר גֶעטרַאַגען,
מַלֹלעוויזֶע, זִינט ער דרוֹיבען, אָל'.דער גַאַלֶּלעריע,
אִיט אַ לַאַכגע פֿפֿיִיל, אוּן טרִינקט אִיטּזי קַאַלֿיָה,

רעקאַ.

אוֹי! דאַז מִיך דִוּ נִיט דער בײַז בִין, טוֹט אִיר לַמַהד !

דִיא מאַגד.

(רײַסט דיא טהירע אוֹיף.)

דוּי קוּאאַט ר' מרדכי דיא גַאַם רוּנטער, מִין גרעט=
טען שטַאַהט.

(אַלֹלע לוֹיפֿען דורֿבֿאַיינאַנדער אוֹיף דִיא טהירע צו.)

רעקאַ.

נו, רעננט זַאַהן מִיבערן הוֹיפֿען, מִיהר שטַאַפֿפֿען !
וואֹ הַאָט דער שטַן דען אַין טאַפֿפֿען ?

צעטולפֿע.

אָ, גַאַטּט ! וואֹ פֿיננע מִיך דען אַין טוֹהך ?
אוֹי ווִיה ! הַאַבע מִיך דאַז אַין רים געבען מִין אַין נִייא טוֹהך !
(זִיא לעסט דאַז טוֹך אָן דער טהירע העענגען, אוּנד לוֹיפֿט
מִיט אַיינעם שוֹה אַם פֿוסע אַב. אַלֹלע אַב.)

————

Sekś Haitukken, wi di Rihsen,

Soi grois, ich kenś gar nit soi sahgen,

Di hemm'n noif in ^{H}.ozer[1] getragen,

Allewaile, sizt er droiben, of der Gallerie,

5 Mit a lange Pfaif, un trinkt mitsi Kofih,

      Reka.

Oi! Das ich doi nit der bai bin, tut mir lahd!

     Di Magd.

    (raiśt di Thire oif.)

Doi kummt <u>R</u>' Mardachai di Gaś runter in greś=
                     ten Staht.

(Alle loifen durchainander oif di Thire zu.)

     Reka.

Nu, rennt ahn ibern Hoifen, ihr Stoffel!

Wu hot der <u>Śoton</u>[2] den main Toffel?

     Zetulpe.

10 O, Gott! Wu finne ich den main Schuhch?

Oi wih! Habe ich da ain Riś geben in main nai Tuhch!

   (Si leśt das Tuch an der Thire hengen, und loift
    mit aineim Schuh am Fuśe ab. Alle ab.)

1. Vorhof.
2. Satan.

ציממער אים פאללאזט.
אפּראָצענע.

זיצט אויף דעם זאָפֿהאַ, איהרע פֿיזע רוהען אויף איינעם
שעמעל. זיא העלט איין הייבלען אין דער האַנד.
דמהו המהסט אַ גיינפֿאַן, דיא בענגדער גיהן.

(התך קאָמט.)

פֿפֿוי, וויא בין איך חיבער דערטרעָקען, שלומיאל!
זמהגט, וואהז האָט דמהז פֿאָר אַ פּירוש?
גיהט אער זוי, איר גיקס, דיר גיקס, רייז לו
אחשורוש?
זייט מוחל, לאָמט מייך אַ גאַנדעראוויל, איהר טאָמאפֿער!
ערטט דרוזען מעגקען אין פֿאָטטאמאפֿער.
מיז דמהז אַ ריוזהן? גיהט אער גאָר זו רייז לו איר?
גוטע לוטט העטט מייך, און וויסטעט מייך דיא טהיר.

התך.

מוי! מוי! מאָאוזען! וואָז מיז דו דער אעהר?
איר קעננע אונג דמך טוין פֿון לענגער העַר.

אסתר.

(קאָמט העריוז פֿאָן איינעם זייטענציממער.)
זמהגט, ליעבער התך! וואָהז דעט מיהר ועגלּוען?
טעט גאָר מייער בעגעהר פֿאַרטטעגלּוען.

התך.

מיך בין אבגטיקט פֿון דיא יודען,

Zimmer im Pallast.

Afrozene.

Sizt oif dem Sopha, ihre Fisse ruhen oif ainem
    Schemel. Si helt ain Haibchen in der Hand.
Dahs hahst a Nainfall, di bender gihl.

(Hathach kommt.)

Pfui, wi bin ich iber aich derschroken, Schlumiel[1]!
Sahgt, wahs hot dahs for a Perusch[2]?
Giht mer soi, mir niks, dir niks rain zu
                       Ahasveros?
5 Sait Mohel[3], lost aich a nandermoil, ihr Schlamper!
Erst droisen melken in Potschamper.

Is dahs a Risuhn? Giht mer nor soi rain zu mir?
Gute Lust hett ich, un waiset aich di Thir.

      Hathach.

Oi! Oi! Mamsel! Was is doi der Mehr?
10 Mir kenne uns doch schoin fun lenger her.

      Esther.

(kommt herois fon ainem Saitenzimmer.)
Sahgt, lieber Hathach! Wahs det ihr wellen?
Tet nor aier Begehr forstellen.

      Hathach.

Ich bin abgschikt fun di Jiden,

---

1. <u>Vid</u>. 16. 5 of text.
2. Erklärung.
3. Ich bitte um Entschuldigung.

זײ לאמסטען זײ אום גאטטעס װיללען ביהטען ;
דאם זײ זאלל ʼריהרדען איט אחשורוש,
דאם איר מנוחה קריגען פאר המן אונד זרש.

אסתר !

וואט, פאר דיא טאל איך מנוחה,
דיא װילל איך אױזראטטען איט מיהר משפחה.
דער װילל איך דיא הונגען אהנריכטען,
דער ניקסמוללען! דער בױזװיכטען !
— אונטער אונז — איין האב איך גמאל בידי.
אױריגג אמך מיך מיהן א גמאלנע סעודה.
און זאהד זין המן עקסטרע דערלו מײן,
און סטעלל דערלו היהן פון בעטטען װײן.
װען זײ דערלויך רעלט שיכור זעננע,
מון מיאוער שיסמען, װעזה זײ טעננע,
רוק מיך איט דער פאריב רוז —
און גיב זין רשע דיהן לעטלטען טטוז.

התך •

דער דו דרויבען װאטט מיהר מאללעם װינע. —
איך װילל מילʼס זאהגען מיהר אונקען און חרבונה!

(אב.)

(חרבונ ה ס װאהנשטיבע. ה ת ך קאממט געלייפען)

התך •

קינדערלױך ! איך װאר בײ דער אסתר דרויבען.
— לאטט אונז גאטט דאנקען אּון לױבען ! —

Si lossen si um Gottes willen bihten:
Das Si soll rihden mit Ahasveros,
Das mir Menu.oh^h^{1} krigen for Haman and Seres.

      Esther.

Wat, for di schaf ich Menu.oh^h^{1},
5 Di will ich oisrotten mit ihr Mischpohoh^2.
Der will ich di Huzzel ahnrichten,
Der niksnuzzen! Der boiswichten!
--Unter uns--main hob ich ganz be-Jodai^3.
Moring mach ich ihn a ganze Se udoh^4.
10 Un lahd sain Haman ekstre derzu ain,
Un stell derzu hihn fun besten Wain.
Wen si dernoich recht Schikkôr^5 senne,
Un nimmer wissen, wahs si tenne,
Ruk ich mit der Farib rois--
15 Un gib sain Roscho ^{6} dihn letzten Stois.

      Hathach.

Der doi droiben watt Ihr alles loine.--
Iz will ich's sahgen Ihr Unkel un Harbona!

     (ab.)

(Harbona's Wohnstube. Hathach kommt geloifen)

      Hathach.

Kinderlich! Ich wor bai der Esther droiben.
--Lost uns Gott danken un loiben!--

1. Ruhe.
2. Familie.
3. in den Händen.
4. Festmahl.
5. betrunken.
6. Bösewicht.

דיא האָט איר דעה: פֿערטפֿרעסלען גיהבען,
המן זאָלל קמען לוועה טאָג אוהר זיהבען.
ער וואכד זיין פֿאַמיליע, וועררען אויזגערמהט.

חרבונה.

איך, התך! זאָמעפֿט גסטווינד לו ר' מרדכי פֿאָטט,
זאַמגט, ער זאָלל גלַייך לו גרייעע מויפֿהיהרען,
און מ ביסאָע בייא איר איר מיינקעהרען.

(חתך אב.)

איך, פֿרמה! לאָמי מויפֿטרמגען כל טוב און כי טוב,
ווייס געטוואע האָט מ וויא מ גוטען סוף. —

צעטולפֿע.

לאָמסען זיא זיך פֿרמגען, ליעבער — טמהטע;
מיז דען קיין בחמה? קיין אמסקערמהטע?

חרבונה.

וי, איין המן! מלוועם איז, רעטטט און בחמה.

צעטולפֿע.

דמהו מיזט וההפעריב, דם האָט אמן דעך דיא וואַהן.
(זיא רייסט איהרען בונד פֿאָם קאָפּפֿע אונד רופֿט.)
צעפֿירעטע! לאָוו זיא גסטווינד לו'ן טניידער און פֿרעסער
סטמנדעביע זאָלען זיא קוואע לו איר הער —
פֿאָר מלוען וויל מיך איין המהר גסטווינד וויקקלע.

חרבונה.

פֿרמה! רילט מהך הער, דיין מיהנטיקקלע,

Di hot mir dahs Fersprechen gihben,

Haman soll kahn zwah Tag mehr lihben.

Er und sain Familie, warren oisgerott.

      Harbona.

Iz, Hathach! Laaft gschwind zu R' Mardachai fott,

5 Saagt, er soll glaich zu graine oifheren,

Un a bisle bai mir ainkehren.

      (Hathach ab.)

Iz, Frah! Los oiftragen kol Tuv=un=ki Tôv[1],

Wails genumme hot soi a guten Sôf[2].

      Zetulpe.

Lassen Sie sich fragen, lieber--Thate:

10 Is den kain Bahl? kain Maskerate?

      Harbona.

Joi, main Haz! Alles is, Retut un Bahl.

      Zetulpe.

Dahs ist suhperib, da hat man doch di Wahl.

      (Si raist ihren Bund fam Kopfe und ruft.)

Zefirete! Laf Si gschwind zu'n Schnaider un Freser

Standenbie sollen si kumme zu mir her--

15 For allen will ich main Hahr gschwind wikkle.

      Harbona.

Frah! Richt ahch her, dain Ihltikkle,

1. "Alles Gute und dass es gut sei." Tendlau, Prov. #524;
likewise Genesis I, 12; however, vid. Stern, M., Daily
Prayers, p. 375 (section dealing with Grace After Meals)--
ve-chol Tôv u-mi-kol Tuv. (Und alles Gute und von jedem Guten).
2. Ende.

גענג 'ס חנוכה ≈ מייזען, מון 'ס הבדלה ∙ העלל רויג,
איר אַלל∙יאיגיהרען, מונזער האיז —

רעקאַ∙

יוי, אער אמאלט דוי זוי מ כוימ∙עהיג, זוי מ געטוה.

חרבונה∙

נמרלי — דיא ליהדען אמאכען איר לו.
(מרדכי קאַממט אין גרעסטען שטאַאט, איהם פֿאָלגען
מעהרערע דער פֿאַרנעהמען ש ו ש 'ס.)

רעקאַ∙

אוי, ווֹיא איז ר' מרדכי געפוצט, ווֹיא 'ס קעטערלֿי
מן דער פֿאַמסעננאַהבֿט.

מרדכי∙

אסתר האַט אחשורוש זיין האן — דערוואַהבֿט;
ער וויֹלל מאַלֿלעמ ניך מיהר ווֹילֿלען טוין.
דאַהו האָט זיא איר זמהֹגען לאָמסען טוין.
דרום לֿאָמט אוני מל פֿראואע ידען
מין טוהן גיהן, מון לו גאָטט ביהטען,
פֿאָר מונזערן מלך זיין לֿאַנג ליהבען,
דאַם ער מיהן זֿאָלל גיהבען
ניקם ווֹיא מזל וברכה,
מיהן און זיין גאַנלע משפחה.
(עז קאָממט איינער אונד פֿערקינדעט.)
מאַללעווֹין ווֹאַטם פובלֿיניהרט,
דאַם המן אמֿרינג נוד ווֹאַטט גֿפיהרט,
מון איט מאַלֿל זיין לֿעהי זיהן

Lang's Ḥannukoh=aisen[1], un's Havdoloh=holz[2] rois,

Mir alliminihren, unser Hois--

       Reka.

Joi, mer macht doi soi a Noifsehi, soi a Getuh.

       Harbona.

Narrli--Di Lihden machen mir zu.

      (Mardachai kommt in gresten Štaat, ihm folgen

        mehrere der vornehmen Susan'ś.)

5   Oi, Wi is R' Mardachai gepuzt, wi 'ś Keterli

                an der Fašenahcht.

      Mardachai.

Esther hot Ahasveros sain Haz--derwahcht:

Er will alleś noich ihr Willen toin,

Dahs hot si mir sahgen lossen schoin.

Drum lost uns als frumme Jiden

10 In Schuhl gihn, un zu Gott bihten,

For unsern Melech[3] sain lang Lihben,

Daś Er ihn soll gihben

Nikś wi Massol u-Berochoh[4],

Ihn un sain ganze Mischpohoh[5].

     (Es kommt ainer und ferkindet.)

15 Allewail watś publizihrt,

Daś Haman moring nois watt gfihrt,

Un mit all sain zehi Sihn

---

1. Menorah: The iron candle stick Menorah of the Hannukoh candles.
2. The wooden candle stick holder for the Saturday and festive nights' candle.
3. König.
4. Glück und Segen.
5. Familie.

געהענקט װאָטט, מעהנער נױך דיהן אַנדערן היהן.
זרש יאַגט איער פֿון היע נױז,
ר' מרדכי קריהגט איהר עשירות און איהר הױז.
און פּוקט מיך נאָר אַלֹלע פּאָר'ן
ער איז שני למלך מיך געװאָרן.

אַללע·

מזל טוב! מזל טוב! איהר עקסעלענן.

צעטולפֿע·

מיך אױס'ן געװיזד בינדען צו פֿאַהר בזואַעעקרעגן —

רעקאָ·

מיך װיֹלֹל גלֹײך צו בעגֹיהבע קוֹבֹען באַװאַבען,
און צו נוקקערהעמאַֹנֹי פּאָר'ן, נון שלח מנות אװאַבען.

חרבונה·

מיך װיֹלֹל נאָר געװיזד איין ראש חרש קֹלאַהד מעהגֹליהבגען.
אָבער זאַהגט, ר מרדכי! װאַז טו מיך פֿאָר איין
טרחה קרײהגען?

מרדכי·

װאָטט איין זֹיעבער חרבונה!
אֹיך װיֹלֹל מיך רעבֿט בעלֹױנע,
אין דער ברכת המגילה לאָם מיך נײן טרײבען לבסוף:
יגם חרבונה זכור לטוב.   (אַללע אַב·)

ענדע·

Gehenkt watt, ahner noich dihn andern hihn.

Seres jagt mer fun hie nois,

R' Mardachai krihgt ihr ʿAschirôs.[1] un ihr Hois.

Un pukt aich nor alle for'n

5   Er is Schêni la-Melech[2] iz geworn.

       Alle.

Massol tôv[3]! Massol tôv[3]! Ihr Exselenz!

       Zetulpe.

Ich mus'n gschwind binden a pahr Blummekrenz--

       Reka.

Ich will glaich a belihbe Kuchen bachen,

Un a Zukkerhazli for'n zu'n Schalah Monôs[4]

                      machen.

       Harbona.

10   Ich will nor gschwind main Rô'sch Hôdesch[5]=Klahd ahnzihgen.

Ober sahgt, R' Mardachai! Was tu ich for main

              Tirhoh[6] krihgen?

       Mardachai.

Watt main lieber Harbona!

Aich will ich recht beloine,

In der Birchas ha-Megiloh[7] los ich nain schraiben le-be-Sôf[8]:

Ve-gam[9] Harbona sochur la-Tôv[10].

                 (alle ab.)

       Ende.

---

1. Reichtümer. 2. der Andere nach dem König. 3. Viel Glück. 4. Austellung der Geschenke. 5. Neumond. 6. Mühe. 7. Blessings before the reading of the scroll of Esther. 8. am Ende. 9. Und auch. 10. behalte gütig im Gedächtnis-- From hymn in prayer book containing prayers for Purim.

PART II

Commentary

COMMON ABBREVIATIONS USED IN THE COMMENTARY

A
A: Analysis
acc.: accusative
auth.: authentic

B

C
C: Commentary
CY: Central Yiddish

D
dat.: dative
delib.: deliberate(ly)
dial.: dialect
dist.: distorted,
       distortion

E
EY: East Yiddish
Eng., Engl.: English
esp.: especially

F
f.: for
f.i.: for instance
FW: Fremdwort, -wörter
    foreign word
fig.: figuratively
Fr.: French

G
G: German
gen.: genitive

H
H: Herz
h: humor(ous)
h c: humoris causa,
     for the sake of humor
HG: High German

HHG: "hyper" HG
Heb., Hebr.: Hebrew

I
inauth.: inauthentic

J

K

L
L: Lexicology
lit.: literally

M
MHG: Middle High German
M.: Mordechai
m c: metri causa, for the
     sake of meter

N
NHG: New High German
nom.: nominative

O
OHG: Old High German
OY: Old Yiddish

P
pers.: person
pl.: plural
prob.: probably

Q

R
R: rhyme
Rz: Reimzwang, forced,
    "impure" R
rev. subst.: reverse sub-
    stitution

S

sc.: supply
SD: stage direction
SEY: South East Yiddish
SG: South German
sg.: singular
Slav.: Slavic

T

U

U: Upper

V

W

WO: word order
WY: West Yiddish

X, Y, Z

Y: Yiddish

Other

<: "came from"
>: "went to"

HEBREWISMS of special interest, where they are found in the
Text, where they are discussed in the Commentary:

Hebrewism-line no.-C page

nebich-1.7-126
Neder-9.10-148
Nekêvôs-7.23-145

samekh--see under 's̈'

Koschor-41.12-253
Kôl (q)-80.3-328

be-ᶜAwônôs-11.7-153
        31.19-228
ᶜÔfôs̈-49.5-271
Kol ᶜÔlom-25.21-208

Pêrôsch-88.3-340
le-Poḥôs̈ Mêoh Alofim-54.20-280
Ponim-36.6-238
pôresch-5.6-137

Zeᵓinoh ve-Roᵓinoh-11.8-154
Zorôs̈-30.4-224
Zorfas̈ Loschôn-44.2-258

qof--see under 'k'

Rabbi-9.10-148
Rôᵓsch Ḥôdesch-92.10-348
Roschoᶜ-43.9-256
Ruḥôs̈-35.2-236

Schadchonus̈-6.1-141
Schabbos̈-11.12-156
Schabbaschon-12.3-156
Schalaḥ Monôs̈-77.21-324
         92.9-348
Schiddich-5.21-140
Schevuᶜôs-27.6-215
Schôteh-76.10-321
Schlemihl-16.5-167-174

S̈eḥôroh-9.11-149, 46.2-264
S̈êchel-41.2-250
S̈echur-50.1-273
S̈êfer-25.22-209

S̈oton-4.16-136, 87.9-339

Tharbus̈-1.4-125
Thaᶜanis̈-67.10-303
Thehilim-11.9-154
Thefiloh-66.7C SD-301
Theḥinoh-67.5-301
Thᵓômar-43.19-257
Thôroh-5.19-140

Introduction

The Yiddish Language

A primary prerequisite for a proper orientation in Judeo-German dialectology[1] are some basic facts about the history of Yiddish.[2] Inextricably interwoven therewith is the story of the Jew in the diaspora.[3] Throughout the diaspora the Jew wrote in Hebrew characters the language of the country in which he settled. Hence there arose Judeo-Persian, Judeo-Greek, Judeo-Spanish, Judeo-French and Judeo-German, the latter the fore-runner of Eastern and Modern Yiddish.

Judeo-German began more than a thousand years ago along the Rhine. This was the home of one of the basic Jewish populations in Europe that came with the Roman legions. The Jewish migrations, which in their onrush stopped at the Rhine,

---

[1] The term Judeo-German is used throughout and properly so only when referring to Western Yiddish, vid. Franz J. Beranek "Die Erforschung der jiddischen Sprache", ZfdPh, Vol. LXX (No. 2, 1947/48) p. 166.

[2] Vid. Max Weinreich, Yiddish, Algemeyne yidishe Entsiklopedye, Vol. Yidn B, pp. 25-90; A.A. Roback, The Story of Yiddish Literature in the Nineteenth Century, New York, 1899.

[3] Heinrich Hirsch Graetz, History of the Jews, 6 vols., Philadelphia, 1891-98; Simon Dubnow, Weltgeschichte des jüdischen Volkes, 10 vols., Berlin, 1925-29; Marvin Lowenthal, The Jews of Germany, New York, 1936.

later preceded eastward to Poland via Southern and Northern Germany. In this continual push to the east through Germany the Jews absorbed to a great degree the varying local German dialectical speech characteristics, to a lesser degree the Slavic speech habits. Modern Yiddish therefore, is fundamentally a composite of German, Hebrew, Aramaic, Slavic and Romance elements, with the German superseding in importance.

The history of Yiddish for the last thousand years has been divided into four periods: (1) Initial Yiddish (1000-1250), (2) Old Yiddish (1250-1500), (3) Middle Yiddish (1500-1700), (4) Modern Yiddish (1700-).[4]

Of the first period, Initial Yiddish, there have as yet been found no linguistic monuments, for the earliest Yiddish manuscript extant, a medical leaflet on phlebotomy, discovered in the archives at Cologne, dates back to only the late fourteenth century.[5] However, in the next period, the Old Yiddish period, there were about one hundred and fifty works written in Yiddish. These works were varied in character. They were mostly stories with biblical themes, religious poetry, religious prayers, mystic works, paraphrased works of original German, Italian, French and English romances, and also a few original romances. In the third period, the Middle Yiddish period, there were two distinct dialectical literatures, Western and Eastern Yiddish. The literature of the former was more varied than that of the latter. In Western

---

[4] Max Weinreich, op. cit., p. 35.

[5] Salomo Birnbaum, "Das älteste datierte Schriftstück in jiddischer Sprache," Beiträge, LVI (1932), pp. 11-32.

Yiddish both religious and secular subjects were emphasized;
in Eastern Yiddish only religious. In Western Yiddish were
written books on morals, translations of the Bible, commentaries on biblical law, paraphrases on biblical subjects e.g.
the books of Judges, Joshua, Kings and Esther; medical books,
histories, books on education, social reflections, and social
novels. In Eastern Yiddish there were mostly religious works
although there was an infiltration of mediaeval German folk-
songs and romances which persisted right up to the end of the
nineteenth century.[6]

Yiddish on the European continent in the nineteenth century was hybrid. It consisted of principally German elements
with some Hebrew, Aramaic, Slavic and Romance. The Hebrew
and Aramaic elements were composed chiefly of religious and
abstract terms taken from the Bible, the Talmud and the Midrash. The Slavic strain consisted of words used in trade
and also to express in a subtle way intimate thoughts and
feelings. The Romance influence, chiefly Italian and French
made itself felt principally in Yiddish names.

The Yiddish language at this time consisted of two main
dialects, Western and Eastern Yiddish. Western Yiddish or
Judeo-German was principally German in character with Hebrew,
Aramaic, Romance and Slavic elements in order of their re-
spective importance. Eastern Yiddish was also essentially
German in character but with greater emphasis, as to be expected, upon the Slavic.

Western Yiddish was the language spoken in German-

---

[6] For information on modern Yiddish literature, vid. the publications of the Yiddish Scientific Institute (Yivo), 535
West 123 Street, New York 27, New York.

speaking territory -- Holland, Germany, Elsass, Switzerland,
Lombardy, Austria and Sudetenland --, Eastern Yiddish in the
Slavic-speaking regions -- Poland, Lithuania, Latvia, Esthonia,
White Russia, East Slovakia, East Hungary, North Rumania and
the Ukraine. Western Yiddish was a complete dialect mixture
with the newly added element of Slavic; Eastern Yiddish, a
development of the Bavarian and East Middle German[7] with the
addition of Russian, Polish, Czech and Lithuanian in order of
importance. Furthermore there were three divisions of
Eastern Yiddish: (1) a northern spoken in the Baltic lands,
White Russia, Lithuania and commonly called the o-dialect
(2) a dialect spoken in Poland known as the u-dialect and
separated from the northern by the old boundary line between
Poland and Lithuania (3) a southern spoken in the Ukraine and
its neighboring lands, East Galicia, Bukowina and Moldavia --
closer to the Polish than to the Lithuanian.

At the beginning of the eighteenth century Yiddish as a
spoken and written language began to decline in Germany, to
rise in the Slavic countries. This decline in Germany was
accelerated at the end of the century so that by the middle
of the nineteenth century Yiddish was almost non-existent in
Germany. On the other hand, while the death knell to Western
Yiddish was sounded in the middle of the nineteenth century,
Eastern Yiddish -- Lithuanian, Polish, Ukrainian -- flourished.
Modern Yiddish has been therefore Eastern Yiddish in character.

Herz's Esther, although written in the early nineteenth
century, must be considered an example of Late Middle Western
Yiddish. Herz reflected in his most popular

---

[7] Franz J. Beranek, op. cit., p. 167.

comedy[8] the language spoken by the Jews of the middle and lower strata of society in the German towns and villages at the beginning of the nineteenth century. This language was fundamentally German with some Hebrew, Aramaic and Romance features. The Slavic strain was negligible, these linguistic characteristics mirrored that period of transition when the Jews emerged from the ghetto into the culture of the new Enlightenment. In this period of change the dramatist, Herz, pilloried through his language the values of Jewish piety, especially the efforts of the pious to prescribe secular literature.

---

[8] J. Herz, Esther, 2nd ed., Fürth, 1854: "Dem fielsaitigen Ferlangen des Publikims zu entsprechen, hat sich der Ferleger entschlossen, dies Werkchen in einer zwaiten Oiflage erschainen zu lassen." -- Preface.

The Language of Herz's <u>Esther</u>

A Yiddish proverb says: "Andere šprachn redt <u>men</u>;
Yiddish redt <u>zich</u>"; i.e.: "Other languages are spoken" (sc.
with some effort), "but Yiddish speaks itself" (sc. without
any effort). The proverb reflects the naive impression of the
native Yiddish speaker that Yiddish is so easy that it need
not even be learned; "it just comes naturally". Another proverb admits that Yiddish does have its difficulties - but only
with respect to its Hebrewisms: Az Got vil štrofn an am-
hoorets, šikt er im a lošn-koideš vort in moil arayn; i.e.:
"When Got wants to punish the ignoramus, He puts a Hebrew word
into his mouth".

Of the Yiddish of Herz just the reverse is true: Its
Hebrewisms are crystal-clear (to the average Yiddish speaker),
but the bulk of the "regular Yiddish" in it (i.e. the over 90%
of the total lexical material which is of German origin) is intelligible neither to the German nor to the Yiddish speaker.

Hence - the need for this introduction and the running
commentary. One need only to try to read the first pages of
the play, whether in the original or in the transliteration, to
be convinced of the basic unintelligibility. But the problem
goes even deeper: after every vocable was traced and its basic
<u>meaning</u> established, the phonology remained more puzzling than
ever: chaos! Each vowel is represented by every other vowel;

consonants are interchanged: the voiced for the unvoiced, the explosives for the fricatives, and vice versa - just the reverse of the expected. And yet, side by side with these puzzling forms one finds the regular HG forms and the equally regular WY forms, with an occasional EY and some G dialect form.

The key to the puzzle is - humor. In the traditional spirit of celebrating Purim as a merry carnival where "anything goes", Herz's Esther is not the simple dramatization of the Biblical Epic (the usual treatment in the religious school), but a sophisticated farce and a comedy of manners of his time, not unlike Gamaliel Bradford's Ole Adam's Chillun. And like Bradford, Herz employs - in addition to comic situations and funny manners - dialect as an integral element of the humor. He goes beyond Bradford in that he does not shrink from the downright obscene - he stretches the liberty afforded by the carnival spirit.[9]

The carnival spirit in the merry-making, not unlike that in the feast of Mardis Gras and Fastnacht and All Fools Day of contemporaneous Europe, often "got out of hand" and exceeded the relatively high degree of permissiveness - in wildness, impertinence and obscenity. The Talmud (Megillah 7b) even tells of the sages Rabbah and Rav Zerah feasting on Purim and getting drunk and Rabbah then "slaying" Rav Zerah, but praying and achieving a miraculous revival.

Parodies[10] on the liturgy and holy lore, especially parodies on the Talmudic tractate dealing with Purim (Megillah),

---

[9] Incidentally, he uses obscenity as humor even where he has no such excuse: in his mock-heroic ballad, "Eine wahre wunderbare und seltsame Geschichte etc.", p. 115 of the 2nd ed., not treated by us in this work.

[10] See: Israel Davidson Parody in Jewish Literature, (New York 1907); A.M. Haberman: "Massechet Purim Mahaduroteha-u-Desfusha" in Areshet 5, (Jerusalem 1972) pp. 136-144.

started as "good, pure fun" with only pretended frivolity for the sake of "innocent merriment", but developed, at times, into excessess that outraged and terrified the Rabbis and induced them to try to stem the tide, with the strictest measures at their disposal, confiscation and burning of the "works", and even excommunicating their authors -- but to no avail.

But the Purim "acting" gave the Rabbis more concern even than the "improper language" in the parodies: the mixing of the sexes; the masquerading in clothes of the opposite sex (forbidden by the Bible: Deut. 22,5); the sin of adultery and bastardization which the Rabbis considered committed by the play acting at marriage by an actress when, in fact, she was legally married and even a mother -- outside of her role on the stage; and above all, extending the playing beyond Purim. The theater had been anathema to the Talmud ever since the Roman gladiator shows, and it considered even really "innocent merriment" as sinful in itself and leading to ever gravér sinning. Again the Rabbis lost their hard-fought battle -- though there were still attempts to suppress the Yiddish theater production here and there in benighted localities as late as after the First World War.[11]

Again, like Bradford, the use of dialect implies the condescension, the "laugh of superiority". Ever since Mendelssohn the Jewish "Intelligentsia" in Germany in this Era of Enlightenment became "assimilationist" in their social philosophy and preached the abandonment of Yiddish (they called their WY "Jüdisch-deutsch") in favor of HG - in a bid for attaining civil rights. WY thus did not die; it was murdered. It became "salonunfähig" - improper for serious or

---

[11] See Sch. Ernst, op. cit. pp. 5-37, especially a photostat of the placard facing p. 32, appealing to the Jews of Ostrov-Mazoviec to boycott the Yiddish theater-troupe because it played on Saturday and thus desecrated the Sabbath.

lofty themes. It could be used only for comedy, to poke fun, to mock the "inferior" with the assumption of superiority by the mocker -- comparable to the prose "comic relief" interspersing high-tragedy verse in Western Classical literature.

Unlike Bradford, though, Herz's dialect is far from authentic. He did his spoofing so well that nobody seems to have caught on till now, that often he coins, invents and distorts forms and dishes them up as Y. While it is hard to decide in some cases, there is a large number of definite distortions that prove that Herz deliberately deviates from HG even in cases where all Y dialects are identical with HG - to get a laugh.

But more than that: Herz uses language as a means of characterization:

1. Herz employs straight HG wherever either he or his characters are serious; thus his title-page, introduction and stage directions (SD) are HG[12];the King and the Court Ladies speak HG, both because of their rank and because it points up their not being Jewish.

---

[12] The transliteration - finished before the insights that resulted in this commentary - does not reflect this fact, and in spelling, at least, the transliteration of Herz's texts is uniform throughout and could mislead one into assuming that Herz meant the text to be Y throughout.

Our Commentary calls special attention, where necessary, to the character of the text. HG is revealed by its specific grammar, which is unmistakably different from Y; mostly also by phonology, though, because of the tradition (since the 18th century) of transliterating the rounded and unrounded vowels alike, when written with Hebrew characters, (cf. Mendelssohn's German translation of the Bible, written with the Hebrew alphabet), Herz writes 'tir', both for 'Tier' and 'Tür'; 'hai' both for 'Heu' and 'hei'; 'lehne' both for

'Löhne' and 'lehne'.

As it is, the transliteration was a most laborious chore and
prone to errors almost in every word: the same word with an
implied identical pronunciation is spelled at times in half a
dozen different ways: sagen, saagen, sahgen, sagn, etc. To
try to redo the transliteration would have resulted in new
errors and in corrections after corrections. It was therefore deemed wiser to leave the original system of transliteration and supplement it in the Commentary. The <u>phonetic</u>
transliteration in the Commentary <u>had</u> to take cognizance of
the Transliteration system of the Play as it is -- so deviation from the I.P.A. <u>had</u> to be made, especially in the case
of the dental fricatives, i.e., the following pairs are
equivalent: 'sch' : 'š', 'ṣ' : 'ss', 's' : 'z',
'z' : 'ts' (or: 'ts'), 'ch' : 'x' -- these have had to
be used at different times, not promiscuously, but as the
logic of clarity and convenience of situation dictated.

It could even be argued that the <u>uniform</u> system of transliteration has the greater merit: it is "diplomatic" and
it uses "consistently" the identical representation of a
Roman letter for a Hebrew letter; it is more suitable for
such "mixed" language patterns as that of Haman and the
"hyper-correct" HG of the snobbish characters - which are
neither "pure" German, nor "pure" Y.

"Misleading" can also be the transliteration of biblical
names. There is absolutely no question but that they were
meant to be pronounced Y: the occasional rhymes prove that.
But as the transliteration was intended for those who
cannot read Y - it was deemed more helpful to use forms
more familiar to them - the forms of Luther's Bible.

Finally, the Hebrewisms are transliterated in their "full"
forms, as they are pronounced in Hebrew prayers but <u>not</u>
in <u>Y speech</u> - where all unaccented vowels are slurred to
'ə'! The Commentary calls attention to this where necessary.

2. Esther speaks Y to Jews; HG to the King.

3. All "old fashioned" Jews speak Y, either authentic WY
   (i.e. the Y spoken in G speech-territory and Herz's own
   dialect), but if that does not deviate from HG then
   "Polish" Y (Central East Y - CEY), or "Galician" Y
   (South East Y - SEY), or some G dialect, or some
   deliberate distortion.

4. The snob, the "high-faluting" climber, the show-off,
   the would-be fashionable HG speaker (who is just too
   ignorant and does not master HG "von rechten von Hause
   aus") uses "hypercorrect" HG (HHG) where "reverse" sound
   substitutions are made, so that they are neither Y nor G,
   (e.g. G weiss - WY waass; therefore WY and G 'wašen'
   became distorted into 'waišen'.

Details

Table of Correspondences: MHG, NHG and Y:

MHG	Kum	koufe	dâ	schôn	ein	Hûs	im	schoenen	süd	Tiutschlant
NHG	Komm	au	"	"	"	au	"	ö	"	Teutschland
WY	Kum	ā	oi	oi	ā(n)	oi		ē	ī	ai
Herz	u	ā	oi	oi	ā(n)	oi		ē(ī)	ī	ai
CEY	i	oi	u	oi	a(ain)	ō		ai	ī	a

that is:

I.	MHG	â	ô	û	î	iu	ê	oe
	NHG	"	"	au	ei	eu	"	ö
	WY	oi	oi	oi	ai	ai	ē	ē
	Herz	"	"	"	"	"	ē(i)	ē(i)
	CEY	u	"	o	ā	ā	ai	ai

With regard to the rest of the vowels, WY is like NHG:
i.e. all short MHG vowels in permanently closed syllables
remain unchanged in both, and such short vowels in openable
syllables are lengthened in both NHG and WY.

All Y, including WY, unrounds round vowels, i.e. ü > i,
ö > e and retain the NHG short high vowel before a nasal or
'1' where standard NHG changes it to a middle vowel: e.g.:
MHG kumen, vul, künic; WY kumen, ful, kinig; HG kommen, voll,
könig; CY kimen, fil, kinig.

CY (unlike WY) changed also the secondary lengthened
vowels (originally short in MHG open syllables) in the identical fashion that it changed the original MHG long vowels:
sagen > sugen, like: dâ > du.

 II. In addition, Herz almost regularly substitutes:
   î for ê(ö): lihben for leben, grihs for HG
    'Gröss'; (and the reverse in Hyper HG)
   û for ô, especially in FW: Kanuhne f. Kanone,
    Mude for Mode
 III. and sometimes (in Hyper HG) ai for a (graid for
   grad)
 IV. and rarely u for â (CEY) in Muhlen for Malen;
   Gruhf for Graf
 V. Any vowel (a, e, i, o, u, ö, ü,) plus rd (rt) or rst
   become 'at' or 'ašt' respectively: HG wartet, werd',
   wird, Wort, wurde', würd' > wat! HG Fürst > Fašt;
   exception: between two labials > o: wirft > woft;
   any vowel plus r before other consonants > ar:
   Hörner > Harrner.
    A reverse phenomenon: HG Narr, nur > ner. In
  an unaccented position it could conceivably be

considered authentic slurring, but since it is used
in rhyme it can only be an inauthentic distortion
for the sake of humor (we abbreviate: inauth.:
h c). In all languages, especially in Y and G, the
'r' tends to lower and not to raise the vowel -
hence the change would not be natural.

VI. There is apocope of -n: sage for sagen, Mendle
for Männlein;

VII. There is apocope instead of HG syncope:
HG lebte (< MHG lebete) Herz: lebet;

VIII. Some frequent items:

HG wir gehen und stehen becomes mir genge un stenne
Herz wir   sind   becomes mir sen,   senne

HG ich habe, tue   wir tun   müssen
Herz ich hon, het tu(b)   tet   mir toin, tenne   messen
                       (authentic)
HG ich hätte   wir haben   wir wollen,   sollen
Herz ich hette, hiebet mir hemme   mir wellen, sellen
Herz 'ihns'   HG 'es'.

IX. There is an almost regular reversal of voiced and
voiceless consonants:

$d <> t$, $g <> k$, $w <> f$, but especially $(z <> s)$
(equals HG -s- $<>$ ss) lihsén - gewihsen equals
HG lesen - gewesen

riht - red (HG Rede, rede)

X. rb $<>$ rw Arwet, (HG Arbeit).

Distortions:

XI. Metanalysis (false division of syllables)
'an' plus vowel becomes 'a' plus 'n' plus vowel:
'an oifen' becomes 'a noiven' (HG Ofen), hence
Nobent from 'an Obent' (HG Abend); a Naffeziehr
(also: Affeziehr - officer), G Offizier; these
distortions are for humorous effect (designated

in the Commentary as h, or h c); all other deviations are found in alphabetical listing of Lexicology (L).

e̅ and i̅ sounds

The most conspicuous deviation of Herz from general WY
is the representation of WY e̅ as i̅ (spelled ה' or ץ' = ih or
ie) - whether < NHG ê, ae, ä-, oe, ö-, e-, ë- ('___'
denotes: open syllable). HG schön, leben = S̆ihn, lieben.
This is most probably a deliberate distortion (not even based
on some existing G dialect), since only originally long
vowels in MHG change in WY; vowels lengthened in NHG are
identical in WY and NHG. (Vogtländisch, for instance,
changes MHG ê and oe to i, but not the other vowels!)
Another indication that Herz is here distorting h c is the
fact of reverse spelling: writing 'le̲ben' (ד) for 'lie̲ben' -
for which there can be no other explantion except Herz's
straining for h effect. Herz is too knowledgeable and
sophisticated to blunder into such a mistake. It is
deliberate.

In fact, his whole system of Yiddish spelling is: "one
big joke" - albeit a rather weak, low-brow joke. He
deviates completely from traditional Y spelling (incidentally
much older and more rational than the NHG spelling he
imitates). Such imitation h c was a common joke among Jews
and rather easily achieved. A Y magazine of humor in
Germany during World War I was called DER S̆CHLEMIEL (S̆
spelled שץה). The point of the joke is: S̆ is represented
in Y by a single letter ש not by the trigraph SCH: שץה
would represent three separate sounds: S̆-TS-H. So Herz
represents the G s, ſ , ſſ with ז or זז even when they are meant

to be voiceless. In Hebrew and Y, ז is laways voiced! He
deviates from HG spelling where it is identical with Y and
hence would not yield a joke: f.i. 'saagen' instead of
'sagen' (in both HG and WY).

All Hebrew is spelled in <u>Square</u> letters, Germanic elements (really non-Hebrew) in cursive (Waiber-šrift or Meschit)
and the separation is carried out even when it means
splitting a stem from its suffix cf. <u>קאס=ת ו ז ע</u> = <u>Asus</u>
= kat. From historical Y spelling Herz retains:

Aleph:[13]   ornans and dividens:

di',   si',   bei',   v'u
דיא   זיא   בייא   ווא7

N.B.   In References, numbers <u>alone</u> refer to page and line of
the play in Part I (a photostat of the original and its
transliteration) -- paginated identically. Numbers with
a preceding 'A' refer to page and/or paragraph in the
unpublished Analysis; with a preceding 'C' to Part II
(the Commentary that follows the pagination of Part I in
referring to page and line of the play); with a preceding 'L' -- to <u>individual</u> <u>entries</u> in the 'Lexicology'
section at the end of Part II.

In the Commentary it was found useful to use German and
English: Herz's Y words are first "converted" into
their corresponding HG <u>forms</u>, and where these are <u>not</u>
identical in meaning, with a more exact HG <u>translation</u>
(thus pointing up not only phono-morphological but also
lexical differences between what H calls his "jüdisch-
deutsche Mundart" and HG). This is followed by English
(translation and/or comment). This may <u>look</u> like a
mishmash on the surface, but its purpose (and we hope:
effect) is greater clarity rather than confusion.

---

[13] Aleph "ornans", or "decorative", so-called because after
the second component of the original diphthong became silent
(ie + uo > ī + ū) and after the dative -e became silent too,
the Aleph representing them was mistakenly explained as due
to 'decoration', then extended to where it never belonged
historically. The Aleph dividens was and still is used as a
diaresis - to divide letters so as to prevent their being
read as digraphs.

Frequent svarabhakti - some authentic Y:

(nakit = G nackt; oreme = G arme; some come ∠ G dialects
and some become deliberate distortions: (פֿאליגט'foligt' =
G folgt). Frequent reversal of <u>voiced</u> and voiceless, h c
Ex: ma<u>ss</u>el for Y ma<u>s</u>el (luck); Kuntiter for Konditor;
apletiren for G applaudieren.

The title page is in "pure" HG, not in Y, in spite of the
impression of our "diplomatic" transliteration of the Hebrew
characters (in which the first nine lines are printed). The
last four lines use the German <u>alphabet</u>. The last <u>three</u>
would normally appear thus in most Jewish prints - they were
intended for the civic authorities and contained place, date
and publisher.

The next unnumbered two pages are also in pure HG - except for the place and date of H's Introduction. Jewish dates
are part of their religion. As already mentioned, the Stage
Directions (SD) are also in HG - an indication of the typical
attitude of his time and place to WY: fit only for comedy.

The List of Characters on the third unnumbered page is
HG - except as noted below.
Line 1 '<u>Ahasveros</u>': Hebrew words and names are printed in
"Square" type; the rest in "Meschit", a sort of
Hebrew "italic" letter, developed from the cursive

On top of the page are the barest aids in rendering the
Text (of the play) intelligible for quick reading. Below
<u>the line</u> are the scholarly comments necessary for a
deeper understanding.

Margin numbers: single numbers refer to lines. A number
followed by a period and another number refer to page and
line.

<u>written</u> forms and used originally mainly for Y
translations of, or commentaries on a Hebrew text -
to set off the Hebrew text from the "rest". Then a
printer's practice evolved and continued for a long
time to print Y books only in Meschit, and since the
main readers of Y were thought to be women (men were
thought to be educated enough in Hebrew not to need
the aid of a translation or commentary in the
vernacular), this type-face came to be known also
as "Waibertaitsch" (Women's translation). Our
printer deviates from the practice in printing the
stage directions also in Square - to set them off
from the "spoken lines" of the play - thereby making
a new application of the old principle - even in
"deviating" from it.

The Hebrewisms are <u>underlined</u> in our Transliteration
to achieve a similar setting-off.

Our transliteration of Biblical names <u>could</u> mislead:
to aid in their instant recognition the forms of
Luther's Bible are used, but the pronunciation was
always, and was meant by H to be, Y! Hence we always indicate it in C. The rhymes prove it - if
proof were needed. Hence pronounce: Achaschvérɔsch.

Line 1 '<u>Kenig</u>': "defective" spelling for König. "Pure" <u>HG</u>,
written with Hebrew characters, had lost the knack
of representing the round vowels ö and ü and wrote
e and i for them. Y requires Kinig. The form
Kenig in MY is a typical recent borrowing from HG -
being a word of "high culture".

Line 3 'Haman': pr. Hɔrmən! In the Purim plays not only a
      vllain, but a comic character.

Line 4 'Mardochai': pr. Mɔrtchə, or in H possibly M>tchə.*

Line 5 'Jehudi': the Hebrew, highly emotional word breaks
      through, instead of the just emotional WY 'Jid'
      (which is avoided because of its tinge of hosti-
      lity).

Line 7 'bai': spelled 'bai', but our transliteration always
      omits the "silent" Aleph (ornans), as the initial
      silent Aleph is also regularly omitted in all
      transliterations (not only our own). In 'bai' the
      aleph was always "ornans" - i.e. had no phonetic
      value whatever, but in a word like 'di•', the aleph
      became silent and therefore ornans, but had had
      originally the value of 'a' and then 'ə'.

Line 9 'Harbona': pr. Charbónə.

Line 10 'Reka' etc.: Non-Biblical, invented by H h c.
      H never passes up an opportunity at "humor",
      therefore one can be sure that each invented name
      also was intended to have humorous connotations -
      even if these are no longer always evident - whe-
      ther his audience "got" the joke or not. And just
      because by their nature names are not usually funny
      per se, H again resorts to sounds that evoke an
      association with the obscene - be that ever so
      slight or far-fetched. He seems to enjoy a "pri-
      vate" joke. (He is not beyond such "suggesting" in

---

*Note: Please supply the spelling "Mordechai" wherever in the
Commentary this name is mentioned and a variant-spelling is
used.

his deliberate distortions of otherwise innocent
words throughout his works.)

'Reka' could conceivably be a diminutive of Rebeca
or even Regina - but it is not. There is Ricke,
Riecke (Friederieke) and Reche (a "backformation"
of Rachel), but no Reka. It is meant to suggest
"Rekel" - "grober, ungeschliffener Faulenzer",
equalling an uncouth, unmannerly, churlish lazy-
bones.

Line 11 'Zetulpe': probably to suggest "Zetuple" - Zertupfelt,
= spotted, pockmarked; more far-fetched: Tulpen-
narr = tulipomaniac.

Line 13 'Zefirete': 'she-goat' in Aramaic, but that probably
escaped most of his audience who probably associated it with 'ze(r)firte" = 'Verführte' - seduced;
H's pretense of innocence is that it is a form of
Zephir. Hebrew 'Zefir' is a synonym of 'seʿir',
which latter has the added meaning of demon, hence
here = She-demon.

Line 14 Jukl: originally diminutive of "Jacob" in Pol.Y,
then "fool", finally h euphemism for the male organ
(cf. English: Jack, Tom, Dick; (Jane); or G Hans,
-hans, hänseln). Highly frequent names tend to such
pejorative semantics.

Line 16: 'Kora': < Greek: girl, virgin.

Line 16: 'Moka': suggests 'Mocke', = Zuchtschwein = breedsow,
and der Mocken = dickes Stück = fat piece.

Line 17: 'Soka': suggests Polish Suka, G dial. Zauk, Zauche,
Zohe = bitch; farther fetched are: socken = beim
Rennen sich faulenzend schleppen = to drag one's
feet when supposed to run, (Badish dial.); or 'der

Sog' = Verführerische Anziehungskraft = seductive
power, and 'soggen' = to suck one's fill.

Col. 2, Line 1: 'Mirza': 'Son of a prince' in Persian, was
mistaken for a female name. Is this the joke?
Allusion to Bodenstedt's "Mirza Schaffy" - Tatar
male poet?

Line 2: 'Zaire': צײרע possibly a phonetic reference to
YHebrew צער 'grief', 'trouble', sometimes pronounced 'tsair'. Voltaire's heroine? Metathesis
for 'Raize'? While "Raize" is not suggestive in Y
and is supposedly a translation of the Hebrew
Hanna (=Grace[ful]), it may have had the connotation
"Titillation" to H.

Line 4: 'Afrozene': suggests Greek "Aphrosyne" = Stupidity,
and G and Y 'Af(fe)' and 'Rotz'=ape and snot.

Line 6: 'Thirze': definitely not the Hebrew 'Thirza' (female
Biblical name), name of a city in Israel, meaning
'Desire[able]' or 'Pleasure' and only recently again
used as a female name (cf. Numbers 26,33; Song 6, 4;
Kings 14, 17), since its spelling is not ת (Tav)
but טה (Teth, He = T, H); though H was surely
conscious of, and deliberately used the connotation;
he seems to combine 'Thier' = animal with 'Hirze'
dial f. Hirschkuh = hind. But where is the joke?

Line 6f: Figši, Fakši: < G 'fick-facken' = cheat; the 'g' in
the first name - just to avoid the obscene spelling,
even though the obscene sound and suggestion inevi-
tably are there - just as intended. The names are
imperative sentences, with the object 'si(e)' (=her)
written together with the verb, which is the vulgar
expression of the sex act. 'Faksi' is less evident-

ly vulgar, but it has the 'k' to make sure the
reader won't fail to get the point: that the first
name, too, is meant to have k - the two (fick-fack)
being related by ablaut, like 'bim-bam', or Eng.
'ding-dong'. In G and Y the voiced g must become
voiceless when followed by voiceless s.

Line 9: Galans: the '-s' plural is Fr. as well as Y and earlier G - though the Fr. has -t, but neither the Y
nor the G would retain the silent 't' at the end:
'galant'.

Line 10: Sidi: an abbr. of Sidonie? meant to suggest Sidian,
Alem. f. Unmensch = brute

Line 11: 'Griben': G Grieben, greaves (= pieces of skin of
fowl left after their rendered fat is poured off -
a Jewish delicacy, the nearest thing to "kosher
fried ham").

Line 12: 'Maline': < Slavic, Raspberry, fig. = good luck,
prosperity; not common as a female name. We have
not found as yet any documentation for our conjecture that 'Raspberry' is also slang for a "girl,
pretty, mature, healthy, and juicy as a berry".
Cf. the E. old hit-song "The darker the berry, the
sweeter the juice".

Line 13: 'Susan'š': pr. Šušanš; 'Šušan' - in "Square" but
the -'s' in "Meschit"; cf. Introduction: C 9.

Text

T E X T

1.1 -Schön fort ist die Verdammte - nicely gone is the
damned woman

.2 -She had a face like a cut-out pumpkin.

N.B. Cf. Introduction on the HG of the Stage Directions (SD)
page 3, #1; single quotes (' ') indicate verbatim
citations from the Text; no quotes -- translations of
the Text; double quotes -- citations other than the
H Text.

1.1 -'Schihn': schön; G $\bar{e}$, + $\bar{e}$ < ö = $\bar{i}$ in H's dialect; herein
he deviates from general WY where they remain $\bar{e}$. How-
ever, H is not consistent and it is at least questionable whether it is authentic Y, or an imitation of a
G dial. (Vogtländisch). 'fott': fort - in H any
vowel plus 'r' plus dental = 'a' and dental; 'schihn
fott' = schön fort. 'is': Y f. ist; 'di' spelled
always 'di ' (with an aleph ornans), always omitted
in the transliteration because meaningless.
'Aruroh': pronounced: 'arurə' - Verfluchte, Verdammte; accursed, damned; Hebrew words in Y were
"Germanized" i.e. fused in their phonology and
grammar with the G components. Thus the 'ultimate'
accent became penult, and the unaccented vowels reduced to ə. They also continued to change semanti-
cally. Hence the Hebrew Dictionary meaning (given in
the notes at the bottom of the transliteration page)
is often only the etymology, not the meaning in our
Text. Hebrewisms have an emotional charge.

.2 -'hot...ghat': hat ... gehabt, Y. The syncope of the 'e'
(in gehat) is not authentic Y but G dial. h c. 'a':
cf. 'ahn' in the next line; MHG ei > WY $\bar{a}$, hence 'ahn'
for ein, but the indefinite article was unaccented and
became reduced to 'a' and 'an'. 'oisg'.: MHG û (NHG
au) WY and NY oi. 'Karpes': Kürbis, pumpkin; substitution of 'p' for 'b', i.e. of voiced and voiceless consonants and vice versa is general in H, though
not typical of WY. It seems to be a deliberate distortion h c - a straining to differ from HG, even
wherever Y is identical with it. A number of dialects

1.4 How is it possible to be so without manners?

.5 'Mahn': Mann, dist. h c.

.6 'brumme': here = grumble, contradict.
'Frah': Frau; MHG ou > WY $\bar{a}$; nicht, Y and dial.

.7 'nebich': bemitleidenswert, "poor thing"; 'doi': da;
MHG $\hat{a}$ > WY oi; in besten: in bester Art (?) in the
best manner, with the best intentions (?)

"oppose" not voiced and voiceless, but soft and hard
(lenis and fortis) and for them it "makes sense" to make
"reverse substitutions" - to indicate that "voice" is not
the criterion. H thus seems to dish up G dialect for Y.
In 'Karpes' there may be an added reason for 'p' - it
alludes thus incongruously to the "Karpas" (the green
herbs of the Passover feast): the pr. is the same now,
only the spelling (Meschit and vowels for Y and G, but
Square and vowellessness for Hebrew) of the two differs.
Pumpkins are commonly used to "cut out" masks in carnivals
(Cf. Halloween in America).

1.4 'Was taitsch': was (be)deut es? What does it mean? How
can such a thing be possible? MY staits̆: a most typical
J. coinage, reflecting J. questioning of the incongruity
of the J. fate.

'Tharbus': Sittlichkeit, Zivilisiertheit, manners,
"civilizedness". There is sarcasm in branding Vashti's
refusing to parade her beauty (in the nude, acc. to post-
Biblical J. legend) before her husband's guests - immoral
and uncivilized! The emended misprint - '-us' (f.'-is')
is probably just a broken type where the Vav (u) without
its stem looks like Yod (i). The rhyme (R) is on the
basis of Karbəs - Tarbəs and therefore really pure:
delib. dist. h c - even at the expense of the R!

.5-6 Reimzwang (Rz = impure, forced rhyme). Even in MHG
the imperative of strong verbs had no final 'e' and
all Y apocopated every final 'e' even where "legitimate":
'e' here = false, H imitation of HG - where it is however: 'komm!'. It is thus a case of hyper-hochdeutsch
(HHG).
'darf': cf. on 17.1.
'brumme': here = widersprechen; apoc. of 'n' of inf. in
some, but not in most, WY and in some G dial. Without

1.8 'bisle': bislein, slightly; 'Gesten': Gästin (female)
guest, here: arrogant pauper (=Vashti).

.9 She sends the King a message: "I'll come when I like."
'Lost'n: lässt ihm; 'mag': sc. komme ich.

.10 Can it be that Vashti (the Gentile!) is "stuck in preparation of 'matso-dough' (unleavened bread) for Passover?"
'gewihš': gewiss, dist. h c.

---

the added 'e' and the subtracted 'n' there could be no
rhyme.

1.7 'doi' : da MHG â > WY oi (EY ɔ/u: NEY: ʊ̄; SEY: u).

'nebich': bemitleidenswert, pitiable; the translations
do not render the emotional charge of this J. coinage.
Again an inevitable creation in Y for the frequent,
typically J. situation. It was introduced even into
WY (on G speech-territory!) as early as the end of the
13th century from Bohemian Y - from Old Czech "nebohi"
- "godless, accursed, unlucky, miserable".

.8 Gesten: Gästin, (female) guest. The word came to be
used often in the context "uninvited, unwelcome guest",
"burdensome beggar" (Schwäb. Wtbch). The meaning
"beggar, poor-man, to be fed and lodged for charity's
sake" was then imparted by G 'Gast' to its Y equivalent
'oirəch' (Heb. 'Oreah' - wayfarer); it was customary
even for poor Jews to bring home Friday eve from the
synagogue "an oirəch for Šabbəš" (Saturday). It is not
likely that G 'Gast' derived this meaning < Y. Every Jew
was familiar with both words (and the Hebrew, as usual,
was the more emotional). The average G was not familiar
with the Y. Hence - the probable direction of the influence. Otherwise one might have argued the 'Oreah' in
Hebrew had already started the development in the direction of "poor stranger" (Cf. the stories of Abraham's
and Lot's hospitality to wayfarers, Exod. 18 and 19 and
Ginsburg Legends of the Jews I; s.v. Abraham and Lot,
p.240-257; 266f; and passim). Here: -"presumptuous,
imposing, arrogant pauper" who does not appreciate the
King's "grace" in condescending to marry her.

.9 'lost'n: MHG 'lâzzen' > Y lɔzn; 'n' f. '-m' f. ihm;
unaccented 'm' > Y 'n': 'mag'; in EY it means only 'to

1.11 'Stus': Unsinn, nonsense; 'ebis doi gehatt'n: etwas da gehabt; had something there.

.12 'Masso' etc.: Unterhandlungen, Geschäfte, negotiations, business. Noit: MHG ô > WY oi.

.13 Hat müssen den Hühnern die Schwänze hinaufbinden, had to tie up the chicken's tails = had some useless, foolish thing (actually therefore: nothing) to do. She could not pretend that she was too busy.

.14 'fersinden': versünden, bring (sin or) guilt upon.

.16 'gezihlt': prob. gezielt, aimed (aimed at her to get her into trouble); improbable: 'gezählt' counted (on her to do something terrible).

---

be allowed to', not 'to like to'.

1.10 gewihs (like 'Mahn' in .5) is inauthentic. No Y lengthens vowels short in NHG! Some G dialects do! As said in our Introduction H strains to make Y sound different than G and thus "funny" and therefore H often resorts to distortions where Y and G are identical. Most of these phenomena are, however, found in G dialects as "regular", authentic developments - only no single G or Y dialect has them all together. None of them has both opposites in his "reverse substitutions"; i.e. none has both unvoicing of the voiced, and voicing of the voiceless consonants at the same time; nor - lengthening of the short and shortening of the long vowels. H, of course, also coins distortions that have no parallel anywhere; 'gstekt': syncope of 'e' G dial. not Y. 'Mazzoh Taag': ungesäuerter Teig, unleavened dough. Leaven on Passover is a capital sin. Pious Jews are extra careful not to run the risk of the dough "leavening" ever so so slightly between the kneading and the baking: the dough is kneaded without interruption until it can be rolled to flatten and put it in the oven. Anyone busy kneading such dough has no time for any interruption. Cf. Tendlau #194. Before Matzo-Factories arose matzo-baking was done privately, the entire community "cooperating", and it started immediately after Purim (=4 weeks before Passover), to allow time to bake for every family a supply for eight days. Harbona therefore asks a rhetorical question: "Surely Vashti couldn't have gotten "stuck" assisting at the communal matzo-baking by kneading the dough?" Why, she is not Jewish!

1.11 'ebis': rev. subst. f. Y 'eppes' < etwas; when 't' and 'w' fuse into <u>one sound</u> (because of unaccentedness) the "resultant" is 'p' - partaking of the labiality of the 'w' and the explosivity of the 't'.

'ghattn': inauth. Rz. Y gehăt. Y favors apocope where SG has syncope.

.12 'noit'.: MHG ô > Gen. Y oi, NEY ey.

.13 'di Hihner': den Hühnern, in MY the pl. is invariable for all the cases, though H <u>at times</u> does use HG inflections even in his WY, and is <u>then</u> inauthentic (it is authentic only in OY).
'noif': (hi)nauf; MHG û > WY and NEY oi, CEY (=Polish Y) ō, SEY (some Ukrainian and Rumanian dial.) u; the apheresis (=cutting off the first, unaccented syllable) is probably G: MY favors the prefix 'her-' (>'ar-') for G 'hin-' and does not apheresize.

2.1 Her arrogance is simply impossible! or; Her arrogance
    will be put an end to!

 .2 Aber jetzt steckt sie schön in der Brühe: but now she
    is caught in her own mess; 'ober': aber, but.

 .3-4 Now (your mood for) laughter is gone for good, isn't
     it? Now Lady Vashti, you are going to crash.

2.1 'Asus-kat': Frechheit, arrogance; one of the rare mis-
    spellings of a Hebrewism '-s' f. '-ṡ! Note the fusion of
    the Hebrew stem 'asus' with the G suffix '-kat'
    (< -keit), typically Y. As always in our Text, the
    Hebrew is printed in Square and the G in Meschit and the
    two are hyphenated. The idiom is ambiguous: lit. "her
    arrogance is really never here" = prob. such arrogance
    does not exist in this world (it's out of this world);
    or: the present is used (as often in Y and G) for the
    future and it means: her arrogance will never be here
    (any more); Der ihr = the dativ (of the demonstr.
    pronoun) plus the possessive adj. - for the possess.
    adj. alone -, frequent in colloquial G (Cf. dem Mann
    sein Gelt, or dem sein Gelt); in MY a possess. suffix
    -s is added to all datives to form the possess.:
    'dems' = that man's, 'ders' = that woman's; 'der frois
    kinder" = the woman's children.

 .2 'ober': aber, but; o = Y; a > â > o- under emphasis; the
    cluster -br prevented further development to oi in WY,
    and to u in CEY. Such clusters often cause shortening
    of vowel (Cf. G Jammer < MHG jâmer).

    iz: old form f. izt (=jetzt); the -t is parasitic. Y
    and G dial.

 .3 Gelt: = it's true isn't it? <(Es) gelte (die Wette),
    let the bet have validity. No longer Y. 'alle weil'
    f. für alleweil = for ever; in G dial. alleweil (like
    'allemal') can also have the meaning: aber jetzt doch
    = but now surely.

    'vergiht': vergeht = (the laughter) will die (on her
    lips).

 .3-4 The lines are addressed (in imagination) to Vashti and
     the 'ihr's' and 'si' are third prs. sg., used f. the

2.6   für ihren Frevel, for her crime.

.10 'Medinôs': Provinzen; provinces.

.11 reden ein paar Wörtlein nur

.12 'Minus': Ketzerei, heresy

---

second prs. sg. formal address among social equals or to inferiors. Not Y. G dialect and archaic (Cf. Herr Meister, leb' er wohl!).

2.4A SD 'Kabnet': office; non-standard form, rare in SD.

.5-8 The King speaks perfect HG and so do those in his retinue who are not deliberately reduced to comic figures. Our Transliteration does not show this sufficiently in that the vowels are rendered mechanically by a uniform system of a one to one correspondence of each letter in the Hebrew and Roman alphabet. It might have been clearer to use two separate systems - one for the Y and another for the G lines. But since it is sometimes difficult to decide, as in the case of the (non-Jewish) comic figures whether the line is Y or G, it was decided to let the old, uniform transliteration stand. The HG grammar is cue enough for the reader to transform the Y vowels into HG; e.g.: .6: 'für' for 'fir'; .7: 'auf' for 'oif'.

.8A SD Harbona: though a non-Jewish chamberlain of the King, H represents him as a comic Jewish figure; the incongruity is h c, but it has a slight "justification" in the case of Harbona: the Purim-hymn ends with "and Harbona also shall be remembered for good". Well, then, he must be a Jew!

.9 'Groiser': -s- for -ŝ- dist. hc to suggest the "lèse majesté" G grauser, gruesome, cruel.

.10 'rihten a baar Wattlich ner' = reden ein paar Wörtlein nur: typical H phonology: G e > i; reverse substitution of voiced and voiceless consonants (d > t; p > b); vowel plus r plus t > 'at' (Wattlich), pl of dimin. = 'lich'; nur = ner (probably pro: 'nər' because it is unaccented), otherwise the isolated shift, if auth., would be hard to explain. Yet, here it is accented in

2.12-13   In me there is no heresy. You hear (from me) God's
          Law.

.13   'hett': hört.

.15   'aier': euer, your.

.18   folgt: befolgt, gehorcht; obeys; Y.

.20   werdet sehen; kein Mann gilt was im Haus; no man is of
      any importance in his own home.

R with Herr! Rz? H uses Rz often enough, but it would
also be a new emphatic form developed from the unaccented 'nər' (Cf. the developmental history of personal pronouns).

2.12 'hett': hört (not hattet! which it sometimes is,):
      syncope of 'höret', came after shift of vowel plus 'rt'
      into 'at' - otherwise it would have become 'hatt'.

.12-13 From me you hear no heretical doctrines (i.e. no
        secular, man-made laws) but the Law of God. Alludes
        to Genesis 3:16 "and he (=Adam, Man) shall rule over
        thee (=Eve, Woman)". In Harbona H satirizes, like the
        typical "Maskil" (follower of "Enlightenment"), the
        obscurantism of the pious.

.15   aier: euer, unrounding of rounded G vowel in Y;
      Ferlange: apocope of n of infin. reg. in H but not
      in MY, and not consistently even in H, Cf. 3.21-22.

.16   gange: Rz and Mz (Metrumzwang) and older form for
      gegangen; not MY.

.18   ihren: here = ac., though '-m' (dat.) in acc. position
      in H > '-n', but 'folgen' in Y means 'obey' and
      governs the ac; Mahn: 'ah' dist h c, here - also Rz.

.20   "double negative" correct in Y and in non-sophisticated,
      colloquial G; niks < nichs (which regularly >G Ks,
      Cf. 'sechs', 'wachs') < nichts in unaccented position;
      WY and G dial.

3.1 from India to Ethiopia

.3 froigen ... noich; fragen ... nach, pay no heed to
"don't give a damn".

.4 werfen nur hinaus, throw out, squander.

.5 For: für.

.7-8 they pinch it (the money for squandering) even from the
poor members of their family (=relatives)! They
sacrifice their children.

3.1 Hôduh: misprinted as: 'Hodəh': it must be the typesetter's error.

.3 froigen ... noich: MHG â > WY oi.

.4 woffen: werfen; G 'a' between labials plus r > o; H.

.5 for: MHG uses 'vor' where NHG uses für; Y = MHG.

.6 Kunzerten ... Trihather; delib. distortion h c - especially with fashionable 'internationalisms'; FW
(foreign word).

.7 Zwacken: Ablaut of 'zwicken', pinch; 'ah': unacc.
form of 'ach', G auch, also; MHG ou > a; 'areme': Y has
svarabhakti 'e'; Gesinder: means "relatives, members
of the family who live in the same house" in Y only.
Pl. -er Y only; in G = "retinue or followers of a
warrior", or "household servants" (including "farm-
hands"). The Y meaning derives from its frequent use in
translating the Biblical Hebrew. 'בית' 'house', >
(people of the house).

.8 Schlagen for a Kapporoh: aufopfern, sacrifice; pron. K
por. Orig. meaning = "Versöhnung", "atonement", then the
"sacrificial animal" through which atonement was achieved, then "victimize", "sacrifice". Already in the
Talmud the pious prayer "may I be his Kappara" meant
"may God accept my death as an atonement for his (the
dear one's) sins". Sometimes in the Gaonic period of
Jewish history (6th to 12th centuries) the ritual arose
that before the Day of Atonement (Yom Kippur) one

3.14 Meš: (Waren) messe, fair; Zihgen: Ziehen, travel.

.15 Doiert: dauert, lasts.

.16 Haben wir, Gott behüte, den grössten... We will, God forbid, have the biggest.

"turned" a chicken over one's head and recited the prayer: "may this be my Kappara". This custom of "underground popular religion" thrived in spite of all efforts of the Rabbinic authorities to root it out. In Hebrew one "does" a Kappara, in Y one hits ("shlugt") Kappara. When chickens are not available, Kappara may be "hit" with money. Thus another custom arose that at any loss or small misfortune the Jew would seek consolation in the prayer: "May it be a Kappara". Then from a pious prayer to a curse: "Be my Kappara" = "Drop dead (instead of me)"; finally, to an expression of malicious joy at the misfortune of a fellow who "deserves it"; Schadenfreude: "a shayne, rayne Kapore" = "good for him", lit.: "a beautiful pure (= 'without a blemish') victim", i.e. "a victim fit for sacrifice".

In EY the idiom is: "Šlogn K. mit di Kinder", but that would be ambiguous: the innocent literal translation could mean: "they help the children perform the Kappara ritual" (by reciting the prayers with them). H's formulation: "for a Kappore" is not ambiguous!

3.9 'dihn Mahn': den Mann; h dist., since 'den' is unacc. and should not develop lengthening and raising of 'e' to 'ī'.

.12 'Wind in Wetter': old, alliterative (Stabreim) formula, where Wetter = Unwetter, bad weather (-no longer so in EY).

.13 ferfrihren, ferbrennen: 'fer-' = zu Tode, to death, a humorous exageration. In both Y and G 'fer-' often adds a pejorative nuance.

.14 'Meš': Messe, auth., but no longer EY where the Hebrew "Yarid (יריד)" is used, probably (partly) because 'mess' in all Y (< Hebr. מת) = 'corpse' - for which very reason H uses it - h c. 'Zihgen': 'Ziehen', H and G dial; not Y.

3.18 unterthinig: untertänig, obediently (humbly).

.19 Dekret.

.20 watt zu spiht: wird zu spät, gets too late.

.21 Da hinein lassen wir stellen, into which (decree) we
will cause to write.

.22 'Was' sc. auch = whatever; haint ahn: heute an, from
today onward; 'wellen': wollen.

.23 'mìššen ... toin': müssen tun.

.24 'Wu nit': wo nicht, in case not, Y; 'jide'; jede;
'ihr loihn': ihren Lohn.

.25 Ihr werdet sehen.

.26 Hat da bald.

3.16 Hem mir: end result of assimilation and umlaut ⟨ hôn wir;
Has ve-Scholôm: Gott behüte, God forbid: lit. "mercy
and peace!"

.21 lesen mir: the 'a' of 'lassen' is umlauted by the 'i'
in mir (wir) and the 'w' in 'wir' ⟩ 'm' by assimilation
to 'n' in 'lassen'; 'mir' f. 'wir' in Y and SG.
Actually the 'n' and 'w' fuse into one sound.

.22 Haint: = Y and SG ⟨MHG hīnt; wellen: Y and MHG!

.23 'toin' the inf. in MHG had many variants which are reflected in both Y and G dial.: 'toin'⟨ 'tan'; EY 'ton'
and 'tun'/'tin'⟨'tuon' and 'tân'.

.25 'sehi': unacc. 'e' is often represented by 'i' in Y and
G dial.

.26 'ball': H sometimes assimilates '-ld' to '-ll' h c.

4.11 Wie wär's denn als Mein(ung)?: What kind of an idea would you think it to) be? or: Lieber, wie wäre es denn = Rather, how would it be?

.12 'abgenge': abgehen.

.13 'hert ... foligt': hört ... folgt

.14 Euer Zorn: your wrath.

.15 ist worden erfüllt

.16 'Zu'n Šoton': Zum Satan.

.17 'Zuguten': Y, unberufen, = knock wood.

4.1-9 N.B. King speaks perfect HG - to the point of an apostrophe in 'schik' for the apocope of the 'e' - something never done for the regular apocope in the Y of his other characters. Notice also the lack of apocope in: 'Wille', 'erstrekke', 'ohne', and 'oisnahme'. Notice: 8 'fon' elsewhere: 'fun'. Hence: 'schehn' = schön; 'Hois', 'ois', 'oif' should all have: 'au'; exception: H slipped twice. He wrote Y 'mus', instead of G 'muš' ('š' = G 'ss') - or was it the typesetter? - and ' in sainen Raich', apparently taking 'Reich' as masc. acc. In MY it would be 'sain Raich' regardless whether masc. or neut., dat. or acc., conceivably H slipped into older WY dative with 'n' for final 'm' - but both the dat. and the 'n' are contrary to HG.

.1-2 Rz - but of a type frequent in HG 'ö' - 'e'.

.10 'falt': fällt, Y and SG leveled out the infin. vowel in the whole present.

.11 'main': < MHG 'meine', is ambiguous = both "idea" and "falsehood"; therefore used by H (Cf. "Meinung" and "Meineid"); here = "rather" Cf. L #14, p. 351.

.13 'abgenge': G dial. not Y.

.14 'foligt': 'i' prob. inauth. h c, though there are Y dial. with such svarabhakti (parasitic) vowels.

4.18 'Kozin': reicher Adliger, here = rich nobleman, gentleman.

.19 'uhzin': uzen, Rz.; here = not "tease" but "torture".

.20 'Jehrlich': liben Jahre, dear years.

4.16 'Zun Šoton': Zum Teufel; 'zu'n' = zu den, acc. f. dat.,
delib. dist. h c. Here all Y and G = 'zum'. Only unacc. 'm' > Y 'n'. The phrase is inauthentic h c; while
usually the Hebrew carries a heavier emotional charge
and is therefore compulsively chosen for curses (Cf. 'a
misse mešune', 'a make', 'a mageyfe', 'a sreyfe', 'ver
geharget', 'a švartsn sof'), just the 'Soton' is avoided because of the taboo (Talmud: 'al tiftah peh le-
Satan' - 'don't give the Satan an opening', i.e. mention
the devil and he comes!). So that just in this curse
Jews took over the G: 'zum Taifel' (or 'Taivel') as a
lesser taboo; and because it is inauthentic it strikes
one as incongruous and h.

.16-17 'Šoton': 'guten': Rz. 'ɔ': 'u', see also 18-19
pron. Kozin-uhzin, but spelled to get a (partial)
graphic R.

.17 'zu guten': Y, sc. 'soll es ausgehen': an adjuration
formula and prayer; that what was mentioned be mentioned 'for good rather than for evil'. i.e. that no
evil eye of the envious should cause the 'good' to
turn to evil by malicious cursing or witchcraft, G;
'unberufen', Engl. knock wood.

.18 'Kozin': in Y: properly 'a Jewish magnate influential
in the Jewish community', or 'a non-Jewish rich nobleman, or official or gentleman; an incongruous word for
a king: h.

.20 'Jehrlich': the dimin. common in Y and in SG to express endearment.

5.1   You have no child, no family.

 .2   'ošur': meiner Seele, upon my soul.

 .4   'Melech': König.

 .5   Wird euch doch öfters.

 .6   'sait ... pôresch', trennt euch, separate yourself.

 .7   'amoil': überhaupt, at all; 'Jôresch': Erbe, heir.

5.1   'hett': = 'habt'. Cf. .10 where it = hätte and .8 and
      .9 where 'hettet' amd 'hiebet' - hätte. H had a
      "field day" with irregular verbs, because they offered
      so many dial. variants, but this plethora of forms was
      not enough and H coined some anomalies of his own;
      Cf. 3.26 'hoit' = hat; MY 'er ir hot'. H is
      deliberately inconsistent. 'kahn Kind un kahn Rind':
      Y, proverbial in this negative form = utterly without
      a family. For the rhyming 'Rind' and its semantics
      cf. the older alliterating (Stabreim) 'Mann und Maus'
      = 'man and mouse'.

 .2   'osur': lit. verboten, forbidden; it is a vestige of
      an adjuration formula like: "may I be forbidden to
      enjoy etc., if I lie." Such an adjuration was the
      equivalent of a religious vow and the liar would be
      incurring a sin each time he did enjoy, etc.; now -
      just an "affirmation".

 .6   'aich sait...pôresch': lit. seid ... trennend; it is
      the most frequent form of using a Hebrew verb in Y;
      especially in older Y: the auxiliary 'sain' plus the
      Hebrew pres. participle analog. to the MHG (and NE)
      "progressive" tenses, but without the 'progressive'
      nuance in meaning.

 .7   'amoil': einmal - omitted in Transliteration.

      'iber hundert Jahr amoil': euphemism; "after you die",
      characteristic of Jewish piety, of taking care of 'not
      to give the Satan an opening'. N.B. H's inconsistency:
      'Jahr' and 'amoil' - in WY the vowels should be 'oi' in
      both; in HG - ā. 'Jôresch': the 'ô' in both 'pôresch'
      and 'Joresch' was pronounced 'ô' in WY even thougn the

5.8 Hätte euer Grossvater auch so gedacht.

.9 Wer hätte dann euren Vater.

MHG 'ô' > 'oi' - because the Hebrew 'o' at that time in
the history of Hebrew pronunciation was no longer (as)
long as the MHG 'ô' and became lengthened in open
syllables together with the (similar) short MHG 'o' in
open syllables and developed like it. Cf. EY (< Hebrew)
'söd': but 'soid s' (= secret(s).) - the sing. and the
plural of the same word being pronounced differently,
because in the sing. the syllable is closed, in the
plural the syllable is open; the development parallels
MHG 'wol' and 'wolle' (NHG 'wohl' and 'Wolle'; EY 'voil'
and 'vol'.) (The G inflectible words - nouns, adjectives and verbs - behaved like open syllables even if
the vowel was followed by a single cons. (only), and
was thus openable by an inflection beginning with a
vowel; here only syllables wherein the vowel was
"closed" by a double consonant and thus remained permanently closed, did the vowels remain short).

5.8 'Harrle': Grossvater WY, (Alsatian Y) and gen. Alem.
and Franc. L #240; 'gedoicht' and .9 'gebroicht') 'oi'
> MHG â; NHG and MY shortened long vowels in permanent-
ly closed syllables! Hence: both HG and EY 'gebracht',
'gedacht'. Since there are also OY forms: 'gedocht'
it is evident that the shortening was not uniform
everywhere and therefore 'oi' could be, probably is not,
authentic.

.9-19 The verbs are all in the pluperfect and imperfect subjunctive expressing unreal conditions in the past and
their hypothetical result in the present. 'Hettet'
(.8) is probably deliberate dist.; maybe also 'hiebet',
which points a weak regular indicative imperfect.
*'habete' which is then umlauted (against the rules for
regular weak verbs!) to *häbete which is then developed
in H's dialect to 'hiebet'; 'ä' ('ē') > 'ī' ('ie') and
final '-e' apocopated probably the only authentic form
is .10 and .12 'hett'.

.9-10 'Taate...Memme': Vater...Mutter, Alsat. Y and gen.
Alem.; MY táte, máme; L 344 and 370. Cf. E daddie,
mammie. MY probably is a re-borrowing from the Slavic,

5.10 'Memme': Mutter.

.11 Woher wäret ihr dann hergekommen?: Whence would you
have come?

.13 'sizet': sässet, would you sit; 'alleweil': jetzt;
'Truhn': Thron.

.14 in den besten Jahren.

.15 'kennt': könnt; 'Sechijoh': "Verdientst" (bei Gott)
und sein belohnendes Glück: "deserts" (from God)
and His rewarding good fortune.

.16 Manneskind; male child.

.17 Jüngling, junger Mann: Youth, young man.
.18 Werdet zum (Vermählungs)altar führen: will lead to the
(marriage) altar.
'Thôroh un Hochmoh': Gotteslehre und weltliche
Bildung; divine lore and secular education.

---

otherwise the final '-e's of the Germanic would be
apocopated in Y. Cf. E dad.

5.12-13 'Suhn'Truhn': Rz. in Y, though not in G (Sohn-
Thron); however, H regularly distorts 'o' in FW to
'u', hence for H it is a pure R; sizet: imperfect
subj.=sässet; as if < *sizete - H makes it a regular
weak verb. Cf. .9 'hiebet'.

.14 Authentic except for '-št'; 'di beste Johr' - thus in
all cases of the plural, invariable; because of -'e' -
apocope, the singular and plural in OY were identical;
MY 'jorn'.

.15 Sechijjoh: pure R with 'unbeschrie'; the apocope of
'n' in the latter is Rz.; Sechijjoh is a typically J
word from the area of piety and is highly charged with
emotion: = "to be privileged by God, as a result of
'works' and/or Grace, to be the recipient of the good
fortune to etc."

.16-17 'Sochor - Bohur': pr. zɔxr-bɔxr = pure R.

.18 "To lead a child under the huppoh" is the most fer-

5.21   'Schiddich': Heiratsantrag, (marriage) matchmaking.

---

   vent wish of every Jewish parent. The 'ḥuppa' is the
   (usually portable) canopy under which a Jewish marriage
   ceremony takes place.

5.19   'Thoroh and Ḥochmoh': the ideal intellectual achieve-
   ments: 'T(h)orah' in the most narrow sense is the
   parchment scroll containing the Pentateuch; in its
   widest - the "revealed word of God from the Bible down
   to the latest loyal disciple"; preoccupation with 'Tora'
   is the highest form of divine worship, the holiest
   activity. 'Ḥochma' = "worldly wisdom and secular education" for the purpose of sustaining life, so it can be
   devoted to Tora.

.15-20   is deliberately anachronistic and incongruous, h c.
   It is extremely "funny" to make Harbona, a non-Jewish
   chamberlain, and Ahasveros, a non-Jewish king, ca.
   400 B.C. talk like an 18th century Jewish person of the
   highest piety with all his values: to be blessed with
   a son who will devote himself to Tora and yet be worldly
   wise too, and to be privileged to see him married.

.21   'Schiddich': (arrangierte) Verlobung, Heiratsantrag
   durch Vermittlung (gewöhnlich): marriage proposal
   (through a broker usually). Another typically Jewish
   "situation": because of the difficulty for a sparsely
   scattered minority to meet up with likely, suitable
   choices for spouses, the profession of the "Shadchen"
   or "marriagebroker" arose. Because of poverty and un-
   employment too many tried to eke out a living by matchmaking and would 'impose' and importune any and every
   'prospect' and pester them -- so people not 'ready'
   would 'scream' at their unceasing propositions. Schiddich is Rz h c, rightly: 'Shidduch' with a hard
   guttural '-ch'; in the mouth of the HG-speaking King
   and in R with 'bitt' 'ich' it is pronounced with a
   soft, palatal 'ch'. The very Hebrewism in his mouth
   is incongruous, hence h; 'von einem': pure HG.

6.1　'Schadchonús': Ehevermittlershonorar, marriagebroker's fees.

.2　'Ne'emonús': Vertrauenswürdigkeit, Ehrlichkeit: trust-worthyness, honesty.

.3　sollte, von ein paar Güldlein.wegen: should, for the sake of a few Gulden.

.4　einen betrügen: deceive somebody.

.6　'dorch Trummel': durch Trommel, by drum.

6.1-4　Reflects the general reputation of marriagebrokers for unconscionably exaggerating and lying about the merits of their 'proteges' in order to earn their fee: the Y proverbs say that the 'brokers can bring together a wall with a wall; - i.e. two opposite walls, that by nature could and should not be together.

.3　'sellet': = imperfect subjunctive < *'söllete' with 'e' apocope and Umlaut, WY and G dial. 'Gildilich': name of a coin, dim. for endearment, but here also for deprecation at the same time.

.4　'betriegen': ie! (for ü) = orig. MHG; NHG ü < spelling mistake of early SG printers who pronounced 'ü' and 'ie' alike (they 'unrounded' round vowels) and were not always sure which is which; the error was aided by a false attribution of its derivation from the noun "Betrug'; 'ahn': einen, not Y but H and G dialect.

.6　'dorch': G 'r' (plus consonant, usually) has the tendency to "lower" the vowel one step in Y:

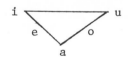

thus i > e;　e > a;　u > o;　o > a.

.8　'Madlich': < 'Maidlin' < 'magetlin'; WY; NEY 'Meydlach', SEY 'maidlech'

6.8 So viel Mädchen nur aufzutreiben sind: as many girls
     as can be gathered up.

.9   'fufzehi': fünfzehn.

.10 'mer': man.

.11 'wat': wird.

.12 'Aagen': Augen; 'Hễn': Anmut, charm.

.13 Die nehmt ihr davon.

.15 Jetzt gebt mal Acht: now just watch.

6.9 'fufzehi': loss of first 'n' is Y; of the last - H;
     'u' (instead of expected 'i') is Y, but anomalous.
     < OHG 'fimf'; probably because the the three labials;
     f, m, f;

.10 'mer': man; a contamination of 'mǝn' and 'mǝr' (< mir
     < wir) in unaccented position; 'dihn': could be
     distorted h c for 'dem' accusative for dative; but it
     could also be the literal rather than the figurative
     meaning, thus not 'vorstellen', to introduce, but
     'stellen vor den könig' = to place before the King.
     The word order distortion, though h, would not surpass
     the accepted 'poetic license' for Rz. The R is pure on
     the basis of 'o' : 'o', but the spelling is Jahr -
     possibly a misprint or defective type.
     .10 'dihn Melech' and .11 'aich' are not switches in
     the form of polite address, but rather .10 = an in-
     direct statement of the text of the Decree and .11 is
     direct address. Cf. on 26,12

.11-12 'schehn' - 'Hễn'; R on the basis of 'e' - 'e'
     since the Hebrew 'Zereh' (in Hễn) is always 'e' even
     in H.

.12 'Hễn': grace - a word highly charged with emotion and
     occurring in every language spoken by Jews.

.13-14 'derfuhn' - 'Truhn': Rz: 'u' is u and 'o' in
     FW > 'u'; dist. h c, R, etc.

6.19 So laufen sie, was sie können; they <u>will</u> run as fast
as they can.

.21 'nakit': nackt, naked.

.23 'aingeschnihrt': sc. 'im Korsett', laced in (in her
corset).

.24 Yet already coiffured in highest style.

6.15 'Iz': jetzt, regular Y development < MHG ie zuo;
> iezue, ieze, iz, iz; the last two forms show the
typically Y apocope of the final e and the shortening
of the long vowel before the double consonant
('z' = ts); 'amoile': einmal, the 'e' suffix inten-
sifies the adverbial force.

.17 j<u>e</u>de: Cf. j<u>i</u>de, 2.24.

.19 w<u>aa</u>s: probably dist. h c, though the vowel <u>was</u> long in
emphasis, hence the EY 'wɔs' and 'wvs'! Cf. 5: 'w<u>a</u>s',
and on 16,8.

.20 'genge un stenne': a contamination = the consonants
from MHG 'gangen' and 'standen' and the vowels from
'gên' and 'stên'; 'nd' = Y (often) 'nn'. Cf. Y 'ge-
finnen, gefunnen, gestannen'.

.22 'nakit': Y older, auth. G form.

.23 'eršt': š (=sch) always spelled by H with ש (= E 'sh')
for every 'sp' and 'st', incl. final '-st'; in G
final '-st' > 'št' only in SG dial. N.B. in SD, H
spells it '-st' not 'št'. i.e. with s (=E 's') and
not ש (=E 'sh'). In Y only final '-rst' > '-ršt'.

7.1 'Wofft': wirft.

.2 in einen (Pan)toffel, in einen Schuh: on one foot a
slipper, on the other a shoe.

.3 'Medinoh': Land, Provinz

.4 'Moro': Furcht.

.5 'Schlihft': schlüpft.

.6 Ins Arbeitsmäntelchen der Magd: into the smock of the
maid.

.7 'Herrenwinkerle': Strohhütlein: little straw hat, Swb.
L 253.

.8 Blumen und verdammtes Zeug: flowers and damned stuff.

.10 Und kümmert sich nicht was es kostet: does not care
what it costs.

.11 'waad': watet.

7.3 'woint': spelled correctly, 'w'oint', with aleph
dividens dividing the three Vavs (ו).

.5-6 Rz: t - d.

.8 'Blumeŝ': -'ŝ'-pl. f. Germanisms in '-e' very rare and
only recent delib. innovation in most-modern Y; but -
correct for '-e' words < Hebrew and Slavic. Hence,
delib. false-analogy pl. h c; all Y and G = Blumen!

'Gesèros ro'ôŝ': lit. böse Dekrete: evil decrees:
stock phrase = 'government decrees designed to oppress
Jews', or 'God's (prior) decree to cause such oppression
as punishment for sin', then euphemism = 'the essence of
evil'.

.9 'fahrt': Y leveled out the vowel in the pres. with the
inf., hence no Umlaut. Pferd: 'pf-' in WY = 'f' in EY;
'-pf' = 'p'. Cf. EY 'ferd' but 'appel'; 'ekstre':
absence of dativ. '-r' would be authentic even in G
since this adjective is a FW ending in '-a' and as such
indecl. Pošt: NB '-št' = SG, not Y!

7.14 'fottbrenge': fortbewegen; go forward.

.15 'kahn': keinen.

.19 'Geplepper': Plappeln; babbling.

.20 'Gebloiter': Geplauder; gossipping; 'Getatter':
     Gezank: quarreling.

.21 'Gelaf': Herumlaufen or Auflauf: running around or
     together (in a crowd).

.22 Lärm; Tummel: noise.

.23 'Nekêwôš': Frauenzimmer: females.

.24 'Port': Ufer: shore, Y.

.26 Werdet Ihr, Mönchlein (?) doch finden eine Braut:
     You monk you! will surely find a bride.

7.10 'estemihrts': 'e' for 'i' h c.

.11 'Di ander': '-e' apocope, not EY though in Lit. Y
     'ander' is indecl. after the indef. art., 'waad':
     '-et' apocope after dental = reg. Y; 'd' f 't' - rev.
     subst.

.12 'Bindele': Bündlein, EY bintele.

.13-14 'genge - brenge': 'gange' - not Y (Cf. L 190) but
     'brengen' is Y, and MHG variant for bringen.

.15-16 Rz: t - d; 'Putzmachers': '-š' pl. not auth. in
     WY even though adopted now by Standard Y; '-š' not
     used with 'Schnaider' to preserve R.

.19-22 The 'ge-' prefix to nouns has the original idea of
     a 'collection', then a 'lot', then 'too much',
     finally just a pejorative nuance in G and even more
     so in Y. Cf. L. p.369-370.

.20 'Gebloiter': 'b' for 'p' to suggest 'Blattern' (MHG
     blâter) boils, carbuncles h c.

.23 'Nekewôš': females, slightly pejorative, hence

8.1 - 2 And even if it isn't so (i.e., even if you should not find one among them fit to be Queen), we will have had our little fun with them.

.8 Man kommt, unbeschrien, <u>um</u>: one (can) die, God forbid, trying to decide what to cook.

.9 'Memme': Mama.

.10 Tell (him) he'll get (his) when I'll catch him.

< Hebrew because of emotion.

7.24 'Menaschke': probably < Slav. 'Monaška (Nönnchen = little <u>nun</u>), because the <u>King</u> refused to marry. H may have misunderstood the Slavic word, or deliberately misused it as a joke. It is spelled as if it were Hebrew (i.e. Square and without vowels) MNŠKH, מנשכה ; gfinne: Y for "finden", except that syncope of '-e' (gf-' for 'gef-') is G.

8.1 - 2 <u>N.B.</u> The present is frequently used to express the future (=good Y <u>and</u> G) and the perfect for the future perfect; 'khat': Cf. 'ghat', both not Y but SG; mit si: acc. f. dat. here authentic Y where third person plural pronoun ('sey') is indecl.; unse<u>r</u>: acc. (without '-n'!) = Y and MHG where possessives have no <u>case</u> decl. si: usually 'si'' (i.e. with aleph ornans).

.3 - 6 King's speech and SD following are basically HG, except for .4: gefallt ('a' for 'ä') and .5: gih ('i' for 'e') and las ('s' for 'š') - all probably "slips" - carried away by habit. But 'i' for 'e' is still of some significance in judging the authenticity of 'e' <u>elsewhere</u> since here the <u>intent</u> was definitely and without any doubt 'e'!

.6 SD '<u>Z</u>tulpe': (sic), elsewhere 'Zetulpe'; names are especially prone to be spelled "defectively" (חסר), i.e., without vowels, analog. to names < Hebr.: H spells <u>all</u> names as if < Hebres, hence he sometimes drops the vowels as well, like in names < Hebrew.

SD Klafir: 'f' for 'v' because even in FW the 'v' is pronounced 'f' by "unknowledgeable" speakers of HG.

9.1 'Sen ... gewiŝen': sind ... gewesen: were.

.3 'geŝn': gegessen.

.4 'taŝt': dürstet; thirsts

.5-6 Nichts als ein Löfflein Suppe und ein paar Zöpflein Wurst: Nothing but a spoonlet of soup and a few rolls of sausage.

.6 'Thire': Tür

.7-8 Das ist ja (wie) Schwein nicht erlaubt, man meint doch man vertaubt Gott behüte = that's (as) forbidden as pork, one can get deaf here, God forbid.

.9 'Worim': Warum. 'Heder': jüdische (religiöse) Schule.

8.8 'unbeschrie rum': h, 'unbeschrie(n)' is just the opposite of what she wants to say - it being used as a prayer that a good, positive condition should continue (unaffected by the evil eye), whereas 'Gott behüte' (the prayer that some feared evil should be averted by God) is what she really wants to say; 'rum' for 'um' (a malapropism: 'rumkommen = to get around a lot, whereas 'umkommen' = to perish, die).

.9 's'Arakstakskserksele': Artaxerxeslein, apparently not understood by typesetter as a name and printed Meschit instead of Square. Dist. h c. 'Artaxerxes' as a name was never used by Jews - neither for naming their children, nor for their dogs, nor for the historic figure, who is always referred to by the Hebrew form: Achaschwerosch. It makes the incongruity ever so much funnier to have the child struggle with the unpronounceable, dist. name. It is also an allusion to the ridiculous practice of Jewish "social climbers" of choosing the most "fancy" foreign (instead of Hebrew) names, or names of current rulers, to stick their children with. H makes the Jewish child bear the name of the Persian King. This time it is not an anachronism, since the very heroes of Purim, Mordecai and Esther, bear names of Persian idols - and the practice has continued up to date.

9.10 Wart_et_; 'Rabbi': Lehrer; 'beli Neder'; ohne Gelübde;
without vowing (to so tell); tu weg deine Ware: Put
away your merchandise.

.12 'un-be-Hesed': ohne Gnade; without Grace; Seroroh:
Herrschaft, sovereign.

8.10 'ibern': über ihn = come across him, find him, catch
him, as well as belabor him (with a stick).

9.1-2 Gasenjungis - gšprunge is: Rz. inauth. '-s' - pl.
(though NG has both Jungs and Jungens, not Junges) and
apocope of '-en' in 'gesprungen', or rather, apocope of
'-n' and elision of '-e'.

.3-6 We have not found the "model" for this song, though
it does sound familiar. One even thinks of Mephisto's
"Song of the Poisoned Rats". As it stands, it is
probably original with H.

.7 'Hasir': Schwein(efleisch): vestige of an adjuration
"as forbidden as pork" and "as truly as I wouldn't eat
Pork", now used to strengthen a negative = "absolutely";
in EY it is still 'osser hazer' = 'forbidden (like) h.';
derlaabt: pref. 'der-' for HG 'er-' = Y and SG.

.9 'Worim': = normally "worum": "for which" "because",
i.e. the relative; 'warum' ("why") = normally warúm in Y
(if used instead of the more authentic 'far vos', the
interrogative. Cf. E 'What for?') Here either authentic contamination of 'Wórum' and 'Warúm' of deliberate
subst. h c; 'i' for 'u' comes only from unaccented
position (< wórum, the relative); the interrogative is
usually oxytone (warúm).

.10 'Watt': Wart_et_, Y; when suffix and stem-ending are
identical, or nearly so, the 'e' is syncopated and the
suffix "lost". 'Rabbi': pron. 'Rebbe' = Lehrer in der
jüdisch-religiösen Schule (Heder) - originally the
only school Jews attended. With "Emancipation" Jews had
to attend secular schools (sometimes "segregated") and
the Heder became the supplementary religious school;
'beli Neder': lit. "without a vow", sc. "do I make
this promise". Pious Jews were especially concerned
about the sin of "breaking one's word", so they took
care of specify each time they promised to do something

9.13 Au! Der ist aber widerwertig!: Wow! Is this fellow
      unpleasant (disgusting)!

 .14 fertig.

---

      that the promise is 'beli Neder', "without vowing" -
      otherwise the mere "word" would be accounted equivalent
      to a vow.

9.11-12 'tub': tue! the 'b' is authentic G dial. < a MHG
      variant 'tuowen', the '-w' > '-b'. Not Y, h c;
      'Seroroh': pure R in WY only where '$\bar{o}$' (Hôlom: ו) fell
      together with 'o' (< '$\bar{a}$') (Kamas: -).˙ In NEY '$\hat{o}$' >
      'ey', in CEY - 'oy'. 'Sehôroh' (Ware) refers to the
      "Linsen" in the SD, but a vulgar insinuation may have
      been intended; 'un-beHesed: lit. "un-in Gnade", "not
      in Grace", "without grace" - either ungracious to-
      wards others, or having fallen out of the grace of
      somebody. 'Seroroh': Herrschaft. The abstract =
      'rule' is used for the concrete "ruler" as in HG.
      'Jich: Text can be read either as '<u>ich</u>' where both 'ich'
      and the apostrophe (') are meaningless; or as 'Jich',
      taking the apostrophe (') to be a 'J' (Jod) that got
      pushed above the line. We know 'jich' as an expression
      of rejection and disgust (=E 'wow' or even 'pu!')
      But it is not documented! The emendation 'Sich' =
      "look" (in WY and MHG), NHG "sieh" is <u>possible</u>, but
      less fitting and against the Text!

 .12-13 The best interpretation seems to be that Reka is
      mocking her husband's order to put <u>her</u> work aside and
      bring him pen and ink, addressing him as a sovereign
      out of sorts and ungracious. The reference <u>could</u> be
      to Vashti, with the meaning of .13: that Vashti fell
      out of the King's grace; and of .12 that something un-
      pleasant happened <u>to</u> Vashti. 'Der' (.13) can be nom.
      msc. (=Harbona) or dat. fem. sg. (=Vashti). But there
      is no other reference to Vashti and .12 and .13 would
      thus be unmotivated and hang in the air.

10.1 'ahns': (ein)<u>mal</u>, <u>do</u> (bring!); adds emphasis; 'Dint':
Tinte.

.4 That (placard) with (the exhortation) not to converse in
the synagogue!

.5 'hostus̈': '-s' = ink and pen; vor eurem Mund liegt auch
kein Brettlein: Your mouths aren't boarded up either.

10.1-2 'Fihder - Dikrihter': Rz. 'd'-'t' and '-er' pl. - FW
pl. = 'n' in Y even f. neut.; 'Dint': 'D' f. 'T' dist.
h c, though common for a time even in "Standard" G;
'Dikrihter': even the unacc. '-e-' which should be
short, is also dist. into 'i'; 'ahns': < MHG 'eines' =
(ein)mal, not Y.

.4 'mi<u>t</u>': could be a misprint for 'mi<u>r</u>' (=we), but <u>dash</u>
before 'sellen' seems to make 'schmuhsen-sellen' a com-
pound verbal noun, and the phrase - the obj. of the
prep. 'mit', and the whole - apposition to 'Dås'; there
is an explanation for the <u>dash</u>; 'mi<u>r</u>' would yield a
less harsh reading.
'Schuhl': Y f. synagogue, which functioned as a house
of learning Tora, as well as of prayer. Tora-learning
as such is considered the highest form of divine worship
and one is exhorted to "pray in the place of learning".
'schmusen': 's' for 'š' though here the reversal is
common in this HG loanword < <u>Hebrew</u> that is no longer
felt as such and is spelled as if a Germanism (Meschit
instead of Square). Cf. L. p. 401 # 500. Conversing
in the synagogue during prayers, especially during the
(long) reading of the Hebrew scriptures, is exceedingly
common, though accounted as a grievous sin and warned
against by placards on the walls of the synagogue and
by ever newly decreed penalties. 'sellen': sollen; Y
and G <u>dialect</u>, umlaut the 'o' in the infinitive of
sollen (and wollen) just as Standard Y and G umlaut
the vowels in the other modal auxiliaries. Originally
none had Umlaut, but in the plural (with the apocope
of '-en!' as a result of enclisis of pron. to preceding vb) the 'i' in the (post-positive) pron. 'wir',
'ir', 'si' caused the Umlaut of the vowel in the
preceding verb (Example: kun-wir > kün-wir); new
infinitives for the 'defective' modals were coined to
resemble the plural (analogy to other verbs).
Standard G stopped at 'wollen' and 'sollen' and left

10. 6 Ihr könnt auch euer Stättlein bestehen: You can maintain your positions (= take care of yourselves).

---

them unumlauted; Standard Y - at sollen. Some dialects
umlauted all modals. Actually 'wollen' < MHG 'wellen'
and 'e' > 'o' because it is between 'w' and 'l' -
(labials) - which can have that effect. When the 'e'
became 'o' the period of the umlaut-activity had already passed. In Y there was a great deal of leveling and putting the same vowel in the entire present
(Cf. ich darf, vil; mir darfen, viln) but the infinitive is 'wellen'. In 'megen' we first had umlaut,
then unrounding; in können there was a contamination
with 'kennen' -- the end result giving two variants,
one with 'e' and the other with 'o' -- used interchangeably. Thus H's 'sellen' < 'söllen" by Y unrounding of 'ö'.

10.5-8 She is apparently handing him the requested ink and
pen; 'for' etc. = lit. "no board lies before your
mouths either, you can maintain yourselves in your
positions too" i.e. You are not lying in a coffin,
you are alive and can speak. .7 'welts': the '-s'
refers apparently to 'conversing in the synagogue'
which, she implies, the men will not admit to, but
(.8) blame the women (only). If this interpretation
is correct then .4 'mit' should read 'mir' and she
would be implying that the 'decree against conversing'
would be directed against women only. The humor would
then be on three levels: 1. poking fun at the "big
fuss" that the pious make about "a little innocent
conversation during divine service"; 2. the
anachronism and incongruity of having the non-Jews,
Reka and Harbona and the Persian King, concern themselves about "propriety and order in Jewish prayer-
houses" - to the point of issuing decrees against
"conversing"; 3. Reka's protest at the implication
that only women do the "talking" and that the
decrees are directed only against them. The Decree
in the Bible is against wives' insubordination to
their husbands (Esther 1, 16-32)!

To .5 Cf. G "sich kein Blatt vor den Mund nehmen" (=
to speak freely and frankly). To .8 - "es einem in
die Schuhe schieben" (= to impute a fault to some one).

10.7 Wollt es nur nicht sein.

.8 schüttet... der Frau in (den) Schuh = blame the woman.

.9 tut

.12 'toin mest': tun müsst

.13 'secht': Seht.

.14 'Huzelstihl': Hutzelstiel, stem of a dried fruit (pear) = nothing.

.15 'Haz': Herz

10.5-6 Brihtle - Stihtle: both long vowels in Y (and G dial.) - but short in Standard G, against the rule that MHG vowels in open syllables > long; (the double consonants in HG are secondary - a spelling device to indicate the brevity).

.7 'nehr': Cf. 9. 'nor': H is inconsistent: Cf. 'mus' (.11) and 'mest' (.12); 'nor' f. 'nur' is authentic Y since when unacc. 'nur' is enclitic and thus read with the next word as sort of unacc. 'prefix', and the 'u' is thus followed by 'r' plus consonant and therefore reduced or lowered to 'o' (according to rule); 'ner' is apparently even more unacc. and reduced to the slurred ə (spelled e). This weak, unacc. form is then used in emphatic positions and is lengthened secondarily to "nehr" by H and even used in R with '-ehr'. Cf. L p. 390 # 400.

.8 'schit': f. schüttet, Y.

.9 'tet' f. tut; H and G dial. not Y.

.10 's watt': es wird; pres. passive f. <u>fut</u>.; pres. f. fut. = Y and G.

.12 An erotic insinuation; also .16.

.13 'Se<u>ch</u>t': 'ch' MHG and OY and G dial, but neither MY nor <u>NHG</u>. Archaization = another way of deviating < HG h c.

11.3   Ihm den Rat gegeben.

.4   'lihben': leben, sc. soll sie.

.5   'a main': lieber: rather.

.6   'ebbes der Mehr': etwas nicht in Ordnung, something
the matter.

.7   Wie sie jetzt leider alle sind.

.8-9   Does she even as much as take a look into our Books
of Edification, Piety and Devotionals?

10.14   'Doi dernoich': da dernach; a pleonasm common in Y and
G dial. (Cf. fun derfun, ʒu derzu - only here the adverb 'da' is repeated instead of the prep.; "Huzelstihl': a stem of a dried fruit, i.e. nothing, not at
all. L. p. 376 #272.

.16   Cf. .12.

11.3   'ihn': acc. f. dat. dist. h c; 'Êzoh': Rat; 'gihben':
gegeben; pref. 'ge-' was originally left out in the
participle of 'perfective' verbs, later extended to all
by analogy (Cf. 'worden' and 'geworden'), except after
an unacc. syllable (Cf. 'alt geworden' and 'veraltet
worden') and the so-called "double=infin. constr."
(habe ihn 'gehen lassen') and in special cases (of
hiatus: ge-essen > gessen; gegeben > geben). Not MY
and probably inauthentic in H h c.

.4   'lihben': elipsis f. "leben möge (or soll) sie" -
typ. J piety to pray for the life of one mentioned by
name. So common is this that it is used in calling
or addressing someone (especially by his first name)
and has almost been reduced to the equivalent of E
'dear' in: Anna dear, mother dear, dear child, Y
Hanne leben, Mame leben, kind leben.

.5-6   'a main': lieber: rather. L p. 351, #14. 'nehr-
mehr: not Rz necessarily, since 'nehr' with '-eh-'
is found in the middle of the line too (Cf. on 10.7)
= 'nur'.

.7   'ba-Awônôs': leider; lit. "durch Sünden": "because
of sins"; more common: 'ba-Awônôsênu' = "through our

11.10   leider aus der Mode: unfortunately not fashinable.

.11-12   I could burst (lit. slit myself open) and still she
would continue to sit over (secular) books on Saturday.

---

sins" (sc.: "have we brought this punishment upon our-
selves") - a constant and typical attitude of the pious
Jew in 'justifying God' in all the ills that befell him.
Mostly used with weakened force = "unfortunately".

11.8   'Z'enoh u-Re'ehnoh': pron. "Tsenne-Renne", a famous Y
paraphrase of the Pentateuch, designed f. women, to
read therein the weekly Biblical portion (Sidrah-
pericope). Published ca. 1618, it has been reprinted
almost annually and was to be found (prior to "Emancipation") in every Jewish family that spoke Y. It
shaped the education of the Jewish home: it was the
"mother's school": devotional, edifying, and her
textbook on Judaism and its ethic, as well as her textbook on Jewish history and anthology of interesting
and entertaining stories.

11.9-10   "Thehillim': Psalms - used by pious Jews to
supplement the obligatory prayers, and for extra
petitions in times of trouble; also those who did not
master enough Hebrew to "worship God by learning
Torah", could substitute "reciting Psalms" for "learning". 'Ma'amôdôs': Psalm-connected special prayers
and Torah-sections. Originally they were used in the
Jerusalem Temple by "representative laymen", while the
priests officiated at the sacrifices. Both Psalms,
and Ma'amôdôs-after-the Psalms, are now prayers "beyond the line of duty" for the specially pious, i.e.
"extra" and not prescribed. There is a separate
"set" for each day of the week. The R is pure:
Ma'amôdôs - Mod(e) is, but H delib. dist. the 'o' in
the FW to 'u' (Mude) even at the expense of the R!
Possibly H intends the R on the basis of '-udes' in
both lines - a pure R in CEY, the pronunciation of
which is at times considered "funny" outside its
territory. Cf. R of 11.19 - 12.1. 'Umstahngesagt':
leider, lit, < "um Stein sei's gesagt", "may it be
said (sc. that it happened) about stone" (and not
about a human being) - an OY prayer of averting an
evil just mentioned, from anybody but stone (which

11.13 'Soton': Satan.

.14 möcht...Schönes... finden.

.15 'Stuš': Unsinn: nonsense, was für ein Unsinn da
alles drinnen steht.

---

cannot be hurt by evil); now weakend to the equivalent
of the sarcastic American slang "big deal", G "auch
mir was"; "leider" is a very poor (one-word) approxi-
mation. Cf. L p. 411 # 596.

11.11 'darf': kann, G not Y; = " I could burst (lit. slit
myself open) with grief (over her behavior) and she
will continue to desecrate the Sabbath with unholy
books". The h is again on several levels: Reka's
(and later Zetulpe's) trying to "climb" to royalty
contrasted with the obvious trashy vulgarity;
Harbona's sentiments like those of most pious Jews
and then his attributing the same sentiments and
values to a non-Jewish King and that King's ideas
about desirable traits in his Queen-to-be; Harbona's
demands on Zetulpe for piety are exaggerated and as
such "funny" even in the most pious Jew, since women
are officially excempt from all religious rites that
require time for their performance - (they worship
God by devoting their time to taking good care of
their families' needs). Hence a woman will be
considered extra pious if she says the daily prayers
obligatory only on a man. If she indulged in
Thehillim and Ma'amodōs too, she would be extra pious.
And while such existed, they were not too numerous,
found at most among the very old, but not to be expected of a young, unmarried girl. Even the
Ze'ehno-u-Re'enoh they were usually expected to start
reading after their marriage - though it might properly be suggested as a substitute for the secular book
(improper) on Saturday. Finally there is h in
Harbona's innocence; his inability to appreciate why
romantic stories should hold an interest for Zetulpe.
Thus in Harbona the secularist Maskil (follower of
"Enlightenment") H pillories the values of Jewish
piety, especially the efforts of the pious to prescribe
secular literature.

11.17 Am End tun sie sich nehmen.

.19 die Geschichte von A bis Z.

12.1 'kelômar...Gruhf': vermeintlich ... Graf; supposedly ... count.

.2 'fašt...Harr': Fürst... Herr: prince... lord.

.3 'Schabbeschon': Taugenichts, Pfuscher: ne'er do well, botcher.

11.12 'Schabbos': To the pious Jew Saturday was not only a day of physical rest but of spiritual fulfillment and meditation of the holy; hence reading of secular books was especially out of place.

.17 'Lebesôf': Am Ende; ungram. Hebrew, but auth. Y; properly (Hebrew): Levasof.

.19 'Ma'aseh': Geschichte: 'A bis Š': pron. "Aleph bis Šof". Tav, Thav respectively (in the NEY pron. Tov, Šov), are the explosive and fricative variants of the same Hebrew letter (T); hence: from Aleph to Tov (or: Šov) = from A to Z. The letters are printed extra large to indicate that their names (and not their sounds) should be pronounced.

.19-21 The R Šof - Gruhf could be pure as 'Šuf-Gruhf') only in CEY, but not in H's WY, where it would be 'Šof - Groif' (MHG â > oi). The NEY R 'Sof-Grof' would be pure and Y, though not WY, but would not sound as "funny" as CEY. Cf. on 11.9-10: both here and there the WY reader would normally pronounce the first R word on the basis of 'ɔ', the 'u' in the second R word would come as a "shock" and thus enhance the h.

12.1 'kelômer': sozusagen, vermeintlich: so-to-speak, supposed(ly). MY elaborates to 'miklomperšt'.

.2 groisen: Cf. on 2.9.

.3 'Schabbeschon': prone to make (spelling) mistakes; a very rare word in late Hebr. unlisted in the most complete Hebr. (and Y) dictionaries, except in Ben Yehuda's and those who follow him: Even Shoshan's,

12.4   '<u>koschoh</u>': schwierig: difficult (to understand).

.5   '<u>hotscheh</u>': sogar: even.

.4-7   What's there so difficult to understand? For all <u>you</u> care, she could even remain an old maid! Hathach proposed a good "match" for her. Why didn't you accept it?

Alkalai's and Stutchkoff's Hebr. "Otzar" (Not in his Y "Oitzer"). It is apparently a J printer's coinage as a curse-word for an error-prone typesetter Hebr. 'Shibbush' = 'error'. H worked for J printers (as an illustrator). None list the meaning: "fool".

12.4   'drahn': may refer to 11.14, i.e. Harbona's inability to understand what is so interesting about "Hansel's getring Gretel"; Reka implies that without the worldly wisdom to be gained from the modern, romantic literture, an old-fashioned Zetulpe would remain an old maid.

.5   'Kennet': könnte; 'hotsche': here = 'even', usually = "at least", < Slav. 'Xotya', the spelling as if it were Hebr. (ח and ה and no <u>vowels</u>), but the print-type (Meschit) indicates that it is not Hebrew. H (and/or the printer) wanted to indicate that the word is neither from the Hebrew nor from the G. i.e., it did not quite 'belong' in his Y. Only EY (on Slavic territory) could "legitimately" contain Slavism, but not WY (on G speech-territory). However, there was constant migration between the two J communities and thus some Slavisms entered even WY.

'groie Zepf': graue Zöpfe. Jewish girls used to cut off their hair after marriage. Jews also had no nunnery. Hence the "horror" of a girl having to plait her hair into braids when already gray, i.e. to remain unmarried.

.6   'geret': geredet, reg. Y syncope of unacc. 'e' (Cf. HG wird < wirdet) when the consonants are (nearly) alike. "A Schiddich redn" = to broker a match proposal between the parties; "a Schiddich tun" = to make (or accept) the match. For R Cf. on 5.20-21.

12.9-10   Nein, Gott behüte! Die taugt für keinen guten
          Juden.

.10   'Pfuzi Kapporah': nichtswürdige Kreatur: worthless
      creature.

.11   'schlinke schlanke': schlendernd: walking indolently.
      'Seroroh': Herrschaft: Lady.

.15   She is not ambitious (enough to <u>do</u> anything).

.17   solch eine verschüttete Gewürzbüchse: such a spilled
      spice-box.

12.7   'hostu': T: 'hottu'.

.10   Jid: auth. Y, derived not < 'Jude' (< late Latin
      'Judeo') but < Hebrew 'Yehudi' > Yudi > Yüd > Yid; an
      example of the principle of the German Umlaut operat-
      ing on even the Hebrew elements of Y! To the old joke,
      the anachronism that both Harbona and the King are
      presumed Jews is added "guter Jid", which in Y (also
      in H's) is not simply a Jew who is 'good', nor even
      one whose Judaism is 'good' (Cf. a "good Catholic");
      it is a technical term for a <u>Jew a Saint</u>, a <u>Miracle-
      worker</u>. A Jew who is only "pious" is: "an <u>ehrlecher</u>
      <u>Jid</u>", lit. "an honest Jew". This semantics, signifi-
      cant as it is in itself, is a source of h for H.

.11   'Pfuzi-Kapporoh': eine unsaubere Nichtswürdige: a
      filthy, unworthy creature. on 'Kapporoh' Cf. on 3.8.
      Pfuze HG Pfütze (mudhole, dirt), with assonance-asso-
      ciation of the word for female sex-organ. To the
      model: "a šêne, raine Kappore", lit. "a beautiful,
      pure sacrificial victim", i.e. "just the right sacri-
      fice" (said, at time maliciously, at a hated person's
      mishap, loss or death) a new expression arose: a
      "filthy Kappore", "not even good enough to die for
      atonement", hence simply: "worthless". Cf. L p. 378
      # 286.

.12   'schlinke schlanke': Y 'schling-schlang':
      schlenkernd: to walk aimlessly. Cf. L p. 401 #495.

.13   ferricht: Y, HG verrichtet.

12.21 Heute Malen – morgen Sticken: today painting tomorrow embroidering.

13.1 'in': "ich nicht": I (do) not like to say (it).

.3 'Grillst': macht grelle Laute: makes shrill sounds. 'unsilige': unselige = "heillose", "damned".

12.14 'wehren': prevented, i.e. stopped from doing what is wrong; drastic for "guide and train".

.15 'begehren': "desire" here in the sense of "pursue the desired goal with ambitious efforts".

.17 Besomin Biks: Spice-box, used to bless over, and smell, the spices in the "havdala" ritual of ushering out the Sabbath. In a spilled box the spices have been wasted and at best there is still an aroma of the spices in it and therefore still looks and smells as if it could be used in the ritual, but it cannot and is therefore of no value. Hence – applied to a person in whom there is an <u>appearance</u> of good qualities, but who is really empty of them, or they are in such disorder that they are wasted. Cf. Tendlau # 153.

.20-21 'ligen – Stiken': Rz g-k, but the vowel <u>is</u> short in 'ligen' in Y and MHG. NB the inconsistent use of 'n' suffix in infinitive.

'ahn': HG 'an', but Y and G dial. < 'ān', hence NEY 'on', CEY 'ūn';

moring: morgen; the metathesis of '-rgen' to '-ring' is regular with H, but not Y; < Swb.

13.1 'in': prob. the MHG fusion 'i'n' f. 'ich ne'; though the spelling does not indicate that, 'i'n mag' is a common MHG phrase,and without this interpretation the line seems to have no meaning.

.3 Grillst: could be misprint f. grillzt < MHG grillezen, Y grilzn; the '-š-' <u>could</u> be authentic too, as there was a variant verbal suffix '-essen'; also '-̇zt' sometimes > '-st' as a result of 'simplifica-tion' (Entlastung): tst > st; it is surely third and not second person singular.

13.4   Cf. below the line.

.5   'os̆ur': bei meiner Seele: upon my soul.

.6   'Fattel Scho'oh: Viertel Stunde

.7   läuft fortwährend herum.

.8   Seiltänzer.

.11-13 Wenn's nach dir ginge, weiss ich, wie sie, armes
       Dinge, ihre Zeit verbrächte. Deinetwegen könnte sie
       weder schreiben noch lesen. If it were up to you, I
       know, how she, poor thing, would spend her time. For
       all you care, she wouldn't know how to write or read.

.14   sonst vor alten Zeiten Mode gewesen.

       'unsilige': unholy, profane, damned.

13.4   lit.: "has all (her) bodices brought (and held)":
       She tries on (or has her maid try on her) all her
       bodices - she is that hard to please (?)

.5   'os̆ur': lit. - 'forbidden'; a vestige of an adjuration
       formula: may all be forbidden to me (to enjoy) if I
       don't tell the truth. Cf. 9.7; 'recht': Y and MHG;
       HG: recht<u>es</u>.

.7   'Schus̆s̆elt': runs around quickly. Cf. L. p.405 # 541.

       'in a lang Klad': Y; in einem lange<u>n</u> Kleid: G; adj.
       undecl. after the indef. article neut.; 'ā saidenen':
       prob. dist. h c, acc. f. dat. Y has 'saidenem̲' even
       for the acc. (dissim. of the two 'n's)! If H did not
       distort even in the monosyllable one might assume that
       even in Y '-nem' first > '-nen' and then '-nem' again.

       'Spenzer': Engl. spencer = a short jacket. Cf. L.
       p.402 # 511.

.10   'gewis': '-s' f. '-s̆' rev. subst.; Cf. .13 and .14
       lihs̆en and gewihs̆en f. lesen und gewesen.

.11-12   '-genget -- brenget': '-et-' = imperf. subj.

13.15   Jetzt gelten die Püpplein nicht mehr.

.16   Jetzt gibt's.

.17   'ahn': einen.

.20   'Loschôn': Sprache.

.21   'Perschoihn': Persön(lichkeit).

13.14   'schunst': sonst, here = "elsewhere"; the reversal of
'sch' and 'š' is probably dist. h c, since H does not
usually change initial 's-' to 'sch'; 'for alters':
in alten Zeiten, analog. to G "von alters her" (=von
alten Zeiten bis jetzt), neither Y nor HG. In 'šunst':
'u' is MHG, remained 'u' in Y, but changed in NHG to
'o' before a nasal. On 'š' f. 'š' Cf. L. p.405 #540.

.15   = It's no longer sufficient to be just a doll (without
education or skill); 'gilden': Y = gilten and gelten,
but 'd' f. 't' = rev. subst.; 'Popperlich': Popperl
is Bavarian f. Püppchen, Marionette; '-lich' is Y pl.;
'nimmer': here with the orig. force: "nie mehr" -
emphatic f. "nicht!"

.16   'gitš': Y, = gibt's; slurring (of the 'b') in such
highly frequent words is not unusual, espec. in dial.
Cf. Scottish "gie's" f. "gives". Conceivably 'gits'
stands f. 'gilts', which would fit even better though
repetitious. The meaning: now only skillful girls
get a mate. The choice of diction ("fast females") is
delib. h c.

.18   'for der Welt': 'for' can mean "für" = "prepared for"
or "vor" = "in the eyes of (the world)"; the dative in
Y - in either case. 'Welt': emphatic!

.17-18   Meaning: What's the trouble here? It does cost a
pretty sum (to keep young ladies up-to-date), but for
that they are world-wise.

.19-20   Rz on the basis of Šušən - Lošən; R impure in
all Y.

Wo. and syntax OY and G dial.; MY iber der Tochters
Gang (i.e. instead of the possessor (Tochter), plus

14.2 'allfott': fortwährend: constantly; 'kihfen':
keifen: rail, reproach, nag.

.3 Es täte Not, sie täte in ein Mausloch schlüpfen, she
would have to run into a mouse-hole.

.4 'arwet': arbeitet.

.10 nicht geredet, mein Mund soll lügen.

.11 miteinander Reue.

.13 Gefallen.

.16 'oisgihben': given away (in marriage).

.19 'Oiszehrung': Tuberkulose

---

the possess. adj. (ihr) in the nomin., plus the thing
possessed (Gang), MY has the dat. of the possessor,
plus '-s' and the thing possessed.

13.21 'Perschoihn': tüchtiger Mensch: skillful person.

14.1 Rz: <u>primary</u> accent with secondary. 'oiffressen':
i.e., aus Liebe; because of love; exaggeration h.

.2 kihfen': either G keifen (=schimpfen, scold) dist. f.
Rz, or MHG kiven, nagen (gnaw) used fig. f. "biting
criticism", (Cf. E "nag"), or MHG giefen = schreien,
lärmen. All three would have the same force here;
('schlihfen': schlüpfen, G dial.)

.3 'tiebet': täte (Cf. 'hiebet' f. hätte), < a variant
infin. MHG tuowen, -w > -b, (Cf. 'tub' = tu!) and to
the new root with -b, a weak imperf. subj. in '-ete'
was formed with a change of vowel (u > ie, perhaps by
way of Umlaut followed by unrounding, or by analog. -
Cf. ruf, rief) and finally by apocope of '-e'. N.B.
H's inconsistency: in the same line he uses 'tet' and
'tiebet' f. "täte"; he also uses 'tet' f. the indicative by the side of 'tut'! Prob. inauth. H coinage
h c.

.4 'arwet': arbeitet; syncop. <u>is</u> Y, but '-rw-' f. '-rb-'
is G dial, and H delib. reverses them h c.

14.20   'Heschek': Lust, desire.

14.9   "Futtrahl": Futteral, a case (or box) to put her in.

.10   'nig': nit; true phonetic rendering of "breath-group"
'nit-geret' where in speech the 't' of 'nit' is assim.
to the 'g' of 'gret'.

.11   'mitanant': Y, miteinander; here simply: beide.

.10-11   Don't talk godlessly. May my prophesy turn out un-
true, but both of you will be sorry (for your impious
attitude).

.13   'Gfalles': Rz f. Gefallen.

.14   'Sorig': Svarabhakti i in dial. betw. guttural 'r'
and palatal 'g'; not particularly typ. of Y dial.,
used by H h c.

.16   'Hest': colloq. f. 'hetst' = hättest.

.17   'oisgihben': f. oisgegeben, dist. h c even if against
meter! "Kinder oisgebn" = Y and G dial., but not HG,
"to give children in marriage" - a most important J
concern!

.19   'ahn': either = 1. einen, or = 2. an; 1. = You can
only give one (us) tuberculosis (with your nagging);
2. = You can only think of the expenses (of education,
dowry and wedding). Cf. L p. 393 #430. Perhaps H is
delib. ambiguous.

.20   Sc. 'di Tochter oisgeben', but the indefiniteness is
delib., the sentence absolutely (without an "object")
has an erotic connotation ("Barkis is willing").

15.3   'be-Choved=e': respectable.

 .5   'Ezoh': Rat: advice; 'Hochom': Kluger, clever fellow.

 .6   'Dihn': Dem; 'roiten': raten.

 .7   ordentlich; ohne Boden.

 .8   'fihlet': fehlte; (I would) need.

 .9   'Soiber': Zuber

.10   'kol-ha-kohol': jederman: everybody.

.11   'Sehoroh - - fahl': Ware - - feil: merchandise -- for
      sale.

.13   'Schambelle': Kauz: queer.

.15   'niber': hinüber.

15.3   'be-Choved=e': lit. = "with honor", hence "respectable",
       "of good family and reputation"; the Hebr. syntactical
       phrase is used and declined like an adj., MY 'bekovedig',
       with 'K' for 'Ch', is "ungrammatical".

 .5   'groiser': 's' instead of 'š' rev. subst. h c suggests
      'grauser' (cruel) instead of 'grosser' (big).

 .7   uhne: the u should be oi in WY (MHG â), CEY un (without
      '-e'), prob. dist. h c.

.6-7   Rz 't' - 'd'.

 .8   'fihlet': fehlte, impf. subj., expressing (sarcastical-
      ly) an unreal wish: (if all my other wishes were ful-
      filled) "I would still need this". 'Daas': (Cf.'waas')
      Y and G dial. lengthen 'a' in the demonstrative because
      of the emphasis, hence EY   u.

 .9   'Soiber' f. Zoiber (MHG Zûber), a "jug with two
      handles", MY Zeber; prob. not a misprint, but delib.
      dist. h c. Malapropism, to suggest G "sauber (-er
      Charakter"), decent character.

.10   'Kohol': 'Kohol' is the only correct form here in the

15.14   May I get crippled on the spot... if I let her make
        one step thither (i.e. to the King's contest-selection
        for beautiful maidens)

  .16   Plaudern . . . Plappeln

  .17   Teufeln . . . Zappeln

  .16f 'Geschmuhš': idle talk, gossip; 'Gebabbel': prattle;
        'Gemaschchiš': deviltry; 'Gezappel': fidgeting.

---

        phrase 'Kol-ha-Kohol', lit. die ganze Gemeinde (the
        whole community) i.e. everybody; but there is the
        "construct" form 'Kehal' and the "fancy" Christian and
        Sephardic pronunciation 'Kahal': one of these in-
        congruous pron. H uses h c Rz. with 'fahl'.

  .11   'Sehôhroh': lit. "Ware": merchandise; ironic and
        euphemistic for a bad person, especially a woman who,
        like a piece of merchandise, is "for sale".

  .12   'sain': auth.; old pl. ending '-e' apocopated, but
        restored analog. in MY.

  .15A NB. The SD are in perfect HG, only the 'ü' is render-
        ed 'i' because that was the common transliterating
        practice of Jews writing G with Hebrew characters --
        the 'ü' and the 'ö' were rendered defectively יי and
        ע i.e. i and e respectively.

  .16f Collective nouns can be formed in G from any stem with
        the prefix Ge- plus (in NG) the suffix -e; when the
        stem is a verb the resulting noun often has a pejora-
        tive, contemptuous nuance; cf. Geheul, Gerede; in EY
        the formantia are 'ge-' plus the suffix '-echts'
        (< G '-icht'), EY 'geredechts' = G Gerede; H is very
        fond of such coinages with just the Prefix 'Ge-',
        ('Ge)schmuš is now in EY a perfectly serious innocent
        word, the best designation for an (extensive) con-
        versation (otherwise 'schmues' or 'schmus' = just
        conversation). Originally 'schmuš' < A Hebr. šmuəs <
        (Hebr. šmuót) meant rumors, gossip -- and it had a
        pejorative, contemptuous nuance even without the
        prefix ge-. It entered G with the meaning of Ge-
        schwätz, 'Schmeichelei', Schöntun (schmeichelndes
        Zureden zu einem Kauf), twaddle, fawning, hypocriti-
        cal persuasion. In WY this perjoritive meaning may

15.18 'Heren': hören.

16.1 'Mecht': möchte.

---

have been preserved through the influence of G. More likely -- H used the word, innocent in Y, with its G connotation and added the prefix to intensify the h. The transliteration is in Meschit, hence H and/or his printer did not consider this word Hebrew any more. SY also disregards its Hebrew origin in spelling! 'Ge-maschchis', like the verb 'maschchisen', may be a H coinage. Not current in EY, < A Hebrew 'mashis', pres. particip. = destroying, destroyer, fig. devil, hence devilish work, deviltry. 'Gezappel': busybody, "nervous" carrying-on because of his suspense.

15.17A 'Zetulpe': comic character, snobbish 'climber' who tries to speak HG, but is too ignorant to do so and only succeeds to distort her WY, so that what she speaks is correct neither in Y nor in G.

.18 'Heren Sie, liebe Mutter': like the typical would-be aristocrat (à la Bourgeois-Gentilhomme) she addresses her mother in the formal form.

16.1 'mecht': typ. Y unrounding of 'ö' and apocope of 'e'.

.2 'koch...soch': cook and get sick; 'soch' is a noun and verb related to the NHG 'siechen' and 'Sucht'; the noun 'Soch' is still current in Y, especially in the combination: 'gele Soch' = jaundice, but the MHG verb 'sochen', though listed in Harkavy, is almost never encountered. NHG has lost 'Soch' and 'sochen' and Y has lost 'Sucht' and 'siechen'. The rhyming curse and the unusual verb have a strong humorous effect. 'Osur': "(Es sei) verboten" - common Y affirmation or mild oath, < Hebrew. Cf. on 13.5.

.3 'ahn nandern': einer andern; OY would require ahner andern; MY both SY and WY, would require (fun)'an-anderer', or 'an anderer'. H is inauth, h c, as usual, here by metanalysis (false syllabification); 'Watt-schaft': Wirtschaft; any vowel plus 'r' plus 't' > 'at' in H's "dialect". There are such dialects, Y and G, very limited geographically, but not common in WY. H dishes them up as Y -- inauth h c.

16.5   'kihl': sc. mein Gemüt: cool (give vent to) my
       anger.

 .6   'Boier kum rois': a figure of speech used to indicate
       challenge.

 .5   'Schlemiel': simpleton, unlucky bungler < the bibli-
       cal name Shelumiel, son of Zuri-Shaddai, chief of the
       tribe of Simeon (Numbers 1, 6). The word is a
       classic example of false etymologizing on the basis of
       "phonetic fracturing", i.e. of twisting the syllables
       of a word to yield an allusion to the current meaning.
       The example is fraught with instructive lessons about
       mistakes in methodology and deserves, therefore, our
       rather lengthy excursion.
       Wasserzieher's Woher 1963 [16] gives the right deriva-
       tion (Shelumiel), but brings in a confusing "contami-
       nation" by attributing erroneously to Shelumiel, as
       its original meaning, "der nicht(s) taugt" (=bungler,
       ne'er-do-well), which is properly the translation
       only of another totally different, offered etymology:
       the pseudo-scientific, artificially reconstructed
       etymon 'šelo'mo‘il'. Wahrig's Deutsches Wörterbuch
       1968, Column 3116, reproduces that false etymon Hebr.
       "selo-mô‘il", "der nicht(s) taugt -- the 's' in
       'nichts' is an added inaccuracy in the translation --
       "Pechvogel, vom Missgeschick Verfolgter" (=never-do-
       well, misfortune's butt); excellent equivalents these
       and an ingeniously reconstructed etymon! Only that
       German lexicologists are not up to the task of examin-
       ing critically the phoniness of etymologies concocted
       for them by Jewish dilettants with but a smattering
       of Hebrew, and illiteracy in historical linguistics.
       The etymology does sound so plausible -- only that it
       is not only demonstrably impossible, but the true
       etymology is available to the scholar willing and
       competent to do the necessary researching of the
       sources:
       Here is the proof:
           1. 'Shelo-mo‘il' is a reconstruction, nowheres
       documented, hence it should at least have been
       starred (*) in Wahrig.
           2. 'Lo-mo‘il', without the 'she-', would still
       be ungrammatical, but a conceivable "folk-creation"
       -- if such were documentable. But with the relative
       prefix 'she-' it could never have been created --

16.5   even by the most ignorant. Except in the most recent
Israeli - coined new "periphrastic hortative", on the
model of Yiddish "zolst gezunt zein", Hebr. "she tehai
bari", 'she-' would be resorted to only to qualify or
define some <u>antecedent</u> noun, or clause, say, "ish shelo
moil" -- a man who cannot do any good. For "Ne'er-do-
well" Lo-moʻil is all anyone knowledgeable enough to
put together the two words would need, and he would
know that he would need, -- i.e. there would be no
occasion and no motivation to use 'she-'; and without
'she-' there is no foundation in the connection for an
etymology for "schlemiel" -- not even an assonance.

    As already hinted: even 'Lo-moʻil' would be "ac-
ceptable" only in the most recent "yiddishized" (colloquial) Hebrew of Israel. A generation ago only the
forms 'aino moʻil', or 'ainenu moʻil' were current.
But, while this would be more correct grammatically
than 'Lo-moʻil', the <u>authentic</u> Hebrew coinage would
require Lo-yoʻil. In fact, there is just such a
coinage in Hebrew and Y on the basis of the Hebrew
root s l h (שׁלח): 'Lo <u>Y</u>utaslach', that is a perfect synonym of the eponym Shlemiel! What is more,
there had been available (< Jer. 22,30), ready-made,
so to speak, 'Lo <u>Y</u>itslach' = "(a man who) does not or
will not prosper", i.e. a "ne'er-do-well", but Jews
deliberately coined 'Lo <u>Y</u>utslach' (the passive of
"Yitslach") to add to the concept of the 'unlucky' that
of the 'unusable', "der Taugenichts".

    The form 'LoYo-ʻil' is actually relatively quite
current: there is an ironic proverb about medicines
and remedies in general that they should be ventured,
because "even if they won't help they cannot hurt" --
"im <u>lo yoʻil</u>, lo yaziq". If therefore a coinage from
this root had even been attempted, the coiner would
have availed himself of the ever-ready 'Lo-Yoʻil'!
But they had already coined 'Lo <u>Y</u>utslach' on the model
of Jeremiah's 'Lo Yitzlach'!

    3. Even if it were granted that the unlikely con-
coction 'Shelomoʻil' <u>was</u> coined, and did gain currency,
its phonetic development could have yielded only one
of the two resultants: 'Shlóimel' or 'Shlemóil' (de-
pending on the accentuation prevailing ultimately:
penult or final), but absolutely never : 'Shlemiel'.

    4. But why <u>should</u> the eponym Shelumiel come to

16.5   mean 'Pechvogel' and 'Taugenichts' (Fortune's Butt or Bungling Ne'er-do-well)?

Thereby hangs a tale -- a curious tale at that.

Number 1,6 lists Shelumiel as the chief of the tribe of Simeon. Numbers 25,6 - 15 tells of the killing of "Zimri, son of Salu, a prince of a chief - house of the Simeonites". The Talmud (Sanhedrin 82), followed by the commentary Baal Haturim (on Num. 1,16 and 25,12), identify Shelumiel with Zimri. Zimri's story is greatly embellished by Talmud (loc. cit.) Targum Jonathan, Midrash Rabba, and Sifre (all ad loc.). But only part of this embellishment gained common currency: the moralizing part -- typically. To the biblical account that Zimri fornicated with Cozbi the Midianite at the idolatrous rites of Baal Peor, post-biblical tradition adds that he challenged Moses at the head of his 24,000 armed tribesmen, brazenly trying to justify his sins and to put Moses in the wrong. It was only then that Phinehas was inspired with holy zeal and killed Zimri. Hence a proverb arose: he acts like Zimri, but claims deserts, like Phinehas. Thus Zimri became an eponym for 'Hypocrite'.

The more lurid details of the elaborated story remained unknown to the "common people" -- so much so that even the would-be "scholars" of Hebrew that furnished the German lexicographers with the false etymology were apparently ignorant of them and so had to go to the trouble of inventing their charmingly persuasive, if utterly impossible, etymon. Had they known the whole story, they could not have failed to arrive at the truth.

It may seem strange that a story extant in so many Sources (even the commentary on Rashi's commentary, the Sifetai Hahamim, cites all the details ad loc., therefore they were actually "in the hands" of every Jewish schoolboy!) -- that such a story should still remain unknown. The fact is though that only the exceptionally gifted student, the real scholar, troubled to "negotiate" any of the cited Sources. They were too difficult.

So only the scholars know that as many as twelve miracles happened to Phinehas in his "holy zeal", (the Talmud lists only six). Two of those were: 1. that he managed to thrust his spear through the very genitals in the very act of fornication; 2. that he was able to expose the pair's guilt to the

16.5 public by carrying the pair out speared and yet in
their original sinful positions with Zimri on top, etc.
      Scholarship in Jewish Holy Lore and piety went
hand in hand. These pious initiates were therefore
reticent about the identity of Shelumiel and Zimri
and would not indulge in dwelling on details of a story
that verged on the pornographic, or in divulging them
to the "unworthy". There are certain things that
"could properly be revealed only to the reliably pious",
(according to the Rabbinic dictum: "Ain megalin ela
litzenuim", based on the Talmudic command: "ain
mosserin oto ela lemi shetzanua" - Kidushim 71a). But
being human after all, these scholars, in spite of their
piety, could not fail to see and "appreciate" the grim
"joke" in Shelumiel's predicament. They then would be
tempted to call anyone in a "funny" predicament
'Shlumiel' -- without revealing the eponym's original
predicament.
      Thus the "joke" as such remained "private". But
nicknames for "luckless fools" are in high demand. And
so Shlemiel passed into common use, without the average
user's appreciating the allusion. But it was just
this ignorance of the esoteric lore behind the contemptuous name that gave rise to all kinds of attemps
at etymologizing and sound associating. Shelumiel as
a name, and therefore as a component of speech (rather
than of the sacramental "full Hebrew", which must be
read to be "letter-perfect", and therefore read almost
mechanically, syllable by syllable) had to be subject
to all phonetic changes of spoken Judeo-German (Y) and
had to develop into 'Shlemihl' (šlɔmi:l). It was thus
associated with G and WY 'schlimm', bad, and especially with WY 'schlimm Masel': luckless fellow, (G
Pechvogel) thus actually another synonym of Shlemiel.
'Masel' means luck in Y (< Hebr. 'mazal' = star, luck)
and thus 'schlimm Masel' means literally 'bad luck' --
but only in WY, where 'schlimm' is still current. EY
lost the word and the phrase 'schlimm Masel' came to
be pronounced 'schlemazel', the 'shle-' prefix was
associated with Hebr. 'shelo' = 'not having', thus =
'not having luck', 'luckless'. The sound clusters
'shle-', 'shme-' and 'shlim- shlam' have, in addition,
pejoritive associations even in G proper, but more so
in Y (Cf. 'Streckformen' in G, and such Y 'Streck-

16.5   formen' as 'gelt-shmelt' used contemtuously of money).
        In MY these synonyms for 'luckless fellow' gained
new individuality by the process of 'division of labor'
or rather differentiation of function. Now each has a
nuance of its own. One of the illustrative anecdotes
tells: a restaurateur, a nebbich, employed a Shlemiel
of a waiter who was prone to spill the hot soup into
the laps of his shlemazel patrons.

Heinrich Heine has a slightly confused version of
this, our etymology of Schlemihl. The German version follows with an English translation of the most
relevant lines:

    "In der Bibel ist zu lesen,
    Als zur Zeit der Wüstenwandrung
    Israel sich oft erlustigt
    Mit den Töchtern Kanaans,

    Da geschah es, dass der Pinhas
    Sahe, wie der edle Simri
    Buhlschaft trieb mit einem Weibsbild
    Aus dem Stamm der Kananiter,

    Und alsbald ergriff er zornig
    Seinen Speer und hat den Simri
    Auf der Stelle totgestochen -
    Also heisst es in der Bibel.

    Aber mündlich überliefert
    Hat im Volke sich die Sage,
    Dass es nicht der Simri war,
    Den des Pinhas Speer getroffen,

    Sondern dass der Blinderzürnte
    Statt des Sünders, unversehens
    Einen ganz Unschuld'gen traf,
    Den Schlemihl ben Zuri Schaddai."

Dieser nun, Schlemihl I.,
Ist der Ahnherr des Geschlechtes
Derer von Schlemihl. Wir stammen
Von Schlemihl ben Zuri Schaddai.

from "Jehuda ben Halevy", Heinrich Heine, Werke, Vol. 1,
p. 413, Reclam, 1924.

"Phineas, blind with fury / In the sinner's place, by
ill luck / Chanced to kill a guiltless person / Named
Schlemihl ben Zuri Shaddai / He, then, this Schlemihl
the First, / Was the ancestor of all the / Race
Schlemihls".

from Joseph L. Baron, Treasury of Jewish Quotations,
1961 (2) #769.1, p. 433.

Heine claims in that poem that he consulted Chamisso,
the famous author of Peter Schemihl for the etymology and that Chamisso referred him to Kriminalrat
Hitzig, to whom he owed this etymology.

That the etymology based on Shelumiel and Zimri being
two different people, and that Shelumiel suffered
innocently the punishment deserved by Zimri is
confused, in fact, impossible - can easily be deduced
from the fact that in numbers 25, 6-15, where the
story of Fornicator's killing by Pinchas is told, only
Zimri is mentioned, never Shelumiel. The fact that
Zimri is here called a "prince of a chief-house of the
Simeonites", that in Deut. 1,6 Shelumiel is also
mentioned as a chief of the Tribe of Simeon - these
facts in themselves would not have given rise to a
story of mistaken identities. And even if they did,
then Zimri, whom the Bible (Deut. 25,14) specifically
names as the victim, should have become the symbol of
the "innocent, luckless by-stander", and not Shelumiel,
whom the Bible does not involve in the Peor story at
all. Shelumiel could at best have been involved by
the supposed "popular legend", if such had ever
really arisen, only in the character of the "lucky
fellow who gets away with everything" -, since thus
the legend would not contradict the specific words of
the Bible (what a Jewish folk legend would not do
unnecessarily) and would still make its point. It

can only be the post-biblical, the Talmudic, identify-
ing the two as one and the same person, with the lurid
elaborations on the one hand, and the mentioned
"reticence of the knowledgeable scholars" on the
other, who deliberately picked the name Shelumiel just
because the Bible does not specifically associate him
with Fornicator's story. It was therefore suitable
for a sort of secret, private joke.

Prof. Dov Sadan, professor emeritus of the
Yiddish Department of the Hebrew University at
Jerusalem and distinguished interpreter of comparative literature, published a wonderfully perceptive
essay on Schlemiel (in Hebrew) in Orlogin (No. I.
1950, pp. 198-203) in which he traces the use of the
name, word and motif of Schlemiel from its origin
to-date in Jewish and German literature. He makes
plausible that after it acquired the meaning of
"luckless fellow" it came to be applied to, and
used about, and by, alienated and would-be emancipated
Jews of Germany to characterize their predicament of
being accepted and at home neither among Jews nor among
Gentiles. This connotation of "homeless Jew cursed
to be eternally wandering" appealed to Adelbert von
Chamisso (1781-1838) who, as a child of a French
aristocrat, had been made homeless by the French
Revolution, became a Prussian patriot and a German
poet - roles in which he felt uncomfortable. He
became restless, a world-traveler, and obsessed with
his homelessness and alienation - what we would call
today - the "loss of his identity". So he came to
write his autobiographic allegory, the novelette
Peter Schlemihl the misadventure of the man who
sold his shadow.

Sadan also uncovered a more recent eponymic
event for giving Schlemiel the connotation of
"luckless": - a discovery that at one and the same
time also accounts for the peculiarity that this
semantic transformation is found in Ashkenazic
Jewry only:

Sadan quotes from Leopold Lef's Lebensalter
(p.54):

". . . In the days of Rabbi Meir of Rothenburg
(ca. 1215-1293) it happened that a [yeshiva] student
left his wife and took up exile for the sake of finding a place of Torah. But when _eleven_ months passed
his wife gave birth to a boy. Yet the Rabbis of the
time handed down the decision that the child was
kosher (=legitimate), basing their opinion on the
precedent of Raba Tosfaah (in Yebamot 80b) when a case
came before him of a woman who gave birth 12 months
after her husband had left her to go overseas, and the
Rabbi declared her "kosher", because of the principle
that a mature fetus could "tarry" in his mother's
womb 3 months beyond his maturation".

(Translated from Sadan's Hebrew)

The name of that Yeshiva student was: Shlumiel!

Sadan cites an additional reference (in Hebrew)
Shor, Joshua Heshil in _Hechalutz_ Vol. 10, p. 101,
Prague 1877.

We maintain that the case of the yeshiva student
started the eponymic reference, but that of itself it
would have died out with the circle initiated into the
details of the event - just as the name of the luckless
husband at Raba Tosfaah's court didn't come down to
us. It was the _biblical_ Shelumiel, identified with
Zimri and his fate at the hands of Pinchas, that kept
the reference permanently alive as the "private joke
of pious scholars".

16.6f   Jetzt gehst du mir nicht gleich da 'naus,
        Kratz ich dir deine Augen gar 'raus.

  .9   'Umstahnsgesagt': leider; 'spiht': spät.

 .11   'mecht': möcht'.

16.6   'iz' G: jetzt, Y (h) iz(t) (er)(t) < MHG nbf. iez
        < iezuo, first shortened in unaccented position,
        then augmented with suffixes, t, -er, -ert, typical
        f. Y adverbs. Cf. L 377 # 276.

  .6f   'nois... rois': apheresis of hinaus...heraus,
        regular in G but not in EY -- where only 'arois'
        < heraus is current; 'hinois' is lost and with it
        the distinction between motion away from the speaker
        and motion toward the speaker. N.B. the delib. dist.
        of '-s' for '-š'; only the prep. but not the adv. in
        Y has voiced 's'; the adv. has voiceless 'š', is both
        Y and G.

        'dain Klozzers': deine Glotzer, your starers; 'dain'
        with 'e'-apocope is delib. dist. h c as both Y and G
        require deine; k in Klozzers is rev. subst. voiceless
        'k' f. voiced 'g' -- here with the added h allusion
        to Klotz: wood, blockhead; even 'Glotzer' would be a
        h coinage as only Glotzauge is listed in HG dictiona-
        ries, but not Glotzer; the '-š' suffix for the pl.
        could be WY (in nouns that in G have no plural diffe-
        rentiation) but as the noun itself is probably a H
        coinage, so the '-š' is an added dist. h c -- at least
        to his would-be G-speaking audience. Cf. L 381,
        # 316, where Glotzer is equated with "blinker" --
        therefore hardly the prototype f. H; it is more
        likely a "natural".

  .7 A-B   SD 1. schütte(1)t ... über... läuft as HG, cf. HG
        'loift (i.e. läuft) fort' against (.10) WY 'laaft...
        fott'.

  .8   'daas': lengthening of 'a' and voicing of 's' are a
        "phonetic contradiction", therefore it is dist. h c.
        the vowel was originally lengthened in emphatic posi-
        tion as demonstrative, hence the further development
        in NEY to 'ɔ' and SEY to 'u; (only the long 'â' de-
        veloped thus). This development must have taken
        place before the demonstrative came to be used as the

definite article -- otherwise the highly frequent 'd́as'
(the article) could not have changed to conform with
the rarer demonstrative 'dās'. The <u>article</u> in Y has
subsequently shortened the ɔ̄/w̄ of the demonstrative to
ɔ̌/ǔ and usually even to ə. The voicing of the 's' (to
'z') can only occur unaccented, therefore in unem-
phatic positions. Therefore H clearly contaminates the
length (authentic only in the demonstrative) with the
voicing (which <u>could</u> be authentic only in the article).
The development was similar for 'waas' (.5): in SEY
'wu: əs' when interrogative (emphatic), 'wus' when
relative.

16.9 'Um̌tahn̦sgesagt': leider, unfortunately; this is an
unusual meaning, coming from the combined use of it with
'nebbich'. It is 'nebbich' that means 'unfortunate(ly)'
(< Bohemian 'nobohy'). Um̌tahn̦sgesagt is a 'warding-
off-prayer (Abwehr-Gebet), so common Y, -- orig. 'um
Štein sei es gesagt', 'may it (i.e. such misfortune) be
reported about stone (only, and not about anything
alive)'. Contracted into WY 'um̌tahnsgesagt' EY
'um̌tainsgezogt', later 'mǐ̧tainsgezogt', it lost the
phonetic cue to its meaning and the only cue left was
its constant "mate" 'nebbich'. Thus it came to be
taken for a synonym of 'nebbich'; finally it lost its
sympathizing, <u>commiserating</u> nuance, instead, assumed a
deprecating, condemning nuance, jeering at the <u>miser-</u>
<u>able</u> <u>unimportance</u> of the affair in question, e.g.:
"hot er dos gegeben a nedoveh, mǐ̧taingezogt" = <u>some</u>
donation he gave, big deal! (said contemptuously).

16.12f 'ihn...dihn': definitely dist. h c -- in Y the dative
'ihm' and 'dem' is used even for the acc. and H substitutes the acc. f. the dat.

   'koschoh': '<u>kosche</u>' and 'schwer' are Y synonyms, but
   while in Hebrew 'kosche' has most of the meaning of Y
   and G 'schwer', (i.e. hard, difficult, incomprehensible,
   questionable, problematical, puzzling), it is not used
   in Y with the meaning '<u>hard</u>'; hence Reka uses the
   wrong synonym = a malapropism.

   'ober': Y '<u>o</u>' < '<u>ā</u>' which was lengthened because of
   occasional emphasis, but the cluster 'br' later
   shortened the resulting long 'ō' to ô, cf. MHG jâmer,

16.12   Was ist ihm aber schwer: But what is so hard for him.

.14   'alah': allein.

17.1   'daf ͭ: (be)darf = muss!; 'ah raisen': einreissen: strain.

NHG Jämmer, also Y tommer (=perhaps) < Hebrew 'tōmar'.

16.14f   'alah - drahn': delib. dist. h c, here even against R - s.r. 'alahn' = allein; the dropping of the final 'n' is < G dial., prob. not WY, at least not general WY, and especially not in an accented syllable.

.14   'Boiswicht': spelled so (oi) for the sake of uniformity of the transliteration, but here the Hebrew characters (וו) are meant to represent G ö, a kind of high-faluting "fancy" G word to be pronounced in <u>G</u>. The emotionally charged concept of 'vicious man' would <u>normally</u> find expression in the Hebrewism 'Roschoh' rather than in the Germanism 'Bös(e)wicht'. In fact, many such emotionally charged Germanisms were completely lost in MY (because of disuse) -- so were the words "Bösewicht" and "Dieb". Hence 'Böswicht' is quasi a "foreign word" in H's Y, otherwise the ö would have been represented as 'ē' or 'i'.

.15   'ligt': Y; the short ĭ is historically correct. NHG 'liegt' is based on a misspelling of the early G printers.
'den': denn; Y spelling - tradition (like Hebrew) does not write double consonants, but H does, only not consistently, and often f. dist. h c.

17.1   'daf': 'r' plus consonant is usually assimilated to double consonant by H (cf. 'watt' f. 'wart' in .2). The spelling is not too consistent to rely on it absolutely, but it seems to indicate that stop-consonants are doubled, or at least the vowel preceding them shortened, while fricatives (here 'f') long by nature, are written undoubled -- though the vowel is still meant to be short; 'darf' in Y = 'must', 'needs', (NHG, '<u>bedarf</u>'), as in MHG. H gives it both the Y and NHG meaning (=to be permitted to); here both are <u>possible</u> but the Y fits better because it is more forceful.

'ah raisen': 'einreissen' and 'anreissen' have become contaminated even in NHG, thus either <u>could</u> be the prototype conceivably, but MY 'zich ainraissen' (sc. dos gezunt) acquired the meaning also of "to (almost) kill oneself with straining at hard work", so also "ainraissen a velt" = "to strain and leave no stone unturned' -- which neither G word can mean; but cf. L p. 397 # 461 = "to tear around" -- which could only with some difficulty be fit here to mean "to tear at" (the chain, like a chained dog).

17.2 'will'n' (sic!) with apostrophe before 'n' to indicate the encliticized 'ihm'; here the 'n' is auth., Y unaccented 'm' tends to become 'n'. '<u>Tharbus</u>': misspelled twice in Text as Tharb<u>is</u>. Misprint? A͞uthor's ignorance? Hebrew oxytones in Y draw back the accent to the penult so that the vowels in final syllables in Y Hebrewisms are weakened and 'u' and 'i' both are weakened to ə. The misspelling can hardly be an attempt to approximate the pronunciation else it would have been spelled Tarbes̆ (תרבת); 'waisen': 's̆' f. 's', rev. sub. h c against R! Cf. the opposite rev. subst. ('s' f. 's̆') in 'gewis' (.4). There is at least some method in this madness of rev. subst. in that it seems to be avoided where it might cause incomprehensibility by confusion with another word. So f.i. 'rais̆en' (.1) is <u>not</u> reversed as it might lead to confusion with 'raisen' (travel); but even confusion is courted if it helps to add to the "humor".

.5 'tub': tu̯! A # 58 for the various forms of 'tun'. the '-b' comes from the intervocalic -w- in the variant 'tuowen', G dial, not Y.

.6 'sich': ich sehe, auth. OWY Cf. A p. 107.
'genge': gehen, G dial. not Y Cf. A p. 117 # 54.

.7 'Ahnsittler': Einsiedler, hermit. Dist. h c.

.8 'sotter': Cf. L p. 407 # 558.

.9 '<u>Lehach'is</u>': zum Trotz, eigentlich = 'um zu trotzen' (i.e. an infinitive phrase, rather than a noun-phrase); 'ich'n: auth. Y, enclitic '-m' (f. ihm) '-n'. In

17.9   'lo$\overset{\bullet}{s}$ ich'n': lasse ich i<u>hm</u>

.12   kauft sie keine schönen Grieben?: won't you buy some nice greaves?

.13   Das sind Zwerglein! Die sind klein!

.15   Was fällt Ihr ein? What ideas you get!

---

some Y dial. the a $>$ $\bar{a}$ $>$ ɔ $>$ u, due to the emotional charge of the word.

.10   'tub': tue, cf. on 17.5

.11A SD '(kommt)': N.B. the HG in SD -- otherwise = 'kumt'!

.9-13 'stihn... gihn... wih': i $<$ $\bar{e}$; 'betrihben': i $<$ ü; 'schihne': i $<$ ö.

.12   'Grihben': cf.C p.121, Y gri<u>v</u>en, and with assimilation of the '-n' to '-m'; 'grivm'.
'kaaft si': third pers. sing. f. second pers. sing. Archaic G, not Y = formal, but less deferential than second pers. pl. (when used to address a <u>single</u> pers. out of politeness), used to equals and social inferiors. The third pers. pl. is HG and reserved by H for "high society" and "climbers".
'kahn schine': auth. Y grammar, G kei<u>ne</u> schö<u>ne</u>n.

.13   '<u>Horeg</u>-lich': here = Zwerglein, "runts". Hebr. 'horeg', SEY 'hoirig' is puzzling in form and meaning. It is supposedly the present <u>active</u> prtcp., ought to mean 'killer', but it actually means 'battered' and/or 'tattered', -- what the <u>passive</u> partcp. 'h$\bar{a}$rug' (= the 'killed', 'corpse') could be expected to develop into by figurativization. It is our conjecture that <u>the</u> <u>st</u>rong emotional charge of the word changed the a to o before the <u>general</u> Y vowel-change. (This varied according to time and place: it started in the SE (Austria) towards the end of the 13th century and ended NW around the end of the 15th.) At the time of the general Y vowel-change 'harug' was already pronounced 'hor<u>ə</u>g' and the first vowel changed with all the other accented '$\bar{o}$'s from its new 'o' position. It fell together with the <u>original</u> 'horeg'

18.4   heute ist Donnerstag;
        'ham kum': heim komme.

 .6   Mutter leben, dear mother.

        (the active partcp.).
            The semantic development: killed > beaten to
        death > beaten and battered to near death > thoroughly
        beaten > weak(ened) > withered > dwarfish > bedraggled.
        H extends the figure to things, to greaves of abnormally
        shriveled size. In Y it can only be used for 'stunted,
        shriveled, freakish' "beat" people.

 .14   'Doi... joi': auth. WY, < MHG 'dâ...jâ'.
        'sen': sind; dial. variants of 'sind' were 'sīn'
        (later = 'sein'), 'sīnen' (later > 'seinen'); these
        > Y 'sinen', 'seinen' and 'sanen' and by contamination
        'senen' and by syncopation 'sen'. In SEY it went even
        further: 'we are' = 'mir (or ints) zemmer'.

 .15   'fallt': G fällt, Y levels out in favor of the vowel
        of the infinitive; 'Ihr': HG 'Ihnen', cf. 'kaaft Si'
        (.12)

 .15-16   'klahne... ahne': '-e' suffix auth.; there is no
        apocope of the '-e' when it has a grammatically im-
        portant function -- here of putting the adjective used
        pronominally in the pl.

 .15A   SD S.r. "Sie hält eine in die Höhe" -- it is meant
        to be HG; WY would read: 'sie halt...der Hehch'.

 .16   'nu': Y; G 'nun'; 'kost': Y, G 'kostet'; Y regularly
        drops the suffix 't' when the stem ends in a '-d' or
        '-t'. G does so only when there is a vowel change in
        the stem (Cf. G er wird -- ihr werdet; er schilt -- ihr
        scheltet, er hält -- ihr haltet); Y does not change
        the stem-vowel!
        'soi ahne' WY: G 'so eine', SY a soine.

18.1   'Memúchantheh': the person is H's creation, the very
        reference to a fictitious wife of the king's chamber-
        lain, Memuchan, is h and so is the construction of the
        word: 'Memuchante' alone (without 'Madam') or 'Madam
        Memuchan' (without the '-te')would be auth. Y. Madam

18.5 'Ihr': Ihnen, you.

'Memuchante' is archaic in Y as Madam Memuchanin would
be in G. The suffix '-te' is a Hebr. and a Y deriva-
tive for feminine nouns derived from the masculine --
cf. G der Müller, die Müllerin, mod. G Frau Müller,
archaic G Frau Müllerin -- with Y: der miler, die
milerte, froi Miler, froi Milerte.

18.2 'Bazzen': "little bear" = a small silver coin of four
Austrian Kreuzer in value, originally of the city of
Bern, Switzerland, whose coat of arms is a bear, later
current in all of Southern Germany. L p. 397, # 46.
'Hot mir wellen ... gihben': auth. WY, but no longer
EY, which gave up the "double infin." construction and
requires 'hot mir gevolt gibn'; 'soi' EY 'azoi'; 'soll
ich lihben': oaths about the value and cost of
merchandise -- common among traders.
'gelossen': '-s̈' f. 's'. rev. subst.

.3 'drum': for it, i.e. at that price, for the Bazzen.

.4 'Donštik': syncopated < Donnerštik; inauth. dist. h c;
'-rst' > Y '-ršt'.

Jewish scholars of old would usually spend all their
time "learning Torah" and their wives would supposedly
deem themselves happy to be privileged to enable them
to engage in their pious and meritorious preoccupation.
The wives would thus keep house, take care of the family, and earn the living at the same time! The names
of these 'women of valor' (Hebr. 'eyšet ḥayil')
therefore often became the surnames of their husbands,
and later, when family names were made obligatory,
these nickname-like surnames became fixed as family
names. Thus Jews developed matronyms as well as
patronyms. Thus an Abraham would be nicknamed
Abraham 'Sarah's', or 'Serkeles', or 'Serkin', or
even 'Sarahsman' and the son might be surnamed
'Sarahson' -- in all their phonetic variations.
These "gainfully employed" wives would have to "close
out" their businesses on Thursdays to be free Fridays
to prepare for the Sabbath -- especially if they were
itinerant peddlers, as Šidi was.

.5 'Ihr' etc.: You; I'll let (have) one (greave) for a
Groschen (- about 1/2 Batzen);

182

18.8 'Goschen': Mund.

.9 Da (hast du's), grosses Unglück, here, (take it) big
misfortune.

.11 'waisen': wissen.

.13 'denen': tun.

'Ihr' - third prs. sg. formal f. second prs. sg. Cf.
on 17.12.

'ahns': 'eins' = das Stück, a piece. 'Griebe' is fem.
and should be so in Y, but "no one eats just a single
greave", hence the noun is heard mostly in the pl. only
and "one is uncertain" of the gender of the sg. Therefore Šidi uses the neuter! Similarly Weinreich's Dictionary lists the plural only ('grivn'), the Harkavy
lists 'griv', the sg., but he does not indicate genders.
Confusion about sg. and pl. of nouns that are usually
used in the plural only, are not uncommon. Cf. the
history of G 'Birne' ('pear') (bir - bire; bire - biren,
biren -- birne, Birne - Birnen), but Cf. (.10) 'ahne'.

.5A SD 'Kohr fon Kindern': the transliteration should not
mislead -- the SD is, as always, meant to be 'perfect'
HG; Y would be 'fun Kinder'; hence 'Kohr' = Chor.

.6 'Joi, Memme lihben': ja, Mutter leben'; Memme: auth.
WY; on 'leben cf. on

.8 'Goschen': vulgar f. mouth. cf. L p. 371, #211.

.9 'groisse Soch': lit. 'great disease' i.e. 'grand mal'
or epilepsy; more auth. Y 'nechpeh' (< Hebr. נכפה),
'epilepsy', fig. 'pain in the neck', 'big trouble',
'misfortune'. Tendlau (# 448) could not figure out
where 'Soch' and 'sochen' came from and guessed wrong.
'groise': 's' f. 'š' to suggest G 'grausam', dist. h c.

.11 'waisen': so in SY, now, but it is a most recent leveling, most Y speakers, and surely WY speakers in 1828
said 'wissen'; hence dist. h c.

.13 'denen': inauth. h c; '-d; f 't' = rev. subst., 'e' f.
'u', and pleonastic suffix '-nen' f. '-n' -- all not Y.

19.1   'iberich': über euch.

.2   Da (habt ihr eine Griebe und so) verreckt! Habt ihr
     eine miteinander, teilt sie; here (is a greave and so)
     drop dead! (Now that) you have one together, divide
     it among yourselves).

.3   gehen Sie (hi)naus in die Küche, meine Magd zahlt
     Ihnen.

.4   'Tets': tut's.

19.1   'iberich': apparently a contraction of 'über euch',
       on the model of 'übern' = 'über ihn', but hardly
       authentic.

.2   'watt main Kapporoh': lit. 'seid mein Versöhnungs-
     opfer', 'be my atonement sacrifice', i.e. 'die in my
     stead for the atonement of my sins', but weakened to
     a simple curse 'drop dead!'. Cf. on 12.10 and L
     p. 378 #286.

     'thaltsi': teilt sie, 'sie' = 'it' the greave;
     written together as a sort of "orthographic humor" à
     la the "spelling gokes" of our Artemus Ward; perhaps
     also to call attention to the richer, feminine
     (dissyllabic) rhyme. There is added h in dividing a
     single greave that is runt-like, among many, whereas
     normally one person eats many greaves.

.3   'giht': Reka is more polite to Sidi than vice versa
     -- she uses the 2nd prs. pl. for the polite sg. (Cf.
     on 17.12); psychologically the opposite would be ex-
     pected -- salespeople are usually more obsequious to
     clients than vice versa; the variation is probably
     not meant to indicate a difference in the social
     standing, or attitudes of the two to one another, but
     it is due rather to H's straining for as much deviation
     from HG as possible. It would be too subtle to assume
     that it is this very psychological reversal of styles
     of address that H intended to base his h on.

     'Kuch': Küche; the omission of the umlaut is UG dial.,
     h c, not Y, where all forms (kich, Kech, Kach)
     derive from Küche, i.e. < 'ü'; one Y dial. 'koch'
     derives < 'kuch'. (Y tends to lower vowels before
     gutturals, G - to prevent the umlauting in such cases.)

19.3   'maad': Magd, < the variant'maid' (with palatalization
        of the '-g', so common in MHG and now in Upper Fran-
        conian (Vogtld.); strangely, this 'ai' < '-age' did
        not develop identically with Germanic 'ai' in EY, where
        it became ɔi/ɔə (like the MHG 'û'), instead of the ex-
        pected ɛi/ai < Germanic 'ai', -- probably because of a
        difference in the operative time of the phonetic changes
        involved.

        'ZahltSi': (sic! -- written together, Cf. on 19.2) =
        zahlt Ihnen, or conceivably 'zahlt Ihr', i.e. either
        3rd pers. pl., or sg. fem.; either is used as formal
        address for second prs. sg.; either is anacoluthic with
        'giht'. All this "incoherence" is delib. dist. h c,
        as is the use of the acc. f. the dat.

  .4   'Tetš': prob. = tut's - tut das, though conceivably
        '-ts' may be Y and G dial. second prs. pl. suffix
        (< Germanic dual) still current in Gal. Y and SG --
        especially since 'das' is unnecessary here. Reka's
        ordering the children to eat bread with the greave is
        "realistic", in that all mothers, especially mothers of
        "modern means", would insist that 'delicacy' should
        serve as "relish" to a whole meal (of bread) rather
        than just as a between-meals "nosh" (snack, "taste")
        that would spoil the appetite, if not the stomach. But
        here it is a fraction of a single, shriveled greave!

  .5   'Frešt': vulgar, because of irritation; 'ešt' is used
        for humans, 'frest' for animals, including "two-legged
        animals".

  .5AB SD are meant to be perfect HG (cf. 'thailt' against
        thalt in .2), but 'Brod' with 'd' is a misprint (?),
        not a Yiddishism, may, of course, be a kind of un-
        conscious HHG of H himself! In final position voiced
        and voiceless consonants are pronounced alike in both
        Y and G, but in G they are still differentiated in
        spelling, but in Y even the spelling is identical in
        permanently final position: cf. Eng. 'death' - dead',
        G 'Tod' - 'tot', Y 'toit'. As 'Brot' rhymes with 'Tod',
        H may have suddenly become 'insecure', uncertain as to
        whether 'Brot' should be spelled with 't' or 'd' and
        since 't' was definitely Y, he decided (unconsciously)
        that G must be 'd'! N.B. SY also differentiates the

19.6   hat man einen Augenblick

.7   'tik': dick

.8   Was steht man aus, mit den Kindern, unbeschrien; what
      one (must) endure with the children, knock wood!

.8A   SD schiebt ... zur Tür

---

spelling when the final <u>does not stay final permanently</u>,
i.e. when the word can add a suffix that begins with a
voiced sound. Cf. tin<u>t</u> - kind (= pure rhyme!), but
tinter - kinder (=impure rhyme). In 'Stuk' u is
"defective" spelling for 'ü' for which in H's time
there no longer existed a precise symbol in Y and writers
vacillated between the 'i' (the unrounded 'ü' -- the most
common rendering), and the 'u' -- the 'defective' (Hebr.
ו) and rarer representation, and וו -- the oldest de-
signation, and the rarest, because <u>it</u> had become too
ambiguous.

.6   '<u>Menuhoh</u>' pronounced mənúxə, stronger than 'Ruh' be-
      cause < Hebr.
      'Nahgenblik': metanalysis, 'an Agenblik' > 'a Nagenblik!
      Cf. Eng. 'newt' and 'apron' < 'an ewt' and ' a napron',
      but in H it is inauth. a delib. dist h c.

.7   'tik': 'dick', 't' f. 'd' - rev. subst.; furthermore,
      here 'dick' suggests "Dickkopf" (stupid), wheres the
      pretended intent is 'voll angespannt' = ' fully tense
      to the point of bursting'.

.8   'umbschrie':   'unbeschrien', more common 'unberu-
      fen' = lit. '(Evil not being) called hither', i.e.
      'knock on wood' (to ward off evil). G, not quite Y,
      which typically prefers here the more emotional
      Hebrewism 'keneynah hore' (kein ayin hore = no evil
      eye). The 'm' for 'n' is auth. Y, a generalization
      of 'um' for 'un' in <u>all</u> positions just from <u>such</u> a
      position as here, i.e. where the dental 'n' <u>is</u>
      assimilated to labial 'b' and thus > 'm'. This
      generalizing is partly due to the fact that 'un'
      < 'und' and 'un-' = 'not' became homophones and 'um-'
      helped to avoice confusion and unintelligibility. In
      SEY the confusion had become even greater: 'un-',
      'in' and 'und' all > 'in'! To further reduce ambiguity
      the prep. 'um' and the prefix 'um-' meaning 'round',

'turn around and change into' respectively, came to be
used in Y much less than in G. The syncope of the 'e'
is prob. delib. dist. h c, and so is the <u>word order</u>,
since 'umbschrie', in spite of the <u>comma</u>, modifies
'stiht mer ois', and Reka is thus 'knocking wood' on
'suffering', as if to prevent the Devil from inter-
fering with <u>it</u>, rather than on 'di Kinder' from whom
she really intends to ward off the evil. 'mit <u>di</u>
Kinder': auth. Y, cf. 5A <u>SD</u> 'unter den Kinde<u>rn</u>',
where HG is intended as always,

19.8   SD 'Schiebt'... 'Türe' are intended. 'zu' is incorrect
f. 'zur' (cf. 'zur' 24.4A), but the idiom <u>is</u> G not Y,
where the normal prep. is not 'zu', but 'durch'.
'Tür<u>e</u>' with the added 'e' <u>is</u> G, but almost HHG, an
archaic form typical now especially of speakers in-
secure in, and not "native" to HG.

.9-11   Zetulpe's speech is a mish-mash of Y and G --
typical of the "climber" and would-be "elegant"
show-off: so .9 '<u>doi fon</u>', .11 '<u>ahns fon</u>'; 'pro<u>wi</u>hren':
is delib. dist., correct <u>G dial</u>., but neither typical
Y nor HG; 'aich' in .11 <u>could</u> stand f. 'euch', since
the rounding of the vowels (and diphthongs) is left
undesignated now and both would be spelled alike. The
questionmark at the end of .11, where we would expect
an exclamation mark, since the sentence is a warning
and threat, and therefore in the nature of a negative
command = something like "should any one of you as much
as stir!" --, this questionmark may be a <u>delib</u>. into-
nation-guide for a high-pitched nervously distorted
screaming of the last word (rihren) and that is probably the purpose also of the four dashes within
which 'rihren' is set: pause and raise the pitch!

'fon Winter': Peter v. Winter (1754-1825), composer of
operas and Singspiele.

.12-15 The song is obviously meant to be HG, hence normally
.13 and .15 'Broich' and 'Boich' should be expected to
be read 'Bräuche' and 'Bäuche' -- in spite of our
transliteration, and in spite of Zetulpe's "faulty"
reproduction of the Text. But 'Boich' is spoken by a
child and would be expected to speak Y, the h would
then come from the destroyed rhyme, or else, with the

20.2   'Hiefele': Töpflein, potty.

.3   langen Sie mir ein Zwiebelchen: hand me a little
       onion.

.4   mach' Sie schnell, ich will eine Tunke schmoren;
       be quick I want to simmer a cream sauce (for the
       soup)

.5   wo sie sind; where they are.

.5A   'zest': zerrt; pulls, treibt an, urges on.

.8   for all I care, let her not (get up).

.9   Eure Gassenstreiche: your street-music; Lausbübereien:
       pranks.

---

       rhyme preserved on the basis of 'oi' from Zetulpe's
       relapse into Y. The former is the more probable. H
       delib. makes her err and say (.13) 'mainen' instead
       of the correct 'mainem' -- to show her ignorance of
       the fine points of HG grammar and her slipping into Y.
        'Folgen' governs the dat. in HG, the acc. in Y;
       however, the Y acc. here would be 'main'; 'mainen' is
       thus incorrect both in Y and G, is HHG and h.

19.20 SD 'fellt ... ein'; = 'chimes in' as well as "suddenly
       interrupts".

20.2   'Hiefele': < dimin. Hafen = Topf, hence Häfelein,
       here = Nachttopf, chamberpot. Cf. Eng. 'potty' in
       child-speech. L p. 375 # 254.

.3   'Zwihfelle': the 'f' is G dial. and Rz, the rev.
       subst. here is "double": a voiceless fricative ('f')
       for a voiced, explosive ('b'). The EY is 'Zwiebel'
       < G, or now more common 'Zibele' < Slavic.
       The whole scene (1-9) of mixing music, cooking, and
       eliminating - problems of a child is typical of the
       'broad', vulgar h of H -- à la Rabelais.

.4   'ainbrenne': to simmer fat, onions (and at times
       flour) for a sauce, to flavor and/or thicken a soup
       with. Y and SG. L p. 350, #7.

20.5 Sarcastic; 'wu': auth. Y.

.5A SD 'zešt': we haven't been able to document the verb,
the context seems to yield the meaning "to urge one
to move on": hardly a printing error f. "zerrt", as
one substitution of one 'r' by 's' is conceivable, but
less so two substitutions.

.6 'ahngenahgelt': the long 'ah' is auth. WY; EY 'ɔ/u'.
The lengthening is due to the extra emphasis on the
adv. and prefix 'an-'; cf. the difference in quantity
of the 'o's in Eng. 'on' and 'of(f)' between them as
prepositions ("on it", "of it") and as adverbs ("put
it on", "take it off"), G dialects lengthen similarly
and even HG does in some adverbs, though not in all.
(Cf. 'in', the prep., and 'ein-' the adv. and prefix
< earlier 'în', < still older 'in-').

.9 'Gassenstraach': prob. = Gassenhauer; streetsong;
perhaps a H coinage in that he expected his audience
to equate 'hauen' with 'streichen' and thereby make
a h slang term even more h, and top the h by having
Reka use it sarcastically for the noise that the
children were making on the street beneath her window
and calling the noise 'street music'. Lit. the
compound means street-pranks-- the sg. and pl. would
be indistinguishable -- but one does not quite 'drive
away' ('fertraiben') a prank or pranks.
Possibly the meaning is to "stop the pranks".
L p. 368 # 177.

21.1   Klimpre nachher weiter; continue your jangling later.

.2   Bete lieber jetzt das Nachmittagsgebet; better pray
        now the afternoon-prayer.

21.1   'noicher': nachher, auth. WY. L p. 390 # 398; it is
        emphatic and contrasted with 'iz' (now) in .2.

.2   'ohr': pray < Latin 'orare': specific technical
        (religious) term in WY for the obligatory prayers.
        This remnant of Judeo-Latin was displaced in EY between
        1720 and 1800 by 'davenen', partly because inner
        phonetic developments made it fall together with
        several other words and it thus became somewhat am-
        biguous. The history and the plethora of offered
        etymologies of the words for prayer in Jewish lan-
        guages, the reasons for their origins and their dis-
        placements make one of the most intriguing chapters
        in linguistic and cultural history.
            Here are some of the results of the research,
        briefly, without the proofs.
            By and large Jewish religious terms are derived
        from Hebrew. Words for praying are not -- because of
        peculiar circumstances: the obligatory public
        prayers require a quorum of ten adult males (='minyan').
        Jews used to live sparsely scattered and the quorum
        was not always easily gotten together. When calling
        another: "Come to prayers" the sacred Hebrew term
        could not be used with "unwashed hands" and the basin
        for hand-washing was far away at the prayer-house!
        The vernacular for 'prayer' was taboo, if it was also
        being used by the "heathens" for prayers to "idols".
        The only "out" of the dilemma was to find a neutral,
        non-cultic vernacular term. The pre-Christian Latin
        'orare, legere, benedicere' were not particularly
        "obligatory" in Roman idolatry, and were therefore
        available for synagogue functions: thus arose WY
        'oren': to pray, 'leyen' (later 'leyenen') to chant
        the Torah-reading, 'bentshen' to utter obligatory
        "blessings". Thus -- the exiles to Rome and their
        descendants.
            The exiles to Hellas similarly picked a neutral
        Hellenic word 'militein', in modern Judesmo (Judeo-
        Spanish) 'meldar'. Strange that the speakers of
        'Ladino" (='Latin'!, but is the older term for
        'Judesmo') should have picked a Greek and not a

21.2 <u>Latin</u> term. Lesson: Sephardic (=Spanish) Jews are
descendants of exiles to Hellas! Their using only one
term, 'meldar' for both 'praying' and 'Torah-reading'
against the two terms of Ashkenazy (=German < Roman)
Jews 'oren' and 'leyenen', is due to a difference in
the style of public worship of these two "ethnic"
groups. In a Sephardic-Spanish congregation the
precentor (prayer-leader) <u>chants all</u> the prayers in
their entirety aloud, i.e. similar to Torah-chanting.

In an Ashkenazy congregation the individual con-
gregants recite and say most of the prayers "to themselves" and with certain small exceptions the precentor only chants aloud the beginnings and endings
of each individual prayer.

In Lithuanian Y 'oren' > 'oyern' and it fell together with the word for 'ears' ('eyern' < G 'Ohren')
for 'honor' (< G 'Ehre'); 'eyer' for 'eggs' (< G
'Eier': 'eyer'). Many Lithuanian Jews in the 18th
century were itinerant peddlers and craftsmen. They
were "caught short" in the afternoons away from a
Jewish house and had to pray "in private" in non-
Jewish homes. They had to beg the host to allow them
to worship <u>undisturbed</u> (one is required to whisper
the Eighteen Blessings - the Amidah - to oneself, while
standing, quasi at attention, facing East, and without
any interruption). To the inquiry of the host what
kind of worship that was, the Jew naively gave the
literal etymologic translation of the Hebrew term for
the 'afternoon-prayer', ('<u>minha</u>' from the meal-'<u>offer-
ing</u>' due in the Jerusalem Temple in the <u>afternoon</u>) and
told him: "I have to perform 'minha' a 'gift offering'
to God." The host did not know that '<u>minha</u>' was only
<u>one</u> of the three obligatory prayers and that its
literary meaning of 'gift' was irrelevant now, and
simply understood that the Jews call their form of
worship 'offering', in Lithuanian: 'dovinati'.
Lithuanian servant-girls in Jewish homes "checked"
whether they could already feed the children, whether
they had already performed their <u>morning</u> prayers -
'dovinati', or called them to those prayers, or even
led them in those prayers (documented!). From the
servant-girl the term spread to the children, from
them to parents who often complained to the teachers
that they did not even succeed to enable their pupils
to 'dovinati', pardon, do 'dovenen', since they were

21.2 speaking Y now and had to use a Y infinitive-suffix and not a Lithuanian. The famous poverty (together with scholarship) of the Lithuanian Jew sent him to his less poor coreligionists to serve as teacher -- all over Eastern Europe, and he promised the not-so scholarly non-Lithuanians that he would teach their children "to more than davenen".

There are over a <u>dozen</u> "seriously" offered etymologies for 'davenen' -- all the way from English 'dawn' through Latin 'divinare' to Arabic-Persian 'divan' to MHG 'doenen', not to speak of the Hebrew etyma --. They are all phony!

'ohr lieber': prayers are obligatory only on <u>adult males</u>. For women to perform the obligatory prayers was an "extra act of piety, beyond the call of duty" -- in which only the elderly, old-fashioned married women indulged for extra "merit". Even they would sooner perform the <u>morning</u> prayer and only more rarely the afternoon and/or evening prayers. The h is that Reka should expect that a girl, a would-be "sophisticated, enlightened" and ambitious Zetulpe, should give up her fashionable singing and piano-playing for such <u>extreme</u> piety. That is just "incongruous"!

'geschaider': 'd' f. 't' rev. subst. even though it is against the R! Dist. h c.

.3 'wer': werde, fut. aux. vaccillates in WY between 'werden' and 'weln'. In G 'werden' as the fut. aux. started in NW Germany ca. 1325 and reached SE ca. 1450 (Cf. Paul, <u>Mhd. Grammatik</u> #278b and 297). EY has 'weln' only. 'wern' < 'werdn' is only the passive aux. in EY.

'f̲attik': '-ar' auth. Y, but cf. .13 f̲ettik! Prob. both 'f̲attik' and 'f̲ettik' are inauth. Y (though auth. G dial.) and H's delib. dist. h c; 'f̲artik' is auth. EY and 'f̲ertik' -- WY.

.4 'schlupperts̓': schlurft, shuffles; SG, not Y. '-s̓' is used "adverbially", it "anticipates" 'nain'. SD 'zu̲r': here -- correct; cf. 19A SD 'zu' -- incorrect.

21.6   H pretends to mean: "I'll be glad to get away from
here for a while", but he suggests: "I'll be glad to
get beside myself" h c.

.7   'amale': einmal, once for all. L p. 351 #15;
'Gekihf': Keiferei, quarreling, L p. 368 #181; on
'Ge-' as a favorite of H for coining abstracts with
pejorative connotations cf. on 15.16.

.9   'send': sind, are; cf. A p. 120 #55.

.10   'worum': warum, why; L p. 415 #628; 'a' 'o' may
be meaningless variations, but originally 'wórum' in
WY meant 'because', while 'warum' meant 'why'. They
fell together and each could mean either. H probably knew the difference and delib. uses the 'wrong'
word h c.

.11   'schenner': schöner, auth. Y. Shortening of the
vowel (hence the doubling of the 'n') occurs sporadically in Y and G before '-er' (but not necessarily
in the same words in the various dialects, but rather
independently). Cf. NHG 'Jammer' and 'Mutter' MHG
'jâmer', 'mǔoter' and Gal. Y 'yumer' (u < â), 'mǔtr'.

.11   Sarcastic!

.12   'sellt': imperfect subjunctive (to express pres. unreality) with umlaut and unrounding of the 'ö' to
'e' Prob. auth. WY. L p. 385, #348.

.13   'ober': WY s.b. 'aber', EY 'ober'; MHG 'ǎ-' > G and
WY 'a', EY 'ɔ/u', but '-er' tended to shorten the
preceding vowel (cf. on 21.11), so that 'ɔ:' < NHG
'a' was shortened before such ɔ: > 'u' in SEY.

.13   'warrn': werden, inauth. general WY, but auth.dial.

21.13-22.1   'fettik - witterwettik': Rz - primary accent
rhymed with secondary accent (many such rhymes cf.
16.10f and passim).

21.13-22.1   The 'e's may represent Zetulpe/s aim to "approach"
HG -- her parents pronounce 'a' in this position!
However, she pronounces 'witter', her parents -

22.1   'widerwertik', disgusting.

  .2   'nain: nicht; 'graid': grad.

  .3   sagt grün ... blau

  .4   'abzapple': abzappeln, to fret, worry, quarrel.

---

correctly 'wi<u>dd</u>er'. H is apparently simply <u>in</u>-<u>consistent</u> and distorts <u>indiscriminately</u> h c. Cf.
for dist. also 'an <u>dihn</u> Thir' (.9) and '<u>das</u> Mund'
(23.4)

22.2   'nain': ungrammatical dist. f. 'nicht' h c.
'graid': grad; delib. dist. inauth. in <u>every</u> Y and
G dial. It is meant to show up the HHG of the
ignorant "climber" Zetulpe on the basis that since
some WY 'ā's < G 'ei', therefore she transposes
(falsely) <u>other</u> WY 'a's (that are also 'ā' in G) into
'ei'.
        The linguistic correspondences are:

Examples	MHG	NHG	WY	NEY	SEY	Engl.
Bein-bone	ei	ei	ā	ey	ay	o
tragen-drag	a-	ā-	ā-	ɔ	u	a
Graf-grave	ā	ā	<u>oi</u>	ɔ	u	a

        Zetulpe exposes her ignorance: she does not
know that 'grad' in G is the same as in her WY.

  .3   'saacht': sagt, auth. in some WY and G <u>dial</u>. but
not general WY; Y 'g' + 't' > '-kt' in <u>pronuncia</u>-<u>tion</u>, but the spelling ignores the loss of the voicing
(here: of the 'g') <u>before</u> a voiceless suffix, just as
Engl. spelling ignores such loss in case of the
suffix '-ed' coming <u>after</u> a voiceless consonant (cf.
Engl.'prized' and 'priced') -- in order to maintain a
uniform, recognizable graphic image for stems of words
and their affixes.
'bloi': blau, auth. WY, even though usually G au >
WY ā, here MHG had 'blā' in non-inflected forms, and
'blâw-' in inflected ones; the WY is derived from the
former, the G from the latter.

  .4   'abzapple': zappeln = to squirm, fidget, toss one's
limbs convulsively (like when hanging), be restless

194

22.6 Tag ... Glück.

.7 zehn Gäule: ten horses.

.8 only I must arrange it with the authorities (tell the
maid).

22.4 and/or worried; 'abzapple' therefore should mean 'work
off' one's 'zappeln' or keep at it till exhausted and
then stop. Here, because of its apparent reference to
the disagreement of the parents (in .2 - .3), H would
seem to use it with a new meaning: either "stop quarreling" or "stop raging (at me)", i.e. ("I let them
vent their anger (at me)" till it dissipates. The original image of violent, convulsive, unavailing "kicking"
endeared the word to H for the humor of it. The
Swabian meaning "to pull and kick one another" (cf. L
p. 350 # 4) might have been intended by H as an added
connotation, but it must have been lost on his
audience.

.5 'was': 's' f. 'š', rev. subst., most frequent with
this word.

.6 Sarcastic: "sure, such a lucky change (i.e. to be
chosen Queen of the Land in a contest) one can have any
day!
'Taach': Tag. 'ch' is G dial. (Frankfurt, among others),
not general WY, though there may have been a WY dial.
with such phonology.

.7 'Nahn -- nain--': the Y and G words for 'no', one after
the other, within the dashes, are probably meant to
indicate a pause, a change of mood to resolute determination, with a concomitant change in intonation, pitch
and pronunciation. The last has the psychological
meaning of giving up her "Yiddishkait" and becoming a
'Goye' and, therefore, speaking like one! On another
level this using first the Y and then G pronunciation
of the same word, with the punctuation indicating the
hesitating pause, might indicate that Zetulpe caught
herself using Y, shifted to G, then, in her disturbance
and her annoyance with herself thought of the Y meaning
of her G 'nain' (which is the number 9) and blurted out
("no, not 9 but) 10 horses!" All of which adds to the
h.

22.10   um Punkt vier Uhr

.11   pompern: hämmern, klopfen.

22.7   'zehe': '-n' – apocope, not WY but G dial; 'Gail':
      auth. > G Gäule, '-e' -- apocope and unrounding of
      'äu' to 'ai'.

.8   'nehr': nur, not Y. EY has 'nor';. this adverb is
      <u>usually</u> unaccented and enclitic, the sequence then
      becomes 'u' plus 'r' plus 'consonant' (from the
      following word) and in such a sequence (vowel plus
      guttural plus consonant) the vowel becomes <u>lowered</u>
      in Y. <u>If</u> 'nehr' is auth. G dial. then it must have
      developed from unaccented position into 'nər' and
      was later lengthened to 'nehr' in very <u>emphatic</u>
      position, which this adverb also has, less usually,
      but not too infrequently. (What it rarely has is
      <u>normal</u> accentuation!)

      'anstellen': arrangieren, not particularly Y in <u>this</u>
      meaning. In addition to a number of other meanings
      (to place -in heaps, -in employment), it connotes 'to
      pretend and masquerade, to cut capers or pranks, play
      tricks, do mischief' -- which connotations are pro-
      bably delib. intended as h <u>associations</u>, though <u>not</u>
      as <u>meanings</u>.

.8-11   The pretended meaning is: "I'll have to arrange with
      the maid that she tell the (house) watchman nicely --
      that exactly about four o'clock he should knock on
      the door". But what it is intended to sound like to
      H's (imaginary) "audience" (H could hardly have ex-
      pected his comedy to be <u>staged</u>) is: "I'll have to
      arrange with the (Government) Authorities that they
      should tell the Guard nicely -- that exactly about
      four he should boom-boom at the door".
      'Maacht': the WY word for 'maid' is 'maad' (so used
      by H in 19.3); 'macht' (on the 'aa' see below) is G
      dial. (Frankfurt, among others) for 'maid', but
      connotes 'Power, Government, Authorities', in HG.
      <u>Here</u> H uses 'Maacht', the ambiguous word, deliberate-
      ly to suggest the HG meaning, and uses the high-
      sounding "anstellen" instead of the simple "sagen",
      to confirm that suggestion, only to pause (- -),
      then finish with the trivial h and slightly obscene

22.8-11   (see below) 'to boom boom' at the door.

       Such surprise endings are very effective as h --
but H is a master of <u>every kind</u> of h and he strains for
more and more h, "doesn't miss a trick". Zetulpe's
monologue here can serve as a "classic" example of the
plethora of the types and levels. It is no exaggeration to say that practically almost every word is "forced" into a h mould -- even articles and prepositions!
That the result may be "too much" and the constant
repetition of the same types of distortion even become
tiresome and make the h appear as obviously forced,
as it <u>actually is</u> -- is unfortunately also true. Yet
there is no denying the wealth, the skill, the virtu-
osity: comic characterizations, intensified by placing
them in comic situations, the queerness hightened by
their funny, "low-class" type of speech, their despe-
rate, hopeless attempts to "hide their inferiority",
the high-faluting, ill-fitting style of supposedly High
Society, the pillorying of obscurantism, the implied
ridiculing of social ills, the clever punning, the
multi-leveled jokes, the double-entendre with its
humorously effective, even though obscene suggestiveness -- and finally the "slapstick" vulgarities and
the forced distortions to suggest "funny" dialect --
all these make H's comedy just <u>packed</u> full of laughs
-- all be it at times lowbrow and forced laughs.

       'anstellen mit der Maacht' - on still another level -
can mean "to do mischief (i.e. to behave improperly)
with the maid"; but for a German the epitome of the
humor is prob. contained in the single moment when
'Maacht' is mistaken for "Government" and 'Wechter' for
"Guard", the agent of the Government, both capital
'G's. and lowly Zetulpe grandiloquently talks of arro-
gating to herself the right to make arrangements for
those august bodies and trouble and use them to boom-
boom at her door!

.8   'maacht': 'aa' dist. h c; in Y <u>and</u> G. '-cht' has the
tendency to shorten originally long vowels and not to
lengthen short ones (Cf. MHG 'gebrächt' >Y and G
'gebrächt'.

.9   'dihn': 'dem' delib. dist. h c, acc. f. dat.
'Wechter': Wächter - watchman; the usual word for
house-watchman is 'Hausknecht'. "Wächter" <u>can</u> also

22.9   mean a Government guard, almost as august as a police-
man in a Polite State -- that's why H prefers it.

.8ff   'fain saacht': say (it) nicely, i.e. "request polite-
ly or respectfully" -- this phrase further strengthens
the suggestion that 'Maacht' and 'Wechter' refer to
Government. On this level the adv. 'fain' would be
misplaced and there would be a h dist. of the word-
order, since it would be Zetulpe who would have to say
it 'fain' to the 'Maacht' and not the 'Maacht' to the
'Wechter'! On still another level, 'fain sacht(e)' is
a very frequent G expression for "very softly, very
gently" -- which the surprise-ending (.11) 'pompern'
(boom-boom) turns into an oxymoron.

.10   'Punkte': in this particular word the '-e- may
possibly come from the slurring of 'punktum' and
another 'um' is added because the '-e' is conceived
as the adverbial suffix '-e' (cf. 'amoile' f. 'einmal');
'a': possibly transposed from 'fire' (conceived as
'fira'); 'ə' is suffixed in SEY to the numbers 1-12
to indicate the hour; this 'ə' may be a remnant of
'uf (dem Saiger)' = 'o'clock'. 'A' before numbers
in Y also means 'approximately' (but not in time-
telling, not to indicate the hour of the day!) and
it is very likely that H concocted another inauth.
oxymoron for Zetulpe 'punkte ...a' to supposedly mean
'exactly ... approximately'.

.11   'pompern': the choice of the unlikely word is due to
its euphemistic use for 'farting'. Not Y! L p. 395
445.

'an dihn Thir': delib. dist. h c -- here the inauthentic (i + h) is exaggerated beyond belief: to our
knowledge there is not a single Y or G dialect in
which 'Tür' is masculine.

.11A   SD 'Poise': pronounce 'Pause'.

.13   The book is a manual on etiquette; by leaving out the
first word of the title ("Ueber") and adding the
adverbial phrase 'in Bett' with a pretended innocent

22.16   Wie man sich bei den Hohen (Kreisen) aufführen soll.

.17   'haint':   heute.

.18   'helfšst':   hilft's;   'toin':   tun.

22.13   meaning (if I could only have the manual to <u>read</u> it in
bed!) H manages to be obscenely suggestive and crack a
"huge joke":   (="If only I could have intercourse with
people in bed tonight").

.14   'in':   Y f. G im, i.e. Y here omits the def. art.
'dorich':   durch; in most Y dialects (exception:
<u>partly</u> NEY) high vowels (u + i) plus guttural conso-
nant (r, ch), plus another consonant, become lowered
(to 'e' and 'o'); in some dialects the heavy consonant cluster ('rch') develops a svarabhakti-vowel
to ease the pronunciation, hence: 'dorich' pronounced
'dɔrəx' OHG and modern G dial. developed similarly
(cf. OHG 'duruch' spelled 'duru̱h') Hebr. too generally
developed such 'parasitic' vowels to ease the pronunciation of clusters -- most penult-accented Hebrew
words with the final closed syllable with the vowel
'ɛ̄' or 'a' (the so-called "segolates") were originally
monosyllabic, heavy clusters.   Cf. Hebr. *'dark' >
'derɛx' but when inflected it is still 'dă̌rki' or that
'qošet' stands side by side with 'qušet'.   In some Y
dial. the svarabhakti-vowel caused umlaut: 'durix' >
'dürich' > 'dirix' > 'derəx' > 'dɛrx'; where lowering
happened before svarabhakti, the development was
'dorix' > *'dörix' > 'derax' etc.   See the vowel-
triangle on C 5.6 for visualizing the meaning of
'lowering' vowels.   While most Y dial. lower only one
step, some lower <u>two</u> steps.   Y speakers of such
dialects are often teased to pronounce their Y for
G 'vierzehn' (14) which is generally Y 'fertsɛn'.   H
vacillates between lowering just one step, or (usually)
two steps; at times he seems to make a distinction
between the two degrees of lowering: the only half-
successful attempts of the climber to abandon Y and
transpose his Y into HG result in one-step lowering.
Cf. on 9.13 and 21.1 (G 'fertig - widerwertig' rendered both 'fa̱ttig - witterwa̱ttik').   <u>Either</u> lowering
is prob. <u>inauth</u>. f. <u>gen</u>. <u>WY</u>. H distorts!   Cf. L p. 351
19.

22.20   'Helling': lichte Stelle.

 .21   'Stelling': Stellungen.

22.16   'Hoiche': Hohe (Leute), high-class people, Y; '-ch'
in 'hoch' was not lost (> 'h') in Y (as it was in HG)
between vowels.

 .18   'helfṡt': = 'helftṡ' = G 'hilfts' metathesis of 't'
and 'ṡ' h c; '<u>e</u>' auth. Y, vowel of the inf. leveled out
throughout the whole pres. Cf. A # 96.

'toin': tun, auth. < 'tân', a MHG variant of 'toun'.

 .20f   'Helling': 'liegt' (as against 'darkness') L p. 374,
#248.
'Stelling': Stellungen, poses; apocope of old sg. and
pl. suffix '-e' left sg. and pl. still alike.
NHG and Y both attempt to introduce distinctions
between sing. and pl. -- distinctions which got lost
in NHG time, due to the leveling down of all unaccented vowels to 'e', and the radical apocope of the final
'-e' (in G only under specific configurations, in Y --
everywhere). G extended the '-en' pl. suffix to most
feminines (especially polysyllables -- because for
<u>such</u> there were no 'models' for umlauting) and also
extended the '-e', umlaut with or without the suffixes
'-e' or '-er' (with umlaut) (Cf. G Macht- Mächte, but
Schlacht - Schlachten; Tag - Tage, but Schlag -
Schläge; Vater - Väter, but Adler (sg. and pl.);
Faden - Fäden, but Kragen (sg. and pl.).
In Y (and SG) where the '-e' apocope was more
thorough, both the '-en', '-er', and the umlaut had to
be extended further than in Standard NHG. So G pl.
Tisch<u>e</u>, Y Tisch<u>en</u>; Y and SG pl. Täg and Krägen; G
pl. Nas<u>en</u>, Y nez (or nezer); G Bäume, Y beymer/
baymer; G pl. Stück<u>e</u>, Y Ꞩtik<u>er</u>. In fact, both Y and
G had to re-organize their pl.-systems and each did it
independently of the other -- with a great deal of
overlapping identities retained from the old pluraliz-
ation devices, or newly extended with identical
"logic".
So both Y and G pl. of 'Stellung' is 'Stellungen',
OY 'Stellung<u>e</u>', MY 'Stellung'. -- Were it not for
'Helling', one might be tempted to see a new-pl.
device in extending umlauting to an <u>unaccented</u> <u>suffix</u>

22.20f (changing '-ung' to '-ing'). But 'Hell<u>ing</u>' and 'Stell-
<u>ing</u>' are also G (not Y!) words in their own right, rare,
not even listed in general G dictionaries. (Sprach-
Brockhaus, 1935), lists both with meanings that do not
fit our context at all, not even as h.

'Helling' was probably locally well-known in the
meaning of "Heller" (=Austrian coin, = 'penny') and
'Stelling' was a distortion for Rz; the h would con-
sist then in using a malapropism 'Helling' (= Heller)
for 'He<u>lle</u>' (= bright light), and the Rz, sg. for pl.
in 'Stell<u>ing</u>'. The fact that the suffixes '-ing' and
'-ung' were "equivalent" in Primitive German (Urger-
manisch) could not have been known to H in 1828. How-
ever, SEY does change every G 'u' to 'i' and <u>old</u>-time
Y '-ung'-words therein <u>are</u> pronounced '-ing', but most
'-ung'-words in Y are <u>recent</u> "cultural" <u>loanwords</u> and
are pronounced as in G: '-ung'.

.22A SD 'gebet': '<u>e</u>' is archaic (Biblical), not quite
HHG, but almost, and typical of an original Y speaker
of that time (1828) "going over" to G.

.22 'Ha<u>rr</u>lich': H<u>e</u>rrlich; a recent cultural loanword in Y
and therefore pronounced '<u>e</u>' even in Y, and just there-
fore given <u>Y</u> phonology by <u>H</u> h c. Y and G both would
require 'herrlich<u>e</u>', unless there were a comma after
it, so that it would be the predicate of an ellipti-
cal sentence: "(= it is) splendid, Zetulpe". As it
stands (without the comma) it is an attributive adj.
and is another dist. h c.

The last line and the two last words in the line
before it, starting with "Adolf von Knigge..." are
not in H's Text.

.24f *Knigges Werk iber den Umgang mit Menschen.- Adolf
von Knigge, 1752-1796. <u>Ueber</u> <u>den</u> <u>Umgang</u> <u>mit</u> <u>Menschen</u>,
1788* is not part of the H Text, but <u>our</u> note.

23.2   Weisszeug, linen.

.3   'Fingerlich': Ringe.

.4   wird...Augen.

.5   'war': werde.

.6f   'schoit - Hoit': schaut - Haut

.8f   'klozzen - ferkozzen': glotzen - verkürzen, stare -
        amuse (make the time pass away fast)

23.1-3 'main': dist. f. 'maine'; the '-e' suffix of the pl.
        ending of the attributive adj. did not suffer apocope
        in Y, or, at the least, it was restored by "System-
        zwang".

.1   'kommen': 'o' G, Y 'u'.

.2   'Waiszaich': 'ch' for 'g' -- G dial. 'ai' for 'eu' --
        auth. Y unrounding L p. 413 # 607.

.3   'Fingerlich': Y and NHG (Fingerlein) f. Ringe.

.4   'wart': the climber's half-successful attempt at G
        pronunciation of 'wird', which in H's (supposedly) WY
        would be 'watt'! 'das Mund': G 'der Mund' = 'dos
        moil' (G das Maul); hence the transfer of the gender
        of the Y to the G word, dist. h c; 'oichen': Augen,
        WY should be 'āgen', which H uses in 14.5 ('Ahg');
        SEY 'oigen' is further distorted to 'oichen' which
        there connotes "groaning" (to sigh: "oi, oi") --
        h c.

.5   'Hafozôs': Contamination of the two Hebrew words in
        the pl. 'Hafozîm' and 'Hafezôs'. The usual Y pl.
        (ungrammatical in Hebr.) is 'Hafézîm'; the meaning is
        not just 'Sachen' (in Hebr. -'devorîm') but
        'Wertsachen', 'jewels' and 'desirabilia', with
        possible erotic suggestion: the contamination and
        newly-coined plural ending in '-fozôs' (pron.
        '-fotzəs') is probably delib. dist. to get the
        sequence '-fótze', an assonance to HG 'Fotze', vulgar,
        for 'female organ', h c.

23.10 malen

.11 'Mariasch': card game; 'Zwikken': boardgame.

.13 'Uberthir': Ouvertüre.

.15 und keine andere mehr ansehen wollen.

.16ff Schnäbel und Giebel verziehen: pull a long nose
       (or: face).

.19 'ball': bald.

23.8f kozzen - ferkozzen: Rz h c; "wird er glozzen" = he will
       stare, but the rev. subst. ('k' f. 'g') makes it sound
       "he'll become a block of wood" (G 'Klotz') or
       "blockhead".

.9 'ferkozzen': < verkürzen = shorten (the time by plea-
    sant entertainment), but it sounds like G 'verkotzen'
    - to make - disgust, - vomit; '-kürzen' should at
    worst become in H's WY '-kazzen', the 'o' is a delib.
    dist. h c. Normal WY would be '-kerzen', though there
    is a new, recent Y coinage 'kortsen', side by side,
    with older 'kirtsen' and 'kertsen' (The last is the
    most general and authentic).

.10 'waiš'n': weise ihm: 'š' f. 's' - dist.; 'n' f. 'm'
     = auth.; 'muhlen': malen, s.b. G 'a' also in WY, but
     H uses the CY 'u' incongruously to get 'dialect' h c.
     'mit'n': mit ihm, auth. Y.

.11 'Mariasch': a card game French 'marriage', i.e. King
     and Queen of the same color = a "winning hand". L
     p. 386 # 361. 'Zwikken': a game, '(zwick)mühle' on a
     board for two players with 9 pieces each, on a system
     of lines in which one tries to build "mills" (figures
     of three pieces next to each other in a row) when one
     can 'take' one piece from the opponent. The games
     chosen by H are suggestive of marriage, pinching
     (zwicken) and 'catching' the play-'mates'.

.13 'Pumpernikkel': apparently the distorted name of a
     composer, but which? Joh. Nepomuk Hummel? (1778-1837);
     Pumpernickel was not an innocent word; the literary
     meaning was 'farting Nick (or devil)' and was later

23.20 Hört nur den Pauker.

.21 Tut nur recht toben.

.23 erheben

.24 nehmen

23.13 applied to the coarse rye bread from unsifted 'un-
bolted' grain that had the reputation for causing
flatulence. <u>That</u> original meaning was probably still
alive for H. (cf. Bon pour Nickel)
'Uberthir': f. Ouvertüre, overture (an introductory
orchestral composition), but suggesting "Untier",
monster, but an "über-Untier", i.e. a "colossal"
monster.

.14 Zetulpe <u>wants</u> to say that the King would be so impressed by her playing that he would become infatuated
with her to the point of being "wild" for her, but
what she <u>is</u> saying is that it will make him "stand
on his head" -- which normally connotes that someone
will stubbornly use every possible trick to oppose
an adversary. She probably meant to say: "Er wird
an mich den Kopf verlieren."
'werd': prob. auth. WY, but if 'watt' is H's <u>real</u>
WY dial., then 'werd' is a 'half-successful' attempt
at HG.
'drieber': darüber, contraction and unrounding, auth.

.15 'ansehi': ansehen, the word is emphatic: '<u>not (even)</u>
<u>look</u>'; the n apocope is G dial., the '-<u>i</u>' certainly
inauth., being unaccented it would just naturally be
lowered to 'e' and finally slurred to ə. L p. 406
#547.

.16f 'Schnieblich': Schnäbel, beaks (='noses'). '-el'
conceived (falsely) as a Y diminutive, hence p.
'-lich'; auth. pl. Schnäbel, or in H's dial. 'Schnie-
bel'. A p. 131f #66 and L p. 401 # 502. 'i' for
'e' and '-lich' pl. are prob. delib. dist. h c.

.16-19 Zetulpe seems to <u>want</u> to say: the other girls
will be thoroughly disappointed and look elsewhere
for a mate; she therefore says "they'll screw their
noses (beaks) to a point" which normally connotes

23.16-19 "they turn up their noses in disdainful rejection",
whereas she means to say they pull a long face and
have a long nose from sad disappointment. Possibly
the image refers to twisting the <u>lips</u> to a sharp point
in determined anger.

.20 'Pohšer': 'Bosser', Klopfer < MHG 'bozen' (Engl. beat),
klopfen, Kegelspielen; here probably drum (or cymbal)
beater. We must then assume that Zetulpe reacts to
a music band or a drummer (about to announce the
"beauty"-contest). The rev. subst. here of 'p' for
'b' may be delib. to suggest the Y Hebr. '<u>Pošer</u>'.
"interpreter of dreams, enigmas and oracles", therefore "prophet". The spelling is like for a non-He-
braic word (Meschit and vowels), yet it would have
been more comprehensible to a <u>listener</u> as the Hebrewism
than as the rare, unlikely, distorted 'Posser'
(Bosser), especially in the sequence: "Hört nur den
<u>Pošer</u>" ("do listen to the oracle"), especially again
since there is <u>no other explicit</u> indication of a
drummer or cymbalist.

.21 'tihben': toben: MHG has 'toüben, toeben' for
blasen, flöten; H contaminated 'toben' = rage with
'toeben' = play a wind instrument -- out of Rz;
'toeben - heben' is a "passable" R in HG too, in WY
it would be a <u>pure</u> R t<u>e</u>ben (unrounded), and f. H
the 'e' > 'i'.

.22 'Grošer': '-er', auth. Y grammar.

.24 'nemme': 'ע' auth. Y; short vowel (hence doubling the
consonant as a spelling-device to indicate the short
quantity) is due to the cluster 'mn' preventing the
modern lengthening of MHG short vowels in openable
syllables; this is also partly the reason for the
short vowels in G genommen (and kommen).

.25 'Triumf<u>h</u>': the final, unnecessary h is an (unnecessary)
imitation of the German (< Greek) spelling 'ph'. It
is almost a spelling-'joke'! In Hebr. and Y the combination of 'p' plus 'h' never yield 'f', therefore
H used 'f' (which is really only a 'p' with a macron
on top of it) plus 'h', <u>prob.</u> h c (for the eye!).

24.1   Freue dich, Vater

.4   'froig...<u>J</u>ingle': frage...J<u>ü</u>nglein.

.6   wartet ich sehe...was man.

.7   werden gekommen sein; probably came.

25.2   Gaukelspielern...Puppenspielern: acrobats...puppeteers

---

23.25-24.2   'Triumfh - Trumpf': not necessarily Rz, since 'mpf' is often simplified ('entlastet') to 'mf' (cf. Y kemfen f. G kämpfen).

24.2A   SD 4-5 'neh<u>e</u>t...steh<u>e</u>t...zeh<u>e</u>n'; the extra 'e's are archaic and "almost" HHG, cf. on 21A SD.

.6   'sich': (ich) sehe (MHG 'sih<u>e</u>', originally pronounced si<u>che</u>, the '-ch' > h (between vowels) and then silent in G; in OY (final) '-e' was apocopated, the 'ch' was no longer <u>between</u> vowels, but final and therefore remained '<u>ch</u>', i.e. unchanged.
'selbst': s̄, not š, because the 't' is secondary (excrescent parasitic) and developed after the 'st' > 'št'.

.7   'warren kumme sain': werden gekommen sein = probably came, as in HG; Y has no fut. perf., and the fut. that it does have cannot be used to express probability either, as in NHG, where fut. and fut. perfect <u>can</u> express pres. and past probability respectively.

25.2   'Kumidianden': 'o' plus 'e' in FW are regularly "raised" by H to 'u' and 'i', possibly because these middle vowels actually articulated somewhat higher in FW, but more likely because distortions in "fashionable" words lend themselves better to poke fun at the "lower-class ignorant climber" attempting to use them.
'Gagel-': Gau<u>k</u>el-: the 'a' f. MHG 'ou' is auth. WY, 'g' for 'k' is "effectively" rev. subst. though actually there was a variant 'gougel-' in MHG -- however, that was hardly known to H's audience.
'Gagelspringerlich' = acrobats. L p. 368 # 173.
'Dokken': SG f. Puppen, here = Puppenspieler,

25.3   'Glokken': bell-shaped dress.

.5   'Nagenblik': Augenblick

.7   Tun dich deine paar Kreuzerlein...are the couple of
     pennies burning a hole in your pocket?

25.2   puppeteers. L p. 360 # 97.

.3   'In der bloie': EY in der bloier; OWY and NHG in der
     bloien (sg.), or in den bloien (pl.); H's 'in der
     bloie' must be delib. dist. h c; 'der bloie' is pos-
     sible only in Nom. masc. sg. in HG. 'In di bloie'
     would be the expected Y (pl.).
     The question mark at the end seems out of place, un-
     less it is meant to indicate a distorted intonation.

.4   'Havél Havólim' is the correct ancient Hebr. accentua-
     tion (in the "construct state"), but this "winged
     phrase" (from Eccl. 1,2), so frequent on the lips of
     otherworldly, pious Jews expressing contempt for the
     "vanity of vanities" of temporal life, is always pro-
     nounced in Y "Hébel Havólim", and only thus can it
     properly rhyme with Halôm on the basis of Havóləm --
     Holəm.

.5   'Nagenblik': metanalysis < an agenblik.

.6   'Stus': fem. as in correct Hebr., but it is now masc.
     in Y.
     'gukken': EY kukken.

.7   'denne': tun, one of the many dialect variants used by
     H from tun, both as verb and auxiliary. A p. 117
     # 54; the '-n' apocope is also G dial. not Y; the 'd'
     for 't' is rev. subst.; the 'e', if auth., would go
     back to the variant 'tun si' where the 'i' of the
     enclitic pronoun umlauted the 'a' to 'e'; the final
     '-e' is due to analogy to most other verbs that have a
     suffix -e(n) added to a stem.
     'baar': 'b' for 'p', rev. subst.
     'Kraizerlich': Kreuzerlein, smallest Austrian coin
     (with a cross on it).

.7A SD 'sihet': sieht, it is meant to be "super" HG! on
     -e- cf. 22.21A SD; in OWY it would be 'sicht'.

25.9-10   Da habt Ihr's schon dort stehen mitten im Lärm.

.12   Was für eine Generation ist das doch?

.13-14   'nikś...nor Wi': nichts a als, nothing but.

.15   wie man recht ausgelassen ist (= sein könnte): how
to be real wanton

25.8ff   is a monologue, but .8, and 'ś' in .9 refer to
"Mädchen" in 24.2E, SD. Mardachai imagines himself
talking to an audience.

.10   'Mit'n': mitten; the apostrophe <u>here</u> indicates that
the   'n' is syllabified (i.e. serves as a <u>vowel</u>),
there being no other vowel between the 't' and the
'n'; elsewhere it = 'mit ihm' or 'ihnen'.
'Gelarreme': lärmendes Gewimmel. On H's fondness for
the prefix 'ge-' cf. on 15.16; the double 'rr' is
probably not accidental, but "Lautmalerei", intensifying the gutturals to express the horror at and
imitation of, the noise and crowd.

.12   'Waas...for': was für; für and vor have almost
changed places from M to NHG times; Y is still like
MHG in this respect. EY 'vos far', which is no
longer separable.
'alleweil': "immer", then "doch". Words for "always" have a tendency to weaken in meaning to a
mere intensifying force.
'Dôr': generation and epoch.

.13   'si': ihnen; not dist., auth. Y. WY 'si' and EY 'sey'
are invariable in all cases; however, it prob. struck
H's audience as h.

.13-14   'nikś...nor Wi': a delib. contamination of two
constructions, 'nikś, nor...' and 'nikś <u>wi</u>' (f. HG
nichts als) h c.

.15   Sarcastic! 'mer is': man ist; the indicative instead of the subjunctive of indirect discourse is
the mark of the unsophisticated speaker -- another
case of characterization by means of speech-style.
'oisgelośśen': the Y is "stronger" than the G "ausgelassen", which can have the "innocent" meaning of

25.15 "frolicsome" or "wild"; in Y it always means wanton, unbridled, immodest, lewd, immoral.

.16 'Woillust': the short 'ŏ' in G Wollust, as against '-ō-' in wohl is due to the fact that in the adj. MHG wŏl was in an openable syllable and was therefore leng- thened in NHG and Y; in the compound 'Wŏllust' the syllable was permanently closed and therefore remained short in NHG. If 'Woillust' were a genuine Y word dating from MHG times, '-ŏ-' would remain short as in G. If it were compounded anew in MY or Modern Y times (from the 16th or the 18th century onward) then it still could not be '-oi-' in WY but only 'ō'; in NEY it would be 'weyllust', in SEY 'woillist', but nowhere in Y 'woillust'. Actually the word was rare in MHG and does not seem to have "reached" Y; at least it is not recorded even in Stutchkoff, who does list thousands of "Germanisms" - as long as they are documented any- where in Y. There is Y 'voiltog' with approximately the same meaning as G Wollust, apparently an inde- pendent Y creation. That G coined the compound with "Lust" and still retains the connotation of lasciviousness, and Y with 'Tog' (day) without such connotation is definitely indicative of the "puritanic", "repressed" Y culture. And so H's 'Woillust' is phony, dist. h c.

.19 'In': prob. a misprint; 'din', i.e. 'dem' acc. f. dat. h c.
'Harr': Herr, auth.; in EY the 'rr' was simplified and the vowel lengthened because of the emotional charge: the word is the "allowed"substitute for the Hebr. names of God, "forbidden" to be taken in vain.

.21 'Kol ʻôlom': here = "the dat. of possession" - 'jedem' = 'jump into everybody's face': lit. = 'der ganzen Welt'; while 'o(i)ləm' is a common Y Hebrewism in the sense of "audience, public, crowd" - it is not so common for "everybody"; and 'kol o(i)ləm' is a "heavy" (and rather ungrammatical) and unlikely Hebrewism in Y -- unlikely, that is, for the "average" Y speaker, but Reb Mordche (Mardochai) is portrayed as the pious scholar, steeped in holy lore, who is properly typified and typed by a style heavy in Hebrewisms; embarrassing him with "impossible" Hebrew

25. 21   grammar adds a gentle, benevolent h touch: "old-
fashioned" Jewish scholars were famed for their
"slovenly" Hebr. grammar -- a "scandal" the Maskilim
(Rationalists) loved to exploit and pillory them for.
The Hebr. grammar problem here is on several levels:
1. "jedermann" ("die ganze Welt") s.b. "kol ho-olom"
(pr. "kol hɔoləm"); "jedem" (der ganzen Welt") s.b.
"lɛxɔl hɔoləm", but while the latter is the correct
Hebr. "dat." it would be bad syntax, as Hebr. does
not use this dat. of possession in this situation,
but a construction more similar to the so-called Engl.
"genitive" (i.e. not like G "springt jedem ins Gesicht
hinein", but rather like the Engl. "jumps into the
face of everybody) -- "sel kɔl hɔoləm"; here, therefore, it would require an additional change of the Y
(and G) word-order to: "špringt in(s) Gesicht šel
kol Hoolom nein", all this requiring a process of
cerebration, not beyond a Reb Mordche, but well
beyond the mood of plaintive righteous indignation he
is in. Incidentally, Hebr. "šel", while today the
equivalent of the Engl. "of", did develop, historically, from a "dative of possession"!

.22   Sarcastic. 'Sêfer': in Y only a 'holy book' (of
Torah, i.e., the Word of God, or of edification) not
just any book (in Hebr.).
'ahnzusehi': WY 'ahn-' can represent both G 'an' and
'ein'; 'an' is the earlier adverbial prefix, 'ein' -
the later, after eyes became near-sighted within a
culture of ever more reading (after Gutenberg's
printing-press); in today's Y therefore: 'in a seyfer
'arainkukn'.
'ʿAvêroh': in Y lit. 'sin', but weakened to mean a
'waste' - of time, effort, etc.

.23   'Gesêroh': in Hebr. lit. a 'decree' of a ruler or
'of God'; as such the word was neutral in feeling,
the holiday-prayer at the opening of the Torah-ark
petitions for "good gesêros"; but in Y the unquali-
fied word came to mean ("God's and/or man's decree
for) Evil, Persecution, Misfortune, Catastrophe" --
a reflection of the rôle of 'Decrees' in the catast-
rophic history of the Jews; here it is weakened and
used sarcastically for a '(bad) innovation in the
social and fashionable requirements (supposedly) that
are a nuisance or a downright curse'.

.24   'Karwe': G dial. (East Franconian) for HG 'Kirch-

26.7   Nein, etwas anderes. Da hört;

25.24 weih" = in meaning to HG Kirmes (< Kirchmesse), ori-
       ginally - "church-dedication" (feast) or church mass
       (and the festivity after it); now - any "festivity",
       so much so that EY has 'kermeš(1)' for "carouse, feast"
       (Harkavy). 'Kermes' comes to EY through the Polish.
       East Franconian 'Kerwe'> f. H 'Karwe'; maybe it is auth.
       WY; we suspect it was chosen for its assonance to EY
       'kurve' (< Polish) = "whore". L. p. 379 #289.

   .24-25 'Krenzle...Kumidie...Tenzle': here = a party or
       feast f. an intimate group...an entertaining show...a
       ball. L p. 382 #324.

26.1   Either 'nimmer' or the question mark would be out of
       place. A "statement of fact" with 'nimmer', or a
       rhetorical question without it (but possibly with its
       opposite 'ja') make "straight" sense. The chance that
       it is an unconscious contamination of the two construc-
       tions -- is unlikely. It can therefore be a delib.
       dist. h c -- either in making Mordechai use a
       malapropism ('nimmer' f. 'ja') or in funnily intoning
       a question instead of a "statement" or -- in both. As
       Mordechai is not meant to be h character, there was
       not much that H could properly do with him to give
       vent to the compulsion to strain for h and still keep
       Mordechai "in characger". A slight sing-song intonation,
       an anacoluth in grammar, a "light" malapropism, added to
       his "naiveté", was as far as H allowed himself to go in
       Reb Morche's distortions. Mordechai was a heroic
       figure, too hallowed by tradition, to be made a butt of
       cheap jokes. The humor had to be subtle, had to pretend
       to follow tradition - even while exaggerating it ever so
       slightly to persiflage it. Post-Biblical tradition
       (Talmud and Midrash) had already reshaped Mordechai into
       a pious, other-worldly, Tora-dedicated rabbi and
       teacher. Y was his proper vehicle; G or HHG in him was
       unbelievable. To manage to make his Y sound h never-
       theless is an achievement -- of sorts!

   .3 'derschaffen': prob. h dist., substituting mechanical-
       ly 'der-' for G 'er-'; auth. Y and MHG for this
       technical term 'create (from nothing)' is 'beschaffen'
       (Mod. Y 'be-').

26.5 'Moring': Swabian dial. dished up as Y h c. L.
p. 388, # 379. Cf. on 12.21.

.6 'Hihngihbetš': Ausverkaus, sale; lit. = 'Hingabe',
i.e., 'wo man Waren hingibt (sc. sehr billig, fast
umsonst)'; the word would be properly coined in EY as
'hingebachts'. L p. 375, # 257.
Landau and Wachstein's conjecture "invitation" could
be plausible (cf. EY "farbétn" to invite -- a calque
of Polish "Zaproszic"), but H's spelling ('gihb-')
clearly shows that he derived it from 'geben' and not
'beten'; the noun-prefix 'ge-' in gebéts would never
be spelled 'gih-' by H, though such spelling is
common in OY and MY.

.7 'ebeš': G etwas > Y and G dial. epes; rev. subst.
h c; cf. on 1.11.
'anderst': G '-res' Y '-rš'; '-t', originally
"parasitic" i.e., a "natural" glide in "relaxed"
pronunciation from the broad fricative (or elsewhere: nasal) articulation to the narrower explosive
(or: oral) one -- this '-t' came to be associated
with adverbs and was later added as an adverbial
suffix also where it was not a natural glide; it is,
however, by no means too common, is low-brow, rather
than just colloquial, and is used h c. Y 'epes
anderš' is the usual translation of the ever so
frequent Y-Hebr. euphemism 'davár ahér' (pr. 'dóvər
axər') used for "unmentionables" = from 'pig' to
'sex-act'. The J ethic is very strict against
"improper language", let alone obscenity. Jewish lore
is full of dire warnings against "foul language".
Here are just a few instances:
The Talmud says (Pes. 3a): "Let man always couch his
story in pure (i.e. euphemistic) language, for (even)
Scripture 'twisted' nine letters to avoid uttering an
ugly word"; and (in Sab. 33a): "On account of the
sin of obscene language many afflictions and hard
evil-decrees are renewed and the youths of the
(enemies of) Israel die, orphans and widows cry and
are not heeded." (The word 'enemies' in the preceding quote is itself an example of euphemism). He
who dirties his mouth (= indulges in obscenity) even
if he was destined (his decree was signed) for 70 good
years, they are turned to evil... his Gehenna is
deepened...the same for the listener...

26.7   Hence, not only pious rabbis but J <u>colloquial</u> <u>speech</u> in
        general became extremely puritanic, so much so, that
        the words of Maimonides that "Hebrew is called the Holy
        Language ("leshon qodeš") because if contains no ob-
        scene vocabulary" could, with equal propriety, have
        been applied to J <u>vernaculars</u> up to the Epochs of
        Emancipation and/or Secularization. The non-J verna-
        cular terms for the "unmentionables" were <u>lost</u> in the
        J adaptations of these <u>same vernaculars</u> and were
        <u>completely</u> displaced by euphemisms -- usually from the
        Hebrew. Hebrew here had a function similar to that of
        Latin in English: to <u>divest</u> the <u>concept</u> of the bad,
        wicked, dirty connotations associated with the vernacu-
        lar vulgarity of "street-language" and invest it with
        the proper atmosphere of scholarship. The functions
        of Hebrew and Latin <u>are</u> <u>similar</u>, but not <u>identical</u>.
        Hebrew connoted not only scholarship, but holiness.
        Holiness in turn is defined in J lore as "restraint in
        chastity" ("geder ervah" -- Vayiqra Rabba, 23). In the
        non-Jewish vernaculars, including English, there has
        always been a <u>choice</u>, the euphemism has existed <u>side</u>
        <u>by side</u> with the vulgarism. In the J vernaculars there
        was no choice. The vulgarism had disappeared because
        of disuse. The curious thing happened that, because of
        the complete absence of the vulgar synonym, the origi-
        nal chaste Hebr. euphemism gradually became a vulgarism
        in its turn, and a new euphemism had to be coined. (Cf.
        the history of Y "arš, toxǝs, hintern"). This curiosity
        misled a would-be historian of Y to write in an Ency-
        clopedia the out-of-focus statement: "If one wants to
        be vulgar in Y, one uses a Hebrewism". The more
        <u>accurate</u> statement would be: "If one wants to be
        refined, polite, or chaste in Y, one uses a Hebrewism;
        however, if one wants to express strong feelings (in-
        cluding feelings of hatred or disgust), since downright
        vulgarisms are rather rare <u>as such</u> in Y, either "foreign
        vulgarisms" are taken over <u>bodily</u> from the socially
        "lower" strata among the neighbors (usually Slavs), or
        the originally euphemistic Hebrewism is pressed into
        vulgar service (cf. "tɔxǝs, nǝkeyyǝ, noiǝf")." Hence
        it is probable that with "ebeš anderšt" H alludes to
        "dóyǝr áxǝr", the sex-act, a sex orgy at the palace.
        Even the 'Hihngihbetš', this rarest of words, probably
        unknown to most of his readers in the sense of 'sale'
        (or 'invitation' - if the accent is - 'hingebéts') H

26.9   morgen...Frühe.

.10   so viel Mädchen (es) sind in Susan hier.

.11   fünfzehn

.12   muss man ihm vorstellen

.13   gefällt ihm

26.7   might have chosen to suggest to the unknowing "putting
to bed en masse", while leaving himself the defense
that he innocently meant: "sale"!

.10   'Soi fiel Maadlich': sc. 'di'; the missing relative
pronoun 'di' is not Y, but is typical of <u>primitive</u>,
"paratactic" style, hence h! 'maad'lich: WY and G
dial. 'sen': sind; cf. A p. 120 # 56.

.11   'In Schloš': f. G in<u>s</u>; Y omits articles in <u>frequent</u>
adverbial phrases (cf. Engl.: "I go to church", but
"...to <u>the</u> synagogue".

.12-14   'for ihn štellen...ihn štellen for': "place before
him...introduce to him" <u>could</u> be the intent of the
repetition, though either phrase could imply either,
and therefore - both.
'ih<u>n</u>': delib. dist. h c, here Y <u>and</u> G require ih<u>m</u>
though NHG does require ih<u>n</u> for "<u>to place before him</u>".

.13   'fufzehi': fünfzehn; 'fufz-' f. 'fünfz-' is NEY
("Lithuanian Y"), but not <u>WY</u>; the final 'n' missing
is <u>G</u> dial., the whole - inauth. Cf. on 6.9.
'bis': a <u>space</u> before 'bis' was left out by <u>typist</u>.

.15   'gfallt'n': sic! with apostrophe before 'n', = gefällt ih<u>m</u>, final 'm' > 'n' in Y when unaccented.

.16   'will': MEY 'vet' < 'veln', with sloughing off of 'l'
before dental in <u>unaccented highly</u> frequent words
(Cf. Engl. will-would).
'for' = both G 'vor' and 'für', NEY 'far' because
enclitization made the 'o' in 'for' follow the rule
that before 'r' plus consonant the 'o' is <u>lowered</u>
to 'a' in MEY. Cf. on 6.6.

27.4 'Gikš': Geck(erei), teasing of fools.

26.17 'Massol': pr. 'Mǎsel'; (the 'ss' is f. Engl. 'zz')
< Hebr. 'mazzāl' f. "star", "planet", then "fate
destined by constellation", then "luck" and finally
"good luck". As usual, the emotionally charged word
comes from the Hebr. The doubling of a consonant in
Hebr. is indicated <u>not</u> by writing it twice, but by
dotting ("dagesh"). But in the usual vowelless text
this doubling-sign (the "dagesh") is omitted and in
<u>modern</u> pronunciation of Hebr. and Y <u>there is no doubl-
ing</u>. Hence, the <u>usual</u> transliteration calls for 'masel'
(or 'mazl').

27.1 Mordechai denies the existence of "luck" or chance: All
that happens is predetermined by God. This is completely in character of his piety and of Jewish tradition. The Talmud states categorically that "no one
stubs his toe Below unless it was decreed thus Above".
Also that "Israel has no <u>mazzal</u>" -- the original meaning of which is "Israel's fate is determined not by con-
stellations, but by the will of God". At first only
cynics injected into the quotation the (latterly possible new) meaning: "a Jew has no luck". Later the
tragic history of the Jews caused this distorted interpretation to be accepted as the <u>true meaning by all</u>
except the erudite scholars!

.4 'Gikš': L p. 370 # 203; "stupid gossip" is plausible,
but "gecken" is also a synonym of "necken" and both
can mean "zum Narren halten", to (try to) make a fool
of someone, and "nix" (and "Nickel") are names of de-
mons who tease and play tricks on humans. It is therefore probable that H used 'nikš' deliberately with the
double meaning of "nothing" and "nix", the latter meaning first emerging as a surprise-climax from 'Gikš'!

.4A SD 'Medchen': HG 'Mädchen' is intended for the SD! In
the <u>Text</u> H uses the <u>WY</u> 'maadlich'!

.5 'Secht': OWY f. "seht".
'dihn': f. dem, dist. h c.
'bloisen': 's' f. 'š', rev. subst. h c; probably
'bloisen' is deliberate malapropism for 'bloien' (= G

27.5   Seht, bei dem blauen

.7   'Horeg=le': Zwerglein, runt.

.9   'taitsch': bedeutet.

.10-11 schwöre es Ihnen bei dem Nudelteig und bei dem
        Wälgerholz.

27.5   blauen), but is actually the WY f. G "blasen" (to blow)
        while the pretended intent is "blossen" (bare).

.6   The Talmud (like the New Testament) enjoins swearing
        even to the truth; the Talmud -- even when refusing to
        swear results in losing in a litigation.

.7   'bist...': indicative f. the imperative, developed
        from a "threat" in the interrogative, i.e., "are you
        going to keep quiet (...or will I have to make you do
        it?") = G "wirst du gleich still sein?" In SY the
        construction is possible only in the interrogative,
        and only in the future tense ("Vest štil zain, tsi
        nit?"). In G the present (with 'gleich') can be used
        for the future and in WY apparently also.
        'Horeg=le': Zwerglein, runt, cf. on 17.13.

.9   'Waas taitsch': G "was bedeutet, was heisst", i.e.,
        "what do you mean by?"; MY "staitš?" developed into
        an exclamation of surprise and/or protest at an un-
        expected wrong, impropriety or incongruity, with the
        meaning: "how come?", "how is such a thing possible?"
        Typical Jewish lexical creation for the typical situa-
        tion Jews so frequently find themselves in.

.10-11 'schwehr'n': schwöre ihm, auth. Y. HG 'ö' is
        secondary development. Y 'e' is like MHG. Text has
        no apostrophe before 'n', but ought to have one. The
        'n' is enclitic for 'm', for "ihm", which > 'n' when
        unaccented. 'n' f. "ihm" is 3rd pers. sg. formal for
        2nd pers. sg., i.e. f. HG "Ihnen".
        'dihn': dist. h c; both Y and G require dem.
        'Frimfelištag': vermicelli (or ladyfinger's) dough.
        'Welkerholz': 'k' f. 'g' rev. subst., definitely in-
        auth. G and Y both require 'g', in fact MHG 'lk'
        would turn into 'lg' in both! dist. h c. SG

27.15   'nehr <u>min</u>...':   die erste Beste.

.16   wäre eine etwas neue Mode.

.17   Lasst...in Ruh, don't bother me.

27.10-11   "Wälgerholz", NHG "Teigrolle", "Nudelholz", Engl. "rolling-pin".
Because of Mordechai's objection to swearing by the name of Heaven, Esther now swears by <u>trivial</u>, non-holy objects -- which would be permissible, were it not for her <u>slip</u>: 'fun Gott'. That she should swear by <u>her</u> rolling-pin and dough in mock-heroic style, the woman's traditional weapon (rolling-pin) and her successful feat (dough) is humorously equal to "by my sword and the enemies I've slain with it!". The incongruous, (because blasphemous) addition of 'fun Gott' is h to H and his rationalist "Enlighteners". It is a h take-off on Jove's thunderbolt or Mercury's club -- but for that very reason simply <u>impossible</u> for the Mordechai or Esther of Tradition: God and His rolling-pin! Cf. L p. 370 # 203.

.12   'fun der <u>ganze</u> G.':   dist. h c; neither Y nor G. HG requires "der ganzen", Y "der ganze<u>r</u>", <u>some</u> G and Y dialects "d<u>i</u> ganz<u>e</u>", but none, absolutely none: 'de<u>r</u> ganze'.

.15   'min...':   "von was immer in seine Hand kommt" = "whatever turns up", "pot luck".

.15-16   'Mude - <u>Jodô</u>':   R is <u>slightly</u> impure whether the pronunciation is auth. "Modə- Jɔdə' or the distorted "Mudə - Jɔdə'. It would be pure only with the dist. 'mudə' and SEY (Galician) "Judə" -- which H prob. meant to suggest.

.17   'Leṡt...gihn': lasst...in Ruh; 'leṡt': the 'e' is dist., h c; G and Y do <u>not</u> umlaut in the <u>imperative</u>. Y does not umlaut even in the indicative, and <u>G</u> does not umlaut in the <u>plural</u> indicative either; and this is the <u>imperative</u> and <u>plural</u>! There <u>is</u> a G <u>dialect</u> that changed the vowel 'a' to 'e' in this verb. H uses it as <u>Y</u> h c.
'Halômôṡ':   Text has '<u>iṡ</u>'; H usually spells Hebrewisms

28.1   Sehen Sie, das ist wieder einmal eine Bekanntmachung;
        this is an announcement again.

 .5   Werden Sie sehen, morgen kommts in Korrespondent.

 .7   Werden Sie sich doch kaum

27.17   traditionally, but seemingly allows himself <u>slight</u>
        variations in final syllables to indicate their
        slurred pronunciation in his Y -- which differs, <u>to</u>
        <u>this day</u>, from the pronunciation of the same words in
        Hebrew <u>qua</u> Hebrew (i.e., liturgy). This spelling is
        still not completely phonetic, but is a hint for such.

 .18   'Worim': cf. on 9.9.
        'Wuchenblettle': 'u' for 'ȣ' dist. h c; 'ȣ' didn't
        change in any Y dialect! But cf. A p. 33-35 # 4,5.

 .19   'Zaitung': Text has '-ing', Urgermanisch '-ing' and
        '-ung' were equivalent, but in HG '-ung' prevailed
        and thence also in Y; only a secondary relatively
        recent shift changed 'u' to 'i' in South EY, but
        not in the WY of H!

28.1   'SichtSi':   printed together in the original, as a
        'spelling joke'; 3rd pers. sg. f. the polite form.
        'Gschaiding': "Bekanntmachung" would fit the context
        best; the meaning "clever person" cited in L p. 372
        # 221 is just barely possible ('daas' should not
        refer to a person). H may have deliberately used it
        as a malapropism for <u>B</u>eschaidung -- Erklärung. On
        '-ing' cf. on 27.19.

 .5   'WatSi': Cf. on .1.
        'Kruȿpendent': dist. of 'Korrespondent', name of a
        newspaper.
        'in': f. 'im' h c, a delib use of inauth. language
        to <u>suggest</u> dialect: Y would require the article or
        the slurred fusion of article with the preposition --
        similar to G.

 .7   'oṡur': here weakened to "kaum", "hardly", cf. on
        13.5.

 .8   'als': Y = immer, pronounced 'alts', cf. R w.
        Schmalz.

28.9 Man wird Ihnen Schmalz einbrennen, i.e., they will make special arrangements just for you, "they'll add fat to your sauce".

.10 Einen König darf man...widerspenstig

.11 'A main': all the more.

.14 Wirtschaft führen.

28.8 Esther is <u>here</u> entirely in the Jewish Tradition; she became the queen of a heathen king <u>against</u> her will. But 28.8 is inconsistent with 26.17 ("Wer da noch das <u>Masol</u> hat") where Esther is made to sigh and yearn for the "luck" of becoming queen. But H does not intend to portray even a semblance of a consistent character. He does not mean to be serious, but to extract from every "situation" all the potential "humorous lines". Similarly in 28.13ff. Esther gives those charmingly naive reasons for not "abandoning her uncle", reasons that make for humor but that are <u>not</u> the reasons Tradition gives (: religious scruples).

.9 'drahnbrenne': "einbrennen", in SG and Y means "to simmer flour in fat" as a thickening sauce for a soup; Hathach sarcastically expresses his annoyance at the extremely haughty hard-to-get and hard-to-please attitude of Esther.
'drahn': = darein, dahinein.

.10 'n': < ein<u>en</u> (by apheresis), f. eine<u>m</u>; acc. f. dat. h c, though in EY 'a' would stand for both cases and, conceivably, unaccented, aphetic 'n' would stand <u>authentically</u> for einem and einen in WY.
'daf': darf = <u>here</u> NHG "must not" and not like Y and MHG "need not".
'widerŠpinig': widerspenstig; the Y forms come f. MHG "spaenic" ("rebellious"), therefore, H - Špin̠ig, EY - Šp̄ēnik(en), terms relatively frequent in Y translations of liturgical text, lost in NHG.

.11 'a main': cf. on 4.11 and L p. 351 # 14. <u>Here</u> = vielmehr, all the more.

.12 'sette': solche. L p. 407 # 558, ultimately < "sotāne".

28.15   Euer...Kaffee...Feuer schüren.

.17   'Bradehoif': Breite Haube, broad cape.

29.2   'Ihfele': Öfe(n)lein.

28.13   'Unkel': 'u' f. 'o' not Y; cf. on 27.17 and L p. 412
        # 600.
        'sellt': subj. of unreality, f. a dial. variant
        *söllte, auth. OY.
        'ferlosšen': '-sš-' auth. OY, MY '-s-', probably also
        '-s-' in H's WY, but the contamination of the Y vowel
        'o' with the G consonant 'š' is a dist. h c.

.16   'nihe': nähen; N.B. the inconsistency here and in
      .18 between '-en' and '-e' as infinitive endings.

.17   'Bradehoif': '_f_' for 'b' in the original. Typist's
      error in the transliteration. L p. 357 # 71.

.18   'weschen, behgle': Rev. of auth. Y and HG h c. Even
      if we were to assume that G $\bar{e}$ > $\bar{i}$ in H's WY, the rev.
      cannot be true -- G 'bügeln' (Y 'bīgeln') could not
      become 'behgeln' or 'behglen'.
      'mangle': mangeln = to smooth lines by rolling with
      a gadget, L p. 386 # 359.

.19-29   Linen and underwear, changed once weekly, used to
      be handed out fresh every Friday afternoon to take
      along to the (ritual) communal bath-house. Also the
      Saturday dinner was brought to the communal oven to
      stay there cooking and baking from Friday about an
      hour before sundown till Saturday (after)noon (or
      dinnertime) -- as the Bible prohibits cooking on
      Saturdays. Such dinner is called "Shalet" in WY or
      "Tsholent" in EY (both ultimately from the Latin
      "calida" or "calenta" -- both calques of the Hebrew
      "Hamim" = "warm" (sc. foods).

29.1   'Schuhlmantel': the long gown used in going to the
      synagogue (= Schuhl). In the eighteenth century Ger-
      man Jews, under the influence of Aufklärung (En-
      lightenment) gradually gave up their peculiarities
      in speech (Yiddish, Jüdisch-deutsch) and dress. They
      gave up their long coats in favor of the shorter
      jacket of their neighbors. But the pious, particu-

29.3 'A, na': ach, nein.

.4 Nudelteig wälgern und Teigbrösel (= Eiergerste) reiben;
roll out noodle-dough and grate dough for egg-barley.

29.1 larly the rabbis, still used the long-coat in the
synagogue. In Eastern Europe a Jew wearing a short
jacket instead of a long coat was considered a "daitsch"
("German").

.2 'Ihfele': i < $\bar{e}$ < ö; EY "eyvale". Both G "oben" and
"Ofen" EY "oyvən" or "oyvm" -- apparently a partial
assimilation to the nasal continuant, i.e. the voiceless
'f' becomes the voiced 'v' and the explosive 'b' becomes
the continuant 'v'. The diminutive may point to the
special "Jewish" invention -- a type of "Dutch oven",
a little, portable metal baking oven, used by Jews in
Western Europe, especially those living in relative
isolation, to prepare their Sabbath food. As the Bible
prohibits cooking on Saturday, the Sabbath-dinner was
kept cooking and/or baking in a specially-designed oven
from Friday about an hour before sundown, till Saturday
dinner-time. Where there were communities of Jews the
food was often "carried" to a communal (usually the
bakery's) oven. Those that baked their own weekly
number of loaves and the Sabbath breads on Fridays in
their own brick baking ovens, would put their Sabbath
food into the still-hot oven immediately after re-
moving the bread and seal it with soft clay. Food so
prepared is called "tsholent" in EY and "shalet" in WY.
("Boston" (or "Yankee") baked beans are supposedly a
dish derived from such "tsholent" -- not of the Jews,
but of the Christian Seventh Day Adventists!)
Thus the diminutive 'Ihfele' suggests the private little
tsholent-oven, but the "tragen" can only connote the
errand with the tsholent to the communal oven. But the
"diminutive" is not absolutely and exclusively used to
designate littleness. It is also used to express endearment and "warm feelings", not completely out of
place in the case of an oven -- if it were one's own
private oven. The most plausible explanation of the
incongruity of the "littleness" of the oven and of
"carrying" the tsholent into it is that it is delib.
h c.

29.5   'waach': weich.

.6   'Schunst': sonst
'Butterwerkkle': Buttersemmel, butter-rolls

.7   'gihbet...aach': gäbe...auch, would give...also.

29.4   'Ewig': as an expression of the most loyal love and
devotion 'ewig' was meant to modify 'bai aich blaiben',
but formally it modifies 'welkern...un...raiben', h c,
as if these drudging chores, usually a source of com-
plaint to the housewife, are Esther's idea of eternal
happiness.
'Frimfel': ultimately "vermicelli"; it went through
numerous phonetic and semantic changes: "vermlis,
frimils, grimils, chrimsel, chremsel", meaning thin
spaghetti, noodles, noodle-cake or -pudding, noodle-
soup, lady-finger, pancake from dough, pancake from
potatoes and eggs. As it is here represented as made
with a rolling-pin, it must mean noodles. Cf. L
p. 366 # 163, Tendlau p. 166 # 552, Mordecal Kosover-
(Jewish) Foods and Beverages p. 61ff (also in Judah
A. Joffe Book, ibidem) -- both YIVO, N.Y. 1958.
'Farbel': dist. h c f. Farfel, G '-rw-' ≶ '-rb-'
in some G dialects; '-rf-' does not alternate so, but
H has his own distortions in rev. subst. of voiced
and voiceless, hence '-rf-' = '-rw-' ≶ '-rb-'; MHG
'varveln' = · "Eiergerste" or "egg-barley", i.e.,
dough made with (at least, some) egg, chopped or
grated into shape of grains (of barley), dried,
roasted, and steamed - used as a soup-filler (like
noodles), or side dish, or a separate delicacy. In
Süsskind's home town (Stropkov, Slovakia) it was also
served late Friday afternoon, after coming home from
the pre-Sabbath.bath in the communal (ritual) bath-
house (Mikveh) and before going to the Synagogue to
"Receive the Sabbath" -- as lunch was not eaten at
Friday noon, to keep the appetite sharp in honor of
the first Sabbath meal on Friday Eve.
Cf. any "Jewish" cookbook, or, for that matter, some
general cookbooks, s.v. "egg-barley" -- for instance,
Mrs. Simon Kander's Settlement Cook-book, Milwaukee,
Wisc., 1930, p. 119.
Ability to prepare noodles and egg-barley (Y "lokshen"
and "farfel") was considered a sine qua non of a good
Jewish housewife, cf. Kosover, op. cit., p. 144.

29.8 Könnte ich dich nur verstecken.

.11 'Graine': Greinen, Heulen.

29.6 'Schunŝt': cf. on 13.14.
'Butterwekkle': '-wekkle': G Wecklein, little roll.

.7 'gihbet': gäbe, would give -- imperfect subjunctive,
prov. coined by H; the strong verb is made weak
("regularized") and just as MHG 'lebete' from 'leben'
yields for H 'lihbet' so 'geben' yields 'gihbet'.
Regularizing the irregular in grammar is a supposed
sign of the ignorant, uneducated, "uncouth", and
therefore a cause for the laugh of superiority by the
"sophisticated".

.8 'ferstekkle': according to Jewish legend Mordechai
wanted to hide Esther, so she would not be in "danger"
of winning the crown. The genuine code of values of
the orthodox Jew, that to become the queen of a pagan
king would be a misfortune, is held up, ever so subtly,
to ridicule.
"Versteckerles" is a children's game of "hide-and-seek";
the diminutivization of the verb "verstecken" to "ver-
steckle" is prob. auth. G and Y baby-talk (perhaps
more frequent in Y than in G) and as such humorous.
The diminutives ('Estherle' and 'verstekkle') are used
primarily, of course, to express Mordechai's emotions
engendered by the instinct for protecting his "little
girl".

.9 'dafŝ': darf's, must not do it. The meaning here is
as in older Y and NHG but not as in SY. MHG and SY
give it the meaning "need'; in the Middle Y period
(ca. 1500-1750) "darf" is used with either meaning,
especially in WY, but also, though less frequently,
in earlier EY. An instructive example would be the
Engl. (mis)translation of the Tze-enoh U-re-ehno (pub.
orig. ca. 1618; repub. by Bloch, N.Y., 1965) on Exodus
6.20: "an uncle "darf" marry a niece, but a nephew
"darf" not marry an aunt" where "darf" = "needs" instead of "is allowed to". Cf. L p. 359, # 86, and on
1.6, 17.1, and 28.10.

.11 'sih': our typist's error. The text has 'sich', auth.
MHG and OY f. NHG "sieh!", Y "se!". Ultimately the

29.13   'Halt...Haz': haltet!...Herz

  .14   'Secht': seht!

  .16   eine Pfütze Tränen...Nudeln Blatt.

  .17   stehen die Haare zu Berg; my hair stands on end

29.11   verb "see" comes from an IE root *seq, the q > ch(x)
in Primitive Germanic, which ultimately became silent
(represented by a silent 'h') between vowels, but
remained 'ch' elsewhere in German. Cf. "sehen" vs.
"Sicht". Analogy to the most frequent forms (infinitive and the plural) leveled out the paradigm in
favor of the forms <u>without</u> the guttural (x), between
MHG and NHG times -- though not in <u>all</u> the dialects.
English "see" had a similar development.
'Graine': disappeared in EY.

  .12A   SD 'Oigen': pronounce "Augen"; it is HG.

  .13   'Halt': auth. Y f. 'haltet'
'z'springt': the apostrophe (') is two type-spaces
away from the rest of the word in the text and seems
to be the remnant of a broken 'e' (ɤ). The 'z' of
'Ha<u>z</u>' is also missing, prob. also because of a broken
type.

  .14   'Secht': cf. on .11.

  .16   'Fezzen': here = Pfütze, puddle, cf. L p. 365
139 C; in HG and Y it means <u>only</u> "rag"; H's audi-
ence prob. didn't get the "joke".
'Frimfelich Plaz': the rolled-out noodle-dough on
the board(?)
'Trehrn': Tränen; Y < MHG variant "treher".

  .17   'Štene': usually 'Štenne' -- G dialect dished up as
Y h c, where Y and HG are identical! Cf. A p. 119;
HG "die Haare stehen mir <u>zu Berg</u>, EY "kapoyer"
(< MHG gê in bor > gê empor > kapoyer) = I am
frightened.
'Bar<u>ig</u>': the parasitic 'i' could have developed only
after G "b<u>er</u>g" became Y "b<u>a</u>rg", or the shift could
not have occurred. This 'i' <u>is</u> auth., but not
general in Y; it would sound "provincial", exaggerated,

30. 1 Zwiebel...beissen...arg.

.3 'tenneš': tun es.

.4 'gemahnt...senneš': gemeint...sind es.

.6 'Haafen': Haufen

.8 'messen': müssen

.14 'Schotcheli, tub...zihren': Närrlein, tue...zierlich; silly, don't act so hard-to-get.

29.17 funny to the majority of Y speakers, and just for that it is used by H.

30.1Af. SD 'Medchen...Oigen': the HG "Mädchen...Augen" are intended.

.1 'Zwihfel': 'f' f. 'b', dist. h c. Cf. C p. 187 on 20.3, and L p. 419 # 654.
'baisen': 's' f. 'š' rev. subst.
'arig': on parasitic 'i' cf. on 29.17; "arg" is current in EY only in the comparative "erger"; the positive "arg", though listed in Harkavy, is no longer listed in Weinreich.

.3 'Secht': Cf. on 29.11.

.3f 'tenneš...senneš': tun es... sind es. Cf. on 17.

.4-9 Hathach and Mädchen are not only not frightened at the chance of Esther's being chosen by the king, they wish it. The "troubles and heartaches" ("Zores" and "Schivre-Lev") that make the Mädchen cry are the heap of cut-up onions, while Hathach supposedly thought that the cause of the tears was real heartache. So he laughs at his "mistake" and all laugh with him. But Mordechai and Esther in 29.5-.18 do cry from Zoreš and Schivre-Lev and could not properly be made to join the laughing at a "mistake" that was no mistake.

.4 'Hob ich': "while".

.8 'messen': Cf. A p. 117 # 52.7.

31.2f wären Sie denn dann noch würdig, dass Sie gingen;
       would you then still be worthy that you should walk.

.5 'sotte': solche

.7 Ein Thron...Brotbrett

30.12 'Hôzo'ôs': pr. "Hotsɔəs" = Ausgaben, Spesen, Un-
kosten, Engl. expenses -- all <u>properly</u> in the plural;
psychologically and actually we rarely "get by" with a
<u>single</u> expense. Note: the 'ô's are broken and look
like 'i's.

.14 'Schotcheli': printed in Meschit, as if it were <u>not</u>
from Hebr., because as a "curse word" or "name-call-
ing", it readily entered G -- as such words are eagerly "picked up"; Hebr. 'šote' = "mad", "crazy",
weakened in Y to "fool" and with the WY diminutive
suffix '-cheli' (a contamination of the NG and SG
diminutives '-che(n)' and '-lei(n)' respectively) it
even has a loving, endearing connotation: "dear
little silly child".
'sich zihren': to put on airs, act important, hard-
to-get, or affectatious. L p. 402 #508.
.15 The sense of the line: One should not depend just on
<u>luck</u> but should <u>do</u> everything possible to attain
success -- this is really out of place here. Esther
supposedly considers becoming the queen a <u>calamity</u>!
But it <u>is</u> a good "funny line".

31.2-4 'wer...tet': wäre...täte, auth. WY imperfect subjunctive, replaced in EY by the conditional "volt
sain" or "volt geven" and "volt (ge)ton"
'den': denn
'mehr': dann noch = adv. of time modifying the verb
and <u>not</u> an adv. of degree to make the adjective comparative.
'genget': ginge; a H-coined imperfect subjunctive, as
if derived from the infinitive "gangen" by the <u>weak</u>
conjugation-suffix '-ete' and in spite of its being a
regular weak, provided with an umlaut; *gängete >
H genget. Cf. on 29.7 'gihbet' and on 5.8-9 'hiebet'
and A p. 121 # 56.

.5 'sotte': solche < 'sô tane', in older EY 'asetige'
< sötig < sot+ig.

31.8   'Mihlkiwelle': Mülleimer

.17   'fersinden': versündigen

31.7   'Barchesbried': prob. = "dough-board" -- the board on
which dough is mixed, kneaded and rolled, in SY "lok-
šenbret", which, however, is used exclusively neither
for noodles, nor for loaves, but for all dough. "Barches" is the regular term in WY for the white, twisted
("braided") loaves of bread used to pronounce the blessings at the three Saturday meals, called in EY "koy-
litš" (< Polish) or "chalə" (Hebr.). The etymology of
"Barches" was moot, but it is most likely derived from
"St. Berchtes bread", a white, cake-like twist that
used to be eaten on this saint's day in some parts of
Germany. Even traces of a Germanic goddess of food,
also Berchta, and remnants of her worship are involved.
Thence it was adopted by Jews for Saturday. While the
derivation from the Heb. "Brāchot" (blessings) is impossible (this would have to yield in WY *brɔxəs) a
popular-etymology may have associated them and helped
to spread and preserve the term. Since Frimfelich,
Farbel, and Werlkerholz are so prominent in Esther's
role, we won't go wrong in assigning "Barches" to the
same sphere, rather than associate it with G "Barchent"
("flannel") and interpret "Barchesbried" as a flannel-
covered ironing-board; but cf. L p. 354 # 43. Possibly
H is deliberately ambiguous, h c; it is not an auth.
term and is used f. Rz too.
'-bried': NHG Brett, with 'e' and 'tt' is an irregular
development of MHG "bret"; whatever the possible reason
for the irregularity in NHG, we should expect NHG
*Brēt (long 'e' and single 't') which Y has, hence H's
further development of 'ē' to 'ī' ('ie', 'ih'); 'd' f.
't' is the usual rev. subst. h c.
On the three obligatory Sabbath meals (Friday eve,
Saturday noon, and before sundown) the blessings have
to be made over two whole loaves to symbolize the
double portion of manna that came down from heaven
each Friday in the desert to provide on Friday food
also for the Sabbath, the rest-day, when no manna fell
(Exodus 16.23). The loaves are placed between two
cloths to symbolize the two layers of dew between

31.19   'be-ʿAwônôs': leider

.21   'als': immer. 'Harrli': Grossvater

.22   'tihglich': täglich.

31.7   which the manna lay. Normally, therefore, a minimum of
four loaves are prepared: the plain loaf is eaten
Friday eve, the twist Sat. noon, and two rolls during
the third meal, before sundown.
Cabbalists and Hassidim have a special loaf made up of
twelve rolls held together by a dough-band to symbolize
the twelve tribes.
On special holidays there are especially-shaped loaves
(e.g., on New Year (Rosh Hashono)) to resemble a spiral,
i.e., a ladder to ascend to heaven with!

.6-16   The meaning seems to be: You, Hathach, think that
if one is good at the dough-board, one is good enough
for the throne, but you ignore the refinements required by a king.

.15   'Heśed': Gunst, Huld -- generally; here perhaps =
Verdienst, deserts.

.16   Obscenely suggestive, though the "innocent" idiom
supposedly means "I am very poor"; cf. "Es reicht
nicht vorn und nicht hinten".

.17   'fersinden': versündigen, prob. a H-coinage, Rz;
not to count one's blessings, but to be dissatisfied
with one's fate is accounted a sin of ingratitude to
God.

.17-18   'nor' and 'nehr' in two consecutive lines!

.18-19   A satirical reference to the "evil" of the dowry
system. There is a Y proverb: "on nadn -- keyn
chasseneh" (= no dowry -- no wedding!). Before the
"Jewish Emancipation" Jews in Christian Europe were
terribly restricted in their occupations (they could
not own land or belong to the guilds of craftsmen).
To support a wife and a family a young husband just
had to have a "nest-egg" of capital to start some
kind of business that would promise the prospect of a
livelihood. Girls of impecunious families had great
difficulty in finding husbands. Every community had a

32.1   Alle "Gott-bewahre" (= Unglücke) sind möglich

31.18-19   charitable society "Hachnoses Kalloh" ("Endowing a
      Bride"). At certain times and places a Jew had to
      buy the "privilege" to marry, and that privilege was
      inheritable only by <u>one</u> son, who was registered as
      "Familiant" -- i.e., having the legal right to raise
      a family.
      After "Emancipation" inertia and custom kept Jews
      mostly in their old occupations and therefore the
      dowry was the <u>sine qua non</u> of most marriages. In
      Israel and America the dowry as an <u>insitution</u> has
      disappeared.
      The implied "social criticism" is h in that it attri-
      butes to Esther a fear that the King won't "consider"
      her because she has no dowry. The h is heightened by
      the anachronism.

  .19   'allewail': = jetzt. G dial. not Y
      'be-ʿAwônôs': lit. "durch Sünden"; the usual ex-
      pression is "ba-ʿAwônôsênu" (durch <u>unsre</u> Sünden) --
      typical of the traditional theodicy of the Jew, whose
      theology and sacred historiography "justified G-d's
      ways to man" and maintained that G-d is perfect in
      His justice and all evil is due punishment for sin.
      Here the expression is perhaps weakened to mean just
      "leider" ("unfortunately").
      'der Welt': the <u>Jewish</u> community in general is meant
      (only in <u>it</u> was dowry a <u>sine qua non</u>), but such is
      the natural egocentrism of <u>all</u> people, that their
      particular group is equated with the world!

  .21   'als': immer, always = Y. 'Harrli': Cf. L p. 373
      # 240.

32.1   'Haš ve--Scholôm': = "G-d forbid", then, euphemisti-
      càlly, by metonomy, the phrase is used as a noun for
      "misfortune", but h here <u>misapplied</u> since Hathach
      means to say, "all <u>good</u> fortunes are possible"!

  .2   'daffen': Cf. on 17.1.
      'ois': delib. dist. h c in word-order, contaminating
      the two idioms (Y and G) "<u>iber</u> epes lachn", and "epes
      <u>oislachn</u>" into "ois epes lachn" (= "to laugh <u>at</u> some-
      thing vs. "to deride something", respectively).

32.2   wir...dürfen über

  .4   Lassen Sie sich nur nicht leid sein

  .5   'brad': breit

  .7   Grafen und Fürsten

  .9   der Feder

  .10   'laient': liest

32.3   The meaning is not <u>quite</u> clear, perhaps it is so
        deliberately. Lit. it says "don't be sorry for your-
        self" (i.e., "you have no reason to be dissatisfied")
        but it apparently means "don't hate yourself", ("you
        are too gifted and blessed for that!").

  .5-6 Not only the Jewish, but apparently also the G
        "primitive" ideal of feminine beauty was "rund und
        saftig", curvacious and soft, and, if one contemplates
        the Valkyries--big-- and therefore a source of humor
        for H and his "sophisticated" audience.

  .6-7 'Kašten - Fašten': a pure rhyme only in H's pseudo-
        dialect.

  .7   Reden mit Grafen und Fürsten: for the phonology cf.
        C p.112f; 'Gruf': the 'u' is auth. only in SEY and even
        there, it being a "higher-culture" word, it would
        normally be "loaned" and therefore pronounced with the
        HG 'ā', instead of the 'ū' of the dialect.

  .7-9 Cf. on 18.4 concerning the role of Jewish women as
        breadwinners of the family. In merchant families the
        daughters were especially educated for their role as
        the business head even to the point of elegance in
        speech and manners and proficiency in foreign lan-
        guages--while the sons were taught Torah and <u>only</u>
        Torah. Excellent examples of this can be found in the
        <u>Memoirs of Glückel of Hameln</u> and in A. Landau and
        B. Wachstein's <u>Jüdische Privatbriefe aus dem Jahre</u>
        <u>1619</u>.

  .8   'boruch ha-Schêm': <u>here</u> = Gott sei Dank!
        'Gelieder': as all Y and SG dialects syncopate, and

32.8 H even more so (cf. 'Gsund'), here he archaizes beyond
HG -- just to be different! Utterly inauth. ('Ge-' -
HHG)

.9 'di': acc. f. dat.

.10 'Ohrt und laient...gut': is <u>proficient</u> in reading the
prayers (in Hebrew!). As women were <u>usually not</u>
educated in Hebrew beyond the ability of reading the
prayers <u>mechanically</u> and without understanding, 'Ohrt
...<u>gut</u>' prob. means that she phrases the Hebrew text
properly, because she, by exception, does understand
it. 'laient' prob. refers to reading the "Tsenoh U
Re-enoh" (cf. on 11.8f), as the word was orig. used
only for "chant-reading"("cantilating") the biblical
texts, and only in 19th cent. EY (and even there not
<u>universally</u>) extended to <u>any</u> reading. An orthodox Jew
is required to chant the weekly pericope to himself
("maavir Zain di Sedreh"), as well as to hear it
chanted at the Sabbath service. Women are not <u>required</u>
to do so, and normally were not proficient enough to
cantilate, though there might have been some rare,
pious soul venturing that far out. There <u>are</u> actually
records of women even insisting on donning phylacteris
("tefillin")! 'Laient' is thus surely a hyperbole to
which it lent itself by its shifting meaning from
"cantilating" to "holy-lore reading" (for edification),
to "reading" in general. Cf. H's similar attempt at h
by over-exaggeration 11.5ff. where he grieves over
Zetulpe's not being proper, since she does not pre-
occupy herself with "Ze-enoh-u Re-enoh", "Thehillim
and Maᶜamodôs". To summarize: the pretended "innocent" meaning of 'laient' is simply "reads"; coupl-
ing it with 'ohrt' connotes at the least "reads Tse-
enoh-u Re-enoh"; with 'recht gut' the suggestion of
knowing Hebrew and cantilating arises, as well as
"<u>professional</u> proficiency" -- in some communities there
was the profession of female precentors ((fir)zogerns)
who lead in prayers and in the reading of edifying
passages from the Techinehs (<u>vernacular</u> prayers for
women) of the Tze-ehnoh-U-Re-chnoh in the Women's
gallery of the synagogue. Cf. L 384 # 340 and p. 391
405.

.11 'Milich': '-<u>i</u>ch' -- the 'i' is parasitic, auth. Y

32.23 'Maad': (Dienst)mädchen

32.11 dial.

.12 'weschen': 'e' f. 'a' is dial. Y and G, but <u>rare</u> in Y.

.13 'allfott': immer; G dial, not Y.

.14 'Gsund': Cf. the severe syncope of the 'e' in "gesund" here with the archaic 'Gelieder' in .8, and cf. both against HG and Y phonology; H thus makes his supposed Y dial. go in <u>opposite</u> directions just to <u>deviate</u> from HG. These deviations are therefore always to be suspected and carefully examined for their authenticity!

.15 'Kiš': the father of Saul, the first king of Israel, hence of royal lineage. H prob. assumed that only the scholars would get the reference -- the others might associate the word with the vulgarism "Kisch mich..." ("kiss me..."), as G "küssen" > Y "kischen", as all Germanic '-ss-' (against Germanic '-t-', > HG and Y '-ss-') > Y '-š-'. There is a similar proverbial Y pun on presumptuous family pedigree: 'mišpachas hassarchi' (a pun on 'hazarchi' (Num. 26.13) and Sarach 26.46 which would <u>have</u> to yield 'Sarchi' -- if a matronym were derived from it, as a patronym Zarchi <u>is</u> derived from 'Zarach') = "stinker" family. Perhaps "Familie Kiš" was a similar contemptuous phrase in H's dial. A <u>third</u> connotation resides in the fact that Kiš (spelled Kisch, Kiss) is a rather common family name among Asutro-Hungarian Jews (as common as 'Klein' is elsewhere - Kiš too means "small"). The joke: "no small matter this family Small!"

.16 'Geseroh': = in Y usually an <u>evil</u> decree, one maliciously and viciously directed to persecute Jews.

.20 'bai Laib': originally = "even if it should cost your life", weakened to "absolutely under no circumstances" -- lost in EY.

33.1 '<u>bi-Semonoh</u>': Transliterated erroneously with 'o' f. 'a'; lit. = "in its (proper) time". Properly and preferably Maᶜariv should be prayed <u>immediately</u> after the appearance of the stars, while the afternoon-prayer (Minḥa) properly should be finished before sunset. To accommodate busy worshippers the synagogue

33.3   Wieso, warum?   How come?   Why?

.9   Sage jemand; somebody tell

.11   probieren (soll)

.18   nehme ihn

.22   Segen

33.1   set the two prayers close to one another so that the
two are performed in <u>one</u> session. The pious usually
make an interval between Minḥa and Maᶜariv, during
which they learn Torah together and thus connect "day
and night" with Torah. The less pious run the two
prayers too close together and risk making Minḥa too
late or Maᶜariv too early. Those who say their prayers
in private, because the proper time in the synagogue
is inconvenient, are usually also remiss in <u>optimum</u>
timing. Ultimately the "obligation is met" even in
non-optimum time -- for Minḥa all afternoon, for
Maᶜariv all night. The point of .1-.3 is the
characterization of Mordche and Hathach by their piety,
which is genuine and spontaneous in Mordche and re-
luctantly assumed in Hathach.

.3   Hathach apparently showed himself less than eager.   In
addition to the anachronisms, the intended h consists
in Mordche "dragging" Hathach to the synagogue the
<u>third</u> time on a plain work-day and not realizing that
(for H, the Maskil, at least) <u>that</u> may be too much.
Mordche is downright <u>surprised</u> at Hathach's reluctance!
'Was taitsch': Cf. on 27.9; 'worim': Cf. C 148 on 9.9.

.4ff   The <u>simple</u> questions are meant to be dubitative, i.e.,
"<u>do</u> I go" f. "<u>should</u> I go."

.9   'ahnṡ': eins, somebody, G dial. not Y; the neuter is
used to express common gender. Cf. G ein<u>s</u> seiner
Eltern ist hier, ich weiss nicht welche<u>s</u>.

.12   'ich'ṡ': '-'ṡ' = the contest.

.15   Then it is a sign of G-d's will.

34.3   habe...anzuziehen

.4   kann ich kein solches Merino(-wollenes)

.5   'eternelleṡ': durable

.6   ellenbreit

.7   taftenes, taffeta

33.17   'gewi<u>nn</u>'ṡ': 'nn' -- (double consonant, so often
found in H) not Y; '-ṡ' = the contest.

.18   'Nemm'n': nehme ihn (den König) ein, win (the king);
EY would more often say <u>here</u> 'nemme<u>m</u>', though 'nemmen',
in spite of aural confusion with the infinitive, is
possible too. In EY the masc. sg. dat. and acc. have
fallen together on the basis of the dat. However,
unaccented '-m' suffix becomes '-n', but not after
nasals!

.19   'binṡ': '-ṡ' = Königin. From .17 on the present
tense is used f. the future, proper and common in G
and Y, and here possible even in Engl.

.20   'maintwihgen': = "I'll accept whatever happens",
"What will be will be".

.20-22   '-wihgen -- Siegen': 'ē' > 'ī' as usual in H.

34. 2   'in de<u>r</u> <u>D</u>unkel': fem. in MHG and Y, neuter in NHG.
In EY only <u>T</u>unkel, in NHG only <u>D</u>unkel, in MHG both,
with 't-' more common.

.3   'ho': auth. Y, though rare when it is a <u>main</u> verb,
and almost unthinkable in this <u>hiatus</u>-position;
fairly common in EY when it is an auxiliary and
spoken fast and without accent; h c. Cf. .6 'hob'.
The unaccented position was aided by "back-forma-
tion" from "ich hon" and "er hot" to yield "ich ho".
'-zih<u>g</u>en': 'g' not EY and prob. not WT either; G
dial. dished up as Y h c, esp. since "zihgen" also
connotes "goats". Cf. L p. 417 # 642.

.4   'Marine': h dist. f. Merino-wollenes Kleid. L
p. 386 # 362.

34.9   'Talie': (gute) Schneiderei, tailoring

.10   'ahn': einem

.11   'H<u>ôreg</u>-le': Krüppel, Pfuscher; cripple, botcher.

.12   verderben

.15   'Tucheṡ': tuchenes (Kleid), cloth (dress).

34.5   'eternelleṡ': Cf. L p. 362 # 113. One is tempted to
motivate H's choice of the word to its stronger suggestion of "eternal", i.e., "burial-shroud", rather
than just"durable" -- the latter meaning would scarcely
have been commonly known. The advice: to dress in
shrouds in the contest to win a queen's crown!

.6   'eihlenbraad': ellenbreit, (many) feet wide; 'ei-' f.
'ell-' is auth. Y < MHG variant 'ėle', the 'ė' of
which regularly developed like MHG 'ê' (in "Gên"). It
therefore sounds WY [e], NEY [ey], SEY [ay] and should
sound [ī] in H! The transliterator's spelling 'eihl'
is somewhat ambiguous, as one might be tempted to
sound the 'ei' as in HG. H consistently spells HG
'ei' (when that's what he wants) as   (two Yods).
Cf. for instance SD 1 A and 1 B 'Zaire' and 'herain',
where he means HG "Zeire" and "herein". The spelling
ה ׳ y is unique, a <u>hapax</u> <u>graphomenon</u>; it must aim at
the NEY phonology [ɛy]; had H aimed at the WY [e] he
have spelled it הy (eh), as he regularly does. H
wanted a deviation from HG phonology (ellen); WY
'Ēlen' would have the connotation of HG "Elentier"
(Elk); his own '<u>Ih</u>lenbraad' might suggest "fried
herring", confusing and ultimately not as funny as the
literal exaggeration; so he chose NEY -- which commu-
nicated clearly and was still different from HG. That
he did <u>not</u> use "his own" '<u>Ih</u>len' might well suggest
that <u>that</u> phonology (NHG ē > ī) was not auth. <u>WY</u> and
would not have been immediately recognized and grasped
by the reader <u>at this point</u>.

.7   'Dafeteṡ': inauth. adj. formed from Taffeta (NHG and
EY noun 'Taft', adj. 'taften') with the usual added
rev. subst. h c. L p. 359 # 85.

34. 9   'Gemach': delight, L p. 369 # 188; no longer Y in
this meaning, and possibly not known to H, let alone
his readers. If "delight" is the meaning here, then
it is, of course, sarcastic. More likely the meaning
is a "bad, botched job" -- the usual pejorative force
of 'Ge-' with H; in EY that would require
'gemachachts'; 'gemach' in EY is restricted to "un-
disturbed". If "delight" is the meaning, then "botch"
is a deliberate connotation anyway.
'Talie': pronounce 'talje'; usually the fashionable
FW for "waist", here prob. = the "tailoring, the cut"
of the dress.

  .10   'mer': man; 'ahn': einem, dat.; the impersonals
'mer ahn sain' (man einem sein) are used for the
personal "er (= der Schneider) mir mein".
'kalieh': pronounce "Kalje"; the Y meaning is
"verderben", "spoil". The R is pure in Y but H's
"sophisticates" prob. pronounced "taje - kalje" and
thus had a funny R!

  .11   'Hôreg-le': "cripple, runt", here prob. also
"botcher", refers to an unmentioned tailor. Cf. on
17.13.
'Worm': 'o' f. G 'u' auth. Y "lowering" of vowel
before guttural plus consonant. Cf. C p.112f.

  .12   'ferdorm': verdorben, spoiled; the assimilation is
auth. colloquial and as such meant to be funny and
is made even funnier by Rz.

  .14   'tut': sc. 'es' (das Kleid); left out delib. h c,
to suggest "going naked".

  .15   'Tucheš': f. 'tuchenes' (Kleid), cotton dress; cf. .7
'Defeteš', both funny adj. formations, delib. dist.
h c, neither HG nor Y nor dial.; with 'Tucheš' the
distortion manages to connote and pronounce the SEY
vulgarism for "arse", < Hebr. euphemism "taxat",
"unten" = HG euphemism "Hintern". The line thus
become obscenely suggestive.

35.2 Nein...für Lumpen

.4 'Kechi': Köchin

.5 Verreckt!

.8 wird ein Aufsehen

.10 Ja -- kurzes Haar ist bald gebürstet; short hair combs fast.

.13 'gihle': gelbe, yellow

.15 Wirst sehen die Schlemihlin ihn verderben.

35.2 'Na': nein; 'Ruhôs': Hebr. "Winde, Geister, Böse Geister, Teufel" then Y "arme Teufel, Lumpen". The last is meant here: "Nein, das (ist ein Kleid darin) Lumpen herumlaufen mögen", "that's a dress fit to be worn by riff-raff". The R Tuches - Ruches is actually pure, but as 'Tuches' is non-existent in HG and WY H's audience and readers are thrown back to the Hebr. Y vulgarism, which in WY is "tɔxəs" and thus Rz and therefore still more "piquant" and supposedly even funnier.

.4 'Kechi': 'Kechin' is auth. Y < G Köchin.

.5 'Wat main Kapporoh': Drop dead! Cf. C p. 132 on 3.8 and L p. 378 # 286.

.6 'hett': habt, prob. inauth. h c. EY 'hot'.

.8 'a Noifsehi': ein Aufsehen; Cf. C p.113,XI.

.9 Did you pack already?

.10 Few possessions don't take long to pack. Cf. L p. 355 # 44.

.10-11 'gebašt - Lašt': gebürstet - Last; 'gebašt' is almost auth. Y (cf. C p.112f.) but in 'Lašt' the 'š' is SG dial. dished up as Y h c. In EY the R would be impure 'gebaršt - lašt'; in 'gebaršt' G '-rst' Y '-ršt', and the 'r' plus consonant "lowers" the pre-

35.10-11   ceding vowel (here -- fully <u>two</u> steps, from'ü'
('i') to 'e', to 'a'); '-tet' is syncopated to '-t' --
all <u>regular</u> Y developments.

.12   'Hihtle': Hütlein; 'kennt'r': '-r' - ihr, Rz to
'Bender'.

.13   'gihle': MHG nom. 'gel', gen. 'gelwes';·Y 'gel' <
nom., NHG 'gel<u>b</u>' < gen.

.15   <u>'Schlumiel</u>-te': (sic! Transliteration to be emended
accordingly!) = Pfuscherin, botcher, and refers to an
unmentioned milliner (cf. on 34.11), who (so the three
warn Moka) is sure to spoil, rather than improve, her
hat.
'Wa<u>st</u>': wirst, we should expect '-š̌-' in auth. Herz!
'Ferschender'n': possibly a <u>pun</u> built on a contamination of 'ferschenner'n' ('verschöner'n') and MHG 'ver-
schenden' (zu Schande machen), coined by H to mean
"spoil in the effort to beautify". The coinage is
drastic, the grammar harsh, the meaning uncertain;
the '-'n' is apparently the encliticized 'ihn' and
refers to an unmentioned "der Hut"; the actual antecedent is (das) 'Hihtlein' and would require 'es
ferschendern', instead of 'verschender (ih)n' -- i.e.,
assuming our analysis to be correct. The curious
grammar is obviously Rz and the Rz is h c!

36.1   'der Zetulpe ihrs': the syntax is good G dial.,
but neither Y nor good HG.

.2   'krumme--Sachen': the dashes (--) indicate a pause,
and 'Sachen' is thus to come supposedly as a surprise,
as if it, the real word, were unmentionable. Yet the
only word which fits with 'krumme' is 'Ideen', ideas,
and the ideas are <u>innocent</u>, and refer to the style of
her little hat!

.3-4   'Bahl - Schahl': Ball - Schal; Rz with delib. dist.
(lengthening the 'a' in 'Ball') h c.

.4   'in ihr': f. G "ihr<u>em</u>", auth. Y, in which poss.
adj. s are <u>invariable</u>, except for the pl. suffix '-e'.

36.8   Das Herz im Leib hat einem

  .10   'Mi'us': ekelig, disgusted.

36.5   'Apripu': (sic! erase the underlining in the transli-
       teration) delib. dist. of FW in fashion -- to "show up"
       the ignorant "nobodies who would ape nobility", "les
       bourgeois gentilshommes".
       'recht': f. 'rechte', apocope is SG dial not Y.
       'gihben': f. 'gegeben'; old perfect participle without
       the prefix 'ge' in perfective verbs, still left out
       sometimes in HG, especially after an unaccented syllable,
       not Y, which tends to extend the 'ge-' beyond the usage
       in HG (cf. 'geŠtudirt'). Cf. A p. 106 # 47.

  .6   'wi?': an exclamation mark would seem more fitting.
       'Ponim--lich': prob. to be pronounced "pénemlech" as
       in EY today: The '-lich' suffix as well as the plura-
       lization caused umlaut in this Hebrewism in MEY. The
       spelling never shows it though. Hence the difficulty
       of determining the incidence of the umlaut. 'Ponim' in
       Hebrew is already plural (an instance of the pluralia
       tantum) and literally means "facings" but in fact has
       the sg. meaning "face". In Y a new pl. had to be
       coined to mean "faces" and it was coined on a German Y
       pattern. i.e., by analogy to "das Gesicht, die Ge-
       sichter": "dos pónem, di pénemer"; "penemlech" =
       "dear, sweet (little) faces".
       'zun': 'n' f. 'm' -- dist. h c.

  .5-6 'gihben - ferlihben': the R is apparently pure in
        the H dial., but Rz in practically all Y dial., hence
        -- "funny". Mrs. Edith Rothenberg, our typist, in-
        forms me that "Hevel Havolim" (cf. on 25.4) was pro-
        nounced by her parents as "Hïvel...". The implication
        of this bomb-shell is that there was so a WY dialect
        in which the short 'ĕ-' in open syllables developed
        first into long 'ē' and then further into 'ī'. The
        phenomenon may have been co-extensive with Vögtländisch
        and touched a relatively small number of WY speakers
        and thus lent itself for that very reason to use as
        "comic relief" by H.

  .7   'dir': not only the person addressed, all are in-
       cluded.
       'Štaat': elegance; still good Y, but obviously a FW

36.7   (cf. 'ā').

.8   'in': Y; G requires 'im' (i.e., syncope f. in <u>dem</u>),
with the article.
'ahn': Y and G require "eine<u>m</u>", the dat. of reference,
where English uses the posse<u>ss</u>ive, e.g.: "I stick <u>my</u>
hand in <u>my</u> pocket", G "Ich stecke <u>mir</u> die Hand in <u>die</u>
Tasche", Y "ix ŝtek <u>mir</u> di hant <u>in</u> taŝ". Y can even
dispense with the "<u>mir</u>". The meaning: "one's heart
within one laughed" f. "it was a sight to rejoice
over". Impersonal f. personal.

.9   'Waaŝ taitsch': here = "Was sagst du?!" Cf. on 27.9.
'nuhbler': eleganter, aristokratischer; the '-uh-' f.
FWs recently borrowed <u>is</u> dist. h c in <u>WY</u> (Cf. H's
'mude', 'Kun<u>t</u>iter', etc.). However, in SEY, i.e., in
"Galitzianer" dial. such '<u>u</u>' <u>is</u> auth. The MHG 'ô'
became 'oi' in both WY and SE<u>Y</u>, but not borrowings
after ca. 1500. However, since MHG 'â' had become Y
'ɔ' by 1500, and that 'ɔ' developed further to 'o'
and ultimately to 'oi' in WY and to 'u' in SEY (around
1725), the new 'o' borrowed after 1500 should have
become 'oi' in WY and 'u' in SEY. The phonology 'u'
('nuhbler', 'mude') did exist among the more traditional, conservative SEY speakers. But just in these
fashionable FWs the 'u' was displaced by the
"cultivated", "correct" 'o' in most speakers. Incidentally, neither Harkavy, nor Weinreich list
"noble", though they do list "mɔdə". Stutchkoff
lists "noble" but only in the sense of "a descendant
of titled nobility", not in its other senses. Yet
it does exist also in the senses of "elegant, well-
mannered, kind-hearted".

.10   '<u>Mi꞊uŝ</u>': a noun in Hebr., meaning "ugliness",
"repulsiveness"; it is used i<u>n</u> Y (and in G: "mies")
as an adj. The Hebr. adj. "ma꞊us" (Y 'mɔəs') fell
into disuse because it became a homophone of Hebr.
"maˤot", "money". It <u>is</u> used when it is combined
with the passive participle for emphasis: "niməs un
mɔəs", because the participle prevents misunder-
standing. Pronounce "mīŝ". This Hebrewism has
completely displaced the Germanic word f. "ugly" in
Y (G "hässlich", the antonym of "schön") as Y prefers
Hebrewisms for words of strong emotional charge. It
even entered G because of the high frequency with

36.10   which G Jews used it. <u>Here</u> its meaning is stronger than just "ugly"; it is "thoroughly disgusted".

.11   'froigen': auth. WY < MHG "frâgen". EY derives from a MHG variant "fregən".

.12   'als oifgezoigen': the pretended "innocent" meaning is prob.: "who raised you (i.e., gave you all your education in elegance?)" H delib. formulates the question ambiguously, so Soka and Moka can <u>misunderstand</u> it as meaning (apparently): "who has kept ('als') teasing you (by keeping you in suspense about inviting you to dance with them)?" Zaire may even be suggesting "who raised you (so bad!)?"

37.1   Dependent-clause word order -- no longer EY.

.2   'Mir hem': SG dial., not Y. 'Hân mir' > 'hammir' > 'hemmir', then also 'mir hem', i.e., the encliticized 'mir' caused the umlaut. "Haben mir" also could yield "hammir" and "hemmer".

.3   'orndlich': auth. Y 'orntlich' f. G "orden(t)lich", the 'd' was lost as a result of "simplification (Entlastung) by dissimilation".

.4   'Triher': Dreher, slow waltz. L p. 409 # 582 and p. 417 # 638.
'a moile Zehi': zehn mal. L p. 385 # 374. 'a moile' apparently had lost its specific meaning of "one time", the suffix '-e' was added, as so often happens to adverbs, and the whole, which was apparently used interchangeably with 'mal' ('moil') for "once upon a time", came to be used also for "mal" in the sense of "(cumulative) repetitions". The word order is G (cf. "mal zehn") <u>not</u> Y.
'missen': müssen; EY has "musn" (s = z) with a secondary shift of the 'ŭ' to 'i' as is to be expected regularly in SEY, i.e., no basic umlaut. H usually has 'messen' from some G dial. and here he uses 'missen', the regular SG dial. form (with unrounding of the HG 'ü'), Rz with 'gerissen'. The "double infinitive construction" with the modal auxiliaries is a relatively recent HG development after the parting of Y and G, and therefore not participated in by EY; WY, that

37.9   'Nafezihr': Offizier, (military) officer

37.4   remained on G speech-territory, did apparently participate, or at least borrow, the construction.
Hence EY has "gemust, gewolt, gekont" for H's
'missen, wellen, kenne' (.4-.7). Originally the
modal auxiliaries, as preterite-presents, had only the
one rigid tense-form and were defective in all other
tenses (as English "must", for instance, still is thus
defective); past tenses, infinitives and participles
were coined anew, gradually, in that order. (In English, only some past tenses were coined, but no infinitives or participles.) Since in HG the new infinitives were coined long before the past participles
(in all verbs in HG, except the verb "sein", the
infinitive is identical with the first and third
person plural present) the "double infinitive construction" became possible long before the "regular
perfect" tense. Since there are so many verbs in HG
where the infinitive and past participle are identical (cf. "vergessen, vergeben, gefallen") and some
more that look like infinitives, because of loss of
the prefix 'ge-' due to their position after an unaccented syllable (cf. "ich habe den Mann gelassen"
against "ich habe den Mann gehen lassen"--here"lassen"
is the past participle without the prefix 'ge-' due to
the unaccented syllable '-en' preceding) modal
auxiliaries with a dependent infinitive were able to
achieve the perfect tense through the double-infini-
tive construction, on the pattern of "habe gehen
lassen", before they developed a perfect participle!

   .5   'wellen': auth. Y and MHG; "wollen" in HG is due to
the secondary influence of the labial ('w'). Cf. its
influence in English on the sound-value of the 'a' in
"war", "wall" against the value in "are", "Al".

   .6   'bain': 'n' d. 'm' h c.
'Fezzen': lit. = "rag", vulgar f. "dress". L p. 365
139B. The boast in 36.9 that the ball could not
have been conducted more "nobly" is coupled with the
"give-away" boast that she was so popular that after
finishing each dance another gentleman would "grab
her by her rag"--to ask her to dance with him.

   .9   'Is...': the inverted word order in Y normally has

37.10 mit ihnen engagiere

 .14 'Hemsin...Huzzer': haben sie ihm...Tritt

 .15 'blait': bleibt (liegen)

 .16 'Iz daf': jetzt muss

37.9 consecutive force, equivalent to the Engl. connectives
"therefore", "and so" (cf. "Er hot nit, ken er nit gebn"
with "He doesn't have, so he can't give.") But here
the whole line is predicate, the "subject" being the
left-out, implied "es" (whether we call it "impersonal"
or "expletive"). The point is the line is not a story
about a student and an officer; they are not the subjects, the centers of interest, about whom information
is predicated. The center of interest is the self-
centered boaster, who can brook no other subject.
Hence student and officer, important as they are to
the boaster, are placed in a construction where they are
the predicate. That is the significance of the difference between 'Is kumme a Študent' and "A Študent is
kumme".
'kumme': "kumen" is the MHG participle, without the
prefix 'ge-' like all perfective verbs; the 'u' is still
Y, the lack of 'ge-' is not. Y has extended the 'ge-'
even beyond HG.
'Nafezihr': by metanalysis (false division) an
'Afezihr' (sic 74.11) Cf. C p.113# XI and L p. 350 # 5.

 .10 'mit si': prob. auth.; in EY "sey" ("they" is an
invariant.
'angaschihr': engagiere(n würde); Kora's innocently
intended meaning is "until I would accept their
request for a dance", but then strict syntax would
require "ich mich ihnen e."; "sich mit einem engagieren"
has the more common euphemistic meaning, "to have a
love affair with someone", and the very rare and
locally limited meaning "to engage oneself to be
married". '-schihr' f. '-giere' is typical of the "uneducated" pronunciation of the French FW, and even
suggests the kitchen and its Geschirr -- coupled with
the bad grammar and syntax and the erotic connotation,
all these enhance the h. L p. 351 # 18.

 .11 'schihn': 'schihn' f. schönen, '-en' ending called in
Y and G.

 .12 'ošur': here = kaum, hardly.

37.13f   The para-, instead of hypo-tactic construction ('Juśt',
instead of "juśt als") makes the style "primitive" and
adds a touch of added humor in that .13 becomes the
<u>cause</u> of .14, i.e., it sounds as if the student was
kicked <u>just because</u> he had "made her compliments".
'Juśt': a "Modewort" which entered G < Latin in the
16th century but didn't "sink" to "lower" levels of
society before it disappeared again in the 19th century; as an <u>adv.</u> it therefore was prob. strictly HG,
neither Y nor dial.; the 'ś' f. 's' is therefore inauth. for added h. EY has 'just' only in the stock-
phrase "a juster balebos", "a well-to-do squire, a
man of means"; WY does have "juśt" = "recht, gerecht",
but apparently only in the stock-phrase "dos is
ni(ś)t juśt". Cf. Tendlau p. 59 # 152.
'Kumplimender' - 'Musikstender' (.14): Rz; linking
accented and unaccented syllables, the 'u' f. 'o',
and the rev. subst. in '-md-' are all H's regular
dist. h c.

.14   'Hemsin': haben sie ih<u>m</u>: the 'n' f. 'm' could be
auth. <u>here</u>, as the encliticized m > n, but the
enclisis itself is of questionable authenticity.
'nebich': cf. C p.126 on 1.7 and L p. 379 # 289.
'Huzzer': Tritt, Stoss, kick, shove -- dial., not Y.
Cf. L p. 376 # 273.

.15   'blait': bleibt; not Y. Cf. L p. 356 # 61.

.16   'Iz daf': jetzt <u>muss</u>; Y and MHG, but elsewhere (e.g.,
1.6) it can also have the meaning "to have permis-
sion". Cf. L p. 357 # 66 and C p.177 on 17.1 and
p.222 on 29.9.
The "officer" and "student" are the "highest society"
these playmates of Esther can conceive of. On the
"historic" level these could be imagined as Jews (in
450 B.C.E.), but on the anachronistic, "realistic"
level, the "officer" definitely could not, and the
"student" also could therefore hardly have been Jews
in the Germany of 1820. Jews had been making efforts
to achieve at least some social and religious
"desegregation" for almost a century, and assimilation
had become the ideal of the upper class of Jewish
Society in Germany (witness the circle around Moses
Mendelssohn ca. 1760) but Legal Emancipation had to
wait till 1871, and real social emancipation was

38.3 '<u>Jôm Tôv</u>-tik': unwohl, unwell

.4   Sie reden...wird auch...Augenblick

37.16 hardly <u>ever</u> achieved. The chemist Fritz Haber had con-
       verted to Christianity. He had invented (along with
       many more useful things) poison gas in 1914, but the
       military kept him from an audience with the Kaiser till
       1915. It is said that the reason given him (for not
       being admitted to an audience with the Kaiser) was that
       (though he was the head of the Chemical Division of the
       Kaiser Wilhelm Institute and also of Chemical Warfare)
       he was only a lieutenant. He was not told <u>why</u> he was
       only a lieutenant. Only one guess is possible: He was
       of Jewish descent. There weren't any Jewish staff-
       officers in the German army even as late as 1918. There
       is a belief among Jews that had Haber attained the rank
       of General in 1914, Germany would have won the war
       before the United States could have entered it.

38.1   'Zetulpe...': = But Zetulpe didn't dance at all.
       'wider': dagegen, on the other hand (compared to us),
       Y.

   .2 The tense is prob. Rz: neither Y nor G require "se-
       quence of tenses".
       'gewelt': 'e' is the older, original vowel, still pre-
       served in some Y and G dial. The 'o' is due to the
       labialization effect of the sequence 'w-l'. In NHG the
       'o' prevailed in all forms except the pres. sg., where
       'i' <u>is</u> the regular Germanic development. In EY today,
       'i' has been extended throughout the pres. by analogy –
       in the <u>modal</u>; in the fut. aux. 'e' prevails, in the past
       participle 'o'. Cf. A p. 117 # 53.

   .3 '<u>Jôm Tôv</u>-tik': lit. = "holiday-like", but more especial-
       ly, "passover-like", as against its antonym "Chometzdik"
       = lit. "leaven-like" and therefore "forbidden on Pass-
       over, unfit for Passover". Cf. C p. 127 on 1.10 about
       the strictness of the no-leaven-on-Passover rule, it
       being a capital sin even just to "harbor" an infinitesi-
       mal amount of leaven on Passover. A special set of
       Passover dishes is guarded throughout the year from be-
       ing as much as touched by anyone who touched leaven-food.
       Hence the "Yomtev'ik" or "Yontevdik" acquired the meaning

38.9   Schlägt...Abend

  .10   'Soch': Plage, Flegel; plague, brat.
        'ebeš der Mehr': etwas los, something wrong.

38.3   of "untouchable" and was used as a humorous euphemism
       for a ritually "unclean" wife (throughout her menstrua-
       tion, and seven "clean" days thereafter, plus a duck-
       ing in a ritual bath after the seven "clean" days) and
       then Y slang for "menstruous"; '-dik' (H '-tik') is an
       adjectival suffix in Y, falsely subtracted by metana-
       lysis from the MHG adj. derived from the pres. parti-
       ciple, e.g., MHG "gehende -- gehendic".

  .4   'rihten': reden

  .4-5 Mirza understands "Jomtevtik" literally as "proper
        and fit for Passover", and she remembers that she
        hasn't as yet collected enough (chicken or goose) fat
        for Passover, even though the holiday was "coming in a
        moment" (that "moment" being exactly one month!). But
        "Passover-fat" was a worrisome problem to a Jewish
        housewife. It still is the most important item in the
        pantry of an orthodox Jew. As all grain- and legume-
        products are forbidden because they can get "leavened"
        when moistened (and, among the "stricter" observers
        even products made from "matzo-meal" -- meal made from
        ground unleavened "matzoh" - wafers are eschewed) the
        menu on Passover is restricted almost exclusively to
        matzoh, eggs, potatoes, beet soup (and meat-- for
        those that could afford meat). To make these palat-
        able large amounts of fat are used. But such fat
        (fit for Passover) didn't use to be on sale. It had
        to be garnered over most of the winter from the
        occasional fowls slaughtered for the Sabbath dinner.
        But this·was a very laborious, care-requiring, burden-
        some procedure: The fowl whose fat was "saved up"
        for Passover, had to be "koshered" "as if for Pass-
        over", i.e., in Passover dishes, that weren't touched
        by anything that had touched "leavened" foods or
        dishes. The hands had to be washed and carefully
        watched; the oven had to be "koshered" for Passover,
        i.e., heated to a glow before the fat could properly
        be rendered on it. Thus collecting Passover-fat was
        quite a chore for the housewife.

38.15 wird's neun Uhr

.16 'tretztsi': neckt sie; she teases.

38.9 'Štrakt': beats; perhaps related to MHG "stragéln" =
to hit, push; more prob. to MHG "stracken", to stretch
outtight (intr.), but used transitively by H ('dich')
in the sense of "drag", perhaps with some erotic connotation; but cf. L p. 405 # 534.

.10 'Soch': lit. = Krankheit, Plage -- sickness, plague;
here used for a person who is a source of trouble, cf.
English "pest", "crank" and the semantics involved when
referring to persons. Prob. an ellipsis f. "groiŝe
Soch" (= epilepsy, grand mal), a synonym of the Y
Hebrewism "nechpe", which means literally "epilepsy"
and figuratively "a 'pesty' or pestiferous (misfortune-
of-a) person". Cf. C p.166 on 16.2 and L p. 407 # 559.
'Mehr': MHG "maere", "story, news, event"; preserved
in Y only in the stock-phrase "(epeŝ, woŝ) der mer" --
"(et)was los", "(what, something) wrong"; "der mer" is
derived from an original MHG gen. pl. (maere), a case
distinction no longer practiced in Y, where the pl. is
identical in all cases. The semantics: Not only is
"no news good news", but for a Jew news usually was
bad news. The meaning of the line: "Is something
wrong with this brat?". L p. 387 # 368.

.11 'For': in der Gegenwart von, in front of.
'alle': auth. Y, though today EY prefers "far alemen".
'be-Herpóh': pronounce "bəxárpə" = "zu Schanden".

.12 'Kol͡Óɫom': lit. = der ganzen Welt, (to) the whole
world.

.13 'Der ihr': tautology; a construction common in G dial.
but not in Y; "der" is the dat. sg. of the fem. pron.
and antecedent of "ihr", the nom. of the poss. adj.;
lit. = "to her her like" f. "her likes", "something
like her"; in EY "ir glaixəniŝ" would suffice.
'is nimmer hie': Rz f. "gibt es nirgends", "doesn't
exist anywhere". Cf. 39.2.

.15 'zun Bett': one should expect "aus dem Bett" or "vom
Bett"; the G idiom "zur Tür hinaus" means "out by way
of the door" and is inapplicable with a bed; dist. h c?

39.1   'Ohren': Beten, prayers.

.3   'Tihg': Tage; 'schnokkle': zieren, to prim

.6   'Schuṡelt...rah': rennt...hinab

.7   'ah': an

.8   'Grihfen': Gräfin

.11   How long will it take you to crawl over?

38.15   'woṭṡ': the 'o' (̣) may be a smeared 'a' (̣), cf.
39.1 'waṭṡ'.
'naine': 'woṭṡ naine' = wird's neun Uhr; on the '-e'
cf. C p.197 on 22.10.

.16   'tretztsi': "tretzen" is a MHG variant of NHG
"trotzen" with the sense of "necken", "tease"; not
Y. L p. 410 # 586.

39.1   'waṭṡ': Cf. 38.15 'woṭṡ', where the 'o', however, may
be a misreading of an ink-smear for a "kamaṣ"
(‿ -'ɔ' in SY pronunciation) for the "pataḧ" (‗ ='a');
H normally changes 'a' to 'ɔ' in-between two labials
(cf. 'wofft' (7.1) f. SY "varft" = G "wirft") but not
just after one labial.

.3   'Tihg': as Y generally apocopated every final G '-e',
the sg. and pl. of all OHG "a-stems" became identical,
so Y (and SG!) had to develop a new pl. and extended
the "i-stem" plural-formation (the umlaut) to many
original a-stems: so HG "Tage" > Y "teg", H 'Tihg'.
'schnokkle': zieren, to prim; G not Y; cf. G dial.
"Schnuki" = "Schatzi" and "nieke" = "Schmuck".

.4   'fatik': fertig; 'guzzen': gucken, L p. 372 # 229.

.5   'Sicht riber...niber': sieht herüber...hinüber.

.6   'Schuṡelt': runs, L p. 405 # 541; 'rah': loss of
final '-b' not Y.

.7   'Kuch': Y; both Y "koch" and "kech" < G dial.
"Kuche" and "Küche".

39.9   'gebihten': a line without rhyme, rare in H.

.10 The Y idiom means "incompetent".

.10A SD 'H<u>o</u>nd-': 'o' seems to be a misprint; the "kamas" ( ) seems too clear to be considered a <u>smear</u> but SDs are always HG, so it is inconceivable for H to intend an 'o' here.

.11 'ihr ich': sic! contraction f. "ihr aich"; 'riber': herüber; 'hokken': G "herüberhocken" could only be an oxymoron, "hocken" implying "squatting in place" and "herüber" implying "moving". The whole line has an unusual structure and is difficult to interpret -- <u>perhaps</u> it means "How long will it take you to <u>crawl</u> home?".

.14 'Iber ahl': sic! (<u>two</u> words) = "überall"; the 'ah' is auth. Y -- the vowel is long because in Germanic (G, Y, and Engl.) the accent in compound <u>adverbs</u> is on the <u>second</u> element and in this adv. this accent is especially strong (cf. G "herúm" and "umhér" consisting of identical components and identical meaning, yet <u>mechanically</u> the accent is shifted to the second element); SEY "iberul".

.15 'a': "ab"; cf. on .6.

.16 Warte, nimm...Lot Käsekücklein -- wait, take along... an ounce of Danish (cheese) pastry.

.16-17 Rz; 'Zwariklich': Y requires "Zware<u>ch</u>lech" (EY "z<u>yo</u>rech") for "little pressed forms of cheese-curds" (then, "cheese-cakes"); the 'k' f. 'ch' may be dist. h c to connote "Zwerglein", "midgets", "runts"; the '-i-'s in the R are dist., svarabhakti vowels, also h c. The usual, traditional "Danish pastry" for the holiday of Purim is called "Homen-tašen" and is filled not with cheese, but with either jam or poppy-seed. Folklore ascribes the "Homentaš" to the commemoration of the legendary event, that Haman's wife, Zereš, was watching the procession in which Haman honored Mordechai by leading him riding on the royal horse, mistook Haman for Mordechai and emptied

39.13　'war': werde

.16　'Zwariklich': Danish cheese pastry

.17　'Wariklich': wirklich, really

40.2　'Gigerigih': Hahn, Geck (Kikeriki); cook, fop
　　　(cock-a-doodle-doo)

.4　'Manschoche': Donnerwetter!; Gosh!
　　　'Gihger': Hahn

.6　Höre! Der Kerl kann aber krähen.

.7　heben Sie ihn. 'Mezi'oh': Gelegenheitskauf; bargain.

39.16-17　her chamber-pot on his head. In order to stop the
　　　drippings, Haman turned up the brim of his hat. Hence
　　　--the three-cornered pastry and its filling! L p. 418
　　　# 652. However, in addition to "Homen-tašen", lots of
　　　other pastries are baked and exchanged as gifts on
　　　Purim.

40.2-4　'Giger(igih)': Cf. L p. 370 # 201f. The "innocent
　　　intent" of the Mädchen is to say that R' Hathach is
　　　coming with a rooster, but she actually says, "R'
　　　Hathach is coming, the rooster", but when 'Gigerigih'
　　　refers to a person, it means "fop", not "rooster"!
　　　Hence R' Mordechai's gentle reproof.
　　　The '-le' in 'Hazufoh-le' (pronounce "Chzúfələ) has
　　　the force of "dear little" (freshie!); his threat to
　　　slap her must be taken to be at least half-humorous.
　　　'Manschoche': G dial. expression of astonishment,
　　　L p. 386 # 360.

.4A　SD 'krehet': the '-e-'is almost HHG, typical for the
　　　native Y speaker "transposing" his WY into G--an
　　　element of h H uses to ridicule his anti-heroes and
　　　uses very heavily, only to fall victim to the same
　　　"tripper", albeit in an attenutated form: After all,
　　　the "fuller" form of the verb is still "correct" in
　　　poetry. That the SD's are meant to be HG is proven
　　　once again by 'krehet' (against 'krihe' in .6).

.7　'Mezi'oh': lit. "Fund", "find", in Y = Gelegenheits-
　　　kauf zum Schleuderpreis; spottbillig, a bargain,
　　　dirt-cheap. In .6-.7 the R is pure.

41.1 'Mokkel': kleine Zuchtsau; little breed-sow

 .2 'Gogel': Gockel(hahn); rooster.

40.8-9 Rz -- "švérīs - məubérəs"; added to the humor of the
Rz is the Hebrewism 'me꜀ubbereš' -- it is not <u>too</u>
current in Y, and would be familiar only to those with
some knowledge of Hebrew, and these would be extra
amused by the incongruity of the <u>feminine form</u> of the
adjective. It is as if someone were to say in G,
"vielleicht ist <u>er</u> gar ein<u>e</u> schwangere" -- only that in
G the predicate adjective is invariant -- whereas in
Hebrew it must agree with its antecedent.

41.1-2 'Mokkel - Gogel': delib. dist. even destroying a
pure R (mɔkl - gɔkl) h c. L p. 388 # 376 and p. 371
209. 'Mokkel' could hardly be WY; EY even lost
"Schwein" and "Sau" and uses the Hebrewism "Chaser"
and even that is often avoided by the pious and displaced by the euphemism "dɔvər axər". Traditionally,
pig and pork have been "abominations" to the Jew, the
embodiment of physical filth and symbol of spiritual
defilement. For a concept so charged emotionally only
a Hebrewism could serve -- both for "pork" and for the
insult "swine". EY uses "Xazər". 'Mokkel', even
though a diminutive, hence less outrageously demeaning,
is still too harsh and insulting to a <u>Jew</u>. Perhaps
therein lies the very reason why H used it: to shock.
Some of H's readers may have been unfamiliar with
'Mokkel' as "piglet", but might have been familiar
with Y "mok", a euphemism for "shmok" (cf. American
Anglo-Y "shmo"), the vulgar, abusive term for "fool".
Y "mok" must be rather limited geographically and is
yet to be recorded. The "accepted" etymology for
"shmok" (G "Schmock") is that it came from Slovenian
"smok" = "fool" -- through the Jewish Ghetto of Prague.
Nobody bothered to enquire why the Prague Ghetto should
have bothered to go to Slovenia for an abusive term.
We suggest what seems to us to be a more probable
etymology: "Shmok"and its synonym "Potz" are both
variants of HG "Schmuck" and "Putz" = "jewelry". Women
handling new-born boys have a habit of examining
their genitals, and, if they are well-proportioned, they
are impressed and they express their joyous admiration.
In Y the expression is "Er hot shaine kalle matones" =
"he has beautiful gifts for the bride". This is a

41.3   lässt er ihn denn laufen?

  .4   tut er ihn wieder verkaufen?

  .8   'git': gibt

 .11   Sind wir denn keine Juden?

 .12   'Koschor': nach Ritus zubereitet; prepared according
        to the ritual laws on foods.

 .15   'Pummer': gross wie eine Bombe

41.1-2   reference to the universal custom of the groom giv-
         ing the bride jewelry and to the equally universal
         problem of the poor groom with the song "I can't give
         you anything but love, Baby".
         Thus, the original literal meaning of the words was
         "jewelry", but from their frequent humorous use for
         the "only gift that the bride will get from her groom"
         they came to be the jocular euphemisms for "penis".
         Cf. C p.211f on 26.7 about the extreme "puritanism"
         of Jewish speech and the consequent loss of all terms
         for the "unmentionables" in all Jewish vernaculars.
         In their absence euphemisms were created, but gradual-
         ly the very euphemisms became "unmentionable" or at
         least "vulgar". From their vulgar meaning they were
         applied figuratively as an abusive term for "fool".
         (Cf. similar American Engl. euphemisms for the penis
         used in slang for "fool": "prick", "stiff", "jerk").
         The spelling 'Gogel' for "Gockel" may have been in-
         tended to allude to "Gog", the powerful king who will
         fight the Messiah (Ez. 38.2) and Og, the king of
         Bashan (Numbers 21.33), the proverbial embodiment of
         gigantism among Jews in Jewish lore. Og, Gog (and
         Magog) are often confused for one another. Thus
         'Gogel' = "little giant", h in itself as an oximoron.
         Also 'Gogel' may allude to G dial. "Gogler", HG
         "Gaukler" in the sense of "circus fool".
         Finally, Y and G dial. "gogel - mogel", HG "gaukeln -
         munkeln" are a humorous reference to "cheating and de-
         ceiving by trickery". There can be no direct relation
         to this meaning in .1-.2, but the humor of the ex-
         pression may have been in the apperception of H.

  .3-4   'LoštEr'n...tutEr'n': auth. Y phonology of "speech

41.3-4   as she is spoke" -- but the running-together of words
         is a kind of spelling joke. There is no other compell-
         ing reason for such spelling, not even the excuse of
         syncopation for the sake of meter: the meter of .4 is
         spoiled by it.

  .5-6   'Scheker - Gihger': apparently H pronounced the 'ĕ-'
         in Hebrewisms as 'ī', just like the 'ĕ-' of MHG (cf.
         MHG "lĕben", H 'lihben'). In HG and all Y except NEY
         (Lithuanian Y) both of these 'ĕ-'s became [e:] but not
         [i:] . Line 5 is a "Flickvers", a "filler", to get a
         R f. 'Gihger'.

  .7-8   'tub - -sub': Rz; on 'tub' cf. C p.149 on 9.11;
         'sub < G Suppe, rev. subst.

  .9   'Dernoichet': '-et': frequent Y adverbial suffix,
         originally an excrescent, "parasitic" 't', only occurr-
         ing after the frequent nasal ('-en') adv.-suffix (cf.
         G irgend, or the pronoun jemand), then extended in
         some Y dial. to every adv.
         'gewihs': 'ih' f. 'ī' = rev. subst.

  .11   'Jiden': the auth. Y f. G "Juden"; G "Jude"< late
         Latin "Judeo", but Y < Hebrew "Jehudi" (cf. C p.125,
         1.5) > "Judi" > "Jüde" (all Y words, regardless of
         etymology, participated in the linguistic changes of
         HG from ca. 900 to ca. 1400 -- thus also the umlauting
         of the 'u' (> 'ü') before an 'i' in the following
         syllable; ca. 1600 Y unrounded the rounded front vowels
         (G 'eu', 'ö', 'ü') -- hence "Jid", which, however, often
         remained spelled   (i.e., "Jud"), partly because of
         the influence of G spelling (it was never pronounced
         'u' in auth. Y after ca. 1100), and partly because Y
         (and even G) often used defective spelling for the
         umlauted vowels, so also a 'u' (Y) for a 'ü' (Y   ).
         As late as between the two World Wars a Y daily appeared
         in Warsaw by the name of   ("Der Jud"), but pro-
         nounced "Yid". Some "backward" printers in New York
         City today spell "Yud, yudiš" when they definitely mean
         the sounds "Yid, yidiš" -- a kind of "cultural lag".

  .12   Pious Jews when traveling take along meats "koshered"
         by themselves, as it is difficult to find reliably

41.12   kosher meat on the road. The naive anachronism here
        makes Esther wrap the meat in paper -- that had not
        been invented yet. There are other naive anachronisms
        in the very "koshering" and in Esther's preparing to
        eat only kosher foods -- she was to keep secret her
        Jewishness!
        'Koschor': foods are "kosher", i.e., "ritually fit
        to eat" for a Jew on three conditions:
        1. They must come only from animals classified as
        "clean" in the Bible (Lev. 11).
        2. These animals must be slaughtered in a prescribed
        way.
        3. After ritual slaughtering the meat must soak for
        half an hour, lie salted "on six sides" and run-off
        blood for an hour (half an hour in a "religious
        emergency"), then the salt is washed off.
        The process is called "koschern" or "kosher machen";
        there also exists "kashern" (with 'a'), apparently an
        older formation. Note:
        1. The oldest Y verbs from the Hebrew used the
        Hebrew consonant-root and uniformly vocalized it with
        the vowel 'a' after the first consonant (e.g.,
        "gazlen", "hargen(en)").
        2. Later Y learned to use a paraphrase of the un-
        changed Hebr. part of speech plus an auxiliary verb
        (e.g., "mechabed zain", "moire hobn").
        3. Latest Y uses the unchanged word with added affixes
        (e.g., "farmishpetn", "soffekn" (= "to doubt")).
        But "kashern" is not used for foods but for utensils,
        dishes, and ovens. These too have to be "kosher",
        free from use with non-kosher foods. Separate dishes
        are required (the most concerned, the "mehadrin",
        keep separate kitchens even) for meat-products as
        against milk-products. If a hot metal ("defiled"
        ceramics cannot be "kashered") utensil or oven
        touched non-kosher foods, or the "meaty" and "milky"
        were interchanged, they can be "kashered", i.e., made
        kosher again, by heating to a glow that which was used,
        with dry heat, and by boiling to overflow in a kettle
        of water with a volume 60 times the displacement-
        (not the container-) volume of the "defiled" ("traife")
        object. This process of making a "traife" utensil
        kosher is called "kashern" (with 'a').
        "Kashern" is Biblical, "kosher-machen" (and "koshern")
        Rabbinical -- hence the difference in age and hence the
        different in spelling!

42.4   'bittich': bitte dich

.5   'mittich': mit dir.

41.13 'Papier': so she can eat it cold with only the paper
       and not the meat touching the "traife" dishes of the
       Court -- a reflex of the habit of kosher-eating Jews.

.15   'Ihr': the so-called "ethical dative" of the 3rd pers.
       sg. "sie" used as the polite form for the 2nd pers. sg.;
       this dative expresses a heightened interest on the part
       of the person.
       'Pummer': not Y, may mean either "bomber", i.e.,
       "very big", or "thick and round".

.16   'Wuch': spelled with the "required" "aleph dividens"
       וװאוך ("Wʼuch"); the 'u', characteristic for H, is
       prob. inauth., dist. h c, but cf. L p. 416 # 632.
       'zu guten': a pious wish, proper only on making a gift
       and wishing the recipient that he should "use it well",
       or while that person is actually using it, but rather
       exaggerated, h c, here, with Hathach using it ob-
       sequiously in an apparent attempt to sell the rooster
       and persuade Esther to buy it.
       'klahn - drahn': a pure R in WY, the 'ei' in G "klein"
       > WY 'ā' and the 'ǎ' in G 'an' > WY 'ā' (EY 'ɔ/uʼ').

42.4f 'bittich - mittich': Rz f. "mit dir"; the misuse of
       the acc. f. the dat. is a frequent dist. of H even
       just h c. The "phonetic" spelling is supposed to be
       an added joke.

.6   '--toin': the dashes are obviously an indication for
       a pause, a hesitation, which "toin", however, does not
       resolve and can therefore make sense only if we assume
       that 'toin' is as specific as Mordechai can properly
       be, i.e., that 'ebeš toin' must be the standing euphem-
       ism for "heeding the call of nature".

.7   C SD 'Haibe': As all SDs are in HG, we should expect
       "Haube"; actually that's what the text does have, ex-
       cept that the stem of the vov(ו) is so faint that
       it looks, at first glance, like a yod (י), and the
       whole digraph (וי) looks like   and therefore 'ai'.

43.1   Man wird, möge es zu Guten geraten, alt; one gets
       old -- may it turn out well.

  .3   'bai Gott': in Gottes Hand

  .4   'ant': Schmerzen, pain.

  .5   'Orndlich': wirklich

  .6   'hihbet': hätte

  .7   'oisgihbet': ausgäbe; would give (her) away (in
       marriage)

  .8   ''in': den König

  .9   Der Bösewicht sollte Augen machen; the fiend (Haman)
       would have <u>some</u> surprise.

43.1   'zu guten': a typical prayer of a pious Jew on men-
       tioning something that <u>may</u> turn out (God forbid!) bad
       (here: 'alt') that it should turn out good.

  .4   'Tut...ant': macht Schmerzen, Sorgen, < MHG "ande",
       "ant", no longer NHG or Y but G dial. NHG has the re-
       lated verb "ahnden" with a slight shift in meaning.

  .5   'Orndlich': auth. Y phonology but NHG semantics! EY
       "orntlex" = "decent" only; in HG it can also mean
       "wirklich", "really". The 't' in HG is parasitic;
       the 'd' in H is metathetic' the 't' in EY is a
       secondary unvoicing of the metathetic 'd'.
       'une': G "ohne", "without"; this should sound "oine"
       in H's WY (< MHG "âne") and "ahne" in NHG; but "ohne"
       is a kind of loanword from Upper G even in NHG and the
       'ō' in H's loanwords becomes 'ū'; 'une' also happens
       to sound like SEY (Galician) "un a", "without a", a
       phonology sometimes used delib. by H to evoke
       laughter. Cf. C p. 229 on 32.7 and p.112f; and L p. 372
       # 220.

  .6   'Sechijjoh': lit. Verdienst (merit), then "Lohn für
       den Verdienst" ("reward for the merit"), then "Gnade"
       ("grace"), then "Privilegium", and finally also "Glück"
       ("good fortune"); but uppermost is still the "pri-
       vilege granted by the Grace of God" -- a typical pious,

43.6   prayerful word, overcharged with emotion; learned
pronunciation: [zəxíə], common pron.: [sxiə]; as a
verb -- "Soiche sain".

.6-7   'hihbet - -gihbet': H's "regular" imperf. subjunctive,
usually used to express an unreality in present time;
here it is equivalent to the "present" (really, future)
conditional to express a wish thought to be unrealiz-
able.
The forms are not auth. Y; they may be borrowed from
some G dial. (there are those which coined new "regular-
weak" subjunctives). Even then, H seems to have not
only adopted them, but to have expanded them h c. He
uses them side by side with the legitimate, auth. subjunctives. Cf. C p.138 on 5.9ff and A p. 112 # 50.

.9   'Roscho^c': Böse, wicked; it has a much stronger emotional charge in Y than even in the original Hebrew!
It is, of course, stronger than the above literal
translations. Eng. "fiend" approaches it. It is the
stock epithet that goes with Haman, in Y "Hɔmən
Hɔrɔ̌šə", and the phrase is used to characterize a person
"thoroughly evil".
'klotsin': glotzen (sic! spelled with ts), rev. subst.
Cf. C p.175 on 16.7.

.10   'nikšnutzige': here it has the force of "incompetent",
"stupid" and alludes to post-biblical legendary
embellishment of her role in adding to Haman's "well-
deserved" woes. Cf. C p. 248 on 39.17 for one such
"fiasco".

.12   'Ganovim': the G "Dieb" died out in Y because the
strong emotional charge favored the exclusive use of
the Hebrewism.
'Levonoh': a word that figures in the liturgy (the new-
moon obligates special prayers: "mechadeš (or: mekadeš)
zain di levɔnə"), usually displaced the equivalent Germanism in Y, though in the 19th century, with the break-
through of the Enlightenment, "Mond" became fashionable
for a time among those who wanted to show off their
secular education, or to conjure up a poetic, romantic
connotation. The curious thing is that today "Mond"
would strike a Y audience as ridiculous as "Levonoh"
struck H's audience then!

43.15   'gitš': gibt's; there are. 'Šôdôs.': Geheimnisse.

.17   'Watt...štellen': wait...pretend

43.13   'efschor': entered Y because of its frequency in Talmudic study.
'Špione': Text has 'Špiune'! H's frequent Rz of 'ɔ' : 'u'; the 'u' here is H's regular representation of an 'o' in a FW.

.15   The dash before 'Sachen' indicates a pause, as if 'Sachen' were funny, an unexpected surprise. We fail to guess what else could have been expected and miss the "fun".

.18   'schnorchen': Y.

.19   'Thᵓômar': also a frequent Talmudic word (cf. on 1.12). Normally languages do not borrow "link-words" (conjunctions, prepositions, adverbs) but Y has borrowed many such from the Talmud -- an indication of the (former) pervasiveness of Talmud-study; it is pronounced now in EY "tɔmər" (instead of the expected "toimər") and is spelled phonetically (unlike H, who spells it correctly, like a Hebrewism is supposed to be) because the shortened vowel destroyed the awareness of its etymology. The ending '-er' causes shortening of the preceding vowel "sporadically" (prob. on the basis of frequency) in G and Y, cf. MHG "muoter, jâmer" NHG "Mutter, Jammer". Actually this phenomenon is only an attenuated, special case of a larger principle that resonants (liquids, semi-vowels, and nasals) caused doubling of preceding consonants and shortening of preceding vowels at various times and under specific circumstances in Germanic languages (cf. Latin "ager", G "Acker"; Lat. "sedeo", Gothic "sitthan", G "sitzen").
'joi': prob. = G "ja", "yes". The frequency of the combinations "tɔmər jɔ, tɔmər nit" (= "if yes, if not", "in (the) case of yes, in (the) case of no") would prompt such a combination here too. The difficulty is that there is no specific antecedent for the 'joi', except a possible loose and not-so-obvious reference to line 15: "where there are secrets, there are no good things" -- then line 19 would say: "and if so, I can hear something".

43.19 Conceivably 'joi' could be an interjection expressing joyous anticipation -- but then it would have to stand between <u>commas</u>, and there are no commas.

20f These two lines are SD! The printer forgot to provide them with the usual <u>parentheses</u>, though the letters are square -- cue enough that they are not part of the "spoken lines". The <u>last</u> line <u>is</u> spoken and should be designated line 20.

44.2f '<u>Loschôn</u> - Susan': pronounce "lɔšn - šušn", Rx in <u>all</u> Y dial. H prob. pronounced "lo:šn'- šusn", as in WY. He seems to use Rz itself as an element óf h and even distorts pure Rs to get Rz. Cf. 43.12f. 'Levónoh - Spiune', where the regular HG "Spione" would yield a perfect R. The 'ō' in <u>recent</u> loanwords is pronounced both 'o' and/or 'u' in Y! Conceivably H meant to "mix" the Y dialects: SEY "lušn" rhyming with general Y "Šusn" also strikes funny.
'Zorfaš Loschôn': funny on several levels:
1. The combination of the two Hebrewisms is "correct" in Y, but absolutely inauthentic! Someone knowledgeable enough to know that "Zorfaš" means France and having good reasons to use the combination "should know" enough to make the whole phrase "authentic" Hebrew: "ləšon Zorfaš" (even that would be rather awkward for "zorfatiš"). Hence this is a subtle "dig" at "Rabbi Reb Mordche's" ignorance of Hebrew "diqduq" (grammar) -- a favorite pastime of the "Haskala intelligentsia". Cf. C p. 210 on 26.1f.
2. The auth. Y for "French" is "frantseyziš"; "Zorfaš" is a scholars' word, used semi-humorously (semi-naively by Reb Mordche) to suggest an ancient, exotic tongue fit for the Persian Emperor over 127 lands some 2200 years ago.
3. The anachronism of making French the "lingua franca" of Persia 400 B.C.E.!
4. Jewish Tradition makes the conspirators speak Tarsian and makes Mordechai "as a member of the Sanhedrin, a master of seventy languages".

.4 'in': enclitic f. "din" (= de<u>n</u>); cf. 25.19 ('in' f. de<u>m</u>) and 'in' in 28.10.

.5 'Liften': dist. in Rz to 'fergiften', though the dat.

44.12   Und immer werden Sie, unbeschrien, dicker und breiter.

44.5   pl. "in (den) Lüften" _is possible_; but the old idiom (still so in Y) uses the _dat. sg._ "in der Luften".

.6   'Galing': Galgen. Some G dial. (not Y) "contract" (metathesize) '-gen' to '-ng'. Cf. the frequent 'moring' f. "morgen" L p. 388 # 379. L p. 368 # 174.

.7   '-brenge': 'e' f. 'i' Y.

.7A   SD The names are obscenely suggestive. Cf. C p. 120 on 6f.

.8f   'Dihner - empfehle': malapropisms of the "ignorant climbers" f. "Dienerin" and "habe die Ehre". "Ich empfehle mich" is proper on "leave taking", not the acknowledgment of a greeting on _meeting_!

.10   The dash indicates that 'Gsundhatt' is an awkward after-thought. The sentence as such is not infrequent in today's colloquial G (or Y), but was apparently considered ungrammatical by the rationalist-purist H. He would use "was macht" with subjects that have volition, not with abstract nouns; '-hatt': the short vowel (with double consonant) is dist. h c.

.11   'umstajnšgsagt': Cf. C p. 154 on 11.9-.10. The "prayer" is slightly inauthentic in _this situation_. It is properly used for a "third person" (or thing), but first and second persons properly say, "nit far aich gedacht" (or the Hebrewism "lo aleychem").

.12   'umbschrie': Cf. C p. 147 on 8. 8 and L p. 411 #595. The h lies in the "primitive" taste, sense of beauty and ideas about health implied in considering 'tik un brader' ("fatter and broader") a blessing and to pray that "envy might not blight it" ('umbschrie' = "knock on wood").
'tik un brader': perfect example of delib. dist. by rev. subst., 't' f. 'd' and vice versa.

45.1 'warren': werden

.2 'mahn...Bahn': meine...Beine

.5 beim Konditor gewesen

.6 Habe mir nur etwas erlangt in den Mund

.7 'hemme': haben

45.1 'main': mein; apocope of <u>every</u> '-e' is UG dial.; it
<u>may</u> have been common in Middle Y. Modern EY <u>has</u> the
pl. '-e' on <u>all</u> adjectives, either preserved or (more
probably) newly restored. MHG poetry allowed the use
of the undeclined adjectives and generally did not
decline the possessive adjectives. The latter EY gives
the pl. '-e' only -- by analogy. H's severe apocope
is prob. <u>not</u> WY.

.2f 'run<u>t</u>er - Wun<u>d</u>er': Rz.

.4f 'genieśen - gewih<u>ś</u>en': '<u>ś</u>' f. 's' dist. (rev. subst.)
f. Rz; 'ih' f. '<u>e</u>' was also dist. for most, if not all,
of H's readers, though it may have been authentic f.
H's own WY dial.; 'genieśen' is "highfalutin" f.
"essen".

.5 'allewail': not only a malapropism but a kind of
"Freudian slip", a substitution for some word like
"eben, erst, unlängst, anderntags", i.e., "just,
recently"; 'allewail' is G dial. meaning "always,
constantly"!
'bain': '-<u>n</u>' is G dial. f. Y (and HG) '-m'. Some G
dial s (again Vogtländisch) use the acc. for <u>both</u>
objective cases.
'Kuntiter': '<u>u</u>' f. 'o', '<u>t</u>' f. 'd' dist. h c.

.6 'Ho': auth. colloquial Y.
'ner': Vogtländisch; 'gelangt': not <u>just</u> "highfalutin"
f. "gekauft" or "gekriegt" ("bought, gotten") but the
use of the simplex "langen" to suggest both "verlangen"
("to yearn, desire") and "erlangen" ("to reach out for
and get"). This vague verb can connote additionally
to "sample and taste just one" (without paying!) and
the surprise (in the next line): she has "taken"

45.8   Nein, nein.

.9   'Mopitigs': Festes (Nahrhaftiges), substantial
        (nourishing)

.10   'Schnekken': Brötchen, rolls

.12   'Nobez': abends, Abende

.15   'Lihkuchen': Lebkuchen, cake

.19   'Hazworrm': Bandwurm, tapeworm

45.6   enough to offer a 'Tutte' to others! Cf. L p. 384
        # 342.
        'in Moil': EY requires "in Moil arayn", HG "ins
        Maul" (HG "Maul" for humans is vulgar and derogatory).
        It may be auth. WY nevertheless. Y tends to drop
        the article in frequent adverbial phrases even more
        than English (cf. HG "geht in die Stadt, die
        Schule, die Kirche", against Eng. ("to town, to school,
        to church", and Y "in štot, in šul").
        'nemme': '-ě-' (HG '-eh-') auth. Y.

.7   'lange Si zu': G, f. the simple Y: "nemt!", Engl.
        "help yourself".
        'aach': the WO (word-order) gives it the force of
        "really", and the clause then means: "if you should
        have..."
        'hemme': prob. inauth. even in G dial., dist. f. Rz
        and h c. 'hemme' is auth. UG dial. only with "wir"
        and is a "legitimate" linguistic development from
        "hân (or: haben) wir". Conceivably "sie hemme" was
        then substituted analogically for *hemse, because
        first and third person pl. had become identical in
        other verbs. Conceivably, but not probably. Just
        because of their so many anomalies the "irregular"
        forms of "sein" and "haben" have resisted regulariza-
        tion by analogy. Cf. L p. 373 #230 and A p. 121
        # 56.

.7A   SD 'Tutte': the vov (ו) is broken off and looks
        more like a yod (י)(i.e., the 'u' looks like an
        'i') with either a slight ink-smear, or possibly
        (but not prob.) the supposed dot ("hiriq") for 'i'.
        The point is that H meant SDs to be "štraight" HG and

45.7A   here we have a confusion of HG "Tutte" (the tit of the breast) with "Tüte" (a paper-bag). In the body of the "spoken lines" H would just relish such a contamination h c, but if it should be deliberate here, it would be the only SD line so used. The 'tt' (f. 't'), however, "argues" for "Tutte"!

.9   'als': immer, Y.
'Mopitigś': something "thick and fat", G dial. Cf. L p. 388 # 377.

.10   'gsunde Schnekken': big rolls, L p. 401 # 501;EY uses the Slavism "Bulkes"; 'gsund', fig. f. "substantial, big" is Y.
'for mir...Mahn': HG "vor" and "für" have "interchanged places" since MHG. Y uses 'far' for both, though there are some traces left of $\overline{\overline{\text{fir}}}$" (< G "für"), especially as an adverb and adverbial prefix; the 'o' > 'a' (was "lowered") due to the enclitization of the preposition to its noun and the resulting sequence of 'r' plus consonant. In EY all prepositions govern the dative. MHG "vor" (in the sense of NHG "für" = "for the benefit of") also takes the dative. H left it in auth. WY and did not distort it into an accusative because 'for mir' differs in both words from HG "für mich"; his usual distortion would have made one word ("mich") identical with HG!

.11   'drahn': Rz f. "darfun".

.12   'Nobez': EY "ovends" G "abends", the genitive used as an adv. of "usual" time, like Engl. "evenings" (the '-s' is now (mis)taken for the pl. '-s'). The 'n-' is due to false metanalysis from "an Obend" > "a Nobend"; "ovends" as an adv. already means G "alle Abend","all evenings", without the "alle" -- "alle", 'N-', '-z' (for '-nds') are all inauth. dist. h c. L p. 391 # 403.

.13   'andert hallem': usually written together, Y "anderthalben", "one and a half", L p. 350 # 7.
'zu'n': sic (with apostrophe) G dial. (Vogtländisch?) use of acc. with prepositions instead of "zum", the dat., as in Y and G.

45.12-13   'Frih - Ḳofih': G "Früh - Kaffee", a pure R only
         in H's dialect where Y and G 'e̅' > 'i̅'; WY "Kafe̅",
         EY "Kavə" (< the Slavic); the 'o' in 'Ḳofih' is an
         additional dist. -- unless it were an Engl. loanword
         with H, instead of the French loanword in HG and
         general WY.

   .14   'Schunŝt': HG "sonst", cf. C p. 161 on 13.14, L p. 405
         # 540, and A p. 79 # 33.2c. From 45.14 to 46.2 H
         satirizes the fat woman who claims "not to eat any-
         thing the whole year except...".

   .15   'Narrenborger': "Nürnberger"; in H's dial. we should
         expect "-barger" with an 'a'! The transposition of
         the phonology in the name of the city yielded "fools'
         city" or "fools-borrowers" -- the pun so precious to
         H. Only a *(Nürn)burg could have yielded "-borg",
         but the auth. name is "-berg".
         'Lihkuchen': auth. Y development < G "Lebkuchen"
         ("ginger-bread"), EY "lekach" (any "cake"). WY
         'e̅' > H's dial. 'i̅'.

   .16-17 'zu guten': prayerful formula = "may it turn out
         to my good"; the prayerbook (passim) Heb. "lətôvo".

   .18   'Kumidie': here = "Theater", a meaning somewhat less
         common in G than in French, and therefore suggestive
         of the climber-snob, esp. with H's usual dist. of the
         'o' into 'u', a development auth. in Y in some FW,
         but not in all, and not in this one.
         'ihnmoil': f. G "einmal"; H usually writes 'emoile';
         'ihn-' can hardly be an error for "ein-", though the
         error would normally be smaller in Y spelling than in
         the Latin transliteration (the omission of the yod
         (י), the "iota"), but G "ein-" is 'aahn', 'aan', or
         'ahn' with H -- we are therefore dealing with the
         addition and not the omission of a yod. Perhaps H
         means 'in Moil' (as in .6) but H deliberately packs in
         three distortions in one "try": He prints the two
         words as one, lengthens the vowel, "forces" the WO.

   .19   'Watŝ': wird es, pres. tense for "usual time" -- not
         the past, which could be identical in form and sound.

   '.20' should be '.21'

46.1 'Gutzelich': Bonbons

.3 Apropos

.5 'war': werde

.6 Mein Maul hinten tut leider flennen

.7 Es reut Sie nicht; you won't regret it.

45.20 'Hazworrm': Bandwurm, tape-worm; the doubling of the second 'r' may throw some light on the omission of the first 'r': they are both inauth. h c -- dialects that weaken, assimilate or vocalize the 'r' before a consonant do not <u>strengthen</u> it intervocalicly, rather, they <u>barely</u> pronounce it! The 'a' (f. 'e') and the 'o' (f. 'u') are auth. Y -- lowering before 'r' plus consonant. L p. 374 # 245. We suspect that 'Hazworrm' is used here figuratively for "hunger-pains" (cf. Engl. "heart-burn").

.21 'gaigt': EY "fidelt"; music without words bores the uncultured and she thus "shows herself up".

46.1 'mi<u>t</u>': Text reads 'mi<u>s</u>', an obvious misprint. 'Gutzelich': goodies, L p. 372 # 228. "Gutsel" is a good Bavarian word, the pl. '-ich' is auth. Y, the whole word -- hardly; though localisms do enter all areas of Y, and this word may have entered <u>parts</u> of WY.

.2 The "innocent", pretended meaning should be: "otherwise I don't waste any money on such goods to indulge my sweet-tooth". 'f<u>or</u>', however, is HHG, Y has 'f<u>ar</u>' though H has 'for' <u>and</u> 'far'. HG would require "f<u>ü</u>r die", Y "far der".
'<u>Sehôroh</u>': can mean "goods", more accurately "me<u>r</u>chandise", and <u>only</u> "merchandise", i.e., only what the seller sells <u>he</u> calls "merchandise", what the consumer buys, the <u>consumer</u> does not designate as "merchandise". But '<u>Sehôroh</u>' is a euphemism for "bought sex" and "verna<u>s</u>chen" in G is a euphemism for a "sex-affair". The line is overlong. For the innocent meaning it should have read: "Schun<u>s</u>t tub ich derfar nik<u>s</u> farnaschen" (or even more preferably: "<u>derfun</u> nik<u>s</u> naschen"). 'Sehôroh...frnaschen' are definitely chosen for their erotic suggestion.

46.3   'Apripu': the underlining is an error of the typist;
it is definitely not a Hebrewism! The text does not
use square type. It is delib. dist. h c; possibly
even some pun is intended; with H the 'o' is usually
distorted into 'u': to suggest "Priapus"? "Aprilkuh"
(= "April fool")?
'in Thiater': All FW are delib. dist. h c; the missing
article is auth. Y.

.4   'is der': f. "is es der", the missing expletive is
inauth. and is meant to suggest primitiveness.

.6   Vulgar: lit. = "my little mouth behind (or: below),
poor thing, is weeping" (= diarrhea); (or, if "hinten"
is a contamination for "unten", then = menses).

.7   'Mihglichkat': = "(Zwang nach) Möglichkeit" (employ as
much force on yourself as) possible. It is doubtful
whether the ellipsis "sich eine Möglichkeit antun" is
possible in G; it is definitely impossible in Y,
though the meaning is clear. L p. 387 # 370.

.8   'rai Ir': sic (printed as one word with apostrophe);
'Ir': dat. f. acc., 'i' f. 'ih', all dist. h c.
L p. 397 # 460.

.13f Malapropisms to show up the pretensions to culture of
the ignorant climber: 'Pumpernikkel' prob. f. Hunper-
dinck, the composer of the operetta Hänsel und
Gretel, is made into a work of Schiller's and the
latter's Louise Müllerin is confused with the
composer Peter Miller; there is not cannonade in
 Louise Müllerin, but there is a cannon-shot, as a
signal for the rebels, at the end of the fourth act
in Fiesko, and there is cannonading on the stage in
some non-Schillerian dramas dealing with the
"Befreiungskriege" (the wars of liberation against
Napoleon, 1813-15); one does not fence ('fecht-')
with cannon but with weapons of stab, cut, or thrust.

.15   'Dekleraziune': f. "Dekorationen"; characteristically
Figsi shows up her lowbrow taste in her being so
impressed by the cannonade and the decorations and in
her "skipping" the music.

47.2   'Pikstuhl': pistol

 .10 'Hôreg-le': Zwerglein

 .16 'Flis': Katarrh

 .17 'wor': war

47.2   'Pikstuhl': contamination of G "Büchse" (H 'Piks') and
"Pistol" -- made easier because of dialects where
'chs' > 's'. L p. 395 # 441.
'Hôlesches': a Hebr. malapropism! -- a substitution of
the pres. participle (meaning "a female dominating or
commanding") for the abstract noun "Haloschus" (pronounce "xalósəs") meaning "fainting". The dist. is
inauth., as the latter is a common Y "household"-word,
whereas the former is rare and would be a "tripper" for
a student of Hebrew.
'schier': beinahe, almost; Y and G. L p. 399 # 485.

 .5 'Kumidianten': in 19th cent. G and Y this is a malapropism for "Schauspieler" (actors), the former having
acquired the exclusive pejorative meaning of "clown".

 .6 Faksi apparently does not understand that "blindschies-
sen" means to "shoot blanks" and wants to say, "what
difference does it make that the actors are blind?";
but actually she "improperly" says the opposite: "for
all I care, let them be blind!" On the significance
of the non-biblical names cf. C p. 118-121.

 .8 'Wu...her': woher; WO auth. WY, but not EY.

 .10 'Hôreg-le': Cf. C p.179 on 17.13. 'derfrihren':
'der-' is auth. Y, f. G 'er-', = "freeze to death".

 .11 'Wen...glaich': "even if"; WY but not EY.

 .12 'gewellt': older form for Y and G "gewollt". HG
requires "wollen" ("double infinitive construction" --
an innovation that is "post Y").

 .13 'bloists...ois': here = "will simply blow through it";
the usual meaning is "to extinguish (a flame)".

48.1   'gǔstepten Unterrok': quilted petticoat

  .2   a hood like bowls used now by lying-in women

  .3   a substantial bodice...hip-cushions

  .4   'Rek': Röcke, skirts

  .5   'gǔstraaften--Flek': gestreifte Schürze (oder Latz);
         striped apron (or bib)

  .6   felt stockings and peasant shoes

  .7   'Tuhch': wrap

  .8   'Fluhtel': chiffon (?)

  .9   'Muthel': Modell, Modebüchlein (?)

47.14   'alle Wail': one word in the text, = adv.

  .16   'Hidusch': Hebr. = an "innovation, novelty", Y =
         "wonder".
         'Fliš...Katahrn': "Flüsse...Katarrhe", sniffles and
         catarrhs; unidiomatic use of the pl. for the "dis-
         tributive" sg. -- dist. h c. L p. 365 # 150.

  .17   'Štok': i.e. "alive", not a "piece of wood"; however,
         the description of 48.1-.14 suggests that she might
         mean not "as thin as a stick" but well-rounded!

48.1   'gǔstepten': here = "quilted", therefore heavy and
         warm.

  .2   'Kindbett-schiššelich': chamber-pots?

  .3   'Kiššelich': Kissenchen, cushions; to make the hips
         wide and round. The '-šš-' correspond, not as the
         usual HG '-ss' to Germanic 't', but to Germanic '-ss',
         Engl. and EY 'š'! L. p. 381 # 307.

  .6   'Schuhch': '-ch': MHG and Y

  .7   'Tuhch': = Überwirftuch, wrap.

  .8-9   'Fluhtel - Muthel': 'Fluhtel' may be a H coinage to

48.12f 'schnizzle - ferbizzle': chop up msall

.16f You cannot really get any (of these children) off your
neck, until you let them do all they want.

.17 WO is due to Rz, = alles was sie wollen

.18 Mine (i.e., my daughter) will make some show (with her
attire) tonight.

.19 "Straight from the (bale of) cloth she has on a dress",
i.e., without fuss. 'ihnŝ': es.

.20f She really has looks tonight, knock wood, but it will
be a pity when the sun will shine on it.

.22 There is something one can say about that hussy.

48.8-9   suggest "light, unsubstantial textiles", evoking
associations with G "Fladen" (SEY "Fluden") -- a
"fluffy" cake, "Flitter(werk)' -- cheap "tinsel",
"Flittchen" -- a girl of easy virtue; "Fladen" is also
used humorously f. "feces". The word is Rz to 'Muthel'
< "Modell" = "Mode(buchlein)". L p. 389 # 383.

.12 'leŝŝen si': G dial., the umlauting of the 'a' in
"lassen" is due to the encliticization of the personal
pronouns with the vowel 'i'; auth. Y requires "lɔsn".

.12-13 'schnizzle - ferbizzle': "chop up small", humorous
f. "zuschneiden", "tailor"; '-bizzle' is related to G
"beissen, beitzen" and Y "pizzeln". L p. 402 # 503
and p. 363 # 123.

.14 'Nahgenblik...nandre': The extra 'n's are due to
metanalysis (cf. C p. 262 on 45.12).
'Gesêroh': the "dictates" of fashion are characterized
by the Y word for the "malevolent decrees" meant deliberately to oppress Jews.

.16 'ahn': einem, dat.

.17 The question mark is due to "attraction" of line 15
and would impart a droll intonation to .16-.17. WO is
due to Rz.

48.18f   Faksi's bragging about her daughter is made to sound funny in that the claimed "merits" are couched in such ambiguous terms that they border on faults: .15-.17 say the parents have no choice since the children pester them so; .18 says her daughter will make some show tonight -- one is at a loss to know whether that's good or bad; .19 says she can get herself a dress directly from the bale of cloth -- is she that skillful or just sloppy?; .20, coming after .19, can only mean: "and she looks really ('aach') accordingly" -- i.e., in accordance with the quality and care of that dress; if not for the 'umbschrie', .20 would be downright negative -- with 'umbschrie', it can still be negative, but funnily so -- "she'll look horrible enough not to provoke an "evil eye by envy". The 'haint' in .18 and .20, esp. in .20, which contrasts with .21, apparently still has the archaic meaning of "tonight", rather than the modern Y meaning of "today" -- and seems to mean that she can "pass" with her looks that night, but the sun's shining on her will bring disaster (.21). The normal meaning of .22 would be: "There's something amiss with this hussy" -- but it has to be taken with .23f. where again her "skills and accomplishments" are sung, and since it is a mother apparently boasting about the good qualities of her daughter, we have to re-interpret .22 as a "gaucherie", i.e., an uncouth and inept "understate-ment". A parent may properly call her child "Flegel" ("brat" or "rascal") in a jocose mood, but not 'Luhder' ("carrion", "hussy"). And since .23f. is unmistakably in praise of her daughter, we must take the intent of .22 also to be in praise and 'ebes der Mehr' to be "forced" into its old original meaning, now no longer in use, not even "archaic use", namely; "there is a story to be told". The tension between vocal intent and achievement is H's special humor.

.22   'Luhder': neut.

.23   ''is...is'n': '-'n' is enclitic for dat. 'm', correct Y, but 'dihn' (.22) is dist. h c (though G dial.).

49.1   Sie sollten sehen wie es malt.

  .2   seinem Vater

  .3   bunte Perlchen

  .4   dass es noch einen solchen hier gäbe.

49.1   'ihnŝ': also in .2 and 48.19, G dial. f. "es", appa-
       rently derived from "jenes", where the 'je-' < 'ie'.
       L p. 377 # 275 and A p. 139 # 70.2.
       'muhlt': the 'u' is SEY and "funny" in WY! L p. 388
       # 380. The WO is exlamatory!

  .2   'Taate': EY, "funny" in most WY; in any Y the 'ǎ' is
       short and the oblique cases (here: the dat.) end in
       'n'; as Y, therefore, it is doubly dist. h c. There
       are G dial.s with 'ā'! The word in EY comes from the
       Slavic, in WY partly through the mediation of G dial.
       L p. 408 # 570.
       'erŝt': eben, neulich; recently.
       'Baitel': usually called "Tallisbaitel"; the simplex
       'Baitel' has all kinds of connotations in G and Y, in-
       cluding "wrong" and therefore h connotations, and for
       that very reason used by H. It is a bag usually made
       of a rich-colored velvet or (less usually) silk, and
       embroidered lovingly with traditional symbolic figures
       and the name of the owner -- by the bride for her
       future husband (here: by the daughter for her beloved
       father -- rather unusual, since the father is presumed
       to have one from his one-time bride!). The bag is
       used for the Tallis, the prayer-shawl, which in most,
       but not all, Jewish congregations is donned only after
       marriage. (In most American congregations, for in-
       stance, it is donned after the 13th birthday -- Bar
       Mitzvah -- the age of becoming "obligated and pri-
       vileged to fulfill God's 613 commandments" to a Jew).
       The bag also accomodates the "Tefillin", the
       "phylacteries", i.e., the leather prayer-capsules
       containing four sections of the Bible and fastened to
       forehead and left biceps with straps. The Tefillin
       are donned for morning prayers on weekdays. The Tallis
       is donned for all morning prayers. The Tefillin also
       are kept in a bag of their own, made with the same
       loving-dedication by a mother (or a sister) for the Bar

49.7   nichts tut es als kichern und lachen

  .8   'hallem': halben

  .9   'rihd': redet

  .14   lasst Euch ('-'ch') (be)fragen

  .16   'nimmer': nicht mehr

49.2   Mitzvah. The Tefillin-bag is much smaller than the
        Talliš-bag and the latter always accommodates the
        former. The capsules of the Tefillin contain parch-
        ments with the passages from Exodus 13 and Deuteronomy
        6 and 11 -- all mentioning the command: "and thou
        shalt bind them (= God's commandments) as a sign on
        your hand and as coronets between your eyes".

  .5   The symbols embroidered on these bags are usually:
        the six-pointed "Star of David" bordered by flowers
        or arabesques. The "crown of the Torah" carried on the
        forelegs of the two lions ("of Judah") and doves
        (symbolizing the Jewish congregation, "Kneses Yisrael")
        are embroidered usually only on Torah "mantlets" and
        curtains of the Torah ark -- not on the Tefillin- or
        Talliš-bags. Although there is no prohibition against
        such extension, and a compulsive show-off might "go to
        town" and even add other 'Hajjôš' and 'ᶜÔfôš', which,
        incidentally, are the only auth. words in Y for "ani-
        mals" and "fowl". The G "Tiere" and "Geflügel", to-
        gether with "Vieh" ("cattle", Y "Bəhɛyməš") died out
        in Y. The Hebrewisms displaced the Germanisms partly
        because of their prominent role in Jewish religious
        doctrine (kosher and non-kosher animals, their ritual
        mode of slaughtering) and partly because of the
        emotional charge of "Xayə" and "Bəhɛymə" in their
        literal and figurative (as words of abuse) meanings.

  .6   'Duhnbach...Mahnhoif': prob. distortions of names of
        popular artists or pictures. We have not been able
        to identify them.

  .7   'foll': HG f. Y "ful" -- typical of the climber's
        transposing Y into G, where her knowledge is adequate
        for it.
        'nikš': sc. "tut si".

49.7   'Kuttern': kichern, G dial. L p. 383 # 337.

  .8   'hallem': a case of extreme assimilation of '-lben' to
       '-lbm', then to '-llm'; prob. not auth. WY.
       'ken': Y f. G kann: A p. 115 # 52.3.

  .9   Pres. f. future, auth. Y and G.

  .10 'Franzesch': almost "natural" syncopation of "Fran-
       zesisch"; the anachronism that kings in Artaxerxes'
       time spoke French is h c.

  .11f Thirze is apparently annoyed by Fakśi's boast about
       her daughter's fluent French. Apparently Thirze's
       daughter does not know French, but her saying she
       doesn't care whether her daughter gets a husband in
       German or in French is inept, h c, since she cannot
       get one in French, so what she intends to say is that
       she would be just as satisfied if she gets him in
       German.

  .13 Fakśi, in her turn, is annoyed at Thirze's snubbing
       her.
       'gstoigen': in Y a traditional humorous rhyme for "ge-
       floigen", but only with "gefloigen", namely in the
       phrase "nit gestoigen -- nit gefloigen", which means
       "a pure fiction, it never happened". Otherwise, the
       past participle is "gestigen", as expected. The phrase
       is supposed to be a Y denial of Jesus' resurrection
       and ascension (= flying) into heaven: "he didn't rise,
       he didn't fly". Tendlau p. 346 # 985 gives a slightly
       "censored" version of the same.

  .14 The overpolite form of address (second pers. pl. instead
       of 3rd pers. sg.) she has been using to her equal (in-
       stead of the expected familiar form, which would be ap-
       propriate for a servant-girl she addresses by first
       name) is due to Fakśi's desire to flatter her and pump
       her for gossip, but it is still incongruous, hyper-
       correct and thus humorous.

  .16-50.1 'hinten' and 'forne' are old, well-known, almost
       hackneyed obscene "jokes". Perhaps they were "new" to
       H's readership. Cf. C p. 265 on 46.6 and C p. 227 on
       31.16.

50.1f   'S̈echur - Bohur': There is no pronunciation "s̈echur";
        the R, pure and auth., is on the basis "sóxər - bóxər"
        'sóxər - bóxər'. The Y word f. G "Lohn" is prob. an
        additional insinuation, but it is suggested only by
        the spelling of the consonants, not by the pronuncia-
        tion of the Y R. The pronunciation of the word f. G
        "Lohn" is, in correct learned Hebrew, "s̈ɔxȯr"; yes,
        but that is also the "correct Hebrew" (liturgical)
        pronunciation of the biblical name Issachar, when
        abbreviated to   . The Y pronunciation is that of
        the R only for the name. The Y pronunciation f. the
        equivalent of G "Lohn" (Engl. "pay, reward") is
        "s̈xar"! i.e., the "construct" instead of the indepen-
        dent form (cf. C p.201 on 23.5). It is therefore
        basically the proper name Issachar and the word for
        "young man" ('Bohur') that are the definite core of
        the R. The motivation for choosing this particular
        name is the "visual" R suggesting Y "s̈xar" ("pay"),
        and the phonetic R, Y "sóxər" (full Hebrew "soher"),
        ר כ שׁ , (= Y "merchant, businessman"), which are
        connoted and insinuated. The SEY basis of the R,
        "s̈úxər - búxər", would be "less rich" by one associa-
        tion, namely "businessman", which in SEY is "s̈óyxər".
        In sum: "sɔxər" is the R word, means Issachar,
        suggests "businessman", and visually (or, in
        correct "full" Hebrew, but not command Y, also
        phonetically) it insinuates "serve ('dihn') for pay".

   .1C SD 'Erster': 's', not 's̈' nor 's̆', i.e., ר not ס
        nor שׁ . This SD is so much HG that it is HHG; i.e.,
        here it even imitates G graphics in spelling 'st'!

   .2f ironical

   .4ı 'hihn...dot': dorthin; WO is awkward or funny in WY,
        impossible in EY.

   .5f 'dir': ethical dat. to include the person addressed
        and involve his interest.
        'Hez...Jacht': chase...hunt; 'Hez' is a hunt with
        dogs, also a very intense hurrying, a "rat-race"; the
        two prob. stand for the compound G "Hetzjagd" --
        hendiadys; the 'Jacht' is a "Schürzen-(H's 'Scharz')
        jagd" -- a skirt-chase.

50.6   Wir haben dir gestern über <u>der</u> wieder

 .13   'barig':   Berge

50.6   'gester': geste<u>rn</u>: the '-n' apocope is G dial. the
       word <u>is</u> WY, f. EY "nechten". 'der': refers to 'Jacht'.
       The language of the 'Galanś' is that expected from
       Galanś: "attempted" HG with "slips into Y, where
       'Erster' in his sarcastic fault-finding uses more Y
       (h c!), and 'Zwaiter', in trying to maintain his
       "dignity", uses more G.

 .10   An insinuation that he is debauching and that it will
       debilitate him.
       'Seften': a "contaminated" pl.: G S<u>ä</u>fte, Y S<u>aften</u>,
       H Seften! Dist. f. Rz and h c.

 .12   'Hendf<u>oll</u>': written together, as a spelling joke, as
       if it were a Y variation f. G "H<u>a</u>ndvoll", whereas it
       means "die Hände - voll"; in addition, in Y it should
       be "f<u>ul</u>"; the dashes after 'Hendfoll' indicate obscene
       insinuation - teasingly evaded by an innocent sub-
       stitute ending.

 .13   "Oqer-Horim", "Berg-oiśraiśer" ("mountain-remover") is
       a complimentary figure for an utterly clever scholar,
       who could prove even the paradoxical by his keen appli-
       cation of Talmudic hermeneutics (e.g., it is used on
       Rabbi Meir in Sanhedrin 24A and Rabbah in Berakhot
       64A) and has become a stock-epithet for a "genius in
       Rabbinic lore".
       "Gott behit' makes it difficult to attribute to 'du
       raiśt <u>B</u>arig (sic, with a capital 'B', contrary to the
       Transliteration) ois' a complimentary meaning; even
       extending the meaning by switching it from the posi-
       tive "<u>most</u> clever", to the negative "over-clever",
       "cunning", "over'reaching" (and there is no evidence
       for such extension!) would not fit too well: i.e.,
       "Are you trying to fool me with cunning?" It prob. is
       intended to mean: "you attempt the impossible and use
       up too much energy" -- all in skirt-chasing!

 .14   'amoil': here in the special G (not Y) sense of "un-
       deniably". 'groi<u>s</u>er': 's' f. 'ś' -- a favorite H
       distortion to suggest G "grauser" ("gruesome, terrible")
       'Spekulant': here prob. = "gambler", i.e., "adventurer"

51.2   'laigenš': leugne es

.4   'in Štaar': a cataract

.5   'derzu weren': turn into cataract (?)

.7   'dafet wihlen': wählen dürfte

.8   'sich': sieh!

50.14   in affairs of love.

.16   'Stiklich': Y, = G "Streiche", "tricks and pranks"
— again an insinuation about "chasing".

51.1   'zu'n: delib. contamination of G "zur Tür" and "aus
dem Zimmer (hinauskommen)".

.2   'laigenš': EY curiously has "k' f. G 'g'; the rhythm
is Y, HG requires "leugne's".

.4   'in': could be misprint for "ain" (HG), Y would
require 'a'; could also be phonetic slurring of G
"ein" to 'n'.

.5   'derzu weren': = "turn into it", i.e., a cataract;
apparently delib., inept expression for "may I get
a cataract"; conceivably 'derzu' could refer to
something Erster whispered — but we couldn't know
then what it is.

.7f   'Sih': Text has 'Sich'! = "Sieh!", also in .8
'dafet': an imperfect subjunctive of G "dürfen", on
the basis of "darfen" (from the sg.; the pl. would
have yielded "dorfen") < intermediate *da(r)fet(e):
= "if I were permitted to choose" — the subjunctive
of "polite request".

.9   'Nekêvôš': the Hebrewism started as a euphemism and
acquired a pejorative nuance.

.10   'Si': = ihren; the 's' should be small! The third
pers. pl. in Y is invariable; EY 'sɛy', H's WY
(apparently) 'si'.
'Kuhr': court(ship), ultimately French "faire la
cour".

52.9 keiner das Klösslein aus dem Hafen; no one will snatch
away your dumpling out of the pot

.10 <u>that</u> bargain won't run away from you

.12 Let's have a brandy

51.13 A cannon is fired to mark an important occasion (royal
arrivals, etc.).

52.1 Our Transliteration minimizes the distortions in the
French - only the rev. subst. of 't' and 'd' ('<u>dreh</u>'
in Y means "twist") and 'e' f. French 'eu' (G 'ȫ'); in
the text every French voiceless 'ṡ' is represented by
the voiced 's' (Engl., Fr. 'z', Y 's').

.9 means: No one will steal your mistress.
'Klihṡle': "Klösslein", EY "Kneydlax", "dumpling"
(usually made of "matzoh"-meal); here = fig. f. "a
round, plump, curvaceous amour". L p. 381 # 312.

.10 The Hebrewisms are normally emotionally charged; here
they are used sarcastically and, therefore, still
emotionally.

.12 'Franzefuhṡ': brandy-drink. L p. 366 #158.

.13 'Maintwihgen': This is the "proper" form; cf. .11
'wihgen mainer', which is archaic, neither Y nor
current HG -- again a sample of H's straining for
forms that deviate from HG.

53.4f Rz, though rev. subst. makes it appear pure: 'ṡ; -
's', G "grüssen - gewesen", EY "gri:ṡn - gəve:zn".

.7 'dihn': <u>not</u> Y, G dial. (Vogtländisch) acc. f. dat.!
h c.

.9 'ṡtift': Y, L p. 404 # 527; 'kuttert': <u>not</u> Y, L
p. 383 # 337.

.12 'Kumuhter': Kommode; dressers (chests of drawers),
L p. 383 # 333; 'u' f. 'o' in "recent" FW-borrowings,
partly auth., partly dist., 't' f. 'd' rev. subst.
'Tischlich': Y, L p. 409 # 575.

53.9   'Ẍtift': Y, scherzt, jokes (is playful)
'kuttert': kichert, giggles

  .12   'Ẍtenne...Kumuhter...Tischlich': stehen...Kommode...
Tischlein

  .13   'Kehrwischlich': Federwische, feather-dusters

  .14   porzellanene Töpflein mit Blumen

  .15   Waschbecken

  .18   könnte man

  .19   elfenbeinerne Stühle...Spitzenbesatz; ivory easy-
chairs...lace border-fringes.

54.1   Eine Uhr...Opernstückchen

  .2   'Milklich': Mücken

  .4   'Hihch': Höhe

  .5   <u>'Scherorôṡ'</u>: Herrschaften

53.13   'Kehrwischlich': EY, HG Flederwisch, L p. 380
298.

  .14   'Schmekken': G dial., h c; lit. "smells". L p. 401
498.
'Hiefelich': not EY; Hafen, "Häfelein" = HG Töpfchen.

  .15   'lefohre': French "lavoir"; EY "ləvúər". L p. 384
344.

  .18   Because it is so clean!

  .19   Apparently a reference to Esther 1:6.

54.1   'A <u>Nuhr</u>': (with capital 'N') metanalysis for 'an
<u>Uhr</u>'.
'Uperẍtikklich': prob. arias played in the music-box
of the clock.

  .2   <u>'sevlen'</u>: Text has <u>'Zev li'</u>! There <u>may</u> be some
spelling joke intended and the division of the word
into two may be deliberate. The '-i' (instead of the

54.6 'štahnige': steinerne

.7 'Un': Text has 'In'! Püppchen von einem Ofen

.8 'Kanebie': Kanapee

.9 'Gemulzeter': Gemälde

.10 The paintings are so vivid and realistic that they could be mistaken for real, living persons, rather than mere human handiwork.

54.2 emended '-en') is auth. H for the infinitive! The verb is a denominative coinage, possibly H's own; "sevel" means "Mist" ("dung") and lit. 'sevli' means "misten" and is a euphemism. Not current in EY: Harkavy lists the noun but not the verb.

.4 'Hihch': 'ch' is not lost in Y because in Y final '-e' was lost before G intervocalic 'ch' was lost. EY "Hêch".

.5 'Şerorôṡ': sic, with 'Ṡ' not 'Sch', = Herrschaften (both abstract and concrete).

.6 'štahnige': A delib. malapropism f. "stahnerne": The former means 1. having some quality of stone, 2. full of stones; the latter means "made of stone". 'Avôdê': auth. Y f. the "correct" Hebr. "Avodoṡ"; the '-e' is spelled with yod (י) and is intended to be pronounced 'ə'. Normal Y spelling would require "Avôdoh", as in such Hebr. compound nouns Y pluralizes only the last component (here Hebrew pluralizes both: "Avôdôṡ Sorôṡ"; "Sorôṡ" is an adj. and "agrees" with the noun; elsewhere Hebrew pluralizes the first element only and Y the last only, e.g., in "construct" compounds cf. "Ṡêfer Tôroh", Hebr. pl.: "Ṡifrê Tôroh", Y pl.: "Ṡêfer Tôrôṡ"). The deviation from Y spelling is partly to indicate the phonetics (H spells the sound 'ə' with a yod passim) and partly, perhaps, as a spelling joke: H was an excellent Hebr. grammarian and despised those less erudite, those who were forced to use the Y analogical "innovations", which he considered signs of an ignoramus. There is also a semantic difference between the Hebr. (= "idolatry" -- i.e., abstract) and Y (=

54.14　'for Woichen': Text has 'for W<u>i</u>chen'! Meaning
　　　　unclear, see below, on C p. 14<u>5</u>.

.21　　Die haben Euch eine Grösse

.22　　'Pummers': balls (?)

54.6　　"idols", "images" -- concrete).

.7　　　Probably: "ein Ofen so nett wie eine Puppe".

.8　　　'Kane<u>b</u>ie': the rev. subst. makes the word for "sofa"
　　　　sound like "can of beer"! This may be delib.! L
　　　　p. 378 # 284.

.9　　　'Gemulzeter': not Y, G dial. L p. 369 # 189.

.11f　For the story cf. Numbers 13.

.13　　'Gschichtiṡ': The '-ṡ' as a plural suffix entered Y
　　　　at its very inception for some G nouns identical in
　　　　the sg. and pl. -- the original source of this suffix
　　　　was Old French (the native language of the first Y
　　　　speakers) and later Low German and Dutch. Still later
　　　　an analogy arose: like the Hebrewism "X̌arpə", pl.
　　　　"X̌arpəṡ (< '-ot'), or the Germanism "Sand ", pl.
　　　　"Šandəṡ", i.e., nouns ending in "schwa" ('ə', the
　　　　unaccented 'e') tended to get the pl. ending '-ṡ'.
　　　　But to this very day there is vacillation in <u>Stan-
　　　　dard</u> Y between the suffix '-ṡ' and '-(e)n', e.g.,
　　　　"legendes", but "Šprachn". All <u>Slavisms</u>, and some
　　　　Germanisms, ending in '-e' get '-ṡ'. Most recently
　　　　the '-ṡ' was added to the unumlautable nouns ending
　　　　in '-er' (e.g., "Šraiber-ṡ"). In <u>WY</u> the substitution
　　　　of the '-ṡ' for the '-n' suffix is unheard of! H is
　　　　using an EY pl. h c.

.14　　'for W<u>oi</u>chen is': Text has 'W<u>i</u>chen'; the 'i' <u>must</u> be
　　　　correct f. the R! But even so, the Rz is harsh. We
　　　　should expect "wicht is". The meaning, too, is
　　　　obscure, i.e., whether "wicht" or 'Wichen", the
　　　　contrast to 'alte Gschichtiṡ', requires the meaning
　　　　"recent events", which is given in 'erst gschehi...
　　　　is'. '<u>for</u> Wichen', if auth., does suggest some
　　　　temporal sense for 'Wichen' -- but no known meaning
　　　　of YG "Wiche, Wieche, Wihe, Wiehe" fits; the perfect
　　　　participle "verwichen" (= "past") <u>could</u> be spelled

55.1 'frihgt': fragt

.3   'maiŝlich': Mäuschen

.6   'oisbruten': ausbrüten

.16 Wir werden

54.14 'for wichen' by H, h c, but the syntax and the Rz
remain harsh.

.15f Delib. anachronism, h c, as are the phonetic dist.

.17, .19   'si': Esther

.18 'schoin': i.e., before formally choosing her.

.19 'Pehrlich': the sg. "Perl" is sometimes misconstrued
as a diminutive in '-l', hence the pl. for diminutives:
'-lich'. EY has both an indeclinable pl. "Perl" (Standard) and "Perlech".

.20 Auth. Y; prices are often quoted in Y with Hebrewisms,
partly from the tradition of "keeping books" in
Hebrew, partly from the habit of "secret language" in
pricing, and, finally, when expressing large sums and
marvelous prices associated with emotion.

.22 'Pummerŝ': Cf. C p. 254 on 41.15; apparently = "something as big and round as Matzoh-dumplings" -- which
can be as big as a large orange! The origin of the
word is uncertain, but one thinks of the interna-
tionalism "bombe", the Eng. "bumper", the EY verb
"bomblen" ("to hang and swing (like a jewel from a
chain)").

The Matzoh-dumpling (EY "Kneydlach") is made from
baked Matzoh, ground up again into flour. It is a
special Passover dish, as no dough-products made of
"virgin flour" is permissible, since they "leaven" (be
it ever so little) in the preparation. Only flour-
products baked once may be "soaked" again in water
without transgressing the prohibition against leaven on
Passover -- and that only "technically". Very pious
Jews refrain even from products made of (baked)
Matzoh-flour soaked in water!

56.1   'det': tut; here = "jammert"

.2   'lihb': leb'!

.3   'nebich': leider

55.1   'frihgt': MHG "frâgen" and "fregn"; WY and NHG forms are derived from "frâgen" (hence WY and H usually show "froigen"); EY has "fregn". H uses EY here f. Rz.

.3   'maiślich': Y, L p. 385 # 351.

.6   'oisbruten': ausbrüten, hatch. L p. 392 # 421. The figure is grotesque; the reference is probably to the "cultivation" that the "contestants" for the Queen's place underwent (Esther 2: 12-16). The missing umlaut is due to Rz and reliance on G dial. EY has "oisbrien" (without the 't') for "hatch". It's not impossible that H is also thinking of SEY "bruten" (G "braten", WY "broiten") = "to roast", figuratively "to cook up", "to prepare" -- somewhat less harsh, because of the frequency of the figure.

.11   A sentiment frequent in Jewish liturgy.

.14A   SD "gelaufen" and "schlägt" are intended; the language of SD's is HG!

.15   'Lost una': EY "lommir", ultimately < "lassen wir".

.16   'merahêm sain': typical Y way of using Hebrew verbs -- the Hebrew participle is compounded with the Y (G) auxiliary. The latter alone is inflected and conjugated, while the Hebrewism remains invariable. The construction is based on and is similar to the MHG (and Engl.) progressive tense.
'warrn': werden; the pres. f. the fut., regular in Y and G; EY "wern".

56.1   'det': a kind of "pro-verb" for the specific "heult" or "jammert", less harsh in G than in Y (cf. .12 'Tet'); possibly H fills 'sehr' also with its archaic meaning of "sorely".

.2   'lihb': leb'! Typically pious Y -- to utter a blessing when a "vocative" is uttered.

56.8   'Krepflich': Kräpfe, (ravioli with) <u>minced meat</u>

.9   'Trepflich': Tröpflein; i.e., "they'll draw our blood
     drop by drop"

.12   'oisgelossen': ausgelassen, unrestrained

.15   'Zepfle': Zäpflein, = 'Trepfle'

56.3   'nebich': cf. C p.126 on 1.7 and L p. 389 # 389.
       'Kapporoh': cf. C p.132 on 3.8, C p.183 on 19.2 and
       L p. 378 # 286.

.4   'Haman, der <u>Roschoˤ</u>': a stock phrase, though '<u>der</u>' is
     an unusual (and unnecessary) translation of the Hebrew
     article 'ho-'; the auth. phrase is "Horoschoˤ".

.5   '<u>Mesirôs</u>': "denunciations" -- a very "bitter" word in
     Y, usually connoting "false, malicious, libelous
     accusations" that so often resulted in terrible per-
     secutions and catastrophes. The original meaning of
     the verbal root (msr) is "deliver up (things, people,
     or, most frequently, information (not <u>necessarily</u>
     incriminating or false information))". Haman's libels
     in Esther 3:3 are elaborated in post-biblical Jewish
     lore. This one verse in Esther is elaborated into
     more than six pages as summarized by Ginzberg (IV,
     pp. 402-408).

.6-16   Pres. used f. future.

.7   'derschossen': an anachronism and distortion of the
     story (which implies "massacre"), Rz -- all h c.

.8-17   All the '-pf-s are WY; EY '-pf-' > 'p'.

.8   'Krepflich': dumplings made from square pieces (about
     2 x 2 in.) of rolled-out (noodle-)dough, folded into
     a triangularly shaped "pocket" and filled with jam,
     cheese or minced meat, then boiled in plain water or
     soup-stock and either fried or baked. The meat-
     "krep(f)lech" are customary on <u>Purim</u>, the Feast of
     Esther, and on <u>Erev Yom Kippur</u>, the day <u>before</u> the Day
     of Atonement.
     'Krepflich' here is due to Rz -- metonomy for "Krepfl-
     fleisch" -- "mince-meat".

56.12   'Tet': cf. rev. subst. in .1 'det'; cf. p. 117 # 54.
'oisgelossen': Rz f. the sake of the "humorous" anachronism in .13; the word was deliberately chosen f.
its conflicting meanings in Y and G: Y = "immodest,
lewd, immoral, indecent", HG "wild, unrestrained, gay,
mischievous". The Y meaning is borrowed from UG
dialects and is an obvious new loanword: the "native"
EY development of HG "ausgelassen" is "oisgelosn"
(with '-os-'; here s = z phonetically); the word f.
"dissolute, indecent" is "oisgelassen" ('-ass-').
Cf. L p. 392 # 423.

.15   'Zepfle': "Zäpflein" = "little tap", by metonomy,
"droplet" (cf. .9 'Trepflich'), i.e., "(reduced to a)
droplet (of blood)" -- but that is said in .16
('Trepfle')! It is just possible the word is used
for its connotations: "voller Zapfen" = "drunkard";
'Zepfle' can mean a "little drunkard"; it is also the
homonym of "Zöpflein", one of whose meanings is
"suppository".

.18   'in der': Y, all prepositions govern the dat.

57.2f   'zamme - Mirmoh': a pure R in H's dial., as a vowel
before 'r + consonant' goes to 'a' and the 'r'
assimilates to the following consonant. Hence, pronounce: "zamme - mamme"! The Hebrewism is not
current in EY; it may have been current in H's dial.,
as it is, unfortunately, an indispensable, emotion-
filled concept of a "false, malicious accusation"
(a "frame-up"), so frequent in our lives. EY uses
the Hebrewism "bilbul" f. "frame-up". WY uses
"bilbul" in its more original, literal meaning of
"mobbing, rioting": 'Mirmoh' is a more likely word
for the concept of "frame-up" because its basic
meaning is "deception".

.3A   SD From here to 58.8A the Text, even though humorous,
is in perfect HG -- as these "Fair Ladies" are conceived of as Gentiles of high education and standing.
The phonology, where possible, and the grammar,
throughout, show that it is meant to be HG. Our
Transliteration distorts the vowels at times for the
sake of a uniform, "one-to-one" representation of
each Hebrew symbol by one unique Roman symbol. Cf.

57.3A C p.109. Hence: "Schöne...Glück...Goethe...Bürger"
etc.
The two "Schöne" are differentiated in character: The
first accepts her "loss" graciously, while the second
-- gracelessly. Finally, the "simple girl" -- fatalistc-
ally, and Zetulpe -- outrageously.

.6 'Rinaldino': Rinaldo was a popular, romantic robber-
hero, a sort of G Robin Hood, the hero of C. A.
Vulpius's picaresque novel "Rinaldo Rinaldini" (1798) --
so popular that it was immediately turned into a drama
(by K. F. Hensler in 1799) and even into farces. If
she cannot win the king, she will enjoy vicariously
adventures with Rinaldo.

.7 'Birgers': Gottfried August Bürger (1747-1794), author
of the famous ballad <u>Lenore</u> (Englished by William
Morris) and other sad, sentimental lyrics of unhappy
love.

.9 'Resignazion': cf. Vogt and Koch's <u>Geschichte der</u>
<u>deutschen Literatur</u>, Vol. 2, p. 308; a "confession"
poem to Charlotte v. Kalb (in 1784), in which Schiller
"resigns" himself to the hopelessness of his love for
a married woman.

.9A SD 'mit...einen': a "lapse" from HG 'einem' because of
the "distance" of the preposition 'mit' (H's Y would
require "a").
'inter': read "unter"; the <u>yod</u> ('i') is a broken <u>vov</u>
('u').

.10 'wohlahn': '-ah-' is phonetically correct for the
oxytone, though HG spelling ignores the phonetics.

58.4 'ferligen': Text has 'ferlihen', HG! The spelling
does deviate from the HG of <u>today</u> ('-ih' f. '-ieh-')
but was an acceptable variant before 1903.

.9-16 Y again.

.13-15 'Stillen - Willen': the first '-n' is <u>archaic</u> Y
and G, dished up as modern Y just because it deviates
from modern G. It is also Rz. The second '-n' is Y
but acceptable also in G, but Y speakers of G would

58.14   'Memme': Mama

.17   Was...verlieben?

.18   'Koreb': Korb

.19   Russpieperlein...gefällt ihm!

.21   mit dem denn los

.22   Von was für...jenes denn

58.13-15   tend to avoid it just because it is Y! The authen-
city of these added '-n's in H's dial. is made especially questionable by H's radical apocope of final
'-n' in the infinitive and pl. of the verb.

.14   'main--Memme': the two dashes indicate a hesitation,
in shy embarrassment about telling to whom she is re-
turning, be it to a lackluster, heaven-destined and
awaited mate, be it "back to mother". Both the hesitation and the ending have a humorous effect.

.16   'messen--nemme': inauth. h c; G "nehmen müssen", Y
"gemust nemmen". To the degree that the double "infinitive" construction is used in WY it is "recent"
HG influence. In an auth. dial. one would expect
the two infinitives to have an identical ending! The
dashes are for the same humorous effect as in .14.

.17   'Waiś...ferleben': cf. C p.186 on 19.9 concerning
Zetulpe's dial. -- the ignorant climber applying
right "substitution" rules -- only wrongly. H's
dial. makes HG 'ei' and 'ē' into 'ā' and 'ī',
respectively; therefore, she turns every Y 'ā' and 'ī'
(even those that are also 'ā' and 'ī' in HG) to a
HHG 'ai' and 'ē'!
'In mir': (f. "mich") Zetulpe's unintentional lapse
into Y syntax -- for which there is no easy "trans-
formational" rule.

.18   'Koreb': parasitic 'e', no more typical of Y than
of G, dist. h c.
'geben': Y and G archaic past participle (without
'ge-' prefix -- the rule for perfective verbs); "Korb
gegeben" would be identical in auth. standard Y and G

58.18 and would have the same rhythm as 'Koreb geben' but would not be as "funny".

.19 'Ruhś-pihpele': "(little) soot-piper", contemptuous for "Blackbirdie", here for Esther, conceived as a petite brunette (against Tradition, which gives her an olive complexion!). Cf. 59.2 L p. 398 # 473.
'gfallt'n': the lack of umlaut is not Y but SG dial.; the '-'n' f. "ihm" is both Y and Vogtländisch. Y generalized the umlaut in the whole pres. and infinitive and in most Y dialects, also in the participle -- prob. because of the frequency of the question and answer: "Vi gefelt dir? Es (Er, Si) gefelt mir". In Zetulpe's dial. the unumlauted 'a' may be HHG.

.20 'Roz-nehśle': vulgar f. "too-young" but also the literal "snot-nose", i.e., the little girl who doesn't even know enough to wipe her nose.
'behalten': in EY = only "hide"! Possibly it has this meaning (in addition to "keen") too in WY -- then it is humorous.

.21 'mit dehn': acc. f. dat. not Y, only G dial. (Vogtländisch), but dished up as Y h c, perhaps also HHG.
'der Mehr': printed together as one word in Text -- a spelling joke.

.22 'ihnś': jenes, that one (refers to Esther, the "Ruhś-pihpele"); in H's dial. 'je-' yields 'jī-' and 'jī-' apparently becomes 'ī-'; apheresis of the semi-vowel before its homorganic vowel 'i' is a common, though not universal, linguistic phenomenon: cf. NEY dial. "jung" but "inger" f. "jinger", "ingl", "Id" f. "jingl", "Jid", and "Goyish" "Israel" f. "Jewish" "Yisrael".

59.1   sind...Hühner...Gänse

.3   'Kiz': Kätzchen

.9   'Zwarechsak': sack in which cheese is pressed

.10   'Nibbeś': stinker

.14   'Nunterschied': Unterschied

.15   'Taig': Tag

.16   Was für eine Weissheit...Haut

.17   'galant': elegant

.19   Mäulchen...Näslein

.20   'Oichen': Augen

.23   'als': alles

.26   'ker': Text; <u>recte</u>: '<u>der</u>'

59.1   'send': a cross between Y "sainen, senen" and G "sind".
'sain': i.e., Esther's -- who are Esther's "pedigreed
parents" or "big-shot" ancestors? The humor lies in
that a "nobody" like Zetulpe questioned the pedigree of
Esther, traditionally of direct royal lineage from the
first Jewish king, Saul. The Talmud identifies Kish,
the ancestor of Mordechai and Esther, with the father
of Saul and motivates Mordechai's commanding Esther to
keep her ancestry a <u>secret</u> by his fear that her royal
descent might induce the king to choose her. This
secrecy then justifies Zetulpe in branding Esther a
"nobody".

.2   "Where does it come from, who knows it?" 'kenn'ś':
f. "kennt's" -- Y contaminates G "können" and "kennen"
and says "er ken" (or "kon") for either; also -- Rz.

.3   'Kiz': "Kätzchen". Y "Er hot dervisht dem Koter" =
"(He got) <u>some</u> big deal". Here it is both figurative
and literal: He got <u>some</u> big bargain in this kitty
(Esther)". L p. 381 # 309.

59.9 'Dreck': prob. less drastic in WY than in EY where it is the height of vulgarity, equivalent therein to Engl. "shit"; in G it only means "dirt".

'Zwarechsak': cheese-sack (from which the whey is still dripping), i.e., Esther is a "worthless, cheap drip". L p. 418 # 652. Though <u>grammatically</u> (as against psychologically) .9 refers to the King!

.10 'Nibbes': "stinker", perhaps with the connotation of the Y Hebrewism "nim'es" = "ekelhaft", "disgusting". L p. 390 # 393.

.11 'den': emphatic

.11A SD 'dem': a slip from HG! Proves that in syntax H was still used to employing his native Y instead of his assumed HG! -- unless we should impute the error (HG requires "den", the acc.) to the typesetter!

.14 '<u>N</u>unterschied': H's regular dist. based on metanalysis -- false syllable division.

.15 'Taig': f. "Tag".

.16 'Wais': f. "was"; cf. on 58. 17. 'Wais for a Waising': a "funny" conundrum, 'Waising' being (probably) a H coinage f. G "Weisse", Y 'vaiskait'.

.17 'galant': a malapropism f. "elegant".

.19 'Maile': prob. inauth. f. "Mail<u>e</u>le", the diminutive of "Moil", of which 'Maile' is the <u>plural</u>!

.20 'Oichen': inauth. WY "āgen", EY "oigen"; here we have a contamination of G dial. '-ch-' f. Y 'g' and EY 'oi' f. WY 'ā'.

.24 'main andre': EY "maine andere"; obscenely suggestive.

.25 'Lareme': dist.? Y "Larem", G "Lärm"; closer to the French etymology "(a)larme"! Auth.?

60.1   'fak̇sen': Possen, Grimassen

 .2   'Allroin': mandrake. 'grihne Bir': grüne Birne

 .5   'wais̈en': zeigen

60.1   'fak̇sen': not Y.

 .2   'Bir': EY "Bar(ne)", ultimately < Lat. Pir(um); the
       orig. pl. "Bire" (< Lat. pira) was soon conceived
       as a sg. and a new pl. "Biren" coined; then <u>it</u>
       "became" sg. and a new pl. "Birn<u>e</u>" was form<u>ed</u>, which
       in turn was conceived of as sg. and the latest pl.
       in G is "Birne<u>n</u>". The most common EY sg. is "Bar"
       (< a <u>sg.</u> "bar<u>n</u>" which was <u>mis</u>construed as a <u>pl.</u>!),
       pl. "bar<u>n</u>". "Bir<u>n</u>" (i.e., 'i' plus 'r' plus con-
       sonant) is the on<u>l</u>y form which could develop into
       th**e** Y "barn". The development of the word in Y has
       a history opposite to that in G; namely, a sg. was
       misconstrued as a plural and a new sg. was produced by
       "backformation", wheres in G each <u>pl.</u> was in turn
       misconstrued as a sg.!
       Cf. on 58.19. "Esther" is a <u>Persian</u> name (= "Star")
       and like most "Jew living in two cultures" she had a
       <u>Jewish</u> name, "Hadassah" (= "Myrtle") -- a name the
       Talmud interprets as pointing to her yellow-greenish
       complexion (Megillah 13A). What American slang calls
       a "peach" (a pretty girl) French slang calls a
       "poire" (pear).
       Zetulpe turns the tradition of Hadassah's being (as
       greenish-yellow as) a <u>myrtle</u> into a "green pear" --
       with all the negative connotations appertaining
       thereto.

 .3   'mes̈sen': EY mes<u>t</u>en.

 .5   'wais̈en': delib. dist., rev. subst. 's̈' f. 's'.

 .5A SD 'Ek̇tas̈e': '-s̈e' f. '-s' is hypercorrect French!

 .7   'dir main': Y.

 .10 'Muroh': ('-oh' = '-eau') apparently a famous (?)
       French milliner.

 .11 'dich': dist., acc. f. dat.

60.9   'Garnetur Spizzen': set of laces

.11 'trezzen': trotzen, spite

.13 'nai Hietle': neu(es) Hütlein

.16 'derhaam': daheim, zuhause

.17 'nahn...koschoh': nein...schwer (zu verstehen)

60.11 'trezzen': MHG "trutzen, trotzen, tratzen, tretzen".
"Tritzen" (< MHG "trutzen") is common in SEY, but the
verb and the noun have practically been displaced by
the Hebrewism (we have in .9) "le-hach‘is (ton)" in
general EY; it is unlisted in either Harkavy or Weinreich, and Stutchkoff has only the noun "Trotz" and
marks it as a "Germanism". The concept "spite" has
such a heavy emotional charge that not only did the
Hebrewism displace the Germanism, but the former has
begun to suffer the lengthening of its short 'ǎ' (in a
closed syllable!) to 'ɔ' and 'u': NEY "ləhɔxəs", SEY
"ləhuxəs"; it even manages to displace the still
current, but dying, preposition "trotz" (also unlisted!),
even though 'Le hach‘is' (sic, unhyphenated) is a
prepositioned infinitive (of purpose) and rather
awkward to use as a preposition: "despite you" = "dir
tzu lehaches".

.13 'nai Hietle': Y; HG requires "neues Hütlein" -- too
much for Zetulpe in her "Ekstase"; the '-es' inflection
is a NHG innovation.

.14 'Kalloh': = Esther, who is imagined to die with envy at
the sight of "Madam Moureau's Hietle" on Zetulpe's
head.
The 'oi's in Zetulpe's speech (f. HG 'o' ("Toit") and
'au' ("ois") are difficult to interpret, since H's
symbol (וֹ) is ambiguous -- 'oi' when Y is intended,
'ay' when G. Zetulpe slips from HG to Y unconsciously.
Note the skillful use of gradations of "dialect" for
subtle (and not so subtle) differentiation of
character.

.15 'Waas is der Ta‘am' is the regular, literal Y translation of the Talmudic Aramaic "Mᵓai Ta‘amoᵓ"! The
alephs are vowel signs and not consonant signs.
N.B. -- The line numbers are wrong on this page in the
Transliteration; .15 should be .18.

61.2   'Mendle': Männlein

  .3   hineingesehen in(s) (Bier?)kännlein

  .7   'Harrn': Herrn

60.13,.15 H anachronistically, though quite in accordance
           with Tradition, makes of Mordechai the pious Rabbi,
           one of whose modes of worship is learning Torah, and
           Torah usually means the "oral Torah", i.e., the
           Talmud (finished some thousand years after Mordechai's
           time). We are supposed to hear the "chant" of such
           learning and the typical, recurring phrase in the
           Babylonian Talmud (more inclusive than the "scantier"
           and, therefore, rather neglected "Jerusalem" Talmud)
           in the original Aramaic and the translation into Y:
           "Mai Ta𝖼amo?" "What's the reason?". Such learning
           "aloud", vocalizing and translating to oneself, is
           a kind of "thinking out loud" of one's argumentation,
           pro and con, of a proposition. Mordechai here is
           chanting: "Nothing more, no, but there still remains
           a difficulty..." In the chant the question mark is
           auth.

61.1   'soi': Text has "doi"!

  .2   According to the Talmud, Haman at this point (when
         ordered to perform the honoring services to Mordechai)
         realizes it was Mordechai's preoccupation with the
         Torah that "merited" Mordechai's triumph over him.
         .2 is therefore said with a mixture of bitter regret
         and envying admiration. Haman has become a comic
         figure in Jewish Tradition and a kind of "Merry
         Andrew" in Purim plays. Hence he talks the "language
         of comedy" (i.e., Y -- in the eyes of G Jews of the
         Enlightenment), though he is obviously a Gentile, and
         this very incongruity added to the humor!
         'flaišigš': Y "flaišig" (no '-š'. cf. 'nai Hietle',
         60.13, and 'klahn Jingle', 61.17), G "fleissiges"
         ('-es'); H's '-gš' is UG dial. -- Haman thus speaks a
         kind of "broken WY", i.e., like a "country bumpkin"
         trying to speak Y but mixing in his "hick" dial., not
         the honorific HG!
         'Mendle': The 'd' is auth. Y (and G dial.), even
         though parasitic.

61.9   'Gaile rait':   "Gäullein" reitet

  .13   Als...Leben ein einziges Mal

61.1,3-5   These lines are whispered, as the SD ('loit') before line .6 shows.

  .7   'Harrn': apparently an "innocent", absolutely regular,
development of G "Herrn" in H's Y: 'e' plur 'r' plus
consonant > 'a' plus consonant. There are only two
difficulties: 1. The Y is usually "Har" without the
added 'rn'; 2. assuming that "Har" is not directly derived from "Herrn", one would expect "Hann" or "Hahn"
in an auth. development, since the 'r' is usually
assimilated.   Perhaps it is auth., nonetheless.
Its choice, however, is definitely due to its homophony
with G "Harn" = "urine".

  .9   'Gaile': "Gäullein", little horse. The spelling with
a single 'l', instead of the double 'll', is prob. due
to an intended pun; namely, by analogy the diminutive
of "Goy" should also yield 'Gaile'!

  .11   The syntax is not Y, prob. not auth.

  .12   'kumme': archaic Y and G and modern G (but not Y) dial.
past participle.
'of': auth. Y as preposition; 'oif' is the adv. But
note the inconsistencies: .14 'oif' used as prep., .15
'nuf' used as adv.

  .13   'a nahnzigš': f. "an ahnzigš" -- even in the venerable
Mordechai's speech H allows an ignorant dist. h c. Note
the inconsistencies in adj. ending ("defective", i.e.,
no ending, used interchangeably with the "strong"
endings '-š'and '-eš'). If it were an isolated phenomenon we might explain it as "transition period" from
the uninflected to the inflected usage, where both
forms are used side by side, but there are too many such
phenomena and they are there as dist. h c.

  .14   'Ho ich': f. "hob" or "hon", but hardly auth. in
pre-vocalic position.
'main Taate sain': The genitive case had died out in
early NHG and was revived by Luther. In the living G

61.14　habe...meines Vaters

.16　'staz 'n Zaam':　anstatt eines Zaumes

.17　'der haam':　zuhause

.18　'a nalter Jid':　ein alter Jude

62.1　'špiet':　spät

.5　'for'n':　für Ihn, for you

.7　(by my coach and) six!

61.14　dialects all kinds of new syntactical substitutions
were coined, the most common of which is exemplified
here:　the <u>nominative</u> plus the possessive adj.　In Y
we have the <u>dative</u> plus '-ṡ' (prob. < the possessive
adj. "sain"), so that against G dial. 'main Taate
sain Pferd'.　Y requires "main tatnṡ ferd".

.16　'Pumṡ':　"oops!"　L p. 396 # 457.

.17　'der haam':　EY "<u>in</u> der haim".

.18　'nalter':　cf. on .13.

62.1　'zu'n':　H's regular dist. of Y and G "zum", even
though he does have <u>G dial</u>, "authority" for 'zu'n'.
'allewail':　G dial. = "immer", the preposition "auf"
of "für" must be "supplied", else we must attribute the
meaning "schon" to 'allewail' -- for which we have no
other evidence.
Tradition tells of Mordechai's being too <u>feeble</u> from
the three days of fasting to <u>mount</u> the horse and Haman
must let Mordechai step on his back to mount.　To
exploit <u>this</u> motive as is would only satisfy the
desire for vengeance on the Enemy.　H, however, strives
f. <u>comedy</u> and so he changes the Tradition (about
Mordechai's <u>not</u> having any difficulty in horseback
riding as <u>such</u>) and extracts the maximum humor from
the pious, unwordly, physically sorry figure of a
hermit-like Rabbi, incapable of horseback riding or
of appreciating the "great honor" and deathly afraid
of the horse, thoroughly despising the ostentation,
depreciating the "Goyish" concept of such "public

62.9   'Bahn': Bein

  .12   'Hudsche': sogar noch, even in addition

  .18   'thut's': Text has 'thut'n' = tut ihm, does for him

62.1   honoring", preferring some simple but useful reward.
      H thus holds up Mordechai's (i.e., the"old-fashioned"
      orthodox Jew's) values to condescending, though good-
      humored, persiflage.

  .2f   For Haman's "dialect" cf. C p. 291 on 61.2. It is not
      HG, even though he was a "Prime Minister", because the
      later Tradition made out of him a carnival-clown, and
      H uses HG only f. what is "serious and/or noble". It
      is conspicuously not Mordechai's Yiddish, since he was
      the "classic enemy" of the Jews. So Haman's dial.
      "had to be" a curious mix, inconsistent and inauth., of
      HG, Y and peasants' G dial. Thus 'aber, ailig, begehrt,
      ehren, gebeten, hab','kains, Kenig, laid, stehn, unter-
      thenig' are practically HG. 'Bai'n, erret, erst, gsagt,
      hett, helft, zihgt, zu'n' could be either "H's Y" or G
      dial.: 'Stiht' (63.12) against "Stehn' (63.11) show
      the degree of inconsistency in two consecutive lines.
      'Oif, daroif, main schente Gailich' can hardly be any-
      thing but WY. 'Oich' is, on the face of it, NEY (WY,
      even H's WY, has "aach"), possibly also some G dial.,
      but because it deviates from both H's WY and from HG
      it is eminently just what H needed for his characteri-
      zation of Haman.

  .7   'mainer Siks': apparently an oath; cf. L p. 406
      # 550.

  .12   'Hudsche': spelled as if it were Hebrew (i.e., in
      square letters), but there is no such Hebrewism in Y;
      there is no such Hebrew word! Apparently the Slavism
      "Chotsche" is meant and H not only mistook its etymolo-
      gy (he was a Hebrew scholar) but almost also its pre-
      cise meaning (Y Slavisms were not native in G and Y
      speakers there guessed their meaning from the context
      in reading. There were no Y dictionaries). Y
      "Chotsch(e)" does mean "wenigstens" ("at least") but
      it also means "sogar" ("even if, although"), but only
      in this sense of "even if" (G "selbst wenn") but not
      "sogar" in the sense of "noch dazu" ("also,

62.12 in addition") and it is in this last sense that H uses it here -- incorrectly!

.15 'Stuš': here = Posse.

.18 'thut's': Text has 'thut'n' = tut ihm, auth. Y. 'Gutš': the R indicates the vowel is long; in EY it is short.

.19 'Gelt': G dial., = "nicht wahr?" "Isn't it so?"

63.1 Mordechai mistakes the "honor" to be the cruel punish-ment he half expected at the hands of Haman for not prostrating himself before him.

.2 'Schlimmer': Frecher, brazen fellow, evil person; a stock G phrase. L p. 400 # 494.

.3 'nimmer': here = noch immer nicht, not yet, G.

.4-5 'hett - gerett': HG hättet - gerettet; the synco-pation is possible in HG m c but unnecessary, hence it is used as a dist. h c; the syncopation is regular in Y and G dial., though auth. EY now uses the Slavic "geratevet", and when it uses the Germanism it most frequently has "gerettet".

.6 'kainš': G dial. f. "keiner" in Y and HG.

.6-7 'gedacht - gsagt': N.B. the inconsistency in spelling the prefix 'ge-' and the sometimes phonetic and some-times historic orthography: 'gsagt' is elsewhere spelled "gsacht" and is here meant to be so pronounced.

.8 'errett': 'er-' is pleonastic because the verb is perfective without the prefix; not Y and rare in HG; it is G dial.

.9 'Trinkgeld': originally a small, trifling reward (= "tip" - namely, to "buy oneself a drink with") given only to "permanent" sleep-in (mostly unmarried) household servants by guests for personal services; sometimes, in an understatement, also a rather big reward, and therefore humorous, esepcially here: a "Trinkgeld" for saving the king's life!

64.1   von meinen schönsten Gäulchen

 .5   einen englischen Reiter, a jockey

 .7   'nem': nähme, would take

63.9   'ihn': G dial. f. "ihm".
      'oich': It is impossible to decide whether the pronun-
      ciation here intended is 'oi' or 'au' (cf. C on 62.2f.)
      but the more probable is 'au'!

 .10 'um...sehn': look around, i.e., investigate. The WO,
      meter, Y and/or G would improve if 'umsehen' were
      printed together at the end, but all are delib. dist.
      h c!

 .11 'als': noch immer, Y. Conceivably it is the Y con-
      junction "as" (= "that") which was contaminated with
      the conjunction "als" (= "when") and now "as" in EY
      means both G "dass" and G "als", and by delib. misuse
      H may be using 'als' for "dass" -- which is neither Y
      nor G.
      The dashes are meant to suggest that Haman is a "ham"
      (actor). He not only quotes the king's direct words,
      but pauses, as if he were acting out the king's
      searching in the book and then exclaiming his heuris-
      tic joy.

 .12 'Bliz Wetter': (here = "Eureka!") -- the humor is in-
      creased by the incongruity of Haman's rejoicing over
      the king's discovery which led to his own ruin! In
      the Bible Haman is not even made aware himself of the
      king's discovery, and H's twist in making Haman report
      it to Mordechai shows an ingenious awareness of the
      "unexploited humor-potential" of situations.

 .14f 'Iz...for': Y; 'ihr guten Lait': HG, the '-ai-' f.
      'eu' is only defective spelling; 'den' (f. "dem") is
      Vogtländisch.

 .21 'des Kenigs Pferd': HG.

 .22f The proclamation ('Dis...begehrt') is in square
      letters.

63.24   '<u>a</u>ber': The spelling (אַ) here deliberately stresses the HG phonology of the king's G, and yet mixes it, in Haman's reporting, with the Y 'Iz'.

64.3   'publizihren': ausschreien, proclaim, L p. 396 # 454.

.6   'dihn': f. Y and G de<u>m</u>, a regular H dist.
'ʿÔlom': here = Publikum, public.
'Pur<u>i</u>m-š̌piel: the fig. meaning in Y is like the contemptuous fig. meaning of Engl. "circus". The point of the joke is, of course, the anachronism in the <u>literal</u> meaning: The Purim-play came <u>afterward</u> to celebrate the triumph of Mordechai (and the Jews) over Haman and yet here the "principals" mention it before the event! And the meaning "comedy, circus, carnival" developed much later still and here Mordechai uses it!

.7   'nem': "nähme", potential subjunctive, (imperfect) f. present unreal: = "I would not take (no matter) how much (I were offered to go through with this).

.8f   God forbid (that I should) etc. The construction is the acme of parataxis and therefore primitive sounding -- as if 'Mach...' were the re-ruminating <u>verbatim</u> of the order actually given him (here: only in Mordechai's <u>interpretation</u> of Haman's <u>implications</u>).

.8   'Mok<u>ôm</u>': here = Flecken, kleines Örtchen; not current in EY.

.9   'Braatehoid': "Breite Haube", Kragenmantel, cape; L p. 350 # 7.
'Zitahkel': Schaufädenträger, "poncho with ritual fringes". L p. 418 # 645 defines it as a "Sedan, a closed carrying-chair". There are contextual difficulties which argue against this: The line seems to deal with <u>clothing</u>; one does not "reit" in a Sedan, but rather "fahr"; Mordechai <u>refuses</u> to ride horseback and <u>pleads in vain</u> for a coach. "Laibzudekl" (SEY "Lăbzidekl") is the <u>auth</u>. Y word for what is more specifically called "arbaʿ Kanfes" or "Tales Koten", i.e., the "little prayer-shawl", a "poncho"-like vest with fringes ("tsitsit") on its four corners, worn by orthodox Jews to fulfil the

64.19 'geroit': gerät, gelingt; i.e., "even if the stupidity
succeeds, turns out well"

64.9 commandment in Numbers 15: 38f. The "Laibzudekl" is
worn by the very pious <u>over</u> their shirt, with the
fringes dangling from <u>under</u> their coat; those dressed in
"modern garb" wear it <u>under</u> their shirt, with the
fringes hidden in their trousers. Reb Mordche would,
of course, wear it over his shirt and, with his
'Braatehoib' of necessity partly unbuttoned for riding
horseback, his "flying tsitses" <u>would</u> make quite a
'Spektahkel'. The curious spelling is perhaps a
<u>delib. dist. to connote</u> "Sedan". Note the Rz.

.11f Rhetorical, ironic question, implying an answer in the
negative.

.12f Rz in WO ('raiten rum') and rhyming a main with a
secondary accent ('rum - Publikum'). N.B., Mordechai's
vocabulary is heavy with Hebrewisms, almost to the
point of being unrealistic (for instance, 'Mokôm'), but,
as for Haman -- "not a one", as is to be expected.

.14 'Paitsch': EY "Baitsch".

.15 Humorous and anachronistic: The proclamation <u>has</u> come
down in Hebrew, in the Book of Esther, but the implication is, of course, that it was made in the language
of the country, Persian, only. But three decrees were
promulgated by the king and each was sent to 127 provinces, to each <u>in its own</u> tongue; the last, or third,
decree (permitting the Jews to defend themselves)
specifically was sent to the Jews too, "in their own
writing and tongue". H twists the story, anticipates
the use of Hebrew, changes the antagonist to G. An
EY humorist would have contrasted <u>Y</u> and G, but to H Y
had not the status of a language!

.16f Meaning: "What's in it for me? I'll remain the
same pauper after the parade that I was before it".

.18 'Th'ômar': pronounce: "tommer", the shortening of
the vowel in this Y Hebrewism is in accordance with an
old Germanic linguistic law that still operates, but
only sporadically, in Y and G (cf. MHG "jâmer" > NHG

64.18   "Jǎmmer"), namely: A resonant (1, m, n, r, w, y) will double a preceding consonant and the double consonant in turn will shorten the preceding vowel. This vowel change so destroyed the awareness of this Y word's Hebrew origin that it has long been spelled phonetically as if it were G. In "full" Hebrew it is pronounced <u>unchanged</u>.

'joi': disturbs the WO -- as the verb should be the second element; the sentence could be "corrected" with one comma after 'joi', but it would give a "pedestrian line", unworthy of H. The line would not be pedestrian and the sentence <u>would</u> be correct with <u>two</u> commas (before and after 'joi'), and we surmise that the meaning is as if the two commas <u>were</u> there, and that they were deliberately <u>not</u> used so as not to give a special intonation, with a sudden screamed 'joi', rather than the intended pauses before and after 'joi'. The whole line is packed, overfull, to express the all-pervasive terror at riding a horse and being killed by it.

.19   'wen...aach': even if; no longer EY.
'geroit': < MHG gerâten; 'â' > WY 'oi'; the infinitive vowel was generalized for the whole pres. (no umlaut); the inflection '-et' (3rd pers. sg.) syncopated after a stem ending in '-t' (or '-d'). L p. 369 # 193.

65.5   'der Kutschen': archaic and dialectal G, neither Y nor HG (cf. .12 'in a Kutsch').

.6   'rutschen': contemptuous, = "move by crawling, showing, rolling", instead of galloping!

.10   'schnoifen': "breathe heavily", as if one had to "hold one's breath" in fearful carefulness; conceivably it means here "snore", but then the h would be broad, rather than subtle.

.11   'hunten': "unten", a contamination of "unten" and "hinten", not uncommon in SEY, but prob. inauth. in WY! SEY has both "<u>hinten</u>" and "<u>inten</u>", and areas of confusion of 'h' and the glottal stop (not unlike cockney Engl. "(h)ear"). Cf. 86.14 and L p. 376 # 270.

65.1   'R<u>ua</u><u>h</u>':   <u>recte</u>:   "Rêvah" = "profit"

  .2   "that I won't be able to go after (attend to) my affairs (nothing) tomorrow (i.e., after a fall from the horse)"

  .9   'Den':   dann

  .10 'schnoifen':   schnaufen

  .14 'neht':   näht, sows

66.1   '<u>apripu</u>':   apropos

65.13 'nerrscher': EY "nahrischer": in WY the '-i-' was syncopated after the lapse of the operative-time of the rule that 'e' followed by a consonant is "lowered" to 'a'. In EY the "i-umlaut" could not operate against a barrier of 'rr' and there was no syncopation but, rather, simplification of the double consonant (after the lapse of the operative-time of the "i-umlaut"), hence "nāriš̌er", with a long 'ā'.

  .14 'halt': "just" -- ironical.

  .15-66.7 Overly naive, h c. H makes Mordechai "fall for" Haman's irony and he even suggests "greater precautionary measures" against his chance of falling off the horse.

  .17 'anderšt': = "otherwise either, except that"; it anticipates .18 as a <u>condition</u>; the '-t' was originally parasitic, but later it became a typical suffix in Y and G dialects for adverbs and prepositions.

  .18 'Schritt for Schritt': "step by step" = "slowly".

66.1   '<u>apripu</u>': dist. h c; cf. C on 36.5.

  .2 'bind': pres. hortatory subjunctive.
      'di<u>hn</u>': de<u>m</u>.

  .3 Completely against Tradition, where Haman is at this point cowering and obsequious, rather impatient and imperious -- which objectively he could not be in his position of "having the tables turned on him". H

67.2   'hareme': (ab)härmen, grieve

  .4   'pfopert': dröhnt, rumbles

  .5   'was...for a': was für ein(e)

  .7   'Hajjas-le': precious life

  .8   'watt': werdet

  .10   'a nariger': ein arger, a bad (difficult)

66.3   could not let an "old-fashioned", non-Enlightened, orthodox Rabbi <u>win</u>. He must lose and be made ridiculous, even if it be against the symbol of the arch-enemy of Israel!

  .6   'n<u>a</u>rrische': Cf. 65.13 where Haman says 'n<u>e</u>rrscher'.

  .7C   SD 'Thefiloh': a Y Hebrewism in the otherwise "pure" HG of the SD's because the emotional charge of 'Thefi-loh' could never be equalled by "Gebetbuch" -- not even for the would-be G-speaking H! In Hebrew and EY the meaning is "prayer" (general, or specifically prescribed); only in WY does it also mean "prayer-<u>book</u>" -- and this usage is a conspicuous earmark of WY (against EY "Siddur").

  .8-9 'Och! - Ach!': the Y and HG monosyllabic exclamations of the various members of the same family is especially "telling" and funny.

67.2   'hareme': "eat one's heart out", not EY; <u>if</u> auth. in WY the svarabhakti 'e' must have developed after the HG 'ä' became 'a' -- or it could not have become 'a'! L p. 373 # 238.

  .4   'pfopert': neither Y nor Standard HG, possibly a contamination of WG "poppern" (= "knock") and its SG variant "pfopfern", or just HHG for "poppern". This rare word must have been chosen for its suggestiveness of the ugly, possibly obscene, sounds "pf prt". L p. 394 # 439.

  .5   'Thehinoh': <u>special</u> <u>Y</u> prayers composed for women. Only

67.5   men are obligated to say the <u>prescribed</u> prayers in
Hebrew (Morning-, Afternoon-, and Evening-prayers, as
well as "additional" holiday-prayers). Women may say
these prayers for extra "merit", but they are exempt
from them, as from all "positive commandments" requiring <u>time</u> in their performance, because <u>their</u> time
is devoted to their family-duties and this is their way
of serving God. But <u>special</u> prayers were composed <u>for</u>
<u>women</u> in the <u>vernacular</u>, so that they could pray with
understanding and be inspired thereby to fervent sin-
cerity (Y-Hebrew "Kavonoh"). These touching prayers
were "tailored" to routine needs as well as all kinds
of emergency occasions. The technical term for these
"women's prayers in the vernacular" is "Techinos" in
Y.

.6   lit.: "now the kitten crawls up your back", an extension of "Kazenbuckel(n)" -- "to bend the back (like
a cat) and be humble". It refers to Zetulpe's <u>sudden</u>
piety and humility before God, in searching for the
fitting prayer.

.7   '<u>Hajjas-le</u>': = life, with the "diminutive" to express
not <u>littleness</u> but <u>endearment</u>, i.e., = "your precious
life"; misspelled 'Hjjt' f. "Hjvt", i.e., "Haj<u>i</u>t" f.
<u>recte</u> "Hajut", prob: to indicate the phonetic Y pro-
nunciation "Xáyəs", rather than the "full" Hebrew
"Xayús"; possibly he even intended the less current,
but more "correct", Y pronunciation "Xíyəs".

.8   Reference to Psalm 69:2, "Save me, O God, for the
waters are come in unto my soul" (Leeser, Moffat:
"...threaten my life"). The verse has become part of
many prayers for help.

.9   '<u>ferkum</u>': EY "kum <u>um</u>".

.10   'a nariger': = "an arger"; the 'i' is dist. h c,
though the parasitic vowel <u>is</u> spoken in <u>some</u>, geographically <u>limited</u>, Y dialects; with the word mis-
division there is an added connotation of "foolish", Y
"narischer" (HG 'ä') because the suffixes '-isch' and
'-ig' have the same meaning! The fast is "difficult"
because it had been ordered for <u>three</u> days (Esther
4:15), and "foolish" because H-Jukl does not believe

68.1   'rumpelt': "boils" noisily

.2   'Rehr': Röhre, enclosed stove compartment

67.10   fasting availas.
    'Tha‘aniṡ': There are four auth. pronunciations f.
this word in Y: "taineṡ > taneṡ > tɔnəṡ > tunəṡ",
the first being the old WY pronunciation, the last --
the Galician. The '-ai-' developed as a compensation
for the loss of the guttural syllable '-‘a-'; the
long 'ā' developed because of the strong emotional
charge of the word: Jews decreed public fasts every
time the community was in trouble, and they assumed
individual fasts when they were in "private" personal
trouble -- and trouble was galore. The pious came
to fast every Monday and Thursday of an ordinary week
-- in addition to four biblically prescribed fast-
days and the non-prescribed fasts on the ten days of
the penitential period (between Rosh Hashonoh (New
Year's) and Yom Kippur (Day of Atonement)) and the
day before the New Moon. Hence Y phrase "every
Monday and Thursday" ("Yedn montik un donerštik") for
an annoyance that occurs too frequently. -- The strong
emotion brings longer stress on the first component
('a') of the diphthong 'ai', lengthens it at the
expense of its second component ('i'), resulting in a
long 'ā', which then developed further, regularly,
to 'ɔ' in NEY and to 'u' in SEY.

.11   "Be my sacrificial animal", i.e., "Drop dead!" Cf.
C p.132 on 3.8 and C p.183 on 19.2 and L p. 378
286.

68.2   'Rehr': Listing L p. 397 # 464 defines this word as
"reed", but the context makes it probable that here
it must mean: "an enclosed compartment in the stove,
not directly over the fire, where pots with already
cooked food are kept hot".

.3   'Schwaigt...štum': vulgar; contamination of "still-
schweigen" and "verstummen".
    'uhn-Ta‘am': 'uhn-': the long vowel is delib. dist.;
the 'u' remains short even in emphasis -- here it is
therefore overemphasized. 'Ta‘am': lit. = "taste",
but here = "charm", a ubiquitous Jewish Hebrewism in
all their adopted vernaculars (like its synonym "Hen"

68.3 'uhn-<u>Ta‘am</u>': "ugly mug!"

  .4 'Schak': Jacques

  .5 That is proper (will "pass") where you come from,
      where you peasants live.

  .6 'Flihgel': Flegel, boor, lout

  .8 Here your obscenities (just) "won't do".

68.3 = "grace, charm") in various combinations and adapta-
      tions, e.g.: "ba ta‘amt" = "charming", "Unta‘am" =
      "ugly person, lack of charm (or taste)".

  .4 'Schak': = Jukl; cf. C p.119 on the possible mockery
      and contempt associated with this form of the name
      "Jacob". 'Schak' is the "fancy", "Frenchified" form
      of it ("Jacques", pronounced "Žak" by "cognoscenti",
      is defectively pronounced "Schak" by the "highfalutin
      climber", ignorant of "genuine" French). Most Jews
      have had two forms for their given names -- ever since
      their first Exile in 486 B.C.E. (In Egypt, the
      Talmud testifies, they kept their Jewish names.) The
      "holy name" is used in all religious functions, whereas
      the <u>civil</u> name is used especially with non-Jewish
      <u>authorities</u> and neighbors (in "assimilated" circles,
      also with all Jews, including family). Thus "Esther"
      herself also has a "holy name": "Hadassah" (cf. Esther
      2:7). In our case here, "Ya‘akov" had as its civic
      form the Latinized "Jacob" (and its later developments:
      "James, Giacomo, Giacopo, etc."); Y developments of the
      name are "Yainkl, Yākef, Yāukef, Yǎkl, Yānkl, Yukl,
      etc." "Yukl", however, became as "common" as "Jack" in
      Engl., and, like it, acquired even a vulgar (= "fool")
      and an obscene (= "penis") connotation -- for which it
      was chosen by H.
      There is something incongruous and therefore funny in
      Zetulpe's calling Jukl by his first name but using the
      "<u>polite</u>" verb forms, yet calling him names like
      'Flihgel'. Note also that her grammar and phonology
      are <u>intended</u> to be G, but she constantly slips into
      Y, and the mixture is also funny. The social gulf
      between "Jacques" and "Jukl" adds to the h. L p. 398
      # 481.

68.4   Supplementary material to C on 68.4 on Jewish names.

There are very many ironies in the history of
Jewish names: both given and family. When Jews
wanted to keep their traditional names, "laws" were
decreed forcing them to assume non-Jewish "civil"
names; when they wanted to assimilate and use their
neighbors' names, they were forbidden and forced to
have recognizable, typically Jewish names. In this
regard, Hitler's "Nürnberg Laws" were only one example
of many. Even the name-changes in Israel have their
story to tell and their ironies!

Sometimes the two names (holy and civil) developed new forms, due both to specific Y phonology and to
mothers' forcing the names into "endearing" forms; for
instance, "Yehuda" and "Judah" would be the first
stage (Latinized biblical names were generally "accepted" by civic authorities). Where and when "Judah"
was "unacceptable" resort was taken to the biblical
symbol of Judah -- "Lion" (Exod. 49:9), which was, in
the various vernaculars: Leo, Lion, Leone, Lewe,
Löwe. The last two developed into Y "Leyb". Then the
diminutive, "endearing" forms yielded: Leybl, Leybale,
Leybuš, and Yidl, Yidale. Finally, the holy and the
civic name, after the latter had assumed a specific
"Jewish-sounding" phonology, were misconceived as a
compound of two separate names ("First" and "Middle"),
and the scholars "retranslated" "Leyb" into Hebrew
"Aryeh", and so arose the holy name "Yehuda-Aryeh".

The Rabbis had their difficulties with this
plethora -- there are many Responsa on the question of
which name is the "real" one and what is its proper
spelling -- of utmost importance in a "bill-of-divorce-
ment", for instance, where a single misspelling would
invalidate the divorce and make a second marriage
impossible, and, if already consummated, invalid and
any children therefrom "illegitimate", with all the
horrible "disabilities" that that meant in a Jewish
community!

.5   Zetulpe suggests that Jukl's uncouthness comes from
his "village" upbringing among peasants and because
of that he lacks "city" refinements.

.6   'Flihgel': lout; L p. 365 # 148.

68.9 - 10   It will surely "kill you" to take your hat off in the house, won't it?

.11   I don't want ever to burden you with the "Hintern" ("behind").

.12   I'd tell you something on the spot, only there are too many witnesses.

.13   'Ahnlihgen':   (Hin)einlegen (into an insane asylum)

68.7   'Mamsel--Harbona':   = Zetulpe; a creation of H, not biblical.

.8   'Unflahtigkaiten':   a malapropism, since Jukl has not as yet been even vulgar, let alone obscene (as he is in .11). He is as yet only not refined. Zetulpe apparently doesn't know the difference. Or she puts on airs. She isn't even familiar with the correct form of the word: '-ä-', not '-a-'.

.9-10   Pious, orthodox Jews don't "go around" bare-headed. Harbona would therefore object to Jukl's baring his head in his house, and yet real refinement would require that Jukl shouldnot bare his head out of respect for the host. Zetulpe's lecturing Jukl on etiquette breaches every rule of it, even in her very act of lecturing! That's the h!

.11   'Hintern':   a pun on 'hindert'n' (.9), here deliberately obscene, but, then, he was provoked to it!

.12   'ball':   G bald, G dial., where final '-ld' > '-ll', not Y! Zetulpe isn't beyond giving tit for tat even in obscenities, but she prefers not to do it in public ('zu hell'). The image is borrowed from the act of love-making -- improper in "bright light". The Talmud (Sabbath 86A) says, "The Israelites are holy: they don't cohabit ("use their beds") by day".

.13   'zu'n Ahnlihgen':   zum (Hin)einlegen (ins Irrenhaus); crazy (enough) to be "put up"; there may be an erotic connotation: "crazy to go to bed".

68.13-69.1   'meschuggoᶜ - Mevukoh':   Rz 'g - k' is common

69.4   'war...': = verrecke, drop dead!

.9   'S̆praz': Spreize

.10   'laaft': läuft

.11   'Secht'ch': Seht Euch

.13   Vielleicht wirft ihn einer

.15   'gihben a Huzzer': gegeben einen Stoss

.16   'Oispuzzer': Verweis, reprimand, punishment ("come-uppance")

68.13-69.1   with H, but 'Mevukoh' is rare enough in Hebrew and is practically never used in Y -- it may be meant as a malapropism for "Mevucho", a slightly more common Y Hebrewism, but uncommon enough to be "difficult" for a woman; both are synonyms of 'Zoroh' ("trouble"): 'Mevukoh' = destruction (by despoiling), "Mevucho" = confusion, perplexity (= "no way out").

69.1   'Ba-ʿAwônôsênu': cf. C p.153 and 11.7.

.2   'Schlim-Massol': pronounce "S̆ləmázl", cf. C p. 167 on 16.5.
'Bai dihn...Bai der': Y uses the dat. with prepositions, while H usually uses the acc. (like Vogtländisch), but apparently not consistently, as a dist. h c.

.3   'anderS̆t': parasitic '-t' is common enough in Y to have become an adverbial suffix (cf. "oich-et, oif-et, op-et") but just with "anders" it is not common due to the heavy clustering.
'Seroroh': sic! Lit. = "Herrschaft", here ironical, = "Lady" or "Princess" (i.e., "too good (aristocratic) to do housework").

.4   'hudsche': pronounce "xɔtS̆ə". Cf. C p. 294 on 62.12.
'Kapporoh': a curse, when emphatic, it = "Drop dead!"; when weaker, it = "Go to hell!". Cf. C p.132 on 3.8 and C p.183 on 19.2 and L p. 378 # 286. The transition from cursing to praying is delib., h c.

70.1   'daft': dürft

  .3   'Wost in di Arwesn': Wurst in die Erbsen

  .4   'Kugel, mit Rezaine': Gugel(napf) mit Rosinen,
       pudding with raisins

  .5   'baišt ahn': break the (your) fast

69.5   It has been aptly said that, instead of "Original Sin",
      Jews believe in and rely on the "Original Merit"
      ('Sechuš Ovôš') of their ancestors.

  .9   A common figure in the "Tehinôš", the Y prayers f.
      women.
      'groise': delib. dist. ('s' f. 'š') h c, to suggest
      "gruesome" -- each time "groiš" occurs.

  .13 'Of ahnmoil': usually = "suddenly", but here =
      "(even though unexpected, yet still) perhaps, by
      chance".

  .14 'ferkum': EY "kum um", perish.

  .15 'Hamôr': sic; 'Huzzer': G dial., not Y, cf. L p. 376
      # 273.

  .16 'Oispuzzer': Cf. L p. 393 # 425.

  .16A SD 'spricht': possibly a printing error f. "springt",
      which would make better sense.

  .17f Possibly an obscene "folksong" -- we haven't been able
      to identify it.

70.1   'daft': here both Y and G meanings fit: "you ought to"
      or "you may".

  .3   'a gesunden Wošt': einen starken (grossen) Wurst.
      'Arwesn': EY "arbes" mistaken for a pl. and a new sg.,
      "arbe", consequently "backformed" -- cf. the similar
      development of Eng. "pea" from "pease" (orig. sg.!).
      The rev. subst. of '-rb-' $\gtrless$ '-rw-' is typical of H.

  .4   'Kugel': special Jewish dish -- a pudding eaten at

70.10   'Zettel': Lotterie

.14   'as': so

.16   'Noich Schuhl': Nach Schuhl, after synagogue
    (prayers)

.18   'Gŝtih': crowd of bystanders; 'Noitel...tupfen':
    add a dot to a note

70.4   the Saturday dinner, part of the "Tscholent" or
    "Schalet", usually made from noodles or potatoes.
    On "special Saturdays", to mark the occasion, extra-
    ordinary Kugels were prepared, whether the "special
    occasion" was private or public. The word is re-
    lated to G "Gugelnapf". Cf. L p. 383 # 329.
    'Resaine': sic!

.7   'Waas...for a': "was für eine": colloquial and good
    Y plural; HG prefers just "was für--", without the
    "eine", f. the pl. EY now has developed the one word
    "wossere".

.8   'oisgelossen': Cf. C p. 283 on 56.12.

.9   On Purim there is a religious command to get drunk to
    the point of not knowing the difference between
    "blessed be Mordechai" and "cursed be Haman".

.10   'Zettel': L p. 617 # 640.

.14   sc. "der Wind" or "nor meglich".

.16   'Schuhl': (sic!) Synagogue; according to the Talmud,
    prayers are especially acceptable if made in a place
    where Torah is learned. Thus the "school" became
    the house of prayer and vice versa.

.18   'Noitel': kleine Note; 'tupfen': betupfen, add a
    dot to. 'Noitel...tupfen' could mean "Nadel...
    durchstossen"; "lautgesetzlich" (according to strict
    rules of linguistic development, which H does not
    always heed) only MHG "Nâdel" could yield, for H,
    "Noitel"; "Note" would (as a FW) yield "Nute", and
    the dimunitive would yield "Nitel". 'tupfen' and
    "ŝtupfen" are synonymous in SG, and "ŝtupfen" (EY

71.2   'blai': blei(be)

  .4   'sich': sehe, look

  .6   'zu špringe': gesprungen, running (galloping)

  .11 'Allewail Štrihlen': immerfort strählen

  .12 'abfihgen': abfegen

  .13 'ahnizihgen': anziehen

  .17 'Frah lihben': Frau, leben (sollt Ihr)!

  .20 'Uffresihrt': Auffrisiert

  .22 'bseššen': besetzt

70.18 "Štuppen") means to "push". "Note<u>paper</u>" (cf. L p. 389
       # 387) hardly fits.

71.6   'zu špringe': Y, HG has "gesprungen"; exaggeration for
       "running (galloping) like a horse".

  .6-7 'Hath<u>a</u>ch - n<u>o</u>ch': <u>not</u> Rz! The Y pronunciation
       (intended for all names) is "Hath<u>o</u>ch". Cf. C p. 109,
       fourth paragraph.

  .9   '<u>Hesed</u>': emotionally very weighty, = "Grace (of God)";
       when coupled with 'mit'n Pferd', one gets a shock of
       humor.

  .10 'hemmsi'n': G dial. f. "haben sie ihn", f. less collo-
       quial HG "hat man ihn"; EY "hobm se nem".

  .11 'Allewail': here = "die ganze Zeit", not EY.
       'Štrihlen': in SG it <u>can</u> be used for "combing <u>down</u>"
       human hair, but in Standard HG it connotes "striegeln",
       "to comb with a horse-brush". That such is the intend-
       ed meaning is proven by .12, which speaks of "rubbing
       with sand and soap and <u>broom</u>". The Maskilim commonly
       libeled the old-fashioned, pious Jew as particularly
       "filthy" -- entirely unjustly, since piety <u>requires</u> a
       Jew to be clean.

  .13 'waiš Hemm<u>e</u>d': auth. Y and MHG; NHG "weiss<u>es</u> Hem<u>d</u>" is

71.13 an innovation.
'ahnzihgen': sic! The extra '-i-' in the Transliteration is a typing error.

.15 The future is used to express present probability, as
in HG, but <u>not</u> EY; = "they are <u>probably</u> finished with
him already".

.16 '<u>Heder</u>': rarely used in Y just for "room" -- it has
tȯ be some "special room", used for holy work. Thus
it became the technical term for a Jewish (religious)
school. Here it is delib. used incongruously for a
bathing and barbering room! The "full" Hebrew pronunciation is "Heder", but in Y it is "Hêder" -- the
emotional chargė caused lengthening of the vowel (cf.
"Pêsach, Mêlech, Nᴐchem (the proper name "Nahum"),
Mᴐśέ).

.18 'heṡt'n': auth. WY; EY "wolṡt'n".
'gekennt', along with .19 'gebrennt': auth. Y.

.20 '<u>Uf</u>-': auth. Y <u>dial</u>., but H usually has the auth.
WY "<u>oif</u>-" for both preposition and adv. prefix;
occasionally he has "of" for the prep. and "uf" for
the adv.
'-f<u>res</u>ihrt': the '-e-' is only a spelling deviation,
a dist. h c, though the unaccented '-i-' <u>could</u> have
had the value of the HG unaccented 'e' -- only that H
does not spell even the suffix '-l<u>i</u>ch' with an '-e-',
where such a shift would have been more natural,
certainly before the palatalization of the 'ch' (from
'x' to 'ç', after 'i'), but even after it. One is
tempted to conjecture that the sequence '-fres-' in
'-fresihrt' tempted the punster in H.

.21 'scharl<u>o</u>ch': sic, with '-o-', dist. h c, to get the
sequence "loch".

.22 'bseṡṡen': Rz, f. "besetzt", with the added intent of
connoting "insane" via the malapropism.

.25 'Blummeṡ': EY, and EY <u>only</u>, has (rather recently)
shifted some G '-n'-plurals to '-s'-plurals on the
pattern of the Hebrewisms and Slavisms ending in
schwa (ə)(e.g., "Tate-s, Charpe-s, Schande-s"), but

72.1   'triben': drüben

.2   'Lewen...Haschen': Löwen...Hirsche

.3   '-schihs̊': -schösse

.4   'Liebens̊grihs̊': Lebensgrösse

.6   'alles Bihs': alles Böse

.7   'Jakrus̊': sic! das Teuerste, the most expensive

.8   'A napfelgrihne atlos̊ene': eine apfelgrüne, atlassene

71.25 Y Germanisms apocopated their final '-e; -- they, therefore, fit the pattern only if they are new borrowings
with the HG '-e'. 'Blum' is OY! And its pl. has been
"blumen" in all Y; hence, delib. dist., h c.

72.1   'ois di': auth. Y.

.2   'gs̊prunge': "in poses of leaping" is the pretended,
"innocent" meaning; what is actually said is the hyperbole that these animals jumped out of Mordechai's
garment-pockets.
'Lewen': the 'e' is MHG and Y; the 'ö' in NHG is an
innovation ('e' between 'l' and the labial 'w'); EY
"leyb", the 'ey' because the MHG '-ê-' in an openable
syllable became long even in NEY (Lithuanian) because
it fell together in quality with the originally long
MHG 'ê' (as in 'gên") and then also in quantity, and
it further developed into a diphthong (SEY 'ay'!); the
'-b' (< '-w') occurs in final position in cases of
heavy emotional charge.
'Haschen': NEY "hirschen", CEY "herschen", H 'Haschen'
-- the last also means HG "Hasen" in the G dial. of
the border-region between South and East Franconian
(between the rivers Main, Kocher, and Neckar; cf. Hans
Reis, "Die deutschen Mundarten", p. 42). Cf. L p. 374
242.

.5   A delib. anachronism, h c: the war between Frederick II
and Maria Theresa, 1756-63.

.6   A prayer to war off evil, normally before it is to be

72.9   'hihbeśt, heśte': hättest, hattest du

.13   'Baiere': Bäuerin

.15   'Bośśer nunter': Ferner unten

.16   'Schaaden...bloist': Schatten...bläst

.19   'Waaden Schoif...Bek': weiden Schafe...Böcke

.21   'fezzen': fetter. 'giht': gibt

.24   'gihle lidere': gelbe lederne

.25   'Nihgelich': Näglein (Nelken)

72.6   mentioned, but frequently also thereafter. Conceiva-
        bly it is an "afterthought" and is deliberately mis-
        placed and should belong immediately after 'Krieg';
        as it stands, it belongs to .7, q.v.

.7   'Jakruś': (sic!) in Y an emotionally charged word
        meaning "Inflation" and "Famine", but it also has the
        literal Hebrew meaning (unemotional) of "expensiveness,
        dearness". Here only the last meaning ("very expen-
        sive" decorations) is intended, but the association
        with the other meaning terrifies Harbona into the
        "misplaced: prayer to ward off the evil. In Luther's
        Bible, too, "Teuring" (corresponding to Y "Yakruś")
        means "famine", but it translates the Hebrew technical
        term for it ("raʿav").

.8   'atlośene': "made of satin or satin-like silk'; the
        'o' f. 'a' is dist., h c; the meter suggests a dis-
        torted accent (on the 'o').

.9   'hihbeśt, heśte': both are, apparently, the imper-
        fect subjunctive of "haben", as the auxiliaries for the
        pluperfect subjunctive, for an unreal condition in past
        time. WY still has all the subjunctive forms, while
        EY has only newly formed conditionals (e.g., "volst
        machn, volst gemacht" = "would make, would have made").
        'hihbeśt' is prob. a simplification of "hihbetst",
        < *häbetest, a novel subjunctive formation on the
        basis of the regular weak verb, even for the imperfect

72.9   subjunctives of the strong and irregular verbs, which
is found in some G dialects (e.g., Bavarian). H uses
<u>all</u> forms: Y, HG, G dialectal, and possibly his own
coinages into the bargain -- and dishes them all up as
Y! 'he<u>s</u>te' is a similar simplification ("Entlastung")
of Y "he<u>t</u>ste", HG "h<u>ä</u>ttest du". Cf. C p.137-40 on 5.1
-.19, and C p.165 on 15.16f.

.11   'allemoil': lit. = "all the time", a "primitive" substitute f. "every" (button).

.12   'Brilljan<u>d</u>': the '-<u>d</u>' is the clearest delib. dist.,
since both Y and HG have '-<u>t</u>' in the sg. and pl., and
both Y and G <u>unvoice final</u> consonants even when they
<u>are</u> voiced in non-final positions!

.13   'Baiere': HG "Bäuerin"; but auth. EY has "poier" for
masc. and "poier<u>te</u>" f. fem. 'Baiere' <u>may</u> be auth. <u>WY</u>,
but, if not, it was chosen f. its connoting "Bavarian
(female)" -- a humorous confusion.

.14   'giht nois': "is going" (haying); the "awkward" construction was chosen deliberately f. its euphemistic
meaning -- "defecates".

.15   'Be<u>ss</u>er nunter': "primitive", incorrect, inept choice
of parts of speech f. HG "ferner unten" and EY "vaiter
arunter(tzu)".
'Schallmai': flute, wind-instrument, L p. 399 # 483.

.16   'Schaa<u>d</u>en': the '-d-' is rev. subst. h c, which makes
it neither Y nor G, but it means "damage" in both WY
and G!
'Tusch': fanfare, L p. 410 # 590.

.21   'fezzen': dist. in sound ('z' f. 't') and grammar
('-en' f. '-er') both in Y and G. The etymology could
yield a form *fetz instead of the regular Y and G "fett",
i.e., a Germanic *faitian, "to fatten", could yield a
past participle in HG *fetz = "fatted". There <u>are</u> such
forms in some HG <u>dialects</u> (cf. L p. 365 # 139A and A
p. 86 # 37.7); correct grammar with this dial. form
would yield a "fet<u>zer</u>" ("fezzer"), but H was determined
to exploit and extract the "last drop" of the humor-
potential: 'fezze<u>n</u>' connotes "rag", "mud-puddle",

73.2   'Gawehlihr': Kavalier

  .3   'schier': beinahe

72.21   "shred", "scrap", "tear to pieces" -- its being ob-
        viously "wrong" only adds to the h.
        'giht': gibt; the 'b' is syncopated here in Y, as it
        is in Eng. and G dialects, and like the 'b' "hat" in
        G (and Y) and the 'v' in "has" in Eng. -- an example of
        the common phenomenon of slurring, reducing the length
        of words of high frequency.
        'Achting': Cf. C p. 199 on 22.20 about '-ing' and
        '-ung'.

  .22   'zu'n Gšpahš': zum Spass; cf. C p.145 on 7.19 and C
        p.165 on 15.16, and L p.369-70 for H's favoring com-
        pounds with the prefix 'Ge-'.

  .23   'fezzen Boich': fetten Bauch -- a H invention, prob.
        copied from carnivals and/or Purim plays, where the
        Comic Figure had an artificial paunch, but it was prob.
        not Mordechai! Only a Maskil like H would dare to go
        even that little a distance in such a direction.
        'bis an der Nahš': where the acc. with the prep. would
        be correct HG H deliberately deviates and uses the
        dat.! The Talmudic idiom is a "belly reading unto
        between the teeth"; the G idiom makes it reach still
        higher -- to the nose!

  .24   'gihle': MHG "gelo-gelwes": Y gel < "gelo", HG
        gelb < "gelw-".
        'lidere': G and Y require "lederne"; there may be a
        G dial. form without the '-n'-formant (to derive adj.s
        from nouns denoting material, cf. Eng. "gold and
        golden") -- but H chose it because of its allusion to
        G "liederlich" = "dissolute, slovenly".

  .24-25 'Hoisen - Roisen': Rz? MHG "hose" should yield
        WY hōse, not 'hoi-'!

  .25   'Runter und runter': = "all the way down".

  .26   'Kuhrierstifelich': more commonly called "Reiterstie-
        fel"; H takes care to define them "with long spurs"
        because his term was the less known because not only
        couriers used spurred boots, but all horseback riders.

73.6   'Haituken': Haiducken

  .9   'gebroicht 'n Goil': gebracht einen Gaul

  .12 'Waas...roiten': Weiss...raten

72.26 H's choice of "Kurier-" must be due to the "spelling-
      joke" lurking in his misspelling 'Kuh-' = "cow"!
      'Spohren': rev. subst. of long and short vowels, h c.

72.26-73.1 'Špohren - geschworen': Rz 'ɔ - o'.

73.2 'Gawehlihr': 'G-' is Y.

  .3 Zetulpe intends to speak HG but in her ignorance she
      reverses the 'ie' and 'e' of "leben" and "verlieben"!
      'in'n': Y = "inem"!

  .5 H's invention

  .6 'Hintin noich': hinten nach, nachher; not Y.
      'Haituken': servants (in Hungarian livery). L p. 373
      # 235.

  .6-7 'Spišen - gewišen': Rz: 's - š' in H; '-īs - -ēs'
      in EY.

  .7 'doten': dort, auth. Y; prob. a contamination of three
      adverbs: "dort: = "there", "dorten" (< '-anna') =
      "thence" (with verbs implying "motion away from"), and
      "dorthin" = "thither" (with verbs implying "motion
      toward"); in EY "dort" and "dorten" are interchangeable
      f. "there", but only "fun dorten" = "from there, thence";
      EY "ahím" (< "ín hin") = G "dorthin", "thereto,
      Thither". Cf. L p. 361 # 100.

  .13 'Štoiten': prob. Low G dial. f. HG "Steiss", "buttocks"
      or f. HG "Schenkel", "things", not HG "Stute", "mare".
      Cf. L p. 405 # 533. Words f. "pudenda" often did not
      participate in the sound-shifts and the "unshifted" Low
      G forms appear also in the HG dial. HG "Stute" would
      be identical in WY, but, while H allowed himself devia-
      tions, the meaning "mare" does not fit the context any-
      way.

  .14 'Fuhse.': printing-error, a period (dot) after 'Fuhse',

73.13 'Štoiten': "Hintern", backside

.14 'Fuhseštihle': Fussstuhl, Schemel

.15 'Pumś': bums! 'Hihch': Höhe. 'Mihiloh': "Pardon!" (a euphemism for "arse").

74.1 'ahn Špringle': einem Sprünglein

.2 'droiben': da oben

.3 'Sechijjoh': Erlebnis

73.14 instead of the required hyphen. 'Štihle': Rz to 'Mehiloh' (pronounced "məxílə"). 'Fuhse-Štihle' is extremely distorted and inauth.; both WY and HG (and even NEY) would require "Fussstuhl", though "Fussben-kel" is the auth. Y form.

.15 'Hihch': EY "Heych", HG "Höhe". The HG (silent) '-h-' developed from the '-ch-' sound (spelled 'h' anyway) in MHG intervocalicly; in Y the final vowel in MHG "hoche" was apocopated and thus the 'x' became final and remained unchanged in pronunciation. Cf. the different pronunciations of HG "hoch" but "hoher" and "höher", Y and G "sehen" but "Sicht", OY ich "sich" but Modern Y and NHG ich "se(he)" -- all of which are due to the same principle.
'Mehiloh': lit. "pardon, forgiveness", a euphemism for "Arsch"; the latter word was completely lost in Y, to-gether with ever so many other Germanisms denoting vul-garities or obscenities. Cf. C p. 211 on 26.7 concern-ing obscenities in Y.

74.3 'Sechijjoh': lit. "deserving (winning) reward from God"; here = "to be privileged to 'experience' some-thing wonderful".

.4 'ebeś': etwas; an idiomatic understatement that ex-presses a high degree; G, not Y.
'fifat': 'f' f. 'v' is here more than just the re-gular rev. subst. of voiced and voiceless; it is to suggest the pronunciation of the "ignoramus:, who is misled by the spelling of this FW into pronouncing this 'v' like a G 'v' (= 'f'); obviously: not Y.

74.4   'ebeš fifat': etwas vivat

  .5   'gejuchzt': gejauchzt

  .8   'geštrozt': (sic!) "crammed, overladen, overloaded"

  .9   'Boigen': Pauken

 .12 'Kumihš': salesmen

 .13 Was für eine Frage? Alle sind sie mit ihm.

 .14 'Kuplimenten': Komplimenten

 .15 'Jenerahlš': Generale

 .16 'Oiber...': musket and sword

 .17 'Galle-schihšen': small, open carriage

 .18 That parade was simply fabulous.

74.5   'gejuchzt': G dial.

 .11 'Affezihr': Offizier; the dist. is to suggest G Affe, Zieher.

 .12 'Kumihš': < Fr. commis voyageur, but auth. in Y and G dialects; however, the spelling (and possibly a shift of accent to the first syllable) is meant to suggest G Kuhmist, "cow manure".

.11-12   Students, store-clerks ('Kumihš'), and army-officers (prob. "cadets") are the acme of High Society to Zetulpe. Note: '-š' plurals were in fashion for FW.

 .13 'daitsch': the 'd-' f. the auth. Y 't-' may be an attempt by Harbona to speak G like his daughter! Cf. C p. 125 on 1.4.

 .15 'Jenerahlš': 'J' f. 'G' is Low G, used here because the Y is identical with HG!

 .16 'Oiber...': anachronism, h c; cf. L p. 391 # 409.

75.2   Wie der Mann, so die Wurst.

  .3   'nor soi': möglichst, (as high) as possible

  .4   'Gsizzen...Dechter': Gesessen...Dächer

  .5   'als': immer (noch), still

  .8   'Ober ahn Gfalleś': aber einen Gefallen

  .9   'oisrihten': ausreden

  .12   'arr...ferzihl': irre...erzähle

74.17   'Galle-schihśen': a H coinage, a "blend" of Fr. "ca-
lèche" and "chaise", to suggest Y "gal-šiśen", an
allusion to the Y "gal-špayen" ("to spit gall").

  .18   'dermehr': (sic!) here = G fabelhaft, "something
special", "fabulous". Now it means "something wrong"!
∠ MHG "der Maere" = "des Erzahlens(wert)".

75.1   'Hasunoh': here used fig. = the "big show" -- which
Jewish marriages, in particular, still notoriously are.
Harbona's "compulsive" thinking of the costs and his
wish that he possessed that much are supposed to
criticize "humorously" Harbona's sense of values.

  .2   "According to the man('s quality is the quality of) the
sausage", = The King gave Mordechai a show befitting
Mordechai's (or the King's?) quality.

  .3   'nor soi': (as high) as they could.

  .5   'als noch nit': immer noch nicht, still not; Y.

  .8   'Gfalleś': '-ś' is dist. h c; cf. C p. 235 on 34.15
and A p. 126 last paragraph.

  .9   'oisrihten': ohne Unterbrechen reden.

  .10   'Ich' and "aach": emphatic.

  .12   'arr': irre, no longer Y, except in "arn", which,
however, means "irritieren" ("annoy, bother").
'ferzihl': erzähle; Y mostly "dertzeylen" (HG 'er-' =

76.2 'a Gelek, a Gekiš': Ein Lecken, ein Küssen

.5 Das (ausserordentliche) Fressen und Servieren

.10 'kihlen': (mein Gemüt) kühlen, avenge myself

.11 von so einem "Wurm" bei der Nase führen

.12 du kommst auch an einen Reichen

.13 sc. "sitzen".

.15 Nachher ist die (Gäste)liste vollständig

75.12 Y and SG dial. 'der-'), though "fertzeylen" too is found; normally, though, "fertzeylen" in both Y and G means "to miscount, make a mistake in counting"; here prob. inauth. and delib. dist. h c. L p. 364 # 137.

76.1 'Ešther': The Hebrew is deliberately misspelled ('š' f. 'ṡ') to indicate unambiguously the intended (mis)-pronunciation. 1. Generally HG changed only initial 'st-' to 'št'; 2. Y changed also medial (and final) 'rst' to 'ršt' (cf. Y eršt and HG erst); 3. most SG dialects also changed medial '-st-' (but not '-st' added as an inflection: 2nd pers. sg. and the super-lative -- thus "hast" but "fašt"); 4. some also changed the inflectional '-st'; 5. finally, one small SG dial. (cf. C p. 312 on 72.2) changed every Germanic 's' (but not the HG 's' that resulted from the shift of Germanic 't'). H in his WY dial. follows "3", and the word may be auth. for a locally limited area, though it is more probable that herein too he dishes up G dial. as Y -- to judge from his practices elsewhere. It is most improbable that '-st' in Hebrewisms ever changed in any Jewish dial. -- though this author does not know enough to make the claim categorically. Hence the 'š' in 'Ešther' is most prob. delib. dist. h c!

.2 'Gekiš': 'ṡ' Rz f. 'š'! Germanic medial '-ss-' became 'ṡ' in "2" and "3" in C above on 76.1.

.3 'Atišhoif': Artus Hof; romances of the King Arthur Cycle were very prominent in Medieval Y literature and also very popular.

76.1-3 With its erotic allusions is a H invention, while .4f. is from Esther 1, as elaborated by the Midrash (esp. the Targum Sheni), but there the reference is to the King's <u>first</u> wedding, with <u>Vashti</u>, not to the second, with Esther!

.6 They must sleep by day because they revel through the night.

.8 'h<u>oi</u>lt': delib. dist. to suggest G "heulen" ("howl, cry"); WY should be identical with HG here: "hōlen" < MHG "hŏln".
'Frischen': sc. "Wain", i.e., a new, <u>additional</u> bottle, or a <u>cooled</u> wine (or possibly even non-fermented grape-juice?). L p. 366 # 164.

.9 'Havru<u>s</u>oh': pronounce "Hevrúsə"; the word is usually used for a religious or "learning"-group (i.e., learning holy lore), but here used f. a drinking-party -- which adds a humorous flavor.
'noich': the emendation is absolutely certain: the 'n' and 'o', when fused because of the ink-run, look like a 't' (i.e., " נ " looks like " ט "); 'tich' yields no meaning and 'noich' fits perfectly.
'ander': "anderer" -- H syncopates the <u>final</u> 'e' in a "dactyl", where HG syncopates the middle 'e'; EY does <u>not</u> syncopate here. In NEY 'ander' is invariable after the indefinite article.

.10 'Schôteh': The Talmud calls Ahasuerus a "fool who killed his wife (Vashti) on the advice of his friend (Memuchan) and killed his friend (Haman) on the advice of his wife (Esther)".
'mich...kihlen': knowing H, we can't help but suspect an erotic insinuation here, as "mich kühlen" does not say the same or mean the same as "mein Mütchen kühlen" ("avenge myself, vent my rage"), which, however, H <u>pretends</u> to want to say.

.11 'Grill...uhzen': 'Grill' can mean a "grasshopper" (as well as "cricket"), which is green. The Talmud ascribes to Esther a <u>green</u> complexion (as well as grace -- rather than <u>beauty</u> -- Megilla 13a). Zetulpe, in her jealous anger, calls Esther a "green worm"; 'uhzen' usually means "to tease, fool" ("necken, foppen"), but

77.2   'saitir': Seid ihr

  .4   'gester': gestern

  .5   'wofft': wirft

  .11 'Kepple': Schlafmütze

76.11 H makes it mean "to make a fool of", in the sense of
       "wind him around her finger", "lead by the nose",
       "manage and control him", rather than just "make him
       the butt of her jokes". (Cf. on 'Schôteh', .10, above.)

  .11-12 'uhzen - Kozin': Rz; 'u - o' in WY and NEY and
          'i - u' elsewhere; actually "uzen" is not current in EY
          and to the degree it entered WY it was a loanword
          (though the word is derived from the biblical name "Uz")
          from G. As such a loanword it would retain the 'u' even
          in SEY, where it then could rhyme 'u - u'. H elsewhere
          uses SEY phonology h c, and whether he intends it here,
          or leaves it as Rz, either is humorous.

  .12   'Kozin': = "ruler, nobleman", when referring to a non-
        Jew, but "man of wealth and 'weight'", when referring
        to a Jew.
        'kehrst': gehörst (mal einem Vornehmen, Reichen), (will)
        come to a magnate (as his wife); "gherst" > "kerst":
        when 'g' and 'h' are pronounced simultaneously, the vo-
        cal cords open to form the 'h' -- and voicing becomes
        impossible since the cords must be stretched tight to
        vibrate -- the result is a fusion of 'g' + 'h' to 'k';
        'kehrst' is auth. Y, the use of the pres. f. the fut.
        is common in G, less so in WY and least in EY -- but
        possible even in EY.

  .13   You won't remain an old maid.

  .15   'Noichet': can really mean only G "nach"; "dernoich(et)"
        means G "nachher" ("afterward") -- which is needed here.
        'Katt': (Gäste)karte, guest list.

  .15-16 'ferfoll - soll': Rz, auth. Y = "full"; 'ferfoll'
          is prob. a H coinage from HG "vervoll(ständigt)" and
          SG dial. "vevolln", "lost, ruined, depraved".

77.14   'hetter'n': hättet ihr ihn, there he is!

.15   'Štehn': listed, entered in the book

.16   'gfinne': finden

.17   'derrett': gerettet

.21   'Schalah Monôš': Purim-gift

77.2   'saitir': the running-together of the words is to
indicate the pronunciation "saitər", so as to rhyme
with (.1) 'waiter'; the pronunciation is auth., but
the spelling becomes "funny".

.4   'gešter': Rz.

.5   'wofft': 'i' + 'r' + cons. yields 'a' + cons. in H,
but 'a' between labials (here: 'w' and 'f') > 'o'.

.8   'Lang': auth. Y "derlang".

.9-10   'hoštuš - nemmtš': hast du (e)s, nimmt (da)s;
running-together of the words h c.
'Brill': anachronism, h c.

.11   'Kepple': "little cap", but a little cap cannot be
pulled over one's ears! The "little" is prob. not
intended as such, but rather as a sleeping cap, and,
because of the personal, intimate association, the
diminutive is used to express endearment. The use
of sleeping caps was general in Germany, but it was
obligatory among pious Jews who considered even
sleeping bare-headed a sin. Thus the 'Kepple' may
be an attempt at another anachronism (making the King
act like a pious Jew in the Germany of 1800) h c.
The pulling of the cap over the ears signifies
readying, determination -- h c, as the King remains
in bed!

.12   'plepple': Rz f. auth. "plapple(n)" = "to say blah-
blah", onomatopoeia f. senseless babbling. The 'e'
f. 'a' in G dial. may have the force of intensifying.
Cf. L p. 395 # 442.

.14   'hetter'n': = hett ihr ihn, HG hättet. This subjunctive,

78.1   'ahn': ei.iem; 'Rachamonus̓': Erbarmen

.2   'ahn': einen; 'estemihren': berücksichtigen, have
       consideration for

.4   'tuhsen': dösen, slumber, doze off

.5   'schmuhṡen': chatter, converse

77.14 thus far supposedly considered unexplained, serves to
       express something <u>incredible but true</u> nonetheless. HG
       "Da wären wir" means "We are here, all right, but who
       would have believed it?!" Admittedly, H uses "hett"
       <u>also</u> as a pres. indicative and not only as an imperfect
       subjunctive (= unreal); however, since "hattet" here
       would be auth., idiomatic HG, it is probable that that
       is what H intended in <u>his</u> dial.

.15   'Štehn': Y and G idiom: "es <u>steht</u> im Buch" = "it is
       <u>written</u> in the book".

.16   A Talmudic proverb from Megilla 6b.

.21   'Schalaḥ Monôṡ': a technical term in Y f. the gifts
       themselves, and f. the religious <u>requirement</u> to send
       these gifts, on Purim, to friends and to the poor, as
       part of the Purim celebration to commemorate the mira-
       culous saving of the Jews from Haman's conspiring to
       destroy them. Here Esther uses the term <u>before</u> the
       event that caused its institution. This naive
       anachronism is delib. h c. The added h lies in offering
       'Trinkgeld' and '<u>Schalah Monôṡ</u>' as an adequate reward
       for saving the King's life.

78.1   Contamination of a Y and a G idiom: Y "<u>oif</u> einem R.
       hobn", G <u>mit</u> einem Mitleid haben", delib. h c.

.2   'eštemihren': slightly "off: in sound and meaning and
       therefore a malapropism and humorous. The "highfalutin"
       FW "estimieren" means "schätzen", but Harbona means to
       let Esther say "Rücksicht haben", "to be considerate
       with".

.4   'wellen': the double infinitive -- not Y.
       'tuhsen': "dösen, duseln" do mean "to doze off", but
       "dusen" <u>usually</u> means "tosen, toben, betäuben" (= "rage,

78.7   'Rôges...': vorgeheuchelter Zorn, pretended anger

 .8   'mach...': marinate him sweet or sour

 .12   'Loster'n': lass' dir ihn

 .15   'Stande bie': stehenden Fusses, immediately.
        'mer'n': man den

 .17   'Spohren straach': spornstreichs, at full gallop

 .19   'boi...Galing...Ihlen': baue...Galgen...Ehlen

78.4   daze"); it is unlikely, but not impossible, that H
       meant also to connote "duhssen", a Galician Y
       euphemism for "to do the unmentionable".

 .4-5 'tuhsen - schmuhsen': Rz 's - s'.

 .7   'kelômar-kihs': sic ('-kihs' is not printed "square",
       i.e., it is a non-Hebrew suffix). The footnote
       reference on this word, given in the Transliteration,
       to Part II is L p. 379 # 292 and Tendlau's explanation,
       cited there, having it mean G "Scheinkäse" ("imitation
       of cheese" put in shop-windows) is not only far-fetched
       but is methodologically untenable: There does not seem
       to exist such an expression in G -- the dictionaries
       list numerous compounds with "Schein-" but no "Schein-
       käse"; there definitely is no such expression in Y (if
       we disregard "Kelomarkehs"). The meaning intended here
       is crystal-clear: "pretended, acted out, but not
       really felt". As an explanation we would venture some-
       thing much simpler: "kelomar" is one of the most common
       "tools" of Rabbinic commentators on "difficult" Hebrew
       passages, and, when rephrasing the difficult texts "in
       other words", more intelligible, "kelomar" literally
       means "like saying, as if to say". Hence it is only
       one step to the meaning, "as if it were to say", "as if
       it were, but really is not." In EY the word has be-
       come so common that the awareness of its Hebrew con-
       nection was lost and it underwent numerous linguistic
       changes and extensions, to change it from a phrase to
       a regular adjective and adverb: "miklomperst"! The
       '-kihs' or '-kehs' must be some Low G dial. suffix
       meaning "Art und Weise", "in the manner of" -- and has
       nothing to do with G "Käse", "cheese". It is a WY

78.7   extension of "kelomar" similar to the EY "(mi)klomperšt".

.8   "For all I care, pickle him" is humorous by itself; H
      adds the distortion of Y "soier", G "sauer" to "soiber"
      (a G dial. form) which in Y and G means "clean", "decent"
      (and sarcastically, "indecent"). The MHG "sûr" > NHG
      "sauer", and, in dialects, > "sawer", "sober"; "sower"
      is also a Y dial. form. H then in rev. subst. has 'w'
      > 'b' -- a "regular" H feature! Cf. .13 'arwet' f.
      "arbet".

.11   'Gfalleš': '-eš' f. '-en' is dist. but not out of Rz,
      since it is used in 75.8 outside the R.

.14-15 'befoilen - hoilen': 'oi' in 'befoilen' is Rz to
      the 'oi' in 'hoilen', which is dist. to allude to G
      "heulen"! In WY both are 'o'!

.15   'štande bie': Latin "stante pede", cf. L p. 403 # 519.

.17   'špohren štraach': Cf. L p. 403 # 515.

.19   'Galing' and (.20) 'moring': the phoneme-cluster '-gen'
      is fused and assimilated into 'əŋ' in some G dialects
      (Bavarian, East Franconian, and East Central G -- H.
      Reis p. 58), but not in auth. Y.
      'Ihlen': Y, < *Elen < MHG êle; NHG < a MHG variant,
      "elle".

77.21-78.22 Harbona quotes Esther's conversation with the
      King while in bed! In the Bible the King is sleeping,
      or, rather, is sleepless, alone. The conversation is
      humorous, even ingeniously charming, but anachronistic,
      impossible for Harbona to know and report, and anti-
      biblical. H makes Esther complain about the King's
      inconsiderateness in waking her about such a trifle as
      Mordechai's reward, pretend not to care about Mordechai,
      and refer the King to Haman, whom she knows is "working
      in the court", presumably on the gallows. The plot is,
      on a human level, more intriguing thus, but in the
      Bible it is Harbona who informs the King about Haman's
      preparing a gallows for Mordechai in Haman's (not the
      King's) court, after Esther's revealing her Jewishness
      and pleading to the King for her people at the end of
      the second banquet, two days after this scene of the

79.1   'brumme': here = whisper!

.3   'Ahn dihn': Einen, den

.5   'ahn den': einem denn

.11   'mahnt': meint

.14   tut ihm auf den...

77.21-78.22   King's sleeplessness, and at the end, instead of at the beginning, of the resolution of the whole "plot".

78.22-79.1   Haman too thinks the King is a fool and says to himself, sarcastically: "that will again be something "clever"".

79.3,.5   'd_ihn, d_en': 'den' is most emphatic here, more so than most of the 'd_ihn' forms. It may be indicative of the _inauthenticity_ of all H's representations of HG 'e̅' by 'i̅'; that is, the 'dihn's are a conscious distortion, whereas the rare 'den' is an unconscious "slip" into the normal and auth.

.13   'schen_sten': the 'e' became shortened in Y in the comparative and superlative of this adj. because of the following consonant clusters, especially '-n(e)r'; a long 'e̅' H would have represented as 'i̅'.

.14-23   'n': stands f. G "ihm" or "ihn"; auth. Y, where an unaccented enclitic '-m' > '-n'.

.16   'in': f. 'im', auth. Y; 'Ott': Ort.

.17   'Hoicher': G Hoher, Hochstehender Adlige (King James Version, Esther 6:9 "one of the king's most noble princes"); the naive 'ganz Hoicher' would normally connote a "very tall" man and is delib. h c.

.19   'der selbst': = 'Hoicher'; here '-st' did _not_ become '-s̆t', because the 't' is only a _recent_ excrescent.

.20   'hie': pronounce "hi̅" (cf. R!), auth. Y; it means not simply _generally_ "here", but "here in this city (or _town_, or _village_)" (not "in this _spot_").

80.2   'Watle der fuhn': Wortlein davon

 .9   'Brumme': here = grumbling

 .10   lange ausblieb, zu spät nach Hause kam

 .11   'Migrune': Migräne

 .14   'di Zait': die (ganze) Zeit

 .15   'izet': jetzt

 .16   'Ba main Lihben': Bei meinem Leben

79.23 'puzt...rois': dist. f. "ois"; "roisputzen" is used
       sarcastically for "to expel, kick (drive, flush) out";
       here it means "to tidy up"; usually it would mean "to
       dress up", but here that would be superfluous as M. is
       to be dressed in the King's raiment. It refers to the
       elaboration on the Esther story in Talmud and Targum
       Sheni that Haman had to bathe and barber M. first, as
       M. had been fasting in sack-cloth and ashes for three
       days.

80.2   'oif der Erd': the phrase is Rz; the Hebrew original
       (Esther 6:11) only speaks of "fallen lassen" ("tappel").
       "omit", but no mention of "Erd"; 'der': auth. Y, dat.
       with the prep. (HG requires the acc. here).

 .3   'Kôl': "great (or: big) voice (or: sound)" is a very
       frequent stock phrase in the Hebrew Bible and liturgy
       meaning "a loud voice (or: sound)" ("Kôl gadôl") -- we
       have the usual dist. spelling 'groisen' ('s' f. 'š') to
       suggest "gruesome", but this phrase too is only a rhyme-
       filler -- the "loud, gruesome voice" is really irrele-
       vant -- it's the:

 .4   'Bukkel foll': that matters! to count out a back-full
       of lashes, i.e., as many as the back can take. It is
       a common G threat to children. For the King to so
       threaten his Prime Minister is -- funny. The whole is
       a H invention: The Bible has no threat.

 .3-4 'Kôl' is a perfect R to 'foll' (in spite of the
       spelling with 'ô'), but 'foll' itself is Rz -- Y is
       "full".

81.3 'honnen': habe ihn

.4 'Ihr': ethical dat., i.e., functioning to indicate an <u>interest</u> by the person referred to ('Ihr') in the action.

.5 In halber Welt gibt nicht ein solchen

.6 'Tikenisch': Korpulenz; 'Pummer': whopper.

.7 <u>Nahas</u>': here = Vergnügen, delight

.11 Sein Vater ist gegen ihn ein Kind (?)

.12 'Schwehrer': Schwören, oath

.13 'Un-<u>taᶜam</u>': here = "ugly mug"

80.5 'woil': WY requires "wohl", like HG; '-oi-' <u>is</u> EY, h c.

.6 'bai Zaiten': Y; there is even a Y Hebrew contamination "betzaitns" f. HG "Zeitig", "on time". Y "Zaitik" = "mature".

.7-15 Another H invention -- to exploit the humor-potential of the situation.

.9f H's persiflage of nagging wives. H was a bachelor!

.11 Reka, herself a "nag", takes the part of Seres: "It was not so bad, she could not have given him a migraine headache". 'Migrune': Rz.

.12 '<u>Schechunoh</u>': not frequent in EY, prob. due to its having fallen together phonetically with "Schechinoh" ("the Divine Presence") for the majority of EY speakers.

81.10 Delib. ambiguous with vulgar insinuation.

.11 ''n': <u>might</u> be an ethical dative, part of the colloquial genitive (= "de<u>m</u> sain Taate"), or a printing error; the construction is very harsh; the meaning <u>may</u> be: "Mordechai's father (though also "big") is a child

82.5   'Pritschebakkel': Hofnarr, court fool

.6   'Di Lait': den Leuten
    'Pritscher': board used by court jester

.7   'Klitscher': Glitscher, slipping

.8   'in ahner lengs': lengthwise, "as tall as he was"

.10   Gehaut auf ihn hinauf

81.11   compared to Mordechai".

.12-13   'Schwehrer', "Gschwehr": awkward substitutes for "Schwur" ("oath"), primitive and ungrammatical, h c. Perhaps there is some additional h intended that escapes us. 'Gschwer' in MHG also meant "pain, carbuncle" (NHG "Geschwür", Y "gešvir" -- which is how H would usually spell HG "Geschwär"!). That these words were deliberately chosen for some purpose is certain; Y normally does not use even the Germanism "Schwur" or "Schwären" f. the noun, but, rather, the Hebrewism "Švuə"! Cf.Lp. 406 # 544.

82-83   The "thing"-vocabulary in 82-83 is a thick concentration of localisms, "heavy" dialect, neither Y nor HG -- in a sense "typing" H's language, albeit in its extreme form.

82.5f   Cf. L p. 395 # 451-2.

.7   'Klitscher': "glitschen" is Y and G; 'K-' f. 'G-' is rev. subst.; '-er' denotes the agent in Y and HG -- in H and G dial. also the action. The periphrastic conjugation (to "do an act" instead of to "act") is most common in G dial., less so in Y, and least in HG. H herein is again on the level of G dial. In Y the periphrastic is used to express the perfective aspect -- "er tut a glitš" = "he suddenly slides (or: slips)", as opposed to "er glitšt", "he slides".

.8   'Putsch': onomatopoetic, "oops"; 'Drek': is very drastic and vulgar in EY, = "feces", not just "dirt" as in G.

.9   'Schleg': EY "Schlek", which would be a perfect rhyme

82.11   'dichtig': tüchtig

.12   'derlacht': aufgelacht, burst out laughing

.13   'Wi'n': Wie dem

.14   '<u>Mirmoh</u>': here = Blendwerk, tricks (of the juggler)

.16   'a Nunterbett, a Dekbettzihch': ein Unterbett...Bett-
deckziech

.17   'Schihch': Schuhe

.18   'runter...a nalte Brik': runder...eine alte Ziegel
(tile)

.19   'Mihlkiwele': Mehlkübel, flour-vat; '-kraiśle':
Krüglein

82.9   to 'Drek'. It is probable that the R was perfect also
in H's dialect but that H distorts, h c. The 'k' in Y
"Ślek" is due to emphatic pronunciation when threaten-
ing to give "Ślek" -- which causes wide opening of the
pharynx and thus prevents the vibration of the vocal
cords.

.12   'derlacht': this <u>may</u> have been an older form in Y f.
G "<u>auflachen</u>", though it is not very probable. Modern
EY requires "<u>zerlachen sich</u>", a calque of the Slavic,
that entered (through Y) even into modern Hebrew (cf.
"hitstaheq").

.15   ''s <u>Jam</u>': the neuter is an influence from HG "<u>das</u>
Meer"; EY requires "<u>der</u> Jam".

.16   'Kopf<u>e</u>-": the 'e' is prob. a dist. h c.
'Nunterbett': lower bed, cf. L p. 391 # 402.

.17   'Schihch': Y.

.19   '-kiwele': HG "Kübel", not Y.
'-kraiśle': HG "Kräuselein" = "Krüglein", not Y; L
p. 358 # 83.

83.2   'Schiwele Hai': Schober Heu, sheaf of hay

  .3   'Bihsen': Besen

  .4   'a Noifegahbel...Suttel Schaf': eine Ofengabel...
        Sudelschaff, "muck-pail"

  .8   'Gensbarig': Gänseberg, (foolish errand?)

  .9   'arig': arg, böse

 .10   'Allewail': jetzt

 .11   'moregrifische Gaṡ': Mariengrabentorsgasse in
        Nürnberg

83.2   'Schiwele': HG Schübel, not Y. L p. 399 # 488.

  .6   'Ninter': the 'i' is not the regular SEY shift of 'u',
        but WY, and the result of a contamination of "hinter"
        and "unter".

  .7   'Meschuvôs': a H coinage (?), an extension of the Y
        Hebrewism "môšov" (pronounce EY: "moyšəv"), originally
        = "settlement", then "(community) settlement (house, for
        the transient poor)", finally, the "slum and dirt and
        disorder" in such a settlement-house, and now simply
        "disarray, garbage, dirt". The extension is prob. the
        pl. suffix 'ôṡ', as if from a sg. "Meschuvoh" (which =
        "backsliding, mischief"!), or the abstraction-suffix
        '-uṡ' -- that is not recorded. "Moyšəv" -- "dirt" --
        is a collective noun and as such needs no pl. In the
        Hebrew sense of "seat and settlement" the auth. pl. is
        "Môšovim", which could be pronounced "məšɔvəm" in WY
        and NEY and "məšuvəm" elsewhere, but even the '-u-'
        would not be spelled with the vov. Besides, Jukl's
        speech is not CY (where 'ɔ' > 'u'). The plausible ex-
        planation remaining is that it is again a delib. dist.
        h c, to show up Jukl's ignorance: a Y Hebrewism is
        apt to "trip" the "Am Ho-orets" ("ignoramus"), cf. C
        p.106. Jukl is presented as a "servant" and on him it
        is supposed to "look good".

  .8   'Gensbarig': Cf. L p. 369 # 191.

 .11   Anachronistically the Nürnberg street of 1820 is trans-

83.12   sieht im Hause Hamans

.14   'Sich...raiten': Sieh...geritten

.15   'sich's dorch'n Spiktihf': seh's durch's Fernrohr

.19   Auf ihn hinunter meinen Nachttopf

83.11   planted to Shushan 400 B.C.E. Cf. L p. 388˙ # 378.

.12   From here to 85.5 the scene is based on a post-biblical elaboration (cf. Ginzberg on the tale: IV. p. 440,
and, for the sources and variants: VI. p. 417, note
173). H makes the burlesque even more vulgar and
drastic by having Seres order her daughter to defecate
into a "pot-for-dessert" (a euphemism f. a chamber-pot)
and "hurry before it's too late".
Typical "dialect" syntax, neither Y nor HG.

.13   'zu'n': Y "ois dem, ois'n"

.14   'Papa': Harbona and Jukl, both, in quoting Gentiles,
sort of quote them "in translation", i.e., in their
own Y, but not without attempting to use "Goyish" (i.e.,
G) now and then -- as they can. Actually WY (being the
result of a fusion of G dialects) is much closer to
HG (also the result of fusion) than many G dialects.
So much so that speakers of EY have mistaken WY to be
G to this very day. Nevertheless, not only Harbona
and Jukl, but even the climber Zetulpe, who is anxious
to speak prestigious HG, are unable to speak "Goyish
like a Goy" in any sustained manner. Actually, that
was true of the generation that preceded H; H's own
generation would have had difficulty speaking sustained Y! Perhaps some of the substitution of G
dial. f. auth. WY is due to H's own limited knowledge!
'Papa' is such an attempt at Goyish. The Y "Tate" had
a positive emotional charge, which "Papa" did not have.
'zu raiten': Y, f. HG "geritten".

.15   'Spiktihf': in EY "Spaktif" < New Latin "(Per)-
spectiv-". L p. 403 # 513.

.18   'Gelarrem': "Lärm", Y "Larem", "hubbub, confusion" --
this 'Ge-' formation does not happen to be current in
Y, though such forms can be freely coined, esp. f. an

84.6 'for'n': vor dem

.7 Gibt...einen Stoss ("poke")

.9 'Kaierai': mess

.10 'Brih': Brüh'

.11 'Zetel': Los, lottery ticket

.18 'Mumfel': Mundvoll

83.18 unpleasant, disturbing activity that is considered "too much" by those annoyed it. L p. 369 # 184.

.19 'Nacht-': H's distortion of the quantity of vowels is the "line of least resistance" for him, when he wants distortion, either to deviate from HG and pretend that that is Y, or h c; such distortions are even too numerous to note; often a pure R is thus "indicated" for destruction, or an actual impure R forced (Rz). Here the emphasis on the scene is to be heightened by the lengthened vowel.
'-scharrem': a confluence and contamination of three words: G "Scherben(topf" = "Nachttopf"; WY "Scharbem, Scharbm"; French "chambre", metonomy for "pot de chambre", and "to be funny", French "charm". The resulting "portmanteau-word" expresses with "charmless" humor: the contents of the chamber-pot as "night-charm".

.20 'Bo-Hori-Of': Moses, "in raging anger", leaves Pharàoh. The phrase became proverbial.
'Kuch': Y "kich, kech" presupposes an earlier "Küch(e)"; Umlaut fails to occur before 'ch' in SG dialects but not in Y! Dist. h c.

84.1 'Zimmes': frequent Y word f. popular Jewish dish: no holiday without "tzimmes" -- the "dessert" that was the crown of the holiday dinner and was sort of specific for each holiday. The word is from OHG (not documented) *zu-muosi = "Zuspeis, Zukost, Nachtisch, dessert".
'Haafen': = Topf. Seres, in tradition, is not a "good housewife" (cf. Reka calling her 'nikšnuzze') and common gossip about slovenly housewives has it that they

84.1   use their regular pots also for such purposes.

.4   'breng': Y.
'<u>Meschuvôs</u>': the 'u' is actually 'i' here, but it is certain that 'u' was intended by H (cf. 83.7) and only an imperfect type-stick with the stem slightly broken makes the 'u' (<u>vov</u>) look like 'i' (<u>yod</u>). It is important to remember this when judging 'i's elsewhere, where 'u' is expected.
'rain': here = "herein", but "rain" also means "clean", and there is h in the juxtaposition of "filth - clean"; it is prob. delib.

.6   'for'n': Y; ''n' = dat. with the prep. where HG requires the acc.

.7   'Pumpf': "Stoss", "poke". L p. 396 # 457.
'Iz schral ois': Tradition tells that Haman lowered the cuff-like brim on his hat to hide his face, so that he would not be recognized. H has Mordechai make him shout out the Proclamation just in front of his (Haman's own) house. 'Iz': jetzt.

.9-10   'Kaierai': "was gekaut wird", vulgar h f. "feces"; similarly, 'Brih' = "soup, brew" -- f. "urine".

.11   'getroffen': = "hit the target, the jackpot"; this can't be imitated as well in Eng.: "That's what I call hitting the jackpot without a lottery-ticket".

.13   "No, wine they'll pour over him" -- sarcastic: "What else but a filth-bath would a scoundrel like Haman deserve?"

.15   '<u>Herpoh</u>': pronounce "Xarpə".

.14-15   Rz 'ɔ - u'; only by mixing Y dialects, i.e., by pronouncing the WY 'ɔ' as 'u' (CY) would the R be pure. Either the hybrid dial. or the Rz would be equally humorous.

.15-16   Alludes to Noah's disgrace as told in Gen. 9:20-26 and elaborated in legends (cf. Ginzberg I. p. 168f. and V. p. 191f.). Noah planted a vineyard, made wine, got drunk, was found naked and abused in his nakedness by

85.1   du Dummkopf...Narr

.6   'gekeht': gekehrt

.7   'derschokkelt': erschaukelt

.8   'saiter': Seid Ihr

.9   Marsch fort! Wir wollen

.11   Haben ihn sechs Würdenträger

84.15-16   his son Ham. Shem and Japhet dutifully and piously
covered the "shame of their father".

.16   'ghatten': neither Y (= "gehat") nor HG, nor consistently H, cf. on "haben", A p. 121 # 56.

.17   'maschhis'n': sic (with small 'm' = verb); EY uses the
noun only, in the original Hebrew sense of "destroyer,
devil, spoiler"; the verb may be H's coinage, and the
context suggests the meaning "wüten" ("rage"), "fluchen"
("curse") and perhaps "drohen" ("threaten").

.18   'Mumfel': sent up a "mouthful" (of reproaches to his
people). L p. 388 # 381.

85.1   'elendsgloie': elendglaue, dumme, L p. 362 # 109.
'Zumpfel': fool; vulgarism sematically similar to Eng.
"stiff, prick". L p. 418 # 649.

.4-5   In order not to spoil the spirit of "fun and comedy"
H deliberately deviates from the legend, i.e., the
daughter only faints, instead of commiting suicide by
jumping out of window. Tradition takes the Heb. word
"avêl" (King James Version: "mourning") in its technical sense: mourning a death in the family (Esther
6:12 and Ginzberg IV. p. 440).
'Hôlesches': misspelled f. "Haloschus". It is prob.
nôt a printing error, but a delib. malapropism -- the
meaning of the former is "dominating, ruling" (pres.
part. fem. sg.).

.6-7   N.B. the omission or retention of 'r' is "inconsistent", or perhaps delib. dist. h c; here the R is pure,
but the spelling insinuates it is not.

85.16   'gschatzte Arwelich': geschürzte Ärmelchen

.17   'karwelich': Körblein

.18-19   'Bendlich - Hendlich': Bändlein - Händlein

.20   'Štehlahsche fun Brihder': Stellage von Brettern

.23   'Poigen...Flihten': Pauken...Flöten

85.7   'derschokkelt': "ins Schaukeln geraten", "got shaken
up (with laughter)"; 'der-': = (SG and) Y prefix f.
HG 'er-'; but here EY would use 'zer-' = HG "auf-
geschaukelt"; akin to MHG "schocken", Y "schokkeln" is
a diminutive-frequentative thereto.

.8   'saiter': prob. Rz f. "ist er", the non-honorific
formal form of address (instead of the familiar form:
"bist du"). Elsewhere Mordechai does not use the
honorific ("seid Ihr") to Haman. Conceivably the '-er'
is not the weakened "Ihr", but the 3rd pers. sg. "Er"
(used f. the non-honorific formal form of address f.
the 2nd pers. sg.) and the "hybrid" "seid Er" used
delib. h c.

.16   "gescha(r)zte": Y, L p. 399 # 486.
'Arwelich': Y "arbl", invariable in the pl., but the
'-1' ending is originally a diminutive suffix and thus
the pl. suffix '-ich' is applied "correctly" by H,
though prob. inauthentically, as the awareness of its
being a diminutive (NHG "Ärmel", OHG "armilo" = "little
arm") has been lost especially in Y, because the sub-
sequent dissimilation of G "Ärmel" to Y "arbl" severed
the connection with "Arm". H's 'rb' ≳ 'rw' is delib.
rev. subst. h c. L p. 352 # 30.

.17   'Blumme-': cf. "Blumeš".

.20   'Štehlahsche': the spelling (and presumably the (mis)-
pronunciation), 'Šteh-', h c, to suggest a supposedly
"false" etymology, turns out to be not so false! Ultimately akin to G "stellen", which is akin to "stehen"!
'Brihder': Y "Brêter", with 'ê'; HG 'ǝ' is due to the
shortening effect of '-er'.

.23   'Flihten': L p. 365 # 149.

86.2   'Postiljuhne...Harrner': Postillione...Hörner

.3   'Tarrner': Türmen

.5   'Tampurš': Trommelschläger, drummers

.6   The guard presented arms.

.8   'g'apletihrt': applaudiert

.14 'Hanswost': "Hans Wurst", jester

.15 'Štiklich': Possen, funny acts

86.3   N.B. Half a line counts as a whole (cf. R).

.4   'Tarrner': MHG "turn, torn"; the R is pure since with
H all vowels + 'r' cons. go to 'a(r)'. EY has '-m',
like HG, but the forms are NEY "turm, turems", CY
"torm - term". Cf. L p. 408 # 569.

.5   'Tampurš': Schweizerisch, not Y. L p. 408 # 567.

.6   'g'ekšezshrt': the 's' is a printer's error f. 'i' --
cf. the R-word 'g'apletihrt'. It is a malapropism f.
the technical term "(das Gewehr) präsentieren!"; 'ge-'
in some Y dialects is used in past participles even
with verbs not accented on the first syllables. In
"Standard Y" "geštudirt" but "telefonirt"!

.8   'g'apletihrt': dist. h c.

.11-12 'raiten - schnaiden': Rz: 't - d'.

.13-15 Part of Esther's supposed "traditional wedding
merriment" -- supposed to last seven days (Y Hebrewisms: "Shivas Yəmey Hasmishteh"), with (at least one)
new guest(s) every day, for pronouncing the "seven (wed-
ding-)blessings" at grace after the meal ("bentshen")
and extra entertainment in honor of the new guest.
Hans Wurst is the (vulgar) vaudeville-like theater-
clown of the primitive G stage -- hardly a fit desig-
nation f. the (chaste) Y wedding-rhymester and jester,
who, in addition to making the wedding guests merry,
had to make the marrying couple "penitently weep for
forgiveness for their sins and pray for future happi-

87.4   'Allewaile': jetzt

  .5   'mitsi Kofih': mit ihnen Kaffee

  .8   'Štoffel': fool; "just run me over, you fools".

  .9   'Toffel': (Pan)toffel

  .10   'Wu finne': Wo finde

  .11   'geben': gegeben

86.13-15 ness"!

  .14   'hunten': h f. "unten"; in some dialects (Y and G,
         as well as generally) the 'h' and the "glottal stop"
         are interchanged (cf. "Cockney Eng."); here we are
         also dealing with contamination of "unten" and "hinten",
         as well as with the syncopation of "hi unten".

86.19-87.1   'schihšen – Rihsen': Rz, 'š – s'.

87.1   'Haitukken': 't' f. 'd', "liveried servants". L
         p. 373 # 235.

  .3   'Hozer': here = Königlichen Hof.

  .5   'mitsi': delib. dist. h c, though in EY it is auth. --
         "mit sey", "sey" being invariable.

  .9   'Soton': this Y Hebrewism is almost taboo and a sub-
         stitute like "Ruah" or the Germanism "Taifel" (or some
         variant thereof) would be expected and "more natural".
         The "incongruity" is h c.

  .10   'finne': '-nn-' in this word is "universal" in all Y
         f. HG '-nd-', but EY has "gefinnen" for HG "finden".
         'Schuhch': '-ch' is Y, and G dial.

  .11   'geben': in older Y and G "perfective" verbs did not
         add the 'ge-' prefix to the perfect participle. They
         were "perfect" without it, by their very meaning.

88 - 92 Practically all the Text from p. 88 to the end is
         H's invention, and where it is based on Tradition,
         Tradition is reversed!

88.1　'Nainfall...gihl': Einfall...gelb

　.6　melden im Vorzimmer

　.7　'Risuhn': "raison", Schicklichkeit, propriety

　.8　'waiset': wiese

88.1　She likes the idea of making the ribbons of the bonnet
　　　yellow -- supposedly a "natural" occupation of Esther's
　　　"social secretary" while "waiting for clients". The
　　　"scene" is to motivate her being scared by Hathach's
　　　sudden entry, or, rather, her abusive reaction to it.

　.3　<u>Pêrôsch</u>: (the 'ô' should be 'û'), pronounce "Pérəš",
　　　in perfect R with (Y) "Axašvérəš". The R-need may be
　　　the <u>pretended</u> reason for the (improper) use of the Y
　　　Hebrewism, a kind of malapropism, and is meant to be
　　　humorous. "Pêruš" does mean "explanation", but in Y
　　　it is used only in the sense of "exegesis and inter-
　　　pretation of a (usually holy and/or difficult) text,
　　　a commentary" -- but <u>not</u> an "explanation of the grounds
　　　of an action or a (mis)conduct". Afrozene, like
　　　Zetulpe, a vulgar "climber" uses her new position as
　　　Esther's chamberlady to "put people down" and to show
　　　off her Hebrew and French -- only to prove her ig-
　　　norance and vulgarity.

　.6　'melken in <u>P</u>otschamper': (f. 'P' Text has 'F'): the
　　　context suggests "melden im Vorzimmer", "to report
　　　(for announcing) in the ante-room". The distortions
　　　here are exaggerated and burlesqued to the point of
　　　unintelligibility, and we are uncertain as to the in-
　　　terpretation, even after long research. 'melken' means
　　　"to milk" and '-schamper' can well be the Fr. word
　　　"chambre" in the usual H dist. with rev. subst. of 'b'
　　　and 'p'.
　　　'Fo<u>t</u>-', with 't', could hardly suggest "Vor-", in the
　　　sense of 'ante-'(room); with a double 'šš' (the 'š' and
　　　't' of Meschit are very similar, yet definitely clearly
　　　distinguishable) there would be a "funny" hybrid word
　　　of G and Fr. It may well be that beside the pretended
　　　innocent meaning, there is an insinuation of some
　　　vulgar humor: In 'Fo<u>t</u>-' the very "disconcerting" 't'
　　　may have been added to suggest Fr. "<u>P</u>ot (de) chambre".

89.6   I'll make it hot for that (family).

 .8   My (husband) I have completely in my hands.

 .14   'Farib': Farbe

88.6   'melken' (f. "melden") is slang for "onanism"; '-scham-
       per' is reminiscent of "Schlamper" (= "slob").

 .7   'Risuhn': "Raison" can mean "propriety" but not in
       isolation, but only with the use of specific verbs
       (e.g., "avoir, entendre, se payer de") -- therefore,
       it is misused and the "funny" malapropism of a climber.

 .8   It would be wrong for an average author to "drag in"
       erotic insinuations in such an innocent line, but not
       for H: in both Hebrew and Latin (H knew both) the
       phrase "zu mir raingên" is a euphemism for "cohabit
       with me".
       'waiset': < *"waisete", a "weak" imperfect subjunctive
       (of a strong verb!), functioning as a present unreal --
       on the model of such new coinages in SG dialects. They
       are inauth. in Y. WY (unlike EY) did preserve the
       imperfect and the subjunctive (EY formed a new condi-
       tional) but didn't abandon the strong in favor of the
       weak forms.

 .10   An insinuation.

 .11-12   'det - Tet': = tut. N.B. H's inconsistency in
       rev. subst.

 .13   In the Bible it is Esther, who is shocked by the news
       of Mordechai's wailing in sack-cloth in front of the
       gate of the Court, and she sends Hathach to him and
       is informed by Mordechai through Hathach of Haman's
       conspiracy and of Mordechai's insistence that she
       plead with the King for the lives of her people.

88.13-89.1   'Jiden - bihten': Rz f. "Jiden - beten"; in H's
       dial. the impurity of the R is "negligible", since the
       vowels have fallen together, and the voiced and voice-
       less alveolar stops ('d' and 't') seem to have fallen
       together too.

89.2-3   The R is pure in WY (and Ukrainian Y); pronounce:

89.2-3 "axašvérəš : zerəš".

.3 'for': EY would require "fun".

.4-5 'Menuhoh – Mischpohoh': Rz 'u – ɔ', pronounce: "mənúxə˙– mišpɔxə", "pure" on the basis of a hybrid dial.: CY "mišpuxə".

.6 'Huzzel ahnrichten': = "Dörrobst herstellen, den Ofen dafür heizen", fig. = "es einem heissmachen", "to make it hot for someone". L p. 376 # 272.

.7 'Der': refers to 'Mischopohoh', dat. fem. sg. 'nikšnuzzen' and 'boiswichten': '-n' = weak declension of the adjectives. In EY there is basically only one (the strong) declension of adjectives, i.e., the endings on the definite article and its following descriptive adjective are identical: G der gute Mann, EY der guter Mann; G der guten Frau (dat. sg.), Y der guter froi; Y and G dem guten Mann -- this may look as if Y too had a weak declension, but the looks are deceiving -- in Y the unaccented '-em' always goes to '-en'. The only real remnant of the weak declension in EY is: dos gute kind.
'boiswichten': Conceivably the two are not nouns (mis)-used as if they were adjectives, but used, rather, as weak nouns. 'bois-' f. G 'bös-' is somewhat difficult in Y, where we should expect 'bês-' and, in H's dial., 'bihs-'; 'bois-' may be a dist. h c, or auth., derived from a variant MHG "bôse".

.8 'main'(en): sc. "Mann" or "Gemahl".
'be-Jodai': the unvocalized Y Hebrewism can be read thus (= pl. "in my hands") or '-jodi' (= sg. "in my hand"); the meaning is identical: "I control my hus-band". The Rz is harsh in any Y dial., including "mixing" dialects (i.e., "be-Júdi -- Súdə"). The Rz is less harsh and the idiom more auth. if we vocalize 'Jodi' ("in der Hand"; Heb. "meiner").
The line has an "auth. ring": the flavor of the Y "se-cret language", i.e., mixing in a "heavy concentration" of Hebrewisms into their vernacular, usually made up of Germanisms, so as to prevent the G from understanding it.

90.3   'warren oisgerott': werden ausgerottet

.11   'Retut un Bahl': Redoute und Ball

.13   'Fešer': Friseur

.16   'Ihltikkle': Öl-lämpchen

89.15   'sain': Y; HG seinem.

.16-17 'loine - Harbona': since H does use impure rhymes,
        we cannot decide whether the Hebr. cholam ('ô') was
        pronounced 'o' or 'oi' (as in EY) by H.

.17A   SD 'kommt geloifen': As ever so often in SD's, the
        fact that they are HG and that our Transliteration may
        be misleading is herewith pointed up for the last time:
        WY requires "kumt zu loifn", hence we must read here
        HG "kommt gelaufen".

90.2   'Tag': pl.; with the Y loss of final 'e', the sg. and
        pl. became identical in all the original "a-stems".
        Therefore, EY had to re-organize its pl. system and
        used umlaut and '-n' far beyond the extent of NHG
        (cf. "Teg" and "tišn").

.5   Mordechai had been fasting in sack-cloth and ashes and
        "went out into the midst of the city and cried a loud
        and bitter cry" (Esther 4:1). 'zu graine oifheren' is
        a Maskil's expression of contempt for the prayers of
        the pious as "whining".

.7   'kol Tuv': 'u', though 'ô' is possible; 'ô' is the
        reading in Gen. 24:10.

.7-8   R is pure as a final 'v' is unvoiced in Y and G
        (= 'f').

.9-10   Rz. "Täte : Maskarād(e)".

.12   'suhperib': superb. 'Wahl': at a "regular" ball a
        lady has to wait to be asked; at a masquerade
        (Redoute) the lady, too, is allowed to choose.

.12A   SD 'fam': sic! but the 'a' is much thicker than
        usual and is therefore surely an 'o'-symbol (komets

91.1   'Lang...rois': reiche...her

.3   'Noifsehi...Getuh': Aufsehen...Getue (or: Getummel)

.4   'Lihden': Läden, shutters

.5   Said by Reka (missing in SD!)

90.12A   alef) that was broken. Hence = 'fom'.

.13   'Freṡer': dist. to suggest "Fresser" ("glutton").

.14   'Standenbie': stehenden Fusses, pronto!

.16   'Ihltikkle': Öltieglein, L p. 362 # 110. But prob. it
       is not a lamp but a jar of oil; cf. end of next item.

91.1   Curious and unusual nomenclature for the "Chanukkah-
        Menorah" and the Havdalah-candle-twist; the simplest
        guess is: '-aisen' and '-holz' were supposedly the
        usual materials of which the Menorah and the Havdalah-
        candle-stick were made. There may be point in using
        different materials for the two: the Menorah used to
        burn wicks dipped directly in cups of oil, hence it
        had to be fire-proof; the Havdalah-candles, or candle-
        twist, are made of tallow and the candles (not the
        twist, though) could be stuck into a wooden candle-
        stick that has a fire-proof, thimble-like, safety-plate
        in its socket. But what is the point of mentioning
        here such use? Besides, Havdalah candles are not
        stuck in candle-sticks at all! They are held up high,
        usually by a little boy (so he'll grow tall) or by a
        little girl (so she'll get a tall groom) and immediately
        after the ritual extinguished in the liquid over which
        the Havdalah "blessings" are made. Therefore, in the
        '-holz' there lurks an older custom of using pine-
        splints (G Kienspan) for a torch to light them, instead
        of tallow or wax candles, or a "torch" made of a candle-
        twist. The Talmud (Pesahim 103b) recommends the
        torch as the most preferred (mitsvah min hamuvhar)
        Havdalah-light. Two candles "stuck-together", to
        imitate a torch, are only a poor substitute for the
        preferred torch. The candle-twist is a torch. A
        cheaper torch were long pine-chips -- long enough to
        last the few minutes it took to perform the Havdalah
        rite.

91.1   As the time of the year is obviously the 13th day of
Adar (the eve of the first Purim) and some 80 days
<u>after</u> the occurrence of Chanukkah, and it is <u>not</u> Sat.
night (needing to usher it out with Havdalah) there
is no <u>proper</u> call for the Menorah or the Havdalah as
such.
Incidentally, anachronisms are a staple element of
H's humor and are used whenever they can be "<u>dragged
in</u>". Chanukkah was instituted about 250 years (ca.
160 B.C.E.) after Purim (ca. 400 B.C.E.).
The curious call for the 'Ihltikkle', '<u>Hannukoh</u>-aisen',
and '<u>Havdoloh</u>-holz' for the illumination of the house
reflects the outburst of the carnival spirit at the
relief felt upon the good tidings of the last-minute
saving from destruction (the Purim-miracle), as if one
said: "Let's celebrate by throwing all into a heap
and make a big bonfire".
The 'Ihltikkle' is prob. the <u>jar with the oil</u> for the
'<u>Hannukoh</u>-aisen'.
'Lang...rois': EY "derlang".

.3-4   Jews used to be required by <u>law</u> (and by their own
prudence) to "keep a low profile". (It is still required of the newly established synagogue in Madrid!)
To be <u>conspicuous</u> was to court the danger of a riot
or massacre. Reka attributes conditions of Jews in
Europe in 1820 to Jews in Shushan in 400 B.C.E.!
Harbona reassures her that he is aware of the danger,
but he has a clever "out": "they'll have all the
illumination they can, but they'll hide it by closing
the window-shutters. The joke is, of course, that
the illumination was meant to <u>advertize</u> God's gracious
<u>miracle</u> and thus glorify God (in the words of the
Talmud: "lefirsumey nissa'" -- to publicize the
miracle).

.5   'Keterli': Käter<u>lein</u>, a <u>sweet</u> tomcat (the diminutive
used as an endearment) -- an allusion to "verliebt wie
ein Kater", hence "dressed up like a dandy in pursuit
of love on carnival night".
'Faṡenahcht': HG Fassnacht, the night before the
beginning of Lent -- a carnival-time in Catholic
countries (here: S Germany). 'Faṡen-' (with 'ṡ'
instrad of 's') is a dist. in that it is neither HG
nor dialect (which has "Fa<u>s</u>en-"). L p. 372 # 299,
p. 363 # 118.

91.5   'Keterli': Käterlein

 .6   'derwahcht': erweicht

 .15 'Allewail watš': Soeben wurde es

 .16 'watt': wird (or: werde)

 .17 'Sihn': Söhne

91.6   'Ahasveros sain Haz': syntax is G dial., <u>not</u> Y (= "Axašꞏ
verošanš harz").
'der<u>wah</u>cht': Y, = erweicht, but many of H's readers
(less knowledgeable of WY) would associate the word with
"derwǎcht" ("awakened"), which is intransitive and therefore "incorrect" here.

 .8   'schoin': WO (with the adv. of time at the end, instead
of after the finite verb) is due to Rz.

 .9-10   Cf. C p. 333 on 88.13.

 .11 Cf. .6.

 .12 'er': should be spelled in <u>capitals</u>. The Text prints
it in "<u>Square</u>" -- an imitation of non-Jewish practice
(in G bibles) of spelling words referring to God in
capitals.

 .13 Pronounce "mǎzl".

 .14 'Ihn': acc. f. dat. not Y, but G dial.

 .15 'Allewail': soeben, just now; not Y.

92.4   'pukt': Y bikt; '<u>pu</u>-' f. HG "bü-" is SG dial.; in EY
"puken" = "burst (with anger, grief, or jealousy)".
If H knew this Y <u>Slavism</u>, then this would be the motivation for his dist.

 .8   'belihb<u>e</u>': the loss of '-n' is not Y; the word <u>may</u>
mean "<u>de</u>licious" (cf. L p. 353 # 33), but it is also
possible that it is a H dist. f. "(be)Lebkuchen",
"gingerbread". Even more intriguing is the possibility
that it may be a H coinage f. WY "minnich", EY "parev(e)".
Jewish dietary laws require the separation of "meaty"

92.4   'pukt...for'n': bückt...vor ihm

 .5   'Schêni la-Melech': Vize-könig

 .8   'belihbe': delicious (or: "pareve"!)

 .9   'Zukkerhazli for'n': Zuckerherzlein für ihn

92.8   and "milky" -- dishes and foods containing milk (or
       its derivatives), or cooked in dishes in which such
       "milky" food had been cooked at any time previously,
       must not be used, cooked, or eaten together with foods
       or dishes containing meat, or its derivative, or with
       foodswhich were cooked in dishes in which such "meaty"
       food had been cooked at any time previously, or cooked
       in or served on such "meaty" dishes. In addition to
       these two sets of meaty and milky dishes, there is
       usually a third set of "neutral" dishes, neither milky
       nor meaty, so that foods prepared in these neutral
       dishes could be eaten together with either milky or
       meaty foods. Such a neutral dish or food is called
       "minnich" in WY. The word is from NHG "beliebig"
       ("optional", i.e., with either milky or meaty). In
       EY "minnich" was displaced by the Slavic "parev(e)"
       = "pairable" (i.e., "combinable" with either milky or
       meaty). For cakes it is especially desirable that
       they be "pareve" - so they could be eaten as dessert
       with any meal, or after all meals, or between meals
       (one must wait six hours after a meaty meal to have
       a milky, and one half-hour minimum -- the extra-
       pious wait longer -- after a milky to have a meaty).
       Even more specially desirable is it in the case of
       cakes sent as gifts -- so the recipient can enjoy them
       all the time. One must remember that before the era
       of commercial bakeries and packaged foods Jews used
       to bake once a week, Friday mornings (or on days be-
       fore the eye of a holiday) and cakes so baked, like
       the bread, were eaten all week with all kinds of foods.

 .9   'Schalah Monôs': gegenseitige Beschenkung, exchanging
       of gifts; one must send a minimum of two food-gifts
       to two friends and two gifts (food and money) to two
       poor strangers -- to fulfill the religious obligation
       on Purim. Cf. Esther 9:22. The joke is that this
       obligation was assumed by all the Jews a year after
       the Purim miracle, to commemorate it on its anniver-

92.9   sary, ever after. Hence the anachronism of having
'Schalah Monôs' sent before it was instituted.

.8-9   'bachen - machen': Rz; 'ch' in 'bachen' is UG, not
Y, L p. 355 # 45.

.10   'Rô'sch Hôdesch': dist. h c; there is no 'Rô'sch
Hôdesch-Ǩlahd' in existence! There are only "Schabbes
Ǩlahder" and (possibly) "Yontef Klahder" (though rare),
but no special clothes to wear on the new-moon only!
Though, of course, new-moon and Purim are Jewish
(minor) holidays and hence holiday dress is appropriate.
Note also that Purim is at full- and not at new-moon.
Furthermore, "Klahd" (is both Y and G) in the sg.
usually can refer to a "dress: for a female only,
whereas the pl. "Kleider" can be used for masculine
clothes.

.12-13   Cf. C p. 343 on 89.16-.17.

.14   'Birchas...': (sic! with short 'a'). Strictly speaking, H is imprecise: the mention of Harbona is not
in the part called the "Blessings of the Megillah",
but in a hymn, "Shoshanas Yaakov" -- composed a
thousand years after the "Blessings", and thousands
of years after the Megillah. But the hymn is a part
of the prayers of which the Blessings forms the other
part.
'le-be-Sôf': an ungrammatical, but common, pronunciation of "livesôf".

.15   'Ve-gam...': = "und auch Harbona sei zum guten gedacht (or: erwähnt)"; this is the last line in the
"Shoshanas Yaakov", i.e., in the Purim prayers. The
humor: Mordechai isn't (and could not have been) the
author of the hymn. The charm of it all, though, is
that the play does end with the same last line as the
Purim service in the synagogue and the singing at home.

Lexicology[1]

---

[1] The symbol § refers to the appropriate sections of the unpublished grammar.

A.

1. â (3, 19); ân (1, 3; 3, 14) – a, an, one – Lex. I, 520:
   ein. For ei : â, vid. §15, 1. n omission and preservation §26, 3; inflection §70, 3.
   A. â : â moile zehi (37, 4) – almost ten times. B. in
   ânem : mir hem getanzt in ânem fott (37, 2) – we continued to dance together –; mit'n Melech (König) in
   ânem fott (49, 10) – on together with the king – Lex. I,
   521 : in ein; Mieses, 160; §70, 4.

2. [abgenge] – go away – abgenge (4, 15) – Lex. I, 3:
   abgân. For form in dialect vid. §54.

3. abštîlen (25, 19 – to rhyme with špîlen 25, 18; abštê-
   len would be the expected form) – steal away from – Lex.
   II, 1173; stëln, stëlen stv. I, 2; no examples in
   Middle High German with the prefix ab; SWb. I 72: ab-
   stelen; DWb. I, 129 abstehlen.

4. abzapple 22, 4 – pull and kick one another – SWb. I 85.
   Cf. zappeln #615.

5. [affezîr]m. – officer – affezîr pl. 74, 11; affezîrs' pl.
   74, 19 – Schulz-Basler II, 236: for uninflected plural
   form superceded by s plural in the eighteenth century;
   – also 861.

6. aier (4, 14, 15; 2, 15, 19) – your – Lex. I, 1464:
   iuwer. For iu : ai vid. §17; uninflected form in attributive position in both the singular and plural §70, 3.

7. ainbrenne 20, 4 – make a brown sauce – SWb. II, 593;
   the usual word throughout the dialect used today as here
   especially without an object.

8.   [ainšnîren] - lace up - aingšnîrt (6, 23) - Lex. II,
   1044: snüeren suv. - no examples with <u>ein</u>. On üe :
   î <u>vid</u>. §19, 1; §21, V.

9.   ainšloifen (77, 4) - fall asleep - Lex. II, 953:
   slâfen - no examples with <u>ein</u>. On â : oi <u>vid</u>. §8, 1.

10.   alân (2, 17); alâ (16, 14) - alone - Lex. I, 36:
   alein. On ei : â <u>vid</u>. 815, 1; ṇ syncope in final unaccented position §26, 2E.

11.   allemoil (39, 1); allemoile (45, 11) - always - Lex.
   I, 33; 2014: al mâl. On â : oi <u>vid</u>. §8, 1.

12.   [alliminîren] - light up in a festive manner - alli-
   minîren (91, 2) - Schulz-Basler I, 282: illuminiren.

13.   allroin (60, 2)m. - mandrake, bottle imp - used here
   to designate a grotesque person or image - <u>Vid</u>.
   Taylor Starck, <u>Die Alraune</u>, Johns Hopkins Dissertation, Baltimore, Maryland, 1916.

14.   a main 4, 11; 28, 11 - all the more - Lex. I, 1414:
   iemêr, iemên. On the interchange of <u>n</u> and <u>r</u>: SWb.
   IV, 1143; Kluge 373; - for appearance in the dialects
   <u>vid</u>. §69.

15.   amale (21, 7) - once for all - DWb. III, 231; amoil
   (5, 7) - once - Rh.Wb. II, 83.

16.   [anbaišen] - have a snack - baiṡt ân (70, 5) - SWb. I,
   176.

17.   anderthallem (45, 13) - one and one-half - Lex. I, 56:
   andert-halben. On lb : ll <u>vid</u>. §24, 3; on numerals
   <u>vid</u>. §70, 4.

18.   [six angašîren] - to be engaged with - hem nit geruht
   bis ix mix mit si angašîr (37, 10) - Schulz-Basler I,
   173.

19.   [anhaben] - wear - di hem anghat (85, 15) - On past

participle in dialect <u>vid</u>. §56.

20. anheren (63, 17) - listen to - Lex. I, 1340; anhoeren.
On oe : e <u>vid</u>. §13; §21, V.

21. anlêgen 68, 13 - stir up trouble - Landau, 47;
anlegens.

22. ânsittler 17, 7 m. - hermit - Lex. I, 528; DWb. III,
296: einsidelaere. On the change ei : â <u>vid</u>. §15, 1.

23. ânzîgen (47, 12; 34, 3) - put on - zîg ân (34, 5, 7) -
Lex. I, 65: anziehen.

24. [apletîren] - applaud - g'apletîrt (86, 7) - On the
preservation of the <u>g</u> in the past participles of
foreign suffixes in the German dialects <u>vid</u>. §47 A. -
Schulz-Basler I, 45: applaudieren.

25. arakśtakśkterkśle (8, 9) n. - jocose reference to the
magnitude of a fly by calling it an Artaxerxes. -
Artaxerxes II, 404 B.C. - 361 B.C. - Hebrew Artakh-
shasta.

26. arem (59, 24)m. - arm - Lex. I, 93: arm stin. On syl-
labic <u>m</u>, <u>vid</u>. §27, 1.

27. [arm] - poor - aremen (4, 21); areme (3, 7; 56, 3) -
Lex. I, 92.

28. arig (30, 1) - badly - Lex. I, 89: arc.

29. arr - err - loś dix fun der nit arr maxen (75, 12) -
Lex. I, 1450: irre. On i : a(r) in dialects <u>vid</u>. §3,
3.

30. [arwele]n. - sleeve - arwelix (85, 16) - DWb. III,
715: erbel m. On <u>lix</u> plural §66; b : w, §30, 2.

31. [arwes]f. - peas - arwesn (70, 3) - Lex. I, 91;
Schmeller I, 135.

32. [arweten] - work - arwet (14, 4; 78, 13) - Lex. I, 88;

arbeiten swv. For b : w vid. §30, 2.

33.   A. aṡ - that - mer soll nit mâne aṡ di sen fun menŝen-
hend (54, 10) - Schmeller I, 1: South East Germany,
Austria, Alpine Lands; Landau and Wachstein 115:
Franken, Elsass, Schweiz, Tirol, Kärnten.

B. as - than - nit lenger as a halbe Scho'oh'[1] (52,
14) - Landau and Wachstein 115: used in all Yiddish
dialects until the eighteenth century.

34.   atiṡhoif (76, 3)m. - Arthur's court - On loss of r
[t] vid. §25, 2 Aa.

35.   [atloṡen] - of resplendent silk material - atloṡene
waste (72, 8) - SWb. I, 347; Roedder 335; Kluge 26:
atlas - oriental material, an Arabian borrowing.

36.   [axting]f. - watch - a fezzen hund gît axting droif
(72, 21) - Lex. I, 32: ahtunge stf., On ung : ing in
unaccented position vid. §40.

---

1.   Stunde.

B.

37. bâ : bâ main lêben (80, 16) - upon my life! - Lex. I,
262: bî. On î : â in unaccented position, and characteristic of Middle Yiddish vid. §12, 1.

38. baiere (72, 13)f. - formerette - Lex. I, 395: bûre,
bûr swm. On û : al vid. 814, 3. DWb. I, 1178:
bäuerin.

39. [baitel]m. - bag - baitel (49, 2) - Lex. I, 290:
biutel stmn. On iu : ai vid. ¦§17, 1b.

40. [bân]n. - leg - bân (45, 2) - Lex. I, 159: bein stn.
On ei : â vid. §15, 1.

41. [bang tun] - to be worried - tuts̓ mir bang (73, 7) -
Lex. I, 121; SWb. I, 608; Landau and Wachstein: very
infrequent in the older language; occurs in the Upper
German dialects.

42. [bɛrig]m - mir štene di hor zu barig (29, 17) - my
hairs stand on edge - Lex. I, 184: bėřc stm. On e :
[a] vid. §2, 3. SWb. I, 865: Berg-ě -, fränk. bis
gegen -ǎ- rg, rəg, rig swäb., rix fränk.

43. barxesbried (31, 7)n. - a board with strong material of
linen and cotton; this fabric has a smooth and a
rough side - SWb. II, 638; DWb. I, 1125: barchatm.
today it appears as barchet, barchant. Middle High
German barkân; Middle Latin borchamus, parchanus.
Explanations of Hebrew provenience, however ingenious,
are fallacious inasmuch as a throne is here likened to
a board with the aforementioned material upon it.
Landau and Wachstein 117: barches̓ plural of Hebrew
Berochoh (blessings); therefore, the bread over which

a blessing is spoken on the eve of Sabbath (bread - a
long white bread with anis seed); this word appears
in North Germany and Austria as <u>barches</u>, in the rest
of Germany as <u>berches</u>. Mieses, 220: <u>barchesbrot</u> has
been looked upon as a West Yiddish word denoting
"Sabbath bread". It cannot be derived from Hebrew
<u>Berochôs</u> (blessings) because the benediction is spoken
over every type of bread. Is it to be associated with
the old Germanic Goddes Perchta-Berchta, the God of
food?

44. [bašten] : koze hor sen ball gebašt (35, 10) -
literally: short hairs are soon brushed, but <u>cf</u>.
Tendlau <u>Prov</u>. #785: insignificant business or
things are soon done.

45. baxen 92, 8 - bake - Lex. I, 136; Kluge 33: Upper
German inform.

46. [bazze]m. - a coin of small value - bazzen (18, 2) -
Lex. I, 136: a small coin of the city of Bern with
its coat of arms.

47. bedaiten 62, 15 - maan - Lex. I, 141: bediuten. On
iu; ai <u>vid</u>. §17,11b.

48. befêlen (39, 9) - command - hot befoilen (78, 14) -
Lex. I, 248: bevëlhen - part. bevoln.

49. bêgle (28, 18) - iron - Kretschmer 379: found especially in Thuringia, Kassel, Fulda, Marburg, West-
phalia, Rhine province, South Germany and Austrian
Alps.

50. beharršer (2, 10)m. - ruler - Lex. I, 1263: hêrscher,
hërscher stm.; Lex. I, 155: behêrren - hërren. On
e : a[r] <u>vid</u>. §2, 3.

51. behîten: gott behît (6, 1) - God forbid! - Lex. I,

156: behüeten swv. On üe : î §19; third singular present volitive subjunctive, §50 A.

52. [bekumme] - receive - hoter...bekumme (82, 9) - Lex. I, 167: bekommen stv. I, 2. part. bekomen, bekumen. On u vocalism [nasals] in past participles in the dialects vid. §47 B Class V.

53. [belîb] - delicious - belîbe (92, 9) - SWz. Wb. III, 991: beliebig.

54. beloine (92, 14) - reward - Lex. I, 175: belônen. On ô : oi vid. §12, 1.

55. berâben (45, 8) - deprive - Lex. I, 197: berouben. On ou : â vid. §16, 1.

56. bês (72, 6) - worthless - Lex. I, 330: boese. On oe : ê vid. §13, 1.

57. betrîben (17, 11) - cast down - Lex. I, 241: betrüben. On üe : î vid. §19, 1.

58. bikken (78, 17) - bend down - Lex. I, 377: bücken. On ü : i vid. §7, 1.

59. bir (60, 2)f. - pear - Lex. I, 280. DWb. II, 37; Kluge, 54.

60. [bixle]n. - little book - bixle (48, 10) - Lex. I, 386: büechelîn. On üe : i vid. §19, 1.

61. [blaiben] - remain - ix blai (71, 2); er blait (37, 15) On b syncope vid. §30, 6. SWb. I, 1190.

62. bloi (22, 3) blue - Lex. I, 294: blâ. On â : oi vid. §8, 1.

63. [bloisen] - blow - bloist (72, 16); gebloisen (85, 22) - Lex. I, 297: blasen. On â : oi vid. §12, 1.

64. [blumme - karwele]n. - flower basket - blummekarwelix (85, 17). On lix plural vid. §66.

65. [boiden]m. - bottom - ûne boiden (15, 8) - Lex. I, 321. On o : oi vid. §4, 2.

66. [boien] - build - ix boi (78, 19); bin ix geboit (59, 16) - Lex. I, 404: bûwen. On û : oi vid. §14, 1.

67. boier (16, 5)m. - "dope" - SWb. I, 699: a foolish, coarse, pigheaded, uneducated individual.

68. [boige]f. - drum - boigen (74, 9) - Lex. I, 305: pûke swf. On û : oi vid. §14, 1. On p, b interchange vid. §30, 1; 31, 1.

69. [boiswixt] - scamp - in den boiswixt (59, 9) - Lex. I, 330: boesewiht. On oe : oi vid. §13, 2.

70. boix (20, 1)m. - stomach - Lex. I, 376: bûch stm. On û : oi vid. §16, 5.

71. [brâtehoib]f. - wide cape - in brâtehoib (64, 9) - Lex. I, 374: breit; Lex. I, 1372 hube swf. On ei : â vid. §15, 1; û : oi vid §14, 1.

72. [brennen] - burn - hem sain bakken gebrennt (71, 19) - Lex. I, 349: brennen, past part. gebrennet, gebrant. On the preservation of e in the past participle in dialects vid. §47 A.

73. briderle (50, 17)n. - buddy - Lex. I, 364: brüederlîn. On üe : i vid. §19, 1.

74. brifle (13, 5)n. - little letter - Lex. I, 353: brievelîn, brievel stn. On le suffix in the dialects vid. §66. On ie : i vid. §20, 1.

75. brik (82, 18)f. - tile - Rh. Wb. I, 975; DWb. II, 379.

76. brillliand(72, 12)m. - cut-face diamond - Heyse 129; Els. Wb. II, 189; Rh. Wb. I, 979; Kluge 69.

77. [bringen] - bring wer hettet gebroixt (5, 9) - Lex. I, 353: bringen, brâhte, brânt. On â : oi vid. §8, 1.

78. [broit]n. - bread - broit (19, 4) - Lex. I, 359: brot stn. On ô : oi vid. §12, 1.

79. [broixen] - need - broix ix (15, 6) - Lex. I, 362:

bruchen. On û : oi <u>vid</u>. §16, 5.

80.   brumme (80, 9) - growl, grumble - Schmeller I, 356.

81.   bukkel (82, 5)m. - humpback - Lex. I, 376; Kluge 83:
         buckel m. Lat. <u>buccula</u>. Old French <u>bouck</u>, Middle High
         German 1200 f. <u>buckel</u>. Since the sixteenth century it
         has adopted the meaning of back, then today hump-back.

82.   [butellic]f. - glass bottle - butellie (76, 8) -
         Schulz-Basler I, 103: Bútell, Butella, Butellʃe - an
         archaic word first occuring in the language at the end
         of the seventeenth century with the import of foreign
         wine in South Germany; Heyse 126; Kluge 90.

83.   butterkraišle (82, 19)n. - butter dish - Lex. I, 401:
         buter swfm.; Lex. I, 1757: krûse swf. On û : ei <u>vid</u>.
         §14, 3.

84.   butterwekkle (29, 6)n. - butter patty - Lex. I, 401;
         Lex. III, 721.

D.

85. [dafeteš]n. - taffeta dress - dafeteš (34, 7) - <u>DWb</u>.
II, 1, 26.

86. [daffen] - to be allowed to - ix daf (17, 1; 29, 10);
darf di frâ (1, 6), daf mer (28, 10); mir daffen (32,
2); îr daft (70, 1). For complete conjugation <u>vid</u>.
§52, 4.

87. [daitšen, taitšen]: wâs daitš (74, 13), was taitš
(1, 4; 27, 9; 33, 3; 37, 1) - how so?, how do you
mean? - Lex. I, 444: diutschen, tiutschen; DWb. II,
1050: deutschen; Kluge 102. On iu : ai <u>vid</u>. 817, 1.
<u>Cf</u>. modern American Yiddish <u>staiš</u> - how do you mean
it? <u>is teutsch</u> - how is that in German?

88. [dax]n. - roof - uf di dexter (75, 4) - Lex. I, 406:
dach stn. pl. dach u. decher. On parasitic or excrescent <u>t</u> in dialect <u>vid</u>. §37, 4b.

89. dekbettzîg (82, 16)n. - down quilt used over a low
bed - DWb. II, 882: deckbett m.; DWb. I, 1739:
bettuch n.

90. [denken]: 'š denken mix gar nit di zaiten (61, 11) -
I can't remember the times (lit. the times do not make
me think) - Kluge 88: denken - the factitive of an
originally strong verb meaning to seem. <u>Cf</u>. modern
German gedenken - to cause one to remember. A.
gedoixt: hettet aier harrle âx soi gedoixt, wer
hiebet den aier tâte, oif di welt gebroixt? - Lex. I,
418: past participle gedâht. On â : oi <u>vid</u>. §8, 1;
on Rückumlaut in the dialects §47 A.

91. der: derbai (30, 12), derfor (85, 13), derfûn (6, 14,

80, 2), dergêgen (13, 18), dermit (76, 12), dernêben
(53, 15), dernieben (18, 1), dernex (22, 5), dernoix
(10, 18; 38, 23; 47, 21), dernoixet (41, 9; 72, 22),
derzu (6, 25; 23, 18), derzwišen (45, 25) - Lex. I,
410: dår : da : der - in unaccented position -
similarly derhâm (60, 15; 61, 17; 65, 3) - at home -
Lex. I, 1216: heim stn. On ei : â vid. §15, 1. A.
derlaxen: hot six derlaxt (82, 12) - he burst out
laughing - Schmeller I, 531: der unaccented Upper
German prefix. Landau and Wachstein 119: corresponds
to Slavic do, - similarly six derbareme (25, 11; 66,
5; 67, 3), derfrîren (47, 10), derhêben (23, 23),
[derlâben] : derlâbt (9, 7), [derretten] : derrett
(77, 17), deršlagen (55, 17), [deršokkeln] : deršokkelt
(85, 7), [derwâxen] : derwâxt (91, 6), [derwišen] :
derwišt (59, 3), derzêlen (38, 12).

92. [dikret]n. - decree - dikrêt (3, 19), dekrete (8, 5;
10, 11), dikrêter (10, 3) - Lex. I, 414: decret stn.
On er plural vid. §64.

93. [dint]f. - ink - dint (10, 1) - Lex. II, 1440: tincte,
tinte swf. On d and t change vid. §37, 3.

94. dixtig - soundly - ix hob ax gšlagen dixtig droif (82,
11) - Lex. II, 1564: tühtec, -ic. On d and t change
vid. §37, 3; on ü - i, §7, 1.

95. doi (1, 7; 1, 11; 21, 5) - then - Lex. I, 445: dâ. On
â : oi vid. §8, 1.

96. [doiern] - last - doiert (3, 15) - Lex. I, 494: dûren.
On û : oi vid. §14, 1.

97. [dokke]f. - puppet - dokken (25, 2) - Lex. II, 1455:
tocke swf. On t and d change vid. §37, 1. Paul 111;
Kluge 108: the usual expression for puppet in South

Germany.

98.   donštik (18, 4)m. – Thursday – Lex. I, 448: doners, donres, dunres – təc stn. SWb. II, 262: dönštig. On loss of r vid. 25, 2 AC.

99.   dorix (22, 14) – through – SWb. II, 479: durix. Lex. I, 477: durch. On u : o vid. §6, 3.

100.   dot (25, 9; 50, 4) – there – Lex. I, 454: dort. A. doten (73, 7) – over there – Schneller I, 544. DWb. II, 1306: dorten. On the r[t] syncope vid. §25, 2Aa.

101.   drâhbrenne: mer watt îr drânbrenne a šmalz (28, 9) – one will get you steamed up (lit. one will burn there-in a piece of lard for you).

102.   droif (7, 8) – upon it – Lex. II, 1687: drûf. On û : oi vid. §14, 1.

103.   droiš : doi laxt er droiš? (65, 7) – cf. Modern German darüber – Lex. II, 2018: drûz. On û : oi vid. §14, 1. A. droisen – outside – Lex. II, 2038: ûze, ouze, adv. bei demonstr. adv.

E.

104.   ebeś (1, 15; 4, 10; 66, 1); ebiś (1, 11) - something -
        DWb. III, 679: eppes - in all Upper and many Middle
        German dialects. Landau and Wachstein 120: in all
        Yiddish dialects.

105.   [êe]f. - marriage - êen (58, 11) - Lex. I, 715.

106.   [êfele]n. - little over - êfele (29, 2) - DWb. VII,
        1154: öfelein. Tirol. das öfele, Nürnb. üfle, Swz.
        öfela.

107.   efterś (5, 5) - often times - Lex. II, 148: öfter.
        On ö > e in dialect vid. §5, 1.

108.   [ekśezsîren] - drill, exercise - hot g'ekśezshrt (86,
        6) - Schulz-Basler I, 186: exerzieren. On the g
        preserved in the past participle of loan words vid.
        §47 A.

109.   elendśgloie (85, 1)f. - "dummy" - Paul 132; DWb. IV,
        1, 7772.

110.   [êltikkle]n. - little oil lamp - êltikkle (90, 17) -
        SWb. V, 58: oeltigel.

111.   erśtlix (41, 8) - in the first place - Paul 149.

112.   [eśśen] - eat - gesn (9, 3) - Lex. I, 718. Weise, §51,
        Grübel, p. 258, §97 b, on form in dialects.

113.   eternelles - name of a dress, so-called on account of
        its durability - zîg ân dain eternelles klâd (34, 5) -
        Heyse 326; Murray, N.E.D., III, 342.

F.

114. [faier]n. - fire - faier (28, 15) - Lex.III, 377:
      viuwer. On iu : ai <u>vid</u>. §17, 1.

115. fâl (15, 11) - for sale - Lex. III, 47: veile, veil.
      On ei : â <u>vid</u>. §15, 1.

116. [farbel]n. - noodles - Lex. III, 26: varvelen pl.
      Schmeller I, 753: fərfelsuppe - a common meal for the
      common folk in Carinthia.

117. [farib]f. - ruk ix mit der farib roiš (89, 14) - I'll
      show my true colors, will confess the truth, - SWb.
      II, 947.

118. [faśenaxt]f. - shrovetide - faśenaxt (91, 5) - DWb.
      III, 1354, Kluge 148.

119. fašt (12, 2)m. - prince - Lex. III, 612: vürste. On
      ü : a <u>vid</u>. §7, 2. On <u>r</u> syncope <u>vid</u>. §25, 2Ac. On <u>s</u>
      š[t] <u>vid</u>. §33, 2.

120. fattel (13, 6)n. - quarter - Lex. III, 342: vierteil,
      viertel stn. On e : a [<u>r</u> + consonant] <u>vid</u>. §20, 3.
      On <u>r</u> syncope <u>vid</u>. §25, 2 A **a.**

121. fatig (71, 15); fattig (73, 4); fattik (9, 14); fettik
      (21, 13) - finished - Lex. III, 266: vertic, vertig.
      On e : a [<u>r</u>] <u>vid</u>. §2, 3. On <u>r</u> syncope <u>vid</u>. §25, 2 A a.

122. fer (4, 4) - for - Lex. III, 583: vür. On ü : e <u>vid</u>.
      §7, 3.

123. ferbizzle (48, 13) - to cut into small pieces - DWb.
      XII, 125: verbisseln - today verbitzeln (Elsass,
      Palatinate, Austria, Upper Saxony).

124. [ferderben] - ruin - hot mir's in grund nain ferdorm
      (34, 12) - Lex. III, 93: verderben stv. -intr.; Lex.
      III, 14: verderben swv. - tr. Here used transitively

- Paul 591.

125. ferfrîren (3, 13) - freeze - Lex. III, 516: vervriesen.
DWb. XII, 355: verfrieren - used today dialectically
(Wetterau, Lausitz, Posen).

126. ferkâfen (41, 4) - sell - Lex. III, 148: verkoufen.
On ou : â vid. §16, 1.

127. ferkozzen (23, 9) - shorten - Lex. III, 151: verkürzen.
On ü : o vid. §7, 3. On r syncope vid. §25, 2 A d.

128. ferkrumme (15, 14) - become deformed - Lex. III, 149.

129. [ferkumme] - perish - ix ferkum (67, 9) - Lex. III, 147;
Paul 598. On u̯ vocalism in dialect vid. §47 B class
IV.

130. ferlêben (36, 6); six ferleben (58, 17); six ferlêben
(60, 5) - fall in love.

131. ferlos̆s̆en (28, 13) - leave - Lex. III, 153: ver-lâzen
stv. On ä : o vid. §8, 3.

132. [fers̆ender]f. - spoiler - fers̆ender'n (35, 22) - to
rhyme with endern (35, 21) - Lex. III, 215: ver-
schenden.

133. fers̆tekkle (29, 8) - hide - DWb. XII, i, 1641: ver-
steckle - Suabia, Elsass and Rhine Franconia.

134. fersinden - cause to sin - soi âne ken dox die ganze
Kehiloh (Gemeinde) fersinden (1, 14) - cf. Tendlau,
Prov. #647.

135. fersuchen 45, 14 - taste - DWb. XII, 1, 1833: used
today in the Upper German dialects.

136. [fertâben] - grow deaf - fertâbt (9, 8) - Lex. III,
272: vertouben. On ou : â vid. §16, 1.

137. [ferzêlen] - tell - ferzêl (75, 12) - Lex. III, 316:
verzeln.

138. ferzîgen (23, 18) - distort, twist - Lex. III, 318:
verziehen.

139. A [fez] - fat - fezzen (72, 21, 72, 23). On t : z <u>vid</u>. §37, 7.

B [fezze]m? - clothes - fezzen (37, 6) - Lex. III, 331; Schmeller I, 781; DWb. III, 1575.

C fezzen (29, 16) f. - pool - Lex. II, 269: phütze stswf. On ü : e <u>vid</u>. §7, 7.

140. fiel : ix weis fiel (20, 5) - an overstatement for "I do not know at all".

141. fifat (74, 4) - hurrah! - Heyse 965; Kluge 349.

142. [fillen] - fill - ix fill (46, 1) - Lex. III, 562: füllen. On ü : i <u>vid</u>. §7, 1.

143. [finden] - find - finne ix (87, 10) - Lex. III, 354: vinden. On nd : nn <u>vid</u>. §36, 6.

144. [fingerle]n. - ring - fingerlix (23, 3) - Lex. III, 356: vingerlîn. DWb. III, 1685. On <u>lix</u> plural <u>vid</u>. §66.

145. fîren (3, 2; 16, 3) - lead - Lex. III, 557: vüeren. On üe : î <u>vid</u>. §19, 1.

146. [fus]m. - foot - fîs (48, 12) - Lex. III, 579: vuoz, pl. vüeze. On üe : î <u>vid</u>. §19, 1.

147. flenne: main maile hinten tut nebix flenne (46, 6) - unfortunately I have a sore throat - literally flenne - make a wry face - DWb. III, 1768 - 1769.

148. flêgel (68, 6)m. - lout - Lex. III, 391: vlegel stw. On e : ê <u>vid</u>. §2, 2. Paul 167; DWb. III, 1747.

149. [flête]f. - flute - flêten (85, 23) - Els. Wb. I, 175: flétl dim.

150. [flis]m. - catarrh - flis (47, 16) - Rh. Wb. II, 627.

151. foigelhaisle (82, 18)n. - little bird cage - SWb. II, 1605, DWb. XII, 2, 412.

152. forois (74, 7) - in front - Lex. III, 483: vorüz. On

ü : oi <u>vid</u>. §14, 1.

153.   fott (1, 1) - away, gone - Lex. III, 482: vort. On <u>r</u> syncope <u>vid</u>. §25, 2 A a.

154.   [fraid]f. - pleasure - fraid (61, 8) - Lex. III, 537: vröude stswf. On öu : ai <u>vid</u>. §16, 2.

155.   [six fraien] - rejoice - frai dix (24, 1) - Lex. III, 542: vröuwen swn. refl. (Engelh. 2707). On öu : ai <u>vid</u>. §16, 2. On <u>w</u> syncope <u>vid</u>. §23, 2.

156.   fraindlix (51, 12) - friendly - Lex. III, 527: vraint-lich. On iu : ai <u>vid</u>. §17, 1.

157.   fraitig (28, 19)m. - Friday - Lex. III, 523: vrîtac -; <u>cf</u>. donštik (18, 4).

158.   [franzefûś]m. - brandy - franzefûś (52, 12) - Rh. Wb. II, 731; franz(en) - fusel m. - brandy from the dregs of wine.

159.   [franześ]n. - French - franzeš (49, 10) - Els. Wb. I, 182. A [franzeš] adj. - fun der franzeše rewulaziûn (54, 16).

160.   [fregen] - ask - frêgt (55, 1) - Lex. III, 495: vrègen. On e : ê <u>vid</u>. §2, 2.

161.   [freśér]m. - hair-dresser - freśér (90, 13) - Heyse 367: friséur.

162.   frî (26, 5) - early - Lex. III, 545: vrüe. On üe : î <u>vid</u>. §19, 1.

163.   [frimfel]n. - "lady finger" dough - frimfel (29, 4); frimfelix (29, 14). A. frimfelištag: ix swêrn bai den frimfelištag (27, 10) - an oath uttered in a jocose manner - <u>cf</u>. modern American Yiddish frimsel; English vermicelli; Rh. Wb. II, 812.

164.   [friše]f. - "cold stuff" - frišen (76, 8) - Lex. III, 521; DWb. IV, 1, 212.

165.   frnašen (46, 2) - eat dainties by stealth or on the sly

- DWb. XII, 907: vernaschen. Lex. II, 37, Paul 373: naschen.

166. froi (21, 6) - happy - Lex. III, 520: vrô. On û : oi vid. §12, 1.

167. [froigen] - ask froigen (3, 3), froig (75, 14) - Lex. III, 487: vrâgen. On ä : oi vid. §8, 1.

168. fun (2, 10; 6, 9) - cf. from - Lex. III, 456: von. On o : u vid. §4, 5.

169. fufzehi (6, 9) - fifteen - Lex. III, 568: vünf-zehen. On ü : u vid. §4, 5. On the dropping of final n vid. §26, 5.

170. fufzig (78, 19) - fifty - Lex. III, 568: vünfzic. On ü : u vid. §4, 5. On n syncope vid. §26, 5.

171. fûsštîle (73, 14)m. - footstool - rhymes with the Hebrew Me.[h]iloh (Arsch) on the following line - DWb. IV, 1, 1050: fussstuhl m. - the foot of a pillar upon which the latter rests.

172. futtrâl (14, 9)n. - covering - Lex. III, 575: vuoterâl stn. On uo : u vid. §18, 1. DWb. IV, 1074; Paul 181.

G.

173. [gâgelšpringer]m. - acrobat - gâgelšpringerlix (25,
      2) - Lex. I, 1059: gougel; Lex. II, 1117: springer.
      On ou : â vid. §16, 3. On lix plural vid. §66.

174. [galing]m. - gallows - galing (44, 6) - Schmeller I,
      901; SWb. III, 26.

175. [galle - šês]f. - msall, open carriage - galle -
      šêšen (74, 17) - Sachs-Villatte I, 208; SWb. I, 208;
      IV, 166 - a blend of French calèche and chaise.

176. [garnetur]f. - cape - garnetur (60, 8) - DWb. IV, 1,
      1371: garnette f.

177. [gaššenstrâx]m. - street prank - gaššenstrâx (20, 9) -
      Lex. II, 1229: strach stm. On ei : â vid. §15, 1.

178. gebabbel (15, 16)n. - prattle - SWb. III, 376.

179. [gêben] - give - git (41, 8; 43, 15) - Lex. I, 750:
      geben. On form in dialect vid. §47 B class V.

180. gebloiter (9, 20)n. - the act of puffing up while en-
      gaged in gossip - Lex. I, 295: blaejan prät blaete,
      blâte, part. geblaet - verbal noun based upon the past
      participle - cf. English bloating. Lex. I, 756: ge-
      bletze stn.

181. gekîf (21, 7)n. - foolish behaviour - Lex. I, 1010;
      DWb. IV, 1, 7343: giefen - preserved in the Alemannic
      and Low Rhine dialect up to the seventeenth century -
      cf. English gape, - cf. # 302 of the glossary.

182. gekiš (76, 2)n. - "smacking" - Lex. I, 804: geküssen
      swv. On ü : i vid. §7, 1.

183. gelâf (7, 21)n. - running together - Lex. I, 824: ge-
      loufe stn. On ou : â vid. §16, 1.

184. gelarme (7, 22)n. - gelarrem (83, 18) - noisy activity - gelarreme (25, 10) - DWb. IV, 1, 2863.

185. gelek (76, 2)n. - happiness - Lex. I, 829: gelücke stn.
On ü : e vid. §7, 6.

186. [gelîd]n. - limb - gelîder (32, 8) - Lex. I, 816:
gelide stn. On i : î vid. §3, 1.

187. [gemân]m. - common soldier, a private - gemâne (74,
15) DWb. IV, 1, 3169; SWb. III, 327.

188. gemax (34, 9)m. - delight - Lex. I, 832.

189. [gemulz]n. - painting - gemulzeter (54, 9) - Lex. I,
835: gemaelze stn. Els. Wb. I, 665: gemälzle pl.
Schmeller I, 1583. On ae : u vid. §9, 4. On er plural
vid. §61.

190. gên (5, 3; 21, 12) - go - genge (7, 13), gange (2, 16),
genget (31, 3) - Lex. I, 733: gân, gên. On e vocalism in Bavarian vid. §54. On g syncope in the past
participle of strong verbs vid. §470 class IV. On t
ending affixed to preterite subjunctive of strong verbs
in the Elsass, Alemannic and Middle Rhine dialects
vid. §50 b.

191. [gensbarig]m. - hill where the geese run around -
gensbarig (83, 8) - DWb. IV, 1, 1267: common throughout Germany e.g. at Grüningen near Giessen.

192. geplapper (7, 19)n. - blabbing - dass watt sain a geplapper (7, 19) - Tendlau, Prov. #114: directed
against gossip and against a person who does not allow
another one to speak.

193. [geroiten] - turn out to be good - geroit (64, 19) -
Lex. I, 871: gerâten. On â : oi vid. §8, 1. SWb. III,
385; Paul 203; Tendlau, Prov. #843: refers to difficult
ventures, though successful, which do not promise special gain - the situation here.

194. gešter (50, 6) - yesterday - Lex. I, 929; Schmeller I, 995; SWb. III, 556. On s : š[t] vid. §33, 2a.

195. getatter (7, 20)n. - tattling - DWb. II, 828; IV, 1, 4359. Schmeller I, 631 - cf. French tête à tête.

196. gethe (57, 7) - Goethe.

197. getimmel (7, 22)n. - tumult, noise - (getummel (86, 7)) -- Lex. I, 950: getümele - tümmel. On ü : i vid. §7, 1. DWb. IV, 1, 4571: oldest forms point to a Bavarian provenience, becomes Middle German only in early New High German.

198. [getû]n. - commotion - getû (91, 3) - DWb. IV, 1, 4382: gethue - usually refers to something bad on the part of the actor.

199. gfreš (76, 5)n. - eating - Lex. I, 965.

200. [giebele]n. - gable - giebelix (23, 17) - Lex. I, 1009: gibel stn. On i : î vid. §3, 1. On lix plural vid. §66.

201. gîgar (40, 4)m. - cook, fop - Kluge 207; Paul 216; Rh. Wb. II, 1230; DWb. IV, 114, 7477.

202. gigerigî (40, 2; 40, 5)m. - cucoo-ru-cu - DWb. IV, 1[4], 7477: gigerligi.

203. gikš (27, 4)n. - stupid gossip - DWb. IV, 1[4], 7320; Rh. Wb. II, 1218, Tendlau Prov. #99.

204. [gildele]n. - small gold coin - gildilix (6, 3) - Lex. I, 1115: guldîn, gulden. DWb. IV, 1, 1054. On u : i vid. §6, 4. On lix plural vid. §66.

205. [glâben] - believe - ix glâb (27, 2; 82, 1), ix gloib (63, 12) - Lex. I, 824: glouben. On ou : â vid. §16, 1; on ou : oi vid. §16, 2.

206. [glik]n. - good luck - glik (22, 6; 57, 4) - Lex. I, 829: glücke stn. On ü : i vid. §7, 1.

207. glikklix (86, 16) - happy - Lex. I, 829: gelückelich.

208. [glokke]f. - bell shaped dress - glokken (25, 3) -
Lex. I, 1036; DWb. IV, 1, 146.

209. gogel (41, 2)m. - rooster - Paul 220; SWb. III, 729.
Rh. Wb. II, 1292.

210. goil (40, 4)m. - horse - oif an šên gaile (61, 9), fon
main šenšte gailix (64, 1) - Lex. I, 1115: gûl stn.
On û : oi vid. §14, 1; on û : ai vid. §14, 3. On lix
plural vid. §66.

211. [gošе]f. - mouth - gošen (18, 8) - Schmeller I, 952;
Paul 220; SWb. III, 752.

212. [gott]m. - si froigen nikš, noix gott un di welt
(3, 3) - they conform neither to divine nor human law,
neither to the religious statutes nor to those of
morality -; also: wider gott nit geret (14, 10) -
when someone foresees a bad turn of affairs and does
not wish to anticipate the divinity by his decision -
Tendlau, Prov. #687.

213. graid (22, 2) - just, as it were - Lex. I, 871:
gerade. On a : aɪ vid. §1, 10.

214. graine (29, 11)n. - weeping - Lex. I, 1086: grînen
stv. II; Paul 222. On î : ai vid. §11, 1.

215. [grellen] - pierce, grate, chirp - grillst mir dên
kopf foll mit unsilige lieder (13, 3) - Lex. I, 1084;
SWb. III, 835: used especially with reference to the
female sex. DWb. IV, 325: found not only in Suabia,
but also in Bavaria.

216. grîn (22, 3), grîne (60, 2) - green - grînen (72, 17)
- Lex. I, 1097: grüene. On üe : î vid. §19, 1.

217. [groi] - gray - groie (12, 5) - Lex. I, 1063: grâ.
On â : oi vid. §8, 1.

218. [groisam] - horrible - groisamen (81, 3) - Lex. I,
1109: gruwesan. On û : oi vid. §14, 1. On w syncope vid. §23, 2.

219. groišer (2, 9), groṡer (23, 22) - great - groise (81,
9) grosen (57, 15), greṡten (3, 16; 6, 24) - Lex. I,
1093: grôz. On ô : oi vid. §12, 1; on ô : o vid.
§12, 3 - also §77, I, 1.

220. [grûf]m. - count - grûf (12, 1), grufen (32, 7) - Lex.
I, 1074: grove. On a : û vid. §1, 8. Els. Wb. I,
270.

221. gšaiding (28, 1)n. - clever person - Lex. I, 902:
geschîde stf. SWb. III, 460: gescheidling m. -; or
oissibly gšaid ding.

222. gšmûs (15, 16)n. - idle chatter - SWb. III, 486; DWb.
IV, 1, 3948: collective to Judeo-German schmus, or
verbal noun to schmusen (empty talk) already in
Middle High German. Cf. #500 of glossary.

223. gšnatter (7, 19)n. - cackling - DWb. IV, 1, 3250; Paul
460.

224. gštê (70, 18)n. - stopping - SWb. III, 552.

225. [gšwêr]n. - swearing - gšwêr (81, 13) - Lex. I, 939:
geswern stv. I, 4.

226. [gsund] - beautiful, fresh - gsunden bruštflek (48, 3),
gsunden wošt (70, 3), gsunde šnekken (45, 10) -
Schmeller II, 307; DWb. IV, 1, 4429.

227. gušte (59, 7)m. - taste - DWb. IV, 1, 1204.

228. [gutzele]n. - goody - gutzelix (46, 1) - SWb. III, 968:
found throughout the Suabian territory with the exception of the South. On lix plural vid. §66.

229. guzzen (39, 4) - gawk - Lex. I, 1110; DWb. IV, 1, 1492:
still preserved in the Upper and Middle German dialects.

H.

230. haben (5, 15) - have - for various dialectical forms
vid. §56 - note also peculiar archaic: ix honnen (81,
3) - Middle High German ix hânin. On â : o Reis, p. 65.

231. hâd (32, 22)m. - heathen - Lex. I, 1207: heiden stm.
On ei : â vid. §15, 1.

232. [hafe]m. - pile - hâfen (30, 6) - Lex. I, 1376: houfe
swm. On ou : â vid. §16, 1.

233. [hai]f. - hay - in hai (72, 14) - Lex. I, 1357: höuwe,
houwe stn. shortened höu, hou, heu. On öu : ai vid.
§16, 2.

234. Haint (3, 23); hait (52, 5) - today - Lex. I, 1222; I,
1292. Schmeller I, 1135; DWb. IV, 2, 887.

235. [haittuke]m. - servant in Hungarian costume - haittuken
(87, 1) - Paul 246: heiduck pl. heiducken. On t, d
interchange vid. §36, 1.

236. hallem: andert-hallem (45, 13) - one and one-half -
Lex. I. ander-halp; ander-halbe; anderthalben. For
phonological development in dialects vid. §24, 3.

237. hâm (38, 6) - home - Lex. I, 1216: heim. On ei : â
vid. §15, 1.

238. hareme: thun si six nit hareme (67, 2) - do not feel
hurt - Lex. I, 1184; Paul 240; Rh. Wb. III, 262:
harmen.

239. Harr (3, 17)m. - sir, man-dên harrn (61, 7) - Lex. I,
1259: hërre swm. On e : a[r] vid. §2, 3.

240. harrle (5, 8)n; harrli (31, 21)n. - grandfather - DWb.
IV, 2, 1146: herrlein n. - found in Franconia and in
the Upper Palatinate. DWb. IV, 2, 1227: herrlein -
found also in Hessen, Bavaria, and the Rhine.

241. [harrn]n. - horn - of îr harrner (86, 3) - Lex. I,
1340: horn stn. pl. hörner. On ö : a [r + consonant]
vid. §5, 3.

242. [haše]m. - hare - hašen (72, 2) - Lex. I, 1192: hase,
swm. On s : š vid. §33, 2 c. SWb. III, 1201.

243. [hâšen] - be called - hâšt (79, 20) - Lex. I, 1126:
heizen stv. red. II. On ei : â vid. §15, 1.

244. haz (10, 15)n. - heart - Lex. I, 1269: herz. On e :
a[r] vid. §2, 3. On r syncope [z] vid. §25, 2 A, d.

245. hazworrm (45, 20)m. - tapeworm - Schmeller I, 1171;
DWb. IV, 2, 1266.

246. [hêben] - raise - hêbsin (40, 7) - Lex. I, 1199: heben.
For contraction vid. §43. A [six hêben] - raise oneself, - hem six gehoiben (75, 3) - Lex. I, 1199: past
part. gehaben. On a : oi vid. §1, 9.

247. [helfebânig] - ivory - helfenbânige (53, 19) - Lex.
II, 231: helfenbeinin. On ei : â vid. §15, 1.

248. [helling]f.: in der helling (22, 20) - while it is
bright - SWb. III, 1413; DWb. IV, 2, 976.

249. [hemmed]n. - shirt - hemmed (71, 13) - Lex. I, 1245;
Schmeller I, 1110; SWb. III, 1415; DWb. IV, 2, 980.

250. hendle (59, 17)n. - little hand - hendlix (85, 19):
Lex. I, 1247: hendelîn stn. On the diminutives in
dialects vid. §66.

251. [henken] - hang - gehenkt watt (92, 1) - Lex. I, 1248:
hengen. On the e vocalism in the past participle in
dialects vid. §47 A.

252. [heren] - hear - hert (4, 13), heren si (15, 17; 68,
1), her (40, 6), gehert (24, 5), ghattn (1, 11),
ghatten (84, 16). Lex. I, 1339: hoeren. On oe : e
vid. §13, 1. On the effect of r + consonant on a
preceding vowel in the German and Yiddish dialects vid.

§21, VI.

253. [herrenwinkerle]n. - little straw hat - herrenwinkerle (7, 7) - SWb. III, 1495.

254. [hiefelle]n. - little pot, toilet bowl - hiefelle (20, 2), hiefelix (53, 14) - Lex. I, 1280: hevelîn stn. On e : ie vid. §2, 4. SWb. III, 1018; Kluge 225; Schmeller I, 1055: found in Upper Palatinate, Upper German dialects.

255. [hifte]f. - hip - hiften kiśśelix (48, 3) - Lex. I, 1376: huf stf. gen. u. pl. hüffe: hüfte. On ü : i vid. §7, 1.

256. hînerštaig (82, 17)f. - hen's cage - Paul 520: steige peculiar to South Germany. Kretschmer 239: used in the Bavarian and Austrian Alpine districts but not at Württemberg - called hühnerkäfig.

257. hîngêbetś (26, 6)n. - invitation, sale - Landau and Wechstein 318: based upon the past participle of beten which throughout all the Yiddish dialects is regularly used for bitten. DWb. IV, 1435: hingeben - to give away. SWb. III, 1634: hingeber m. vendor. The first mentioned meaning seems to be the more appropriate one.

258. hinne (19, 5) - inside - Lex. I, 1438; inne. On prothetic h vid. §39, 2.

259. [hintern]m. - buttocks - hintern (68, 11) - Schmeller I, 1137.

260. [hîtle]n. - little hat - hîtle (35, 12), hietle (60, 12) - Lex. I, 1375: hüetlîn. On üe : î vid. §19, 1.

261. [hoib]f. - cape - hoib (48, 2) - Lex. I, 1372: hûbe swf.; Paul 241. On û : oi vid. §14, 1.

262. [hoif]m. - court yard - in hoif (78, 13) ibern hoifen (87, 8) - Lex. I, 1320: hof stm. On o : oi vid. §4,2.

263. hoilen (78, 15) - fetch - hoilt (76, 8) - Lex. I,
1326: holen. On o : oi <u>vid</u>. §4, 2.

264. hoisen (57, 2) - outside - DWb. IV, 2, 699: hauszen.

265. hoit (59, 15) f. - skin - hoit (23, 7) - Lex. I, 1408:
hût. On û : oi <u>vid</u>. §14, 1.

266. hokken (39, 11) - squat - DWb. IV, 2, 1649; Lex. I,
1373: hûchen.

267. hopsa (69, 17) - hallo! - DWb. IV, 2, 1800.

268. hor (35, 11)n. - hair - Lex. I, 1182: hâr. On â : o
<u>vid</u>. Reis, p. 65ff.

269. [hûn]n. - chicken - hîner (59, 1) - Lex. I, 1391: huon
stn. pl. hüener. On üe : î <u>vid</u>. §19, 1.

270. hunten (65, 11; 86, 14) - below - Lex. II, 1777: unden.
On inorganic h <u>vid</u>. §39, 2.

271. hutš : hutš!'ṡ is kalt (42, 8) - brrr! it is cold, -
Lex. I, 1409: hutsch interj. - raschen schwung in die
höhe bezeichnend.

272. [huzzel]f.: der will ix di huzzel ânrixten (89, 6) - I
will repay her - SWb. III, 1938. Tendlau, <u>Prov</u>. #251.
A. [huzzelstîl]n. - nothing at all (lit. a pit of a
pear) - huzzelstîl (10, 14).

273. [huzzer]m. - kick (37, 15; 69, 15) - DWb. IV, 2,
2001ff.: used mostly in the Franconian dialects with
the meaning of falling upon a person in an hostile
manner.

I.

274.   iber (11, 12) - over - Lex. II, 1606: über. On ü : i
           <u>vid</u>. §7, 1. A. ibern (8, 10) - over him. B. iberich
           (19, 1) - over you - <u>vid</u>. §70, 1.
275.   îns (48, 19; 49, 1; 49, 2; 49, 8; 58, 22; 59, 2) - that
           one, one, it - <u>vid</u>. §70, 2.
276.   itzt (13, 1), is (13, 16), izt (48, 2), izet (80, 15) -
           now - DWb. IV, 2, 2317.

J.

277.   jaxt (50, 5)f. - hunt - SWb. IV, 58; DWb. IV, 2, 2199.
278.   jingle (74, 2)n. - young man - Lex. I, 1489: jungelîn.
           On u : i <u>vid</u>. §6, 4.
279.   [johr]n, - year - johr (5, 14; 26, 13; 45, 14; 52, 2) -
           Lex. I, 1472: jâr. On ä : o[r] <u>vid</u>. §8, 2.
280.   joi (38, 3) - yes - Lex. I, 1466: jâ. On â : oi <u>vid</u>.
           §8, 1.

K.

281.   kâfen (18, 10) - buy - koif ix (60, 8), kâft (17, 11)
- Lex. I, 1695: koufen. On ou : â, oi <u>vid</u>. §16, 2.

282.   [kaierai]f. - mess, masticated material - kaierai (84,
9) - Lex. I, 1594: kiuwe. On iu : ai <u>vid</u>. §17, 1a.
SWb. IV, 287: käuer - he who chews. SWb. Wb. II, 1111
keierei, f. - unpleasantness caused by gossip - note
identity in form but difference in meaning.

283.   kân (2, 20) - no - Lex. I, 1536: kein. On ei : â <u>vid</u>.
§15, 1.

284.   kanebie (54, 8)n. - canopy - Heyse 141: canapé n.

285.   [kanûne]f. - canon - kanûne (46, 16) - SWb. IV, 194:
kanû -ne: Frk.; Heyse 491: kanóne f.

286.   A. kappore n.: doi watt main kappore (19, 2; 35, 5;
67, 11) - may all my sins be upon you - Tendlau, <u>Prov</u>.
#445: "werde für mich dahin genommen!"; if the curse
is not expressed, then "wer 'meines'". B. pfuzi -
kappore n.: di fîrt six dox oif a pfuzi - kappore
(12, 10) - she acts like a horrible thing - Avé-
Lallement, <u>Das deutsche Gaunertum</u>, vol. 4, p. 392ff.;
Tendlau, <u>Prov</u>. p. 69: to designate something as
worthlessly bad - usually futze kappore - in the place
of an expiatory sacrifice. The inference is that one
does not always give the best as an expiatory sacrifice;
hence it refers to something tainted. C. kappore n.:
šlagen for a kappore di kinder (3, 8) - Tendlau, <u>Prov</u>.
p. 69: "Ich schlag Dich für e Kappore!" - "wie man
das Versöhnungshuhn sich um den Kopf schlägt". - In
general kappore may have the following meanings:

(1) expiatory sacrifice (2) good-for-nothing (3)
scape-goat.

287. karl (40, 14)m. - fellow - Lex. I, 1520.

288. [karpeś]m. - pumpkin - Lex. I, 1791: kürbiz stm.
On ü : a [r] vid. §7, 2. On b : p vid. §30, 1b.
Paul 309; DWb. V, 2927.

289. karwe (25, 24)f. - church dedication festival - Lex.
I, 1587: kirchwîhe stf.; Heyse II, 346: a church
festival - appears in dialect today in Upper Germany.

290. [katârn]m. - catarrh - katârn (47, 16) - Schulz-
Basler I, 340: katarrh - in the medical books of the
sixteenth century -, a synonym for fliś on the same
line.

291. katt (76 , 15) - program - Les. I, 1524: karte. On
r syncope [t] vid. §25, 2 A a.

292. [kelômer-kês]m. - pretending - kelômer-kês (78, 7) -
Tendlau, Prov. #303: "So zu sagen: käse-Scheinkäse".
Die Redensart ist fon den hölzerren Käsen von den
Spezereilläden hergenommen und soll jeden falschen
Schein, jede Verstellung bezeichnen. Nahm jemand z.b.
den Schein an, als sei ihm etwas unlieb, indes man
vom Gegenthal überzeugt war, so hiess es: Das send
(sind) "kloomer-käs".

293. [kendle]n. - jug - Lex. I, 1547: kendelîn stn.
On le diminutive vid. §66. DWb. V, 176. Paul 279:
a predominantly South German word.

294. kenig (63, 7)m. - king - kenigś (63, 22); kenig (2,
19; 3, 17) - Lex. I, 1774: künic. On ü : e, i vid.
§7, 6.

295. [kenne] - be able - Lex. I, 1778: kunnen, künnen.
For the many forms with the emphasis on the e vocalism

and its parallels in the German dialects vid. §52, 3.

296. kepfle (56, 17)n. - poor little head - Lex. I, 1676:
köpfelîn. On ö : e vid. §5, 1. On le suffix vid.
§66.

297. [kêren] - sweep up - du kêrst (76, 12) - Lex. I, 1552.
A. [six kêren] - turn to, pay attention to - hot six
... gekêt (85, 6) -; On r syncope [t] vid. §25,
2 A a.

298. [kerwišle]n. - feather duster - kerwišlix (53, 13) -
DWb. IX, 429; SWb. IV, 347: kehrwisch. On lix
plural vid. §66.

299. keterli (91, 5)n. - tomcat. On li suffix vid. §66.

300. kexi (35, 4)f. - cook - Lex. I, 1661: köchinne stf.
On ö : e vid. §5, 1.

301. kezle n.: krîxt dir 'š kezle in bukkel noif (67, 6) -
you act in a humble fashion - DWb. V, 292: katzen-
buckel - originally referred to cats who bow when
they go around a person in a fawning manner - then
applied to the humble bows and gestures of subservient
people.

302. kîfen (14, 2) - gape - DWb. IV, 1, 7343: giefn - dialectical word preserved especially in the Alemannic
and Low Rhine dialects.

303. [six kîlen] - to vent one's rage, to "let off steam" -
max nit, daš ix mix an dir kîl (16, 4), mext ix mix...
kîlen (76, 10) - Lex. I, 1764: küelen. On üe - î
vid. §19, 1.

304. [kindbettsišsele]n. - childbirth bowl - kindbettsišse-
lix (48, 2) - SWb. IV, 377: kindbetterschüssel f. -
bowls in which food is brought to women about to give
birth (Balingen, Stadt u. Oberamt). On lix plural

vid §66.

305. [kinderle]n. - boy, oh boy! - kinderlix (70, 1) - vid.
§66.

306. kirzlix (63, 4) - recently - Lex. I, 1799: kurzlîche.
On u : i vid. §5, 4.

307. [kisšele]n. - cushion placed on hips to fill out
figure - hiften kisšelix (48, 3) - Lex. I, 1801:
küssen. On ü : i vid. §7, 1; on lix plural vid. §66.

308. [kittele]n. - smock, frock - kittele (7, 6) - Lex. I,
1590: kitel, kittel stm.; DWb. V, 862.

309. [kiz]f. - kid - kiz (59, 3) - Lex. I, 1595: kitze,
kiz stn. DWb. V, 868: n. Upper German word; Paul 286:
Upper German and East Franconian.

310. [klâd]n. - dress - klâd (13, 7; 92, 14), klâder (3, 5;
48, 12), klaidr (23, 1), klaider (63, 20), klâdlix
(85, 15) - Lex. I, 1618: kleit stn. pl. kleit u.
kleider - vid. ei : â §15, 1. On lix plural vid. §66.

311. klânigkat (30, 16)f. - trifle - Lex. I, 1615: kleineg-
heit stf. On ei : â vid. §15, 1.

312. [klêšle]n. - dumpling - klêšle (52, 9) - Lex. I, 1683:
kloezel stn. On oe : ê vid. §13, 1. DWb. V, 1248;
Paul 290.

313. [klimpern] - "tickle the ivories" - klimper (21, 1) -
Paul, 289; DWb. V, 1169.

314. [klitšer]m. - tumble by sliding, slipping - Rh. Wb. II,
1276; DWb. IV, 1, 131: glitscher m. On g and k interchange vid. §40, 2.

315. klozzen (23, 8) - gape - klitsin (43, 9) - Lex. I,
1039: glotzen. On g and k interchange vid. §40, 2.

316. [klozzer]m. - "blinker" - klozzerš (16, 7) - SWb. III,
709; glotzerm; Schmeller I, 979. On š plural vid. §64.

317. [kofê]n. - coffee - Heyse 179. Schulz-Basler I, 317:
up to late in the eighteenth century the forms were
both koffee and kaffee.

318. [kofêkrîgle]n. - coffee pitcher - kofêkrîgle (68, 3) -
Lex. I, 1753: krügelin stn. On üe : î vid. §19, 1.

319. [kopf]m. - head - kopf (13, 19) - Lex. I, 1676: kopf
stn. pl. köpfe. On ö : e vid. §5, 1.

320. kopfekišen (82, 16)n. - pillow - Lex. I, 1676: kopf-
küssen. On ü : i vid. §7, 1.

321. [korb]n.: mir hot er ain koreb gebe (58, 18) - he
refused my proposal of marriage. DWb. V, 1800:
different explanations (1) A basket was placed in the
way of an unwelcome suitor as an allegorial answer.
(2) The girl gave instead of an answer a real basket
without a bottom to it. (3) Originally a lover was
hoisted up to the window of his beloved one in the
night in a basket and in case of a refusal of love was
let down with such force to the earth that the bottom
broke and he had to fall through. This phrase was in
frequent use in the seventeenth and eighteen century.

322. [koze] - short - koze (35, 10) - Lex. I, 1797: kurz.
On u : o[r] vid. §6, 3. On r syncope vid. §25, 2 A d.

323. [kraizerle]n. - little coin - kraizerlix (25, 7) -
Lex. I, 1742: kriuzelîn stn. On iu : ai vid. §17, 1.
On lix plural vid. §66.

324. krenzle (25, 24)n. - club - Sanders I, 1016.

325. krepfle (56, 14)n. - triangular shaped dumpling of
dough with liver inside - krepflix (56, 8) - DWb. V.
2065: kräpfel n. (Thur.) f. (Wetterau - kräppel);
Bav. - Aust. krapfl for kräpflein. Kretschmer 358:
kräpel, kräppel - Middle German form. Paul 303.

Throughout Germany and America today this dumpling is
eaten by Jews on Friday nights and holidays. It is
a delicacy.

326. krippel (59, 25)m. – mole – DWb. IV, 1, 253: griebel;
SWb. II, 829. On g and k interchange vid. §40, 2.

327. krist (32, 21)m. – Christian – Lex. I, 1737: kristen
stswmf. DWb. II, 619.

328. [kruŝpendent]m. – name of a newspaper – kruŝpendent
(28, 5) – Heyse 218: Correspondent.

329. [kugel]n. – raisin pudding – kugel (70, 4) – SWb. IV,
823; Schmeller I, 1231.

330. kumîs (74, 12)n. – salesman – Heyse 187: commis.

331. kumme (1, 8) – come – Lex. I, 1668: komen str. I, 2.
For the various forms with the predominance of the u
forms in the German dialects vid. §47 B class IV.

332. [kumpliment]n. – compliment – kumplimendr (37, 13),
kuplimenten (74, 14) – Heyse 191: compliment n. pl.e.

333. [kumûter]n. – counter – kumûter (53, 12) – Heyse 192:
comptoir or comtoir.

334. [kuntiter]n. – confectioner – kuntiter (45, 5) – Heyse
197: conditor; Rh. Wb. IV, 1184: konditor, kunditer.
DWb. II, 634: conditor.

335. [kunzert]n. – concert – kunzerten (3, 6) – Els. Wb. II,
453.

336. [kûr] f.: max si a bisle di kûr (51, 10) – flirt a
little. Cf. French cour.

337. kuttern (49, 8)n. – giggling. A. si kuttert (53, 9) –
she giggles – Lex. I, 1804.

L.

338.   lâd: loš si six nêr nit sain so lâd (32, 4) – "don't
be so difficult to get along with" – Lex. I, 1871:
leit. On ei : â vid. §15, 1.

339.   lâfen (3, 11; 83, 20) – run lâft (16, 10), lâf (90, 13),
lâft (69, 10) – Lex. I, 1967: loufen. On ou : â vid.
§16, 1.

340.   [laienen] – read, especially in prayer – laient (32,
10) Bischoff...
leien, leyen: lesen (ein Gebet usw. im vorgeschrie-
benen Tonfalle) hersagen – cf. Latin legere. Landau
and Wachstein 126: common in all Yiddish dialects 'to
read'; Mieses, p. 238: leien – older form, laynen used
today – both in the sense of to read; DWb. VI, 779:
lesen – to read a prescribed prayer–used in old Bavarian and even today in this sense.

341.   [lait]f. – people – lait (31, 1) – Lex. I, 1942: liut
stm. On iu : ai vid. §17, 1.

342.   lange (28, 19) – reach out to get something – gelangt
(45, 6) – Lex. I, 1820; DWb. VI, 171.

343.   [leffele]n. – little spoon – leffele (9, 5) – Lex. I,
1886: leffel stm. On le suffix vid. §66. Kluge 362;
Paul 331; SWb. IV, 1273.

344.   lefohre (53, 15) – dark yellow – Heyse 532: liver.

345.   [lêkux]m. – honey cake – lêkuxen (45, 15) – DWb. VI,
487; Kluge 207; Paul 330: South and West German word
for honey cake; Mieses, p. 241: traces lejkix (näsche-
rei) to Ital. lecco and Bavarian leckkich as a popular
adaptation of a foreign loan – a most questionable hypo-
thesis.

346.   [lider] - leather - lidere (72, 24) - Lex. I, 1901:
       liderên.

347.   loiben (10, 9) - praise - Lex. I, 1947: loben. On
       o : oi vid. §4, 2.

348.   [loin]m. - reward - loin (3, 24; 52, 15; 63, 1), lohn
       (2, 6) - Lex. I, 1953: lôn stem. On ô : oi vid. §12,
       1.

349.   loine (89, 16) - reward - Lex. I, 1953: lônen. On ô
       : oi vid. §12, 1.

350.   [loit]n. - one-half ounce - loit (39, 16) - Lex. I,
       1961: lôt stn. On ô : oi vid. §12, 1. Kluge 365;
       SWb. IV, 1303.

351.   [lûder]n. - wretch, bitch - lûder (48, 22) - Lex. I,
       1985: luoder stn. On ou : û vid. §18, 1. Paul 333;
       DWb. VI, 1233.

352.   [luft]m. - breeze, air - in liften (44, 5) - Lex. I,
       1977 luft stm. pl. lufte u lüfte. On ü : i vid. §7,
       1.

M.

353.   mâd (19, 3)f. - girl - Lex. I, 2007: maget, magt stf.
contr. meit, mait. On ei : â <u>vid</u>. §15, 1.

354.   mâdle (9, 3)n. - little girl - mâdlix (15, 1) - Lex. I,
2008: magetlîn, megetlîn dem. to maget. SWb. IV, 1376:
mädlein. On the diminutive suffix <u>vid</u>. §66.

355.   mâg: itzt hot si in mâg nit sagen (13, 1) - now she
has the devil - Tendlau, <u>Prov</u>.#436, 439.

356.   maile (46, 6)n. - mouth - Lex. I, 2220: mûle stn. On
û : ai <u>vid</u>. §14, 3. Schmeller I, 1585.

357.   main aid (62, 2)m. - I swear - Schmeller I, 36.

358.   maišlix: maišlix still (55, 3) - as quiet as a mouse -
Lex. I, 2258: mûslîehen. On û : ai <u>vid</u>. §14, 3. SWb.
IV, 1568; Roedder p. 459.

359.   mange (28, 18) - mangle i.e. smooth with a mangle (a
machine for smoothing linen) - Lex. I, 2030. Kretschmer 392: used in South Germany (Elsass, Freiburg,
Württemburg, Bavaria and Luxembourg - a word older than
rollen).

360.   mânšoxe (40, 4) - dear me!; imagine that! - SWb. IV,
1579: mein - used as an interjection; SWb. V, 1092;
Schmeller II, 364: schoch - an expression of astonishment. On ei : â <u>vid</u>. §15, 1.

361.   [mariaš]f.? - card game like Pinochle or Sixty-six -
Schmeller I, 1637; SWb. IV, 1474.

362.   [marine]m. - merino: a fine French all-wool dress fabric for women, twilled on both sides - originally made
of merino wool - marine (34, 4) - Heyse 571.

363.   [maxerloin]n. - payment for work - maxerloin (7, 18) -

Lex. I, 2003: machlôn stmn. On ô : oi vid. §12, 3.
Kluge 368.

364. [memme]f. - mother - memme (5, 10) - Vilmar p. 268:
used in Hessen by Jewish children when calling their
mother. The word was in general use in Elsass. Paul
340: mamá, from French mamen, but in South Germany
máma, mámme and used thus in the speech of the common
folk. DWb. VI, 1517.

365. mendle (61, 2)n. - little man (ironically, scornfully)
- SWb. IV, 1446; SWz. Wb. IV, 320; Schmeller II, 578.
Lex. I, 2102: mennelîn stn. On nn : nd vid. §36, 5.
On le suffix vid. §66. DWb. VI, 1595.

366. mêlkiwelle (31, 8; 82, 19)n. - vat for flour - DWb. VI,
1869: mehlkübelein; Els. Wb. I, 418: mëlkkübel.

367. mer (1, 4) - one - Schmeller I, 1641 - vid. §70, 3
for dialectical diffusion.

368. [mêr]f.: ebbeŝ der mêr (11, 6), ebeŝ der mêr (74, 18) -
something the matter - Tendlau, Prov. #150; - was is
nox der mêr (13, 17) - what is the matter - Tendlau,
Prov. #150.

369. [mîder]n. - bodice - mîder (13, 4) - Lex. I, 2238:
mooder, müeder stn.; Kluge 390; SWb. IV, 1781. On
üe : î vid. §19, 1.

370. [mîglixkât]f.: tu si six an mîglixkât ân (46, 7) -
do what you can - Lex. I, 2218: mügelichkeit stf.
On ü : i vid. §7, 1.

371. [milix]f. - milk - milix (32, 11) - Lex. I, 2136; SWb.
IV, 1665.

372. mir (8, 2; 10, 12; 10, 14) - we - Schmeller I, 1641.
Vid. also §70, 1.

373. miŝŝen (37, 4) - have to, be obliged to - Lex. I,
2217; müezen. On üe : i vid. §191.

374.   [moil]n. - mouth - for aier moil (10, 5) - Lex. I,
2220: mûle, mûle stn. On û : oi <u>vid</u>. §14, 1. A
[moil]n. - time - a nânzigś moil (61, 13) - Lex. I,
2014: mâl stn. On â : oi <u>vid</u>. §8, 1.

375.   [moislox]n. - mousehole - moislox (14, 3) - Lex. I,
2192: miuseloch stn. On iu : oi <u>vid</u>. §17, 1b.

376.   mokkel (41, 1)m. - sow - Lex. I, 2193; SWb. IV, 1721,
1722.

377.   [mopitigs]n. - substatial food - mopitigś (45, 9) -
DWb. VI, 2525: mops m. - first appearing at the of
the sixteenth century, of Middle and Low German origin
- refers to the stupid expression of a person - <u>cf</u>.
Middle English moppe, New English mope - allusion is
to a face with a pug nose; then the name was applied
to a bull dog - very popular throughout Germany in
the seventeenth and eighteen century. In the Upper
German dialects appeared mopper and moppel to designate this type of animal. Its popularity lead the
common people to deduce figurative expressions based
upon its form and peculiarities. Hence, the allusion
may be to something to eat that is staple, substantial.

378.   moregrifiśe gaś (83, 11) - name of street in the
eastern section of Nürnberg, running at a right angle
to Marienthorgraben; and better known as Marienstrasse,
the main street in Marienvorstadt.

379.   moring (12, 21; 34, 3) - tomorrow - SWb. IV, 1756.

380.   mûlen (12, 21)n. - painting - Lex. I, 2019: malen.
On a : û <u>vid</u>. §1, 8.

381.   [mumfel]m. - mouthful - mumfel (84, 18) - SWb. IV,
1807; DWb. VI, 2668: mumpfel.

382.   [musikśtand]n. - music stand - musikstender (37, 14) -
DWb. X, 2, 740.

383. [muthel]m. - pattern - muthel (48, 9) – Els. Wb. I, 652.

N.

384. nâ (45, 8), nân (46, 5; 47, 3), nain (18, 11) - no - Lex. II, 51: nein. On ei : â vid. §15, 1.

385. [nai] - new - nai (60, 12), naie (3, 5), naien (37, 4) - Lex. II, 92: niuwe. On iu : ai vid. §17, 1.

386. nân : nikš mêr nân (60, 16) - it does not go any deeper into the subject - nân - New High German hinein.

387. narrenborger (15, 15) - Nürnberg.

388. [naxt - šarrem]m. - (1) night-chamber, French pot de chambre (2) a euphemism for excrement - naxt - šarrem (83, 19). The Jewish legend favors the latter interpretation - cf. Heyse 163: charme m. - literally charm.

389. nebix (1, 7; 3, 10) - alas - Bisdhoff p. 61: nebbich, nebboch - unfortunately - presumably from Slavic ne bohu (nicht bei (nit) Gott) or more particularly from Bohemian ne bohy; Landau and Wachstein, p. 128: common in all Yiddish dialects - related to Čech. nebohý - wretched, Little Russian neboha - poor devil; Tendlau, Prov. #633: from ne bi uch (cf. Hebrew parallel: lo alechem). This latter conjecture is fallacious.

390. [nêgele]n. - carnation - nêgelix (72, 25) - Lex. II,

47: negelkîn. On e : ê vid. §2, 2. On lix plural
vid. §66.

391. nêhe (28, 16; 32, 12) - sew - Lex. II, 29: naejen.
On ae : ê vid. §9, 2. On loss of intervocalic j vid.
§22, 3.

392. nemme (11, 2; 58, 16) - take - Lex. II, 52. For various forms vid. §47 B class IV.

393. [nibbeš]m. - "stinker" - nibbeš (59, 9) - DWb. VII,
851: nipp m. - das nippen; DWb. VII, 852: nippen -
to nip.

394. [nikšnuzze]f. - good-for-nothing - der nikšnuzzen
(89, 7) - DWb. VII, 729: Nichtsnutzm.

395. nit : nit wi fiel (64, 7) - not much - wi pleonistic
- common to all German dialects - vid. §86; Lex. II,
831, niht, nit, nihts. A. nig: wider gott nig
geret - vid. #212 of glossary. B. nikš (2, 20). On
ht : ks in the German dialects vid. §38, 3.

396. noifegâbel f.: mit a noifegâbel (83, 4) - with an
oven fork - DWb. VII, 1159: ofengabel f. - hence
false syllable division - vid. 826, 3.

397. [noitel]n. - piece of paper - noitel (70, 18) - SWb.
IV, 2067: notel.

398. noixer (21, 1); noixet (76, 15) - afterwards - SWb. IV,
1887: nach-her adv. shortened to nacher, nocher,
noxərt.

399. [noixgenge] - be of interest to, or affect an individual - Lex. II, 4: nâchgân. On â : oi vid. §8, 1;
Schmeller I, 921: gengen = gehen. Vid. §50 B; §54.

400. nor (32, 18), nêr (11, 5) - only, just - Lex. II, 122;
III, 800: nûr. On û : e, e in dialects vid. §14, 4.

401. nûbler (36, 9) - more elegant - Kluge 418: nobel.

402. nunterbett (82, 16)n. - a lower bed. For false syllable division vid. §26, 3.

O.

403. [obend]m. - evening - obendŝ (41, 14) nobez (45, 12), in ganzen nobend (38, 9) - Lex. I, 10: âbent stm. On â : o vid. §8, 1; on false syllable division vid. §26, 3; on s plural vid. §61, 64.

404. odentlix (11, 13); ondtlix (15, 7); orndlix (37, 3) - regularly, usually - Lex. II, 161: ordenlich. On loss of r before dental vid. §25, 2 A b.

405. [ohren] - pray - ohr (21, 20, ohrt (32, 10); ohren (39, 1) - Schmeller I, 134: oren (jüdisch; Wetterau) - to pray loudly and in a sing-song fashion - related to Latin orare. Mieses p. 239: common throughout the entire West Yiddish dialect.

406. oi (9, 12; 26, 17; 56, 13; 88, 9) - oh! - SWb. V, 51.

407. oib (5, 4) - although - Lex. II, 127: obe, ob. On o : oi vid. §4, 3.

408. oiben (48, 5; 54, 3) - above, to the top - Lex. II, 131: obene, oben. On o: oi vid. §4, 3.

409. [oiber - un untergewêr]n. - musket and sword - oiber - un untergewêr (74, 16) - DWb. VII, 1087; DWb. XI, 3, 1580.

410. oif (1, 16), of (61, 12), uf (69, 13) - upon - Lex. II, 1687: ûf. On û : oi, o, u vid. §14, 2.

411. [oifdriken] - stamp upon - oifgedrikt - Lex. I, 470: drücken. On ü : i <u>vid</u>. §7, 1.

412. six oiffîren (22, 16) - behave - Lex. II, 1707: ûvrü-eren. On ü : oi <u>vid</u>. §14, 2; on üe : i <u>vid</u>. §19, 1.

413. oiffreŝŝen (14, 1) - eat up - Lex. III, 107: vrēzzen.

414. oifgetrag (76, 5)n. - serving of food - SWb. I, 427: auf-trage - to serve food on tables - used only in Franconia.

415. oifheren (90, 5) - stop - Lex. II, 1694: ûfhoeren. On û : oi <u>vid</u>. §14, 2; on oe : e <u>vid</u>. §13, 1.

416. [oifkraxen]: wi'n pritŝebakkel der bukkel is oifge-kraxt - burst, snap open - Lex. I, 1700: krachen; DWb. I, 678: aufkrachen.

417. oifraisen (23, 4) - tear open - Lex. II, 1699: ûfrîsen. On û : oi <u>vid</u>. §14, 2; on î : ai <u>vid</u>. §15, 1.

418. oiftraiben (6, 8) - round up - SWb. I, 428; DWb. I, 762: auftreiben.

419. oifzêlen (80, 4) - measure out; count up - Lex. II, 1708: ûfzaln, ûfzeln. On û : oi <u>vid</u>. §14, 2; DWb. I, 782: schläge aufzählen.

420. ois (2, 19; 23, 13) - throughout, out of - Lex. II, 2018: ûz. On û : oi <u>vid</u>. §14, 1.

421. oisbruten (55, 6) - hatch - Lex. II, 2020: ûzbrüeten. On û : oi <u>vid</u>. §14, 1. SWb. I, 459; ausbruten - used transitively - lack of umlaut generally common in Suabia.

422. [oisgêben] - marry off - du heŝt si oisgêben (14, 17) - Lex. II, 2018; ûzgeben. On û : oi <u>vid</u>. §14, 1. On verb form in dialect <u>vid</u>. §47 B class IV.

423. oisgeloŝŝen (25, 15) - wild, dissolute - Lex. II, 2025: ûzgelâzen. SWb. I, 484: ausgelassen - refers es-pecially to children. DWb. I, 873.

424.   oisklingle (24, 3) – make known by ringing a bell –
Lex. II, 2924: ûzklingelen. DWb. I, 894: ausklingeln.
On û : oi <u>vid</u>. §14, 1.

425.   [oispuzzer]m. – "polishing off" – oispuzzer (69, 16) –
DWb. I, 927.

426.   oisrêten (75, 9) – finish speaking – Lex. II, 2027:
ûz-e-reden. On û : oi <u>vid</u>. §14, 1; on e : ê <u>vid</u>. §2,
2; on d : t <u>vid</u>. §36, 1.

427.   [oisrotten] –exterminate – oisrotten (89, 5) – Lex. II,
2028: Middle German ûzroten. DWb. I, 940: ausrotten.
On û : oi <u>vid</u>. §14, 1.

428.   [oišnaiden] – carve out – ân oisgsnittner karpes (1,
3) – Lex. II, 1035: snîden – no examples with <u>ûz</u>.

429.   [oisštên] – endure – ix oisštê (38, 14) – Lex. II,
2032: ûzstân, – stên, SWb. I, 525; DWb. I, 984:
ausstehen. On û : oi <u>vid</u>. §14, 1; on ê vocalism in
dialects <u>vid</u>. §54.

430.   [oiszêrung]f. – expenditure of money – oiszêrung (14,
19) – Lex. III, 1091: zerung stf.; SWb. I, 541:
auszerung f.

431.   oix (62, 5), âx (5, 8; 90, 16) – also – Lex. II, 181:
ouch. On ou : oi, â <u>vid</u>. §16, 3.

432.   [oix]n. – eye – oixen (23, 4; 59, 19) – Lex. II, 182:
ouge. On ou : oi <u>vid</u>. §16, 3; on g : x <u>vid</u>. §40, 3.
SWb. I, 442: āx (Frk.).

433.   [ott]m. – place – in ganzen ott (79, 16) – Lex. II,
169: ort stnm. On <u>r</u> syncope <u>vid</u>. §25, 2 A a.

434.   ox (66, 8) – oh! an interjection indicating sudden
pain – DWb. VII, 1729; SWb. V, 28.

P.

435.   pápa (83, 14)m. - father, daddy, papa - Paul 392:
         papá from the French like mamá; however, in South
         Germany among the common folk the pronunciation is
         pápa which leads also to a páppe form as a result of
         the change in accent - a similar phenomenon in Ameri-
         can Yiddish.

436.   [pâr, bâr]n. - few - pâr (9, 6; 10, 2; 22, 21), bâr
         (2, 11) - Lex. II, 204: pâr. On p : b vid. §31, 1a.

437.   [pêrlix]h. - bead - kûlêrte pêrlix (49, 3) - Lex. II,
         218: pêrle stf. On lix plural vid. §66.

438.   peršoihn (13, 21)f. - beauty - Paul 394: Middle High
         German persone from Latin persona which originally
         referred to a mask worn by an actor; then it designated
         the role of the actor; with all this was associated
         the exterior appearance of the actor - hence, an ex-
         ternal quality of beauty. Like the French it refers
         to the feminine sex. DWb. VII, 1561; SWb. I, 880:
         perschon.

439.   [pfopern] - rumble - pfopert (67, 4) - DWb. VII, 1814:
         pfupfern - a provincial word indicating a restless
         movement (Bavarian); pfopfern (Wtz.).

440.   pfuzi - kappore (12, 10)n. - a horrible thing - vid.
         # 280, B.

441.   [pikštûl]f. - pistol - pikštûl (47, 2) - Heyse 701:
         pistole. Els. Wb. II, 110: pistûl; Els. Wb. II, 12:
         pikso, pikš f.; Kluge 347. Our form is the result of
         the contamination of two forms in dialects in which ks
         : s regularly (Hessen, Thüringia, Mittelfranken,

Südelsass, Westschwaben) - Weise p. 33.

442.   plepple (77, 12) - babble - DWb. VII, 1897: pläppern, plappern - an iterative verb to plappen - onomatopoetic meaning - to blab... It is difficult to account for the alliterative or assimilative changes of the liquid consonant l.

443.   [pohs̓er]m. - faker - pohs̓er (23, 20) - SWb. I, 1311: boser m. Vid. §30, 31 for sound value of b in Upper German dialects. Cf. English poser, French poseur.

444.   [poige]f. - drum - mit poigen (85, 23) - Lex. II, 305: pûke swf. On û : oi vid. §14, 1. On k: g vid. §33.

445.   pompern (22, 11) - hammer - Lex. II, 307: pumpern. On u : o in Suabian vid. §6, 6.

446.   poppele (54, 7)n. - puppet - DWb. VII, 2251: püpplein.

447.   [popperle]n. - ugly, misshapen creature - popperlix (13, 15) - SWb. I, 1293: poperle; Schmeller I, 400; DWb. VII, 2000: popel, pöpel. On lix plural vid. §66.

448.   [portrett]n. - portrait - portretter (54, 5) - Heyse 718: portrait pl. s. SWz. Wb. IV, 1634: port(e)rett pl. unchanged or portretter (Thurgau, Zürich). On er plural vid. §61.

449.   [pots̓amper]m. - pot de chambre, i.e. chamber pot - Els. Wb. II, 124; SWb. I, 1326: potschamber m.

450.   praxt (36, 7)f. - splendid affair - Paul 401.

451.   prits̓e - bakkel (82, 5)m. - court jester; a personification in a comical manner of the wielder of a broad stick. SWz. Wb. IV, 1105; Kluge 34; SWb. IV, 564.

452.   [prits̓er]f. - broad wooden board used by court jester - Kluge 457: pritsche f.

453.   prowîren (19, 10; 22, 7) - attempt, try out - Lex. II,

299: probieren. On b : w <u>vid</u>. §30, 2.

454. publizîren (64, 3) – announce – publizîrt (91, 15),
puplizîrt (28, 3).

455. [pumpernikkel]m. – operetta – pumpernikkel (23, 13) –
DWb. VII, 2231: originally a popualr folk song.

456. [pumpeln] – pound, pump – pumpelt (68, 4) – DWb. VII,
2228.

457. [pumpf]m. – poke – pumpf (84, 7) – SWb. I, 1520:
bumpf m. <u>Cf</u>. English <u>bump</u>.

458. pumš (73, 15) – cops! – SWb. I, 1520: <u>bumps</u>.

459. putš̌ (84, 9) – bang! – SWb. I, 1560; Els. Wb. II, 124;
Swz. Wb. IV, 1936.

R.

460.	[raien]: 'š rait 'ir nit (46, 8) - you will not regret it - Lex. II, 774: riuwen, riwen (Middle German also with the dative). On iu : ai vid. §17.

461.	raišen: â raišen (17, 1) - "tear around" - Lex. II, 447: rîzen stv. II intr. On î : ai vid. §11, 1. DWb. VIII, 754.

462.	[râisig]n. - branches - fun raisig (85, 12) - Lex. II, 456: rîsach, rîsech stn. On î : ai vid. §11, 1. DWb. VIII, 774: limited to High German.

463.	[raiter]m.: a nenglišen raiter (64, 5) - an English jockey, i.e. a skilled rider - cf. ein lateinischer Reiter - a clumsy rider - Wander III, p. 1654.

464.	[rêr]f. - reed used as a spoon - in der rêr (68, 2) - Lex. II, 486 rore, roere stswf. On ô : ê vid. §13, 1.

465.	[six resolfîren] - make up one's mind - six resolfîrt (28, 2) - Heyse 796.

466.	rêsûn, f, a rêsûn (88, 7) - a sensible thing - Heyse 769.

467.	rêten (2, 11) - speak - hot ir geret a guten Schiddich (Verlobung) - has arranged a good marriage for her - Lex. II, 367: reden, past part, geret. Vid. §36, 1 for pronunciation of t in dialects.

468.	retut (90, 11)n. - masquerade ball - Heyse 780.

469.	six rîren (19, 11) - move - si six rîrt (54, 23) - Lex. II, 529: rüeren swv. On üe : i vid. §19, 1.

470.	roit (72, 21) - red - Lex. II, 502: rôt. On ô : oi vid. §12, 1.

471.   roiten (15, 6) – save – Lex. II, 411; retten. On e
        : oi vid. §2, 6.

472.   [rokšôš]m. – coat tail – rok-šêš (72, 3) – DWb. VIII,
        1106: rockschoss m. – Viennese rockschezl.

473.   rûs-pîpele (58, 18)n. – soot cinderelle – DWb. VII,
        2251; Kluge 460.

                                S.

474.   [sâf]f. – soap – sâf (71, 12) – Lex. II, 854:   seife,
        swf. On ei : â vid. §15, 1.

475.   [sâgen] – say – sâxt (22, 3; 22, 9) – Lex. II, 711:
        sagen.   On g : x in the dialects vid. §40, 3.

476.   [sâltenzer]m. – rope dancer – sâltenzer (13, 8) – Lex.
        II, 856: seil stn; Lex. II, 1425: tenzer stm. On
        ei : â vid. §15, 1.

477.   sain (5, 7) – to be. For forms and parallels in the
        German dialects vid. §55.

478.   [šâde]m. – shade – in šâden (72, 16) – Lex. II, 671:
        schate stswm. In the sound value of d in the Upper
        German dialects vid. §37, 3.

479.   [šaf]m.: suttel šaf (83, 4) – saddle bucket used for
        coal – Lex. II, 628.

480.   šaiden (57, 10) – depart – Lex. II, 684 scheiden – se-
        parate; with reflexive – to go away.

481.   šak (68, 4) – another name for jukl – vid. dramatis

personae.

482. [šâl]n. - kerchif - šâl (36, 4) -. SWb. V, 667; Els.
Wb. II, 406; Swz. Wb. VIII, 534.

483. [šallmai]f. - pipe - sallmai (72, 15) - Lex. II, 645:
schalmîe. On î : ai vid. §11, 1.

484. [šambelle]m. - sullen, queer fellow - mit dên šambelle
(15, 13) - SWb. V, 681: schampeler m.

485. šarlox (71, 21) - scarlet - Lex. II, 663: scharlachîn.

486. [šatzen] - roll up - gšatzte arwelix (85, 16) - DWb.
VIII, 2281.

487. šên (5, 2) - beautiful, fine - comp. šenner (21, 11),
superl. šenšte (64, 1), šenšten (79, 13); šên (1, 1) -
already - vid. §13, 1.

484. šinden (39, 15) - skin one - Paul 444.

485. šîr (47, 2) - almost - Lex. II, 726; Kluge 517.

486. šîren (28, 15) - clean - Lex. II, 762; Kluge 515; DWb.
VIII, 2621: in the Middle Rhine of the fifteenth
century as schiuren (polish through rubbing) - a
terminus technicus used by metal artisans.

487. [šitten]: šitt alleš der frâ in šûx nain (10, 8) - un-
load everything upon the wife; make her be responsible
- Lex. II, 833: schütten. On ü : i vid. §7, 1.

488. šiwele (83, 2)n. - bushel, pile - Lex. II, 808:
schübel; Schmeller II, 362. On ü : i vid. §7, 1; on
b : w vid. §30, 2.

489. [six slaixen] - steal away - hot er six gšlixen (80,
13) - Lex. II, 973: slîchen stv. p.p. geslichen.

490. [slamper]m. - dirty, squalid man - îr šlamper (88, 5) -
Paul 445; DWb. IX, 439: schlamper m. - parallel form
schlammer - unkempt man - in Upper German dialects as
f. schlampere - dirty woman - cf. modern American
Yiddish schlump - a filthy person; schlumperai -

filthiness.

491. šlemîl (16, 5); slumuêl (88, 2)m. - an awkward "Jonah"
- Tendlau, Prov. #625: schlemiel - possibly of Hebrew
or of German origin. If from the German, it is related to the word schlim (askew). It refers to a
person all of whose activities always go wrong. If
from the Hebrew there is a name Schelumiel which
corresponds to the German Gottfried. The South German
Jews use with the same significance: schlemóchem,
schlemśchemte! schlem-och-ihm! (ach ihm), Mieses,
p. 223: schlemiehl: "schlymosl" (schlimm + masal)
among the Eastern Jews. Šlemîl is a West Yiddish
shortening of this "schlymosl" of it may be a trans-
formed Slavic word Szalawila (a stupid, good-for-
nothing). Tendlau's Hebrew explanation is preferable
- vid. also Numbers I, 6: Schelumiel, the son of
Zarishaddai.

492. šlîfen (14, 3) - slip - šlîft (7, 5) - Lex. II, 974:
sliefen. On ie : î vid. §20, 1.

493. [šlim-massol]m. - misfortune - šlim-massol (69, 2) -
Tendlau, Prov. p. 140: massal - planet or star;
massal tob - good star; schlimm-massel - an unlucky
star. It may be related to Italian schiamazzo, and
also a corruption of schlimmsal like trübsal -; common
adjectiye form is schlimmassiltig. Paul 451: Middle
High German slimp - fundamental concept of askew still
preserved sporadically in the eighteenth century.
Then the word assumed the meanings of bad, sick,
insignificant.

494. šlimmer (63, 2)m. - evil person, malefactor - DWb. IX,
721: schlimmerer.

495. šlinke šlanke (12, 11) - in an indolent, aimless
manner - Lex. II, 980: slinc s. linc, lenc -kes,
adj. - awkward, unknowingly; Lex. II, 981: slingen
stv. I, 3 - move back and forth - cf. English to
slink. DWb. IX, 743: schlinken verb - a parallel
form to schlingen. DWb. IX, 480: schlanken verb -
to walk around indolently. The phrase is typically
Bavarian. Schmeller II, 528.

496. šloifen (43, 17; 54, 8; 65, 9) - sleep - Lex. II,
953: slâfen. On â : oi vid. §8, 1.

497. [šluppern] - shuffle - šlupperts (21, 4) - Lex. II,
992.

498. [šmekke]f. - flowers - šmekken (53, 14) - DWb. IX,
961: common in Upper Germany. SWb. V, 986.

499. šmunzle (79, 7) - smirk - Lex. II, 1019: smunzeln swv.
s.v.a. smutzeln, smonzeln. Lex. II, 1020: smutzen -
to force oneself to laugh. Kluge 533: note n infix
already prevalent since the beginning of the eighteenth century in schmerzen; l appears first in the fifteenth century. DWb. IX, 1133.

500. šmûsen (10, 4); šmûsen (78, 5) - gossip, chatter
idly - DWb. IX, 1135: to speak, relate - a widely
spread dialectical word (Upper and Middle Germany) of
Yiddish provenience. The verb is formed from the
noun schmus, m. - talk, derived from Hebrew schmûôth
(tales). Kluge 532; Tendlau, Prov. #108.

501. [šnekkè]m. - roll - šnekken (45, 10) - Schmeller II,
567.

502. [šniebele]n. - mouth - šniebelix (23, 16) - Lex. II,
1027: snebelîn stn. DWb. IX, 1144: schnabel - used
in a humorous vein for a person's mouth; DWb. IX,
1146: schnäbelchen n. - refers to the mouth of a girl

or woman.

503. šnizzle (48, 12) - cut into small pieces - Lex. II,
1039; Lex. III, 240; Lex. III, 1449; DWb. IX, 1361.

504. šnoifen (65, 10) - breathe heavily, pant - Lex. II,
1044: snûfen. On û : oi vid. §14, 2 - DWb. IX, 1206:
schnaufen - used in the Upper German dialects - of Low
German provenience into the Upper German dialects in
the sixteenth century. Kluge 534.

505. šnokkle (39, 3) - primp - DWb. IX, 1156: schnackeln -
an Upper German word - originally to make a resounding
loud noise, then a quick movement. It is an iterative
formation to schnacken - snatch for something quickly
DWb. IX, 1387: schnickeln - an iterative formation to
schnicken (Thuringian) - to make a short motion with
one's fingers.

506. [šoif]n. - sheep - šoif (72, 19) - Lex. II, 628:
schaf stn. On â : oi vid. §8, 1.

507. šon (2, 5) - already - Lex. II, 768: schône, schôn.
On ô : o vid. §12, 3.

508. šotxeli (30, 14)n. - little fool - Kluge 511: schaute
m. - ridiculous fool, from Hebrew šôte (stupid, foolish)
- came into West Middle German of the sixteenth century.
DWb. IX, 1606: schote (schaute) - fool - especially
the merchant who allows himself to be robbed at his
store counter. Harkavy p. 491.

509. [špektakel]m. - spectacle - špektakel (64, 8) - Kluge
573; Paul 503.

510. špekulant (50, 14)m. - thinker - Heyse 866.

511. [špenzer]m. - spencer - špenzer (13, 7) - DWb. X,
2157: used especially in Bavaria, in Württemberg.

512. špiet (62, 1) - late - Lex. II, 1072: spaete.

513. [špiktîf]m. - lorgnette - špiktîf (83, 15) - Sachs-
Villate II, 1629 spektivi - South German provincial-
ism used in familiar style.

514. [špizze]f. - lace - špizzen (60, 8) - Roedder p. 531;
cf. Fr. dentelles.

515. [špohr]f.: špohren štrâx (78, 17) - "lickity split" -
DWb. X, 1, 2686: spornstracks. Lex. II, 1125: spür,
spur stn. f. - trail, tracks. Lex. II, 1220: stroc,
strock adj., adv. - at once.

516. [šprâzen] - spread - šprâz (69, 9) - Kluge 580:
spreizen wk. verb - since the sixteenth century with
ei; parallel form eu with it until the seventeenth
century. Schmeller II, 708: spreizen (Franken.)
Paul 508.

517. [špringle]n. - hop - in ân špringle (74, 1) - DWb. X,
2, 205: sprünglein. On le suffix vid. §66.

518. [štân]m. - stone - iber štân (6, 21) - Lex. II, 1161:
stein. On ei : â vid. 815, 1. A. [stônig] - made
of rock - stânige (54, 6) - Lex. II, 1164: stelac,
-ic.

519. štande bie (78, 15; 90, 14) - at once, immediately -
Heyse 872: stante, Ital. (Latin and Italian stare -
to stand). In business correspondence to designate
the current month - stante ɔede 'stehenden fusse' -
at once. SWb. V, 1639: stantepede - štandes-ɓɔ
(Kaufbeuren: Stadt u. Bezirk) - unconditionally, at
once.

520. [štâr]m. - cataarac - host in štâr (51, 4) - you are
blind - Lex. II, 1142; Kluge 587.

521. štaz (61, 16) - instead of - Lex. II, 1144; Kluge 587.

522. [štêlaše]f. - platform - of a štêlaše (85, 20) -
Heyse 874.

523. [štelling]f. - line, except - štelling (22, 21) - Lex.
II, 1131: stallunge stf.; DWb. X, 2, 2266.

524. štên (17, 9; 22, 15) - stand - Lex. I, 1135. For various forms in the dialects vid. §54.

525. [štêpen] - stitch - gštepten (48, 1) - Lex. II, 1177;
Paul 522.

526. štêtle (10, 6)n. - little city - Lex. II, 1184: stet-
lîn. On e : ê vid. §2, 2; on le suffix vid. §66.

527. [štifen] - tease - štift (53, 19) - DWb. X, 2, 2793:
stiefeln - of unclear origin: Suabian stiften - to
stir up; Swiss stiefeln - to spur on; Middle German
stifeln, stiebeln - to chase away. Harkavy p. 497:
to sport, to play, to frolic.

528. [štîge]m. - step - štîgen (39, 6) - Lex. II, 1185.

529. [štik]n. - play - in dên štik (46, 17) - Lex. II, 1259:
stück. A. [štikkle]n. - piece, act - štikkle (41, 14),
štiklix (50, 16) - Lex. II, 1260: stückelîn. On ü :
i vid. §7, 1. On le, lix suffix vid. §66.

530. [štille]f.: in der stillen (58, 13) - in silence -
Lex. II, 1196.

531. [štoffel]m. - stupid - îr stoffel (87, 8) - DWb. X,
3, 163ff.: stoffel - shortened form of Christoffel,
nickname for Christopher, Christoph - a favorite name
used by peasants. St. Christopher, of giant size and
very awkward, carries the Christ child through the raging water, supporting himself on a tree trunk - patron
of boatsmen and treasure hunters - coarse peasant-like
face was the cause for farcical comments. His picture
hung in many homes.

532. [štois]m. - thrust - štois (89, 15) - Lex. II, 1217:
stôz stm. On ô : oi vid. §12, 1.

533. [štoite]f. - steed - štoiten (73, 13) - Lex. II, 1273: stuot stf. uo : oi vid. §18, 3. Kluge 604.

534. [štraken] - strike - štrakt (38, 9) - DWb. X, 3, 599: strackel - a cudgel with which to strike; strackeln vb. - to push, to kick, to strike.

535. [štrêlen] - comb - strêlen (71, 11) - Lex. II, 1223; Schmeller II, 813: strelen (schwäb.).

536. [štrozen] - strut - gštrozt (74, 18) - Lex. II, 1251: Paul 531.

537. štuš (1, 11)m. - stupidity - Kluge 604: Hebrew šetûth, Judeo-German štuss - used dialectically in German.

538. [šûl]f. - synagogue - šûl (10, 5; 91, 10) - SWb. V, 1174; SWb. V, 119. The Jewish synagogue of today, as well as of ancient time, has a three-fold function: (1) a place of learning and study (2) social purposes (3) prayer. Today the first named is the most important.

539. [šûlmantel]m. - long cloak that extended over one's knees - worn by the Jews as they went to their synagogue - šûlmantel (29, 1) - DWb. IX, 1958.

540. šunst (13, 14; 29, 5) - in such a manner, so - Lex. II, 1327: sunst. On s: š vid. §33, 2 C. Kluge 570. DWb. X, 1, 1736.

541. [šusseln] - move around quickly in a frivolous, light-hearted thoughtless fashion - šusselt (13, 7) - Schmeller II, 480; schoszeln, schosseln - to run thoughtlessly back and forth; DWb. IX, 2071: schusel f. - a thoughtless, empty-headed woman who moves about quickly; - especially in the eastern districts - Austrian schuserl, schussel, schuselig; schuseln, schusln, a verb - to run or act quickly - used in

Carinthia.

542. [šwanz]m.: hot mešn di hîner di šwenz noif binden (1,
13) - Tendlau, Prov. #191: "Als Spott auf den Einwand
eines Trägen, dass er zu irgend etwas keine Zeit habe:
Torheit! er hat Wichtigeres zu tun? hat den Hühnern
die Schwänze hinaufzubinden, damit sie dieselben nicht
schmutzig machen und tragen sie doch schon von selbst
oben".

543. šwaz (35, 12) - black - Lex. II, 1343: swarz. On r
syncope vid. §25, 2 A d.

544. [šwêrer]m. - oath - šwêrer (81, 12) - DWb. IX, 2746:
schwörer - jurator; also an oath.

545. [šwern] - swear - ix šwern (27, 10) - Lex. II, 1363:
swern. On n as an ending of the first singular of
the present in the dialects vid. §42.

546. [šwezen] - gossip, chatter - šwezt (15, 7) - Kluge 550.

547. sehi (2, 20; 3, 25; 28, 5) - see - Lex. II, 851:
sehen. On the various forms vid. §47 B class V.

548. sellen (10, 4) - be obliged to, ought to, have to -
Lex. II, 1053: soln. On the e vocalism in the dialects vid. §52, 5.

549. sêr (56, 1) - pained - Lex. II, 888; Kluge, 556:
schwäb; bair.

550. [siks]f.: er muš reiten, mainer siks (62, 7) - he
must driye my coach and six - DWb. IX, 2276.

551. simpel (12, 3)m. - stupid - Heyse 851. Kluge 564:
Upper German simpel first in Württemberg in 1626.
DWb. X, 1, 1061: weak-minded - especially in High
German dialects.

552. sîs (78, 8) - sweet - Lex. II, 1287: süeze. On üe :
î vid. §19, 1.

553.   [sizzen] - sit - gsizzen sen si (75, 4) - Lex. I,
       994: sitzen. On the i vocalism vid. §47 B class V;
       on the auxiliary in South German dialects vid. §81, 1.

554.   šo (9, 4; 57, 10; 57, 14) - so - SWb. V, 1428;
       Roedder 528.

556.   soifen (25, 18) - "lap up" - Lex. 1289: sûfen. On ü :
       oi vid. §14, 1; DWb. VIII, 1877; Paul 432.

557.   [sorig]f. - care, worry - sorig (14, 14) - Lex. II,
       1057 sorge stswf. DWb. X, 1, 1756: the i appearing
       after r in many German dialects is secondary in nature.

558.   [sot] - such - sotter (17, 8), sotte (31, 5), sette
       (28, 12) - DWb. X, 1, 1428 - based upon Middle High
       German sôtân - related to solch; cf. Mittelschwaben -
       a sötteger, Schlesisch - setter; cf. modern American
       Yiddish asetike... There is a possibility that these
       words may be associated with Middle High German sot
       Lex. II, 1058 - foolish adj.; cf. likewise DWb. X, 1,
       1819, but it does not fit the context throughout -
       vid. 31, 5.

559.   sox f.: doi groise sox! (18, 9) - there you big soak!
       - mit der sox is ebeš mêr (38, 10) - something is the
       matter with that soak - sox dir (16, 2) - go soak for
       yourself. Tendlau Prov. #448: "Was sochst Du da
       unthust nix?" - "Die grosse Soch! (Tochter) geht den
       ganzen Tag schlinke, schleife!" von einer erwachsenen
       Tochter, die immer müssig umherschlendert. DWb. X,
       1, 1388: sochen vb. - dialectical, especially Upper
       German.

560.   [summer]m. - sommer - summer (81, 7) - Lex. II, 1297;
       DWb. X, 1, 1509.

561.   [sûn]m. - son - sûn (5, 12) - DWb. X, 1, 1420.

562.   sûperib (90, 12) - splendid - Heyse 887.

563.   [suttel]m. - saddle - suttel šâf (83, 4) - Lex. II,
        612: satel stm. On a: u vid. §1, 8.

564.   [suxen]: wer suxt tut gfinne (77, 16) - Wander IV,
        954.

T.

565.   taig (59, 14)m. - day - Lex. II, 1384: tac. On a :
        ai vid. §1, 10.

566.   talie (34, 9)f. - cut of a dress - Heyse 899: taille
        (spr. talj).

567.   [tampur]m. - drummer - tampurs (86, 5) - DWb. XI, 1,
        102. For a plural vid. §61.

568.   tarrik (52, 22)m. - Turk ‑ Lex. II, 1580: turc-kes.
        türke, turke stswm. Els. II, 713. On u[rr] : ü : ö
        : e : a in the dialects vid. §6, 5; 21, VI.

569.   [tarrn]m.- tower - tarrner - Lex. II, 1582: turn stm.
        Schmeller I, 622: der turn. On u : a vid. §7, 2.

570.   tâte (90, 9)m. - father - Lex. II, 1408: tate swm.
        On a : â vid. §1, 2. DWb. XI, 1, 160; Elsa II, 726;
        Ochs: datte etc. Cf. English dad, daddy.

571.   [tendlen] - have fun; joke, play - tendle (19, 14) -
        DWb. XI, 4, 105: tändeln.

572.   [tieben] - steal away - tiebet (14, 3) - DWb. II,
        1091: dieben. Schmeller I, 480; Rh. Wb. I, 1349.

573.   tikniš (81, 6)f. - something big - Schmeller I, 488:

dickisch (Nürnberg). SWb. II, 190: dicke and dickne.
Els. Wb. II, 672: dicke (Unterelsass), dickere
(Münstertal).

574. [tir]f. - door - thir (88, 8) - Lex. II, 1579: tür stf.
on ü : i vid. §7, 1.

575. [tišle]n. - table cloth - tišlix (53, 12) - Lex. II,
1443: tischlach stn. DWb. XI, 1, 517: tischlach - in
the Upper German dialects. Vid. §66 on lix plural.

576. [toffel]m. - slipper - toffel (7, 2; 87, 9) - DWb.
XI, 1, 630; Schmeller I, 590; Kluge 431; Paul 543; Els.
Wb. II, 657.

577. [toigen] - be of use - toigt (12, 9) - Lex. II, 1559:
tugen, tügen; pres. touc. On ou : oi vid. §16, 3.
DWb. XI, 1, 196.

578. toin (3, 23; 29, 9) - do - Lex. II, 1575: tuon. On
the various forms in the dialects vid. §54.

579. toisend (58, 4) - thousand - Lex. II, 1590: tûsent.
On û : oi vid. §14, 1.

580. [toit]m. - death - zu toit (60, 10) - Lex. II, 1470:
tôt. On ô : oi vid. §12, 1.

581. [trêather]n. - theater - trêather (37, 4) - common
throughout all Yiddish dialects.

582. [trêer] - slow waltz - trêer (37, 4) - Lex. II, 1503:
treiros. DWb. II, 1366; Paul 112. Cf. Modern German
dreher.

583. trepfle (56, 16)n. - drop - trepflix (56, 9) - Lex. II,
1525: tröpfelîn. On ö : e vid. §5, 1. SWb. II, 402.

584. [trêr]m. - tear - trêrn (29, 16), treren (29, 18) -
Lex. II, 1149: treher. For plural vid. §61.

585. [tresše]m. - counter - tresšen (53, 19) - Weise. p. 112:
tresen from French tresoir, an Old French loan in Low

German – common in Switzerland, Elsass, Palatinate and the Rhine province.

586. trezzen (39, 7) – tease – tretztsi (38, 16) – DWb. XI, 1, 1115: Upper German trutzen since the sixteenth century regularly appears in the form tratzen, trätzen – no examples in Old High German; in Middle High German it appears in Bavarian – Austrian. The original meaning was to harass, annoy; very frequently in the sixteenth century in the Upper German dialects – to tease.

587. triben (72, 1) – over there.

588. [troibe]m. – grape – troiben (71, 25) – Lex. II, 1533: trûbe swm; swstf. On û : oi <u>vid.</u> §14, 1.

589. [trûn]m. – throne – trûn (5, 13) – Lex. II, 1524: trôn, thrône stm.

590. [tuš]m. – joyful sound, flourish – tuš (72, 16) – Kluge 636: popular word found at the borders of the Slavic speaking peoples; often in Carinthia and Austria in the meaning of loud noise – Schmeller I, 628: Bavarian dialect word.

591. tûsen (78, 4) – doze – Lex. II, 1592; DWb. II, 1760.

592. [uberthir]f. - opening - uberthir (23, 13) - Heyse 643.
593. [ûffresîren] - dress hair - ûffresîrt (71, 20) -
      Schulz-Basler I, 227.
594. [ufzug]m. - scene - mit dền ufzug (74, 18) - SWb. I,
      436: aufzug.
595. Umbšrie (19, 8); unbšrie (5, 14; 8, 18) - "knock on
      wood" - DWb. XI, 3, 350: unbeschrieen - used especial-
      ly as an absolute participle. Els. Wb. II, 514: un-
      b^{e}schröue^n - an exclamation to ward off evil from
      something praised or mentioned.
596. umštânsgsagt (11, 10; 12, 16; 16, 9) - unfortunately -
      Landau and Wachstein p. 130: "stein: dem stein ge-
      sagt: abwehrungsformel bei erwähnung eines übels um
      seiner übertragen, auf den angeredeten vorzubeugen" -
      common in North Germany. At the mention of a sorrow or
      a misfortune the Northern German Jews say: "stein 's
      geklagt"; the Polish Jews say: "im steins gesagt".
      Gerzon p. 128, #26: mištêns gesagt, imštêns gesagt -
      unfortunately - found in Elsass Yiddish. Tendlau,
      Prov. #641: "dem staan sei es geklagt" - God forbid
      that it happen to you or to me...or perhaps by
      metathesis: staan = satan. We believe the latter in-
      terpretation to be incorrect.
597. [umwenden] - change around - umgewend (21, 8) - Lex.
      III, 759: wenden swv., p.p. gewants seltener gewendet.
      On e vocalism in the past participle in the dialects
      vid. §47 A.
598. unferdrossen (58, 9) - eagerly - Lex. II, 1952; DWb.

412

XI, 3, 2021.

599. [unflâtigkait]f. - filthy doing - unflâtigkaiten (68,
8) - Lex. II, 1976: unvlaeticheit stf.; DWb. XI, 3,
563: unflätigkeit - represents the condition or
characteristic of filth rather than the action which
is represented rather by unfläteri. In the text, however, the activities are stressed.

600. unkel (28, 13)m. - uncle - Els. Wb. I, 55.

601. [unsilig] - unblissful - mit unsilige lieder (13, 3) -
Lex. II, 1930: unsaelic, saelic.

602. [ûz]n. - delight, fun - ûz (8, 2) - DWb. XI, 3, 2618:
started in Southwest Germany where the nickname was
especially popular. The fundamental concept was that
of a contemtible, foolish person who is given over to
drink. Gradually there evolved from this idea of
disdain good-natured sarcasm, irony - especially in
the dialects. In Elsass it assumes the notion of
outwitting a person on account of his stupidity. It
also goes so far as to adopt the meaning of cheating
a person.

603. ûzen: das er six fon soi ain grill last ûzen (76, 11);
ûzin: wellen mir uns ûzin (4, 19) - have fun - Kluge
646: a widely spread dialectical word (from Switzerland to Hessen, from the Rhine Palatinate to Bavaria);
- used as a nickname for Ulrich -; by 1570 in Suabian
literature only; in common use only in the middle of
the eighteenth century.

W.

604. wâden (72, 19) – graze – wâd (7, 11) – Lex. III, 704:
weiden. On ei : â vid. §15, 1.

605. [waintroibe]m. – bunch of grapes – waintroiben (54, 12)
– Lex. III, 919: wîntrûbe swstmf. On î : ai vid.
§11, 1; on û : oi vid. §14, 1.

606. [waiśing]f. – cleanliness – waising (59, 15) – Lex.
III, 701; waschunge. On a : ai vid. §1, 10; on s :
ś vid. §35, 2. DWb. XIII, 2269: waschung f. : in
poetry it refers as here to physical cleanliness.
This explanation is preferable to that of "whiteness"
– Lex. III, 958: wîze, wîz stn. – pale color as a
symbol of guilt.

607. [waiśzaix]n. – linen – waisjaix (23, 2) – DWb. XIV,
1, 1229: weisszeug.

608. [walken] – press solidly – gewalke (48, 6) – DWb. XIII,
1244: walken. In Middle and Upper German the word is
preserved in the technical language of cloth makers.
It refers to the beating, the rolling of woolen
material to make it solidly pressed.

609. [wârem] – warm – wâreme rek (48, 4) – Lex. III, 692:
warm.

610. wariklix (39, 17) – really – Lex. III, 928: wirke-lich.
Els. Wb. II, 853: weriklich. On i : a[r] vid. §3, 3;
21, VI.

611. warrn (76, 18) – become – Lex. III, 775: werden stv.
I, 3. On a vocalism vid. §2, 3; on all forms and use
with the infinitive to form the future vid. §48.

612. watle: daś doi kân watle der fûn fallt oif der erd
(80, 2) – the matter is to be followed to the letter –

414

SWb. II, 926: Meine Worte sind auf den Boden gefallen - "Er erkennt die Wertlosigkeit der Sache". A. watt-lix: lošt mix rêten, a bâr wattlix new - let me speak only a few words (2, 11) - Lex. III, 979: wörtelîn. On o : a <u>vid</u>. §5, 3; on <u>lix</u> plural <u>vid</u>. §66.

613. watten (9, 14) - wait - watt (20, 9; 24, 6) - Lex. III, 697: warten. On <u>r</u> syncope <u>vid</u>. §25, 2 A a.

614. [wattšaft]f. - household - wattšaft (16, 3) - Lex. III, 934: wirtschaft stf. On i : a[r] <u>vid</u>. §3, 3; on <u>r</u> syncope §25, 2 A a.

615. [wattšhois]n. - inn - wattšhois (25, 17) - Lex. III, 936: wirtshûs stn. On i : a[r] <u>vid</u>. §3, 3; on <u>r</u> syncope §25, 2 A a; on û : oi §14, 1.

616. wâx (29, 5) - soft - Lex. III, 736: weich. On ei : â <u>vid</u>. §15, 1.

617. [welkerholz]n. - rolling pin; used in an oath in a jocose manner - ix šwêrn bai den frimpelištag un bai den welkerholz fun gott (27, 10-11) - DWb. XIII, 1235; Gerzon, p. 102; Tendlau, <u>Prov</u>. #552.

618. welkern (29, 4) - to roll: in the sense of rolling dough - DWb. XIII, 1236: wälgern.

619. weren (51, 5) - guarantee - Lex. III, 788; SWb. XIII, 785.

620. wešen (28, 18) - wash - Lex. III, 701; DWb. XIII, 2225: the <u>a</u> in waschen becomes umlauted under the influence of the <u>sch</u> sound in the Rhine and Middle Franconian, the Alemannic-Suabian dialects.

621. widerwattik (9, 13), witterwettik (22, 1) - unpleasant, obnoxious - Lex. III, 871; widerwertic. On <u>r</u> syncope <u>vid</u>. §25, 2 A a.

622. [wind]m.: <u>Mešchoreš</u> (Diener), max wind (81, 10) -

Tendlau, <u>Prov</u>. #250: "Um ein anmassendes hoffartiges
Begehr mit Spott und Verachtung zurückzuweisen... Ich
bin dein Diener nicht, dass Du mir zuherrschen könntest:
Fächle mir ein wenig! Wart nur auf!"

623.   winterklâd (35, 1)n. - winter dress - Lex. III, 916:
winterkleit stn.   On ei : â <u>vid</u>. §15, 1.

624.   [wirdigen] - consider worthy - gewirdigt (58, 6) -
Lex. III, 928.

625.   [woffen] - throw - wofft (7, 1), gewoffen (82, 15) -
Lex. III, 777: wёrfen.   On e : o <u>vid</u>. §2, 3;   on
<u>r</u> syncope <u>vid</u>. §25, 2 A a.

626.   woil (80, 5) - well, Lex. III, 964: wol.   On o : oi
<u>vid</u>. §4, 2.

627.   woilluŠt (25, 16)f. - pleasure; voluptuous enjoyment.
Lex. III, 973: wollust stmf.   On o : oi <u>vid</u>. §4, 2;
on st : Št §33, 2 a.

628.   worim (9, 9); worum (21, 10) - why - Lex. III, 621;
warumbe; DWb. XIII, 2188: variations between <u>a</u> and
<u>o</u> in the first syllable (worim - Albrecht 6; worumbe
- Brant, <u>Narrenschiff</u>, 1, 20; warim - Gerbet (140);
worüm - Gerbet (140).   In the Middle German dialects ü
in the second syllable was widespread.

629.   worm (34, 11)m. - worm - Lex. III, 1008: wurm stm.;
md. auch worm; SWb. VI, 989; Roedder 578.

630.   woŠt m.: dernoix der man, dernoix der woŠt! (75, 2)
- You can tell a man by what he eats. - Wander V,
466; Lex. III, 1010: wurst stf.   On u : o <u>vid</u>. §6,
3; on <u>r</u> syncope §25, 2 A a; on st : Št §53, 2 a.
Paul 667.

631.   [wott]n. - word - wott (27, 2) - Lex. III, 977: wort
stn.   On <u>r</u> syncope <u>vid</u>. §25, 2 A a.

632. [wux]f. - weak - wux (61, 16) - Lex. III, 963: woche
      swf. On o : u <u>vid</u>. §4, 5.

633. [wuxenblettle]n. - weekly newspaper - wuxenblettle (27,
      18) - DWb. XIV, 2, 936ff.: wochenblättlein. Kluge
      696.

                              X.

634. xotše (12, 5) - at least - Landau and Wachstein: chot-
      sche - common throughout Yiddish - <u>cf</u>. poln. choc,
      kleinruss. choč, chočá.

Z.

635. [zaiting] f. - newspaper - in der zaiting (27, 19) -
Lex. III, 1141: zitunge stswf. On î : ai vid. §11,
1.

636. [zâm] m. - bridle - ho ix ghatt, 'n šwanz štaz 'n zâm
(61, 16) - Lex. I, 1158: zoùm stm. On ou : â in the
German dialects and especially in Suabian, vid. Moser
Frühnhd. Gramm, p. 161, 877, note 9.

637. zapple (16, 14) - flounder - DWb. XV, 275: zappeln -
found in the Suabian, Elsass and Rhine Franconian
dialects.

638. zehe (22, 7), zehi (37, 4; 39, 1) - ten - Lex. III,
1042: zehn. On n syncope vid. §26, 2.

639. zepfle (56, 15)n. - tap - a play on zapft (56, 9) -
Lex. III, 1060: zepfelîn, zepfel stn.; DWb. XV, 265;
SWb. VI, 1048; Schmeller II, 1143: zepflein. On le
suffix vid. §66.

640. zettel n.: hot unser zettel getroffen? (70, 10) -
refers to lottery - DWb. XV, 816: used provincially
eyen today in Austria. A. kân zetel, un dox getroffen
(84, 11) - refers to a lottery, in which a person does
not participate, but as a result of which he must
endure its bad results. Tendlau, Prov. #628.

641. [zimmes] m. - pudding - zimmes (84, 1) - SWb. VI, 1212
from zu - imbiss - with the loss of b. Cf. Schmeller
I, 192: z 'imbis', - another possible explanation:
zu + mûs - Lex. I, 2225: mûs stn. - food.

642. zîgen (3, 14; 25, 17) - go - Lex. III, 1103: ziehen
stv. III.

418

643. [zipfele]n. - pinch - zipfelix (9, 6) - Lex. III, 1131:
zipfel(1)în stn. On lix plural vid. 866.

644. [zišpringen] - burst into pieces - zišpringt (29, 13) -
Lex. III, 1085: zerspringen str.

645. [zitâkel]n. - sedan - zitâkel (64, 9) - Murray, N.E.D.
VIII, part II, p. 371 - a closed vehicle to seat one
person, borne on two poles by two bearers, one in front
and one in behind; in fashionable use during the
seventeenth, eighteenth and nineteenth centuries.
Benoist-Goelzer p. 1385: sedecula - petite chaise.

646. [zoiber]m. - two-handled bucket - zoiber (15, 9) -
Lex. III, 1162: zûber stm. On û : oi vid. §14, 1.
Kluge 716; Paul 684. DWb. XVI, 239: originally in
the Upper German dialects and then a loan into the
North Italian dialects.

647. [zopf]m. - pig-tail - zepf (12, 5) - Lex. III, 1159:
zopf stm. pl. zöpfe. On ö : e vid. §5, 1; 21, V.

648. [zukkerhazli]n. - sugar heart - zukkerhazli (92, 9) -
Lex. III, 1166: zucker stm., Lex. I, 1269: hërzelîn.
On e : a vid. §2, 3; on r syncope vid. §25, 2 A d; on
le suffix vid. §66.

649. zumpfel (85, 1)m. - a term of abuse directed to a
woman - Lex. III, 1174; Schmeller II, 1125; DWb. XVI,
541.

650. zurik (22, 7) - back - Lex. III, 1091: zerücke. On
ü : i vid. §7, 1.

651. [zwaken] - tug - zwaken (3, 7) - Lex. III, 1203; DWb.
XVI, 927.

652. [zwarexsak]m. - a sack containing farmer's cheese
from which the liquid is excreted - zwarexsak (59, 8)
- Lex. II, 1596: twarc, quarc stm. On tw : zw vid.

§37, 6; on k : x <u>vid</u>. §41, 4.   DWb. XVI, 954 zwarg m.
- East Middle German dwarg, twarg from Polish tvarog -
High German form regularly quark. DWb. VII, 2318:
quarksack - a sack of strong linen filled with cheese,
which is weighed down by a stone so that the whey
might drip off.

653.   [zwikken]n. - card game - zwikken (23, 11) - SWb. VI,
1452; DWb. XVI, 1119: zwicken - to get into a tight
place. The reference here is to an ancient game
"Mühlenspiel"; - for description <u>vid</u>. DWb. VI, 2638,
2640.

654.   [zwîfel]m. - onion - zwîfel (30, 1); diminutive -
zwîfelle (20, 3) - Lex. III, 1212: zwibolle swm. On
i : î <u>vid</u>. §6, 2; on b : f <u>vid</u>. §30, 3. SWb. VI,
1446: zwifel. Paul 687.

A Selected Bibliography

Adelung, Johann Christoph: Wörterbuch der hochdeutschen
        Mundart, 4 vols., Leipzig, 1793-1801.

Altman, A.: Moses Mendelssohn, University of Alabama Press,
        University, Alabama, 1973.

Archiv far Geshichte, Teater un Drame, I, New York, 1930.

Avé-Lallement, Fr. Chr. B.: Das deutsche Gaunertum, Part. III
        & IV, Leipzig, 1862.

Bach, Adolph: Geschichte der deutschen Sprache, 4th ed.,
        Heidelberg, 1950.

Baron Salo Wittmayer: A Social and Religious History of the
        Jews, II, III, XI, Jewish Publication Society,
        Philadelphia, 1952-1969.

--------------------: "The Modern Age", in L. Schwarz, ed.,
        Great Ages and Ideas of the Jewish People, New
        York, Random House, 1956, pp. 315-484, also Modern
        Library, 1965.

Eisenstein: see Barzilay.

Barzilay, Isaac E.: "The Ideology of the Berlin Haskalah",
        in Proceedings of the American Association of
        Jewish Research, XXV, (1956), pp. 1-37.

------------------: "The Treatment of the Jewish Religion
        in the Literature of the Berlin Haskalah", ibid.,
        XXIV, (1955), pp. 39-68.

------------------: Shelomo Yehuda Rapoport (Shir) and his
        Contemporaries, Tel Aviv, 1969.

Behaghel, Otto: Deutsche Syntax, 4 vols., Heidelberg,
        1923-1932.

--------------: Die deutsche Sprache, Leipzig, 1930.

Behaghel, Otto: Geschichte der deutschen Sprache, 5th ed.,
        Berlin, 1928.   (Behaghel).

Beiträge zur Geschichte der deutschen Sprache und Literatur,
        Halle, 1874 ff.   (Beiträge).

Ben-Yehuda, Elieser: Thesaurus Totius Hebraitatis (=Complete
        Dictionary of Ancient and Modern Hebrew),
        Jerusalem-Berlin, 1910-1958, 16 vols.

Benecke-Zarncke-Müller: Mittelhochdeutsches Wörterbuch,
        vols. I-IV, Leipzig, 1854-1861.

Benoist-Goelzer: Nouveau Dictionaire, Latin-Français,
        Paris, 1934?   (Benoist-Goelzer).

Beranek, Franz J.: "Die Erforschung der jiddischen Sprache",
        ZfdPh, vol. LXX, (No. 2, 1947/48), pp. 163-74.

----------------: "Jiddish", in W. Stammler (ed.), Deutsche
        Philologie im Aufriss, 2nd ed., vol. I, Berlin,
        1957, 1555-2000.

----------------: Die jiddische Mundart Nordostungarns,
        Brno-Leipzig, 1941.

----------------: Das Pinsker Yiddisch, Berlin, 1958.

----------------: "Sprachgeographie des Jiddischen in der
        Slowakei", Zeitschrift für Phonetik und allge-
        meine Sprachwissenschaft, III, (1949), 25-46.

Bernfeld, Simon: Dor Tahapuchot, (=A Perverse Generation),
        2 vols., Warsaw, 1914.

Birnbaum, Salomo: "Das älteste datierte Schriftstück in
        jiddischer Sprache", Beiträge, LVI, (1932),
        pp. 11-22.

Birnbaum, Salomo: Das hebräische und aramäische Element in der jiddischen Sprache, Leipzig, 1922.

----------------: "Jiddish", in Encyclopaedia Judaica, vol. IX, Berlin, 1932, pp. 112-127.

----------------: "Jewish Languages", in Essays in Honour of . . . J.H. Hertz, London, 1944, pp. 51-67.

----------------: "Jiddische Psalmenübersetzungen", in H. Vollmer, F. Jülicher and W. Lüdtke (eds.), Die Psalmenverdeutschung . . . bis Luther, Potsdam, 1932, pp. 4f., 8f., 19, and Tables I and II.

----------------: "Die jiddische Sprache", Germanisch-Romanische Monatsschrift 11 (1923), 149ff.

----------------: Praktische Grammatik der jiddischen Sprache, Vienna-Leipzig (1918).

----------------: "Die Stellung der jiddischen Sprache", Mitteilungen der Akademie zur wissenschaftlichen Erforschung des Deutschtums, 1930, No. 6.

----------------: "Uebersicht über den jiddischen Vokalismus", Zeitschrift für deutsche Mundarten, XVIII, (1923), pp. 122-130.

----------------: "Die Umschrift des ältesten datierten jiddischen Schriftstücks", Teuthonista, VIII, (1931-32), pp. 197-207.

----------------: "Die Umschrift des Jiddischen", Teuthonista, IX, (1933), pp. 90-105.

---------------- and Joffe Judah A.: "Yiddish", in Universal Jewish Encyclopedia, New York, vol. X, 1943, 598-602.

----------------: "Yiddish and Jewishness", in Yubileumbukh tsum zekhtsikstn geburtstog fun Dr. Natan Birnbaum, Warsaw, 1925, pp. 147-157.

Bischoff, Erich: Wörterbuch der Wichtigsten Geheim- und Berufssprachen, Leipzig, 1916. (Bischoff).

426

Blanc, Heim: The Yiddish Language.   A Brief Survey of
    its Slavic Elements.   (Honors Thesis in Compara-
    tive Philology - unpublished), Cambridge, Mass.,
    April 1, 1948.

Borokhov, B.: "The Tasks of Yiddish Philology", in Der
    Pinkes.   pp. 1-22, (in Yiddish).

------------: (The Library of the Yiddish Philologist), in
    Der Pinkes, Vilna, 1913, (end - separate pagina-
    tion), 1-65.

Cassirer, Ernst: The Philosophy of Enlightment, Boston,
    1955.

Crecelius, Wilhelm: Oberhessisches Wörterbuch, vols. I &
    II, Darmstadt, 1897-1899.

Curme, George O.:   A Grammar of the German Language, re-
    vised edition, New York, 1922.

Davidson, I.:   Parody in Jewish Literature, New York, 1907.

Dubnow, Simon: Weltgeschichte des jüdischen Volkes, VII-IX,
    Berlin, 1929-1930.

--------------:   History of the Jews I-IV, New York, Yoseloff,
    1967.

Efroykin, Y.:   Oyfkum un umkum fun yidishe golesshprakhn un
    dialektn, Paris, 1951.

Folkovitsh, E.:   Yidish: fonetik, grafik, leksik, gramatik,
    Moscow, 1940.

Field of Yiddish: see Weinreich, U.

Filologische shriftn (fun YIVO), 1-5, Vilna, Yiddish Scien-
    tific Institute - YIVO, 1926-1938.

Fischer, Hermann: Schwäbisches Wörterbuch, vol. I-VI,
    Tübingen, 1901-1924. (Swb).

Erik, Max: Geshikhte fun der Yidisher Literatur, Warsaw,
    1928.

Erik, Max: Vegn Altyidishn Roman un Novele ..., Warsaw, 1926.

Fischer, Jechiel: Das Jiddische und sein Verhältnis zu den deutschen Mundarten, Leipzig, 1936.

Freehof, S.B.: "Devotional Literature in the Vernacular", Yearbook of the Central Conference of American Rabbis, XXXIII (1923), 375-424.

Friedländer, David: "Sendschreiben an die deutsche (sic!) Juden". (Hebrew alphabet). Supplement to Ha-Meassef, IV (1788)(=an appeal to the Jews to give up their Judisch-Deutsch and so gain respect of their neighbors, and equality.)

Fuks, L.: The Oldest Known Literary Documents of Yiddish Literature, (c. 1382), Leiden, 1957.

--------: ed. Das altjiddishe Epos, Melokim-Buk, 2 vols., Assen, 1965.

--------: Das Schmuelbuch des Mosche Esrim Wearba, 2 vols., ibid. 1961.

Gebhardt, August: Grammatik der Nürnberger Mundart, Leipzig, 1901. (Gebhardt).

Gerzon, Jacob: Die jüdisch-deutsche Sprache, Frankfurt-am-Main, 1912. (Gerzon).

Gesenius, Wilhelm: Handwörterbuch über das Alte Testament, Leipzig, 1886.

Gininger, C.: "Sainean's Accomplishments in Yiddish Linguistics", The Field of Yiddish, I, 147-178.

Ginzberg, Louis: The Legends of the Jews, Jewish Publication Society, Philadelphia, 7 vols., 1947.

Glatzer, Nahum N.ed.: Dynamics of Emancipation, Boston, 1965.

Gorin, B.: Di Geschichte fun Idishen Teater New York, 1918, 2 vols.

Graetz, Heinrich: Geschichte der Juden, XI, Leipzig, 1900.

Greenstone, Julius H.: Jewish Feasts and Fasts, Phil., 1945.

Grimm, Jacob und Wilhelm: Deutsches Wörterbuch, Leipzig,
       1854 ff. (DWb.).

Grubel, Johann Konrad: Sämmtliche Werke, ed. Fromann,
       Nürnberg, 1873. (Grubel).

Grünbaum, Max: Jüdischdeutsche Chrestomathie, Leipzig,
       1862.

Grünwald, Moritz: Über den jüdisch-deutschen Jargon,
       Prague, 1858.

Haberman, A.M.: "Massechet Purim Mahaduroteha u-Defuseha",
       Areshet, 5, (Jerusalem, 5732).

Harkavy, Alexander: Yiddish-English-Hebrew Dictionary, New
       York, 1925. (Harkavy).

Hertel, Ludwig: Die Salzinger Mundart, Inaugural-disser-
       tation, Jena, Meiningen, 1888.

Herz, Joseph: Esther, 2nd ed., Fürth, 1854.

Heyne, Moriz: Deutsches Wörterbuch, 3 vols., Leipzig,
       1890-1895.

Heyse, J.C.A.: Allgemeines verdeutschendes und erklärendes
       Fremdwörterbuch, 12th ed., Hannover, 1859.
       (Heyse).

Hirt, Hermann: Etymologie der neuhochdeutschen Sprache,
       Munich, 1921.

Jastrow, Marcus: A Dictionary of the Targumim, the Talmud...
       and the Midrashic Literature, New York - Berlin,
       1926, (Horeb Reprint).

Jofen, J.B.: The Dialectological Makeup of East European
       Yiddish: Phonological and Lexicological Criteria,
       Microfilm Dissertation no. 6639 (Columbia University,
       1954); abstract in Dissertation Abstracts XIV (1953),
       140; resumé (Y. Yofen) in Yidishe shprakh XIII
       (1953), 157-160, reprinted in Yudah A. Yofe-bukh,
       232-235.

-----------: A Linguistic Atlas for Eastern European Yid-
       dish, Ann Arbor, Mich., 1964.

Joffe, Judah A. and Mark, Yudel: Great Dictionary of the Yiddish Language, New York - Jerusalem, 1961 f. (3 vols. of 13 planned).

Yuda A. Yofe-bukh, ed. Y. Mark, New York, 1958. (Studies in honor of Judah A. Joffe.)

Joffe, Judah A.: "The Slavic Element in Yiddish", Pinkes fun Anopteyl fun Yivo, I-II (1927-28), 235-256, 296-312.

----------------: Elia Bachur's Poetical Works, (Bovobuch), N.Y., 1949.

Kaufmann, D.: Die Memoiren der Glückel von Hameln, Frankfurt-am-Main, 1896.

Keyserling, M.: Moses Mendelssohn, sein Leben und seine Werke, Leipzig, 1862.

Kehrein, J.: Grammatik der deutschen Sprache des XV bis XVII Jh., vol. 3, Leipzig, 1856.

Klausner, Joseph: Historia shel ha-Sifrut ha-Ivrit ha-Chadasha, Jerusalem, 1952, 2nd ed.

----------------: History of Modern Hebrew Literature, London, 1932.

Klitzke, Carl Paul: The German Household Poem, Dissertation, University of Chicago, 1936.

Kluge, Friedrich: Etymologisches Wörterbuch der deutschen Sprache, 11th ed. rev. by Alfred Götze, Berlin, 1934. (Kluge).

Kretschmer, Paul: Wortgeographie der hochdeutschen Umgangsprache, Göttingen, 1918. (Kretschmer).

Landau, Alfred: "Das Deminutivum der galizisch-jüdischen Mundart", Deutsche Mundarten, Zeitschrift für Bearbeitung des Mundartlichen Materials, ed. by J.W. Nagl, vol. I, Vienna, 1895, pp. 46-58; 126-132. (Landau, Das Deminutivum).

Landau, Alfred: "Die Sprache der Mémoiren Glückels von Hameln",
   Mitteilungen der Gesellschaft für jüdische Volkskunde,
   7, Hamburg, 1901. (Landau).

Landau, A., Wachstein, B.: _Jüdische Privatbriefe aus dem
   Jahre 1619_, Vienna, 1911. (Landau and Wachstein).

Landau, Leo: "Arthurian Legends", _Teutonia_, No. 21, Part I,
   Leipzig, 1912.

-----------: "A Hebrew-German (Judeo-German) Paraphrase of the
   Book of Esther of the Fifteenth Century", _Journal
   of English and Germanic Philology_, XVIII (1919),
   497-555.

Leibowitz, N.: "Die Übersetzungstechnik der jüdisch-deutschen
   Bibelübersetzungen des 15. u. 16. Jahrhunderts darge-
   stellt an den Psalmen", _Beiträge_, IV, (1931),
   pp. 377-463.

Levy, Jacob: _Neuhebräisches und Chaldäisches Wörterbuch über
   die Talmudim und Midraschim_, vol. I-IV, Leipzig,
   1876-1889.

Lexer, M.: "_Mittelhochdeutsches Handwörterbuch_, vol. I-III,
   Leipzig, 1872-78. (Lex.).

Lingvistishe zamlung, 1-3, Minsk, Belorussian Academy of
   Sciences, Institute for Jewish Proletarian Culture,
   1933-36.

Liptzin, Sol: _A History of Yiddish Literature_, New York,
   1972.

Loewe, H.: _Die Sprachen der Juden_, Cologne, 1911.

Lowenthal, M.: _The Jews of Germany_, New York, 1936.

Mahler, Raphael: _A History of Modern Jewry_, London, 1971.

----------------: _Divre Yeme Yisrael: Dorot Achronim_,
   (=History of the Jewish People: Last Generations),
   II, Merchavya, 1954.

Martin, E., Lienhart, H.: _Wörterbuch der elsässischen
   Mundarten_, vol. I-II, Strassburg, 1899, 1907.

(Els. Wb.).

Meisinger, Othmar: Wörterbuch der Rappenauer Mundart, Dortmund, 1906.

Meisel, N.: Dos Yidishe Shafn . . .in Sovetnfarband, New York, 1954.

Meyer, Michael A.: The Origins of the Modern Jew, Jewish Identity and European Culture in Germany, 1749-1824, Wayne State University Press, 1967.

Metcalf, George J.: "Forms of Address in German (1500-1800)", Washington University Studies, New Series. Languages and Literature, No. 7, St. Louis, 1938. (Metcalf).

Midrash Rabbah: Esther, tr. by Maurice Simon, London, 1939.

Mieses, M.: Die jiddische Sprache, Berlin-Vienna, 1924. (Mieses).

Mitteilungen des Arbeitskreises für Jiddistik, Butzbach, 1955-date.

Montefiore, C.C., Loewe, M.: A Rabbinic Anthology, London, 1938.

Moser, Virgil: Frühneuhochdeutsche Grammatik, vol. I, Heidelberg, 1929.

Müller, Joseph: Rheinisches Wörterbuch, vol. I-III, Bonn, Berlin, 1928-44.

Muret-Sanders: Encyclopädisches Wörterbuch der englischen und deutschen Sprache, 4 vols., Berlin, London, New York, 1899-1901.

Murray, James A.: A New English Dictionary, vols. III, VIII, Oxford, 1891-1914. (NED).

Niger, Sh.: Yidische Shrayber in Sovet Rusland, New York, 1958.

Noble, S.: Khumesh-taytsh: an oysforshung vegn der traditsye fun taytshn khumesh in di khadorim, New York, 1943 (with English summary), (=Pentateuch-

Translation Tradition in Yidish Religious Schools).

Ochs, Ernst: Badisches Wörterbuch, Lahn in Baden, 1951.

Paul, Hermann: Deutsche Grammatik, vol. III-IV, Halle a.S.,
     1919-1920.

------------: Deutsches Wörterbuch, 4th ed. revised by K.
     Euling, Halle, 1935. (Paul).

Paul, H., Gierach, E.: Mittelhochdeutsche Grammatik, 14th
     ed. Halle, 1944. (Paul-Gierach).

Perles, F.: "Zur Erforschung des Jüdischdeutschen", Bei-
     träge, XLIV, (1920), pp. 182-184.

Pfister, Hermann v.: Mundartliche und stammhaftliche Nach-
     träge zu E.F.C. Vilmars Idiotikon von Hessen,
     Marburg, 1886.
 Der Pinkes, ed. S. Niger, Vilna, 1913.

Pinkes fun Amopteyl fun YIVO, I, II, New York, 1927-28.

Pomerantz, A.: Di Sovetishe Harugey Malkhus, Buenas Aires,
     1962.

Prilutski, N.: Yidishe Dialektologishe Forshungen, 1-5:
     Warsaw 1917-1924, includes "Tzum Yidishen Konso-
     nantizm"; tzum Yidishen Vokalizm",; "Dialektologishe
     Paraleln" (="Noyakh Prilutski's Zamlbikher,etc.");
     Mameloshn".

------------: Dialektologishe Forarbetn (="Mameloshn" II),
     Vilna, 1937.

Reis, Hans: Die deutsche Mundartdichtung, Sammlung Göschen,
     1915.

------------: Die deutschen Mundarten, Sammlung Göschen,
     1920.

Raisen, Z.: Fun Mendelson bis Mendele, Warsaw, 1923.

----------: Grammatik fun der jiddischer Sprache, Vilna,
     1921. (Raisen).

Ritter, Immanuel: Geschichte der jüdischen Reformation, Pt.

II, David Friedländer: sein Leben und Wirken,
Berlin, 1861.

Roback, A.A.: The Story of Yiddish Literature, New York,
1940.

--------------: "The Yiddish Language", in Contemporary
Jewish Record, vol. VII, No. VI, New York, December
1944.

Roedder, Edwin: Volkssprache und Wortschatz des badischen
Frankenlands, New York, 1936.

Rudavsky, D.: Emancipation and Adjustment, New York, 1969.

Sachs, K.; Villatte, C.: Encyclopädisches Wörterbuch der
französischen und deutschen Sprache, 2 vols., Berlin,
1881. (Sachs-Villatte).

Sadan, Dov: (On Shlemiel), Orlogin, I, (1950), 198ff.,
(in Hebrew).

Saineau, L.: "Essai sur le Judéo-Allemand", in Mémoires de
la société de Linguistique de Paris, 1903.

Sanders, D.: Wörterbuch der deutschen Sprache, Leipzig,
1860. (Sanders).

Sapir, E.: "Notes on Judeo-German Phonology", Jewish
Quarterly Review, New Series, vol. VI, Philadelphia, 1915. (Sapir).

Schauss, Hayyim: The Jewish Festivals, Cincinnati, 1938.

Schmeller, J.A.: Bayrisches Wörterbuch, revised by J.K.
Fromann, 2 vols., Munich, 1872. (Schmeller).

Schulman, Elazar: Sefat Yehudit Ashkenazit Y'Sifruta, etc.
(=Yiddish Language and Literature", (1500-1800),
Riga, 1913.

Schulman, Elias: Di Sovet-Yidishe Literatur, New York, 1971.

Schulz, H.; Basler, O.: Deutsches Fremdwörterbuch, vol. I,
Strassburg, 1913; vol. II, Berlin, 1942.

Schwarz, Ernst: Die deutschen Mundarten, Göttingen, 1950.

434

Selig, Gottfried: Lehrbuch der jüdisch-deutschen Sprache,
        Leipzig, 1792.

Seligmann, Caesar: Geschichte der jüdischen Reformbewegung
        von Mendelssohn bis zur Gegenwart, Frankfurt-am-Main,
        1922.

Shipper, I.: "The Beginnings of Old Yiddish", in Yidishe
        Filologye, vol. I, no. 2, pp. 272-287, Warsaw, 1924,
        (in Yiddish).

Shklyar, H.: (Yiddish Dialectological Research in the Soviet
        Union), "Tsum fuftsntn yortog . . .", pp. 141-163,
        (in Yiddish).

Shmeruk, H., ed.: Jewish Pulications in the Soviet Union,
        1917-1960, Jerusalem, 1961, (in Hebrew).

------------------: A shpigl oif a Shteyn, Anthology of
        Twelve Liquidated Yiddish Writers in the Soviet
        Union, Tel Aviv, 1964.

Shriftn Kiev: Ukrainian Academy of Sciences, Chair for
        Yiddish Culture, 1928. (Only vol. I published).

Simon, Max; Cohen L.: Ein neuer Maphteach, Berlin, 1897.

Staerck, W.; Leitzmann, A.: Die jüdisch-deutschen Bibel-
        übersetzungen, von den Anfängen bis zum Ausgang des
        18 Jahrhunderts, Frankfurt-am-Main, 1923.

Staub, Friedrich, Tobler, Ludwig: Schweizerisches Idioti-
        kon - Wörterbuch der schweizerdeutschen Sprache,
        vol. I-IX, Frauenfeld, 1881-1925.

Strack, H.L.: Jüdisches Wörterbuch, Leipzig, 1916.

Stutchkoff, Nahum: Thesaurus of the Yiddish Language,
        New York, 1950.

------------------: Thesaurus of the Hebrew Language, New
        York, 1968.

Süsskind, Nathan: "How Yiddish Originated", (in Yiddish),
        (Thoughts on the History of Yiddish), Yidishe
        Shprakh, XIII, 4, Oct.-Dec. 1953, pp. 97-108,
        (in Yiddish).

435

Süsskind, Nathan: "Guidelines for the Study of Jewish Languages", ibid, XXI, 1, June 1965, pp. 1-17.

----------------: "Old and Middle Yiddish", (Brief Introduction), ibid XXIX, nos. 1-3, 1969-70, pp. 43-64.

Tendlau, A.: Sprichwörter und Redensarten deutsch-jüdischer
Vorzeit, Frankfurt-am-Main, 1860. (Tendlau-Prov.).

Tsaytshrift (far yidisher geshikhte, demografye un ekonomik,
literatur-forshung, shprakh-visnshaft un etnografye),
1-5, Minsk, Institute for Belorussian Culture,
Jewish Section, 1926-31.

Tsum fuftsntn yortog oktyaber-revolutsye; literarish-
lingvistisher zamlbukh, Minsk, 1932.

Veynger, M.: Yidishe dialektologye, Minsk, 1929.

Vilenkin, L.: Yidisher shprakhatlas fun Sovetn-farband,
Minsk, 1931.

Vilmar, A.F.C.: Idiotikon von Kurhessen, Marburg, Leipzig,
1883. (Vilmar).

Viner, M. and Zaretski, A.: ed. Fragn fun yidisher
shprakh, Moscow, 1938.

Vollmer, Gottfried: Vollständiges jüdisch-deutsches und
deutsch-jüdisches Wörterbuch, Hamburg, n.d.

Wahrig, Gerhard: Deutsches Wörterbuch, Gütersloh, 1960.

Wallach, Luitpold: Liberty and Letters: the Thoughts of
Leopold Zunz, London, 1959.

Wander, Karl Friedrich Wilhelm: Deutsches Sprichwörter-
lexikon, vol. III-V, Leipzig, 1873-1880. (Wander).

Waxman, Meyer: History of Jewish Literature, New York-
London, 1966, 2nd ed., 6 vols.

Weigand, Fr. L.K.: Deutsches Wörterbuch, 2 vols., Giessen,
1909-1910. (Weigand-Hirt).

Weinhold, K.: Alemannische Grammatik, Berlin, 1863.

Weinhold, K.: <u>Bairische Grammatik</u>, Berlin, 1867. (Weinhold).

------------: <u>Mittelhochdeutsche Grammatik</u>, 2nd ed., Padeborn, 1883.

Weinreich, Max: Bibliography in (Festshrift) <u>For Max Weinreich</u>, Mouton, The Hague, 1964, pp. 287-305.

--------------: <u>Bilder fun der Yidisher Literaturgeshikhte</u> (till Mendele), Vilna, 1928.

--------------: <u>History of the Yiddish Language</u>, 4 vols., YIVO, New York, 1973, (in Yiddish).

--------------: "Outlines of Western Yiddish", in <u>Yidishe Shprakh</u>, XIII (1953) 35-69, reprinted in <u>Judah A. Joffe - Book</u>, 158-194, (=Bibliography #349), (in Yiddish).

--------------: <u>Staplen</u>, Berlin, 1923.

--------------: "Vos iz der mer?", <u>Yidische Filologye</u>, vol. I, pp. 2, 3, 229.

--------------: "Yiddish", <u>Algemeyne yidische Entsiklopedye</u>, vol. Yidn B, New York, 1940.

--------------: "Prehistory and Early History of Yiddish", in <u>Field of Yiddish</u>, I, 1954, pp. 73-101; (=Bibliography # 324).

--------------: "Yidishkayt and Yiddish": On the Impact of Religion on Language in Ashkenazic Jewry in <u>Mordecai M. Kaplan Jubilee Volume</u>, New York, 1953, pp. 481-514 (=Bibliography #323).

Weinreich, Uriel: <u>College Yiddish: An Introduction to the Yiddish Language and to Jewish Life and Culture</u>, New York, 1949.

----------------: (ed.) <u>Field of Yiddish</u>, I, New York, 1954; II, 1966.

----------------: <u>Modern Yiddish-English-Yiddish Dictionary</u>, YIVO, New York, 1968.

----------------; Herzog, M. and Ravid, W.: <u>Language and</u>

Culture Atlas of Ashkenazic Jewry, (on-going project at Columbia University, New York, cf. "Goldene Keyt", no. 37; Proceedings of the Meeting of the American Ethnological Society, Spring 1962, Seattle 1963, pp. 27-39; Anthropological Linguistics, IV, 1962.

Weinreich, Uriel and Beatrice: Yiddish Language and Folklore, a Selected Bibliography, Mouton, The Hague, 1959.

Weinryb, Bernard D.: "Aaron Wolfsohn's Dramatic Writings in their Historical Setting", Jewish Quarterly Review, XLVIII (1957-58), 35-50.

Weiss, Th.: "Das elsässer Judendeutsch", Jahrbuch für Geschichte, Sprache und Literatur Elsass-Lothringens, XII, Jahrgang, pp. 121-183, Strassburg, 1896.

Weise, Oscar: Unsere Mundarten, Leipzig, Berlin, 1919.

Wiener, Leo: History of Yiddish Literature in the Nineteenth Century, New York, 1899.

-----------: "On the Judeo-German Spoken by the Russian Jews", American Journal of Philology, vol. XIV, no. 4, pp. 456-482, 1893.

Wilmanns, W.: Deutsche Grammatik, vol. III, Strassburg, 1906. (Wilmanns).

Wisse, Ruth: The Schlemiel as Modern Hero, Chicago University Press, 1971.

Wolf, Siegmund A.: Jiddisches Wörterbuch, Mannheim, 1962.

Wrede, F., Mitzka, W.: Deutscher Sprachatlas, Marburg, 1926 f.

Yidishe filologye, Warsaw, 1924-26 (only vol. I published).

Yidishe shprakh, New York, YIVO, 1941-date.

Di yidishe shprakh, Kiev, 1927-31; continued as "Afn shprakhfront", (second and third series), 1934-39.

YIVO = "Yidish Scientific Institute", now, "Yivo Institute for Jewish Research", with a Graduate School, and

438

with unequaled Archives, Collections, Library and Publications specializing in (though not limited to) Yiddish and the Civilization of Eastern European Jewry the World over.

Of course to us, additionally, are:

Yivo-Annual of Jewish Social Science, 1946f.
Yivo-bibliografye, New York, 1943f.
Guides to Jewish Subjects in Social Humanistic Research, 1966f.
Yivo-Bleter, (in Yiddish), I-XIV, Vilna, 1931-39, XV, New York, 1940f.

Zaretski, A.: Praktishe yidishe gramatik, Moscow, 1926, 2nd ed., Vilna, 1929.

Zeitschrift für deutsche Philologie, Halle, 1867ff. (ZfdPh.)

Zinberg, I.: Di Geshichte fun der Literatur bei Yidn, Vilna, 1929, 12 vols. (The Berlin Enlightment - in vol. VII.)

-----------: A History of Jewish Literature, Case Western University Press, Cleveland and London, 1972-4, (5 of 12 vols.).

-----------: Toledot Sifrut Yisrael, 7 vols., Tel Aviv, 1956.

A WORD OF EXPLANATION:

      The inconsistency in transliterating Yiddish titles and
names in this bibliography: it was found impractical to reduce
some four conflicting systems of transliteration by adopting
one of them (YIVO's) as a standard, and rewriting the others:
if for no other reason than that the works and authors have
been listed, known and quoted, each according to its time and
place of origin: thus YIVO's Journal YIDISHE SHPRAKH (in
English speech-territory - even though in English proper the
language is spelled "Yi<u>dd</u>ish", with "dd" - but Yiddish spelling
following Hebrew tradition, does not <u>write</u> the consonants
double); <u>that</u> - against the same title "<u>j</u>iddi<u>sh</u>c<u>e</u> <u>S</u>pra<u>ch</u>"
(Birnbaum's), whose name is listed doubly in <u>Uriel</u> Weinreich's
Bibliography: for his listings in English and German: as
"S. Birnbaum", for those in Yiddish as "Sholyme Birnboym";
ditto for Weinreich himself, who listed his own name for
Yiddish items only as "Vaynraykh".

      So we have: Yidish, Yiddish, jiddisch and even
Idish! Could not help it !